THE

COMPLETE WORKS

OF

SAMUEL TAYLOR COLERIDGE.

WITH AN INTRODUCTORY ESSAY

UPON HIS

PHILOSOPHICAL AND THEOLOGICAL OPINIONS.

EDITED BY

PROFESSOR SHEDD.

IN SEVEN VOLUMES.

VOL. II.

NEW YORK:
HARPER & BROTHERS, PUBLISHERS,
Nos. 329 AND 331 PEARL STREET,
FRANKLIN SQUARE.
1853.

THE COMPLETE WORKS OF SAMUEL TAYLOR COLERIDGE,

VOL. II.

THE FRIEND.

NEW YORK:
HARPER & BROTHERS.
1853.

THE FRIEND:

A SERIES OF ESSAYS

TO AID IN THE FORMATION OF FIXED PRINCIPLES

IN POLITICS, MORALS, AND RELIGION,

WITH LITERARY AMUSEMENTS INTERSPERSED.

BY SAMUEL TAYLOR COLERIDGE.

WITH THE AUTHOR'S LAST CORRECTIONS AND AN APPENDIX, AND WITH A SYNOPTICAL TABLE OF THE CONTENTS OF THE WORK,

BY HENRY NELSON COLERIDGE, ESQ., M.A.

NEW YORK:
HARPER & BROTHERS.
1853.

Now for the writing of this werke,
I, who am a lonesome clerke,
Purposed for to write a book
After the world, that whilome took
Its course in oldè days long passed:
But for men sayn, it is now lassed
In worser plight than it was tho,
I thought me for to touch also
The world which neweth every day—
So as I can, so as I may,
Albeit I sickness have and pain,
And long have had, yet would I fain
Do my mind's hest and besiness,
That in some part, so as I guess,
The gentle mind may be advised.

GOWER, *Pro. to the Confess. Amantis.*

ADVERTISEMENT.

THE present edition of THE FRIEND comprises all the corrections, and most of the notes, found in the author's handwriting in an interleaved copy of the work, bequeathed by him to his daughter-in-law. The Editor has revised the text with as much care as circumstances would permit, and has added a preliminary sketch of the plan and details of the whole, with an appendix, containing several passages, parts of the scattered essays originally published in 1809, and omitted in the recast of the work in 1818, but which seem worthy of separate preservation. It is earnestly hoped that what has thus been done may further the more general acceptance of a work, which, with all its imperfections, is, perhaps, the most vigorous of Mr. Coleridge's compositions; and which, if it had contained nothing but the essays, in the first volume, on the duty and conditions of communicating truth, and those in the third, on the principles of scientific method, with the reconcilement of the Platonic and Baconian processes of investigation, would still, as the Editor conceives, have constituted one of the most signal benefits conferred in this age on the cause of morals and sound philosophy.

Lincoln's Inn,
11th Sept. 1837.

OBJECT AND PLAN OF THE WORK.

THE FRIEND consists of a methodical series of essays, the principal purpose of which is to assist the mind in the formation for itself of sound, and therefore permanent and universal, principles in regard to the investigation, perception, and retention of truth, in what direction soever it may be pursued; but pre-eminently with reference to the three great relations in which we are placed in this world,—as citizens to the state, as men to our neighbors, and as creatures to our Creator,—in other words, to politics, to morals, and to religion. The author does not exhibit any perfect scheme of action or system of belief in any one of these relations; and that he has not done so, nor meant to do so, are points which must be borne in mind by every reader who would understand and fairly appreciate the work. For its scope is to prepare and discipline the student's moral and intellectual being,—not to propound dogmas or theories for his adoption. The book is not the plan of a palace, but a manual of the rules of architecture. It is a προπαίδευμα,—something to set the mind in a state of pure recipiency for the specific truths of philosophy, and to arm its faculties with power to recognize and endure their presence.

In pursuing, however, this main design, the author has examined with more or less minuteness many particular systems and codes of opinion lying in his way; and in stating the grounds of his rejection of some, and entire or partial admission of others of them, he has in effect expressed his own convictions upon several of the most important questions, yet disputed in moral and political philosophy. But it is not so much to any given conclusion so expressed that the reader's attention seems to be invited, as to the reasoning founded on principles of universal application, by which such conclusion has been evolved;—the primary and prevailing aim throughout the work being, as well under the forms of criticism, biography, local description, or personal anecdote, as of direct moral, political, or metaphysical disquisition, to lay down and illustrate certain fundamental distinctions and rules of intellectual action, which, if well grounded and thoroughly taken up and appropriated, will give to every one the power of working out, under any circumstances, the conclusions of truth for himself. The game from time to time started and run down may be rich and curious; but still at the end of the day it is the chase itself, the quickened eye, the lengthened breath, the firmer nerve, that must ever be the huntsman's best reward.

The Friend is divided into two main sections; the first comprising a discussion of the principles of political knowledge; the second treating of the grounds of morals and religion, and revealing the systematic discipline of mind requisite for a true understanding of the same. To these is prefixed a general introduction, for the greater part devoted to a statement of the duty of communicating the truth, and of the conditions under which it may be communicated safely; and three several collections of essays, in some degree miscellaneous and called Landing-Places—interposed in different places for amusement, retrospect, and preparation—complete the work.

TABLE OF CONTENTS.

The following synoptical view of the plan and contents of "The Friend" may prove useful to those who read the work for the first time in the present edition.

GENERAL INTRODUCTION.

ESSAYS I—XVI. pp. 19–118.

FIRST LANDING-PLACE.

FIRST SECTION.

ON THE PRINCIPLES OF POLITICAL KNOWLEDGE.

SECOND LANDING-PLACE.

ESSAYS I–IV. pp. 311–343.

SECOND SECTION.

ON THE GROUNDS OF MORALS AND RELIGION, AND THE DISCIPLINE OF THE MIND REQUISITE FOR A TRUE UNDERSTANDING OF THE SAME.

ESSAYS I–XI. pp. 347–472.

THIRD LANDING-PLACE.

*Friend! were an author privileged to name his own judge,—in addition to moral and intellectual competence I should look round for some man, whose knowledge and opinions had for the greater part been acquired experimentally; and the practical habits of whose life had put him on his guard with respect to all speculative reasoning, without rendering him insensible to the desirableness of principles more secure than the shifting rules and theories generalized from observations merely empirical, or unconscious in how many departments of knowledge, and with how large a portion even of professional men, such principles are still a *desideratum*. I would select, too, one who felt kindly, nay, even partially, toward me; but one whose partiality had its strongest foundations in hope, and more prospective than retrospective would make him quick-sighted in the detection, and unreserved in the exposure, of the deficiencies and defects of each present work, in the anticipation of a more developed future. In you, honored friend! I have found all these requisites combined and realized: and the improvement, which these essays have derived from your judgment and judicious suggestions, would, of itself, have justified me in accompanying them with a public acknowledgment of the same. But knowing, as you can not but know, that I owe in great measure the power of having written at all to your medical skill, and to the characteristic good sense which directed its exertion in my behalf; and whatever I may

* Dedication to the second edition.—*Ed.*

have written in happier vein to the influence of your society and to the daily proofs of your disinterested attachment ;—knowing, too, in how entire a sympathy with your feelings in this respect the partner of your name has blended the affectionate regards of a sister or daughter with almost a mother's watchful and unwearied solicitudes alike for my health, interest, and tranquillity ; —you will not, I trust, be pained,—you ought not, I am sure, to be surprised—that

TO

MR. AND MRS. GILLMAN,

OF HIGHGATE,

These Volumes are dedicated,

IN TESTIMONY OF HIGH RESPECT AND GRATEFUL AFFECTION,

BY THEIR FRIEND,

S. T. COLERIDGE.

October 7, 1818.
Highgate.

THE FRIEND.

ESSAY I.

Crede mihi, non est parvæ fiduciæ, polliceri opem decertantibus, consilium dubiis, lumen cæcis, spem dejectis, refrigerium fessis. Magna quidem hæc sunt, si fiant; parva, si promittantur. Verum ego non tam aliis legem ponam, quam legem vobis meæ propriæ mentis exponam; quam qui probaverit, teneat; cui non placuerit, abjiciat. Optarem, fateor, talis esse, qui prodesse possem quam plurimis. PETRARCH. *De vita solitaria.**

Believe me, it requires no little confidence, to promise help to the struggling, counsel to the doubtful, light to the blind, hope to the despondent, refreshment to the weary. These are indeed great things, if they be accomplished; trifles if they exist but in a promise. I, however, aim not so much to prescribe a law for others, as to set forth the law of my own mind; which let the man, who shall have approved of it, abide by; and let him, to whom it shall appear not reasonable, reject it. It is my earnest wish, I confess, to employ my understanding and acquirements in that mode and direction, in which I may be enabled to benefit the largest number possible of my fellow-creatures.

ANTECEDENTLY to all history, and long glimmering through it as a holy tradition, there presents itself to our imagination an indefinite period, dateless as eternity; a state rather than a time. For even the sense of succession is lost in the uniformity of the stream.

It was toward the close of this golden age (the memory of which the self-dissatisfied race of men have everywhere preserved and cherished) when conscience acted in man with the ease and uniformity of instinct; when labor was a sweet name for the activity of sane minds in healthful bodies, and all enjoyed

* Lib. I. tract. iv. c. 4. Some clauses in the original are omitted, and one or two changes of words have been made, by the Author, in this quotation.—*Ed.*

in common the bounteous harvest produced, and gathered in, by common effort; when there existed in the sexes, and in the individuals of each sex, just variety enough to permit and call forth the gentle restlessness and final union of chaste love and individual attachment, each seeking and finding the beloved one by the natural affinity of their beings; when the dread Sovereign of the universe was known only as the universal parent, no altar but the pure heart, and thanksgiving and grateful love the sole sacrifice.——

In this blest age of dignified innocence, one of their honored elders, whose absence they were beginning to notice, entered with hurrying steps the place of their common assemblage at noon, and instantly attracted the general attention and wonder by the perturbation of his gestures, and by a strange trouble both in his eyes and over his whole countenance. After a short but deep silence, when the first buzz of varied inquiry was becoming audible, the old man moved toward a small eminence, and having ascended it, he thus addressed the hushed and listening company:—

"In the warmth of the approaching mid-day, as I was reposing in the vast cavern, out of which, from its northern portal, issues the river that winds through our vale, a voice powerful, yet not from its loudness, suddenly hailed me. Guided by my ear, I looked toward the supposed place of the sound for some form, from which it had proceeded. I beheld nothing but the glimmering walls of the cavern. Again, as I was turning round, the same voice hailed me: and whithersoever I turned my face, thence did the voice seem to proceed. I stood still, therefore, and in reverence awaited its continuation. 'Sojourner of earth!' (these were its words) 'hasten to the meeting of thy brethren, and the words which thou now hearest, the same do thou repeat unto them. On the thirtieth morn from the morrow's sunrising, and during the space of thrice three days and thrice three nights, a thick cloud will cover the sky, and a heavy rain fall on the earth. Go ye therefore, ere the thirtieth sun arise, retreat to the cavern of the river, and there abide, till the clouds have passed away, and the rain be over and gone. For know ye of a certainty that whomever that rain wetteth, on him, yea, on him and on his children's children will fall—the spirit of madness.'

Yes! madness was the word of the voice: what this be, I know not! But at the sound of the word trembling came upon me, and a feeling which I would not have had; and I remained even as ye beheld and now behold me."

The old man ended, and retired. Confused murmurs succeeded, and wonder, and doubt. Day followed day, and every day brought with it a diminution of the awe impressed. They could attach no image, no remembered sensations, to the threat. The ominous morn arrived, the prophet had retired to the appointed cavern, and there remained alone during the appointed time. On the tenth morning, he emerged from his place of shelter, and sought his friends and brethren. But alas! how affrightful the change! Instead of the common children of one great family, working toward the same aim by reason, even as the bees in their hives by instinct, he looked and beheld, here a miserable wretch watching over a heap of hard and innutritious small substances, which he had dug out of the earth, at the cost of mangled limbs and exhausted faculties. This he appeared to worship, at this he gazed, even as the youths of the vale had been accustomed to gaze at their chosen virgins in the first season of their choice. There he saw a former companion speeding on and panting after a butterfly, or a withered leaf whirling onward in the breeze; and another with pale and distorted countenance following close behind, and still stretching forth a dagger to stab his precursor in the back. In another place he observed a whole troop of his fellow-men famished and in fetters, yet led by one of their brethren who had enslaved them, and pressing furiously onward, in the hope of famishing and enslaving another troop moving in an opposite direction. For the first time, the prophet missed his accustomed power of distinguishing between his dreams and his waking perceptions. He stood gazing and motionless, when several of the race gathered around him, and inquired of each other, Who is this man? how strangely he looks! how wild!—a worthless idler! exclaims one: assuredly, a very dangerous madman! cries a second. In short, from words they proceeded to violence: till harassed, endangered, solitary in a world of forms like his own, without sympathy, without object of love, he at length espied in some foss or furrow a quantity of the maddening water still unevaporated, and uttering the last words of reason, IT IS IN VAIN TO BE SANE IN A

WORLD OF MADMEN, plunged and rolled himself in the liquid poison, and came out as mad as, and not more wretched than, his neighbors and acquaintances.

The plan of The Friend is comprised in the motto to this essay. This tale or allegory seems to me to contain the objections to its practicability in all their strength. Either, says the skeptic, you are the blind offering to lead the blind, or you are talking the language of sight to those who do not possess the sense of seeing. If you mean to be read, try to entertain, and do not pretend to instruct. To such objections it would be amply sufficient, on my system of faith, to answer, that we are not all blind, but all subject to distempers of the mental sight, differing in kind and in degree; that though all men are in error, they are not all in the same error, nor at the same time; and that each, therefore, may possibly heal the other, even as two or more physicians, all diseased in their general health, yet under the immediate action of the disease on different days, may remove or alleviate the complaints of each other. But in respect to the entertainingness of moral writings, if in entertainment be included whatever delights the imagination or affects the generous passions, so far from rejecting such a mean of persuading the human soul, my very system compels me to defend not only the propriety, but the absolute necessity, of adopting it, if we really intend to render our fellow-creatures better or wiser.

But it is with dullness as with obscurity. It may be positive, and the author's fault; but it may likewise be relative, and if the author has presented his bill of fare at the portal, the reader has himself only to blame. The main question then is, of what class are the persons to be entertained?—" One of the later school of the Grecians (says Lord Bacon) examineth the matter, and is at a stand to think what should be in it that men should love lies, where neither they make for pleasure, as with poets; nor for advantage, as with the merchant; but for the lie's sake. But I can not tell: this same truth is a naked and open daylight, that doth not show the masques and mummeries and triumphs of the world half so stately and daintily, as candle-lights. Truth may perhaps come to the price of a pearl, that showeth best by day; but it will not rise to the price of a diamond or carbuncle, that showeth best in varied lights. A mixture of a lie doth ever add pleasure. Doth any man doubt, that if there were taken from men's minds, vain opinions, flattering hopes, false valuations, imaginations as one would, and the like, but it would leave the minds of a number of men, poor shrunken things, full of melancholy and indisposition, and unpleasing to themselves?"*

A melancholy, a too general, but not, I trust, a universal truth!—and even where it does apply, yet in many instances not irremediable. Such at least must have been my persuasion; or the present volumes must have been wittingly written to no purpose. If I believed our nature fettered to all this wretchedness of head and heart by an absolute and innate necessity, at least by a necessity which no human power, no efforts of reason or eloquence, could remove or lessen; I should deem it even presumptuous to aim at other or higher object than that of amusing a small portion of the reading public.

And why not? whispers worldly prudence. To amuse, though only to amuse, our visitors is wisdom as well as good-nature, where it is presumption to attempt their amendment. And truly it would be most convenient to me in respects of no trifling importance, if I could persuade myself to take the advice. Released by these principles from all moral obligation, and ambitious of procuring pastime and self-oblivion for a race, which could have nothing noble to remember, nothing desirable to anticipate, I might aspire even to the praise of the critics and *dilettanti* of the higher circles of society; of some trusty guide of blind fashion; some pleasant analyst of taste, as it exists both in the palate and the soul; some living gauge and mete-wand of past and present genius. But alas! my former studies would still have left a wrong bias! If instead of perplexing my common sense with the flights of Plato, and of stiffening over the meditations of the imperial Stoic, I had been laboring to imbibe the gay spirit of a Casti, or had employed my erudition, for the benefit of the favored few, in elucidating the interesting deformities of ancient Greece and India, what might I not have hoped from the suffrage of those, who turn in weariness from the Paradise Lost, because compared with the prurient heroes and grotesque monsters of Italian romance, or even with the narrative dialogues of the melodious Metastasio, that adventurous song,

Which justifies the ways of God to man,—

---

* Essays. I. Of Truth.—*Ed.*

has been found a poor substitute for a Grimaldi, a most inapt medicine for an occasional propensity to yawn! For, as hath been decided, to fill up pleasantly the brief intervals of fashionable pleasures, and above all to charm away the dusky gnome of *ennui*, is the chief and appropriate business of the poet and the novelist! This duty unfulfilled, Apollo will have lavished his best gifts in vain; and Urania henceforth must be content to inspire astronomers alone, and leave the sons of verse to more amusing patronesses. And yet—and yet—but it will be time to be serious, when my visitors have sat down.

ESSAY II.

Sic oportet ad librum, presertim miscellanei generis, legendum accedere lectorem, ut solet ad convivium conviva civilis. Convivator annititur omnibus satisfacere: et tamen si quid apponitur, quod hujus aut illius palato non respondeat, et hic et ille urbane dissimulant, et alia fercula probant, ne quid contristent convivatorem. Quis enim eum convivam ferat, qui tantum hoc animo veniat ad mensam, ut carpens quæ apponunter, nec vescatur ipse, nec alios vesci sinat? Et tamen his quoque reperias inciviliores, qui palam, qui sine fine damnent ac lacerent opus, quod nunquam legerint. Ast hoc plusquam sycophanticum est damnare quod nescias. ERASMUS.

A reader should sit down to a book, especially of the miscellaneous kind, as a well-behaved visitor does to a banquet. The master of the feast exerts himself to satisfy all his guests; but if after all his care and pains there should still be something or other put on the table that does not suit this or that person's taste, they politely pass it over without noticing the circumstance, and commend other dishes, that they may not distress their kind host, or throw any damp on his spirits. For who could tolerate a guest that accepted an invitation to your table with no other purpose but that of finding fault with every thing put before him, neither eating himself, nor suffering others to eat in comfort. And yet you may fall in with a still worse set than even these, with churls that in all companies and without stop or stay, will condemn and pull to pieces a work which they have never read. But this sinks below the baseness of an informer, yea, though he were a false witness to boot! The man, who abuses a thing of which he is utterly ignorant, unites the infamy of both—and in addition to this, makes himself the pander and sycophant of his own and other men's envy and malignity.

THE musician may tune his instrument in private, ere his audience have yet assembled; the architect conceals the foundation of his building beneath the superstructure. But an author's harp must be tuned in the hearing of those, who are to understand its after-harmonies; the foundation stones of his edifice must lie open to common view, or his friends will hesitate to trust themselves beneath the roof.

From periodical literature the general reader deems himself

entitled to expect amusement, and some degree of information, and if the writer can convey any instruction at the same time, and without demanding any additional thought (as the Irishman, in the hackneyed jest, is said to have passed off a light guinea between two good halfpence), this supererogatory merit will not perhaps be taken amiss. Now amusement in and for itself may be afforded by the gratification either of the curiosity or of the passions. I use the former word as distinguished from the love of knowledge, and the latter in distinction from those emotions which arise in well-ordered minds, from the perception of truth or falsehood, virtue or vice :—emotions, which are always preceded by thought, and linked with improvement. Again, all information pursued without any wish of becoming wiser or better thereby, I class among the gratifications of mere curiosity, whether it be sought for in a light novel or a grave history. We may therefore omit the word information, as included either in amusement or instruction.

The present work is an experiment; not whether a writer may honestly overlook the one, or successfully omit the other, of the two elements themselves, which serious readers at least persuade themselves that they pursue; but whether a change might not be hazarded of the usual order, in which periodical writers have in general attempted to convey them. Having myself experienced that no delight either in kind or degree is equal to that which accompanies the distinct perception of a fundamental truth, relative to our moral being; having, long after the completion of what is ordinarily called a learned education, discovered a new world of intellectual profit opening on me—not from any new opinions, but lying, as it were, at the roots of those which I had been taught in childhood in my catechism and spelling-book; there arose a soothing hope in my mind that a lesser public might be found, composed of persons susceptible of the same delight, and desirous of attaining it by the same process. I heard a whisper too from within, (I trust that it proceeded from conscience, not vanity) that a duty was performed in the endeavor to render it as much easier to them, than it had been to me, as could be effected by the united efforts of my understanding and imagination.

Actuated by this impulse, the writer wishes, in the following essays, to convey not instruction merely, but fundamental instruction; not so much to show the reader this or that fact, as to kindle his own torch for him, and leave it to himself to choose the particular objects, which he might wish to examine by its light. The Friend does not indeed exclude from his plan occasional interludes, and vacations of innocent entertainment and promiscuous information, but still in the main he proposes to himself the communication of such delight as rewards the march of truth, rather than to collect the flowers which diversify its track, in order to present them apart from the homely, yet foodful or medicinal herbs, among which they had grown. To refer men's opinions to their absolute principles, and thence their feelings to the appropriate objects, and in their due degrees; and finally, to apply the principles thus ascertained, to the formation of steadfast convictions concerning the most important questions of politics, morality, and religion—these are to be the objects and the contents of his work.

Themes like these not even the genius of a Plato or a Bacon could render intelligible, without demanding from the reader thought sometimes, and attention generally. By thought I here mean the voluntary production in our own minds of those states of consciousness, to which, as to his fundamental facts, the writer has referred us: while attention has for its object the order and connection of thoughts and images, each of which is in itself already and familiarly known. Thus the elements of geometry require attention only; but the analysis of our primary faculties, and the investigation of all the absolute grounds of religion and morals, are impossible without energies of thought in addition to the effort of attention. The Friend will not attempt to disguise from his readers that both attention and thought are efforts, and the latter a most difficult and laborious effort; nor from himself, that to require it often or for any continuance of time, is incompatible with the nature of the present publication, even were it less incongruous than it unfortunately is with the present habits and pursuits of Englishmen. Accordingly I shall be on my guard to make the essays as few as possible, which would require from a well-educated reader any energy of thought and voluntary abstraction.

But attention, I confess, will be requisite throughout, except in the excursive and miscellaneous essays that will be found interposed between each of the three main divisions of the work. On whatever subject the mind feels a lively interest, attention, though always an effort, becomes a delightful effort. I should be quite at ease, could I secure for the whole work as much of it, as a card party of earnest whist-players often expend in a single evening, or a lady in the making-up of a fashionable dress. But where no interest previously exists, attention (as every school-master knows) can be procured only by terror: which is the true reason why the majority of mankind learn nothing systematically, except as school-boys or apprentices.

Happy shall I be, from other motives besides those of self-interest, if no fault or deficiency on my part shall prevent the work from furnishing a presumptive proof, that there are still to be found among us a respectable number of readers who are desirous to derive pleasure from the consciousness of being instructed or meliorated: and who feel a sufficient interest as to the foundations of their own opinions in literature, politics, morals, and religion, to afford that degree of attention, without which, however men may deceive themselves, no actual progress ever was or ever can be made in that knowledge, which supplies at once both strength and nourishment.

ESSAY III.

Αλλ' ὡς παρέλαβον τὴν τέχνην παρὰ σοῦ, τὸ πρῶτον μὲν εὐθὺς
Οἰδοῦσαν υπὸ κομπασμάτων, καὶ ῥημάτων ἐπαχθῶν,
Ἴσχνανα μὲν πρώτιστον αὐτὴν, καὶ τὸ βάρος ἀφεῖλον,
Ἐπυλλίοις καὶ περιπάτοις καὶ τευτλίοισι μικροῖς
Χυλὸν διδοὺς στωμυλμάτων, ἀπὸ βιβλίων, ἀπ' ἠθῶν.

ARISTOPH. RANÆ. 939.

IMITATION.*

When I received the Muse from you, I found her puffed and pampered,
With pompous sentences and terms, a cumbrous huge virago.
My first attention was applied to make her look genteelly,
And bring her to a moderate bulk by dint of lighter diet,
I fed her with plain household phrase, and cool familiar salad,
With water-gruel episode, with sentimental jelly,
With moral mince-meat: till at length I brought her within compass.

FRERE.

IN the preceding essay I named the present undertaking an experiment. The explanation will be found in the following letter, written to a correspondent during the first attempt, and before the plan was discontinued from an original error in the mode of circulation.

TO ———.

When I first undertook the present publication for the sake and with the avowed object of referring men in all things to principles or fundamental truths, I was well aware of the obstacles which the plan itself would oppose to my success. For in

* This imitation is printed here by permission of the author, from a series of free translations of selected scenes from Aristophanes: a work, of which (should the author be persuaded to make it public) it is my deliberate judgment, that it will form an important epoch in English literature, and open out sources of metrical and rhythmical wealth in the very heart of our language, of which few, if any, among us are aware.

order to the regular attainment of this object, all the dryest and least attractive essays must appear in the beginning, and thus subject me to the necessity of demanding effort or soliciting patience in that part of the work, where it was most my interest to secure the confidence of my readers by winning their favor. Though I dared warrant for the pleasantness of the journey on the whole; though I might promise that the road would, for the far greater part of it, be found plain and easy, that it would pass through countries of various prospect, and that at every stage there would be a change of company; it still remained a heavy disadvantage, that I had to start at the foot of a high and steep hill: and I foresaw, not without occasional feelings of despondency, that during the slow and laborious ascent it would require no common management to keep my passengers in good-humor with the vehicle and its driver. As far as this inconvenience could be palliated by sincerity and previous confession, I have no reason to accuse myself of neglect. In the prospectus* of The Friend, which for this cause I reprinted and annexed to the first essay, I felt it my duty to inform such as might be inclined to patronize the publication, that I must submit to be esteemed dull by those who sought chiefly for amusement: and this I hazarded as a general confession, though in my own mind I felt a cheerful confidence that it would apply almost exclusively to the earlier essays. I could not therefore be surprised, however much I may have been depressed, by the frequency with which you hear The Friend complained of for its abstruseness and obscurity; nor did the highly flattering expressions, with which you accompanied your communication, prevent me from feeling its truth to the whole extent.

An author's pen, like children's legs, improves by exercise. That part of the blame which rests on myself, I am exerting my best faculties to remove. A man long accustomed to silent and solitary meditation, in proportion as he increases the power of thinking in long and connected trains, is apt to lose or lessen the talent of communicating his thoughts with grace and perspicuity. Doubtless too, I have in some measure injured my style, in respect to its facility and popularity, from having almost confined my reading, of late years, to the works of the ancients and those of the elder writers in the modern languages. We insensibly imitate

* See Appendix A.—*Ed.*

what we habitually admire; and an aversion to the epigrammatic unconnected periods of the fashionable Anglo-Gallican taste has too often made me willing to forget, that the stately march and difficult evolutions, which characterize the eloquence of Hooker, Bacon, Milton, and Jeremy Taylor, are, notwithstanding their intrinsic excellence, still less suited to a periodical essay. This fault I am now endeavoring to correct; though I can never so far sacrifice my judgment to the desire of being immediately popular, as to cast my sentences in the French moulds, or affect a style which an ancient critic would have deemed purposely invented for persons troubled with the asthma to read, and for those to comprehend who labor under the more pitiable asthma of a short-witted intellect. It can not but be injurious to the human mind never to be called into effort: the habit of receiving pleasure without any exertion of thought, by the mere excitement of curiosity and sensibility, may be justly ranked among the worst effects of habitual novel reading. It is true that these short and unconnected sentences are easily and instantly understood: but it is equally true, that wanting all the cement of thought as well as of style, all the connections, and (if you will forgive so trivial a metaphor) all the hooks-and-eyes of the memory, they are easily forgotten: or rather, it is scarcely possible that they should be remembered.—Nor is it less true, that those who confine their reading to such books dwarf their own faculties, and finally reduce their understandings to a deplorable imbecility: the fact you mention, and which I shall hereafter make use of, is a fair instance and a striking illustration. Like idle morning visitors, the brisk and breathless periods hurry in and hurry off in quick and profitless succession; each indeed for the moments of its stay prevents the pain of vacancy, while it indulges the love of sloth; but all together they leave the mistress of the house (the soul, I mean) flat and exhausted, incapable of attending to her own concerns, and unfitted for the conversation of more rational guests.

I know you will not suspect me of fostering so idle a hope, as that of obtaining acquittal by recrimination; or think that I am attacking one fault, in order that its opposite may escape notice in the noise and smoke of the battery. On the contrary, I shall do my best, and even make all allowable sacrifices, to render my manner more attractive and my matter more generally interesting. In the establishment of principles and fundamental doctrines, I must of necessity require the attention of my reader to become my fellow-laborer. The primary facts essential to the intelligibility of my principles I can prove to others only as far as I can prevail on them to retire into themselves and make their own minds the objects of their steadfast attention. But, on the other hand, I feel too deeply the importance of the convictions, which first impelled me to the present undertaking, to leave unattempted any honorable means of recommending them to as wide a circle as possible.

Hitherto I have been employed in laying the foundation of my work. But the proper merit of a foundation is its massiveness and solidity. The conveniences and ornaments, the gilding and stucco work, the sunshine and sunny prospects, will come with the superstructure. Yet I dare not flatter myself, that any endeavors of mine, compatible with the duty I owe to truth and the hope of permanent utility, will render The Friend agreeable to the majority of what is called the reading public. I never expected it. How indeed could I, when I was to borrow so little from the influence of passing events, and when I had absolutely excluded from my plan all appeals to personal curiosity and personal interests? Yet even this is not my greatest impediment. No real information can be conveyed, no important errors rectified, no widely injurious prejudices rooted up, without requiring some effort of thought on the part of the reader. But the obstinate (and toward a contemporary writer, the contemptuous) aversion to intellectual effort is the mother evil of all which I had proposed to war against, the queen bee in the hive of our errors and misfortunes, both private and national. To solicit the attention of those, on whom these debilitating causes have acted to their full extent, would be no less absurd than to recommend exercise with the dumb-bells, as the only mode of cure, to a patient paralytic in both arms. You well know, that my expectations were more modest as well as more rational. I hoped, that my readers in general would be aware of the impracticability of suiting every essay to every taste in any period of the work; and that they would not attribute wholly to the author, but in part to the necessity of his plan, the austerity and absence of the lighter graces in the first fifteen or twenty numbers. In my cheerful moods I sometimes flattered myself, that a few even among those, who foresaw that my lucubrations would at all times require more attention than from the nature of their own employments they could afford them, might yet find a pleasure in supporting The Friend during its infancy, so as to give it a chance of attracting the notice of others, to whom its style and subjects might be better adapted. But my main anchor was the hope, that when circumstances gradually enabled me to adopt the ordinary means of making the publication generally known, there might be found throughout the kingdom a sufficient number of meditative minds, who, entertaining similar convictions with myself, and gratified by the prospect of seeing them reduced to form and system, would take a warm interest in the work from the very circumstance, that it wanted those allurements of transitory interests, which render particular patronage superfluous, and for the brief season of their blow and fragrance attract the eye of thousands, who would pass unregarded

————————flowers
Of sober tint, and herbs of med'cinable powers.

In these three introductory essays, the Friend has endeavored to realize his promise of giving an honest bill of fare, both as to the objects and the style of the work. With reference to both I conclude with a prophecy of Simon Grynæus, from his premonition to the candid reader, prefixed to Ficinus's translation of Plato, published at Leyden, 1557. How far it has been gradually fulfilled in this country since the Revolution in 1688, I leave to my candid and intelligent readers to determine :—

Ac dolet mihi quidem deliciis literarum inescatos subito jam homines adeo esse, præsertim qui Christianos se profitentur, ut legere nisi quod ad presentem gustum *facit, sustineant nihil: unde et disciplinæ et philosophia ipsa jam fere prorsus etiam a doctis negliguntur. Quod quidem propositum studiorum nisi mature corrigetur, tam magnum rebus incommodum dabit, quam dedit barbaries olim. Pertinax res barbaries est, fateor; sed minus potest tamen, quam illa persuasa prudentia literarum si ratione caret, sapientiæ virtutisque specie misere* lectores *circumducens.* * * *

Succedet igitur, ut arbitror, haud ita multo post, pro rusti-

*cana sæculi nostri ruditate, captatrix illa blandiloquentia, robur animi virilis omne, omnem virtutem masculam, profligatura, nisi cavetur.**

In very truth, it grieveth me that men, those especially who profess themselves to be Christians, should be so taken with the sweet baits of literature that they can endure to read nothing but what gives them immediate gratification, no matter how low or sensual it may be. Consequently, the more austere and disciplinary branches of philosophy itself are almost wholly neglected, even by the learned.—A course of study (if such reading, with such a purpose in view, could deserve that name) which, if not corrected in time, will occasion worse consequences than even barbarism did in the times of our forefathers. Barbarism is, I own, a wilful headstrong thing; but with all its blind obstinacy it has less power of doing harm than this self-sufficient, self-satisfied plain good common sense sort of writing, this prudent saleable popular style of composition, if it be deserted by reason and scientific insight pitiably decoying the minds of men by an imposing show of amiableness, and practical wisdom, so that the delighted reader knowing nothing knows all about almost every thing. There will succeed, therefore, in my opinion, and that too within no long time, to the rudeness and rusticity of our age, that ensnaring meretricious popularness in literature, with all the tricksy humilities of the ambitious candidates for the favorable suffrages of the judicious public, which if we do not take good care will break up and scatter before it all robustness and manly vigor of intellect, all masculine fortitude of virtue.

* In the original of this passage, the words *gulam* and *mortales* stand respectively for *præsentem gustum* and *lectores.—Ed.*

ESSAY IV.

Si modò quæ natura et ratione concessa sint, assumpserimus, præsumptionis suspicio a nobis quam longissime abesse debet. Multa antiquitati, nobismet nihil, arrogamus. Nihilne vos? Nihil mehercule, nisi quod omnia omni animo veritati arrogamus et sanctimoniæ.

ULR. RINOV. De Controversiis.

If we assume only what nature and reason have granted, with no shadow of right can we be suspected of presumption. To antiquity we arrogate many things, to ourselves nothing. Nothing? Aye, nothing: unless indeed it be, that with all our strength we arrogate all things to truth and moral purity.

IT has been remarked by the celebrated Haller, that we are deaf while we are yawning. The same act of drowsiness that stretches open our mouths, closes our ears. It is much the same in acts of the understanding. A lazy half-attention amounts to a mental yawn. Where then a subject, that demands thought, has been thoughtfully treated, and with an exact and patient derivation from its principles, we must be willing to exert a portion of the same effort, and to think with the author, or the author will have thought in vain for us. It makes little difference for the time being, whether there be an *hiatus oscitans* in the reader's attention, or an *hiatus lacrymabilis* in the author's manuscript. When this occurs during the perusal of a work of known authority and established fame, we honestly lay the fault on our own deficiency, or on the unfitness of our present mood; but when it is a contemporary production, over which we have been nodding, it is far more pleasant to pronounce it insufferably dull and obscure. Indeed, as charity begins at home, it would be unreasonable to expect that a reader should charge himself with lack of intellect, when the effect may be equally well accounted for by declaring the author unintelligible; or that he should accuse his own inattention, when by half a dozen phrases of abuse, as "heavy stuff, metaphysical jargon," &c., he can at once excuse his laziness, and gratify his pride, scorn, and envy. To similar impulses we must attribute the praises of a true modern reader, when he meets with a work in the true modern taste: namely, either in skipping, unconnected, short-winded, asthmatic sentences, as easy to be understood as impossible to be remembered, in which the merest common-place acquires a momentary poignancy, a petty titillating sting, from affected point and wilful antithesis; or else in strutting and rounded periods, in which the emptiest truisms are blown up into illustrious bubbles by help of film and inflation. "Aye!" (quoth the delighted reader) "this is sense, this is genius! this I understand and admire! I have thought the very same a hundred times myself!" In other words, this man has reminded me of my own cleverness, and therefore I admire him. Oh! for one piece of egotism that presents itself under its own honest bare face of I myself I, there are fifty that steal out in the mask of *tu-isms* and *ille-isms!*

It has ever been my opinion, that an excessive solicitude to avoid the use of our first personal pronoun, more often has its source in conscious selfishness than in true self-oblivion. A quiet observer of human follies may often amuse or sadden his thoughts by detecting a perpetual feeling of purest egotism through a long masquerade of disguises, the half of which, had old Proteus been master of as many, would have wearied out the patience of Menelaus. I say, the patience only: for it would ask more than the simplicity of Polypheme, with his one eye extinguished, to be deceived by so poor a repetition of Nobody. Yet I can with strictest truth assure my readers that with a pleasure combined with a sense of weariness, I see the nigh approach of that point of my labors, in which I can convey my opinions and the workings of my heart, without reminding the reader obtrusively of myself. But the frequency with which I have spoken in my own person, recalls my apprehensions to the second danger, which it was my hope to guard against; the probable charge of arrogance, or presumption, both for daring to dissent from the opinions of great authorities, and, in my following numbers perhaps, from the general opinion concerning the true value of certain authorities deemed great. The word presumption, I appropriate to the internal feeling, and arrogance to the way and manner of outwardly expressing ourselves.

As no man can rightfully be condemned without reference to some definite law, by the knowledge of which he might have avoided the given fault, it is necessary so to define the constituent qualities and conditions of arrogance, that a reason may be assignable why we pronounce one man guilty and acquit another. For merely to call a person arrogant or most arrogant, can convict no one of the vice except perhaps the accuser. I remember, when a young man who had left his books and a glass of water to join a convivial party, each of whom had nearly finished his second bottle, was pronounced very drunk by the whole party—he looked so strange and pale! Many a man, who has contrived to hide his ruling passion or predominant defect from himself, will betray the same to dispassionate observers, by his proneness on all occasions to suspect or accuse others of it. Now arrogance and presumption, like all other moral qualities, must be shown by some act or conduct: and this too must be an act that implies, if not an immediate concurrence of the will, yet some faulty constitution of the moral habits. For all criminality supposes its essentials to have been within the power of the agent. Either, therefore, the facts adduced do of themselves convey the whole proof of the charge, and the question rests on the truth or accuracy with which they have been stated; or they acquire their character from the circumstances. I have looked into a ponderous review of the corpuscular philosophy by a Sicilian Jesuit, in which the acrimonious Father frequently expresses his doubt, whether he should pronounce Boyle or Newton more impious than presumptuous, or more presumptuous than impious. They had both attacked the reigning opinions on most important subjects, opinions sanctioned by the greatest names of antiquity, and by the general suffrage of their learned contemporaries or immediate predecessors. Locke was assailed with a full cry for his presumption in having deserted the philosophical system at that time generally received by the universities of Europe; and of late years Dr. Priestley bestowed the epithets of arrogant and insolent on Reid, Beattie, &c., for presuming to arraign certain opinions of Mr. Locke, himself repaid in kind by many of his own countrymen for his theological novelties. It will scarcely be affirmed, that these accusations were all of them just, or that any of them were fit or courteous. Must we therefore say, that in order to avow doubt or disbelief of a popular persuasion without arrogance, it is required that the dissentient should know himself to possess the genius, and foreknow that he should acquire the reputation, of Locke, Newton, Boyle, or even of a Reid or Beattie? But as this knowledge and prescience are impossible in the strict sense of the words, and could mean no more than a strong inward conviction, it is manifest that such a rule, if it were universally established, would encourage the presumptuous, and condemn modest and humble minds alone to silence. And as this silence could not acquit the individual's own mind of presumption, unless it were accompanied by conscious acquiescence; modesty itself must become an inert quality, which even in private society never displays its charms more unequivocally than in its mode of reconciling moral deference with intellectual courage, and general diffidence with sincerity in the avowal of the particular conviction.

We must seek then elsewhere for the true marks, by which presumption or arrogance may be detected, and on which the charge may be grounded with little hazard of mistake or injustice. And as I confine my present observations to literature, I deem such *criteria* neither difficult to determine nor to apply. The first mark, as it appears to me, is a frequent bare assertion of opinions not generally received, without condescending to prefix or annex the facts and reasons on which such opinions were formed; especially if this absence of logical courtesy is supplied by contemptuous or abusive treatment of such as happen to doubt of, or oppose, the decisive *ipse dixi*. But to assert, however nakedly, that a passage in a lewd novel, in which the Sacred Writings are denounced as more likely to pollute the young and innocent mind than a romance notorious for its indecency—to assert, I say, that such a passage argues equal impudence and ignorance in its author, at the time of writing and publishing it—this is not arrogance; although to a vast majority of the decent part of our countrymen it would be superfluous as a truism, if it were exclusively an author's business to convey or revive knowledge, and not sometimes his duty to awaken the indignation of his reader by the expression of his own.

A second species of this unamiable quality, which has been often distinguished by the name of Warburtonian arrogance, betrays itself, not as in the former, by proud or petulant omission of proof or argument, but by the habit of ascribing weakness of intellect, or want of taste and sensibility, or hardness of heart, or corruption of moral principle, to all who deny the truth of the doctrine, or the sufficiency of the evidence, or the fairness of the reasoning adduced in its support. This is indeed not essentially different from the first, but assumes a separate character from its accompaniments: for though both the doctrine and its proofs may have been legitimately supplied by the understanding, yet the bitterness of personal crimination will resolve itself into naked assertion. We are, therefore, authorized by experience, and justified on the principle of self-defence and by the law of fair retaliation, in attributing it to a vicious temper arrogant from irritability, or irritable from arrogance. This learned arrogance admits of many gradations, and is aggravated or palliated, accordingly as the point in dispute has been more or less controverted, as the reasoning bears a smaller or greater proportion to the virulence of the personal detraction, and as the person or parties, who are the objects of it, are more or less respected, more or less worthy of respect.*

Lastly, it must be admitted as a just imputation of presumption

* Had the author of the Divine Legation of Moses more skilfully appropriated his coarse eloquence of abuse, his customary assurances of the idiocy, both in head and heart, of all his opponents; if he had employed those vigorous arguments of his own vehement humor in the defence of truths acknowledged and reverenced by learned men in general; or if he had confined them to the names of Chubb, Woolston, and other precursors of Thomas Paine; we should perhaps still characterize his mode of controversy by its rude violence, but not so often have heard his name used, even by those who have never read his writings, as a proverbial expression for learned arrogance. But when a novel and doubtful hypothesis of his own formation was the citadel to be defended, and his mephitic hand-granados were thrown with the fury of lawless despotism at the fair reputation of a Sykes and a Lardner, we not only confirm the verdict of his independent contemporaries, but cease to wonder, that arrogance should render men objects of contempt in many, and of aversion in all, instances, when it was capable of hurrying a Christian teacher of equal talents and learning into a slanderous vulgarity, which escapes our disgust only when we see the writer's own reputation the sole victim. But throughout his great work, and the pamphlets in which he supported it, he always seems to write as if he had deemed it a duty of decorum to publish his fancies on the Mosaic Law as the Law itself was delivered, that is, in thunders and lightnings: or as if he had applied to his own book instead of the sacred mount, the menace,—*There shall not a hand touch it but he shall surely be stoned or shot through.*

when an individual obtrudes on the public eye, with all the high pretensions of originality, opinions and observations, in regard to which he must plead wilful ignorance in order to be acquitted of dishonest plagiarism. On the same seat must the writer be placed, who in a disquisition on any important subject proves, by falsehoods either of omission or of positive error, that he has neglected to possess himself, not only of the information requisite for this particular subject; but even of those acquirements, and that general knowledge, which could alone authorize him to commence a public instructor. This is an office which can not be procured *gratis*. The industry, necessary for the due exercise of its functions, is its purchase-money; and the absence or insufficiency of the same is so far a species of dishonesty, and implies a presumption in the literal as well as the ordinary sense of the word. He has taken a thing before he had acquired any right or title thereto.

If in addition to this unfitness which every man possesses the means of ascertaining, his aim should be to unsettle a general belief closely connected with public and private quiet; and if his language and manner be avowedly calculated for the illiterate, and perhaps licentious, part of his countrymen; disgusting as his presumption must appear, it is yet lost or evanescent in the close neighborhood of his guilt. That Hobbes translated Homer into English verse and published his translation, furnishes no positive evidence of his self-conceit, though it implies a great lack of self-knowledge and of acquaintance with the nature of poetry.* A strong wish often imposes itself on the mind for an actual power: the mistake is favored by the innocent pleasure derived from the exercise of versification, perhaps by the approbation of intimates; and the candidate asks from more impartial readers that sentence, which nature has not enabled him to anticipate. But when the philosopher of Malmesbury waged war with Wallis and the fundamental truths of pure geometry, every instance of his gross ignorance and utter misconception of the very elements of the science he proposed to confute, furnished an unanswerable fact in

* At the time I wrote this essay, and indeed till the present month, December, 1818, I had never seen Hobbes' translation of the Odyssey, which, I now find, is by no means to be spoken of contemptuously. It is doubtless as much too ballad-like, as the later versions are too epic; but still, on the whole, it leaves a much truer impression of the original.

proof of his high presumption; and the confident and insulting language of the attack leaves the judicious reader in as little doubt of his gross arrogance. An illiterate mechanic, who mistaking some disturbance of his nerves for a miraculous call proceeds alone to convert a tribe of savages, whose language he can have no natural means of acquiring, may have been misled by impulses very different from those of high self-opinion; but the illiterate perpetrator of the 'Age of Reason' must have had his very conscience stupefied by the habitual intoxication of presumptuous arrogance, and his common sense over-clouded by the vapors from his heart.

As long therefore as I obtrude no unsupported assertions on my readers; and as long as I state my opinions and the evidence which induced or compelled me to adopt them, with calmness and that diffidence in myself, which is by no means incompatible with a firm belief in the justness of the opinions themselves; while I attack no man's private life from any cause, and detract from no man's honors in his public character, from the truth of his doctrines, or the merits of his compositions, without detailing all my reasons and resting the result solely on the arguments adduced; while I moreover explain fully the motives of duty, which influenced me in resolving to institute such investigation; while I confine all asperity of censure, and all expressions of contempt, to gross violations of truth, honor, and decency, to the base corrupter and the detected slanderer; while I write on no subject, which I have not studied with my best attention, on no subject which my education and acquirements have incapacitated me from properly understanding; and above all while I approve myself, alike in praise and in blame, in close reasoning and in impassioned declamation, a steady friend to the two best and surest friends of all men, truth and honesty; I will not fear an accusation of either presumption or arrogance from the good and the wise, I shall pity it from the weak, and welcome it from the wicked.

ESSAY V.

In eodem pectore nullum est honestorum turpiumque consortium: et cogitare optima simul ac deterrima non magis est unius animi quam ejusdem hominis bonum esse ac malum. QUINCTILIAN.*

There is no fellowship of honor and baseness in the same breast; and to combine the best and the worst designs is no more possible in one mind, than it is for the same man to be at the same instant virtuous and vicious.

Cognitio veritatis omnia falsa, si modo proferantur, etiam quæ prius inaudita erant, et dijudicare et subvertere idonea est. AUGUSTIN.

A knowledge of the truth is equal to the task both of discerning and of confuting all false assertions and erroneous arguments, though never before met with, if only they may freely be brought forward.

I HAVE said, that my very system compels me to make every fair appeal to the feelings, the imagination, and even the fancy. If these are to be withholden from the service of truth, virtue, and happiness, to what purpose were they given? In whose service are they retained? I have indeed considered the disproportion of human passions to their ordinary objects among the strongest internal evidence of our future destination, and the attempt to restore them to their rightful claimants, the most imperious duty and the noblest task of genius. The verbal enunciation of this master truth could scarcely be new to me at any period of my life since earliest youth; but I well remember the particular time, when the words first became more than words to me, when they incorporated with a living conviction, and took their place among the realities of my being. On some wide common or open heath, peopled with ant-hills, during some one of the gray cloudy days of late autumn, many of my readers may have noticed the effect of a sudden and momentary flash of sunshine on all the countless

* XII. 1. 4.—*Ed.*

little animals within his view, aware too that the self-same influence was darted co-instantaneously over all their swarming cities as far as his eye could reach; may have observed, with what a kindly force the gleam stirs and quickens them all, and will have experienced no unpleasurable shock of feeling in seeing myriads of myriads of living and sentient beings united at the same moment in one gay sensation, one joyous activity! But awful indeed is the same appearance in a multitude of rational beings, our fellow-men, in whom too the effect is produced not so much by the external occasion as from the active quality of their own thoughts. I had walked from Göttingen in the year 1799, to witness the arrival of the Queen of Prussia, on her visit to the Baron Von Hartzberg's seat, five miles from the University. The spacious outer court of the palace was crowded with men and women, a sea of heads, with a number of children rising out of it from their fathers' shoulders. After a buzz of two hours' expectation, the avant-courier rode at full speed into the court. At the loud cracks of his long whip and the trampling of his horse's hoofs, the universal shock and thrill of emotion—I have not language to convey it—expressed as it was in such manifold looks, gestures, and attitudes, yet with one and the same feeling in the eyes of all! Recovering from the first inevitable contagion of sympathy, I involuntarily exclaimed, though in a language to myself alone intelligible, "O man! ever nobler than thy circumstances! Spread but the mist of obscure feeling over any form, and even a woman incapable of blessing or of injuring thee shall be welcomed with an intensity of emotion adequate to the reception of the Redeemer of the world!"

To a creature so highly, so fearfully gifted,—who, alienated as he is by a sorcery scarcely less mysterious than the nature on which it is exercised, yet, like the fabled son of Jove in the evil day of his sensual bewitchment, lifts the spindles and distaffs of Omphale with the arm of a giant—to such a creature truth is self-restoration: for that which is the correlative of truth, the existence of absolute life, is the only object which can attract toward it the whole depth and mass of his fluctuating being, and alone therefore can unite calmness with elevation. But it must be truth without alloy and unsophisticated. It is by the agency of indistinct conceptions, as the counterfeits of the ideal and transcendant, that evil and vanity exercise their tyranny on the feelings of man. The powers of darkness are politic if not wise; but surely nothing can be more irrational in the pretended children of light, than to enlist themselves under the banners of truth, and yet rest their hopes on an alliance with delusion.

As one among the numerous artifices, by which austere truths are to be softened down into palatable falsehoods, and virtue and vice, like the atoms of Epicurus, to receive that insensible *clinamen* which is to make them meet each other half-way, I have an especial dislike to the expression, pious frauds. Piety indeed shrinks from the very phrase, as an attempt to mix poison with the cup of blessing: while the expediency of the measures which the words were intended to recommend or palliate, appears more and more suspicious, as the range of our experience widens, and our acquaintance with the records of history becomes more extensive and accurate. One of the most seductive arguments of infidelity grounds itself on the numerous passages in the works of the Christian Fathers, asserting the lawfulness of deceit for a good purpose. For how can we rely on their testimony concerning the supernatural facts? That the Fathers held, almost without exception, that "wholly without breach of duty it is allowed to the teachers and heads of the Christian Church to employ artifices, to intermix falsehoods with truths, and especially to deceive the enemies of the faith, provided only they hereby serve the interests of truth and the advantage of mankind,"* is the unwilling confession of RIBOF. St. Jerome, as is shown by the citations of this learned theologian, boldly attributes this management—*falsitatem dispensativam*—even to the Apostles themselves. But why speak I of the advantage given to the opponents of Christianity? Alas!

* *De œconom. Patrum. Integrum omnino doctoribus et cœtus Christiani antistitibus esse, ut dolos versent, falsa veris intermisceant, et imprimis religionis hostes fallant, dummodo veritatis commodis et utilitati inserviant.*—I trust, I need not add, that the imputation of such principles of action to the first inspired propagators of Christianity, is founded on a gross misconstruction of those passages in the writings of St. Paul, in which the necessity of employing different arguments to men of different capacities and prejudices, is supposed and acceded to. In other words, St. Paul strove to speak intelligibly, willingly sacrificed indifferent things to matters of importance, and acted courteously as a man, in order to win attention as an Apostle. A traveller prefers for daily use the coin of the nation through which he is passing, to bullion or the mintage of his own country: and is this to justify a succeeding traveller in the use of counterfeit coin?

to this doctrine chiefly, and to the practices derived from it, we must attribute the utter corruption of the religion itself for so many ages, and even now over so large a portion of the civilized world. By a system of accommodating truth to falsehood, the pastors of the Church gradually changed the life and light of the Gospel into the very superstitions which they were commissioned to disperse, and thus paganized Christianity in order to christen Paganism. At this very hour Europe groans and bleeds in consequence.

So much in proof and exemplification of the probable expediency of pious deception, as suggested by its known and recorded consequences. An honest man, however, possesses a clearer light than that of history. He knows, that by sacrificing the law of his reason to the maxim of pretended prudence, he purchases the sword with the loss of the arm that is to wield it. The duties which we owe to our own moral being, are the ground and condition of all other duties; and to set our nature at strife with itself for a good purpose, implies the same sort of prudence, as a priest of Diana would have manifested, who should have proposed to dig up the celebrated charcoal foundations of the mighty temple of Ephesus, in order to furnish fuel for the burnt-offerings on its altars. Truth, virtue, and happiness, may be distinguished from each other, but can not be divided. They subsist by a mutual co-inherence, which gives a shadow of divinity even to our human nature. *Will ye speak wickedly for God; and talk deceitfully for him?** is a searching question, which most affectingly represents the grief and impatience of an uncorrupted mind at perceiving a good cause defended by ill means: and assuredly if any temptation can provoke a well-regulated temper to intolerance, it is the shameless assertion, that truth and falsehood are indifferent in their own natures; that the former is as often injurious (and therefore criminal) as the latter, and the latter on many occasions as beneficial (and consequently meritorious) as the former.

I feel it incumbent on me, therefore, to place immediately before my readers in the fullest and clearest light, the whole question of moral obligation respecting the communication of truth, its extent and conditions. I would fain obviate all apprehensions either of my incaution on the one hand, or of any insincere

* Job xiii. 7.—*Ed.*

reserve on the other, by proving that the more strictly we adhere to the letter of the moral law in this respect, the more completely shall we reconcile that law with prudence; thus securing a purity in the principle without mischief from the practice. I would not, I could not dare, address my countrymen as a friend, if I might not justify the assumption of that sacred title by more than mere veracity, by open-heartedness. Pleasure, most often delusive, may be born of delusion. Pleasure, herself a sorceress, may pitch her tents on enchanted ground. But happiness (or, to use a far more accurate as well as more comprehensive term, solid well-being) can be built on virtue alone, and must of necessity have truth for its foundation. Add, too, the known fact that the meanest of men feels himself insulted by an unsuccessful attempt to deceive him; and hates and despises the man who has attempted it. What place then is left in the heart for virtue to build on, if in any case we may dare practise on others what we should feel as a cruel and contemptuous wrong in our own persons? Every parent possesses the opportunity of observing how deeply children resent the injury of a delusion; and if men laugh at the falsehoods that were imposed on themselves during their childhood, it is because they are not good and wise enough to contemplate the past in the present, and so to produce by a virtuous and thoughtful sensibility that continuity in their self-consciousness, which nature has made the law of their animal life. Ingratitude, sensuality, and hardness of heart, all flow from this source. Men are ungrateful to others only when they have ceased to look back on their former selves with joy and tenderness. They exist in fragments. Annihilated as to the past, they are dead to the future, or seek for the proofs of it everywhere, only not (where alone they can be found) in themselves. A contemporary poet has expressed and illustrated this sentiment with equal fineness of thought and tenderness of feeling:—

My heart leaps up when I behold
  A rainbow in the sky!
So was it, when my life began;
So is it now I am a man;
So let it be, when I grow old,
  Or let me die.
The child is father of the man,

And I would wish my days to be
Bound each to each by natural piety.*

WORDSWORTH.

Alas! the pernicious influence of this lax morality extends from the nursery and the school to the cabinet and senate. It is a common weakness with men in power, who have used dissimulation successfully, to form a passion for the use of it, dupes to the love of duping! A pride is flattered by these lies. He who fancies that he must be perpetually stooping down to the prejudices of his fellow-creatures, is perpetually reminding and re-assuring himself of his own vast superiority to them. But no real greatness can long co-exist with deceit. The whole faculties of man must be exerted in order to noble energies; and he who is not earnestly sincere, lives in but half his being, self-mutilated, self-paralyzed.

The latter part of the proposition, which has drawn me into this discussion, that, I mean, in which the morality of intentional falsehood is asserted, may safely be trusted to the reader's own moral sense. Is it a groundless apprehension, that the patrons and admirers of such publications may receive the punishment of their indiscretion in the conduct of their sons and daughters? The suspicion of Methodism must be expected by every man of rank and fortune, who carries his examination respecting the books which are to lie on his breakfast-table, farther than to their freedom from gross verbal indecencies, and broad avowals of Atheism in the title-page. For the existence of an intelligent

* I am informed, that these very lines have been cited, as a specimen of despicable puerility. So much the worse for the citer. Not willingly in his presence would I behold the sun setting behind our mountains, or listen to a tale of distress or virtue; I should be ashamed of the quiet tear on my own cheek. But let the dead bury the dead! The poet sang for the living. Of what value indeed, to a sane mind, are the likings or dislikings of one man, grounded on the mere assertions of another? Opinions formed from opinions—what are they, but clouds sailing under clouds, which impress shadows upon shadows?

Fungum pelle procul, jubeo; nam quid mihi fungo?
Conveniunt stomacho non minus ista suo.

I was always pleased with the motto placed under the figure of the rosemary in old herbals:—

Apage, sus! Haud tibi spiro.

First Cause may be ridiculed in the notes of one poem, or placed doubtfully as one of two or three possible hypotheses, in the very opening of another poem, and both be considered as works of safe promiscuous reading *virginibus puerisque:* and this, too, by many a father of a family, who would hold himself highly culpable in permitting his child to form habits of familiar acquaintance with a person of loose habits, and think it even criminal to receive into his house a private tutor without a previous inquiry concerning his opinions and principles, as well as his manners and outward conduct. How little I am an enemy to free inquiry of the boldest kind, and in which the authors have differed the most widely from my own convictions and the general faith, provided only, the inquiry be conducted with that seriousness, which naturally accompanies the love of truth, and be evidently intended for the perusal of those only, who may be presumed capable of weighing the arguments,—I shall have abundant occasion of proving in the course of this work. *Quin ipsa philosophia talibus e disputationibus non nisi beneficium recipit. Nam si vera proponit homo ingeniosus veritatisque amans, nova ad eam accessio fiet: sin falsa, refutatione eorum priores tanto magis stabilientur.**

The assertion, that truth is often no less dangerous than falsehood, sounds less offensively at the first hearing, only because it hides its deformity in an equivocation, or double meaning of the word truth. What may be rightly affirmed of truth, used as synonymous with verbal accuracy, is transferred to it in its higher sense of veracity. By verbal truth, we mean no more than the correspondence of a given fact to given words. In moral truth, we involve likewise the intention of the speaker, that his words should correspond to his thoughts in the sense in which he ex-

* GALILÆI, *Syst. Cosm.* p. 42.—Moreover, philosophy itself can not but derive benefit from such discussions. For if a man of genius and a lover of truth brings just positions before the public, there is a fresh accession to the stock of philosophic insight; but if erroneous positions, the former truths will by their confutation be established so much the more firmly.

The original is in the following words:—

La filosofia medesima non può se non ricever benefizio dalle nostre dispute; perchè se i nostri pensieri saranno veri, nuovi acquisti si saranno fatti; se falsi, col ributtargli, maggiormente verranno confermate le prime dottrine.

Dial. I. 44. Padov. 1774.—*Ed.*

pects them to be understood by others: and in this latter import we are always supposed to use the word, wherever we speak of truth absolutely, or as a possible subject of moral merit or demerit. It is verbally true, that in the sacred Scriptures it is written: *As is the good, so is the sinner, and he that sweareth as he that feareth an oath. A man hath no better thing under the sun, than to eat, and to drink, and to be merry. There is one event unto all: the living know they shall die, but the dead know not any thing, neither have they any more a reward.** But he who should repeat these words, with this assurance, to an ignorant man in the hour of his temptation, lingering at the door of the alehouse, or hesitating as to the testimony required of him in the court of justice, would, spite of this verbal truth, be a liar, and the murderer of his brother's conscience. Veracity, therefore, not mere accuracy; to convey truth, not merely to say it, is the point of duty in dispute: and the only difficulty in the mind of an honest man arises from the doubt, whether more than veracity, that is, the truth and nothing but the truth—is not demanded of him by the law of conscience; whether it does not exact simplicity; that is, the truth only, and the whole truth. If we can solve this difficulty, if we can determine the conditions under which the law of universal reason commands the communication of the truth independently of consequences, we shall then be enabled to judge whether there is any such probability of evil consequences from such communication, as can justify the assertion of its occasional criminality, as can perplex us in the conception, or disturb us in the performance, of our duty.

The conscience, or effective reason, commands the design of conveying an adequate notion of the thing spoken of, when this is practicable: but at all events a right notion, or none at all. A schoolmaster is under the necessity of teaching a certain rule in simple arithmetic empirically,—(do so and so, and the sum will always prove true);—the necessary truth of the rule—that is, that the rule having been adhered to, the sum must always prove true—requiring a knowledge of the higher mathematics for its demonstration. He, however, conveys a right notion, though he can not convey the adequate one.

* Eccles. viii. 15; ix. 2, 5.—*Ed.*

ESSAY VI.

Πολυμαθίη κάρτα μὲν ὠφελέει, κάρτα δὲ βλάπτει τὸν ἔχοντα. Ὠφελέει μὲν τὸν δεξιὸν ἄνδρα, βλάπτει δὲ τὸν ῥηϊδίως φωνεῦντα πᾶν ἔπος καὶ ἐν παντὶ δήμῳ. Χρὴ δὲ καιροῦ μέτρα εἰδέναι· σοφίης γὰρ οὗτος ὅρος. Εἰ δὲ οἱ ἔξω καιροῦ ῥῆσιν μουσικὴν πεπνυμένως ἀείσουσιν, οὐ παρα δέχονται ἐν ἀργίῃ γνώμην, αἰτίην δ' ἔχουσι μωρίας.

ANAXARCHUS, apud Stobæum, Serm. xxxiv.*

General knowledge and ready talent may be of very great benefit, but they may likewise be of very great disservice to the possessor. They are highly advantageous to the man of sound judgment, and dexterous in applying them; but they injure your fluent holder-forth on all subjects in all companies. It is necessary to know the measures of the time and occasion: for this is the very boundary of wisdom—(that by which it is defined, and distinguished from mere ability). But he, who without regard to the unfitness of the time and the audience, will soar in the high region of his fancies with his garland and singing robes about him, will not acquire the credit of seriousness amidst frivolity, but will be condemned for his silliness, as the greatest idler of the company, because the most unseasonable.

THE moral law, it has been shown, permits an inadequate communication of unsophisticated truth, on the condition that it alone is practicable, and binds us to silence when neither an adequate, nor even a right, exposition of the truth is in our power. We must first inquire then,—what is necessary to constitute, and what may allowably accompany, a right though inadequate notion,—and, secondly, what are the circumstances, from which we may deduce the impracticability of conveying even a right notion; the presence or absence of which circumstances it therefore becomes our duty to ascertain. In answer to the first question, the conscience demands: 1. That it should be the wish and design of the mind to convey the truth only; that if in addition to the negative loss implied in its inadequateness, the notion communicated should lead to any positive error, the cause should lie in

* Edit. Gaisford.—*Ed.*

the fault or defect of the recipient, not of the communicator, whose paramount duty, whose inalienable right, it is to preserve his own integrity,* the integral character of his own moral being. Self-respect; the reverence which he owes to the presence of humanity in the person of his neighbor; the reverential upholding of the faith of man in man; gratitude for the particular act of confidence; and religious awe for the divine purposes in the gift of language; are duties too sacred and important to be sacrificed to the guesses of an individual, concerning the advantages to be gained by the breach of them. 2. It is further required, that the supposed error shall not be such as will pervert or materially vitiate the imperfect truth, in communicating which we had unwillingly, though not perhaps unwittingly, occasioned it. A barbarian so instructed in the power and intelligence of the infinite Being as to be left wholly ignorant of his moral attributes, would have acquired none but erroneous notions even of the former. At the very best, he would gain only a theory to satisfy his curiosity with; but more probably, would deduce the belief of a Moloch or a Baal. For the idea of an irresistible, invisible Being, naturally produces terror in the mind of uninstructed and unprotected man, and with terror there will be associated whatever has been accustomed to excite it, anger, vengeance, &c.; as is proved by

* The best and most forcible sense of a word is often that which is contained in its etymology. The author of the poems, the Synagogue, frequently affixed to Herbert's Temple, gives the original purport of the word "integrity," in the following lines of the fourth stanza of the eighth poem:*

> Next to sincerity, remember still,
> Thou must resolve upon integrity.
> God will have all thou hast, thy mind, thy will,
> Thy thoughts, thy words, thy works.—

And again, after some verses on constancy and humility, the poem concludes with—

> He that desires to see
> The face of God, in his religion must
> Sincere, entire, constant, and humble be.

Having mentioned the name of Herbert, that model of a man, a gentleman, and a clergyman, let me add, that the quaintness of some of his thoughts, not of his diction, than which nothing can be more pure, manly, and unaffected, has blinded modern readers to the great general merit of his poems, which are for the most part exquisite in their kind.

* Church-Porch.—*Ed.*

the mythology of all barbarous nations. This must be the case with all organized truths; the component parts derive their significance from the idea of the whole. Bolingbroke removed love, justice, and choice, from power and intelligence, and yet pretended to have left unimpaired the conviction of a Deity. He might as consistently have paralyzed the optic nerve, and then excused himself by affirming, that he had, however, not touched the eye.

The third condition of a right though inadequate notion is, that the error occasioned be greatly outweighed by the importance of the truth communicated. The rustic would have little reason to thank the philosopher, who should give him true conceptions of the folly of believing in ghosts, omens, dreams, &c. at the price of abandoning his faith in divine providence, and in the continued existence of his fellow-creatures after their death. The teeth of the old serpent planted by the Cadmuses of French literature, under Lewis XV., produced a plenteous crop of philosophers and truth-trumpeters of this kind, in the reign of his successor. They taught many truths, historical, political, physiological, and ecclesiastical, and diffused their notions so widely, that the very ladies and hair-dressers of Paris became fluent encyclopedists: and the sole price which their scholars paid for these treasures of new information, was to believe Christianity an imposture, the Scriptures a forgery, the worship, if not the belief, of God superstition, hell a fable, heaven a dream, our life without providence, and our death without hope. They became as gods as soon as the fruit of this Upas tree of knowledge and liberty had opened their eyes to perceive that they were no more than beasts—somewhat more cunning, perhaps, and abundantly more mischievous. What can be conceived more natural than the result,—that self-acknowledged beasts should first act, and next suffer themselves to be treated, as beasts. We judge by comparison. To exclude the great is to magnify the little. The disbelief of essential wisdom and goodness, necessarily prepares the imagination for the supremacy of cunning with malignity. Folly and vice have their appropriate religions, as well as virtue and true knowledge: and in some way or other fools will dance round the golden calf, and wicked men beat their timbrels and kettle-drums to,—

—Moloch, horrid king, besmeared with blood
Of human sacrifice and parents' tears.

My feelings have led me on, and in my illustration I had almost lost from my view the subject to be illustrated. One condition yet remains: that the error foreseen shall not be of a kind to prevent or impede the after acquirement of that knowledge which will remove it. Observe, how graciously nature instructs her human children. She can not give us the knowledge derived from sight without occasioning us at first to mistake images of reflection for substances. But the very consequences of the delusion lead inevitably to its detection; and out of the ashes of the error rises a new flower of knowledge. We not only see, but are enabled to discover by what means we see. So, too, we are under the necessity, in given circumstances, of mistaking a square for a round object: but ere the mistake can have any practical consequences, it is not only removed, but in its removal gives us the symbol of a new fact, that of distance. In a similar train of thought, though more fancifully, I might have elucidated the preceding condition, and have referred our hurrying enlighteners and revolutionary amputators to the gentleness of nature, in the oak and the beech, the dry foliage of which she pushes off only by the propulsion of the new buds, that supply its place. My friends! a clothing even of withered leaves is better than bareness.

Having thus determined the nature and conditions of a right notion, it remains to consider the circumstances which tend to render the communication of it impracticable, and oblige us of course, to abstain from the attempt—oblige us not to convey falsehood under the pretext of saying truth. These circumstances, it is plain, must consist either in natural or moral impediments. The former, including the obvious gradations of constitutional insensibility and derangement, preclude all temptation to misconduct, as well as all probability of ill-consequences from accidental oversight, on the part of the communicator. Far otherwise is it with the impediments from moral causes. These demand all the attention and forecast of the genuine lovers of truth in the matter, the manner, and the time of their communications public and private; and these are the ordinary materials of the vain and the factious, determine them in the choice of their audiences and of their arguments, and to each argument give powers not its own. They are distinguishable into two sources, the streams from which, however, most often become confluent, namely, hindrances from ignorance,—(I here use the word in relation to the habits of reasoning as well as to the previous knowledge requisite for the due comprehension of the subject,)—and hindrances from predominant passions.*

From both these the law of conscience commands us to abstain, because such being the ignorance and such the passions of the supposed auditors, we ought to deduce the impracticability of conveying not only adequate but even right notions of our own convictions: much less does it permit us to avail ourselves of the causes of this impracticability in order to procure nominal proselytes, each of whom will have a different, and all a false, conception of those notions that were to be conveyed for their truth's sake alone. Whatever is, or but for some defect in our moral character would have been, foreseen as preventing the conveyance of our thoughts, makes the attempt an act of self-contradiction: and whether the faulty cause exist in our choice of unfit words or our choice of unfit auditors, the result is the same and so is the guilt. We have voluntarily communicated falsehood.

Thus, without reference to consequences,—if only one short digression be excepted—from the sole principle of self-consistence or moral integrity, we have evolved the clue of right reason, which we are bound to follow in the communication of truth. Now then let me appeal to the judgment and experience of the reader, whether he who most faithfully adheres to the letter of the law of conscience will not likewise act in strictest correspondence to the maxims of prudence and sound policy. I am at least unable to recollect a single instance, either in history or in my personal experience, of a preponderance of injurious consequences from the publication of any truth, under the observance of the moral conditions above stated: much less can I even imagine any case, in which truth, as truth, can be pernicious. But if the assertor of the indifferency of truth and falsehood in their own natures, attempt to justify his position by confining the word truth, in the first instance, to the correspondence of given words to given facts, without reference to the total impression left by such words,—what is this more than to assert, that articulated sounds are things of moral indifferency;—and that we may relate a fact accurately, and nevertheless deceive grossly and wickedly? Blifil related accurately Tom Jones's riotous joy

* See Lay Sermon addressed to the higher and middle classes. VI.

during his benefactor's illness, only omitting that this joy was occasioned by the physician's having pronounced him out of danger. Blifil was not the less a liar for being an accurate matter-of-fact liar. Tell-truths in the service of falsehood we find everywhere, of various names and various occupations, from the elderly young women that discuss the love affairs of their friends and acquaintances at the village tea-tables, to the anonymous calumniators of literary merit in reviews, and the more daring malignants, who dole out discontent, innovation and panic, in political journals: and a most pernicious race of liars they are! But who ever doubted it?—Why should our moral feelings be shocked, and the holiest words with all their venerable associations be profaned, in order to bring forth a truism! But thus it is for the most part with the venders of startling paradoxes. In the sense in which they are to gain for their author the character of a bold and original thinker, they are false even to absurdity; and the sense in which they are true and harmless, conveys so mere a truism, that it even borders on nonsense. How often have we heard—"The rights of man—hurra!—The sovereignty of the people—hurra!"—roared out by men who, if called upon in another place and before another audience, to explain themselves, would give to the words a meaning, in which the most monarchical of their political opponents would admit them to be true, but which would contain nothing new, or strange, or stimulant, nothing to flatter the pride, or kindle the passions, of the populace!

ESSAY VII.

At profanum vulgus lectorum quomodo arcendum est? Librisne nostris jubeamus, ut coram indignis obmutescant? Si linguis, ut dicitur, emortuis utamur, eheu! ingenium quoque nobis emortuum jacet: sin aliter,—Minervæ secreta crassis ludibrium divulgamus, et Dianam nostram impuris hujus sæculi Actæonibus nudam proferimus. Respondeo: ad incommoditates hujusmodi evitandas, nec Græce nec Latine scribere opus est. Sufficiet, nos sicca luce usos fuisse et strictiore argumentandi methodo. Sufficiet, innocenter, utiliter scripscisse: eventus est apud lectorem. Nuper emptum est a nobis Ciceronianum istud De Officiis, opus quod semper pæne Christiano dignum putabamus. Mirum! libellus factus fuerat famosissimus. Credisne? Vix: at quomodo? Maligno quodam, nescio quem, plena margine et super tergo, annotatum est, et exemplis, calumniis potius, superfœtatum! Sic et qui introrsum uritur inflammationes animi vel Catonianis (ne dicam, sacrosanctis) paginis accipit. Omni aura mons, omnibus scriptis mens ignita, vescitur.

RUDOLPHI LANGII, Epist. ad amicum quemdam Italicum, in qua linguæ patriæ et hodiernæ usum defendit et eruditis commendat.

Nec me fallit, ut in corporibus hominum sic in animis multiplici passione affectis, medicamenta verborum multis inefficacia visum iri. Sed nec illud quoque me præterit, ut invisibiles animorum morbos, sic invisibilia esse remedia. Falsis opinionibus circumventi veris sententiis liberandi sunt, ut qui audiendo ceciderant audiendo consurgant.

PETRARCH. Prefat. in lib. de remed. utriusque fortunæ, sub fin.

But how are we to guard against the herd of promiscuous readers? Can we bid our books be silent in the presence of the unworthy? If we employ what are called the dead languages, our own genius, alas! becomes flat and dead: and if we embody our thoughts in the words native to them or in which they were conceived, we divulge the secrets of Minerva to the ridicule of blockheads, and expose our Diana to the Actæons of a sensual age. I reply: that in order to avoid inconveniences of this kind, we need write neither in Greek nor in Latin. It will be enough, if we abstain from appealing to the bad passions and low appetites, and confine ourselves to a strictly consequent method of reasoning.

To have written innocently, and for wise purposes, is all that can be required of us: the event lies with the reader. I purchased lately Cicero's work, *De Officiis*, which I had always considered as almost worthy of a Christian. To my surprise it had become a most flagrant libel. Nay! but how?—Some one, I know not who, out of the fruitfulness of his own malignity, had filled all the margins and other blank spaces with annotations—a true superfætation of examples, that is, of false and slanderous tales! In like manner, the slave of impure desires will turn the pages of Cato, not to say, Scripture itself, into occasions and excitements of wanton imaginations. There is no wind but fans a volcano, no work but feeds a combustible mind.

I am well aware, that words will appear to many as inefficacious medicines when administered to minds agitated with manifold passions, as when they are muttered by way of charm over bodily ailments. But neither does it escape me, on the other hand, that as the diseases of the mind are invisible, invisible must the remedies likewise be. Those who have been entrapped by false opinions are to be liberated by convincing truths: that thus having imbibed the poison through the ear they may receive the antidote by the same channel.

THAT our elder writers to Jeremy Taylor inclusively quoted to excess, it would be the very blindness of partiality to deny. More than one might be mentioned, whose works are well characterized in the words of Milton, as a paroxysm of citations, pampered metaphors, and aphorisming pedantry. On the other hand, it seems to me that we now avoid quotations with an anxiety that offends in the contrary extreme. Yet it is the beauty and independent worth of the citations far more than their appropriateness which have made Johnson's Dictionary popular even as a reading book—and the mottos with the translations of them are known to add considerably to the value of the Spectator. With this conviction I have taken more than common pains in the selection of the mottos for The Friend: and of two mottos equally appropriate prefer always that from the book which is least likely to have come into my readers' hands. For I often please myself with the fancy, now that I may have saved from oblivion the only striking passage in a whole volume, and now that I may have attracted notice to a writer undeservedly forgotten. If this should be attributed to a silly ambition in the display of various reading, I can do no more than deny any consciousness of having been so actuated: and for the rest, I must console myself by the reflection, that if it be one of the most foolish, it is at the same time one of the most harmless, of human vanities.

The passages prefixed lead at once to the question, which will probably have more than once occurred to the reflecting reader of the preceding essay. How will these rules apply to the most important mode of communication? to that, in which one man may utter his thoughts to myriads of men at the same time, and to myriads of myriads at various times and through successions of generations? How do they apply to authors, whose foreknowledge assuredly does not inform them who, or how many, or of what description, their readers will be? How do these rules apply to books, which once published, are as likely to fall in the way of the incompetent as of the judicious, and will be fortunate indeed if they are not many times looked at through the thick mists of ignorance, or amid the glare of prejudice and passion?—I answer in the first place, that this is not universally true. The readers are not seldom picked and chosen. Relations of certain pretended miracles performed a few years ago, at Holywell, in consequence of prayers to the Virgin Mary, on female servants, and these relations moralized by the old Roman Catholic arguments without the old Protestant answers, have to my knowledge been sold by travelling pedlers in villages and farm-houses, not only in a form which placed them within the reach of the narrowest means, but sold at a price less than their prime cost, and doubtless, thrown in occasionally as the make-weight in a bargain of pins and stay-tape. Shall I be told, that the publishers and reverend authorizers of these base and vulgar delusions had exerted no choice as to the purchasers and readers? But waiving this, or rather having first pointed it out, as an important exception, I further reply,—that if the author have clearly and rightly established in his own mind the class of readers, to which he means to address his communications; and if both in this choice, and in the particulars of the manner and matter of his work, he conscientiously observe all the conditions which reason and conscience have been shown to dictate, in relation to those for whom the work was designed; he will, in most instances, have effected his design and realized the desired circumscription. The posthumous work of Spinoza—(*Ethica ordine geometrico demonstrata*)—may, indeed, accidentally fall into the hands of an incompetent reader. But (not to mention, that it is written in a dead language), it will be entirely harmless, because it must needs be utterly unintelligible. I venture to assert, that the whole first book, *De Deo*, might be read in a literal English translation to any congregation in the kingdom, and that no individual who had not been habituated to the strictest and most laborious processes of reasoning, would even suspect its orthodoxy or piety, however heavily the few who listened might complain of its obscurity and want of interest.

This, it may be objected, is an extreme case. But it is not so for the present purpose. I am speaking of the probability of injurious consequences from the communication of truth. This I have denied, if the right means have been adopted, and the necessary conditions adhered to, for its actual communication. Now the truths—that is, the positions believed by the author to be truths—conveyed in a book are either evident of themselves, or such as require a train of deductions in proof: and the latter will be either such truths as are authorized and generally received; or such as are in opposition to received and authorized opinions; or lastly, positions presented as truths for the appropriate test of examination, and still under trial, *adhuc in lite*. Of this latter class I affirm, that in no one of the three sorts can an instance be brought of a preponderance of ill-consequences, or even of an equilibrium of advantage and injury from a work, in which the understanding alone has been appealed to, by results fairly deduced from just premises, in terms strictly appropriate. Alas! legitimate reasoning is impossible without severe thinking, and thinking is neither an easy nor an amusing employment. The reader, who would follow a close reasoner to the summit and absolute principle of any one important subject, has chosen a chamois-hunter for his guide. Our guide will, indeed, take us the shortest way, will save us many a wearisome and perilous wandering, and warn us of many a mock road that had formerly led himself to the brink of chasms and precipices, or at best in an idle circle to the spot from which he started. But he can not carry us on his shoulders: we must strain our own sinews, as he has strained his; and make firm footing on the smooth rock for ourselves, by the blood of toil from our own feet. Examine the journals of our humane and zealous missionaries in Hindostan. How often and how feelingly do they describe the difficulty of making the simplest chain of reasoning intelligible to the ordinary natives: the rapid exhaustion of their whole power of attention, and with what pain and distressful effort it is exerted, while it lasts. Yet it is amongst individuals of this class, that the hideous practices of self-torture chiefly, indeed almost exclusively, prevail. O! if folly were no easier than wisdom, it being often so very much more grievous, how certainly might not these miserable men be converted to Christianity? But alas! to swing by hooks passed through the back, or to walk on shoes with nails of iron pointed upward on the soles, all this is so much less difficult, demands so very inferior an exertion of the will than to think, and by thought to gain knowledge and tranquillity!

It is not true, that ignorant persons have no notion of the advantages of truth and knowledge. They see and confess those advantages in the conduct, the immunities, and the superior powers of the possessors. Were these attainable by pilgrimages the most toilsome, or penances the most painful, we should assuredly have as many pilgrims and as many self-tormentors in the service of true religion and virtue, as now exist under the tyranny of Papal or Brahman superstition. This inefficacy of legitimate reason, from the want of fit objects,—this its relative weakness, and how narrow at all times its immediate sphere of action must be,—is proved to us by the impostors of all professions. What, I pray, is their fortress, the rock which is both their quarry and their foundation, from which and on which they are built?—The desire of arriving at the end without the effort of thought and will, which are the appointed means. Let us look backward three or four centuries. Then, as now, the great mass of mankind were governed by the three main wishes, the wish for vigor of body, including the absence of painful feelings;—for wealth, or the power of procuring the external conditions of bodily enjoyment,—these during life; and security from pain and continuance of happiness after death. Then, as now, men were desirous to attain them by some easier means than those of temperance, industry, and strict justice. They gladly therefore applied to the priest, who could insure them happiness hereafter without the performance of their duties here; to the lawyer who could make money a substitute for a right cause; to the physician, whose medicines promised to take the sting out of the tail of their sensual indulgences, and let them fondle and play with vice, as with a charmed serpent; to the alchemist, whose gold-tincture would enrich them without toil or economy; and to the astrologer, from whom they could purchase foresight without knowledge or reflection. The established professions were, without exception, no other than licensed modes of witchcraft. The wizards, who would now find their due reward in Bridewell, and their appropriate honors in the pillory, sat then on episcopal thrones, candidates for saintship, and already canonized in the belief of their deluded contemporaries ; while the one or two real teachers and discoverers of truth were exposed to the hazard of fire and fagot,—a dungeon the best shrine that was vouchsafed to a Roger Bacon* and a Galileo !

ESSAY VIII.

Pray, why is it, that people say that men are not such fools now-a-days as they were in the days of yore? I would fain know, whether you would have us understand by this same saying, as indeed you logically may, that formerly, men were fools, and in this generation are grown wise? How many and what dispositions made them fools? How many and what dispositions were wanting to make 'em wise? Why were those fools? How should these be wise? Pray, how came you to know that men were formerly fools? How did you find that they are now wise? Who made them fools? Who in Heaven's name made us wise? Who d'ye think are most, those that loved mankind foolish, or those that love it wise? How long has it been wise? How long otherwise? Whence proceeded the foregoing folly? Whence the following wisdom? Why did the old folly end now and no later? Why did the modern wisdom begin now and no sooner? What were we the worse for the former folly? What the better for the succeeding wisdom? How should the ancient folly have come to nothing? How should this same new wisdom be started up and established? Now answer me, an't please you!

RABELAIS' *Preface to his 5th Book.*

MONSTERS and madmen canonized and Galileo blind in a dungeon!† It is not so in our times. Heaven be praised, that in this respect, at least, we are, if not better, yet better off, than our

* "It is for his country, not his order, to glory in the man whom that order condemned to imprisonment, not for his supposed skill in magic, but for those opinions which he derived from studying the Scriptures, wherein he was versed beyond any other person of his age."

SOUTHEY'S *Colloquies*, viii.

And see the note there.—*Ed.*

† This is not strictly accurate. Galileo was sentenced by the Inquisition at Rome, on the 22d of June, 1633; and, although his right eye had been formerly affected, he did not become blind till the end of 1637. His confinement, likewise, in the proper prison of the Inquisition, was merely nominal, although the restrictions under which he was kept to the end of his life, were of the most distressing and injurious description.—*Ed.*

forefathers. But to what, and to whom (under Providence) do we owe the improvement? To any radical change in the moral affections of mankind in general? Perhaps the great majority of men are now fully conscious that they are born with the god-like faculty of reason, and that it is the business of life to develop and apply it?—The Jacob's ladder of truth, let down from heaven, with all its numerous rounds, is now the common highway, on which we are content to toil upward to the objects of our desires?—We are ashamed of expecting the end without the means?—In order to answer these questions in the affirmative, I must have forgotten the animal magnetists;* the proselytes of Brothers, and of Joanna Southcote; and some thousand fanatics less original in their creeds, but not a whit more rational in their expectations; I must forget the infamous empirics, whose advertisements pollute and disgrace all our newspapers, and almost paper the walls of our cities; and the vending of whose poisons and poisonous drams—with shame and anguish be it spoken—supports a shop in every market-town! I must forget that other reproach of the nation, that mother-vice, the lottery! I must forget, that a numerous class plead prudence for keeping their fellow-men ignorant and incapable of intellectual enjoyments, and the revenue for upholding such temptations as men so ignorant will not withstand,—yes! that even senators and officers of state put forth the revenue as a sufficient reason for upholding, at every fiftieth door throughout the kingdom, temptations to the most pernicious vices, which fill the land with mourning, and fit the laboring classes for sedition and religious fanaticism! Above all I must forget the first years of the French revolution, and the millions throughout Europe who confidently expected the best and choicest results of knowledge and virtue, namely, liberty and universal peace, from the votes of a tumultuous assembly—that is, from the mechanical agitation of the air in a large room at Paris—and this too in the most light, unthinking, sensual, and profligate, of the European nations,—a nation, the very phrases of whose language are so composed, that they can scarcely speak without lying!—No! Let us not deceive ourselves. Like the man who used to pull off his hat with great demonstration of respect whenever he spoke of himself, we are

* Recanted since 1817. After subtracting all exaggerated or doubtful testimonies, the undeniable facts are as important as they are surprising.

fond of styling our own the enlightened age: though as Jortin, I think, has wittily remarked, the golden age would be more appropriate. But in spite of our great scientific discoveries, for which praise be given to whom the praise is due, and in spite of that general indifference to all the truths and all the principles of truth, that belong to our permanent being, and therefore do not lie within the sphere of our senses,—that same indifference which makes toleration so easy a virtue with us, and constitutes nine tenths of our pretended illumination,—it still remains the character of the mass of mankind to seek for the attainment of their necessary ends by any means rather than the appointed ones; and for this cause only, that the latter imply the exertion of the reason and the will. But of all things this demands the longest apprenticeship, even an apprenticeship from infancy; which is generally neglected, because an excellence, that may and should belong to all men, is expected to come to every man of its own accord.

To whom then do we owe our meliorated condition?—To the successive few in every age,—more indeed in one generation than in another, but relatively to the mass of mankind always few,—who by the intensity and permanence of their action have compensated for the limited sphere, within which it is at any one time intelligible; and whose good deeds posterity reverences in their results; though the mode, in which we repair the inevitable waste of time, and the style of our additions, too generally furnish a sad proof, how little we understand the principles. I appeal to the histories of the Jewish, the Grecian, and the Roman republics, to the records of the Christian Church, to the history of Europe from the treaty of Westphalia, 1648. What do they contain but accounts of noble structures raised by the wisdom of the few, and gradually undermined by the ignorance and profligacy of the many? If therefore the deficiency of good, which everywhere surrounds us, originate in the general unfitness and aversion of men to the process of thought, that is, to continuous reasoning, it must surely be absurd to apprehend a preponderance of evil from works which can not act at all except as far as they call the reasoning faculties into full co-exertion with them.

Still, however, there are truths so self-evident, or so immediately and palpably deduced from those that are, or are acknowledged for such, that they are at once intelligible to all men, who possess the common advantages of the social state; although by sophistry, by evil habits, by the neglect, false persuasions, and impostures of an anti-Christian priesthood joined in one conspiracy with the violence of tyrannical governors, the understandings of men may become so darkened and their consciences so lethargic, that a necessity will arise for the republication of these truths, and this too with a voice of loud alarm, and impassioned warning. Such were the doctrines proclaimed by the first Christians to the Pagan world; such were the lightnings flashed by Wickliff, Huss, Luther, Calvin, Zuinglius, Latimer, and others, across the Papal darkness; and such in our own times the agitating truths, with which Thomas Clarkson, and his excellent confederates, the Quakers, fought and conquered the legalized *banditti* of men-stealers, the numerous and powerful perpetrators and advocates of rapine, murder, and (of blacker guilt than either) slavery. Truths of this kind being indispensable to man, considered as a moral being, are above all expedience, all accidental consequences: for as sure as God is holy, and man immortal, there can be no evil so great as the ignorance or disregard of them. It is the very madness of mock prudence to oppose the removal of a poisoned dish on account of the pleasant sauces or nutritious viands which would be lost with it! The dish contains destruction to that, for which alone we ought to wish the palate to be gratified, or the body to be nourished.

The sole condition, therefore, imposed on us by the law of conscience in these cases is, that we employ no unworthy and heterogeneous means to realize the necessary end,—that we intrust the event wholly to the full and adequate promulgation of the truth, and to those generous affections which the constitution of our moral nature has linked to the full perception of it. Yet evil may, nay it will, be occasioned. Weak men may take offence, and wicked men avail themselves of it; though we must not attribute to the promulgation, or to the truth promulgated, all the evil, of which wicked men—predetermined, like the wolf in the fable, to create some occasion—may choose to make it the pretext. But that there ever was, or ever can be, a preponderance of evil, I defy either the historian to instance, or the philosopher to prove. "Let it fly away, all that chaff of light faith that can fly off at any breath of temptation; the cleaner will the true grain be stored up in the granary of the Lord,"—we are entitled to say with Tertullian :* and to exclaim with heroic Luther,— "Scandal and offence! Talk not to me of scandal and offence. Need breaks through stone walls, and recks not of scandal. It is my duty to spare weak consciences as far as it may be done without hazard of my soul. Where not, I must take counsel for my soul, though half or the whole world should be scandalized thereby."†

Luther felt and preached and wrote and acted, as beseemed a Luther to feel and utter and act. The truths, which had been outraged, he re-proclaimed in the spirit of outraged truth, at the behest of his conscience and in the service of the God of truth. He did his duty, come good, come evil! and made no question, on which side the preponderance would be. In the one scale there was gold, and impressed thereon the image and superscription of the universal Sovereign. In all the wide and ever-widening commerce of mind with mind throughout the world, it is treason to refuse it. Can this have a counter-weight? The other scale indeed might have seemed full up to the very balance-yard; but of what worth and substance were its contents? Were they capable of being counted or weighed against the former? The conscience, indeed, is already violated when to moral good or evil we oppose things possessing no moral interest. Even if the conscience dared waive this her preventive *veto*, yet before we could consider the twofold results in the relation of loss and gain, it must be known whether their kind is the same or equivalent. They must first be valued, and then they may be weighed or counted, if they are worth it. But in the particular case at present before us, the loss is contingent and alien; the gain essential and the tree's own natural produce. The gain is permanent, and spreads through all times and places; the loss but temporary, and owing its very being to vice or ignorance, vanishes at the approach of knowledge and moral improvement. The gain reaches all good men, belongs to all that love light and de-

* *Avolent, quantum volent, paleæ leves fidei quocunque afflatu tentationum! eo purior massa frumenti in horrea Domini reponetur.* De Præscript. advers. Hæretic. I. c. 3.—*Ed.*

† *Aergerniss hin, Aergerniss her! Noth bricht Eisen, und hat kein Aergerniss. Ich soll der schwachen Gewissen schonen so fern es ohne Gefahr meiner Seelen geschehen mag. Wo nicht, so soll ich meiner Seelen rathen, es aergere sich daran die ganze oder halbe Welt.*

sire an increase of light: to all and of all times, who thank Heaven for the gracious dawn, and expect the noon-day; who welcome the first gleams of spring, and sow their fields in confident faith of the ripening summer and the rewarding harvest-tide! But the loss is confined to the unenlightened and the prejudiced—say rather, to the weak and the prejudiced of a single generation. The prejudices of one age are condemned even by the prejudiced of the succeeding ages: for endless are the modes of folly, and the fool joins with the wife in passing sentence on all modes but his own. Who cried out with greater horror against the murderers of the Prophets, than those who likewise cried out, Crucify him! Crucify him!—Prophet and Saviour, and Lord of life, Crucify him! Crucify him!—The truth-haters of every future generation will call the truth-haters of the preceding ages by their true names: for even these the stream of time carries onward. In fine, truth considered in itself and in the effects natural to it, may be conceived as a gentle spring or water-source, warm from the genial earth, and breathing up into the snow drift that is piled over and around its outlet. It turns the obstacle into its own form and character, and as it makes its way increases its stream. And should it be arrested in its course by a chilling season, it suffers delay, not loss, and waits only for a change in the wind to awaken and again roll onwards:—

I semplici pastori
Sul Vesolo nevoso
Fatti curvi e canuti,
D' alto stupor son muti,
Mirando al fonte ombroso
Il Po con pochi umori;
Poscia udendo gli onori
Dell' urna angusta e stretta,
Che 'l Adda, che'l Tesino
Soverchia in suo cammino,
Che ampio al mar 's affretta,
Che si spuma, e si suona,
Che gli si da corona! *

* *Chiabrera Rime,* xxviii. "But falsehood," continues Mr. C., "is fire in stubble; it likewise turns all the light stuffs around it into its own substance for a moment, one crackling blazing moment,—and then dies; and all its converts are scattered in the wind, without place or evidence of their existence, as viewless as the wind which scatters them."

'The simple shepherds grown bent and hoary-headed on the snowy Vesolo, are mute with deep astonishment, gazing in the overshadowed fountain on the Po with his scanty waters; then hearing of the honors of his confined and narrow urn, how he receives as a sovereign the ADDA and the TESINO in his course, how ample he hastens on to the sea, how he foams, how mighty his voice, and that to him the crown is assigned.'

ESSAY IX.

Great men have liv'd among us, heads that plann'd
And tongues that utter'd wisdom—better none.
*   *   *   *   *
Even so doth Heaven protect us! WORDSWORTH.

IN the preceding essay I have explained the good, that is, the natural consequences of the promulgation to all of truths which all are bound to know and to make known. The evils occasioned by it, with few and rare exceptions, have their origin in the attempts to suppress or pervert it; in the fury and violence of imposture attacked or undermined in her strongholds, or in the extravagances of ignorance and credulity roused from their lethargy, and angry at the medicinal disturbance—awaking, not yet broad awake, and thus blending the monsters of uneasy dreams with the real objects, on which the drowsy eye had alternately half-opened and closed, again half-opened and again closed. This re-action of deceit and superstition, with all the trouble and tumult incident, I would compare to a fire which bursts forth from some stifled and fermenting mass on the first admission of light and air. It roars and blazes, and converts the already spoilt or damaged stuff, with all the straw and straw-like matter near it, first into flame, and the next moment into ashes. The fire dies away, the ashes are scattered on all the winds, and what began in worthlessness ends in nothingness. Such are the evil, that is, the casual consequences of the same promulgation.

It argues a narrow or corrupt nature to lose sight of the general and lasting consequences of rare and virtuous energy, in the brief accidents which accompanied its first movements—to set lightly by the emancipation of the human reason from a legion of devils, in our complaints and lamentations over the loss of a herd of swine! The Cranmers, Hampdens, and Sidneys,—the counsellors of our Elizabeth, and the friends of our other great deliverer, the third William,—is it in vain that these have been our countrymen? Are we not the heirs of their good deeds? And what are noble deeds but noble truths realized? As Protestants, as Englishmen, as the inheritors of so ample an estate of might and right, an estate so strongly fenced, so richly planted, by the sinewy arms and dauntless hearts of our forefathers, we of all others have good cause to trust in the truth, yea, to follow its pillar of fire through the darkness and the desert, even though its light should but suffice to make us certain of its own presence. If there be elsewhere men jealous of the light, who prophesy an excess of evil over good from its manifestation, we are entitled to ask them, on what experience they ground their bodings? Our own country bears no traces, our own history contains no records to justify them. From the great æras of national illumination we date the commencement of our main national advantages. The tangle of delusions which stifled and distorted the growing tree, have been torn away; the parasite weeds, that fed on its very roots, have been plucked up with a salutary violence. To us there remain only quiet duties, the constant care, the gradual improvement, the cautious, unhazardous labors of the industrious though contented gardener—to prune, to engraft, and one by one to remove from its leaves and fresh shoots the slug and the caterpillar. But far be it from us to undervalue with light and senseless detraction the conscientious hardihood of our predecessors, or even to condemn in them that vehemence, to which the blessings it won for us leave us now neither temptation nor pretext. That the very terms, with which the bigot or the hireling would blacken the first publishers of political and religious truth, are, and deserve to be, hateful to us, we owe to the effects of its publication. We ante-date the feelings in order to criminate the authors of our tranquillity, opulence, and security. But let us be aware. Effects will not, indeed, immediately disappear with their causes; but neither can they long continue without them. If by the reception of truth in the spirit of truth, we became what we are; only by the retention of it in the same spirit, can we remain what we are. The narrow seas that form our boundaries,—what were they in times of old? The convenient highway for Danish and Norman pirates. What are they now? Still but "a span of waters." Yet they roll at the base of the inisled Ararat, on which the ark of the hope of Europe and of civilization rested!

> Even so doth God protect us, if we be
> Virtuous and wise. Winds blow and waters roll,
> Strength to the brave, and power and deity:
> Yet in themselves are nothing! One decree
> Spake laws to them, and said that by the soul
> Only the nations shall be great and free! WORDSWORTH.

ESSAY X.

I deny not but that it is of greatest concernment in the church and commonwealth to have a vigilant eye how books demean themselves as well as men; and thereafter to confine, imprison, and do sharpest justice on them as malefactors. For books are not absolutely dead things, but do contain a potency of life in them to be as active as that soul was whose progeny they are; nay, they do preserve as in a vial the purest efficacy and extraction of that living intellect that bred them. I know they are as lively and as vigorously productive as those fabulous dragon's teeth: and being sown up and down may chance to spring up armed men. And yet on the other hand, unless wariness be used, as good almost kill a man as kill a good book. Who kills a man, kills a reasonable creature, God's image; but he who destroys a good book, kills reason itself, kills the image of God, as it were in the eye. Many a man lives a burthen to the earth; but a good book is the precious life-blood of a master-spirit, embalmed and treasured up on purpose to a life beyond life.

MILTON'S *Speech for the liberty of unlicensed printing.*

THUS far then I have been conducting a cause between an individual and his own mind. Proceeding on the conviction, that to man is intrusted the nature, not the result, of his actions, I have presupposed no calculations; I have presumed no foresight. —Introduce no contradiction into thy own consciousness. Acting, or abstaining from action, delivering or withholding thy thoughts, whatsoever thou doest, do it in singleness of heart. In all things, therefore, let thy means correspond to thy purpose, and let the purpose be one with the purport.—To this principle I have referred the supposed individual, and from this principle solely I have deduced each particular of his conduct. As far, therefore, as the court of conscience extends,—and in this court alone I have been pleading hitherto—I have won the cause. It has been decided, that there is no just ground for apprehending mischief from truth communicated conscientiously,—that is, with a strict observance of all the conditions required by the conscience;—that what is not so communicated, is falsehood, and that to the falsehood, not to the truth, must the ill consequences be attributed.

Another and altogether different cause remains now to be pleaded; a different cause, and in a different court. The parties concerned are no longer the well-meaning individual and his conscience, but the citizen and the state—the citizen, who may be a fanatic as probably as a philosopher, and the state, which concerns itself with the conscience only as far as it appears in the action, or still more accurately, in the fact; and which must determine the nature of the fact not merely by a rule of right formed from the modification of particular by general consequences,—not merely by a principle of compromise, that reduces the freedom of each citizen to the common measure in which it becomes compatible with the freedom of all; but likewise by the relation which the facts bear to its—the state's—own instinctive principle of self-preservation. For every depository of the supreme power must presume itself rightful: and as the source of law not legally to be endangered. A form of government may indeed, in reality, be most pernicious to the governed, and the highest moral honor may await the patriot who risks his life in order by its subversion to introduce a better and juster constitution; but it would be absurd to blame the law by which his life is declared forfeit. It were to expect, that by an involved contradiction the law should allow itself not to be law, by allowing the state, of which it is a part, not to be a state. For, as Hooker has well observed, the law of men's actions is one, if they be respected only as men; and another, when they are considered as parts of a body politic.*

But though every government subsisting in law,—for pure lawless despotism grounding itself wholly on terror precludes all consideration of duty—though every government subsisting in law must, and ought to, regard itself as the life of the body politic, of

* Eccl. Pol. I. xvi. 6.—*Ed.*

which it is the head, and consequently must punish every attempt against itself as an act of assault or murder, that is, sedition or treason; yet still it ought so to secure the life as not to prevent the conditions of its growth, and of that adaptation to circumstances, without which its very life becomes insecure. In the application, therefore, of these principles to the public communication of opinions by the most efficient mean,—we have to decide, whether consistently with them there should be any liberty of the press; and if this be answered in the affirmative, what shall be declared abuses of that liberty, and made punishable as such; and in what way the general law shall be applied to each particular case.

First, then, ought there to be any liberty of the press? I do not here mean, whether it should be permitted to print books at all;—for this essay has little chance of being read in Turkey, and in any other part of Europe it can not be supposed questionable—but whether by the appointment of a censorship the government should take upon itself the responsibility of each particular publication. In governments purely monarchical,—that is, oligarchies under one head—the balance of advantage and disadvantage from this monopoly of the press will undoubtedly be affected by the general state of information; though after reading Milton's 'Speech for the liberty of unlicensed printing'* we shall probably be inclined to believe, that the best argument in favor of licensing under any constitution is that, which supposing the ruler to have a different interest from that of his country, and even from himself as a reasonable and moral creature, grounds itself on the incompatibility of knowledge with folly, oppression, and degradation. What our prophetic Harrington said of religious, applies equally to literary, toleration:—"If it be said that in France there is liberty of conscience in part, it is also plain that while the hierarchy is standing, this liberty is falling, and that if ever it comes to pull down the hierarchy, it pulls down that monarchy also: wherefore the monarchy or hierarchy will be

* *Il y a un voile qui doit toujours couvrir tout ce que l'on peut dire et tout ce qu'on peut croire du droit des peuples et de celui des princes, qui ne s'accordent jamais si bien ensemble que dans le silence.*

Mém. du Card. de Retz.

How severe a satire where it can be justly applied! how false and calumnious if meant as a general maxim!

beforehand with it, if they see their true interest."*—On the other hand, there is no slight danger from general ignorance: and the only choice, which Providence has graciously left to a vicious government, is either to fall by the people, if they are suffered to become enlightened, or with them, if they are kept enslaved and ignorant.

The nature of our constitution, since the Revolution, the state of our literature and the wide diffusion, if not of intellectual, yet of literary, power, and the almost universal interest in the productions of literature, have set the question at rest relatively to the British press. However great the advantages of previous examination might be under other circumstances, in this country it would be both impracticable and inefficient. I need only suggest in broken sentences—the prodigious number of licensers that would be requisite—the variety of their attainments, and—inasmuch as the scheme must be made consistent with our religious freedom—the ludicrous variety of their principles and creeds—their number being so great, and each appointed censor being himself a man of letters, *quis custodiet ipsos custodes?* If these numerous licensers hold their offices for life, and independently of the ministry *pro tempore*, a new, heterogeneous, and alarming power is introduced, which can never be assimilated to the constitutional powers already existing:—if they are removable at pleasure, that which is heretical and seditious in 1809, may become orthodox and loyal in 1810;—and what man, whose attainments and moral respectability gave him even an endurable claim to this awful trust, would accept a situation at once so invidious and so precarious? And what institution can retain any useful influence in so free a nation when its abuses have made it contemptible? Lastly, and which of itself would suffice to justify the rejection of such a plan—unless all proportion between crime and punishment were abandoned, what penalties could the law attach to the assumption of a liberty, which it had denied, more severe than those which it now attaches to the abuse of the liberty, which it grants? In all those instances at least, which it would be most the inclination—perhaps the duty—of the state to prevent, namely, in seditious and incendiary publications,—(whether actually such, or only such as the existing government chose so to denominate, makes no difference in the argument).

* Syst. of Politics, vi. 10.—*Ed.*

the publisher, who hazards the punishment now assigned to seditious publications, would assuredly hazard the penalties of unlicensed ones, especially as the very practice of licensing would naturally diminish the attention to the contents of the works published, the chance of impunity therefore be so much greater, and the artifice of prefixing an unauthorized license so likely to escape detection. It is a fact, that in many of the former German states in which literature flourished, notwithstanding the establishment of censors or licensers, three fourths of the books printed were unlicensed—even those, the contents of which were unobjectionable, and where the sole motive for evading the law, must have been either the pride and delicacy of the author, or the indolence of the bookseller. So difficult was the detection, so various the means of evasion, and worse than all, from the nature of the law and the affront it offers to the pride of human nature, such was the merit attached to the breach of it—a merit commencing perhaps with Luther's Bible, and other prohibited works of similar great minds, published with no dissimilar purpose, and thence by many an intermediate link of association finally connected with books, of the very titles of which a good man would wish to remain ignorant. The interdictory catalogues of the Romish hierarchy always present to my fancy the muster-rolls of the two hostile armies of Michael and of Satan printed promiscuously, or extracted at haphazard, save only that the extracts from the former appear somewhat the more numerous. And yet even in Naples, and in Rome itself, whatever difficulty occurs in procuring any article catalogued in these formidable folios, must arise either from the scarcity of the work itself, or the absence of all interest in it. Assuredly there is no difficulty in obtaining from the most respectable booksellers the vilest provocatives to the basest crimes, though intermixed with gross lampoons on the heads of the church, the religious orders, and on religion itself. The stranger is invited into an inner room, and the proscribed wares presented to him with most significant looks and gestures, implying the hazard, and the necessity of secrecy. A creditable English bookseller would deem himself insulted, if such works were even inquired after at his shop. It is a well-known fact, that with the mournful exception indeed of political provocatives, and the titillations of vulgar envy provided by our anonymous critics, the loathsome articles are among us vended and offered for sale almost exclusively by foreigners. Such are the salutary effects of a free press, and the generous habit of action imbibed from the blessed air of law and liberty, even by men who neither understand the principle, nor feel the sentiment, of the dignified purity, to which they yield obeisance from the instinct of character. As there is a national guilt which can be charged but gently on each individual, so are there national virtues, which can as little be imputed to the individuals,—nowhere, however, but in countries where liberty is the presiding influence, the universal *medium* and *menstruum* of all other excellence, moral and intellectual. Admirably doth the admirable Petrarch admonish us :—

Nec sibi vero quisquam falso persuadeat, eos qui pro libertate excubant, atque hactenus desertæ reipublicæ partes suscipiunt, alienum agere negotium; suum agunt. In hac una reposita sibi omnia norint omnes, securitatem mercator, gloriam miles, utilitatem agricola. Postremo, in eadem religiosi cærimonias, otium studiosi, requiem senes, rudimenta disciplinarum pueri, nuptias puellæ, pudicitiam matronæ, gaudium omnes invenient. * * * * *Huic uni reliquæ, cedant curæ! Si hanc omittitis, in quantalibet occupatione nihil agitis: si huic incumbitis, etsi nihil agere videmini, cumulate tamen et civium et virorum implevistis officia.**

Nor let any one falsely persuade himself, that those who keep watch and ward for liberty, are meddling with things that do not concern them, instead of minding their own business. For all men should know, that all blessings are stored and protected in this one, as in a common repository. Here is the tradesman's security, the soldier's honor, the agriculturist's profit. Lastly, in this one good of liberty the religious will find the permission of their rites and forms of worship, the students their learned leisure, the aged their repose, boys the rudiments of the several branches of their education, maidens their chaste nuptials, matrons their womanly honor and the dignity of their modesty, fathers of families the dues of natural affection and the sacred privileges of their ancient home, every one their hope and their joy. To this one

* *Petrarch. Epist.* 45, *ad Nicolaum tribunum urbis almæ novissimum et ad populum Romanum.* The translation contains clauses referring to expressions, which in the second edition, were inserted in the Latin quotation by Mr. C. himself.—*Ed.*

solicitude, therefore, let all other cares yield the priority. If you omit this, be occupied as much and sedulously as you may, you are doing nothing: If you apply your heart and strength to this, though you seem to be doing nothing, you will, nevertheless, have been fulfilling the duties of citizens and of men, yea, in a measure pressed down and running over.

I quote Petrarch often in the hope of drawing the attention of scholars to his inestimable Latin writings. Let me add, in the wish likewise of recommending to the London publishers a translation of select passages from his treatises and letters. If I except the German writings and original letters of the heroic Luther, I do not remember a work from which so delightful and instructive a volume might be compiled.

To give the true bent to the above extract, it is necessary to bear in mind, that he who keeps watch and ward for freedom, has to guard against two enemies, the despotism of the few and the despotism of the many—but especially in the present day against the sycophants of the populace.

License they mean, when they cry liberty!
For who loves that, must first be wise and good.

ESSAY XI.

Nemo vero fallatur, quasi minora sint animorum contagia quam corporum. Majora sunt; gravius lædunt; altius descendunt, serpuntque latentius.
PETRARCH. De Vit. Solit. L. 1. tract. 3. c. 4.

And let no man be deceived as if the contagions of the soul were less than those of the body. They are yet greater; they convey more direful diseases; they sink deeper, and creep on more unsuspectedly.

WE have abundant reason then to infer, that the law of England has done well and concluded wisely in proceeding on the principle so clearly worded by Milton: "that a book should be as freely admitted into the world as any other birth; and if it prove a monster, who denies but that it may justly be burnt or sunk into the sea?" We have reason then, I repeat, to rest satisfied with our laws, which no more prevent a book from coming into the world unlicensed, lest it should prove a libel, than a traveller from passing unquestioned through our turnpike-gates, because it is possible he may be a highwayman. Innocence is presumed in both cases. The publication is a part of the offence, and its necessary condition. Words are moral acts, and words deliberately made public the law considers in the same light as any other cognizable overt act.

Here, however, a difficulty presents itself. Theft, robbery, murder, and the like, are easily defined: the degrees and circumstances likewise of these and similar actions are definite, and constitute specific offences, described and punishable each under its own name. We have only to prove the fact and identify the offender. The intention too, in the great majority of cases, is so clearly implied in the action, that the law can safely adopt it as its universal maxim, that the proof of the malice is included in the proof of the fact; especially as the few occasional exceptions have their remedy provided in the prerogative of pardon intrusted to the supreme magistrate. But in the case of libel, the degree makes the kind, the circumstances constitute the criminality; and both degrees and circumstances, like the ascending shades of color or the shooting hues of a dove's neck, die away into each other, incapable of definition or outline. The eye of the understanding, indeed, sees the determinate difference in each individual case, but language is most often inadequate to express what the eye perceives, much less can a general statute anticipate and pre-define it. Again: in other overt acts a charge disproved leaves the accused either guilty of a different fault, or at best simply blameless. A man having killed a fellow-citizen is acquitted of murder;—the act was manslaughter only, or it was justifiable homicide. But when we reverse the iniquitous sentence passed on Algernon Sidney, during our perusal of his work on government; at the moment we deny it to have been a traitorous libel, our beating hearts declare it to have been a benefaction to our country, and under the circumstances of those times the performance of an heroic duty. From this cause, therefore, as well as from a libel's being a thing made up of degrees and circumstances,—and these too, discriminating offence from merit by such dim and ambulant boundaries,—the intention of the agent, wherever it can be independently or inclusively ascertained, must be allowed a great share in determining the character of the action, unless the law is not only to be divorced from moral justice, but to wage open hostility against it.*

* According to the old adage: you are not hanged for stealing a horse,

Add too, that laws in doubtful points are to be interpreted according to the design of the legislator, where this can be certainly inferred. But the laws of England, which owe their own present supremacy and absoluteness to the good sense and generous dispositions diffused by the press more, far more, than to any other single cause, must needs be presumed favorable to its general influence. Even in the penalties attached to its abuse, we must suppose the legislature to have been actuated by the desire of preserving its essential privileges. The press is indifferently the passive instrument of evil and of good: nay, there is some good even in its evil. "Good and evil we know," says Milton, in the Speech from which I have selected the motto of the preceding essay, "in the field of this world, grow up together almost inseparably: and the knowledge of good is so involved and interwoven with the knowledge of evil, and in so many cunning resemblances hardly to be discerned, that those confused seeds which were imposed on Psyche as an incessant labor to cull out and sort asunder, were not more intermixed."—"As, therefore, the state of man now is, what wisdom can there be to choose, what continence to forbear, without the knowledge of evil? He that can apprehend and consider vice with all her baits and seeming pleasures, and yet abstain, and yet distinguish, and yet prefer that which is truly better, he is the true way-faring Christian. I can not praise a fugitive and cloistered virtue, unexercised and unbreathed, that never sallies out and sees her adversary."—"That virtue, therefore, which is but a youngling in the contemplation of evil, and knows not the utmost that vice promises to her followers, and rejects it, is but a blank virtue, not a pure."—"Since, therefore, the knowledge and survey of vice is in this world so necessary to the constituting of human virtue, and the scanning of error to the confirmation of truth, how can we more safely and with less danger scout into the regions of sin and falsity, than by reading all manner of tractates, and hearing all manner of reason?"—Again—but, indeed the whole treatise is one strain of moral wisdom and political prudence:—"Why should we then affect a rigor contrary to the manner of God and of nature, by abridging or scanting those means, which books, freely permitted, are both to the trial of virtue and the

but that horses may not be stolen. To what extent this is true, I shall have occasion to examine hereafter.

exercise of truth? It would be better done to learn, that the law must needs be frivolous, which goes to restrain things uncertainly, and yet equally, working to good and to evil. And were I the chooser, a dram of well-doing should be preferred before many times as much the forcible hindrance of evil-doing. For God, sure, esteems the growth and completion of one virtuous person, more than the restraint of ten vicious."

The evidence of history is strong in favor of the same principles, even in respect of their expediency. The average result of the press from Henry VIII. to Charles I. was such a diffusion of religious light as first redeemed and afterwards saved this nation from the spiritual and moral death of Popery; and in the following period it is to the press that we owe the gradual ascendency of those wise political maxims, which casting philo sophic truth in the moulds of national laws, customs, and existing orders of society, subverted the tyranny without suspending the government, and at length completed the mild and salutary revolution by the establishment of the house of Brunswick. To what must we attribute this vast over-balance of good in the general effects of the press, but to the over-balance of virtuous intention in those who employed the press? The law, therefore, will not refuse to manifest good intention a certain weight even in cases of apparent error, lest it should discourage and scare away those, to whose efforts we owe the comparative infrequency and weakness of error on the whole. The law may, however, nay, it must demand, that the external proofs of the author's honest intentions should be supported by the general style and matter of his work, and by the circumstances and mode of its publication. A passage, which in a grave and regular disquisition would be blameless, might become highly libellous and justly punishable if it were applied to present measures or persons for immediate purposes, in a cheap and popular tract. I have seldom felt greater indignation than at finding in a large manufactory a sixpenny pamphlet, containing a selection of inflammatory paragraphs from the prose-writings of Milton, without a hint given of the time, occasion, state of government, and other circumstances under which they were written—not a hint, that the freedom which we now enjoy, exceeds all that Milton dared hope for, or deemed practicable; and that his political creed sternly excluded the populace, and indeed the majority of the population, from all pretensions to political power. If the manifest bad intention would constitute this publication a seditious libel, a good intention equally manifest can not justly be denied its share of influence in producing a contrary verdict.

Here then is the difficulty. From the very nature of a libel it is impossible so to define it, but that the most meritorious works will be found included in the description. Not from any defect or undue severity in the particular law, but from the very nature of the offence to be guarded against, a work recommending reform by the only rational mode of recommendation, that is, by the detection and exposure of corruption, abuse, or incapacity, might, though it should breathe the best and most unadulterated English feelings, be brought within the definition of libel equally with the vilest incendiary pamphlet, that ever aimed at leading and misleading the multitude. Not a paragraph in the Morning Post during the Peace of Amiens, (or rather the experimental truce so called,)—though to the immortal honor of the then editor, that newspaper was the chief secondary means of producing the unexampled national unanimity, with which the war recommenced and has since been continued,—not a paragraph warning the nation, as need was and most imperious duty commanded, of the perilous designs and unsleeping ambition of our neighbor, the mimic and caricaturist of Charlemagne, but was a punishable libel. The law of libel is a vast aviary, which encages the awakening cock and the geese whose alarum preserved the Capitol, no less than the babbling magpie and ominous screech-owl. And yet will we avoid this seeming injustice, we throw down all fence and bulwark of public decency and public opinion; political calumny will soon join hands with private slander; and every principle, every feeling, that binds the citizen to his country and the spirit to its Creator, will be undermined—not by reasoning, for from that there is no danger; but—by the mere habit of hearing them reviled and scoffed at with impunity. Were we to contemplate the evils of a rank and unweeded press only in its effect on the manners of a people, and on the general tone of thought and conversation, the greater the love which we bore to literature and to all the means and instruments of human improvement, the greater would be the earnestness with which we should solicit the interference of law: the more anxiously should we wish for some Ithuriel spear, that might remove from the ear of the public, and expose in their own fiendish shape those reptiles, which inspiring venom and forging illusions as they list,

————————thence raise
At least distempered, discontented thoughts,
Vain hopes, vain aims, inordinate desires.

PARADISE LOST.

ESSAY XII.

Quomodo autem id futurum sit, ne quis incredibile arbitretur, ostendam. Imprimis multiplicabitur regnum, et summa rerum potestas per plurimos dissipata et concisa minuetur. Tunc discordiæ civiles in perpetuum serentur, nec ulla requies bellis exitialibus erit, donec reges decem pariter existant qui orbem terræ, non ad regendum, sed ad consumendum, partiantur. Hi exercitibus in immensum coactis, et agrorum cultibus destitutis, quod est principium eversionis et cladis, disperdent omnia, et comminuent, et vorabunt. Tum reperite adversus eos hostis potentissimus ab extremis finibus plagæ septentrionalis orietur, qui tribus ex eo numero deletis qui tunc Asiam obtinebunt, assumetur in societatem a cæteris, ac princeps omnium constituetur. Hic insustentabili dominatione vexabit orbem; divina et humana miscebit; infanda dictu et execrabilia molietur; nova consilia in pectore suo volutabit, ut proprium sibi constituat imperium; leges commutabit, suas sanciet; contaminabit, diripiet, spoliabit, occidet. Denique immutato nomine, atque imperii sede translata, confusio ac perturbatio humani generis consequetur. Tum vere detestabile, atque abominandum tempus existet, quo nulli hominum sit vita jucunda. LACTANTIUS de Vitâ Beatâ, Lib. vii. c. 16.

But lest this should be deemed incredible, I will show the manner in which it is to take place. First, there will be a multiplication of independent sovereignties, and the supreme magistracy of the empire, scattered and cut up into fragments, will be enfeebled in the exercise of power by law and authority. Then will be sown the seeds of civil discords, nor will there be any rest or pause to wasteful and ruinous wars; while the soldiery kept together in immense standing armies, the kings will crush and lay waste at their will;—until at length there will rise up against them a most puissant military chieftain of low birth, who will have conceded to him a fellowship with the other sovereigns of the earth, and will finally be constituted the head of all. This man will harass the civilized world with an insupportable despotism, he will confound and commix all things spiritual and temporal. He will form plans and preparations of the most execrable and sacrilegious nature. He will be forever restlessly turning over new schemes in his imagination, in order that he may fix the imperial power over all in his own name and possession. He will change the former laws, he will sanction a code of his own, he will contaminate, pillage, lay waste and massacre. At length, when he has succeeded in the change of names and titles, and in the transfer of the seat of empire, there will follow a confusion and perturbation of the human race; then will there be for a while an era of horror and abomination, during which no man will enjoy his life in quietness.*

I INTERPOSE this essay as an historical comment on the words "mimic and caricaturist of Charlemagne," as applied to the despot, whom since the time that the words were first printed, we have, thank Heaven! succeeded in encaging. The motto contains one of the most striking instances of an uninspired prophecy fulfilled even in many of its *minutiæ*, that I recollect ever to have met with: and it is hoped, that as a curiosity it will reconcile my readers to its unusual length. But though my chief motive was that of relieving, by the variety of an historical parallel, the series of argument on this most important of all subjects, the communicability of truth, yet the essay is far from being a digression. Having given utterance to *quicquid in rem tam maleficam indignatio dolorque dictarent*, concerning the mischiefs of a lawless press, I held it an act of justice to give a portrait no less lively of the excess to which the remorseless ambition of a government might go in accumulating its oppressions in the one instance before the discovery of printing, and in the other during the suppression of its freedom.

I have translated the following from a voluminous German work, Michael Ignaz Schmidt's History of the Germans, from Charles the Great to Conrade I.; in which this extract forms the conclusion of the second chapter of the third book. The late tyrant's close imitation of Charlemagne was sufficiently evidenced by his assumption of the iron crown of Italy, by his imperial coronation with the presence and authority of the Holy Father; by his imperial robe embroidered with bees in order to mark him as a successor of Pepin, and even by his ostentatious revocation of Charlemagne's grants to the Bishop of Rome. But that the differences might be felt likewise, I have prefaced the translation with the few following observations.

* This translation has expressions referring to some words inserted by the author in the Latin quotation in the previous editions.—*Ed.*

Let it be remembered then, that Charlemagne, for the greater part, created for himself the means of which he availed himself; that his very education was his own work, and that unlike Peter the Great, he could find no assistants out of his own realm; that the unconquerable courage and heroic dispositions of the nations he conquered, supplied a proof positive of real superiority, indeed the sole positive proof of intellectual power, in a warrior: for how can we measure force but by the resistance to it? But all was prepared for Bonaparte; Europe weakened in the very heart of all human strength, namely, in moral and religious principle, and at the same time accidentally destitute of any one great or commanding mind: the French people, on the other hand, still restless from revolutionary fanaticism; their civic enthusiasm already passed into military passion and the ambition of conquest; and alike by disgust, terror, and characteristic unfitness for freedom, ripe for the reception of a despotism. Add too, that the main obstacles to an unlimited system of conquest, and the pursuit of universal monarchy had been cleared away for him by his pioneers the Jacobins, namely, the influence of the great landholders, of the privileged and of the commercial classes. Even the naval successes of Great Britain, by destroying the trade, rendering useless the colonies, and almost annihilating the navy of France, were in some respects subservient to his designs by concentrating the powers of the French empire in its armies, and supplying them out of the wrecks of all other employments, save that of agriculture. France had already approximated to the formidable state so prophetically described by Sir James Steuart, in his Political Economy, in which the population should consist chiefly of soldiers and peasantry: at least the interests of no other classes were regarded. The great merit of Bonaparte has been that of a skilful steersman, who with his boat in the most violent storm still keeps himself on the summit of the waves, which not he, but the winds had raised. I will now proceed to my translation.

"That Charles was a hero, his exploits bear evidence. The subjugation of the Lombards, protected as they were by the Alps, by fortresses and fortified towns, by numerous armies, and by a great name; of the Saxons, secured by their savage resoluteness, by an untamable love of freedom, by their desert plains and enormous forests, and by their own poverty; the humbling of the

Dukes of Bavaria, Aquitania, Bretagne, and Gascony; proud of their ancestry as well as of their ample domains; the almost entire extirpation of the Avars, so long the terror of Europe; are assuredly works which demanded a courage and a firmness of mind such as Charles only possessed.

"How great his reputation was, and this too beyond the limits of Europe, is proved by the embassies sent to him out of Persia, Palestine, Mauritania, and even from the Khalifs of Bagdad. If at the present day an embassy from the Black or Caspian Sea comes to a prince on the Baltic, it is not to be wondered at, since such are now the political relations of the four quarters of the world, that a blow which is given to any one of them is felt more or less by all the others. Whereas in the time of Charlemagne, the inhabitants in one of the known parts of the world scarcely knew what was going on in the rest. Nothing but the extraordinary, all-piercing report of Charles's exploits could bring this to pass. His greatness, which set the world in astonishment, was likewise, without doubt, that which begot in the Pope and the Romans the first idea of the re-establishment of their empire.

"It is true, that a number of things united to make Charles a great man—favorable circumstances of time, a nation already disciplined to warlike habits, a long life, and the consequent acquisition of experience, such as no one possessed in his whole realm. Still, however, the principal means of his greatness Charles found in himself. His great mind was capable of extending its attention to the greatest multiplicity of affairs. In the middle of Saxony he thought on Italy and Spain, and at Rome he made provisions for Saxony, Bavaria, and Pannonia. He gave audience to the ambassadors of the Greek emperor and other potentates, and himself audited the accounts of his own farms, where every thing was entered even to the number of the eggs. Busy as his mind was, his body was not less in one continued state of motion. Charles would see into every thing himself, and do every thing himself, as far as his powers extended and even this it was, too, which gave to his undertakings such force and energy.

"But with all this the government of Charles was the government of a conqueror, that is splendid abroad and fearfully oppressive at home. What a grievance must it not have been for the people, that Charles for forty years together dragged them now to the Elbe, then to the Ebro, after this to the Po, and from thence back again to the Elbe, and this not to check an invading enemy, but to make conquests which little profited the French nation! This must prove too much, at length, for a hired soldier: how much more for conscripts, who did not live only to fight, but who were fathers of families, citizens, and proprietors? But above all, it is to be wondered at, that a nation, like the French, should suffer themselves to be used as Charles used them. But the people no longer possessed any considerable share of influence. All depended on the great chieftains, who gave their willing suffrage for endless wars, by which they were always sure to win. They found the best opportunity, under such circumstances, to make themselves great and mighty at the expense of the freemen resident within the circle of their baronial courts; and when conquests were made, it was far more for their advantage than that of the monarchy. In the conquered provinces there was a necessity for dukes, vassal kings, and different high offices: all this fell to their share.

"I would not say this if we did not possess incontrovertible original documents of those times, which prove clearly to us that Charles's government was an unhappy one for the people, and that this great man, by his actions, labored to the direct subversion of his first principles. It was his first pretext to establish a greater equality among the members of his vast community, and to make all free and equal subjects under a common sovereign. And, from the necessity occasioned by continual war, the exact contrary took place. Nothing gives us a better notion of the interior state of the French monarchy, than the third capitular of the year 811.* All is full of complaint, the bishops and earls clamoring against the freeholders, and these in their turn against the bishops and earls. And, in truth, the freeholders had no small reason to be discontented and to resist, as far as they dared, even the imperial levies. A dependant must be content to follow his lord without further questioning: for he was paid for it. But a free citizen, who lived wholly on his own property, might reasonably object to suffer himself to be dragged about in all quarters of the world, at the fancies of his lord: especially as there was so much injustice intermixed. Those who gave up

* Compare with this the four or five quarto volumes of the French Conscript Code.

their properties entirely, or in part, of their own accord, were left undisturbed at home, while those, who refused to do this, were forced so often into service, that at length, becoming impoverished, they were compelled by want to give up, or dispose of, their free tenures to the bishops or earls.*

"It almost surpasses belief to what a height, at length, the aversion to war rose in the French nation, from the multitude of the campaigns, and the grievances connected with them. The national vanity was now satiated by the frequency of victories: and the plunder which fell to the lot of individuals, made but a poor compensation for the losses and burthens sustained by their families at home. Some, in order to become exempt from military service, sought for menial employments in the establishments of the bishops, abbots, abbesses, and earls. Others made over their free property to become tenants at will of such lords, as from their age or other circumstances, they thought would be called to no further military services. Others even privately took away the life of their mothers, aunts, or other of their relatives, in order that no family residents might remain through whom their names might be known, and themselves traced; others voluntarily made slaves of themselves, in order thus to render themselves incapable of the military rank."

When this extract was first published, namely, September 7, 1809, I prefixed the following sentence: "This passage contains so much matter for political anticipation and well-grounded hope, that I feel no apprehension of the reader's being dissatisfied with its length." I trust, that I may now derive the same confidence from his genial exultation, as a Christian, and from his honest pride as a Briton, in the retrospect of its completion. In this belief I venture to conclude the essay with the following extract from a "Comparison of the French republic, under Bonaparte, with the Roman empire under the first Cæsars," published by me in the Morning Post, 21st September, 1802.

If, then, there be no counterpoise of dissimilar circumstances, the prospect is gloomy indeed. The commencement of the public slavery in Rome, was in the most splendid era of human genius. Any unusually flourishing period of the arts and sci-

* It would require no great ingenuity to discover parallels, or at least equivalent hardships to these, in the treatment of, and regulations concerning, the reluctant conscripts.

ences in any country, is, even to this day, called the Augustan age of that country. The Roman poets, the Roman historians, the Roman orators, rivalled those of Greece; in military tactics, in machinery, in all the conveniences of private life, the Romans greatly surpassed the Greeks. With few exceptions, all the emperors, even the worst of them, were, like Bonaparte,* the liberal encouragers of all great public works, and of every species of public merit not connected with the assertion of political freedom:

——— O juvenes, circumspicit atque agitat vos,
Materiamque sibi Ducis indulgentia quærit.†

It is even so, at this present moment, in France. Yet, both in France and in Rome, we have learned, that the most abject dispositions to slavery rapidly trod on the heels of the most outrageous fanaticism for an almost anarchical liberty. *Ruere in servitium consules, patres, eques: quanto quis illustrior, tanto magis falsi ac festinantes.*‡ Peace and the coadunation of all the civilized provinces of the earth were the grand and plausible pretexts of Roman despotism: the degeneracy of the human species itself, in all the nations so blended, was the melancholy effect. To-morrow, therefore, we shall endeavor to detect all those points and circumstances of dissimilarity, which, though

* Imitators succeed better in copying the vices than the excellences of their archetypes. Where shall we find in the First Consul of France a counterpart to the generous and dreadless clemency of the first Cæsar? *Acerbe loquentibus satis habuit pro concione denunciare, ne perseverarent. Aulique Cæcinæ criminosissimo libro, et Pitholai carminibus maledicentissimis laceratam existimationem suam civili animo tulit.*—(Sueton. I. 75.—*Ed.*)

It deserves translation for English readers. "To those who spoke bitterly against him, he held it sufficient to signify publicly, that they should not persevere in the use of such language. His character had been mangled in a most libellous work of Aulus Cæcina, and he had been grossly lampooned in some verses by Pitholaus; but he bore both with the temper of a good citizen."

For this part of the First Consul's character, if common report speaks the truth, we must seek a parallel in the dispositions of the third Cæsar, who dreaded the pen of a paragraph writer, hinting aught against his morals and measures, with as great anxiety, and with as vindictive feelings, as if it had been the dagger of an assassin lifted up against his life. From the third Cæsar, too, he adopted the abrogation of all popular elections.

† Juvenal. Sat. vii. 20.—*Ed.*

‡ Tacit. Ann. i. 7.—*Ed.*

they can not impeach the rectitude of the parallel, for the present, may yet render it probable, that as the same constitution of government has been built up in France with incomparably greater rapidity, so it may have an incomparably shorter duration. We are not conscious of any feelings of bitterness towards the First Consul; or, if any, only that venial prejudice, which naturally results from the having hoped proudly of an individual, and the having been miserably disappointed. But we will not voluntarily cease to think freely and speak openly. We owe grateful hearts, and uplifted hands of thanksgiving to the Divine Providence, that there is yet one European country—and that country our own—in which the actions of public men may be boldly analyzed, and the result publicly stated. And let the Chief Consul, who professes in all things to follow his fate, learn to submit to it, if he finds that it is still his fate to struggle with the spirit of English freedom, and the virtues which are the offspring of that spirit;—if he finds, that the genius of Great Britain, which blew up his Egyptian navy into the air, and blighted his Syrian laurels, still follows him with a calm and dreadful eye; and in peace, equally as in war, still watches for that liberty, in which alone the genius of our isle lives, and moves, and has its being; and which being lost, all our commercial and naval greatness would instantly languish, like a flower, the root of which had been silently eaten away by a worm; and without which, in any country, the public festivals, and pompous merriments of a nation present no other spectacle to the eye of reason, than a mob of maniacs dancing in their fetters.

ESSAY XIII.

Must there be still some discord mix'd among
The harmony of men, whose mood accords
Best with contention tun'd to notes of wrong?
That when war fails, peace must make war with words,
With words unto destruction arm'd more strong
Than ever were our foreign foemen's swords;
Making as deep, tho' not yet bleeding wounds?
What war left scarless, calumny confounds.

Truth lies entrapp'd where cunning finds no bar:
Since no proportion can there be betwixt
Our actions which in endless motions are,
And ordinances which are always fixt.
Ten thousand laws more can not reach so far,
But malice goes beyond, or lives commixt
So close with goodness, that it ever will
Corrupt, disguise, or counterfeit it still.

And therefore *would our glorious Alfred,* who
Join'd with the king's the good man's majesty,
Not leave law's labyrinth without a clue—
Gave to deep skill its just authority,—
*　　*　　*　　*　　*　　*
But the last judgment—this his jury's plan—
*Left to the natural sense of work-day man.**

I recur to the dilemma stated in the eighth essay. How shall we solve this problem? Its solution is to be found in that spirit which, like the universal *menstruum* sought for by the old alchemists, can blend and harmonize the most discordant elements;—it is to be found in the spirit of a rational freedom diffused and become national, in the consequent influence and control of public opinion, and in its most precious organ, the jury. It

* Daniel. Epistle to Sir Thomas Egerton. The lines in italics are substituted by the author for the original, and there are a few other verbal alterations.—*Ed.*

is to be found, wherever juries are sufficiently enlightened to perceive the difference, and to comprehend the origin and necessity of the difference, between libels and other criminal overt-acts, and are sufficiently independent to act upon the conviction, that in a charge of libel, the degree, the circumstances, and the intention, constitute—not merely modify—the offence, give it its being, and determine its legal name. The words maliciously and advisedly, must here have a force of their own, and a proof of their own. They will consequently consider the law as a blank power provided for the punishment of the offender, not as a light by which they are to determine and discriminate the offence. The understanding and conscience of the jury are the judges *in toto*: the law a blank *congê d'êlire.* The law is the clay, and those the potter's wheel. Shame fall on that man, who shall labor to confound what reason and nature have put asunder, and who at once, as far as in him lies, would render the press ineffectual and the law odious: who would lock up the main river, the Thames, of our intellectual commerce; would throw a bar across the stream, that must render its navigation dangerous or partial, using as his materials the very banks, which were intended to deepen its channel and guard against its inundations! Shame fall on him, and a participation of the infamy of those, who misled an English jury to the murder of Algernon Sidney.

But though the virtuous intention of the writer must be allowed a certain influence in facilitating his acquittal, the degree of his moral guilt is not the true index or mete-wand of his condemnation. For juries do not sit in a court of conscience, but of law; they are not the representatives of religion, but the guardians of external tranquillity. The leading principle, the pole-star, of the judgment in its decision concerning the libellous nature of a published writing, is its more or less remote connection with after overt-acts, as the cause or occasion of the same. Thus the publication of actual facts may be, and most often will be, criminal and libellous, when directed against private characters: not only because the charge will reach the minds of many who can not be competent judges of the truth or falsehood of facts to which themselves were not witnesses, against a man whom they do not know, or at best know imperfectly; but because such a publication is of itself a very serious overt-act, by which the author without authority and without trial, has inflicted punishment on a fellow-subject, himself being witness and jury, judge and executioner. Of such publications there can be no legal justification, though the wrong may be palliated by the circumstance that the injurious charges are not only true, but wholly out of the reach of the law. But in libels on the government there are two things to be balanced against each other : first, the incomparably greater mischief of the overt-acts, if we suppose them actually occasioned by the libel—(as for instance, the subversion of government and property, if the principles taught by Thomas Paine had been realized, or if even an attempt had been made to realize them, by the many thousands of his readers) ; and second, the very great improbability that such effects will be produced by such writings. Government concerns all generally, and no one in particular. The facts are commonly as well known to the readers, as to the writer : and falsehood therefore easily detected. It is proved, likewise, by experience, that the frequency of open political discussion, with all its blamable indiscretions, indisposes a nation to overt-acts of practical sedition or conspiracy. They talk ill, said Charles V. of his Belgian provinces, but they suffer so much the better for it. His successor thought differently : he determined to be master of their words and opinions, as well as of their actions, and in consequence lost one half of those provinces, and retained the other half at an expense of strength and treasure greater than the original worth of the whole. An enlightened jury, therefore, will require proofs of more than ordinary malignity of intention, as furnished by the style, price, mode of circulation, and so forth ; or of punishable indiscretion arising out of the state of the times, as of dearth, for instance, or of whatever other calamity is likely to render the lower classes turbulent, and apt to be alienated from the government of their country. For the absence of a right disposition of mind must be considered both in law and in morals, as nearly equivalent to the presence of a wrong disposition. Under such circumstances the legal paradox that a libel may be the more a libel for being true, becomes strictly just, and as such ought to be acted upon.

Concerning the right of punishing by law the authors of heretical or deistical writings, I reserve my remarks for a future essay, in which I hope to state the grounds and limits of toleration more accurately than they seem to me to have been hitherto traced. There is one maxim, however, which I am tempted to seize as it passes across me. If I may trust my own memory, it is indeed a very old truth: and yet if the fashion of acting in apparent ignorance thereof be any presumption of its novelty, it ought to be new, or at least have become so by courtesy of oblivion. It is this: that as far as human practice can realize the sharp limits and exclusive proprieties of science, law and religion should be kept distinct. There is, in strictness, no proper opposition but between the two polar forces of one and the same power.* If I say then, that law and religion are natural opposites, and that the latter is the requisite counterpoise of the former, let it not be interpreted, as if I had declared them to be contraries. The law has rightfully invested the creditor with the power of arresting and imprisoning an insolvent debtor, the farmer with the power of transporting, mediately at least, the pillagers of his hedges and copses; but the law does not compel him to exercise that power, while it will often happen that religion commands him to forego it. Nay, so well was this understood by our grandfathers, that a man who squares his conscience by the law was a common paraphrase or synonyme of a wretch without any conscience at all. We have all of us learnt from history, that there was a long and dark period, during which the powers and the aims of law were usurped in the name of religion by the clergy and the courts spiritual: and we all know the result. Law and

* Every power in nature and in spirit must evolve an opposite as the sole means and condition of its manifestation: and all opposition is a tendency to re-union. This is the universal law of polarity or essential dualism, first promulgated by Heraclitus, 2000 years afterwards re-published, and made the foundation both of logic, of physics, and of metaphysics by Giordano Bruno. The principle may be thus expressed. The identity of *thesis* and *antithesis* is the substance of all being; their opposition the condition of all existence or being manifested; and every thing or *phenomenon* is the exponent of a *synthesis* as long as the opposite energies are retained in that *synthesis*. Thus water is neither oxygen nor hydrogen, nor yet is it a commixture of both; but the *synthesis* or indifference of the two: and as long as the *copula* endures, by which it becomes water, or rather which alone is water, it is not less a simple body than either of the imaginary elements, improperly called its ingredients or components. It is the object of the mechanical atomistic philosophy to confound *synthesis* with *synartesis*, or rather with mere juxtaposition of corpuscules separated by invisible interspaces. I find it difficult to determine, whether this theory contradicts the reason or the senses most: for it is alike inconceivable and unimaginable.

religion thus interpenetrating, neutralized each other; and the baleful product, or *tertium aliquid*, of this union retarded the civilization of Europe for centuries. Law splintered into the *minutiæ* of religion, the awful function and prerogative of which it is to take account of every *idle word*, became a busy and inquisitorial tyranny: and religion substituting legal terrors for the ennobling influences of conscience remained religion in name only. The present age appears to me approaching fast to a similar usurpation of the functions of religion by law: and if it were required, I should not want strong presumptive proofs in favor of this opinion, whether I sought for them in the charges from the bench concerning wrongs, to which religion denounces the fearful penalties of guilt, but for which the law of the land assigns damages only: or in sundry statutes—and all praise to the late Mr. Wyndham, *Romanorum ultimo*—in a still greater number of attempts towards new statutes, the authors of which displayed the most pitiable ignorance, not merely of the distinction between perfect, and imperfect obligations, but even of that still more sacred distinction between things and persons. What the son of Sirach advises concerning the soul, every senator should apply to his legislative capacity:—reverence it in meekness, knowing how feeble and how mighty a thing it is!*

From this hint concerning toleration, we may pass by an easy transition to the, perhaps, still more interesting subject of tolerance. And here I fully coincide with Frederic H. Jacobi, that the only true spirit of tolerance consists in our conscientious toleration of each other's intolerance. Whatever pretends to be more than this, is either the unthinking cant of fashion, or the soul-palsying narcotic of moral and religious indifference. All of us without exception, in the same mode though not in the same degree, are necessarily subjected to the risk of mistaking positive opinions for certainty and clear insight. From this yoke we can not free ourselves, but by ceasing to be men; and this too not in order to transcend, but to sink below, our human nature. For if in one point of view it be the mulct of our fall, and of the corruption of our will; it is equally true, that contemplated from another point, it is the price and consequence of our progressiveness. To him who is compelled to pace to and fro within

* The reference, probably, is to Ecclus. x. 28. *My son, glorify thy soul in meekness, and give it honor according to the dignity thereof.—Ed.*

the high walls and in the narrow court-yard of a prison, all objects may appear clear and distinct. It is the traveller journeying onward full of heart and hope, with an ever-varying horizon on the boundless plain, who is liable to mistake clouds for mountains, and the *mirage* of drouth for an expanse of refreshing waters.

But notwithstanding this deep conviction of our general fallibility, and the most vivid recollection of my own, I dare avow with the German philosopher, that as far as opinions, and not motives, principles, and not men,—are concerned ; I neither am tolerant, nor wish to be regarded as such. According to my judgment, it is mere ostentation, or a poor trick that hypocrisy plays with the cards of nonsense, when a man makes protestation of being perfectly tolerant in respect of all principles, opinions, and persuasions, those alone excepted which render the holders intolerant. For he either means to say by this, that he is utterly indifferent towards all truth, and finds nothing so insufferable as the persuasion of there being any such mighty value or importance attached to the possession of the truth as should give a marked preference to any one conviction above any other ; or else he means nothing, and amuses himself with articulating the pulses of the air instead of inhaling it in the more healthful and profitable exercise of yawning. That which doth not withstand, hath itself no standing place. To fill a station is to exclude or repel others,—and this is not less the definition of moral, than of material solidity. We live by continued acts of defence, that involve a sort of offensive warfare. But a man's principles, on which he grounds his hope and his faith, are the life of his life. *We live by faith*, says the philosophic Apostle ; and faith without principles is but a flattering phrase for wilful positiveness, or fanatical bodily sensation. Well, and of good right therefore, do we maintain with more zeal, than we should defend body or estate, a deep and inward conviction, which is as the moon to us ; and like the moon with all its massy shadows and deceptive gleams, it yet lights us on our way, poor travellers as we are, and benighted pilgrims. With all its spots and changes and temporary eclipses, with all its vain halos and bedimming vapors, it yet reflects the light that is to rise on us, which even now is rising, though intercepted from our immediate view by the mountains that inclose and frown over the vale of our mortal life.

This again is the mystery and the dignity of our human nature, that we can not give up our reason, without giving up at the same time our individual personality. For that must appear to each man to be his reason which produces in him the highest sense of certainty; and yet it is not reason, except so far as it is of universal validity and obligatory on all mankind. There is a one heart for the whole mighty mass of humanity, and every pulse in each particular vessel strives to beat in concert with it. He who asserts that truth is of no importance except in the signification of sincerity, confounds sense with madness, and the word of God with a dream. If the power of reasoning be the gift of the supreme Reason, that we be sedulous, yea, and militant in the endeavor to reason aright, is his implied command. But what is of permanent and essential interest to one man must needs be so to all, in proportion to the means and opportunities of each. Woe to him by whom these are neglected, and double woe to him by whom they are withholden; for he robs at once himself and his neighbor. That man's soul is not dear to himself, to whom the souls of his brethren are not dear. As far as they can be influenced by him, they are parts and properties of his own soul, their faith his faith, their errors his burthen, their righteousness and bliss his righteousness and his reward—and of their guilt and misery his own will be the echo. As much as I love my fellow-men, so much and no more will I be intolerant of their heresies and unbelief—and I will honor and hold forth the right hand of fellowship to every individual who is equally intolerant of that which he conceives such in me. We will both exclaim—'I know not what antidotes among the complex views, impulses and circumstances, that form your moral being, God's gracious providence may have vouchsafed to you against the serpent fang of this error,—but it is a viper, and its poison deadly, although through higher influences some men may take the reptile to their bosom, and remain unstung.'

In one of those poisonous journals, which deal out profaneness, hate, fury, and sedition through the land, I read the following paragraph. "The Brahmin believes that every man will be saved in his own persuasion, and that all religions are equally pleasing to the God of all. The Christian confines salvation to the believer in his own Vedas and Shasters. Which is the more humane and philosophic creed of the two?" Let question answer question. Self-complacent scoffer! Whom meanest thou by God? The God of truth?—and can He be pleased with falsehood, and the debasement or utter suspension of the reason which he gave to man that he might receive from him the sacrifice of truth? Or the God of love and mercy?—and can He be pleased with the blood of thousands poured out under the wheels of Juggernaut, or with the shrieks of children offered up as fire offerings to Baal or to Moloch? Or dost thou mean the God of holiness and infinite purity?—and can He be pleased with abominations unutterable and more than brutal defilements,—and equally pleased too as with that religion, which commands us that we have no fellowship with the unfruitful works of darkness but to reprove them;—with that religion, which strikes the fear of the Most High so deeply, and the sense of the exceeding sinfulness of sin so inwardly, that the believer anxiously inquires: *Shall I give my first-born for my transgression, the fruit of my body for the sin of my soul?*—and which makes answer to him,—*He hath showed thee, O man, what is good; and what doth the Lord require of thee, but to do justly, and to love mercy, and to walk humbly with thy God?** But I check myself. It is at once folly and profanation of truth, to reason with the man who can place before his eyes a minister of the Gospel directing the eye of the widow from the corpse of her husband upward to his and her Redeemer,—(the God of the living and not of the dead)—and then the remorseless Brahmin goading on the disconsolate victim to the flames of her husband's funeral pile, abandoned by, and abandoning, the helpless pledges of their love—and yet dare ask, which is the more humane and philosophic creed of the two?—No! No! when such opinions are in question I neither am, nor will be, nor wish to be regarded as, tolerant.

* Micah vi. 7, 8.—*Ed.*

ESSAY XIV.

Knowing the heart of man is set to be
The centre of this world, about the which
These revolutions of disturbances
Still roll; where all the aspects of misery
Predominate; whose strong effects are such,
As he must bear, being powerless to redress:
And that unless above himself he can
Erect himself, how poor a thing is man! DANIEL.*

I HAVE thus endeavored, with an anxiety which may perhaps have misled me into prolixity, to detail and ground the conditions under which the communication of truth is commanded or forbidden to us as individuals, by our conscience; and those too, under which it is permissible by the law which controls our conduct as members of the state. But is the subject of sufficient importance to deserve so minute an examination? O that my readers would look round the world, as it now is, and make to themselves a faithful catalogue of its many miseries! From what do these proceed, and on what do they depend for their continuance? Assuredly, for the greater part, on the actions of men, and those again on the want of a vital principle of action. *We live by faith.* The essence of virtue consists in the principle. And the reality of this, as well as its importance, is believed by all men in fact, few as there may be who bring the truth forward into the light of distinct consciousness. Yet all men feel, and at times acknowledge to themselves, the true cause of their misery. There is no man so base, but that at some time or other, and in some way or other, he admits that he is not what he ought to be, though by a curious art of self-delusion, by an effort to keep at peace with himself as long and as much as possible, he will throw off the blame from the amenable part of his na-

* Epistle to the Countess of Cumberland.—*Ed.*

ture, his moral principle, to that which is independent of his will, namely, the degree of his intellectual faculties. Hence, for once that a man exclaims, how dishonest I am! on what base and unworthy motives I act! we may hear a hundred times, what a fool I am! curse on my folly! and the like.*

Yet even this implies an obscure sentiment, that with clearer conceptions in the understanding, the principle of action would become purer in the will. Thanks to the image of our Maker not wholly obliterated from any human soul, we dare not purchase an exemption from guilt by an excuse, which would place our melioration out of our own power. Thus the very man, who will abuse himself for a fool but not for a villain, would rather, spite of the usual professions to the contrary, be condemned as a rogue by other men, than be acquitted as a blockhead. But be this as it may, in and out of himself, however, he sees plainly the true cause of our common complaints. Doubtless, there seem many physical causes of distress, of disease, of poverty and of desolation—tempests, earthquakes, volcanos, wild or venomous animals, barren soils, uncertain or tyrannous climates, pestilential swamps, and death in the very air we breathe. Yet when do we hear the general wretchedness of mankind attributed to these? Even in the most awful of the Icelandic and Sicilian eruptions, when the earth has opened and sent forth vast rivers of fire, and the smoke and vapor have dimmed the light of heaven for months, how small has been the comparative injury to the human race;—and how much even of this injury might be fairly attributed to combined imprudence and superstition! Natural calamities that do indeed spread devastation wide (for instance, the marsh fever), are almost without exception, voices of nature in her all-intelligible language—do this! or cease to do that! By the mere absence of one superstition, and of the sloth engendered by it, the plague would probably cease to exist throughout Asia and Africa. Pronounce meditatively the name of Jenner, and ask what might we not hope, what need we deem unattainable, if all the time, the effort, the skill, which we waste in making

* I do not consider as exceptions the thousands that abuse themselves by rote with lip-penitence, or the wild ravings of fanaticism; for these persons at the very time they speak so vehemently of the wickedness and rottenness of their hearts, are then commonly the warmest in their own good opinion, covered round and comfortable in the wrap-rascal of self-hypocrisy.

ourselves miserable through vice, and vicious through misery, were embodied and marshalled to a systematic war against the existing evils of nature! No, It is a wicked world! This is so generally the solution, that this very wickedness is assigned by selfish men, as their excuse for doing nothing to render it better, and for opposing those who would make the attempt. What have not Clarkson, Granville Sharp, Wilberforce, and the Society of the Friends, effected for the honor, and if we believe in a retributive Providence, for the continuance of the prosperity of the English nation, imperfectly as the intellectual and moral faculties of the people at large are developed at present! What may not be effected, if the recent discovery of the means of educating nations (freed, however, from the vile sophistications and mutilations of ignorant mountebanks) shall have been applied to its full extent! Would I frame to myself the most inspiring representation of future bliss, which my mind is capable of comprehending, it would be embodied to me in the idea of Bell receiving, at some distant period, the appropriate reward of his earthly labors, when thousands and ten thousands of glorified spirits, whose reason and conscience had, through his efforts, been unfolded, shall sing the song of their own redemption, and pouring forth praises to God and to their Saviour, shall repeat his *new name* in heaven, give thanks for his earthly virtues, as the chosen instruments of divine mercy to themselves, and not seldom perhaps turn their eyes toward him, as from the sun to its image in the fountain, with secondary gratitude and the permitted utterance of a human love! Were but a hundred men to combine a deep conviction that virtuous habits may be formed by the very means by which knowledge is communicated, that men may be made better, not only in consequence, but by the mode, and in the process, of instruction;—were but a hundred men to combine that clear conviction of this, which I myself at this moment feel, even as I feel the certainty of my being, with the perseverance of a Clarkson or a Bell, the promises of ancient prophecy would disclose themselves to our faith, even as when a noble castle hidden from us by an intervening mist, discovers itself by its reflection in the tranquil lake, on the opposite shore of which we stand gazing.* What an awful duty, what a nurse of all other, the fairest vir-

* This is, I fear, too complex, too accidental an image to be conveyed by words to those, who have not seen it themselves in nature. 1830.

tues, does not hope become! We are bad ourselves, because we despair of the goodness of others.

If then it be a truth, attested alike by common feeling and common sense, that the greater part of human misery depends directly on human vices, and the remainder indirectly, by what means can we act on men so as to remove or preclude these vices, and purify their principle of moral election? The question is not by what means each man is to alter his own character—in order to this, all the means prescribed and all the aidances given by religion, may be necessary for him. Vain, of themselves, may be

> —— the sayings of the wise
> In ancient and in modern books enrolled
> *   *   *   *   *
> Unless he feel within
> Some source of consolation from above,
> Secret refreshings, that repair his strength
> And fainting spirits uphold.*

This is not the question. Virtue would not be virtue, could it be given by one fellow-creature to another. To make use of all the means and appliances in our power to the actual attainment of rectitude, is the abstract of the duty which we owe to ourselves: to supply those means as far as we can, comprises our duty to others. The question then is, what are these means? Can they be any other than the communication of knowledge, and the removal of those evils and impediments which prevent its reception? It may not be in our power to combine both, but it is in the power of every man to contribute to the former, who is sufficiently informed to feel that it is his duty. If it be said, that we should endeavor not so much to remove ignorance, as to make the ignorant religious;—religion herself, through her sacred oracles, answers for me, that all effective faith pre-supposes knowledge and individual conviction. If the mere acquiescence in truth, uncomprehended and unfathomed, were sufficient, few indeed would be the vicious and the miserable, in this country at least, where speculative infidelity is, God be praised! confined to a small number. Like bodily deformity, there is one instance here and another there; but three in one place are already an undue proportion. It is highly worthy of observation, that the

* Samson Agonistes.

inspired writings received by Christians are distinguishable from all other books pretending to inspiration, from the scriptures of the Brahmins, and even from the Koran, in their strong and frequent recommendations of truth. I do not here mean veracity, which can not but be enforced in every code which appeals to the religious principle of man; but knowledge. This is not only extolled as the crown and honor of a man, but to seek after it is again and again commanded us as one of our most sacred duties. Yea, the very perfection and final bliss of the glorified spirit is represented by the Apostle as a plain aspect, or intuitive beholding, of truth in its eternal and immutable source. Not that knowledge can of itself do all! The light of religion is not that of the moon, light without heat; but neither is its warmth that of the stove, warmth without light. Religion is the sun, the warmth of which indeed swells, and stirs, and actuates the life of nature, but who at the same time beholds all the growth of life with a master-eye, makes all objects glorious on which he looks, and by that glory visible to all others.

But though knowledge be not the only, yet that it is an indispensable and most effectual agent in the direction of our actions, one consideration will convince us. It is an undoubted fact of human nature, that the sense of impossibility quenches all will. Sense of utter inaptitude does the same. The man shuns the beautiful flame, which is eagerly grasped at by the infant. The sense of a disproportion of certain after-harm to present gratification, produces effects almost equally uniform: though almost perishing with thirst, we should dash to the earth a goblet of wine in which we had seen a poison infused, though the poison were without taste or odor, or even added to the pleasures of both. Are not all our vices equally inapt to the universal end of human actions, the satisfaction of the agent? Are not their pleasures equally disproportionate to the after-harm? Yet many a maiden, who will not grasp at the fire, will yet purchase a wreath of diamonds at the price of her health, her honor, nay, —and she herself knows it at the moment of her choice,—at the sacrifice of her peace and happiness. The sot would reject the poisoned cup, yet the trembling hand with which he raises his daily or hourly draught to his lips, has not left him ignorant that this too is altogether a poison. I know it will be objected, that the consequences foreseen are less immediate; that they are diffused over a larger space of time; and that the slave of vice hopes where no hope is. This, however, only removes the question one step further: for why should the distance or diffusion of known consequences produce so great a difference? Why are men the dupes of the present moment? Evidently because the conceptions are indistinct in the one case, and vivid in the other; because all confused conceptions render us restless; and because restlessness can drive us to vices that promise no enjoyment, no not even the cessation of that restlessness. This is indeed the dread punishment attached by nature to habitual vice, that its impulses wax as its motives wane. No object, not even the light of a solitary taper in the far distance, tempts the benighted mind from before; but its own restlessness dogs it from behind, as with the iron goad of destiny. What then is or can be the preventive, the remedy, the counteraction, but the habituation of the intellect to clear, distinct, and adequate conceptions concerning all things that are the possible object of clear conception, and thus to reserve the deep feelings which belong, as by a natural right, to those obscure ideas* that are necessary to the moral perfection of the human being, notwithstanding, yea, even in consequence, of their obscurity—to reserve these feelings, I repeat, for objects, which their very sublimity renders indefinite, no less than their indefiniteness renders them sublime,—namely, to the ideas of being, form, life, the reason, the law of conscience, freedom, immortality, God! To connect with the objects of our senses the obscure notions and consequent vivid feelings, which are due only to immaterial and permanent things, is profanation relatively to the heart, and superstition in the understanding. It is in this sense, that the philosophic Apostle calls covetousness idolatry. Could we emancipate ourselves from the bedimming influences of custom, and the transforming witchcraft of early

* I have not expressed myself as clearly as I could wish. But the truth of the assertion, that deep feeling has a tendency to combine with obscure ideas, in preference to distinct and clear notions, may be proved by the history of fanatics and fanaticism in all ages and countries. The *odium theologicum* is even proverbial: and it is the common complaint of philosophers and philosophic historians, that the passions of the disputants are commonly violent in proportion to the subtlety and obscurity of the questions in dispute. Nor is this fact confined to professional theologians: for whole nations have displayed the same agitations, and have sacrificed national policy to the more powerful interest of a controverted obscurity.

associations, we should see as numerous tribes of *fetisch*-worshipers in the streets of London and Paris, as we hear of on the coasts of Africa.

ESSAY XV.

A palace when 'tis that which it should be
Leaves growing, and stands such, or else decays;
With him who dwells there, 'tis not so: for he
Should still urge upward, and his fortune raise.

Our bodies had their morning, have *their* noon,
And shall not better—*the* next change is night;
But *their* far larger guest, t' whom sun and moon
Are sparks and short-lived, claims another right.

The noble soul by age grows lustier,
Her appetite and her digestion mend;
We must not starve nor hope to pamper her
With woman's milk and pap unto the end.

Provide you manlier diet! DONNE.*

I AM fully aware, that what I am writing and have written (in these latter essays at least) will expose me to the censure of some, as bewildering myself and readers with metaphysics; to the ridicule of others as a school-boy declaimer on old and worn-out truisms or exploded fancies; and to the objection of most as obscure. The last real or supposed defect has already received an answer both in the preceding essays, and in the appendix to my first Lay-Sermon, entitled The Statesman's Manual. Of the former two, I shall take the present opportunity of declaring my sentiments; especially as I have already received a hint that my idol, Milton, has represented metaphysics as the subject which the bad spirits in hell delight in discussing. And truly, if I had exerted my subtlety and invention in persuading myself and others that we are but living machines, and that, as one of the late followers of Hobbes and Hartley has expressed the system, the as-

* Letter to Sir Henry Goodere. The words in italics are substituted for the original.—*Ed.*

sassin and his dagger are equally fit objects of moral esteem and abhorrence; or if with a writer of wider influence and higher authority, I had reduced all virtue to a selfish prudence eked out by superstition,*—for, assuredly, a creed which takes its central point in conscious selfishness, whatever be the forms or names that act on the selfish passion, a ghost or a constable, can have but a distant relationship to that religion, which places its essence in our loving our neighbor as ourselves, and God above all,—I know not, by what arguments I could repel the sarcasm. But what are my metaphysics?—Merely the referring of the mind to its own consciousness for truths indispensable to its own happiness! To what purpose do I, or am I about to, employ them? To perplex our clearest notions and living moral instincts? To deaden the feelings of will and free power, to extinguish the light of love and of conscience, to make myself and others worthless, soulless, God-less? No! to expose the folly and the legerdemain of those who have thus abused the blessed machine of language; to support all old and venerable truths; and by them to support, to kindle, to project the spirit; to make the reason spread light over our feelings, to make our feelings, with their vital warmth, actualize our reason:—these are my objects, these are my subjects; and are these the metaphysics which the bad spirits in hell delight in?

But how shall I avert the scorn of those critics who laugh at the oldness of my topics, evil and good, necessity and arbitrament, immortality and the ultimate aim? By what shall I regain their favor? My themes must be new, a French constitution; a balloon; a change of ministry; a fresh batch of kings on the Continent, or of peers in our happier island; or who had the best of it of two parliamentary gladiators, and whose speech, on the subject of Europe bleeding at a thousand wounds, or our own country struggling for herself and all human nature, was cheered

* "And from this account of obligation it follows, that we are obliged to nothing but what we ourselves are to gain or lose something by; for nothing else can be a violent motive to us. As we should not be obliged to obey the laws, or the magistrate, unless rewards or punishments, pleasure or pain, somehow or other, depended upon our obedience; so neither should we, without the same reason, be obliged to do what is right, to practise virtue, or to obey the commands of God."—Paley, Moral and Political Philosophy, B. II. c. 2, *et passim.*—*Ed.*

by the greatest number of "laughs," "loud laughs," and "very loud laughs:"—(which, carefully marked by italics, form most conspicuous and strange parentheses in the newspaper reports.) Or if I must be philosophical, the last chemical discoveries,—provided I do not trouble my reader with the principle which gives them their highest interest, and the character of intellectual grandeur to the discoverer; or the last shower of stones, and that they were supposed, by certain philosophers, to have been projected from some volcano in the moon,—care being taken not to add any of the cramp reasons for this opinion! Something new, however, it must be, quite new and quite out of themselves! for whatever is within them, whatever is deep within them, must be as old as the first dawn of human reason. But to find no contradiction in the union of old and new, to contemplate the Ancient of days with feelings as fresh, as if they then sprang forth at his own *fiat*—this characterizes the minds that feel the riddle of the world, and may help to unravel it! To carry on the feelings of childhood into the powers of manhood, to combine the child's sense of wonder and novelty with the appearances which every day for perhaps forty years has rendered familiar,

> With sun and moon and stars throughout the year,
> And man and woman ———

this is the character and privilege of genius, and one of the marks which distinguish genius from talent. And so to represent familiar objects as to awaken the minds of others to a like freshness of sensation concerning them—that constant accompaniment of mental, no less than of bodily, health—to the same modest questioning of a self-discovered and intelligent ignorance, which, like the deep and massy foundations of a Roman bridge, forms half of the whole structure—(*prudens interrogatio dimidium scientiæ*, says Lord Bacon)—this is the prime merit of genius, and its most unequivocal mode of manifestation. Who has not, a thousand times, seen it snow upon water? Who has not seen it with a new feeling, since he has read Burns's comparison of sensual pleasure,

> To snow that falls upon a river,
> A moment white—then gone forever!*

* Tam O'Shanter.—*Ed.*

In philosophy equally, as in poetry, genius produces the strongest impressions of novelty, while it rescues the stalest and most admitted truths from the impotence caused by the very circumstance of their universal admission. Extremes meet;—a proverb, by the by, to collect and explain all the instances and exemplifications of which, would constitute and exhaust all philosophy. Truths, of all others the most awful and mysterious, yet being at the same time of universal interest, are too often considered as so true that they lose all the powers of truth, and lie bed-ridden in the dormitory of the soul, side by side with the most despised and exploded errors.

But as the class of critics, whose contempt I have anticipated, commonly consider themselves as men of the world, instead of hazarding additional sneers by appealing to the authorities of recluse philosophers,—for such, in spite of all history, the men who have distinguished themselves by profound thought, are generally deemed, from Plato and Aristotle to Cicero, and from Bacon to Berkeley—I will refer them to the darling of the polished court of Augustus, to the man, whose works have been in all ages deemed the models of good sense, and are still the pocket companion of those who pride themselves on uniting the scholar with the gentleman. This accomplished man of the world has given us an account of the subjects of conversation between himself and the illustrious statesmen who governed, and the brightest luminaries who then adorned, the empire of the civilized world:

Sermo oritur non de villis domibusve alienis,
Nec male, necne, lepus saltet. Sed quod magis ad nos
Pertinet, et nescire malum est, agitamus: utrumne
Divitiis homines, an sint virtute beati?
Quidve ad amicitias, usus rectumne, trahat nos;
Et quæ sit natura boni, summumque quid ejus.—HOR.*

Berkeley indeed asserts, and is supported in his assertion by Lord Bacon and Sir Walter Raleigh, that without an habitual in-

* Serm. II. vi. 71. Conversation arises not concerning the country seats or families of strangers, nor whether the dancing hare performed well or ill. But we discuss what more nearly concerns us, and which it is an evil not to know: whether men are made happy by riches or by virtue: whether interest or a love of virtue should lead us to friendship; and in what consists the nature of good, and what is the ultimate or supreme good—*the summum bonum.*

terest in these subjects, a man may be a dexterous intriguer, but never can be a statesman. Would to Heaven that the verdict to be passed on my labors depended on those who least needed them! The water-lily in the midst of waters lifts up its broad leaves, and expands its petals at the first pattering of the shower, and rejoices in the rain with a quicker sympathy, than the parched shrub in the sandy desert.

God created man in his own image. To be the image of his own eternity created he man! Of eternity and self-existence what other likeness is possible, but immortality and moral self-determination? In addition to sensation, perception, and practical judgment—instinctive or acquirable—concerning the notices furnished by the organs of perception, all which in kind at least, the dog possesses in common with his master; in addition to these, God gave us reason, and with reason he gave us reflective self-consciousness; gave us principles, distinguished from the maxims and generalizations of outward experience by their absolute and essential universality and necessity; and above all, by superadding to reason the mysterious faculty of free-will and consequent personal amenability, he gave us conscience—that law of conscience, which in the power, and as the indwelling word, of a holy and omnipotent legislator commands us—from among the numerous ideas mathematical and philosophical, which the reason by the necessity of its own excellence creates for itself,—unconditionally commands us to attribute reality, and actual existence, to those ideas and to those only, without which the conscience itself would be baseless and contradictory, to the ideas of soul, of free-will, of immortality, and of God. To God, as the reality of the conscience and the source of all obligation; to free-will, as the power of the human being to maintain the obedience which God through the conscience has commanded, against all the might of nature; and to the immortality of the soul, as a state in which the weal and woe of man shall be proportioned to his moral worth. With this faith all nature,

———all the mighty world
Of eye and ear———*

presents itself to us, now as the aggregated material of duty, and now as a vision of the Most High revealing to us the mode, and

* Wordsworth. Lines near Tintern Abbey.—*Ed.*

time, and particular instance of applying and realizing that universal rule, pre-established in the heart of our reason.

"The displeasure of some readers," to use Berkeley's words,* "may, perhaps, be incurred by my *having surprised* them into certain reflections and inquiries, for which they have no curiosity. But perhaps some others may be pleased to find *themselves* carried into ancient times, *even though they should consider* the hoary maxims, *defended* in these essays, barely as hints to awaken and exercise the inquisitive reader, on points not beneath the attention of the ablest men. Those great men, Pythagoras, Plato, and Aristotle, men the most consummate in politics, who founded states, or instructed princes, or wrote most accurately on public government, were at the same time the most acute at all abstracted and sublime speculations;—the clearest light being ever necessary to guide the most important actions. And whatever the world *may opine*, he who hath not much meditated upon God, the human mind, and the *summum bonum*, may possibly make a thriving earth-worm, but will most indubitably make a *blundering* patriot and a sorry statesman."

ESSAY XVI.

Blind is that soul which from this truth can swerve,
No state stands sure, but on the grounds of right,
Of virtue, knowledge; judgment to preserve,
And all the pow'rs of learning requisite:
Though other shifts a present turn may serve,
Yet in the trial they will weigh too light. DANIEL.†

I EARNESTLY entreat the reader not to be dissatisfied either with himself or with the author, if he should not at once understand every part of the preceding essay; but rather to consider it as a mere annunciation of a magnificent theme, the different parts of which are to be demonstrated and developed, explained, illustrated, and exemplified in the progress of the work. I like-

* Siris, 350. The words in italics are substituted for the original.—*Ed.*
† *Musophilus.* The line in italics is substituted.—*Ed.*

wise entreat him to peruse with attention and with candor, the weighty extract from the judicious Hooker, prefixed as the motto to a following essay.* In works of reasoning, as distinguished from narrations of events or statements of facts; but more particularly in works, the object of which is to make us better acquainted with our own nature, a writer whose meaning is everywhere comprehended as quickly as his sentences can be read, may indeed have produced an amusing composition, nay, by awakening and re-enlivening our recollections, a useful one; but most assuredly he will not have added either to the stock of our knowledge, or to the vigor of our intellect. For how can we gather strength, but by exercise? How can a truth, new to us, be made our own without examination and self-questioning—any new truth, I mean, that relates to the properties of the mind, and its various faculties and affections? But whatever demands effort, requires time. Ignorance seldom vaults into knowledge, but passes into it through an intermediate state of obscurity, even as night into day through twilight. All speculative truths begin with a postulate, even the truths of geometry. They all suppose an act of the will; for in the moral being lies the source of the intellectual. The first step to knowledge, or rather the previous condition of all insight into truth, is to dare commune with our very and permanent self. It is Warburton's remark, not the Friend's, that of all literary exercitations, whether designed for the use or entertainment of the world, there are none of so much importance, or so immediately our concern, as those which let us into the knowledge of our own nature. Others may exercise the understanding or amuse the imagination; but these only can improve the heart and form the human mind to wisdom.

> *The* recluse hermit ofttimes *more doth* know
> *Of the world's inmost wheels*, than worldlings can.
> As man is of the world, the heart of man
> Is an epitome of God's great book
> Of creatures, and men need no farther look. DONNE.†

The higher a man's station, the more arduous and full of peril his duties, the more comprehensive should his foresight be, the more rooted his tranquillity concerning life and death. But these

* Essay IV. Sect. On the Principles of Political Knowledge. See Eccl. Pol. I. c. I. 2.—*Ed.*

† Eclogue. The words in italics are substituted.—*Ed.*

are gifts which no experience can bestow, but the experience from within: and there is a nobleness of the whole personal being, to which the contemplation of all events and *phænomena* in the light of the three master ideas, announced in the foregoing pages, can alone elevate the spirit. *Anima sapiens*, says Giordano Bruno,—and let the sublime piety of the passage excuse some intermixture of error, or rather let the words, as they well may, be interpreted in a safe sense—*anima sapiens non timet mortem, immo interdum illam ultro appetit, illi ultro occurrit. Manet quippe substantiam omnem pro duratione eternitas, pro loco immensitas, pro actu omniformitas. Non levem igitur ac futilem, atqui gravissimam perfectoque homine dignissimam contemplationis partem persequimur, ubi divinitatis, naturæque splendorem, fusionem, et communicationem, non in cibo, potu, et ignobiliore quadam materia cum attonitorum seculo perquirimus; sed in augusta Omnipotentis regia, immenso ætheris spatio, in infinita naturæ geminæ omnis fientis et omnia facientis potentia, unde tot astrorum, mundorum, inquam, et numinum, uni altissimo concinentium atque saltantium absque numero atque fine juxta propositos ubique fines atque ordines contemplamur. Sic ex visibilium æterno, immenso et innumerabili effectu sempiterna immensa illa majestas atque bonitas intellecta conspicitur, proque sua dignitate innumerabilium deorum (mundorum dico) adsistentia, concinentia, et gloriæ ipsius enarratione, immo ad oculos expressa concione glorificatur. Cui immenso mensum non quadrabit domicilium atque templum;—ad cujus majestatis plenitudinem agnoscendam atque percolendam, numerabilium ministrorum nullus esset ordo. Eia igitur ad omniformis Dei omniformem imaginem conjectemus oculos, vivum et magnum illius admiremur simulacrum!—Hinc miraculum magnum a Trismegisto appellabatur homo, qui in Deum transeat quasi ipse sit Deus, qui conatur omnia fieri sicut Deus est omnia; ad objectum sine fine, ubique tamen finiendo, contendit, sicut infinitus est Deus, immensus, ubique totus.**

* *De monade, &c.* A wise spirit does not fear death, nay, sometimes—as in cases of voluntary martyrdom—seeks and goes forth to meet it, of its own accord. For there awaits all actual beings, for duration eternity, for place immensity, for action omniformity. We pursue, therefore, a species of contemplation not light or futile, but the weightiest and most worthy of

If this be regarded as the fancies of an enthusiast, by such as

> ———deem themselves most free,
> When they within this gross and visible sphere
> Chain down the winged soul, scoffing ascent,
> Proud in their meanness, ———*

by such as pronounce every man out of his senses who has not lost his reason; even such men may find some weight in the

an accomplished man, while we examine and seek for the splendor, the interfusion, and communication of the Divinity and of nature, not in meats or drink, or any yet ignoble matter, with the race of the thunder-stricken; but in the august palace of the Omnipotent, in the illimitable ethereal space, in the infinite power, that creates all things, and is the abiding being of all things.

There we may contemplate the host of stars, of worlds, and their guardian deities, numbers without number, each in its appointed sphere, singing together, and dancing in adoration of the One Most High. Thus from the perpetual, immense, and innumerable goings on of the visible world, that sempiternal and absolutely infinite Majesty is intellectually beheld, and is glorified according to his glory, by the attendance and choral symphonies of innumerable gods, who utter forth the glory of their ineffable Creator in the expressive language of vision! To him illimitable, a limited temple will not correspond—to the acknowledgment and due worship of the plenitude of his majesty there would be no proportion in any innumerable army of ministrant spirits. Let us then cast our eyes upon the omniform image of the attributes of the all-creating Supreme, nor admit any representation of his excellency but the living universe, which he has created! Thence was man entitled by Trismegistus, the great miracle, inasmuch as he has been made capable of entering into union with God, as if he were himself a divine nature; tries to become all things, even as in God all things are; and in limitless progression of limited states of being, urges onward to the ultimate aim, even as God is simultaneously infinite, and everywhere all!

Giordano Bruno, the friend of Sir Philip Sidney and Fulk Greville, was burnt under pretence of atheism, at Rome, on the 17th of February, 1599–1600 (Scioppio ends his narrative in these words: *Sic ustulatus misere periit, renunciaturus, credo, in reliquis illis, quos finxit, mundis, quonam pacto homines blasphemi et impii a Romanis tractari solent. Hic itaque modus in Roma est, quo contra homines impios et monstra hujusmodi procedi à nobis solet.*—Ed.) His works are perhaps the scarcest books ever printed. They are singularly interesting as portraits of a vigorous mind struggling after truth, amid many prejudices, which from the state of the Romish Church, in which he was born, have a claim to much indulgence. One of them (entitled Ember Week) is curious for its lively accounts of the rude state of London, at that time, both as to the streets and the manners of the citizens.

---

* Poetical Works, VII. p. 83.—*Ed.*

historical fact that from persons, who had previously strengthened their intellects and feelings by the contemplation of principles—principles, the actions correspondent to which involve one half of their consequences, by their ennobling influence on the agent's own soul, and have omnipotence, as the pledge for the remainder—we have derived the surest and most general maxims of prudence. Of high value are they all. Yet there is one among them worth all the rest, which in the fullest and primary sense of the word is, indeed, the maxim, that is, *maximum*, of human prudence; and of which history itself, in all that makes it most worth studying, is one continued comment and exemplification. It is this: that there is a wisdom higher than prudence, to which prudence stands in the same relation as the mason and carpenter to the genial and scientific architect; and it is from the habits of thinking and feeling, which in this wisdom had their first formation, that our Nelsons and Wellingtons inherit that glorious hardihood, which completes the undertaking, ere the contemptuous calculator, who has left nothing omitted in his scheme of probabilities, except the might of the human mind, has finished his pretended proof of its impossibility. You look to facts, and profess to take experience for your guide. Well! I too appeal to experience: and let facts be the ordeal of my position! Therefore, although I have in this and the preceding essays quoted more frequently and copiously than I shall permit myself to do in future, I owe it to the cause I am pleading not to deny myself the gratification of supporting this connection of practical heroism with previous habits of philosophic thought, by a singularly ap-

(*La cena de le ceneri.* See particularly the second dialogue.—*Ed.*) The most industrious historians of speculative philosophy, have not been able to procure more than a few of his works. Accidentally I have been more fortunate in this respect, than those who have written hitherto on the unhappy philosopher of Nola; as out of eleven works, the titles of which are preserved to us, I have had an opportunity of perusing six. I was told, when in Germany, that there is a complete collection of them in the royal library at Copenhagen. If so, it is unique.

(Wagner has collected and published seven of the Italian works of Bruno: Leipzig, 1830. These are, *Il Candelajo; La cena de le ceneri; De la causa, principio et uno; De l'infinito, universo e mondi; Spaccio de la bestia trionfante; Cabala del caballo Pegaseo;* and *De gli eroici furori.* Two others are mentioned by Bruno, himself in the *Cena*, &c.; namely, *L'arca di Noè* and *Purgatorio dell' inferno.* Wagner could not discover these. The titles of twenty-three works in Latin are given by Wagner.—*Ed.*)

propriate passage from an author whose works can be called rare only from their being, I fear, rarely read, however commonly talked of. It is the instance of Xenophon, as stated by Lord Bacon, who would himself furnish an equal instance, if there conld be found an equal commentator.

"It is of Xenophon the philosopher, who went from Socrates' school into Asia, in the expedition of Cyrus the younger, against King Artaxerxes. This Xenophon, at that time, was very young, and never had seen the wars before; neither had any command in the army, but only followed the war as a volunteer, for the love and conversation of Proxenus, his friend. He was present when Falinus came in message from the great King to the Grecians, after that Cyrus was slain in the field, and they, a handful of men, left to themselves in the midst of the King's territories, cut off from their country by many navigable rivers, and many hundred miles. The message imported, that they should deliver up their arms and submit themselves to the King's mercy. To which message, before answer was made, divers of the army conferred familiarly with Falinus, and amongst the rest Xenophon happened to say: 'Why, Falinus! we have now but these two things left, our arms and our virtue; and if we yield up our arms, how shall we make use of our virtue?' Whereto Falinus, smiling on him, said, 'If I be not deceived, young gentleman, you are an Athenian, and I believe you study philosophy, and it is pretty that you say; but you are much abused, if you think your virtue can withstand the King's power.' Here was the scorn: the wonder followed;—which was, that this young scholar or philosopher, after all the captains were murdered in parley, by treason, conducted those ten thousand foot through the heart of all the King's high countries from Babylon to Græcia, in safety, in despite of all the King's forces, to the astonishment of the world, and the encouragement of the Grecians, in time succeeding, to make invasion upon the kings of Persia; as was after purposed by Jason the Thessalian, attempted by Agesilaus the Spartan, and achieved by Alexander the Macedonian, all upon the ground of the act of that young scholar."*

Often have I reflected with awe on the great and disproportionate power, which an individual of no extraordinary talents or attainments may exert, by merely throwing off all restraint of

* Advancement of Learning. B. I.—*Ed.*

conscience. What then must not be the power, where an individual, of consummate wickedness, can organize into the unity and rapidity of an individual will all the natural and artificial forces of a populous and wicked nation? And could we bring within the field of imagination, the devastation effected in the moral world, by the violent removal of old customs, familiar sympathies, willing reverences, and habits of subordination almost naturalized into instinct; of the mild influences of reputation, and the other ordinary props and aidances of our infirm virtue, or at least, if virtue be too high a name, of our well-doing; and above all, if we could give form and body to all the effects produced on the principles and dispositions of nations by the infectious feelings of insecurity, and the soul-sickening sense of unsteadiness in the whole edifice of civil society; the horrors of battle, though the miseries of a whole war were brought together before our eyes in one disastrous field, would present but a tame tragedy in comparison. Nay it would even present a sight of comfort and of elevation, if this field of carnage were the sign and result of a national resolve, of a general will, so to die, that neither deluge nor fire should take away the name of country from their graves, rather than to tread the same clods of earth, no longer a country, and themselves alive in nature, but dead in infamy. What is Greece at this present moment? It is the country of the heroes from Codrus to Philopæmen; and so it would be, though all the sands of Africa should cover its cornfields and olive-gardens, and not a flower were left on Hymettus for a bee to murmur in.

If then the power with which wickedness can invest the human being be thus tremendous, greatly does it behoove us to inquire into its source and causes. So doing we shall quickly discover that it is not vice, as vice, which is thus mighty; but systematic vice. Vice self-consistent and entire; crime corresponding to crime; villany entrenched and barricadoed by villany; this is the condition and main constituent of its power. The abandonment of all principle of right enables the soul to choose and act upon a principle of wrong, and to subordinate to this one principle all the various vices of human nature. For it is a mournful truth, that as devastation is incomparably an easier work than production, so may all its means and instruments be more easily arranged into a scheme and system: even as in a siege every building and garden, which the faithful governor must destroy, as impeding the defensive means of the garrison, or furnishing means of offence to the besieger, occasions a wound in feelings which virtue herself has fostered: and virtue, because it is virtue, loses perforce part of her energy in the reluctance with which she proceeds to a business so repugnant to her wishes, as a choice of evils. But he, who has once said with his whole heart, Evil, be thou my good! has removed a world of obstacles by the very decision, that he will have no obstacles but those of force and brute matter. The road of justice

> Curves round the corn-field and the hill of vines,
> Honoring the holy bounds of property;—*

but the path of the lightning is straight; and straight the fearful path

> Of the cannon-ball. Direct it flies and rapid,
> Shatt'ring that it may reach, and shatt'ring what it reaches.†

Happily for mankind, however, the obstacles which a consistently evil mind no longer finds in itself, it finds in its own unsuitableness to human nature. A limit is fixed to its power: but within that limit, both as to the extent and duration of its influence, there is little hope of checking its career, if giant and united vices are opposed only by mixed and scattered virtues; and those too, probably, from the want of some combining principle, which assigns to each its due place and rank, at civil war with themselves, or at best perplexing and counteracting each other. In our late agony of glory and of peril, did we not too often hear even good men declaiming on the horrors and crimes of war, and softening or staggering the minds of their brethren by details of individual wretchedness? Thus under pretence of avoiding blood, they were withdrawing the will from the defence of the very source of those blessings without which the blood would flow idly in our veins! Thus lest a few should fall on the bulwarks in glory, they were preparing us to give up the whole state to baseness, and the children of free ancestors to become slaves, and the fathers of slaves!

Machiavelli has well observed, *Sono di tre generazioni cervelli: l'uno intende per se; l'altro intende quanto da altri gli è*

* Poetical Works, VII. p. 480.—*Ed.*

† Ibid. p. 480.—*Ed.*

*mostro ; e il terzo non intende nè per se stesso, nè per dimostrazione di altri.** "There are brains of three races. The one understands of itself; the second understands as much as is shown it by others; the third neither understands of itself nor what is shown it by others."† I should have no hesitation in placing that man in the third class of brains, for whom the history of the last twenty years has not supplied a copious comment on the preceding text. The widest maxims of prudence are like arms without hearts, disjoined from those feelings which flow forth from principle as from a fountain. So little are even the genuine maxims of expedience likely to be perceived or acted upon by those who have been habituated to admit nothing higher than expedience, that I dare hazard the assertion, that in the whole chapter of contents of European ruin, every article might be unanswerably deduced from the neglect of some maxim which has been repeatedly laid down, demonstrated, and enforced with a host of illustrations, in some one or other of the works of Machiavelli, Bacon, or Harrington. Indeed I can remember no one event of importance which was not distinctly foretold, and this not by a lucky prize drawn among a thousand blanks out of the lottery wheel of conjecture, but legitimately deduced as certain consequences from established premises. It would be a melancholy, but a very profitable employment, for some vigorous mind, intimately acquainted with the recent history of Europe, to collect the weightiest aphorisms of Machiavelli alone, and illustrating by appropriate facts the breach or observation of each, to render less mysterious the present triumph of lawless violence. The apt motto to su cha work would be,—*The children of darkness are wiser in their generation than the children of light.*

So grievously, indeed, have men been deceived by the showy theories of unlearned mock thinkers, that there seems a tendency in the public mind to shun all thought, and to expect help from

* *Il Principe*, c. xxii.—*Ed.*

† *Οὗτος μὲν πανάριστος, ὃς αὐτῷ πάντα νοήσῃ,*
Φρασσάμενος τά κ' ἔπειτα καὶ ἐς τέλος ᾖσιν ἀμείνω·
'Εσθλὸς δ' αὖ κἀκεῖνος, ὃς εὖ εἰπόντι πίθηται.
"Ος δέ κε μήτ' αὐτὸς νοέῃ, μήτ' ἄλλου ἀκούων
Εν θυμῷ βάλληται, ὁ δ' αὖτ' ἀχρήϊος ἀνήρ.
Op. et Dies. 293, &c.

Cic, p. Cluent. c. 31. Liv. xxii. 29. Diog. Laer. vii. 1. 21.—*Ed.*

any quarter rather than from seriousness and reflection; as if some invisible power would think for us, when we gave up the pretence of thinking for ourselves. But in the first place, did those, who opposed the theories of innovators, conduct their untheoretic opposition with more wisdom, or to a happier result? And secondly, are societies now constructed on principles so few and so simple, that we could, if even we wished it, act as it were by instinct, like our distant forefathers in the infancy of states? Doubtless, to act is nobler than to think: but as the old man doth not become a child by means of his second childishness, as little can a nation exempt itself from the necessity of thinking which has once learnt to think. Miserable was the delusion of the late mad realizer of mad dreams, in his belief that he should ultimately succeed in transforming the nations of Europe into the unreasoning hordes of a Babylonian or Tartar empire, or even in reducing the age to the simplicity—so desirable for tyrants—of those times, when the sword and the plough were the sole implements of human skill. Those are epochs in the history of a people, which, having been, can never more recur. Extirpate all civilization and all its arts by the sword, trample down all ancient institutions, rights, distinctions, and privileges, drag us backward to our old barbarism, as beasts to the den of Cacus—deem you that thus you could recreate the unexamining and boisterous youth of the world, when the sole questions were—"What is to be conquered? and who is the most famous leader?"

In an age in which artificial knowledge is received almost at the birth, intellect and thought alone can be our upholder and judge. Let the importance of this truth procure pardon for its repetition. Only by means of seriousness, and meditation, and the free infliction of censure in the spirit of love, can the true philanthropist of the present time, curb-in himself and his contemporaries; only by these can he aid in preventing the evils which threaten us, not from the terrors of an enemy so much as from our own fear of, and aversion to, the toils of reflection. For all must now be taught in sport—science, morality, yea, religion itself. And yet few now sport from the actual impulse of a believing fancy and in a happy delusion. Of the most influential class, at least, of our literary guides—the anonymous authors of our periodical publications—the most part assume this character from cowardice or malice, till having begun with studied ignorance and a premeditated levity, they at length realize the lie, and end indeed in a pitiable destitution of all intellectual power.

To many I shall appear to speak insolently, because the public,—(for that is the phrase which has succeeded to The Town, of the wits of the reign of Charles II.)—the public is at present accustomed to find itself appealed to as the infallible judge, and each reader complimented with excellencies, which, if he really possessed, to what purpose is he a reader, unless, perhaps, to remind himself of his own superiority! I confess that I think very differently. I have not a deeper conviction on earth, than that the principles of taste, morals, and religion, which are taught in the commonest books of recent composition, are false, injurious, and debasing. If these sentiments should be just, the consequences must be so important, that every well-educated man, who professes them in sincerity, deserves a patient hearing. He may fairly appeal even to those whose persuasions are most opposed to his own, in the words of the philosopher of Nola:—*Ad isthæc quæso vos, qualiacunque primo videantur aspectu, adtendite, ut qui vobis forsan insanire videar, saltem quibus insaniam rationibus cognoscatis.* What I feel deeply, freely will I utter. Truth is not detraction; and assuredly we do not hate him to whom we tell the truth. But with whomsoever we play the deceiver and flatterer, him at the bottom we despise. We are, indeed, under a necessity to conceive a vileness in him, in order to diminish the sense of the wrong we have committed, by the worthlessness of the object.

Through no excess of confidence in the strength of my talents, but with the deepest assurance of the justice of my cause, I bid defiance to all the flatterers of the folly, and foolish self-opinion of the half-instructed many;—to all who fill the air with festal explosions and false fires sent up against the lightnings of heaven, in order that the people may neither distinguish the warning flash nor hear the threatening thunder! How recently did we stand alone in the world? And though the one storm has blown over, another may even now be gathering: or haply the hollow murmur of the earthquake within the bowels of our own commonweal may strike a direr terror than ever did the tempest of foreign warfare. Therefore, though the first quatrain is no longer applicable, yet the moral truth and the sublime exhortation of the following sonnet can never be superannuated. With it I conclude this essay, thanking God that I have communed with, honored, and loved its wise and high-minded author. To know that such men are among us, is of itself an antidote against despondence:—

Another year!—another deadly blow!
Another mighty empire overthrown!
And we are left, or shall be left, alone;
The last that dares to struggle with the foe.
'Tis well! from this day forward we shall know
That in ourselves our safety must be sought;
That by our own right hands it must be wrought;
That we must stand unpropt or be laid low.
O dastard! whom such foretaste doth not cheer!
We shall exult, if they, who rule the land,
Be men who hold its many blessings dear,
Wise, upright, valiant; not a venal band,
Who are to judge of danger which they fear,
And honor, which they do not understand. WORDSWORTH.

THE LANDING-PLACE:

OR ESSAYS INTERPOSED FOR AMUSEMENT, RETROSPECT, AND PREPARATION.

MISCELLANY THE FIRST.

Etiam a Musis si quando animum paulisper abducamus, apud Musas nihilominus feriamur: at reclines quidem, at otiosas, at de his et illis inter se libere colloquentes.

THE LANDING-PLACE.

ESSAY I.

O blessed letters! that combine in one
All ages past, and make one live with all:
By you we do confer with who are gone,
And the dead-living unto council call!
By you the unborn shall have communion
Of what we feel and what doth us befall.

Since writings are the veins, the arteries,
And undecaying life-strings of those hearts,
That still shall pant and still shall exercise
Their mightiest powers when nature none imparts:
And the strong constitutic.. of their praise
Wear out the infection of distemper'd days.

DANIEL'S MUSOPHILUS.

THE intelligence, which produces or controls human actions and occurrences, is often represented by the Mystics under the name and notion of the supreme harmonist. I do not myself approve of these metaphors: they seem to imply a restlessness to understand that which is not among the appointed objects of our comprehension or discursive faculty. But certainly there is one excellence in good music, to which, without mysticism, we may find or make an analogy in the records of history. I allude to that sense of recognition, which accompanies our sense of novelty in the most original passages of a great composer. If we listen to a symphony of Cimarosa, the present strain still seems not only to recall, but almost to renew, some past movement, another and yet the same! Each present movement bringing back as it were, and embodying the spirit of some melody that had gone before, anticipates and seems trying to overtake something that is to come: and the musician has reached the summit of his art, when having thus modified the present by the past, he at the same time weds the past in the present to some prepared and corresponsive future. The auditor's thoughts and feelings move under the same influence : retrospection blends with anticipation, and hope and memory, a female Janus, become one power with a double aspect. A similar effect the reader may produce for himself in the pages of history, if he will be content to substitute an intellectual complacency for pleasurable sensation. The events and characters of one age, like the strains in music, recall those of another, and the variety by which each is individualized, not only gives a charm and poignancy to the resemblance, but likewise renders the whole more intelligible. Meantime ample room is afforded for the exercise both of the judgment and the fancy, in distinguishing cases of real resemblance from those of intentional imitation, the analogies of nature, revolving upon herself, from the masquerade figures of cunning and vanity.

It is not from identity of opinions, or from similarity of events and outward actions, that a real resemblance in the radical character can be deduced. On the contrary, men of great and stirring powers, who are destined to mould the age in which they are born, must first mould themselves upon it. Mohammed born twelve centuries later, and in the heart of Europe, would not have been a false prophet ; nor would a false prophet of the present generation have been a Mohammed in the seventh century. I have myself, therefore, derived the deepest interest from the comparison of men, whose characters at first view appear widely dissimilar, who yet have produced similar effects on their different ages, and this by the exertion of powers which on examination will be found far more alike, than the altered drapery and costume would have led us to suspect. Of the heirs of fame few are more respected by me, though for very different qualities, than Erasmus and Luther ; scarcely any one has a larger share of my aversion than Voltaire ; and even of the better-hearted Rousseau I was never more than a very lukewarm admirer. I should perhaps too rudely affront the general opinion, if I avowed my whole creed concerning the proportions of real talent between the two purifiers of revealed religion, now neglected as obsolete, and the two modern conspirators against its authority, who are still the Alpha and Omega of continental genius. Yet when I abstract the questions of evil and good, and measure only the effects produced and the mode of producing them, I have repeatedly found the names of Voltaire, Rousseau, and Robespierre, recall in a similar cluster and connection those of Erasmus, Luther, and Muncer.

Those who are familiar with the works of Erasmus, and who know the influence of his wit, as the pioneer of the Reformation; and who likewise know, that by his wit, added to the vast variety of knowledge communicated in his works, he had won over by anticipation so large a part of the polite and lettered world to the Protestant party; will be at no loss in discovering the intended counterpart in the life and writings of the veteran Frenchman. They will see, indeed, that the knowledge of the one was solid through its whole extent, and that of the other extensive at a cheap rate, by its superficiality; that the wit of the one is always bottomed on sound sense, peoples and enriches the mind of the reader with an endless variety of distinct images and living interests; and that his broadest laughter is everywhere translatable into grave and weighty truth: while the wit of the Frenchman, without imagery, without character, and without that pathos which gives the magic charm to genuine humor, consists, when it is most perfect, in happy turns of phrase, but far too often in fantastic incidents, outrages of the pure imagination, and the poor low trick of combining the ridiculous with the venerable, where he, who does not laugh, abhors. Neither will they have forgotten that the object of the one was to drive the thieves and mummers out of the temple, while the other was propelling a worse banditti, first to profane and pillage, and ultimately to raze it. Yet not the less will they perceive, that the effects remain parallel, the circumstances analogous, and the instruments the same. In each case the effects extended over Europe, were attested and augmented by the praise and patronage of thrones and dignities, and are not to be explained but by extraordinary industry and a life of literature; in both instances the circumstances were supplied by an age of hopes and promises—the age of Erasmus restless from the first vernal influences of real knowledge, that of Voltaire from the hectic of imagined superiority. In the voluminous works of both, the instruments employed are chiefly those of wit and amusing erudition, and alike in both the errors and evils, real or imputed, in religion and politics are the objects of the battery. And here we must stop. The two men were essentially different. Exchange mutually their dates and spheres of action, yet Voltaire, had he been ten-fold a Voltaire, could not have made up an Erasmus; and Erasmus must have emptied himself of half his greatness and all his goodness, to have become a Voltaire.

Shall I succeed better or worse with the next pair, in this our new dance of death, or rather of the shadows which I have brought forth—two by two—from the historic ark? In our first couple I have at least secured an honorable retreat, and though I failed as to the agents, I have maintained a fair analogy in the actions and the objects. But the heroic Luther, a giant awaking in his strength, and the crazy Rousseau, the dreamer of love-sick tales, and the spinner of speculative cobwebs; shy of light as the mole, but as quick-eared too for every whisper of the public opinion; the teacher of stoic pride in his principles, yet the victim of morbid vanity in his feelings and conduct! From what point of likeness can we commence the comparison between a Luther and a Rousseau? And truly had I been seeking for characters that, taken as they really existed, closely resemble each other, and this, too, to our first apprehensions, and according to the common rules of biographical comparison, I could scarcely have made a more unlucky choice: unless I had desired that my parallel of the German *son of thunder* and the visionary of Geneva, should sit on the same bench with honest Fluellen's of Alexander the Great and Harry of Monmouth. Still, however, the same analogy would hold as in my former instance: the effect produced on their several ages by Luther and Rousseau, were commensurate with each other, and were produced in both cases by what their contemporaries felt as serious and vehement eloquence, and an elevated tone of moral feeling: and Luther, not less than Rousseau, was actuated by an almost superstitious hatred of superstition, and a turbulent prejudice against prejudices. In the relation too which their writings severally bore to those of Erasmus and Voltaire, and the way in which the latter co-operated with them to the same general end, each finding its own class of admirers and proselytes, the parallel is complete.

I can not, however, rest here. Spite of the apparent incongruities, I am disposed to plead for a resemblance in the men themselves, for that similarity in their radical natures, which I abandoned all pretence and desire of showing in the instances of Voltaire and Erasmus. But then my readers must think of Luther not as he really was, but as he might have been, if he had been born in the age and under the circumstances of the Swiss philosopher. For this purpose I must strip him of many advantages which he derived from his own times, and must contemplate him in his natural weaknesses as well as in his original strength. Each referred all things to his own ideal. The ideal was indeed widely different in the one and in the other: and this was not the least of Luther's many advantages, or, to use a favorite phrase of his own, not one of his least favors of preventing grace. Happily for him he had derived his standard from a common measure already received by the good and wise; I mean the inspired writings, the study of which Erasmus had previously restored among the learned. To know that we are in sympathy with others, moderates our feelings as well as strengthens our convictions: and for the mind, which opposes itself to the faith of the multitude, it is more especially desirable, that there should exist an object out of itself, on which it may fix its attention, and thus balance its own energies.

Rousseau, on the contrary, in the inauspicious spirit of his age and birth-place,* had slipped the cable of his faith, and steered by the compass of unaided reason, ignorant of the hidden currents that were bearing him out of his course, and too proud to consult the faithful charts prized and held sacred by his forefathers. But the strange influences of his bodily temperament on his understanding; his constitutional melancholy pampered into a morbid excess by solitude; his wild dreams of suspicion; his hypochondriacal fancies of hosts of conspirators all leagued against him and his cause, and headed by some arch-enemy, to whose machinations he attributed every trifling mishap—all as much the creatures of his imagination, as if instead of men he had conceived them to be infernal spirits and beings preternatural—these, or at least the predisposition to them, existed in the ground-work of his nature: they were parts of Rousseau himself. And what corres-

* Infidelity was so common in Geneva about that time, that Voltaire in one of his letters exults, that in this, Calvin's own city, some half-dozen only of the most ignorant believed in Christianity under any form. This was, no doubt, one of Voltaire's usual lies of exaggeration: it is not, however, to be denied, that here, and throughout Switzerland, he and the dark master in whose service he employed himself, had ample grounds of triumph.

ponding in kind to these, not to speak of degree, can we detect in the character of his supposed parallel? This difficulty will suggest itself at the first thought, to those who derive all their knowledge of Luther from the meagre biography met with in the Lives of eminent Reformers, or even from the ecclesiastical histories of Mosheim or Milner: for a life of Luther, in extent and style of execution proportioned to the grandeur and interest of the subject, a life of the man Luther, as well as of Luther the theologian, is still a *desideratum* in English literature, though perhaps there is no subject for which so many unused materials are extant, both printed and in manuscript.*

ESSAY II.

Is it, I ask, most important to the best interests of mankind, temporal as well as spiritual, that certain works, the names and number of which are fixed and unalterable, should be distinguished from all other works, not in degree only but even in kind?† And that these, collectively, should form THE BOOK, to which in all the concerns of faith and morality the last recourse is to be had, and from the admitted decisions of which no man dare

---

* The affectionate respect in which I hold the name of Dr. Jortin—one of the many illustrious nurslings of the college to which I deem it no small honor to have belonged—Jesus, Cambridge—renders it painful to me to assert, that the above remark holds almost equally true of a life of Erasmus. But every scholar well read in the writings of Erasmus and his illustrious contemporaries, must have discovered, that Jortin had neither collected sufficient, nor the best, materials for his work: and—perhaps from that very cause—he grew weary of his task, before he had made a full use of the scanty materials which he had collected.

† This is one of the hinges on which the gate of egress from the spiritual Rome turns. Historically, the affirmative to the question has been the constant and close companion of Protestantism:—but whether it be likewise its indispensable support, remains yet to be discussed, at the tribunal of sound philosophy. Hitherto both the ay and the no have been, as it appears to me, but very weakly and superficially argued. But I confess that Chillingworth makes me half a Roman Catholic on this point; lest in acceding to the grounds of his arguments against the Romanists, I should become less than half a Christian, and lose the substantive in my earnestness to tear off its parasitical and suffocating epithet:—that is, cease to be a Catholic in aversion to the Papal *bull* of Roman Catholic. 1830.

appeal?—If the mere existence of a book so called and charactered be, as the Koran itself suffices to evince, a mighty bond of union, among nations whom all other causes tend to separate; if moreover the book revered by us and our forefathers has been the foster-nurse of learning in the darkest, and of civilization in the rudest, times; and lastly, if this so vast and wide a blessing is not to be founded in a delusion, and doomed therefore to the impermanence and scorn in which sooner or later all delusions must end; how, I pray you, is it conceivable that this should be brought about and secured, otherwise than by God's special vouchsafement to this one book, exclusively, of that divine MEAN, that uniform and perfect middle way, which in all points is at safe and equal distance from all errors whether of excess or defect? But again, if this be true—and what Protestant Christian worthy of his baptismal dedication will deny its truth?—if in the one book we are entitled, or even permitted, to expect the golden mean throughout;—surely we ought not to be hard and over-stern in our censures of the mistakes and infirmities of those, who pretending to no warrant of extraordinary inspiration have yet been raised up by God's providence to be of highest power and eminence in the reformation of his Church. Far rather does it behoove us to consider, in how many instances the peccant humor native to the man had been wrought upon by the faithful study of that only faultless model, and corrected into an unsinning, or at least a venial, predominance in the writer or preacher. Yea, that not seldom the infirmity of a zealous soldier in the warfare of Christ has been made the very mould and ground-work of that man's peculiar gifts and virtues. Grateful too we should be, that the very faults of famous men have been fitted to the age, on which they were to act: and that thus the folly of man has proved the wisdom of God, and been made the instrument of his mercy to mankind.

WHOEVER has sojourned in Eisenach, will assuredly have visited the Warteburg, interesting by so many historical associations, which stands on a high rock, about two miles to the south from the city gate. To this castle Luther was taken on his return from the imperial Diet, where Charles V. had pronounced the ban upon him, and limited his safe convoy to one and twenty days. On the last but one of these days, as he was on his way to Waltershausen, a town in the duchy of Saxe Gotha, a few leagues to the south-east of Eisenach, he was stopped in a hollow behind the castle Altenstein, and carried to the Warteburg. The Elector of Saxony, who could not have refused to deliver up Luther, as one put in the ban by the Emperor and the Diet, had ordered John of Berleptsch, the governor of the Warteburg, and Burckhardt von Hundt, the governor of Altenstein, to take Luther to one or the other of these castles, without acquainting him which; in order that he might be able, with safe conscience, to declare, that he did not know where Luther was. Accordingly they took him to the Warteburg, under the name of the Chevalier (*Ritter*) George.

To this friendly imprisonment the Reformation owes many of Luther's most important labors. In this place he wrote his works against auricular confession, against Jacob *Latronum*, the tract on the abuses of masses, that against clerical and monastic vows, composed his exposition of the 22, 27, and 68 Psalms, finished his declaration of the *Magnificat*, began to write his Church homilies, and translated the New Testament. Here too, and during this time, he is said to have hurled his inkstand at the devil, the black spot from which yet remains on the stone wall of the room he studied in; which, surely, no one will have visited the Warteburg without having had pointed out to him by the good Catholic who is, or at least some few years ago was, the warden of the castle. He must have been either a very supercilious or a very incurious traveller if he did not, for the gratification of his guide at least, inform himself by means of his penknife, that the said marvellous blot bids defiance to all the toils of the scrubbing brush, and is to remain a sign forever; and with this advantage over most of its kindred, that being capable of a double interpretation, it is equally flattering to the Protestant and the Papist, and is regarded by the wonder-loving zealots of both parties, with equal faith.

Whether the great man ever did throw his inkstand at his Satanic Majesty, whether he ever boasted of the exploit, and himself declared the dark blotch on his study wall in the Warteburg, to be the result and relict of this author-like hand-grenado,—(happily for mankind he used his inkstand at other times to better purpose, and with more effective hostility against the arch-fiend)—I leave to my reader's own judgment; on condition, however, that he has previously perused Luther's Table Talk, and other writings of the same stamp, of some of his most illustrious contemporaries, which contain facts still more strange and whimsical, related by themselves and of themselves, and accompanied with solemn protestations of the truth of their statements. Luther's Table Talk, which to a truly philosophic mind, will not be less interesting than Rousseau's Confessions, I have not myself the means of consulting at present, and can not therefore say, whether this ink-pot adventure is, or is not, told or referred to, in it;* but many considerations incline me to give credit to the story.

Luther's unremitting literary labor and his sedentary mode of life, during his confinement in the Warteburg, where he was treated with the greatest kindness, and enjoyed every liberty consistent with his own safety, had begun to undermine his former unusually strong health. He suffered many and most distressing effects of indigestion and a deranged state of the digestive organs. Melancthon, whom he had desired to consult the physicians at Erfurth, sent him some de-obstruent medicines, and the advice to take regular and severe exercise. At first he followed the advice, sate and labored less, and spent whole days in the chase; but like the younger Pliny, he strove in vain to form a taste for this favorite amusement of the gods of the earth, as appears from a passage in his letter to George Spalatin, which I translate for an additional reason;—to prove to the admirers of Rousseau, who perhaps will not be less affronted by this biographical parallel, than the zealous Lutherians will be offended, that if my comparison should turn out groundless on the whole, the failure will not have arisen either from the want of sensibility in our great reformer, or of angry aversion to those in high places, whom he regarded as the oppressors of their rightful equals. "I have been," he writes, "employed for two days in the sports of the field, and was willing myself to taste this bitter-sweet amusement of the great heroes: we have caught two hares, and one brace of poor little partridges. An employment this which does not ill suit quiet leisurely folks: for even in the midst of the ferrets and dogs, I have had theological fancies. But as much pleasure as the general appearance of the scene and the mere looking-on occasioned me, even so much it pitied me to think of the mystery and emblem which lies beneath it. For what does this symbol signify, but that the devil, through his godless huntsmen and dogs, the bishops and theologians to wit, doth privily chase and catch the innocent poor little beasts? Ah! the simple and credulous souls came thereby far too plain before my eyes. Thereto comes a yet more frightful mystery: as at my earnest entreaty we had saved alive one poor little hare, and I had concealed it in the sleeve of my great coat, and had strolled off a short distance from it, the dogs in the mean time found the poor

* It is not.—*Ed.*

hare. Such, too, is the fury of the Pope with Satan, that he destroys even the souls that had been saved, and troubles himself little about my pains and entreaties. Of such hunting then I have had enough." In another passage he tells his correspondent, "You know it is hard to be a prince, and not in some degree a robber, and the greater a prince the more a robber." Of our Henry VIII. he says, "I must answer the grim lion that passes himself off for king of England. The ignorance in the book is such as one naturally expects from a king; but the bitterness and impudent falsehood is quite leonine." And in his circular letter to the princes, on occasion of the peasants' war, he uses a language so inflammatory, and holds forth a doctrine which borders so near on the holy right of insurrection, that it may as well remain untranslated.

Had Luther been himself a prince he could not have desired better treatment than he received during his eight months' stay in the Warteburg; and in consequence of a more luxurious diet than he had been accustomed to, he was plagued with temptations both from the flesh and the devil. It is evident from his letters* that he suffered under great irritability of his nervous system, the common effect of deranged digestion in men of sedentary habits, who are at the same time intense thinkers; and this irritability added to, and revivifying, the impressions made upon him in early life, and fostered by the theological systems of his manhood, is abundantly sufficient to explain all his apparitions and all his nightly combats with evil spirits. I see nothing improbable in the supposition, that in one of those unconscious half-sleeps, or rather those rapid alternations of the sleeping with the half-waking state, which is the true witching time,

> ——————————the season
> Wherein the spirits hold their wont to walk,

the fruitful *matrix* of ghosts—I see nothing improbable, that in some one of those momentary slumbers, into which the suspen-

* I can scarcely conceive a more delightful volume than might be made from Luther's letters, especially from those that were written from the Warteburg, if they were translated in the simple, sinewy, idiomatic, hearty, mother-tongue of the original. A difficult task I admit—and scarcely possible for any man, however great his talents in other respects, whose favorite reading has not lain among the English writers from Edward VI. to Charles I.

sion of all thought in the perplexity of intense thinking so often passes, Luther should have had a full view of the room in which he was sitting, of his writing-table and all the implements of study, as they really existed, and at the same time a brain-image of the devil, vivid enough to have acquired apparent outness, and a distance regulated by the proportion of its distinctness to that of the objects really impressed on the outward senses.

If this Christian Hercules, this heroic cleanser of the Augean stable of apostasy, had been born and educated in the present or the preceding generation, he would, doubtless, have holden himself for a man of genius and original power. But with this faith alone, he would scarcely have removed the mountains which he did remove. The darkness and superstition of the age, which required such a reformer, had moulded his mind for the reception of impressions concerning himself, better suited to inspire the strength and enthusiasm necessary for the task of reformation, impressions more in sympathy with the spirits whom he was to influence. He deemed himself gifted with supernatural influxes, an especial servant of heaven, a chosen warrior, fighting as the general of a small but faithful troop, against an army of evil beings, headed by the prince of the air. These were no metaphorical beings in his apprehension. He was a poet indeed, as great a poet as ever lived in any age or country; but his poetic images were so vivid, that they mastered the poet's own mind! He was possessed with them, as with substances distinct from himself: Luther did not write, he acted poems. The Bible was a spiritual, indeed, but not a figurative armory in his belief: it was the magazine of his warlike stores, and from thence he was to arm himself, and supply both shield and sword, and javelin, to the elect. Methinks I see him sitting, the heroic student, in his chamber in the Warteburg, with his midnight lamp before him, seen by the late traveller in the distant plain of Bischofsroda, as a star on the mountain! Below it lies the Hebrew Bible open, on which he gazes, his brow pressing on his palm, brooding over some obscure text, which he desires to make plain to the simple boor and to the humble artisan, and to transfer its whole force into their own natural and living tongue. And he himself does not understand it! Thick darkness lies on the original text: he counts the letters, he calls up the roots of each separate word, and questions them as the familiar spirits of an oracle. In vain; thick darkness continues to cover it; not a ray of meaning dawns through it. With sullen and angry hope he reaches for the Vulgate, his old and sworn enemy, the treacherous confederate of the Roman anti-Christ, which he so gladly, when he can, rebukes for idolatrous falsehoods, that had dared place

> Within the sanctuary itself their shrines,
> Abominations! ———

Now—O thought of humiliation—he must entreat its aid. See! there has the sly spirit of apostasy worked-in a phrase, which favors the doctrine of purgatory, the intercession of saints, or the efficacy of prayers for the dead; and what is worst of all, the interpretation is plausible. The original Hebrew might be forced into this meaning: and no other meaning seems to lie in it, none to hover above it in the heights of allegory, none to lurk beneath it even in the depths of cabala! This is the work of the tempter; it is a cloud of darkness conjured up between the truth of the sacred letters and the eyes of his understanding, by the malice of the evil one, and for a trial of his faith! Must he then at length confess, must he subscribe the name of Luther to an exposition which consecrates a weapon for the hand of the idolatrous hierarchy? Never! never!

There still remains one auxiliary in reserve, the translation of the Seventy. The Alexandrine Greeks, anterior to the Church itself, could intend no support to its corruptions—the Septuagint will have profaned the altar of truth with no incense for the nostrils of the universal bishop to snuff up. And here again his hopes are baffled! Exactly at this perplexed passage had the Greek translator given his understanding a holiday, and made his pen supply its place. O honored Luther! as easily mightest thou convert the whole city of Rome, with the Pope and the conclave of cardinals inclusively, as strike a spark of light from the words, and nothing but words, of the Alexandrine version. Disappointed, despondent, enraged, ceasing to think, yet continuing his brain on the stretch in solicitation of a thought; and gradually giving himself up to angry fancies, to recollections of past persecutions, to uneasy fears and inward defiances and floating images of the evil being, their supposed personal author; he sinks without perceiving it, into a trance of slumber; during which his brain retains its waking energies, excepting that what would have been mere thoughts before, now—the action and counterweight of his senses and of their impressions being withdrawn—shape and condense themselves into things, into realities. Repeatedly half-wakening, and his eyelids as often reclosing, the objects which really surround him form the place and scenery of his dream. All at once he sees the arch-fiend coming forth on the wall of the room, from the very spot, perhaps, on which his eyes had been fixed vacantly during the perplexed moments of his former meditation: the inkstand which he had at the same time been using, becomes associated with it: and in that struggle of rage, which in these distempered dreams almost constantly precedes the helpless terror by the pain of which we are finally awakened, he imagines that he hurls it at the intruder, or not improbably in the first instant of awakening, while yet both his imagination and his eyes are possessed by the dream, he actually hurls it. Some weeks after, perhaps, during which interval he had often mused on the incident, undetermined whether to deem it a visitation of Satan to him in the body or out of the body, he discovers for the first time the dark spot on his wall, and receives it as a sign and pledge vouchsafed to him of the event having actually taken place.

Such was Luther under the influences of the age and country in and for which he was born. Conceive him a citizen of Geneva, and a contemporary of Voltaire: suppose the French language his mother-tongue, and the political and moral philosophy of English free-thinkers re-modelled by Parisian *fort esprits*, to have been the objects of his study;—conceive this change of circumstances, and Luther will no longer dream of fiends or of anti-Christ—but will he have no dreams in their place? His melancholy will have changed its drapery; but will it find no new costume wherewith to clothe itself? His impetuous temperament, his deep working mind, his busy and vivid imaginations—would they not have been a trouble to him in a world, where nothing was to be altered, where nothing was to obey his power, to cease to be that which it had been, in order to realize his pre-conceptions of what it ought to be? His sensibility, which found objects for itself, and shadows of human suffering in the harmless brute, and even in the flowers which he trod upon—might it not naturally, in an unspiritualized age, have wept, and trembled, and dissolved, over scenes of earthly passion, and the struggles of love with duty? His pity, that so easily passed into rage, would it not have found in the inequalities of mankind, in the oppressions of governments and the miseries of the governed, an entire instead of a divided object? And might not a perfect constitution, a government of pure reason, a renovation of the social contract, have easily supplied the place of the reign of Christ in the new Jerusalem, of the restoration of the visible Church, and the union of all men by one faith in one charity? Henceforward then, we will conceive his reason employed in building up anew the edifice of earthly society, and his imagination as pledging itself for the possible realization of the structure. We will lose the great reformer, who was born in an age which needed him, in the philosopher of Geneva, who was doomed to misapply his energies to materials the properties of which he misunderstood, and happy only that he did not live to witness the direful effects of his own system.

ESSAY III.

Pectora cui credam? quis me lenire docebit
Mordaces curas, quis longas fallere noctes,
Ex quo summa dies tulerit Damona sub umbras?

Omnia paulatim consumit longior ætas,
Vivendoque simul morimur, rapimurque manendo.

Ite tamen, lacrymæ! purum colis æthera, Damon!
Nec mihi conveniunt lacrymæ. Non omnia terræ
Obruta! vivit amor, vivit dolor! ora negatur
Dulcia conspicere: flere et meminisse relictum est.

MILTON: PETRARCH: MILTON.

THE two following essays I devote to elucidation, the first of the theory of Luther's apparitions stated perhaps too briefly in the preceding essay; the second for the purpose of removing the only obstacle, which I can discover in the next section of The Friend, to the reader's ready comprehension of the principles, on which the arguments are grounded. First, I will endeavor to make my ghost theory more clear to those of my readers, who are fortunate enough to find it obscure in consequence of their own good health and unshattered nerves. The window of my library at Keswick is opposite to the fire-place, and looks out on the very large garden that occupies the whole slope of the hill on which the house stands. Consequently, the rays of light transmitted through the glass, that is, the rays from the garden, the opposite mountains, and the bridge, river, lake, and vale interjacent, and the rays reflected from it, of the fire-place, &c., enter the eye at the same moment. At the coming on of evening, it was my frequent amusement to watch the image or reflection of the fire, that seemed burning in the bushes or between the trees in different parts of the garden or the fields beyond it, according as there was more or less light; and which still arranged itself among the real objects of vision, with a distance and magnitude proportioned to its greater or lesser faintness. For still as the darkness increased, the image of the fire lessened and grew nearer and more distinct; till the twilight had deepened into perfect night, when all outward objects being excluded, the window became a perfect looking-glass: save only that my books on the side shelves of the room were lettered, as it were, on their backs with stars, more or fewer as the sky was less or more clouded, the rays of the stars being at that time the only ones transmitted. Now substitute the phantom from Luther's brain for the images of reflected light, the fire for instance, and the forms of his room and its furniture for the transmitted rays, and you have a fair resemblance of an apparition, and a just conception of the manner in which it is seen together with real objects. I have long wished to devote an entire work to the subject of dreams, visions, ghosts, and witchcraft, in which I might first give, and then endeavor to explain, the most interesting and best attested fact of each, which has come within my knowledge, either from books or from personal testimony. I might then explain in a more satisfactory way the mode in which our thoughts, in states of morbid slumber, become at times perfectly dramatic,—for in certain sorts of dreams the dullest weight becomes a Shakspeare,—and by what law the form of the vision appears to talk to us its own thoughts in a voice as audible as the shape is visible; and this too oftentimes in connected trains, and not seldom even with a concentration of power which may easily impose on the soundest judgments, uninstructed in the optics and acoustics of the inner sense, for revelations and gifts of prescience. In aid of the present case, I will only remark, that it would appear incredible to persons not accustomed to these subtle notices of self-observation, what small and remote resemblances, what mere hints of likeness from some real external object, especially if the shape be aided by color, will suffice to make a vivid thought consubstantiate with the real object, and derive from it an outward perceptibility. Even when we are broad awake, if we are in anxious expectation, how often will not the most confused sounds of nature be heard by us as articulate sounds? For instance, the babbling of a brook will appear for a moment the voice of a friend, for whom we are waiting, calling out our own names. A short meditation, therefore, on the great law of the imagination, that a likeness in part tends to become a likeness of the whole, will make it not only conceivable but probable, that the inkstand itself, and the dark-colored stone on the wall, which Luther perhaps had never till then noticed, might have a considerable influence in the production of the fiend, and of the hostile act by which his obtrusive visit was repelled.

A lady once asked me if I believed in ghosts and apparitions. I answered with truth and simplicity: No, madam! I have seen far too many myself. I have indeed a whole memorandum-book filled with records of these *phænomena*, many of them interesting as facts and *data* for psychology, and affording some valuable materials for a theory of perception, and its dependence on the memory and imagination. *In omnem actum perceptionis imaginatio influit efficienter*, says Wolfe. But he* is no more, who would have realized this idea; who had already established the foundations and the law of the theory; and for whom I had so often found a pleasure and a comfort, even during the wretched and restless nights of sickness, in watching and instantly recording these experiences of the world within us, of the *gemina natura, quæ fit et facit, et creat et creatur!* He is gone, my friend; my munificent co-patron, and not less the benefactor of my intellect!—He who, beyond all other men known to me, added a fine and ever-wakeful sense of beauty to the most patient accuracy in experimental philosophy and the profounder researches of metaphysical science; he who united all the play and spring of fancy with the subtlest discrimination and an inexorable judg-

* Thomas Wedgwood.

ment; and who controlled an almost painful exquisiteness of taste by a warmth of heart, which in the practical relations of life made allowances for faults as quickly as the moral taste detected them; a warmth of heart, which was indeed noble and pre-eminent, for alas! the genial feelings of health contributed no spark toward it. Of these qualities I may speak, for they belonged to all mankind.—The higher vitues, that were blessings to his friends, and the still higher that resided in and for his own soul, are themes for the energies of solitude, for the awfulness of prayer!—virtues exercised in the barrenness and desolation of his animal being; while he thirsted with the full stream at his lips, and yet with unwearied goodness poured out to all around him, like the master of a feast among his kindred in the day of his own gladness! Were it but for the remembrance of him alone and of his lot here below, the disbelief of a future state would sadden the earth around me, and blight the very grass in the field.

ESSAY IV.

Χαλεπὸν, ὦ δαιμόνιε, μὴ παραδείγμασι χρώμενον, ἱκανῶς ἐνδείκνυσθαί τι τῶν μειζόνων. κινδυνεύει γὰρ ἡμῶν ἕκαςος, οἷον ὄναρ, εἰδὼς ἅπαντα, πάντ' αὖ πάλιν ὥσπερ ὕπαρ ἀγνοεῖν. PLATO, Politicus.

It is difficult, excellent friend! to make any comprehensive truth completely intelligible, unless we avail ourselves of an example. Otherwise we may, as in a dream, seem to know all, and then, as it were awaking, find that we know nothing.

AMONG my earliest impressions I still distinctly remember that of my first entrance into the mansion of a neighboring baronet, awfully known to me by the name of the great house,* its exterior having been long connected in my childish imagination with the feelings and fancies stirred up in me by the perusal of the Arabian Nights' Entertainments.† Beyond all other objects,

* Escot, near Ottery St. Mary, Devon, then the seat of Sir George Young, and since burnt down, in 1808.—*Ed.*

† As I had read one volume of these tales over and over again before my fifth birth-day, it may be readily conjectured of what sort these fancies

I was most struck with the magnificent staircase, relieved at well-proportioned intervals by spacious landing-places, this adorned with grand or showy plants, the next looking out on an extensive prospect through the stately window, with its side-panes of rich blues and saturated amber or orange tints: while from the last and highest the eye commanded the whole spiral ascent with the marble pavement of the great hall, from which it seemed to spring up as if it merely used the ground on which it rested. My readers will find no difficulty in translating these forms of the outward senses into their intellectual analogies, so as to understand the purport of The Friend's landing-places, and the objects I proposed to myself, in the small groups of essays interposed under this title between the main divisions of the work.

My best powers would have sunk within me, had I not soothed my solitary toils with the anticipation of many readers—(whether during my life, or when my grave shall have shamed my detractors into a sympathy with its own silence, formed no part in this self-flattery—) who would submit to any reasonable trouble rather than read, 'as in a dream seeming to know all, to find on awaking that they know nothing.' Having, therefore, in the three preceding essays selected from my conservatory a few plants, of somewhat gayer petals and a livelier green, though like the geranium tribe of a sober character in the whole physiognomy and odor, I shall first devote a few sentences to a catalogue of my introductory lucubrations, and the remainder of the essay to the prospect, as far as it can be seen distinctly from our present site. Within a short distance, several ways meet: and at that point only does it appear to me that the reader will be in danger of mistaking the road. Dropping the metaphor, I would say that there is one term, reason, the meaning of which has become unsettled. To different persons it conveys a different notion, and not seldom to the same person at different times; while the force, and to a certain extent, the intelligibility of the follow-

and feelings must have been. The book, I well remember, used to lie in a corner of the parlor-window at my dear father's vicarage-house: and I can never forget with what a strange mixture of obscure dread and intense desire I used to look at the volume and watch it, till the morning sunshine had reached and nearly covered it, when, and not before, I felt the courage given me to seize the precious treasure and hurry off with it to some sunny corner in our play-ground.

ing sections depend on its being interpreted in one sense exclusively.

Essays I. to IV. inclusively convey the design and contents of the work; my judgment respecting the style, and my defence of myself from the charges of arrogance and presumption. Say rather, that such are the personal threads of the discourse: for it will not have escaped the reader's observation, that even in these prefatory pages principles and truths of general interest form the true contents, and that amid all the usual compliments and courtesies of a first presentation to the reader's acquaintance the substantial object is still to assert the practicability, without disguising the difficulties, of improving the morals of mankind by a direct appeal to their understandings; to show the distinction between attention and thought, and the necessity of the former as a habit or discipline without which the very word, thinking, must remain a thoughtless substitute for dreaming with our eyes open; and lastly, the tendency of a certain fashionable style with all its accommodations to paralyze the very faculties of manly intellect by a series of petty stimulants. After this preparation, I proceed at once to lay the foundations common to the whole work by an inquiry into the duty of communicating truth, and the conditions under which it may be communicated with safety, from essay V. to XVI. inclusively. Each essay will, I believe, be found complete in itself, yet an organic part of the whole considered as one disquisition. First, the inexpediency of pious frauds is proved from history, the shameless assertion of the indifference of truth and falsehood exposed to its deserved infamy, and an answer given to the objection derived from the impossibility of conveying an adequate notion of the truths, we may attempt to communicate. The conditions are then detailed, under which, right though inadequate notions may be taught without danger, and proofs given, both from facts and from reason, that he, who fulfils the conditions required by conscience, takes the surest way of answering the purposes of prudence. This is, indeed, the main characteristic of the moral system taught by The Friend throughout, that the distinct foresight of consequences belongs exclusively to the infinite Wisdom which is one with that Almighty Will, on which all consequences depend; but that for man—to obey the simple unconditional commandment of eschewing every act that implies a self-contradiction, or, in other words, to produce and maintain the greatest possible harmony in the component impulses and faculties of his nature, involves the effects of prudence. It is, as it were, prudence in short-hand or cipher. A pure conscience, that inward something, that *θεὸς οἰκεῖος*, which being absolutely unique no man can describe, because every man is bound to know, and even in the eye of the law is held to be a person no longer than he may be supposed to know it—the conscience, I say, bears the same relation to God, as an accurate time-piece bears to the sun. The time-piece merely indicates the relative path of the sun, yet we can regulate our plans and proceedings by it with the same confidence as if it was itself the efficient cause of light, heat, and the revolving seasons: on the self-evident axiom, that in whatever sense two things—for instance, A. and $\overline{\text{C. D. E.}}$,—are both equal to a third thing, B., they are in the some sense equal to each other. Cunning is circuitous folly. In plain English, to act the knave is but a roundabout way of playing the fool; and the man, who will not permit himself to call an action by its proper name without a previous calculation of all its probable consequences, may be indeed only a coxcomb, who is looking at his fingers through an opera-glass; but he runs no small risk of becoming a knave. The chances are against him. Though he should begin by calculating the consequences with regard to others, yet by the mere habit of never contemplating an action in its own proportions and immediate relations to his moral being, it is scarcely possible but that he must end in selfishness: for the 'you,' and the 'they' will stand on different occasions for a thousand different persons, while the 'I' is one only, and recurs in every calculation. Or grant that the principle of expediency should prompt to the same outward deeds as are commanded by the law of reason; yet the doer himself is debased. But if it be replied, that the reaction on the agent's own mind is to form a part of the calculation, then it is a rule that destroys itself in the very propounding, as will be more fully demonstrated in the second or ethical division of The Friend, when I shall have detected and exposed the equivoque between an action and a series of motions, by which the determinations of the will are to be realized in the world of the senses. What modification of the latter corresponds to the former, and is entitled to be called by the same name, will often depend on time, place, persons and circumstances, the consideration of which requires an exertion of the judgment; but the action itself remains the same, and like all other ideas pre-exists in the reason, or, in the more expressive and perhaps more precise and philosophical language of St. Paul, in the spirit, unalterable because unconditional, or with no other than that most awful condition, *as sure as God liveth, it is so!*

These remarks are inserted in this place, because the principle admits of easiest illustration in the instance of veracity and the actions connected with the same, and may then be intelligibly applied to other departments of morality, all of which Woollston indeed considers as only so many different forms of truth and falsehood. So far I treated of oral communication of the truth. The applicability of the same principle is then tried and affirmed in publications by the press, first as between the individual and his own conscience, and then between the publisher and the state: and under this head I have considered at large the questions of a free press and the law of libel, the anomalies and peculiar difficulties of the latter, and the only possible solution compatible with the continuance of the former: a solution rising out of and justified by the necessarily anomalous and unique nature of the law itself. I confess that I look back on this discussion concerning the press and its limits with a satisfaction unusual to me in the review of my own labors: and if the date of their first publication (September, 1809) be remembered, it will not perhaps be denied on an impartial comparison, that I have treated this most important subject, so especially interesting in the present time, more fully and more systematically than it had up to that time been. *Interim tum recti conscientia, tum illo me consolor, quod optimis quibusque certe non improbamur, fortassis omnibus placituri, simul atque livor ab obitu conquieverit.*

Lastly, the subject is concluded even as it commenced, and as beseemed a disquisition placed as the steps and vestibule of the whole work, with an enforcement of the absolute necessity of principles grounded in reason as the basis or rather as the living root of all genuine expedience. Where these are despised or at best regarded as aliens from the actual business of life, and consigned to the ideal world of speculative philosophy and Utopian politics, instead of state wisdom we shall have state-craft, and for the talent of the governor the cleverness of an embarrassed spendthrift—which consists in tricks to shift off difficulties and dangers when they are close upon us, and to keep them at arm's length, not in solid and grounded courses to preclude or subdue them. We must content ourselves with expedient-makers—with fire-engines against fires, life-boats against inundations; but no houses built fire-proof, no dams that rise above the water-mark. The reader will have observed that already has the term, reason been frequently contradistinguished from the understanding and the judgment. If I could succeed in fully explaining the sense in which the word reason is employed by me, and in satisfying the reader's mind concerning the grounds and importance of the distinction, I should feel little or no apprehension concerning the intelligibility of these essays from first to last. The following section is in part founded on this distinction: the which remaining obscure, all else will be so as a system, however clear the component paragraphs may be, taken separately. In the appendix* to my first Lay Sermon, I have, indeed, treated the question at considerable length, but chiefly in relation to the heights of theology and metaphysics. In the next number I attempt to explain myself more popularly, and trust that with no great expenditure of attention the reader will satisfy his mind, that our remote ancestors spoke as men acquainted with the constituent parts of their own moral and intellectual being, when they described one man as "being out of his senses," another as "out of his wits," or "deranged in his understanding," and a third as having "lost his reason." Observe, the understanding may be deranged, weakened, or perverted; but the reason is either lost or not lost, that is, wholly present or wholly absent.

ESSAY V.

Man may rather be defined a religious than a rational creature, in regard that in other creatures there may be something of reason, but there is nothing of religion. HARRINGTON.

IF the reader will substitute the word "understanding" for "reason," and the word "reason" for "religion," Harrington has here completely expressed the truth for which I am contending. Man may rather be defined a rational than an intelligent creature, in regard that in other creatures there may be something of understanding, but there is nothing of reason. But that this was Harrington's meaning is evident. Otherwise, instead of comparing two faculties with each other, he would contrast a faculty with one of its own objects, which would involve the same absurdity as if he had said, that man might rather be defined an astronomical than a seeing animal, because other animals possessed the sense of sight, but were incapable of beholding the satellites of Saturn, or the *nebulæ* of fixed stars. If further confirmation be necessary, it may be supplied by the following reflections, the leading thought of which I remember to have read in the works of a continental philosopher. It should seem easy to give the definite distinction of the reason from the understanding, because we constantly imply it when we speak of the difference between ourselves and the brute creation. No one, except as a figure of speech, ever speaks of an animal reason;*

* I have this moment looked over a translation of Blumenbach's Physiology, by Dr. Elliotson, which forms a glaring exception, p. 45. I do not know Dr. Elliotson, but I do know Professor Blumenbach, and was an assiduous attendant on the lectures, of which this classical work was the text-book; and I know that that good and great man would start back with surprise and indignation at the gross materialism mortised on to his work: the more so because during the whole period, in which the identification of man with the brute in kind was the fashion of naturalists, Blumenbach

but that many animals possess a share of understanding, perfectly distinguishable from mere instinct, we all allow. Few persons have a favorite dog without making instances of its intelligence an occasional topic of conversation. They call for our admiration of the individual animal, and not with exclusive reference to the wisdom in nature, as in the case of the στοϱγὴ, or maternal instinct of beasts; or of the hexangular cells of the bees, and the wonderful coincidence of this form with the geometrical demonstration of the largest possible number of rooms in a given space. Likewise, we distinguish various degrees of understanding there, and even discover from inductions supplied by the zoologists, that the understanding appears, as a general rule, in an inverse proportion to the instinct. We hear little or nothing of the instincts of the "half-reasoning elephant," and as little of the understanding of caterpillars and butterflies.* But reason is wholly denied, equally to the highest as to the lowest of the brutes; otherwise it must be wholly attributed to them, and with it therefore self-consciousness, and personality, or moral being.

I should have no objection to define reason with Jacobi,† and with his friend Hemsterhuis, as an organ bearing the same relation to spiritual objects, the universal, the eternal, and the necessary, as the eye bears to material and contingent *phenomena*. But then it must be added, that it is an organ identical with its appropriate objects. Thus, God, the soul, eternal truth, &c., are

remained ardent and instant in controverting the opinion, and exposing its fallacy and falsehood, both as a man of sense and as a naturalist. I may truly say, that it was uppermost in his heart and foremost in his speech. Therefore, and from no hostile feeling to Dr. Elliotson (whom I hear spoken of with great regard and respect, and to whom I myself give credit for his manly openness in the avowal of his opinions), I have felt the present animadversion a duty of justice as well as gratitude. April 8, 1817.

* Note, that though "reasoning" does not in our language, in the lax use of words natural in conversation or popular writings, imply scientific conclusion, yet the phrase "half-reasoning" is evidently used by Pope as a poetic hyperbole.

† *Von den Göttlichen Dingen, Beilage A.* Jacobi, in this passage, speaks of reason in man as being recipient rather than originant, and of this as the true Platonic doctrine. The affirmation of identity rather than pre-conformity between the finite and infinite Reason, by Coleridge, in this passage, is more than Jacobi is ready to affirm, as Coleridge evidently means to indicate by his criticism. A better statement of the doctrine may be found in an extract from John Smith, I. p. 264, note.—*Am. Ed.*

the objects of reason; but they are themselves reason. We name God the Supreme Reason; and Milton says,—

—whence the soul
Reason receives, and reason is her being.*

Whatever is conscious self-knowledge is reason: and in this sense it may be safely defined the organ of the supersensuous; even as the understanding wherever it does not possess or use the reason, as its inward eye, may be defined the conception of the sensuous, or the faculty by which we generalize and arrange the *phenomena* of perception; that faculty, the functions of which contain the rules and constitute the possibility of outward experience. In short, the understanding supposes something that is understood. This may be merely its own acts or forms, that is, formal logic; but real objects, the materials of substantial knowledge, must be furnished, I might safely say revealed, to it by organs of sense. The understanding of the higher brutes has only organs of outward sense, and consequently material objects only; but man's understanding has likewise an organ of inward sense, and therefore the power of acquainting itself with invisible realities or spiritual objects. This organ is his reason.

Again, the understanding and experience may exist† without reason. But reason can not exist without understanding; nor does it or can it manifest itself but in and through the understanding, which in our elder writers is often called discourse, or the discursive faculty, as by Hooker, Lord Bacon, and Hobbes: and an understanding enlightened by reason Shakspeare gives as the contradistinguishing character of man, under the name 'discourse of reason.' In short, the human understanding possesses two distinct organs, the outward sense, and the mind's eye, which is reason: wherever we use that phrase, the 'mind's eye,' in its proper sense, and not as a mere synonyme of the memory or the

* P. L. v. 486.—*Ed.*

† Of this no one would feel inclined to doubt, who had seen the poodle dog, whom the celebrated BLUMENBACH,—a name so dear to science, as a physiologist and comparative anatomist, and not less dear as a man to all Englishmen who have ever resided at Göttingen in the course of their education,—trained up, not only to hatch the eggs of the hen with all the mother's care and patience, but to attend the chickens afterwards, and find the food for them. I have myself known a Newfoundland dog, who watched and guarded a family of young children with all the intelligence of a nurse, during their walks.

fancy. In this way we reconcile the promise of revelation that the blessed will see God, with the declaration of St. John, *No man hath seen God at any time.**

I will add one other illustration to prevent any misconception, as if I were dividing the human soul into different essences, or ideal persons. In this piece of steel I acknowledge the properties of hardness, brittleness, high polish, and the capability of forming a mirror. I find all these likewise in the plate glass of a friend's carriage; but in addition to all these I find the quality of transparency, or the power of transmitting, as well as of reflecting, the rays of light. The application is obvious.

If the reader therefore will take the trouble of bearing in mind these and the following explanations, he will have removed beforehand every possible difficulty from The Friend's political section. For there is another use of the word, reason, arising out of the former indeed, but less definite, and more exposed to misconception. In this latter use it means the understanding considered as using the reason, so far as by the organ of reason only we possess the ideas of the necessary and the universal; and this is the more common use of the word, when it is applied with any attempt at clear and distinct conceptions. In this narrower and derivative sense the best definition of reason, which I can give, will be found in the third member of the following sentence, in which the understanding is described in its three-fold operation, and from each receives an appropriate name. The sense,—*vis sensitiva vel intuitiva*—perceives: *vis regulatrix*—the understanding, in its own peculiar operation—conceives: *vis rationalis*—the reason or rationalized understanding—comprehends. The first is impressed through the organs of sense; the second combines these multifarious impressions into individual notions, and by reducing these notions to rules, according to the analogy of all its former notices, constitutes experience: the third subordinates both of them, the notions, namely, and the rules of experience, to absolute principles or necessary laws: and thus concerning objects, which our experience has proved to have real existence, it demonstrates, moreover, in what way they are possible, and in doing this constitutes science. Reason therefore, in this secondary sense, and used, not as a spiritual organ, but as a

* 1 *Ep.* iv. 12.—*Ed.*

faculty, namely, the understanding or soul enlightened by that organ,—reason, I say, or the scientific faculty, is the intellection of the possibility or essential properties of things by means of the laws that constitute them. Thus the rational idea of a circle is that of a figure constituted by the circumvolution of a straight line with its one end fixed.

Every man must feel, that though he may not be exerting different faculties, he is exerting his faculties in a different way, when in one instance he begins with some one self-evident truth,—that the *radii* of a circle, for instance, are all equal,—and in consequence of this being true sees at once, without any actual experience, that some other thing must be true likewise, and that, this being true, some third thing must be equally true, and so on till he comes, we will say, to the properties of the lever, considered as the spoke of a circle ; which is capable of having all its marvellous powers demonstrated even to a savage who had never seen a lever, and without supposing any other previous knowledge in his mind, but this one, that there is a conceivable figure, all possible lines from the middle to the circumference of which are of the same length : or when, in another instance, he brings together the facts of experience, each of which has its own separate value, neither increased nor diminished by the truth of any other fact which may have preceded it ; and making these several facts bear upon some particular project, and finding some in favor of it, and some against it, determines for or against the project, according as one or the other class of facts preponderate : as, for example, whether it would be better to plant a particular spot of ground with larch, or with Scotch fir, or with oak in preference to either. Surely every man will acknowledge, that his mind was very differently employed in the first case from what it was in the second ; and all men have agreed to call the results of the first class the truths of science, such as not only are true, but which it is impossible to conceive otherwise : while the results of the second class are called facts, or things of experience : and as to these latter we must often content ourselves with the greater probability, that they are so or so, rather than otherwise—nay, even when we have no doubt that they are so in the particular case, we never presume to assert that they must continue so always, and under all circumstances. On the contrary, our conclusions depend altogether on contingent circumstances.

Now when the mind is employed, as in the case first mentioned, I call it reasoning, or the use of the pure reason; but, in the second case, the understanding or prudence.

This reason applied to the motives of our conduct, and combined with the sense of our moral responsibility, is the conditional cause of conscience, which is a spiritual sense or testifying state of the coincidence or discordance of the free will with the reason. But as the reasoning consists wholly in a man's power of seeing, whether any two conceptions which happen to be in his mind, are, or are not in contradiction to each other, it follows of necessity, not only that all men have reason, but that every man has it in the same degree. For reasoning, or reason, in this its secondary sense, does not consist in the conceptions themselves or in their clearness, but simply, when they are in the mind, in seeing whether they contradict each other or no.

And again, as in the determinations of conscience the only knowledge required is that of my own intention—whether in doing such a thing, instead of leaving it undone, I did what I should think right if any other person had done it; it follows that in the mere question of guilt or innocence, all men have not only reason equally, but likewise all the materials on which the reason, considered as conscience, is to work. But when we pass out of ourselves, and speak, not exclusively of the agent as meaning well or ill, but of the action in its consequences, then of course experience is required, judgment in making use of it, and all those other qualities of the mind which are so differently dispensed to different persons, both by nature and education. And though the reason itself is the same in all men, yet the means of exercising it, and the materials,—that is, the facts and conceptions—on which it is exercised, being possessed in very different degrees by different persons, the practical result is, of course, equally different—and the whole ground-work of Rousseau's philosophy ends in a mere nothingism.—Even in that branch of knowledge, where the conceptions, on the congruity of which with each other, the reason is to decide, are all possessed alike by all men, namely in geometry;—for all men in their senses possess all the component images, namely simple curves and straight lines; yet the power of attention required for the perception of linked truths, even of such truths, is so very different in A and in B, that Sir Isaac Newton professed that it was in this power only that he was superior to ordinary men. In short, the sophism is as gross as if I should say,—the souls of all men have the faculty of sight in an equal degree—forgetting to add, that this faculty can not be exercised without eyes, and that some men are blind and others short-sighted,—and should then take advantage of this my omission to conclude against the use or necessity of spectacles, and microscopes,—or of choosing the sharpest-sighted men for our guides.

Having exposed this gross sophism, I must warn against an opposite error—namely, that if reason, as distinguished from prudence, consists merely in knowing that black can not be white—or when a man has a clear conception of an inclosed figure, and another equally clear conception of a straight line, his reason teaches him that these two conceptions are incompatible in the same object, that is, that two straight lines can not include a space— — the reason must therefore be a very insignificant faculty. For a moment's steady self-reflection will show us, that in the simple determination 'black is not white'—or, 'that two straight lines can not include a space'—all the powers are implied, that distinguish man from animals;—first, the power of reflection—2d, of comparison—3d, and therefore of suspension of the mind—4th, therefore of a controlling will, and the power of acting from notions, instead of mere images exciting appetites; from motives, and not from mere dark instincts. Was it an insignificant thing to weigh the planets, to determine all their courses, and prophesy every possible relation of the heavens a thousand years hence? Yet all this mighty chain of science is nothing but a linking together of truths of the same kind, as, the whole is greater than its part;—or, if A and B $=$ C, then A $=$ B: or $3+4=7$, therefore $7+5=12$, and so forth. X is to be found either in A or B, or C or D: it is not found in A, B, or C; therefore it is to be found in D. What can be simpler? Apply this to a brute animal. A dog misses his master where four roads meet;—he has come up one, smells to two of the others, and then with his head aloft darts forward to the fourth road without any examination. If this were done by a conclusion, the dog would have reason;—how comes it then, that he never shows it in his ordinary habits? Why does this story excite either wonder or incredulity?—If the story be a fact, and not a fiction, I should say—the breeze brought his master's scent down the fourth road to the dog's nose, and that therefore he did not put it down to the road, as in the two former instances. So awful and almost miraculous does the simple act of concluding, that 'take three from four, there remains one,' appear to us, when attributed to one of the most sagacious of all brute animals.

THE FRIEND.

SECTION THE FIRST.

ON THE PRINCIPLES OF POLITICAL KNOWLEDGE.

Hoc potissimum pacto felicem ac magnum regem se fore judicans, non si quam plurimis sed si quam optimis imperet. Proinde parum esse putat justis præsidiis regnum suum muniisse, nisi idem viris eruditione juxta ac vitæ integritate præcellentibus ditet atque honestet. Nimirum intelligit hæc demum esse vera regni decora, has veras opes.

ERASMUS: EPIST. AD EPISC. PARIS.

THE FRIEND.

ESSAY I.

Dum politici sæpiuscule hominibus magis insidiantur quam consulunt, potius callidi quam sapientes; theoretici e contrario se rem divinam facere et sapientiæ culmen attingere credunt, quando humanam naturam, quæ nullibi est, multis modis laudare, et eam, quæ re vera est, dictis lacessere norunt. Unde factum est, ut nunquam politicam conceperint quæ possit ad usum revocari; sed quæ in Utopia vel in illo poetarum aureo sæculo, ubi scilicet minime necesse erat, institui potuisset. At mihi plane persuadeo, experientiam omnia civitatum genera, quæ concipi possunt ut homines concorditer vivant, et simul media, quibus multitudo dirigi, seu quibus intra certos limites contineri debeat, ostendisse: ita ut non credam, nos posse aliquid, quod ab experientia sive praxi non abhorreat, cogitatione de hac re assequi, quod nondum expertum compertumque sit.

Cum igitur animum ad politicam applicuerim, nihil quod novum vel inauditum est; sed tantum ea quæ cum praxi optime conveniunt, certa et indubitata ratione demonstrare aut ex ipsa humanæ naturæ conditione deducere, intendi. Et ut ea quæ ad hanc scientiam spectant, eadem animi libertate, qua res mathematicas solemus, inquirerem, sedulo curavi humanas actiones non ridere, non lugere, neque detestari; sed intelligere. Nec ad imperii securitatem refert quo animo homines inducantur ad res recte administrandas, modo res recte administrentur. Animi enim libertas, seu fortitudo, privata virtus est; at imperii virtus securitas. SPINOSA Op. Post. p. 267.

While the mere practical statesman too often rather plots against mankind, than consults their interest, crafty, not wise; the mere theorists, on the other hand, imagine that they are employed in a glorious work, and believe themselves at the very summit of earthly wisdom, when they are able, in set and varied language, to extol that human nature, which exists nowhere, except indeed in their own fancy, and to accuse and vilify our nature as it really is. Hence it has happened, that these men have never conceived a practicable scheme of civil policy, but, at best, such forms of government only, as might have been instituted in Utopia, or during the golden age of the poets: that is to say, forms of government excellently adapted for those who need no government at all. But I am fully persuaded, that experience has already brought to light all conceivable sorts of political institutions under which human society can be maintained in concord, and likewise the chief means of directing the multitude, or retaining them within given boundaries: so that I can hardly believe, that on this subject the deepest research would arrive at any result, not abhorrent from experience and practice, which has not been already tried and proved.

When, therefore, I applied my thoughts to the study of political philosophy, I proposed to myself nothing original or strange as the fruits of my reflections; but simply to demonstrate from plain and undoubted principles, or to deduce from the very condition and necessities of human nature, those plans and maxims which square the best with practice. And that in all things which relate to this province, I might conduct my investigations with the same freedom of intellect with which we proceed in questions of pure science, I sedulously disciplined my mind neither to laugh at, nor bewail, nor detest, the actions of men; but to understand them. For to the safety of the state it is not of necessary importance what motives induce men to administer public affairs rightly, provided only that public affairs be rightly administered.* For moral strength, or freedom from the selfish passions, is the virtue of individuals; but security is the virtue of a state.

ON THE PRINCIPLES OF POLITICAL PHILOSOPHY.

All the different philosophical systems of political justice, all the theories on the rightful origin of government, are reducible in the end to three classes, correspondent to the three different points of view, in which the human being itself may be contemplated. The first denies all truth and distinct meaning to the words, right and duty; and affirming that the human mind consists of nothing but the manifold modifications of passive sensation, considers men as the highest sort of animals indeed, but at the same time the most wretched; inasmuch as their defenceless nature forces them into society: while such is the multiplicity of wants engendered by the social state, that the wishes of one are sure to be in contradiction to those of some other. The assertors of this system consequently ascribe the origin and continuance of government to fear, or the power of the stronger, aided by the force of custom. This is the system of Hobbes. Its statement is its confutation. It is, indeed, in the literal sense

* I regret, that I should have given, by thus selecting it for my motto, an implied consent to this very plausible, but false and dangerous position. 1830.

of the word, preposterous: for fear pre-supposes conquest, and conquest a previous union and agreement between the conquerors. A vast empire may perhaps be governed by fear; at least the supposition is not absolutely inconceivable, under circumstances which prevent the consciousness of a common strength. A million of men united by mutual confidence and free intercourse of thoughts form one power, and this is as much a real thing as a steam-engine; but a million of insulated individuals is only an abstraction of the mind, and but one told so many times over without addition, as an idiot would tell the clock at noon—one, one, one. But when, in the first instances, the descendants of one family joined together to attack those of another family, it is impossible that their chief or leader should have appeared to them stronger than all the rest together; they must therefore have chosen him, and this as for particular purposes, so doubtless under particular conditions, expressed or understood. Such we know to be the case with the North American tribes at present; such, we are informed by history, was the case with our own remote ancestors. Therefore, even on the system of those who, in contempt of the oldest and most authentic records, consider the savage as the first and natural state of man, government must have originated in choice and an agreement. The apparent exceptions in Africa and Asia are, if possible, still more subversive of this system: for they will be found to have originated in religious imposture, and the first chiefs to have secured a willing and enthusiastic obedience to themselves as delegates of the Deity.

But the whole theory is baseless. We are told by history, we learn from our experience, we know from our own hearts, that fear, of itself, is utterly incapable of producing any regular, continuous, and calculable effect, even on an individual; and that the fear, which does act systematically upon the mind, always pre-supposes a sense of duty, as its cause. The most cowardly of the European nations, the Neapolitans and Sicilians, those among whom the fear of death exercises the most tyrannous influence relatively to their own persons, are the very men who least fear to take away the life of a fellow-citizen by poison or assassination; while in Great Britain, a tyrant, who has abused the power, which a vast property has given him, to oppress a whole neighborhood, can walk in safety unarmed and unattended, amid a hundred men, each of whom feels his heart burn with rage and indignation at the sight of him. It was this man who broke my father's heart; or, it is through him that my children are clad in rags, and cry for the food which I am no longer able to provide for them. And yet they dare not touch a hair of his head! Whence does this arise? Is it from a cowardice of sensibility that makes the injured man shudder at the thought of shedding blood? Or from a cowardice of selfishness which makes him afraid of hazarding his own life? Neither the one nor the other! The field of Waterloo, as the most recent of a hundred equal proofs, has borne witness that,—

——bring a *Briton* frae his hill,
* * * * * *
Say, such is royal George's will,
An' there's the foe,
He has nae thought but how to kill
Twa at a blow.
Nae cauld, faint-hearted doubtings tease him;
Death comes, wi' fearless eye he sees him;
Wi' bluidy hand, a welcome gies him;
And when he fa's,
His latest draught o' breathin' leaves him
In faint huzzas.*

Whence then arises the difference of feeling in the former case? To what does the oppressor owe his safety? To the spirit-quelling thought;—the laws of God and of my country have made his life sacred! I dare not touch a hair of his head!—'Tis conscience that makes cowards of us all,—but oh! it is conscience too which makes heroes of us all.

* Burns.—*Ed.*

ESSAY II.

Le plus fort n'est jamais assez fort pour être toujours le maître, s'il ne transforme sa force en droit et l'obeissance en devoir. ROUSSEAU.

Viribus parantur provinciæ, jure retinentur. Igitur breve id gaudium, quippe Germani victi magis, quam domiti. FLORUS, iv. 12.*

The strongest is never strong enough to be always the master, unless he transforms his power into right, and obedience into duty.

Provinces are taken by force, but they are kept by right. This exultation therefore was of brief continuance, inasmuch as the Germans had been overcome, but not subdued.

A TRULY great man,† the best and greatest public character that I had ever the opportunity of making myself acquainted with,—on assuming the command of a man of war, found a mutinous crew, more than one half of them uneducated Irishmen, and of the remainder no small portion had become sailors by compromise of punishment. What terror could effect by severity and frequency of acts of discipline, had been already effected. And what was this effect? Something like that of a polar winter on a flask of brandy. The furious spirit concentered itself with tenfold strength at the heart; open violence was changed into secret plots and conspiracies; and the consequent orderliness of the crew, as far as they were orderly, was but the brooding of a tempest. The new commander instantly commenced a system of discipline as near as possible to that of ordinary law;—as much as possible, he avoided, in his own person, the appearance of any will or arbitrary power to vary, or to remit, punishment. The rules to be observed were affixed to a conspicuous part of the ship, with the particular penalties for the breach of each particular rule; and care was taken that every individual of the ship should know and understand this code. With a single exception in the case of mutinous behavior, a space of twenty-four hours

* Slightly altered.—*Ed.*

† Sir Alexander Ball.—*Ed.*

was appointed between the first charge and the second hearing of the cause, at which time the accused person was permitted and required to bring forward whatever he thought conducive to his defence or palliation. If, as was commonly the case—for the officers well knew that the commander would seriously resent in them all caprice of will, and by no means permit to others what he denied to himself,—no answer could be returned to the three questions—Did you not commit the act? Did you not know that it was in contempt of such a rule, and in defiance of such a punishment? And was it not wholly in your own power to have obeyed the one and avoided the other?—the sentence was then passed with the greatest solemnity, and another, but shorter, space of time was again interposed between it and its actual execution. During this space the feelings of the commander, as a man, were so well blended with his inflexibility, as the organ of the law; and how much he suffered previously to and during the execution of the sentence was so well known to the crew, that it became a common saying with them when a sailor was about to be punished, the captain takes it more to heart than the fellow himself. But whenever the commander perceived any trait of pride in the offender, or the germs of any noble feeling, he lost no opportunity of saying, "It is not the pain that you are about to suffer which grieves me! You are none of you, I trust, such cowards as to turn faint-hearted at the thought of that! but that, being a man, and one who is to fight for his king and country, you should have made it necessary to treat you as a vicious beast,—it is this that grieves me."

I have been assured, both by a gentleman who was a lieutenant on board that ship at the time when the heroism of its captain, aided by his characteristic calmness and foresight, greatly influenced the decision of the most glorious battle recorded in the annals of our naval history; and very recently by a gray-headed sailor, who did not even know my name, or could have suspected that I was previously acquainted with the circumstances—I have been assured, I say, that the success of this plan was such as astonished the oldest officers, and convinced the most incredulous. Ruffians, who, like the old Buccaneers, had been used to inflict torture on themselves for sport, or in order to harden themselves beforehand, were tamed and overpowered, how or why they themselves knew not. From the fiercest spirits were heard the most earnest entreaties for the forgiveness of their commander: not before the punishment, for it was too well known that then they would have been to no purpose, but days after it, when the bodily pain was remembered but as a dream. An invisible power it was, that quelled them, a power, which was therefore irresistible, because it took away the very will of resisting. It was the awful power of law, acting on natures pre-configured to its influences. A faculty was appealed to in the offender's own being: a faculty and a presence, of which he had not been previously made aware,—but it answered to the appeal; its real existence therefore could not be doubted, or its reply rendered inaudible; and the very struggle of the wilder passions to keep uppermost counteracted their own purpose, by wasting in internal contest that energy which before had acted in its entireness on external resistance or provocation. Strength may be met with strength; the power of inflicting pain may be baffled by the pride of endurance; the eye of rage may be answered by the stare of defiance, or the downcast look of dark and revengeful resolve; and with all this there is an outward and determined object to which the mind can attach its passions and purposes, and bury its own disquietudes in the full occupation of the senses. But who dares struggle with an invisible combatant,—with an enemy which exists and makes us know its existence—but where it is, we ask in vain?—No space contains it—time promises no control over it—it has no ear for my threats—it has no substance, that my hands can grasp, or my weapons find vulnerable—it commands and can not be commanded—it acts and is insusceptible of my reaction—the more I strive to subdue it, the more am I compelled to think of it—and the more I think of it, the more do I find it to possess a reality out of myself, and not to be a phantom of my own imagination; that all, but the most abandoned men, acknowledge its authority, and that the whole strength and majesty of my country are pledged to support it; and yet that for me its power is the same with that of my own permanent self, and that all the choice, which is permitted to me, consists in having it for my guardian angel or my avenging fiend! This is the spirit of law! the lute of Amphion, the harp of Orpheus! This is the true necessity, which compels man into the social state, now and always, by a still-beginning, never-ceasing, force of moral cohesion.

Thus is man to be governed, and thus only can he be governed. For from his creation the objects of his senses were to become his subjects, and the task allotted to him was to subdue the visible world within the sphere of action circumscribed by those senses, as far as they could act in concert. What the eye beholds, the hand strives to reach; what it reaches, it conquers, and makes the instrument of further conquest. We can be subdued by that alone which is analogous in kind to that by which we subdue: therefore by the invisible powers of our nature; whose immediate presence is disclosed to our inner sense, and only as the symbols and language of which all shapes and modifications of matter become formidable to us.

A machine continues to move by the force which first set it in motion. If only the smallest number in any state, properly so called, hold together through the influence of any fear that does not itself pre-suppose the sense of duty, it is evident that the state itself could not have commenced through animal fear. We hear, indeed, of conquests; but how does history represent these? Almost without exception as the substitution of one set of governors for another: and so far is the conqueror from relying on fear alone to secure the obedience of the conquered, that his first step is to demand an oath of fealty from them, by which he would impose upon them the belief, that they become subjects; for who would think of administering an oath to a gang of slaves? But what can make the difference between slave and subject, if not the existence of an implied contract in the one case, and not in the other? And to what purpose would a contract serve, if, however it might be entered into through fear, it were deemed binding only in consequence of fear? To repeat my former illustration—where fear alone is relied on, as in a slave ship, the chains that bind the poor victims must be material chains: for these only can act upon feelings which have their source wholly in the material organization. Hobbes has said, that laws without the sword are but bits of parchment. How far this is true, every honest man's heart will best tell him, if he will content himself with asking his own heart, and not falsify the answer by his notions concerning the hearts of other men. But were it true, still the fair answer would be—Well! but without the laws the sword is but a piece of iron. The wretched tyrant, who disgraces the present age and human nature itself, had exhausted the whole magazine of animal terror, in order to consolidate his truly Satanic government. But look at the new French catechism, and in it read the misgivings of his mind, as to the sufficiency of terror alone! The system, which I have been confuting, is indeed so inconsistent with the facts revealed to us by our own mind, and so utterly unsupported by any facts of history, that I should be censurable in wasting my own time and my reader's patience by the exposure of its falsehood, but that the arguments adduced have a value of themselves independently of their present application. Else it would have been an ample and satisfactory reply to an assertor of this bestial theory—Government is a thing which relates to men, and what you say applies only to beasts.

Before I proceed to the second of these systems, let me remove a possible misunderstanding that may have arisen from the use of the word contract: as if I had asserted, that the whole duty of obedience to governors is derived from, and dependent on, the fact of an original contract. I freely admit, that to make this the cause and origin of political obligation, is not only a dangerous but an absurd theory; for what could give moral force to the contract? The same sense of duty which binds us to keep it, must have pre-existed as impelling us to make it. For what man in his senses would regard the faithful observation of a contract entered into to plunder a neighbor's house, but as a treble crime? First the act, which is a crime of itself; secondly, the entering into a contract which it is a crime to observe, and yet a weakening of one of the main pillars of human confidence not to observe, and thus voluntarily placing ourselves under the necessity of choosing between two evils;—and thirdly, the crime of choosing the greater of the two evils, by the unlawful observance of an unlawful promise. But in my sense, the word contract is merely synonymous with the sense of duty acting in a specific direction, that is, determining our moral relations, as members of a body politic. If I have referred to a supposed origin of government, it has been in courtesy to a common notion: for I myself regard the supposition as no more than a means of simplifying to our apprehension the ever-continuing causes of social union, even as the conversation of the world may be represented as an act of continued creation. For, what if an original contract had really been entered into, and formally recorded?

Still it could do no more than bind the contracting parties to act for the general good in the best manner, that the existing relations among themselves (state of property, religion, and so forth), on the one hand, and the external circumstances on the other (ambitious or barbarous neighbors, and the like), required or permitted. In after-times it could be appealed to only for the general principle, and no more, than the ideal contract, could it affect a question of ways and means. As each particular age brings with it its own exigencies, so must it rely on its own prudence for the specific measures by which they are to be encountered.

Nevertheless, it assuredly can not be denied, that an original, —more accurately, an ever-originating,—contract is a very natural and significant mode of expressing the reciprocal duties of subject and sovereign. We need only consider the utility of a real and formal state contract,—the Bill of Rights for instance, —as a sort of *est demonstratum* in politics; and the contempt lavished on this notion, though sufficiently compatible with the tenets of a Hume, will seem strange to us in the writings of a Protestant clergyman,* who surely owed some respect to a mode of thinking which God himself had authorized by his own example, in the establishment of the Jewish constitution. In this instance there was no necessity for deducing the will of God from the tendency of the laws to the general happiness: his will was expressly declared. Nevertheless, it seemed good to the divine wisdom, that there should be a covenant, an original contract, between himself as sovereign, and the Hebrew nation as subjects. This I admit was a written and formal contract; but the relations of mankind, as members of a body spiritual, or religious commonwealth, to the Saviour, as its head or regent;—is not this, too, styled a covenant, though it would be absurd to ask for the material instrument that contained it, or the time when it was signed or voted by the members of the church collectively.†

* See Paley's Moral and Political Philosophy. B. vi. c. 3.—*Ed.*

† It is perhaps to be regretted, that the words, Old and New Testament, —they having lost the sense intended by the translators of the Bible,— have not been changed into the Old and New Covenant. We can not too carefully keep in sight a notion, which appeared to the Primitive Church the fittest and most scriptural mode of representing the sum of the contents of the sacred writings.

With this explanation, the assertion of an original or a perpetual contract is rescued from all rational objection; and however speciously it may be urged, that history can scarcely produce a single example of a state dating its primary establishment from a free and mutual covenant, the answer is ready: if there be any difference between a government and a band of robbers, an act of consent must be supposed on the part of the people governed.

ESSAY III.

Human institutions can not be wholly constructed on principles of science, which is proper to immutable objects. In the government of the visible world the Supreme Wisdom itself submits to be the author of the better; not of the best, but of the best possible in the subsisting relations. Much more must all human legislators give way to many evils rather than encourage the discontent that would lead to worse remedies. If it is not in the power of man to construct even the arch of a bridge that shall exactly correspond in its strength to the calculations of geometry, how much less can human science construct a constitution except by rendering itself flexible to experience and expediency: where so many things must fall out accidentally, and come not into any compliance with the preconceived ends: but men are forced to comply subsequently, and to strike in with things as they fall out, by after applications of them to their purposes, or by framing their purposes to them. SOUTH.

THE second system corresponds to the second point of view under which the human being may be considered, namely, as an animal gifted with understanding, or the faculty of suiting measures to circumstances. According to this theory, every institution of national origin needs no other justification than a proof, that under the particular circumstances it is expedient. Having in my former essays expressed myself,—so at least I am conscious I shall have appeared to do to many persons;—with comparative slight of the understanding considered as the sole guide of human conduct, and even with something like contempt and reprobation of the maxims of expedience, when represented as the only steady light of the conscience, and the absolute foundation of all morality; I shall perhaps seem guilty of an inconsistency, in declaring myself an adherent of this second system, a zealous advocate for deriving the various forms and modes of government from human prudence, and of deeming that to be just which experience has proved to be expedient. From this charge of inconsistency* I shall best exculpate myself by the full statement of the third system, and by the exposition of its grounds and consequences.

* Distinct notions do not suppose different things. When I make a threefold distinction in human nature, I am fully aware, that it is a distinction, not a division, and that in every act of mind the man unites the properties of sense, understanding, and reason. Nevertheless it is of great practical importance, that these distinctions should be made and understood, the ignorance or perversion of them being alike injurious; as the first French constitution has most lamentably proved. It was the fashion in the profligate times of Charles II. to laugh at the Presbyterians, for distinguishing between the person and the king; while in fact they were ridiculing the most venerable maxims of English law;—the king never dies—the king can do no wrong,—and subverting the principles of genuine loyalty, in order to prepare the minds of the people for despotism.

Under the term "sense," I comprise whatever is passive in our being, without any reference to the question of materialism or immaterialism; all that man is in common with animals, in kind at least—his sensations, and impressions, whether of his outward senses, or the inner sense of imagination. This, in the language of the schools, was called the *vis receptiva*, or recipient property of the soul, from the original constitution of which we perceive and imagine all things under the forms of space and time. By the "understanding," I mean the faculty of thinking and forming judgments on the notices furnished by the sense, according to certain rules existing in itself, which rules constitute its distinct nature. By the pure "reason," I mean the power by which we become possessed of principles,—the eternal verities of Plato and Descartes, and of ideas, not images—as the ideas of a point, a line, a circle, in mathematics;* and of justice, holiness, free-will, and the like, in morals. Hence in works of pure science the definitions of necessity precede the reasoning, in other works they more aptly form the conclusion.

To many of my readers it will, I trust, be some recommendation of these distinctions, that they are more than once expressed, and everywhere supposed, in the writings of St. Paul. I have no hesitation in undertaking to prove, that every heresy which has disquieted the Christian Church, from Tritheism to Socinianism, has originated in and supported itself by arguments rendered plausible only by the confusion of these faculties, and thus demanding for the objects of one, a sort of evidence appropriated to those of another faculty.—These disquisitions have the misfortune of being in ill-report, as dry and unsatisfactory; but I hope, in the course of the work, to gain them a better character—and if elucidations of their practical impor-

* In the severity of logic, the geometrical point, line, surface, circle, and so forth, are theorems, not ideas.

The third and last system, then, denies all rightful origin to government, except as far as it is derivable from principles contained in the reason of man, and judges all the relations of man in society by the laws of moral necessity, according to ideas. I here use the word in its highest and primitive sense, and as nearly synonymous with the modern word ideal,—according to archetypal ideas co-essential with the reason, the consciousness of these ideas being indeed the sign and necessary product of the full development of the reason. The following then is the fundamental principle of this theory: Nothing is to be deemed rightful in civil society, or to be tolerated as such, but what is capable of being demonstrated out of the original laws of the pure reason. Of course, as there is but one system of geometry, so according to this theory there can be but one constitution and one system of legislation, and this consists in the freedom, which is the common right of all men, under the control of that moral necessity, which is the common duty of all men. Whatever is not everywhere necessary, is nowhere right. On this assumption the whole theory is built. To state it nakedly is to confute it satisfactorily. So at least it should seem. But in how winning and specious a manner this system may be represented even to minds of the loftiest order, if undisciplined and unhumbled by practical experience, has been proved by the general impassioned admiration and momentous effects of Rousseau's *Du Contrat Social*, and the writings of the French economists, or, as they more appropriately entitled themselves, physiocratic philosophers: and in how tempting and dangerous a manner it may be represented to the populace, has been made too evident in our own country by the temporary effects of Paine's Rights of Man. Relatively, however, to this latter work it should be observed, that it is not a legitimate offspring of any one theory, but a confusion of the immortality of the first system with the misapplied universal principles of the

tance from the most momentous events of history, can render them interesting, to give them that interest at least. Besides, there is surely some good in the knowledge of truth, as truth—we were not *made to live by bread alone*—and in the strengthening of the intellect. It is an excellent remark of Scaliger's—*Harum indagatio subtilitatum, etsi non est utilis ad machinas farinarias conficiendas, exuit animum tamen inscitiæ rubigine, acuitque ad alia.*—Exerc. 307. §§ 3. The investigation of these subtleties, though of no use to the construction of machines for grinding corn, yet clears the mind from the rust of ignorance, and sharpens it or other things.

last: and in this union, or rather lawless alternation, consists the essence of Jacobinism, as far as Jacobinism is any thing but a term of abuse, or has any meaning of its own distinct from democracy and sedition.

A constitution equally suited to China and America, or to Russia and Great Britain, must surely be equally unfit for both, and deserve as little respect in political, as a quack's panacea in medical, practice. Yet there are three weighty motives for a distinct exposition of this theory,* and of the ground on which its pretensions are bottomed: and I dare affirm, that for the same reasons there are few subjects which in the present state of the world have a fairer claim to the attention of every serious Englishman, who is likely, directly or indirectly, as partisan or as opponent, to interest himself in schemes of reform.

The first motive is derived from the propensity of mankind to mistake the abhorrence occasioned by the unhappy effects or accompaniments of a particular system for an insight into the falsehood of its principles. And it is the latter only, a clear insight, not any vehement emotion, that can secure its permanent rejection. For by a wise ordinance of nature our feelings have no abiding-place in our memory; nay, the more vivid they are in the moment of their existence, the more dim and difficult to be remembered do they make the thoughts which accompanied them. Those of my readers, who at any time of their life have been in the habit of reading novels, may easily convince themselves of this truth, by comparing their recollections of those stories which most excited their curiosity, and even painfully affected their feelings, with their recollections of the calm and meditative pathos of Shakspeare and Milton. Hence it is that human experience, like the stern lights of a ship at sea, illumines only the path which we have passed over. The horrors of the Peasants' War in Germany, and the direful effects of the Anabaptist tenets, which were only nominally different from those of

* As metaphysics are the science which determines what can, and what can not, be known of being and the laws of being, *à priori*,—that is, from those necessities of the mind or forms of thinking, which, though first revealed to us by experience, must yet have pre-existed in order to make experience itself possible, even as the eye must exist previously to any particular act of seeing, though by sight only can we know that we have eyes—so might the philosophy of Rousseau and his followers not inaptly be entitled, metapolitics, and the doctors of this school metapoliticians

Jacobinism by the substitution of religious for philosophical jargon, struck all Europe for a time with affright. Yet little more than a century was sufficient to obliterate all effective memory of those events: the same principles budded forth anew, and produced the same fruits from the imprisonment of Charles I. to the restoration of his son. In the succeeding generations, to the follies and vices of the European courts, and to the oppressive privileges of the nobility, were again transferred those feelings of disgust and hatred, which for a brief while the multitude had attached to the crimes and extravagances of political and religious fanaticism: and the same principles, aided by circumstances and dressed out in the ostentatious garb of a fashionable philosophy, once more rose triumphant, and effected the French revolution. That man has reflected little on human nature who does not perceive that the detestable maxims and correspondent crimes of the existing French despotism, have already dimmed the recollections of the democratic phrenzy in the minds of men; by little and little, have drawn off to other objects the electric force of the feelings, which had massed and upholden those recollections; and that a favorable concurrence of occasions is alone wanting to awaken the thunder and precipitate the lightning from the opposite quarter of the political heaven. The true origin of human events is so little susceptible of that kind of evidence which can compel our belief even against our will; and so many are the disturbing forces which modify the motion given by the first projection; and every age has, or imagines it has, its own circumstances which render past experience no longer applicable to the present case; that there will never be wanting answers and explanations, and specious flatteries of hope. I well remember, that when the examples of former Jacobins, Julius Cæsar, Cromwell, &c. were adduced in France and England at the commencement of the French Consulate, it was ridiculed as pedantry and pedants' ignorance, to fear a repetition of such usurpation at the close of the enlightened eighteenth century. Those who possess the *Moniteurs* of that date will find set proofs, that such results were little less than impossible, and that it was an insult to so philosophical an age, and so enlightened a nation, to dare direct the public eye towards them as lights of admonition and warning.

It is a common weakness with official statesmen, and with

those who deem themselves honored by their acquaintance, to attribute great national events to the influence of particular persons, to the errors of one man and to the intrigues of another, to any possible spark of a particular occasion, rather than to the true cause, the predominant state of public opinion. I have known men who, with most significant nods, and the civil contempt of pitying half-smiles, have declared the natural explanation of the French revolution, to be the mere fancies of garreteers, and then, with the solemnity of cabinet ministers, have proceeded to explain the whole by anecdotes. It is so stimulant to the pride of a vulgar mind, to be persuaded that it knows what few others know, and that it is the important depository of a sort of state secret, by communicating which it confers an obligation on others! But I have likewise met with men of intelligence, who at the commencement of the revolution were travelling on foot through the French provinces, and they bear witness, that in the remotest villages every tongue was employed in echoing and enforcing the doctrines of the Parisian journalists ; that the public highways were crowded with enthusiasts, some shouting the watchwords of the revolution, others disputing on the most abstract principles of the universal constitution, which they fully believed, that all the nations of the earth were shortly to adopt ; the most ignorant among them confident of his fitness for the highest duties of a legislator ; and all prepared to shed their blood in the defence of the inalienable sovereignty of the self-governed people. The more abstract the notions were, with the closer affinity did they combine with the most fervent feelings, and all the immediate impulses to action. The Lord Chancellor Bacon lived in an age of court intrigues, and was familiarly acquainted with all the secrets of personal influence. He, if any man, was qualified to take the gauge and measurement of their comparative power ; and he has told us, that there is one, and but one infallible source of political prophecy, the knowledge of the predominant opinions and the speculative principles of men in general, between the age of twenty and thirty. Sir Philip Sidney,—the favorite of Queen Elizabeth, the paramount gentleman of Europe, the nephew, and—as far as a good man could be—the confidant of the intriguing and dark-minded Earl of Leicester,—was so deeply convinced that the principles diffused through the majority of a nation are the true oracles from whence statesmen are to learn wisdom, and that when the people speak loudly it is from their being strongly possessed either by the godhead or the dæmon, that in the revolution of the Netherlands he considered the universal adoption of one set of principles, as a proof of the divine presence. 'If Her Majesty,' says he, 'were the fountain, I would fear, considering what I daily find, that we should wax dry. But she is but a means which God useth.' But if my readers wish to see the question of the efficacy of principles and popular opinions for evil and for good proved and illustrated with an eloquence worthy of the subject, I can refer them with the hardiest anticipation of their thanks to the late work concerning the relations of Great Britain, Spain, and Portugal, by my honored friend, William Wordsworth, *quem quoties lego, non verba mihi videor audire, sed tonitrua.**

* I consider this reference to, and strong recommendation of, the work above mentioned, not as a voluntary tribute of admiration, but as an act of mere justice both to myself and to the readers of The Friend. My own heart bears me witness, that I am actuated by the deepest sense of the truth of the principles, which it has been and still more will be my endeavor to enforce, and of their paramount importance to the well-being of society at the present juncture: and that the duty of making the attempt, and the hope of not wholly failing in it, are, far more than the wish for the doubtful good of literary reputation, or any yet meaner object, my great and ruling motives. Mr. Wordsworth I deem a fellow-laborer in the same vineyard, actuated by the same motives and teaching the same principles, but with far greater powers of mind, and an eloquence more adequate to the importance and majesty of the cause. I am strengthened too by the knowledge, that I am not unauthorized by the sympathy of many wise and good men, and men acknowledged as such by the public, in my admiration of his pamphlet.—*Neque enim debet operibus ejus obesse, quod vivit. An si inter eos, quos numquam vidimus, floruisset, non solum libros ejus, verum etiam imagines conquireremus, ejusdem nunc honor præsentis, et gratia quasi satietate languescet? At hoc pravum, malignumque est, non admirari hominem admiratione dignissimum, quia videre, alloqui, audire, complecti, nec laudare tantum, verum etiam amare, contingit.* PLIN. Epis. Lib. I. 16.

It is hardly possible for a man of ingenuous mind to act under the fear that he shall be suspected by honest men of the vileness of praising a work to the public, merely because he happens to be personally acquainted with the author. That this is so commonly done in reviews, furnishes only an additional proof of the morbid hardness produced in the moral sense by the habit of writing anonymous criticisms, especially under the further disguise of a pretended board or association of critics, each man expressing himself, to use the words of Andrew Marvel, as a synodical *individuum.* With regard, however, to the probability of being warped by partiality, I can only

That erroneous political notions—they having become general and a part of the popular creed—have practical consequences, and these, of course, of a most fearful nature, is a truth as certain as historic evidence can make it: and that when the feelings excited by these calamities have passed away, and the interest in them has been displaced by more recent events, the same errors are likely to be started afresh, pregnant with the same calamities, is an evil rooted in human nature in the present state of general information, for which we have hitherto found no adequate remedy. It may, perhaps, in the scheme of Providence, be proper and conducive to its ends, that no adequate remedy should exist: for the folly of men is the wisdom of God. But if there be any means, if not of preventing, yet of palliating, the disease, and, in the more favored nations, of checking its progress at the first symptoms; and if these means are to be at all compatible with the civil and intellectual freedom of mankind; they are to be found only in an intelligible and thorough exposure of the error, and, through that discovery, of the source, from which it derives its speciousness and powers of influence on the human mind. This therefore is my first motive for undertaking the disquisition.

The second is, that though the French code of revolutionary principles is now generally rejected as a system, yet everywhere in the speeches and writings of the English reformers, nay, not seldom in those of their opponents, I find certain maxims asserted

say that I judge of all works indifferently by certain fixed rules previously formed in my mind with all the power and vigilance of my judgment; and that I should certainly of the two apply them with greater rigor to the production of a friend than to that of a person indifferent to me. But wherever I find in any work all the conditions of excellence in its kind, it is not the accident of the author's being my contemporary or even my friend, or the sneers of bad-hearted men, that shall prevent me from speaking of it, as in my inmost convictions I deem it deserves.

——————————— no, friend!
Though it be now the fashion to commend,
As men of strong minds, those alone who can
Censure with judgment, no such piece of man
Makes up my spirit: where desert does live,
There will I plant my wonder, and there give
My best endeavors to build up his glory,
That truly merits!

Recommendatory Verses to one of the old plays.

or appealed to, which are not tenable, except as constituent parts of that system. Many of the most specious arguments in proof of the imperfection and injustice of the present constitution of our legislature will be found, on closer examination, to presuppose the truth of certain principles, from which the adducers of these arguments loudly profess their dissent. But in political changes no permanence can be hoped for in the edifice, without consistency in the foundation.

The third motive is, that by detecting the true source of the influence of these principles, we shall at the same time discover their natural place and object; and that in themselves they are not only truths, but most important and sublime truths; and that their falsehood and their danger consist altogether in their misapplication. Thus the dignity of human nature will be secured, and at the same time a lesson of humility taught to each individual, when we are made to see that the universal necessary laws, and pure ideas of reason, were given us, not for the purpose of flattering our pride, and enabling us to become national legislators; but that, by an energy of continued self-conquest, we might establish a free and yet absolute government in our own spirits.

ESSAY IV.

Albeit therefore, much of that we are to speak in this present cause, may seem to a number perhaps tedious, perhaps obscure, dark, and intricate (for many talk of the truth, which never sounded the depth from whence it springeth: and therefore, when they are led thereunto, they are soon weary, as men drawn from those beaten paths, wherewith they have been inured); yet this may not so far prevail, as to cut off that which the matter itself requireth, howsoever the nice humor of some be therewith pleased or no. They unto whom we shall seem tedious, are in no wise injured by us, because it is in their own hands to spare that labor which they are not willing to endure. And if any complain of obscurity, they must consider, that in these matters it cometh no otherwise to pass, than in sundry the works both of art, and also of nature, where that which hath greatest force in the very things we see, is, notwithstanding, itself oftentimes not seen. The stateliness of houses, the goodliness of trees, when we behold them, delighteth the eye: but that foundation which beareth up the one, that root which ministereth unto the other nourishment and life, is in the bosom of the earth concealed; and if there be at any time occasion to search into it, such labor is then more necessary than pleasant, both to them which undertake it and for the lookers-on. In like manner, the use and benefit of good laws, all that live under them, may enjoy with delight and comfort, albeit the grounds and first original causes from whence they have sprung, be unknown, as to the greatest part of men they are. But when they who withdraw their obedience, pretend that the laws which they should obey are corrupt and vicious; for better examination of their quality, it behooveth the very foundation and root, the highest well-spring and fountain of them to be discovered. Which, because we are not oftentimes accustomed to do, when we do it, the pains we take are more needful a great deal than acceptable, and the matters which we handle, seem by reason of newness (till the mind grow better acquainted with them), dark, intricate, and unfamiliar. For as much help whereof, as may be in this case, I have endeavored throughout the body of this whole discourse, that every former part might give strength unto all that follow, and every latter bring some light unto all before: so that if the judgments of men do but hold themselves in suspense, as touching these first more general meditations, till in order they have perused the rest that ensue; what may seem dark at the first, will afterwards be found more plain, even as the latter particular decisions will appear, I doubt not, more strong when the other have been read before.

HOOKER.*

ON THE GROUNDS OF GOVERNMENT AS LAID EXCLUSIVELY IN THE PURE REASON; OR A STATEMENT AND CRITIQUE OF THE THIRD SYSTEM OF POLITICAL PHILOSOPHY,—THE THEORY OF ROUSSEAU AND THE FRENCH ECONOMISTS.

I PROCEED to my promise of developing from its embryo principles the tree of French liberty, of which the declaration of the rights of man, and the constitution of 1791 were the leaves, and the succeeding and present state of France the fruits. Let me not be blamed, if, in the interposed essays, introductory to this section, I have connected this system, though only in imagination, though only as a possible case, with a name so deservedly reverenced as that of Luther. It is some excuse, that to interweave with the reader's recollections a certain life and dramatic interest, during the perusal of the abstract† reasonings that are to fol-

* Eccl. Pol. B. I. c. 1, 2.—*Ed.*

† I have been charged in The Friend with a novel and perplexing use of the word *abstract*, both as verb and noun. Novel it certainly is not; it being authorized by Lord Bacon, Des Cartes, and others. The fact is this: I take the word in its proper meaning, as *abstraho*, I draw from. The image, by which I represent to myself an oak-tree, is no *fac simile* or ade-

low, is the only means I possess of bribing his attention. We have, most of us, at some period or other of our lives, been amused with dialogues of the dead. Who is there, that wishing to form a probable opinion on the grounds of hope and fear for an injured people warring against mighty armies, would not be pleased with a spirited fiction, which brought before him an old Numantian discoursing on that subject in Elysium, with a newly-arrived spirit from the streets of Saragoza or the walls of Gerona?

But I have a better reason. I wished to give every fair advantage to the opinions, which I deemed it of importance to confute. It is bad policy to represent a political system as having no charm but for robbers and assassins, and no natural origin but in the brains of fools or madmen, when experience has proved, that the great danger of the system consists in the peculiar fascination it is calculated to exert on noble and imaginative spirits; on all those who, in the amiable intoxication of youthful benevolence, are apt to mistake their own best virtues and choicest powers for the average qualities and attributes of the human character. The very minds, which a good man would most wish to preserve or disentangle from the snare, are by these angry misrepresentations rather lured into it. Is it wonderful that a man should reject the arguments unheard, when his own heart proves the falsehood of the assumptions by which they are prefaced; or that he should retaliate on the aggressors their own evil thoughts? I am well aware, that the provocation was great, the temptation almost inevitable; yet still I can not repel the conviction from my mind, that in part to this error, and in part to a certain inconsistency in his own fundamental principles, we are to attribute the small number of converts made by Burke

quate *icon* of the tree, but is abstracted from it by my eye. Now this appears to me a more natural as well as more grammatical and philosophical use of the word, than that elliptic construction, by which an accusative noun, and the preposition following it are to be understood, namely, I draw (*my attention from*) the, &c. Thus:—I give the outline of a flower on a slate with a slate pencil.—Now, I would say, I abstract the shape from the flower, or of the flower. But the objector would express the same thing by saying, I abstract the color, &c. (that is, my attention from the color, &c.)

Perhaps the latter might be better in familiar writing; but I continue to prefer the former on subjects that require precision. 1830.

during his life-time. Let me not be misunderstood. I do not mean, that this great man supported different principles at different æras of his political life. On the contrary, no man was ever more like himself. From his first published speech on the American colonies to his last posthumous tracts, we see the same man, the same doctrines, the same uniform wisdom of practical counsels, the same reasoning and the same prejudices against all abstract grounds, against all deduction of practice from theory. The inconsistency to which I allude, is of a different kind: it is the want of congruity in the principles appealed to in different parts of the same work; it is an apparent versatility of the principle with the occasion. If his opponents are theorists, then every thing is to be founded on prudence, on mere calculations of expediency; and every man is represented as acting according to the state of his own immediate self-interest. Are his opponents calculators? Then calculation itself is represented as a sort of crime. God has given us feelings, and we are to obey them;—and the most absurd prejudices become venerable, to which these feelings have given consecration. I have not forgotten, that Burke himself defended these half-contradictions, on the pretext of balancing the too much on the one side by a too much on the other. But never can I believe but that the straight line must needs be the nearest; and that where there is the most, and the most unalloyed truth, there will be the greatest and most permanent power of persuasion. But the fact was, that Burke in his public character found himself, as it were, in a Noah's ark, with a very few men, and a great many beasts. He felt how much his immediate power was lessened by the very circumstance of his measureless superiority to those about him: he acted, therefore, under a perpetual system of compromise—a compromise of greatness with meanness; a compromise of comprehension with narrowness; a compromise of the philosopher,—who, armed with the twofold knowledge of history and the laws of spirit, looked, as with a telescope, far around and into the remote distance,—with the mere men of business, or with yet coarser intellects, who handled a truth, which they were required to receive, as they would handle an ox, which they were desired to purchase. But why need I repeat what has been already said in so happy a manner by Goldsmith of this great man:—

Who too deep for his hearers, still went on refining,
And thought of convincing, while they thought of dining.*

And if in consequence it was his fate to "cut blocks with a razor," I may be permitted to add, that in respect of truth, though not of genius, the weapon was injured by the misapplication.

For myself, however, I act and will continue to act under the belief, that the whole truth is the best antidote to falsehoods, which are dangerous chiefly because they are half-truths: and that an erroneous system is best confuted, not by an abuse of theory in general, nor by an absurd opposition of theory to practice, but by a detection of the errors in the particular theory. For the meanest of men has his theory, and to think at all is to theorize. With these convictions I proceed immediately to the system of the economists, and to the principles on which it is constructed, and from which it must derive all its strength.

The system commences with an undeniable truth, and an important deduction therefrom equally undeniable. All voluntary actions, say they, having for their objects, good or evil, are moral actions. But all morality is grounded in the reason. Every man is born with the faculty of reason: and whatever is without it, be the shape what it may, is not a man or person, but a thing. Hence the sacred principle, recognized by all laws, human and divine, the principle indeed, which is the ground-work of all law and justice, that a person can never become a thing, nor be treated as such without wrong. But the distinction between person and thing consists herein, that the latter may rightfully be used, altogether and merely, as a mean; but the former must always be included in the end, and form a part of the final cause. We plant the tree and we cut it down, we breed the sheep and we kill it, wholly as means to our own ends. The wood-cutter and the hind are likewise employed as means, but on an agreement of reciprocal advantage, which includes them as well as their employer in the end. Again: as the faculty of reason implies free-agency, morality,—that is, the dictate of reason,—gives to every rational being the right of acting as a free agent, and of finally determining his conduct by his own will, according to his own conscience: and this right is inalienable except by guilt, which is an act of self-forfeiture, and the conse-

* Retaliation.—*Ed.*

quences therefore to be considered as the criminal's own moral election. In respect of their reason* all men are equal. The measure of the understanding and of all other faculties of man, is different in different persons: but reason is not susceptible of degree. For since it merely decides whether any given thought or action is or is not in contradiction with the rest, there can be no reason better, or more reason, than another.

Reason! best and holiest gift of God and bond of union with the giver;—the high title by which the majesty of man claims precedence above all other living creatures;—mysterious faculty, the mother of conscience, of language, of tears, and of smiles;—calm and incorruptible legislator of the soul, without whom all its other powers would 'meet in mere oppugnancy;'—sole principle of permanence amid endless change,—in a world of discordant appetites and imagined self-interests the one only common measure, which taken away,—

> Force should be right; or, rather right and wrong,—
> Between whose endless jar justice resides,—
> Should lose their names, and so should justice too.
> Then every thing includes itself in power,
> Power into will, will into appetite;
> And appetite a universal wolf,
> So doubly seconded with will and power,
> Must make perforce a universal prey!

Thrice blessed faculty of reason! all other gifts, though goodly and of celestial origin, health, strength, talents, all the powers and all the means of enjoyment, seem dispensed by chance or sullen caprice;—thou alone, more than even the sunshine, more than the common air, art given to all men, and to every man alike. To thee, who being one art the same in all, we owe the privilege, that of all we can become one, a living whole,—that we have a country. Who then shall dare prescribe a law of moral action for any rational being, which does not flow immediately from that reason, which is the fountain of all morality? Or how without breach of conscience can we limit or coerce the powers of a free agent, except by coincidence with that law in his own mind, which is at once the cause, the condition, and the

* This position has been already explained, and the sophistry grounded on it detected and exposed, in Essay V. of the First Landing-Place. II. pp. 143–150.

measure of his free agency? Man must be free; or to what purpose was he made a spirit of reason, and not a machine of instinct? Man must obey; or wherefore has he a conscience? The powers, which create this difficulty, contain its solution likewise: for their service is perfect freedom. And whatever law or system of law compels any other service, disennobles our nature, leagues itself with the animal against the god-like, kills in us the very principle of joyous well-doing, and fights against humanity.

By the application of these principles to the social state there arises the following system, which, as far as its first grounds are concerned, is developed the most fully by J. J. Rousseau in his work *Du Contrat Social.* If then no individual possesses the right of prescribing any thing to another individual, the rule of which is not contained in their common reason, society, which is but an aggregate of individuals, can communicate this right to no one. It can not possibly make that rightful which the higher and inviolable law of human nature declares contradictory and unjust. But concerning right and wrong, the reason of each and every man is the competent judge: for how else could he be an amenable being, or the proper subject of any law? This reason, therefore, in any one man, can not even in the social state be rightfully subjugated to the reason of any other. Neither an individual, nor yet the whole multitude which constitutes the state, can possess the right of compelling him to do any thing, of which it can not be demonstrated that his own reason must join in prescribing it. If therefore society is to be under a rightful constitution of government, and one that can impose on rational beings a true and moral obligation to obey it, it must be framed on such principles that every individual follows his own reason while he obeys the laws of the constitution, and performs the will of the state while he follows the dictates of his own reason. This is expressly asserted by Rousseau, who states the problem of a perfect constitution of government in the following words: *trouver une forme d'association—par laquelle chacun s'unissant à tous, n'obéisse pourtant qu' à lui même, et reste aussi libre qu' auparavant,*—that is, to find a form of society according to which each one uniting himself with the whole shall yet obey himself only and remain as free as before. This right of the individual to retain his whole natural independence, even in the social state, is absolutely inalienable. He can not possibly concede or compromise it: for this very right is one of his most sacred duties. He would sin against himself, and commit high treason against the reason which the Almighty Creator has given him, if he dared abandon its exclusive right to govern his actions.

Laws obligatory on the conscience, can only therefore proceed from that reason which remains always one and the same, whether it speaks through this or that person: like the voice of an external ventriloquist, it is indifferent from whose lips it appears to come, if only it be audible. The individuals indeed are subject to errors and passions, and each man has his own defects. But when men are assembled in person or by real representatives, the actions and reactions of individual self-love balance each other; errors are neutralized by opposite errors; and the winds rushing from all quarters at once with equal force, produce for the time a deep calm, during which the general will arising from the general reason displays itself. 'It is fittest,' says Burke himself,* 'that sovereign authority should be exercised where it is most likely to be attended with the most effectual correctives. These correctives are furnished by the nature and course of parliamentary proceedings, and by the infinitely diversified characters which compose the two Houses. The fulness, the freedom, and publicity of discussion, leave it easy to distinguish what are acts of power, and what the determinations of equity and reason. There prejudice corrects prejudice, and the different asperities of party zeal mitigate and neutralize each other.'

This, however, as my readers will have already detected, is no longer a demonstrable deduction from reason. It is a mere probability, against which other probabilities may be weighed: as the lust of authority, the contagious nature of enthusiasm, and other of the acute or chronic diseases of deliberative assemblies. But which of these results is the more probable, the correction or the contagion of evil, must depend on circumstances and grounds of expediency: and thus we already find ourselves beyond the magic circle of the pure reason, and within the sphere of the understanding and the prudence. Of this important fact Rousseau was by no means unaware in his theory, though with gross inconsistency he takes no notice of it in his application of the the-

* Note on his motion relative to the Speech from the Throne, vol. ii. p. 647, 4to Edit.

ory to practice. He admits the possibility, he is compelled by history to allow even the probability, that the most numerous popular assemblies, nay even whole nations, may at times be hurried away by the same passions, and under the dominion of a common error. This will of all is then of no more value, than the humors of any one individual: and must therefore be sacredly distinguished from the pure will which flows from universal reason. To this point then I entreat the reader's particular attention: for in this distinction, established by Rousseau himself, between the *volonté de tous* and the *volonté générale*,—that is, between the collective will, and a casual overbalance of wills—the falsehood or nothingness of the whole system becomes manifest. For hence it follows, as an inevitable consequence, that all which is said in the *Contrat Social* of that sovereign will, to which the right of universal legislation appertains, applies to no one human being, to no society or assemblage of human beings, and least of all to the mixed multitude that makes up the people: but entirely and exclusively to reason itself, which, it is true, dwells in every man potentially, but actually and in perfect purity is found in no man and in no body of men. This distinction the latter disciples of Rousseau chose completely to forget, and,—a far more melancholy case—the constituent legislators of France forgot it likewise. With a wretched parrotry they wrote and harangued without ceasing of the *volonté générale*—the inalienable sovereignty of the people: and by these high-sounding phrases led on the vain, ignorant, and intoxicated populace to wild excesses and wilder expectations, which entailing on them the bitterness of disappointment cleared the way for military despotism, for the Satanic government of horror under the Jacobins, and of terror under the Corsican.

Luther lived long enough to see the consequences of the doctrines into which indignant pity and abstract principles of right had hurried him—to see, to retract and to oppose them. If the same had been the lot of Rousseau, I doubt not, that his conduct would have been the same. In his whole system there is beyond controversy much that is true and well reasoned, if only its application be not extended farther than the nature of the case permits. But then we shall find that little or nothing is won by it for the institutions of society; and least of all for the constitution of governments, the theory of which it was his wish to ground on it. Apply his principles to any case, in which the sacred and inviolable laws of morality are immediately interested, all becomes just and pertinent. No power on earth can oblige me to act against my conscience. No magistrate, no monarch, no legislature, can without tyranny compel me to do any thing which the acknowledged laws of God have forbidden me to do. So act that thou mayest be able, without involving any contradiction, to will that the maxim of thy conduct should be the law of all intelligent beings—is the one universal and sufficient principle and guide of morality.* And why? Because the object of morality is not the outward act, but the internal maxim of our actions. And so far it is infallible. But with what show of reason can we pretend, from a principle by which we are to determine the purity of our motives, to deduce the form and matter of a rightful government, the main office of which is to regulate the outward actions of particular bodies of men, according to their particular circumstances? Can we hope better of constitutions framed by ourselves, than of that which was given by Almighty Wisdom itself? The laws of the Hebrew commonwealth, which flowed from the pure reason, remain and are immutable; but the regulations dictated by prudence, though by the divine prudence, and though given in thunder from the mount, have passed away; and while they lasted, were binding only for that one state, the particular circumstances of which rendered them expedient.

Rousseau indeed asserts, that there is an inalienable sovereignty inherent in every human being possessed of reason: and from this the framers of the constitution of 1791 deduce, that the people itself is its own sole rightful legislator, and at most dare only recede so far from its right as to delegate to chosen deputies the power of representing and declaring the general will. But this is wholly without proof; for it has already been fully shown, that according to the principle out of which this consequence is attempted to be drawn, it is not the actual man, but the abstract reason alone, that is the sovereign and rightful lawgiver. The confusion of two things so different is so gross an error, that the Constituent Assembly could scarcely proceed a step in their declaration of rights, without some glaring inconsistency. Children are excluded from all political power;—are they not human

* Kant's *Grundlegung zur Metaphysik der Sitten*, pp. 46, 47. Leipsic, 1838. Am. Ed.

beings in whom the faculty of reason resides? Yes! but in them the faculty is not yet adequately developed. But are not gross ignorance, inveterate superstition, and the habitual tyranny of passion and sensuality, equally preventives of the development, equally impediments to the rightful exercise, of the reason, as childhood and early youth? Who would not rely on the judgment of a well-educated English lad, bred in a virtuous and enlightened family, in preference to that of a brutal Russian, who believes that he can scourge his wooden idol into good-humor, or attributes to himself the merit of perpetual prayer, when he has fastened the petitions, which his priest has written for him, on the wings of a windmill?—Again: women are likewise excluded—a full half, and that assuredly the most innocent, the most amiable half, of the whole human race, is excluded, and this too by a constitution which boasts to have no other foundations but those of universal reason! Is reason then an affair of sex? No! But women are commonly in a state of dependence, and are not likely to exercise their reason with freedom. Well! and does not this ground of exclusion apply with equal or greater force to the poor, to the infirm, to men in embarrassed circumstances, to all in short whose maintenance, be it scanty or be it ample, depends on the will of others? How far are we to go? Where must we stop? What classes should we admit? Whom must we disfranchise? The objects concerning whom we are to determine these questions, are all human beings, and differenced from each other by degrees only, these degrees, too, oftentimes changing. Yet the principle on which the whole system rests is, that reason is not susceptible of degree. Nothing, therefore, which subsists wholly in degrees, the changes of which do not obey any necessary law, can be subjects of pure science, or determinable by mere reason. For these things we must rely on our understandings, enlightened by past experience and immediate observation, and determining our choice by comparisons of expediency.

It is therefore altogether a mistaken notion, that the theory which would deduce the social rights of man, and the sole rightful form of government from principles of reason, involves a necessary preference of the democratic, or even the representative, constitutions. Accordingly, several of the French economists, although devotees of Rousseau and the physiocratic system, and assuredly not the least respectable of their party either in morals or in intellect,—and these, too, men who lived and wrote under the limited monarchy of France, and who were therefore well acquainted with the evils connected with that system,—did yet declare themselves for a pure monarchy in preference to the aristocratic, the popular, or the mixed form. These men argued, that no other laws being allowable but those which are demonstrably just, and founded in the simplest ideas of reason, and of which every man's reason is the competent judge, it is indifferent whether one man, or one or more assemblies of men, give form and publicity to them. For being matters of pure and simple science, they require no experience in order to see their truth ; and among an enlightened people, by whom this system had been once solemnly adopted, no sovereign would dare to make other laws than those of reason. They further contend, that if the people were not enlightened, a purely popular government could not co-exist with this system of absolute justice : and if it were adequately enlightened, the influence of public opinion would supply the place of formal representation, while the form of the government would be in harmony with the unity and simplicity of its principles. This they entitle *le despotisme légal sous l'empire de l'évidence.* The best statement of the theory thus modified, may be found in *Mercier de la Rivière, l'ordre naturel et essentiel des sociétés politiques.* From the proofs adduced in the preceding paragraph, to which many others might be added, I have no hesitation in affirming that this latter party are the more consistent reasoners.

It is worthy of remark, that the influence of these writings contributed greatly, not indeed to raise the present emperor, but certainly to reconcile a numerous class of politicians to his unlimited authority : and as far as his lawless passion for war and conquest allows him to govern according to any principles, he favors those of the physiocratic philosophers. His early education must have given him a predilection for a theory conducted throughout with mathematical precision ; its very simplicity promised the readiest and most commodious machine for despotism, for it moulds a nation into as calculable a power as an army ; while the stern and seeming greatness of the whole, and its mock elevation above human feelings, flattered his pride, hardened his conscience, and aided the efforts of self-delusion. Reason is the sole sovereign, the only rightful legislator: but reason to act on man must be impersonated. The Providence which had so marvellously raised and supported him, had marked him out for the representative of reason, and had armed him with irresistible force, in order to realize its laws. In him, therefore, might becomes right, and his cause and that of destiny (or, as he now chooses to word it, exchanging blind nonsense for staring blasphemy), his cause and the cause of God are one and the same. Excellent postulate for a choleric and self-willed tyrant! What avails the impoverishment of a few thousand merchants and manufacturers? What even the general wretchedness of millions of perishable men, for a short generation? Should these stand in the way of the chosen conqueror, the *innovator mundi, et stupor sæculorum*, or prevent a constitution of things, which erected on intellectual and perfect foundations groweth not old, but like the eternal justice, of which it is the living image,

> ——————————may despise
> The strokes of fate, and see the world's last hour?

For justice, austere, unrelenting justice, is everywhere holden up as the one thing needful; and the only duty of the citizen, in fulfilling which he obeys all the laws, is not to encroach on another's sphere of action. The greatest possible happiness of a people is not, according to this system, the object of a governor; but to preserve the freedom of all, by coercing within the requisite bounds the freedom of each. Whatever a government does more than this, comes of evil: and its best employment is the repeal of laws and regulations, not the establishment of them. Each man is the best judge of his own happiness, and to himself must it therefore be intrusted. Remove all the interferences of positive statutes, all monopoly, all bounties, all prohibitions, and all encouragements of importation and exportation, of particular growth and particular manufactures: let the revenues of the state be taken at once from the produce of soil; and all things will then find their level, all irregularities will correct each other, and an indestructible cycle of harmonious motions take place in the moral equally as in the natural world. The business of the governor is to watch incessantly, that the state shall remain composed of individuals, acting as individuals, by which alone the freedom of all can be secured. Its duty is to take care that itself remain the sole collective power, and that all the citizens should enjoy the same rights, and without distinction be subject to the same duties.

Splendid promises! Can any thing appear more equitable than the last proposition, the equality of rights and duties? Can any thing be conceived more simple in the idea? But the execution—! Let the four or five quarto volumes of the Conscript Code be the comment! But as briefly as possible I shall prove, that this system, as an exclusive total, is under any form impracticable; and that if it were realized, and as far as it were realized, it would necessarily lead to general barbarism and the most grinding oppression; and that the final result of a general attempt to introduce it, must be a military despotism inconsistent with the peace and safety of mankind. That reason should be our guide and governor is an undeniable truth, and all our notion of right and wrong is built thereon: for reason is one of the two fountain-heads in which the whole moral nature of man originated and subsists. From reason alone can we derive the principles which our understandings are to apply, the ideal to which by means of our understandings we should endeavor to approximate. This, however, gives no proof that reason alone ought to govern and direct human beings, either as individuals or as states. It ought not to do this, because it can not. The laws of reason are unable to satisfy the first conditions of human society. We will admit that the shortest code of the law is the best, and that the citizen finds himself most at ease where the government least intermeddles with his affairs, and confines its efforts to the preservation of public tranquillity; we will suffer this to pass at present undisputed, though the examples of England, and before the late events, of Holland and Switzerland,—surely the three happiest nations of the world—to which perhaps we might add the major part of the former German free towns, furnish stubborn facts in presumption of the contrary,—yet still the proof is wanting that the first and most general applications and exertions of the power of man can be definitely regulated by reason unaided by the positive and conventional laws in the formation of which the understanding must be our guide, and which become just because they happen to be expedient.

The chief object for which men first formed themselves into a state was not the protection of their lives, but of their property.

Where the nature of the soil and climate precludes all property but personal, and permits that only in its simplest forms, as in Greenland, men remain in the domestic state and form neighborhoods, but not governments. And in North America the chiefs appear to exercise government in those tribes only which possess individual landed property. Among the rest the chief is their general; but government is exercised only in families by the fathers of families. But where individual landed property exists, there must be inequality of property: the nature of the earth and the nature of the mind unite to make the contrary impossible. But to suppose the land the property of the state, and the labor and the produce to be equally divided among all the members of the state, involves more than one contradiction: for it could not subsist without gross injustice, except where the reason of all and of each was absolute master of the selfish passions of sloth, envy, and the like; and yet the same state would preclude the greater part of the means by which the reason of man is developed. In whatever state of society you would place it, from the most savage to the most refined, it would be found equally unjust and impossible; and were there a race of men, a country, and a climate, that permitted such an order of things, the same causes would render all government superfluous.

To property, therefore, and to its inequalities all human laws directly or indirectly relate, which would not be equally laws in the state of nature. Now it is impossible to deduce the right of property* from pure reason. The utmost which reason could give would be a property in the forms of things, as far as the forms were produced by individual power. In the matter it could give no property. We regard angels and glorified spirits as beings of pure reason: and who ever thought of property in heaven? Even the simplest and most moral form of it, namely, marriage (we know from the highest authority), is excluded from the state of pure reason. Rousseau himself expressly admits that property can not be deduced from the laws of reason and nature; and he ought therefore to have admitted at the same time that his whole theory was a thing of air. In the most respectable point of view

* I mean, practically and with the inequalities inseparable from the actual existence of property. Abstractedly, the right to property is deducible from the free-agency of man. If to act freely be a right, a sphere of action must be so too.

he could regard his system as analogous to geometry. If indeed it be purely scientific, how could it be otherwise? Geometry holds forth an ideal which can never be fully realized in nature, even because it is nature; because bodies are more than extension, and to pure extension of space only the mathematical theorems wholly correspond. In the same manner the moral laws of the intellectual world, as far as they are deducible from pure intellect, are never perfectly applicable to our mixed and sensitive nature, because man is something besides reason; because his reason never acts by itself, but must clothe itself in the substance of individual understanding and specific inclination, in order to become a reality and an object of consciousness and experience. It will be seen hereafter that together with this, the key-stone of the arch, the greater part and the most specious of the popular arguments in favor of universal suffrage fall in and are crushed. I will mention one only at present. Major Cartwright,—in his deduction of the rights of the subject from principles "not susceptible of proof, being self-evident, if one of which be violated all are shaken,"—affirms (Principle 98th; though the greater part indeed are moral aphorisms or blank assertions, not scientific principles) "that a power which ought never to be used ought never to exist." Again he affirms that "laws to bind all must be assented to by all, and consequently every man, even the poorest, has an equal right to suffrage;" and this for an additional reason, because "all without exception are capable of feeling happiness or misery, accordingly as they are well or ill governed." But are they not then capable of feeling happiness or misery accordingly as they do or do not possess the means of a comfortable subsistence? and who is the judge, what is a comfortable subsistence, but the man himself? Might not then, on the same or equivalent principles, a leveller construct a right to equal property? The inhabitants of this country without property form, doubtless, a great majority; each of these has a right to a suffrage, and the richest man to no more; and the object of this suffrage is, that each individual may secure himself a true efficient representative of his will. Here then is a legal power of abolishing or equalizing property: and according to Major C. himself, a power which ought never to be used ought not to exist.

Therefore, unless he carries his system to the whole length of common labor and common possession, a right to universal suffrage can not exist; but if not to universal suffrage, there can exist no natural right to suffrage at all. In whatever way he would obviate this objection, he must admit expedience founded on experience and particular circumstances, which will vary in every different nation, and in the same nation at different times, as the maxim of all legislation and the ground of all legislative power. For his universal principles, as far as they are principles and universal, necessarily suppose uniform and perfect subjects, which are to be found in the ideas of pure geometry and, I trust, in the realities of heaven, but never, never, in creatures of flesh and blood.

ESSAY V.

ON THE ERRORS OF PARTY SPIRIT: OR EXTREMES MEET.

And it was no wonder if some good and innocent men, especially such as he (Lightfoot) who was generally more concerned about what was done in Judea many centuries ago, than what was transacted in his own time in his own country—it is no wonder if some such were for a while borne away to the approval of opinions which they, after more sedate reflection, disowned. Yet his innocency from any self-interest or design, together with his learning, secured him from the extravagances of demagogues, the people's oracles.—LIGHTFOOT'S *Works, Publisher's Preface to the Reader.*

I HAVE never seen Major Cartwright, much less enjoy the honor of his acquaintance; but I know enough of his character, from the testimony of others and from his own writings, to respect his talents, and revere the purity of his motives. I am fully persuaded that there are few better men, few more fervent or disinterested adherents of their country or the laws of their country, of whatsoever things are lovely, of whatsoever things are honorable. It would give me great pain should I be supposed to have introduced, disrespectfully, a name, which from my early youth I never heard mentioned without a feeling of affectionate admiration. I have indeed quoted from this venerable patriot, as from the most respectable English advocate for the theory, which derives the rights of government, and the duties of obedience to it, exclusively from principles of pure reason. It was of consequence to my cause that I should not be thought to have been waging war against a straw image of my own setting up, or even against a foreign idol that had neither worshipers nor advocates in our own country; and it was not less my object to keep my discussion aloof from those passions, which more unpopular names might have excited. I therefore introduced the name of Cartwright, as I had previously done that of Luther, in order to give every fair advantage to a theory, which I thought it of importance to confute; and as an instance that though the system might be made tempting to the vulgar, yet that, taken unmixed and entire, it was chiefly fascinating for lofty and imaginative spirits, who mistook their own virtues and powers for the average character of men in general.

Neither by fair statements nor by fair reasoning should I ever give offence to Major Cartwright himself, nor to his judicious friends. If I am in danger of offending them, it must arise from one or other of two causes; either that I have falsely represented his principles, or his motives and the tendency of his writings. In the book from which I quoted, "The People's Barrier against undue Influence" (the only one of Major Cartwright's which I possess), I am conscious that there are six foundations stated of constitutional government. Therefore, it may be urged, the author can not be justly classed with those who deduce our social rights and correlative duties exclusively from principles of pure reason, or unavoidable conclusions from such. My answer is ready. Of these six foundations three are but different words for one and the same, namely, the law of reason, the law of God, and first principles: and the three that remain can not be taken as indifferent, inasmuch as they are afterwards affirmed to be of no validity except as far as they are evidently deduced from the former; that is, from the principles implanted by God in the universal reason of man. These three latter foundations are, the general customs of the realm, particular customs, and acts of Parliament. It might be supposed that the author had not used his terms in the precise and single sense in which they are defined in my former essay; and that self-evident principles may be meant to include the dictates of manifest expedience, the inductions of the understanding as well as the prescripts of the pure reason. But no; Major Cartwright has guarded against the possibility of this interpretation, and has expressed himself as decisively, and with as much warmth, against founding governments on grounds of expedience, as I have done against founding morality on the same. Euclid himself could not have defined his words more sternly within the limits of pure science; for instance, see the 1st, 2d, 3d, and 4th primary rules:—'A principle is a manifest and simple proposition comprehending a certain truth. Principles are the proof of every thing: but are not susceptible of external proof, being self-evident. If one principle be violated, all are shaken. Against him, who denies principles, all dispute is useless, and reason unintelligible, or disallowed, so far as he denies them. The laws of nature are immutable.'—Neither could Rousseau himself, nor his predecessors, the Fifth-monarchy men, have more nakedly or emphatically identified the foundations of government in the concrete with those of religion and morality in the abstract: see Major Cartwright's primary rules from 31 to 39, and from 44 to 83. In these it is affirmed;—that the legislative rights of every citizen are inherent in his nature; that, being natural rights, they must be equal in all men; that a natural right is that right which a citizen claims as being a man, and that it hath no other foundation but his personality or reason; that property can neither increase nor modify any legislative right; that every one man shall have one vote however poor, and for any one man, however rich, to have more than one vote, is against natural justice, and an evil measure; that it is better for a nation to endure all adversities, than to assent to one evil measure; that to be free is to be governed by laws, to which we have ourselves assented, either in person or by representative, for whose election we have actually voted: that all not having a right of suffrage are slaves, and that a vast majority of the people of Great Britain are slaves! To prove the total coincidence of Major Cartwright's theory with that which I have stated, and I trust confuted, in the preceding essay, it only remains for me to prove, that the former, equally with the latter, confounds the sufficiency of the conscience to make every person a moral and amenable being, with the sufficiency of judgment and experience requisite to the exercise of political right. A single quotation will place this out of all doubt, which from its length I shall insert in a note.*

* 'But the equality' (observe, that Major Cartwright is here speaking of the natural right to universal suffrage, and consequently of the univer-

Great stress, indeed, is laid on the authority of our ancient laws, both in this and the other works of our patriotic author; and whatever his system may be, it is impossible not to feel, that the author himself possesses the heart of a genuine Englishman. But still his system can neither be changed nor modified by these appeals: for among the primary maxims, which form the groundwork of it, we are informed not only that law in the abstract is the perfection of reason; but that the law of God and the law of the land are all one! What! The statutes against witches; or those against papists, the abolition of which gave rise to the infamous riots in 1780! Or, in the author's own opinion, the statutes of disfranchisement and for making Parliaments septen-

sal right of eligibility, as well as of election, independently of character or property)—'the equality and dignity of human nature in all men, whether rich or poor, is placed in the highest point of view by St. Paul, when he reprehends the Corinthian believers for their litigations one with another, in the courts of law where unbelievers presided; and as an argument of the competency of all men to judge for themselves, he alludes to that elevation in the kingdom of heaven which is promised to every man who shall be virtuous, or in the language of that time, a saint. *Do ye not know,* says he, *that the saints shall judge the world? And if the world shall be judged by you, are ye unworthy to judge the smallest matters? Know ye not that ye shall judge the angels? How much more things that pertain to this life?* If after such authorities, such manifestations of truth as these, any Christian through those prejudices, which are the effects of long habits of injustice and oppression, and teach us to *despise the poor*, shall still think it right to exclude that part of the commonalty, consisting of tradesmen, artificers, and laborers, or any of them from voting in elections of members to serve in Parliament, I must sincerely lament such a persuasion as a misfortune both to himself and his country. And if any man,—not having given himself the trouble to consider whether or not the Scripture be an authority, but who, nevertheless, is a friend to the rights of mankind—upon grounds of mere prudence, policy, or expediency, shall think it advisable to go against the whole current of our constitutional and law maxims, by which it is self-evident that every man, as being a man, is created free, born to freedom, and, without it, a thing, a slave, a beast; and shall contend for drawing a line of exclusion at freeholders of forty pounds a year, or forty shillings a year, or householders, or pot-boilers, so that all who are below that line shall not have a vote in the election of a legislative guardian,—which is taking from a citizen the power even of self-preservation, —such a man, I venture to say, is bolder than he who wrestled with the angel; for he wrestles with God himself, who established those principles in the eternal laws of nature, never to be violated by any of his creatures.' Pp. 23, 24.

nial!—Nay! but (Principle 28) an unjust law is no law: and (P. 22) against the law of reason neither prescription, statute, nor custom, may prevail; and if any such be brought against it, they be not prescriptions, statutes, nor customs, but things void: and (P. 29) what the Parliament doth shall be holden for naught whensoever it shall enact that which is contrary to a natural right! I dare not suspect a grave writer of such egregious trifling, as to mean no more by these assertions, than that what is wrong is not right; and if more than this be meant, it must be that the subject is not bound to obey any act of Parliament, which according to his conviction entrenches on a principle of natural right; which natural rights are, as we have seen, not confined to the man in his individual capacity, but are made to confer universal legislative privileges on every subject of every state, and of the extent of which every man is competent to judge, who is competent to be the object of law at all, that is, every man who has not lost his reason.

In the statement of his principles, therefore, I have not misrepresented Major Cartwright. Have I then endeavored to connect public odium with his name, by arraigning his motives, or the tendency of his writings? The tendency of his writings in my inmost conscience I believe to be perfectly harmless, and I dare cite them in confirmation of the opinions which it was the object of my introductory essays to establish, and as an additional proof, that no good man communicating what he believes to be the truth for the sake of truth, and according to the rules of conscience, will be found to have acted injuriously to the peace or interests of society. The venerable state-moralist,—for this is his true character, and in this title is conveyed the whole error of his system,—is incapable of aiding his arguments by the poignant condiment of personal slander, incapable of appealing to the envy of the multitude by bitter declamation against the follies and oppressions of the higher classes. He would shrink with horror from the thought of adding a false and unnatural influence to the cause of truth and justice, by details of present calamity or immediate suffering, fitted to excite the fury of the multitude, or by promises of turning the current of the public revenue into the channels* of

* I must remind the reader, that this essay was written in October, 1809. If Major Cartwright has ever since then acted in a different spirit, and tampered personally with the distresses, and consequent irritability of the

individual distress and poverty, so as to bribe the populace by selfish hopes. It does not belong to men of his character to delude the uninstructed into the belief that their shortest way of obtaining the good things of this life, is to commence busy politicians, instead of remaining industrious laborers. He knows, and acts on the knowledge, that it is the duty of the enlightened philanthropist to plead for the poor and ignorant, not to them.

No.—From works written and published under the control of austere principles, and at the impulse of a lofty and generous enthusiasm,—from works rendered attractive only by the fervor of sincerity, and imposing only by the majesty of plain dealing, no danger will be apprehended by a wise man, no offence received by a good man. I could almost venture to warrant our patriot's publications innoxious, from the single circumstance of their perfect freedom from personal themes in this age of personality, this age of literary and political gossiping, when the meanest insects are worshiped with a sort of Egyptian superstition, if only the brainless head be atoned for by the sting of personal malignity in the tail; when the most vapid satires have become the objects of a keen public interest purely from the number of contemporary characters named in the patch-work notes,—which possess, however, the comparative merit of being more poetical than the text,—and because, to increase the stimulus, the author has sagaciously left his own name for whispers and conjectures! —In an age, when even sermons are published with a double appendix stuffed with names—in a generation so transformed from the characteristic reserve of Britons, that from the ephemeral sheet of a London newspaper to the everlasting Scotch professorial quarto, almost every publication exhibits or flatters the epidemic distemper; that the very last year's rebuses in the Lady's Diary, are answered in a serious elegy 'On my father's death,' with the name and *habitat* of the elegiac Œdipus subscribed;—and other ingenious solutions are likewise given to the said rebuses—not, as heretofore, by Crito, Philander, A B, X Y, &c., but by fifty or sixty plain English surnames at full length, with their several places of abode! In an age, when a bashful

ignorant, the inconsistency is his, not mine. If what I then believed and avowed should now appear a severe satire in the shape of a false prophecy, any shame I might feel for my lack of penetration would be lost in the sincerity of my regret.—1818.

Philalethes or *Phileleutheros* is as rare on the title-pages and among the signatures of our magazines, as a real name used to be in the days of our shy and notice-shunning grandfathers! When—more exquisite than all—I see an epic poem—spirits of Maro and Mæonides, make ready to welcome your new compeer! —advertised with the special recommendation, that the said epic poem contains more than a hundred names of living persons! No—if works as abhorrent, as those of Major Cartwright, from all unworthy provocatives to vanity, envy, and the selfish passions, could acquire a sufficient influence on the public mind to be mischievous, the plans proposed in his pamphlets would cease to be altogether visionary: though even then they could not ground their claims to actual adoption on self-evident principles of pure reason, but on the happy accident of the virtue and good sense of that public, for whose suffrages they were presented. Indeed with Major Cartwright's plans I have no present concern; but with the principles, on which he grounds the obligations to adopt them.

But I must not sacrifice truth to my reverence for individual purity of intention. The tendency of one good man's writings is altogether a different thing from the tendency of the system itself, when seasoned and served up for the unreasoning multitude, as it has been by men whose names I would not honor by writing them in the same sentence with Major Cartwright's. For this system has two sides, and holds out very different attractions to its admirers who advance towards it from different points of the compass. It possesses qualities, that can scarcely fail of winning over to its banners a numerous host of shallow heads and restless tempers, men who, without learning,—or, as one of my friends has forcibly expressed it, strong book-mindedness,—live as alms-folks on the opinions of their contemporaries, and who,—well pleased to exchange the humility of regret for the self-complacent feelings of contempt,—reconcile themselves to the *sans culotterie* of their ignorance, by scoffing at the useless fox-brush of pedantry.* The attachment of this numerous class is owing neither to

* He (*Charles Brandon, Duke of Suffolk*) knowing that learning hath no enemy but ignorance, did suspect always the want of it in those men who derided the habit of it in others: like the fox in the fable, who, being without a tail, would persuade others to cut off theirs as a burthen. But he liked well the philosopher's division of men into three ranks—some who

the solidity and depth of foundation in this theory, nor to the strict coherence of its arguments; and still less to any genuine reverence for humanity in the abstract. The physiocratic system promises to deduce all things, and every thing relative to law and government, with mathematical exactness and certainty, from a few individual and self-evident principles. But who so dull, as not to be capable of apprehending a simple self-evident principle, and of following a short demonstration? By this system, 'the system' as its admirers were wont to call it, even as they named the writer who first applied it in systematic detail to the whole constitution and administration of civil policy,—Du Quesnoy—*le docteur*, or 'the teacher;'—by this system the observation of times, places, relative bearings, history, national customs and character, is rendered superfluous;—all, in short, which, according to the common notion, makes the attainment of legislative prudence a work of difficulty and long-continued effort, even for the acutest and most comprehensive minds. The cautious balancing of comparative advantages, the painful calculation of forces and counterforces, the preparation of circumstances, the lynx-eyed watching for opportunities, are all superseded; and by the magic oracles of certain axioms and definitions it is revealed how the world with all its concerns should be mechanized, and then let go on of itself. All the positive institutions and regulations, which the prudence of our ancestors had provided, are declared to be erroneous or interested perversions of the natural relations of man; and the whole is delivered over to the faculty, which all men possess equally, namely, the common sense or universal reason. The science of politics, it is said, is but the application of the common sense, which every man possesses, to a subject in which every man is concerned. To be a musician, an orator, a painter, a poet, an architect, or even to be a good mechanist, presupposes genius; to be an excellent artisan or mechanic, requires more than an average degree of talent; but to be a legislator requires nothing but common sense. The commonest human intellect, therefore, suffices for a perfect

knew good and were willing to teach others; these he said were like gods among men—others who though they knew not much, yet were willing to learn; these he said were like men among beasts—and some who knew not good and yet despised such as should teach them; these he esteemed as beasts among men.—*Lloyd's State Worthies*, p. 33.

insight into the whole science of civil polity, and qualifies the possessor to sit in judgment on the constitution and administration of his own country, and of all other nations. This must needs be agreeable tidings to the great mass of mankind. There is no subject, which men in general like better to harangue on than politics; none, the deciding on which more flatters the sense of self-importance. For as to what Johnson calls 'plebeian envy,'* I do not believe that the mass of men are justly chargeable with it in their political feelings; not only because envy is seldom excited except by definite and individual objects, but still more because it is a painful passion, and not likely to co-exist with the high delight and self-complacency with which the harangues on states and statesmen, princes and generals, are made and listened to in ale-house circles or promiscuous public meetings. A certain portion of this is not merely desirable, but necessary in a free country. Heaven forbid that the most ignorant of my countrymen should be deprived of a subject so well fitted to

impart
An hour's importance to the poor man's heart!†

But a system which not only flatters the pride and vanity of men, but which in so plausible and intelligible a manner persuades them, not that this is wrong and that ought to have been managed otherwise; or that Mr. X. is worth a hundred of Mr. Y. as a minister or Parliament man; but that all is wrong and mistaken,—nay, almost unjust and wicked,—and that every man is competent, and in contempt of all rank and property, on the mere title of his personality, possesses the right, and is under the most solemn moral obligation, to give a helping hand toward overthrowing all;—this confusion of political with religious claims, this transfer of the rights of religion disjoined from the austere duties of self-denial, with which religious rights exercised in their proper sphere can not fail to be accompanied; and not only disjoined from self-restraint, but united with the indulgence of those passions,—self-will, love of power,—which it is the principal aim and hardest task of religion to correct and restrain;—

* I now more than fear that Dr. Johnson was in the right: and that I must recant my opinion with 'Coleridge! thy wish was father to that thought, not a clearer insight into the nature of man, not a wider experience of men.'—October 20th, 1818.

† Deserted Village.—*Ed.*

this, I say, is altogether different from the village politics of yore, and may be pronounced alarming and of dangerous tendency by the boldest advocates of reform not less consistently, than by the most timid eschewers of popular disturbance.

Still, however, the system had its golden side for the noblest minds: and I should act the part of a coward, if I disguised my convictions, that the errors of the aristocratic party were full as gross, and far less excusable. Instead of contenting themselves with opposing the real blessings of English law to the splendid promises of untried theory, too large a part of those, who called themselves anti-Jacobins, did all in their power to suspend those blessings; and thus furnished new arguments to the advocates of innovation, when they should have been answering the old ones. The most prudent, as well as the most honest, mode of defending the existing arrangements would have been, to have candidly admitted what could not with truth be denied, and then to have shown that, though the things complained of were evils, they were necessary evils; or if they were removable, yet that the consequences of the heroic medicines recommended by the revolutionists would be far more dreadful than the disease. Now either the one or the other point, by the double aid of history and a sound philosophy, they might have established with a certainty little short of demonstration, and with such colors and illustrations as would have taken strong hold of the very feelings which had attached to the democratic system all the good and valuable men of the party. But instead of this they precluded the possibility of being listened to even by the gentlest and most ingenuous among the friends of the French revolution, by denying or attempting to palliate facts, which were equally notorious and unjustifiable, and by supplying the lack of brain by an overflow of gall. While they lamented with tragic outcries the injured monarch and the exiled noble, they displayed the most disgusting insensibility to the privations, sufferings, and manifold oppressions of the great mass of the continental population, and a blindness or callousness still more offensive to the crimes and unutterable abominations of their oppressors.* Not only was the

* I do not mean the sovereigns, but the old nobility of both Germany and France. The extravagantly false and flattering picture, which Burke gave of the French nobility and hierarchy, has always appeared to me the greatest defect of his, in so many respects, invaluable work.

Bastile justified, but the Spanish Inquisition itself;—and this in a pamphlet passionately extolled and industriously circulated by the adherents of the then ministry. Thus, and by their infatuated panegyrics on the former state of France, they played into the hands of their worst and most dangerous antagonists. In confounding the conditions of the English and the French peasantry, and in quoting the authorities of Milton, Sidney, and their immortal compeers, as applicable to the present times and the existing government, the demagogues appeared to talk only the same language as the anti-Jacobins themselves employed. For if the vilest calumnies of obsolete bigots were applied against these great men by the one party, with equal plausibility might their authorities be adduced, and their arguments for increasing the power of the people be re-applied to the existing government, by the other. If the most disgusting forms of despotism were spoken of by the one in the same respectful language as the executive power of our own country, what wonder if the irritated partisans of the other were able to impose on the populace the converse of the proposition, and to confound the executive branch of the English sovereignty with the despotisms of less happy lands? The first duty of a wise advocate is to convince his opponents, that he understands their arguments and sympathizes with their just feelings. But instead of this, these pretended constitutionalists recurred to the language of insult, and to measures of persecution. In order to oppose Jacobinism they imitated it in its worst features; in personal slander, in illegal violence, and even in the thirst for blood. They justified the corruptions of the state in the same spirit of sophistry, by the same vague arguments of general reason, and the same disregard of ancient ordinances and established opinions, with which the state itself had been attacked by the Jacobins. The wages of state dependence were represented as no less sacred than the property won by industry or derived from a long line of ancestors.

It was, indeed, evident to thinking men, that both parties were playing the same game with different counters. If the Jacobins ran wild with the rights of man, and the abstract sovereignty of the people, their antagonists flew off as extravagantly from the sober good sense of our forefathers, and idolized as mere an abstraction in the rights of sovereigns. Nor was this confined to sovereigns. They defended the exemptions and privileges of all privileged orders, on the presumption of their inalienable right to them, however inexpedient they might have been found, as universally and abstractly as if these privileges had been decreed by the Supreme Wisdom, instead of being the offspring of chance or violence, or the inventions of human prudence. Thus, while they deemed themselves defending, they were in reality blackening and degrading the uninjurious and useful privileges of our English nobility, which rest on nobler and securer grounds. Thus too, the necessity of compensations for dethroned princes was affirmed as familiarly, as if kingdoms had been private estates: and no more disapprobation was expressed at the transfer of five or ten millions of men from one proprietor to another, than of as many score head of cattle. This most degrading and superannuated superstition, or rather this ghost of a defunct absurdity, raised up by the necromancy of a violent re-action,—such as the extreme of one system is sure to occasion in the adherents of its opposite,—was more than once allowed to regulate our measures in the conduct of a war, on which the integrity of the British empire and the progressive civilization of all mankind depended. I could mention possessions of paramount and indispensable importance to first-rate national interests, the nominal sovereign of which had delivered up all his sea-ports and strongholds to the French, and maintained a French army in his dominions, and had therefore, by the law of nations, made his territories French dependencies—which possessions were not to be touched, though the natural inhabitants were eager to place themselves under our permanent protection—and why?—They were the property of the king of Naples! All the grandeur and majesty of the law of nations, which taught our ancestors to distinguish between a European sovereign and the miserable despots of oriental barbarism, and to consider the former as the representative of the nation which he governed, and as inextricably connected with its fortunes as sovereign, were merged in the basest personality. Instead of the interests of mighty nations, it seemed as if a mere law-suit were carrying on between John Doe and Richard Roe! The happiness of millions was light in the balance, weighed against a theatric compassion for one individual and his family, who,—I speak from facts that I myself know,—if they feared the French more, hated us worse. Though the restoration of good sense commenced during the interval of the peace of Amiens, yet it was not till the Spanish insurrection that Englishmen of all parties recurred, *in toto*, to the old English principles, and spoke of their Hampdens, Sidneys, and Miltons with the old enthusiasm. During the last war, an acquaintance of mine—least of all men a political zealot—had named a vessel which he had just built—The Liberty ; and was seriously admonished by his aristocratic friends to change it for some other name. What ? replied the owner very innocently—should I call it The Freedom ? That (it was replied) would be far better, as people might then think only of freedom of trade ; whereas Liberty had a jacobinical sound with it ! Alas ! (and this is an observation of Denham and of Burke) is there then no medium between an ague-fit and a frenzy-fever ?

I have said that to withstand the arguments of the lawless, the anti-Jacobins proposed to suspend the law, and by the interposition of a particular statute to eclipse the blessed light of the universal sun, that spies and informers might tyrannize and escape in the ominous darkness. Oh ! if these mistaken men, intoxicated with alarm and bewildered by that panic of property, which they themselves were the chief agents in exciting, had ever lived in a country where there was indeed a general disposition to change and rebellion ! Had they ever travelled through Sicily, or through France at the first coming on of the revolution, or even, alas ! through too many of the provinces of a sister-land, they could not but have shrunk from their own declarations concerning the state of feeling and opinion at that time predominant throughout Great Britain. There was a time—Heaven grant that that time may have passed by !—when by crossing a narrow strait they might have learned the true symptoms of approaching danger, and have secured themselves from mistaking the meetings and idle rant of such sedition as shrank appalled from the sight of a constable, for the dire murmuring and strange consternation which precedes the storm or earthquake of national discord. Not only in coffee-houses and public theatres, but even at the tables of the wealthy, they would have heard the advocates of existing government defend their cause in the language and with the tone of men, who are conscious that they are in a minority. But in England, when the alarm was at the highest, there was not a city, no, not a town, in which a man suspected of holding democratic principles could move abroad without receiving some unpleasant proof of the hatred in which his supposed opinions were held by the great majority of the people: and the only instances of popular excess and indignation, were on the side of the government and the established church. But why need I appeal to these invidious facts? Turn over the pages of history, and seek for a single instance of a revolution having been effected without the concurrence of either the nobles, or the ecclesiastics, or the moneyed classes, in any country in which the influences of property had ever been predominant, and where the interests of the proprietors were interlinked! Examine the revolution of the Belgic provinces under Philip II.; the civil wars of France in the preceding generation, the history of the American revolution, or the yet more recent events in Sweden and in Spain; and it will be scarcely possible not to perceive, that in England, from 1791 to the peace of Amiens, there were neither tendencies to confederacy nor actual confederacies, against which the existing laws had not provided both sufficient safeguards and an ample punishment. But alas! the panic of property had been struck in the first instance for party purposes; and when it became general, its propagators caught it themselves, and ended in believing their own lie;—even as the bulls in Borodale are said sometimes to run mad with the echo of their own bellowing. The consequences were most injurious. Our attention was concentred on a monster which could not survive the convulsions in which it had been brought forth,—even the enlightened Burke himself too often talking and reasoning as if a perpetual and organized anarchy had been a possible thing! Thus while we were warring against French doctrines, we took little heed whether the means by which we attempted to overthrow them were not likely to aid and augment the far more formidable evil of French ambition. Like children, we ran away from the yelping of a cur, and took shelter at the heels of a vicious war-horse.

The conduct of the aristocratic party was equally unwise in private life and to individuals, especially to the young and inexperienced, who were surely to be forgiven for having had their imagination dazzled, and their enthusiasm kindled, by a novelty so specious, that even an old and tried statesman, Mr. Fox, had pronounced it a stupendous monument of human wisdom and human happiness. This was indeed a gross delusion, but assuredly for young men at least, a very venial one. To hope too boldly of human nature is a fault which all good men have an interest in forgiving. Nor was it less removable than venial, if the party had taken the only way by which the error could be, or even ought to have been removed. Having first sympathized with the warm benevolence and the enthusiasm for liberty, which had consecrated it, they should have then shown the young enthusiasts that liberty was not the only blessing of society; that, though desirable, even for its own sake, it yet derived its main value as the means of calling forth and securing other advantages and excellences, the activities of industry, the security of life and property, the peaceful energies of genius and manifold talent, the development of the moral virtues, and the independence and dignity of the nation in its relations to foreign powers: and that neither these nor liberty itself could subsist in a country so various in its soils, so long inhabited, and so fully peopled as Great Britain, without difference of ranks and without laws which recognized and protected the privileges of each. But instead of thus winning them back from the snare, they too often drove them into it by angry contumelies, which being in contradiction with each other could only excite contempt for those that uttered them. To prove the folly of the opinions, they were represented as the crude fancies of unfledged wit and school-boy statesmen; but when abhorrence was to be expressed, the self-same unfledged school-boys were invested with all the attributes of brooding conspiracy and hoary-headed treason. Nay, a sentence of absolute reprobation was passed on them; and the speculative error of Jacobinism was equalized to the mysterious sin in Scripture, which in some inexplicable manner excludes not only mercy but even repentance. It became the watch-word of the party, once a Jacobin always a Jacobin. And wherefore?* I will suppose this question asked by an individual, who in his youth or earliest manhood had been enamored of a system, which for him had combined at once the austere beauty of science with all the light and colors of imagination, and with all the warmth of wide religious charity, and who, overlooking its idèal essence, had dreamed of actually building a government on personal and natural rights

* The passage which follows was first published in the Morning Post, in the year 1800, and contained, if I mistake not, the first philosophical appropriation of a precise import to the word Jacobin, as distinct from republican, democrat, and demagogue. [The article appeared Oct. 21, 1802. S. C.]

alone.—And wherefore? Is Jacobinism an absurdity, and have we no understanding by which to detect it? Is it productive of all misery and all horrors, and have we no natural humanity to make us turn away with indignation and loathing from it? Uproar and confusion, insecurity of person and of property, the tyranny of mobs or the domination of a soldiery; private houses changed to brothels, the ceremony of marriage but an initiation to harlotry, and marriage itself degraded to mere concubinage—these, the wiser advocates of aristocracy have said, and truly said, are the effects of Jacobinism! In private life, an insufferable licentiousness, and abroad an intolerable despotism. Once a Jacobin, always a Jacobin—O wherefore? Is it because the creed which we have stated is dazzling at first sight to the young, the innocent, the disinterested, and to those, who judging of men in general from their own uncorrupted hearts, judge erroneously, and expect unwisely? Is it, because it deceives the mind in its purest and most flexible period? Is it, because it is an error, that every day's experience aids to detect? An error against which all history is full of warning examples? Or is it because the experiment has been tried before our eyes and the error made palpable?

From what source are we to derive this strange *phænomenon*, that the young and the enthusiastic, who, as our daily experience informs us, are deceived in their religious antipathies, and grow wiser; in their friendships, and grow wiser; in their modes of pleasure, and grow wiser; should, if once deceived in a question of abstract politics, cling to the error forever and ever? And this too, although in addition to the natural growth of judgment and information with increase of years, they live in the age in which the tenets have been acted upon; and though the consequences have been such, that every good man's heart sickens, and his head turns giddy at the retrospect.

ESSAY VI.

> Truth I pursued, as fancy sketched the way,
> And wiser men than I went worse astray.

I WAS never myself, at any period of my life, a convert to the Jacobinical system.* From my earliest manhood, it was an axiom in politics with me, that in every country where property prevailed, property must be the grand basis of the government; and that that government was the best, in which the power or political influence of the individual was in proportion to his property, provided that the free circulation of property was not impeded by any positive laws or customs, nor the tendency of wealth to accumulate in abiding masses unduly encouraged. I perceived, that if the people at large were neither ignorant nor immoral, there could be no motive for a sudden and violent change of government; and if they were, there could be no hope but of a change for the worse. The temple of despotism, like that of the Mexican God, would be rebuilt with human skulls, and more firmly, though in a different style of architecture.† Thanks to the excellent education which I had received, my reason was too clear not to draw this circle of power round me, and my spirit too honest to attempt to break through it. My feelings, however, and imagination did not remain unkindled in this general conflagration; and I confess I should be more inclined to be ashamed than proud of myself, if they had. I was a sharer in the general vortex, though my little world described the path of its revolution in an orbit of its own. What I dared not expect from constitutions of government and whole nations, I hoped from religion and a small company of chosen individuals. I formed a plan, as harmless as it was extravagant, of trying the experiment of human

* See Essay XVI. of this volume.—*Ed.*

† To the best of my recollection, these were Mr. Southey's words in the year 1794.

perfectibility on the banks of the Susquehanna ; where our little society, in its second generation, was to have combined the innocence of the patriarchal age with the knowledge and genuine refinements of European culture ; and where I dreamed that in the sober evening of my life, I should behold the cottages of independence in the undivided dale of industry,—

> And oft, soothed sadly by some dirgeful wind,
> Muse on the sore ills I had left behind!

Strange fancies, and as vain as strange! yet to the intense interest and impassioned zeal, which called forth and strained every faculty of my intellect for the organization and defence of this scheme, I owe much of whatever I at present possess, my clearest insight into the nature of individual man, and my most comprehensive views of his social relations, of the true uses of trade and commerce, and how far the wealth and relative power of nations promote or impede their welfare and inherent strength. Nor were they less serviceable in securing myself, and perhaps some others, from the pitfalls of sedition: and when we at length alighted on the firm ground of common sense from the gradually exhausted balloon of youthful enthusiasm, though the air-built castles, which we had been pursuing, had vanished with all their pageantry of shifting forms, and glowing colors, we were yet free from the stains and impurities which might have remained upon us, had we been travelling with the crowd of less imaginative malcontents, through the dark lanes and foul by-roads of ordinary fanaticism.

But oh! there were thousands as young and as innocent as myself who, not like me, sheltered in the tranquil nook or inland cove of a particular fancy, were driven along with the general current! Many there were, young men of loftiest minds, yea, the prime stuff out of which manly wisdom and practical greatness are to be formed, who had appropriated their hopes and the ardor of their souls to mankind at large, to the wide expanse of national interests, which then seemed fermenting in the French republic as in the main outlet and chief crater of the revolutionary torrents; and who confidently believed, that these torrents, like the lavas of Vesuvius, were to subside into a soil of inexhaustible fertility on the circumjaçent lands, the old divisions and mouldering edifices of which they had covered or swept away—enthusiasts of kindliest temperament, who to use the words of the poet, having already borrowed the meaning and the metaphor, had approached

> the shield
> Of human nature from the golden side,
> And would have fought even to the death to attest
> The quality of the metal which they saw.

My honored friend Mr. Wordsworth has permitted me to give a value and relief to the present essay, by a quotation from one of his unpublished poems, the length of which I regret only from its forbidding me to trespass on his kindness by making it yet longer. I trust there are many of my readers of the same age with myself, who will throw themselves back into the state of thought and feeling in which they were when France was reported to have solemnized her first sacrifice of error and prejudice on the bloodless altar of freedom, by an oath of peace and good-will to all mankind.

> Oh! pleasant exercise of hope and joy!
> For mighty were the auxiliars, which then stood
> Upon our side, we who were strong in love.
> Bliss was it in that dawn to be alive,
> But to be young was very heaven;—Oh! times,
> In which the meagre stale forbidding ways
> Of custom, law, and statute, took at once
> The attraction of a country in romance;
> When reason seem'd the most to assert her rights,
> When most intent on making of herself
> A prime enchanter to assist the work,
> Which then was going forward in her name.
> Not favor'd spots alone, but the whole earth
> The beauty wore of promise—that which sets
> (To take an image which was felt no doubt
> Among the bowers of paradise itself)
> The budding rose above the rose, full blown.
> What temper at the prospect did not wake
> To happiness unthought of? The inert
> Were roused, and lively natures rapt away.
> They who had fed their childhood upon dreams,
> The play-fellows of fancy, who had made
> All powers of swiftness, subtilty, and strength
> Their ministers, used to stir in lordly wise
> Among the grandest objects of the sense,
> And deal with whatsoever they found there
> As if they had within some lurking right

To wield it;—they too, who of gentle mood
Had watch'd all gentle motions, and to these
Had fitted their own thoughts, schemers more mild
And in the region of their peaceful selves;——
Now was it that both found, the meek and lofty
Did both find helpers to their heart's desire
And stuff at hand, plastic as they could wish—
Were call'd upon to exercise their skill
Not in Utopia, subterraneous fields,
Or some secreted island, Heaven knows where,
But in the very world, which is the world
Of all of us, the place where in the end
We find our happiness, or not at all.

The peace of Amiens deserved the name of peace, for it gave us unanimity at home, and reconciled Englishmen with each other. Yet it would be as wild a fancy as any of which I have treated, to expect that the violence of party spirit is never more to return. Sooner or later the same causes, or their equivalents, will call forth the same opposition of opinion, and bring the same passions into play. Ample would be my recompense, could I foresee that this present essay would be the means of preventing discord and unhappiness in a single family; if its words of warning, aided by its tones of sympathy, should arm a single man of genius against the fascinations of his own ideal world, a single philanthropist against the enthusiasm of his own heart. Not less would be my satisfaction, dared I flatter myself that my lucubrations would not be altogether without effect on those who deem themselves men of judgment, faithful to the light of practice, and not to be led astray by the wandering fires of theory;—if I should aid in making these aware, that in recoiling with too incautious an abhorrence from the bugbears of innovation, they may sink all at once into the slough of slavishness and corruption. Let such persons recollect that the charms of hope and novelty furnish some palliation for the idolatry to which they seduce the mind; but that the apotheosis of familiar abuses and of the errors of selfishness is the vilest of superstitions. Let them recollect, too, that nothing can be more incongruous than to combine the pusillanimity, which despairs of human improvement, with the arrogance, supercilious contempt, and boisterous anger, which have no pretensions to pardon, except as the overflowing of ardent anticipation and enthusiastic faith. And finally, and above all, let it be remembered by both parties, and indeed by controversialists on all subjects, that every speculative error which boasts a multitude of advocates, has its golden as well as its dark side ; that there is always some truth connected with it, the exclusive attention to which has misled the understanding, some moral beauty which has given it charms for the heart. Let it be remembered that no assailant of an error can reasonably hope to be listened to by its advocates, who has not proved to them that he has seen the disputed subject in the same point of view, and is capable of contemplating it with the same feelings as themselves ; for why should we abandon a cause at the persuasions of one who is ignorant of the reasons which have attached us to it ? Let it be remembered, that to write, however ably, merely to convince those who are already convinced, displays but the courage of a boaster ; and in any subject to rail against the evil before we have inquired for the good, and to exasperate the passions of those who think with us, by caricaturing the opinions and blackening the motives of our antagonists, is to make the understanding the pander of the passions ; and even though we should have defended the right cause, to gain for ourselves ultimately from the good and wise no other praise than the supreme Judge awarded to the friends of Job for their partial and uncharitable defence of his justice : *My wrath is kindled against* you, *for ye have not spoken of me the thing that is right.**

* Job xlii. 7.—*Ed.*

ESSAY VII.

ON THE VULGAR ERRORS RESPECTING TAXES AND TAXATION.

"Οπερ γὰρ οἱ τὰς ἐγχέλεις θηρώμενοι πέπονθας·
"Οταν μὲν ἡ λίμνη καταςῆ, λαμβάνουσιν οὐδέν·
'Εάν δ' ἄνω τε καὶ κάτω τὸν βόρβορον κυκῶσιν,
Αἱροῦσι· καὶ σὺ λαμβάνεις, ἢν τὴν πόλιν ταράττῃς.*

It is with you as with those that are hunting for eels. While the pond is clear and settled, they take nothing; but if they stir up the mud high and low, then they bring up the fish:—and you succeed only as far as you can set the state in tumult and confusion.

In a passage in the last essay, I referred to the second part of the "Rights of Man," in which Paine assures his readers that their poverty is the consequence of taxation: that taxes are rendered necessary only by wars and state corruption; that war and corruption are entirely owing to monarchy and aristocracy; that by a revolution and a brotherly alliance with the French republic, our land and sea forces, our revenue officers, and three fourths of our pensioners, placemen, and other functionaries, would be rendered superfluous; and that a small part of the expenses thus saved, would suffice for the maintenance of the poor, the infirm, and the aged, throughout the kingdom. Would to God that this infamous mode of misleading and flattering the lower classes were confined to the writings of Thomas Paine! But how often do we hear, even from the mouths of our parliamentary advocates for popularity, the taxes stated as so much money actually lost to the people; and a nation in debt represented as the same both in kind and consequences, as an individual tradesman on the brink of bankruptcy! It is scarcely possible, that these men should be themselves deceived; that they should be so ignorant of history as not to know that the freest nations, being at the same time

* Aristoph. Equites, v. 864, &c.—*Ed.*

commercial, have been at all times the most heavily taxed: or so void of common sense as not to see that there is no analogy in the case of a tradesman and his creditors, to a nation indebted to itself. Surely, a much fairer instance would be that of a husband and wife playing cards at the same table against each other, where what the one loses the other gains. Taxes may be indeed, and often are, injurious to a country: at no time, however, from their amount merely, but from the time or injudicious mode in which they are raised. A great statesman, lately deceased, in one of his anti-ministerial harangues against some proposed impost, said,—'the nation has been already bled in every vein, and is faint with loss of blood.' This blood, however, was circulating in the mean time through the whole body of the state, and what was received into one chamber of the heart was instantly sent out again at the other portal. Had he wanted a metaphor to convey the possible injuries of taxation, he might have found one less opposite to the fact, in the known disease of aneurism, or relaxation of the coats of particular vessels, by a disproportionate accumulation of blood in them, which sometimes occurs when the circulation has been suddenly and violently changed, and causes helplessness, or even mortal stagnation, though the total quantity of blood remains the same in the system at large.

But a fuller and fairer symbol of taxation, both in its possible good and evil effects, is to be found in the evaporation of waters from the surface of the planet. The sun may draw up the moisture from the river, the morass, and the ocean, to be given back in genial showers to the garden, the pasture, and the corn-field; but it may likewise force away the moisture from the fields of tillage, to drop it on the stagnant pool, the saturated swamp, or the unprofitable sand-waste. The gardens in the south of Europe supply, perhaps, a not less apt illustration of a system of finance judiciously conducted, where the tanks or reservoirs would represent the capital of a nation, and the hundred rills hourly varying their channels and directions under the gardener's spade, give a pleasing image of the dispersion of that capital through the whole population, by the joint effect of taxation and trade. For taxation itself is a part of commerce, and the government may be fairly considered as a great manufacturing house, carrying on in different places, by means of its partners and overseers, the trades of the ship-builder, the clothier, the iron-founder, and the like.

There are so many real evils, so many just causes of complaint in the constitution and administration of governments, our own not excepted, that it becomes the imperious duty of every well-wisher of his country, to prevent, as much as in him lies, the feelings and efforts of his compatriots from losing themselves on a wrong scent. Whether a system of taxation is injurious or beneficial on the whole, is to be known, not by the amount of the sum taken from each individual, but by that which remains behind. A war will doubtless cause a stagnation of certain branches of trade, and severe temporary distress in the places where those branches are carried on; but are not the same effects produced in time of peace by prohibitory edicts and commercial regulations of foreign powers, or by new rivals with superior advantages in other countries, or in different parts of the same? Bristol has, doubtless, been injured by the rapid prosperity of Liverpool and its superior spirit of enterprise; and the vast machines of Lancashire have overwhelmed and rendered hopeless the domestic industry of females in the cottages and small farm-houses of Westmoreland and Cumberland. But if peace has its stagnation as well as war, does not war create or re-enliven numerous branches of industry as well as peace? Is it not a fact, that not only our own military and naval forces, but even a part of those of our enemy are armed and clothed by British manufacturers? It can not be doubted, that the whole of our immense military force is better and more expensively clothed, and both these and our sailors better fed than the same persons would be in their individual capacities: and this forms one of the real expenses of war. Not, I say, that so much more money is raised, but that so much more of the means of comfortable existence are consumed, than would otherwise have been. But does not this, like all other luxury, act as a stimulus on the producing classes, and this in the most useful manner, and on the most important branches of production, on the tiller, on the grazier, the clothier and the maker of arms? Had it been otherwise, is it possible that the receipts from the property tax should have increased, instead of decreased, notwithstanding all the rage of our enemy?

Surely, never from the beginning of the world was such a tribute of admiration paid by one power to another, as Buonaparte within the last few years has paid to the British empire. With all the natural and artificial powers of almost the whole of continental Europe, with all the fences and obstacles of all public and private morality broken down before him, with a mighty empire of fifty millions of men, nearly two thirds of whom speak the same language, and are as it were fused together by the intensest nationality; with this mighty and swarming empire, organized in all its parts of war, and forming one huge camp, and himself combining in his own person the two-fold power of monarch and commander-in-chief;—with all these advantages, with all these stupendous instruments and inexhaustible resources of offence, this mighty being finds himself imprisoned by the enemy whom he most hates, and would fain despise, insulted by every wave that breaks upon his shores, and condemned to behold his vast flotillas as worthless and idle as the sea-weed that rots around their keels! After years of haughty menace and expensive preparations for the invasion of an island, the trees and buildings of which are visible from the roofs of his naval store-houses, he is at length compelled to make open confession, that he possesses one mean only of ruining Great Britain. And what is it? The ruin of his own enslaved subjects. To undermine the resources of one enemy, he reduces the continent of Europe to the wretched state in which it was before the wide diffusions of trade and commerce, deprives its inhabitants of comforts and advantages to which they and their fathers had been for more than a century habituated, and thus destroys, as far as his power extends, a principal source of civilization, the origin of a middle class throughout Christendom, and with it the true balance of society, the parent of international law, the foster-nurse of general humanity, and, to sum up all in one, the main principle of attraction and repulsion, by which the nations were rapidly, though insensibly, drawn together into one system, and by which alone they could combine the manifold blessings of distinct character and national independence, with the needful stimulation and general influences of intercommunity, and be virtually united, without being crushed together by conquest, in order to waste away under the *tabes* and slow putrefaction of a universal monarchy. This boasted pacificator of the world, this earthly

Providence,* as his Roman Catholic bishops blasphemously call him, professes to entertain no hope of purchasing the destruction of Great Britain at a less price than that of the barbarism of all Europe. By the ordinary war of government against government, fleets against fleets, and armies against armies, he could effect nothing. His fleets might as well have been built at his own expense in our dockyards, as tribute offerings to the masters of the ocean : whilst his army of England lay encamped on his coasts like wolves baying the moon !

Delightful to humane and contemplative minds was the idea of countless individual efforts working together by a common instinct and to a common object, under the protection of an unwritten code of religion, philosophy, and common interest, which made peace and brotherhood co-exist with the most active hostility. Not in the untamed plains of Tartary, but in the very bosom of civilization, and himself indebted to its fostering care for his own education and for all the means of his elevation and power, did this genuine offspring of the old serpent warm himself into the fiend-like resolve of waging war against mankind and the quiet growth of the world's improvement—in an emphatic sense the enemy of the human race. By these means only he deems Great Britain assailable,—a strong presumption, that our prosperity is built on the common interest of mankind ;—this he acknowledges to be his only hope—and in this hope he has been utterly baffled.

To what then do we owe our strength and our immunity ? To the sovereignty of law,—the incorruptness of its administration,—our national church,—our religious sects,—the purity, or at least the decorum, of private morals, and the independence, activity, and weight, of public opinion ?—These and similar advantages are doubtless the materials of the fortress, but what has been the cement ? What has bound them together ? What has rendered Great Britain, from the Orkneys to the rocks of Scilly, indeed and with more than metaphorical propriety, a body politic,—our

* It has been well remarked, that there is something far more shocking in Buonaparte's pretensions to the gracious attributes of the Supreme Ruler, than in his most remorseless cruelties. There is a sort of wild grandeur, not ungratifying to the imagination, in the answer of Timur Khan to one who remonstrated with him on the inhumanity of his devastations: *cur me hominem putas, et non potius iram Dei in terris agentem ob perniciem humani generis?* Why do you deem me a man, and not rather the incarnate wrath of God acting on the earth for the ruin of mankind?

roads, rivers, and canals being so truly the veins, arteries, and nerves, of the state, that every pulse in the metropolis produces a correspondent pulsation in the remotest village on its extreme shores? What made the stoppage of the national bank the conversation of a day without causing one irregular throb, or the stagnation of the commercial current, in the minutest vessel? I answer without hesitation, that the cause and mother principle of this unexampled confidence, of this system of credit, which is as much stronger than mere positive possessions, as the soul of man is than his body, or as the force of a mighty mass in free motion, than the pressure of its separate component parts in a state of rest—the main cause of this, I say, has been our national debt. What its injurious effects on the literature, the morals, and religious principles of this country, have been, I shall hereafter develop with the same boldness. But as to our political strength and circumstantial prosperity, it is the national debt which has wedded in indissoluble union all the interests of the state, the landed with the commercial, and the man of independent fortune with the stirring tradesman and reposing annuitant. It is the national debt, which, by the rapid nominal rise in the value of things, has made it impossible for any considerable number of men to retain their own former comforts without joining in the common industry, and adding to the stock of national produce; which thus first necessitates a general activity and then by the immediate and ample credit, which is never wanting to him, who has any object on which his activity can employ itself, gives each man the means not only of preserving but of increasing and multiplying all his former enjoyments, and all the symbols of the rank in which he was born. It is this which has planted the naked hills and inclosed the bleak wastes in the lowlands of Scotland not less than in the wealthier districts of South Britain: it is this, which, leaving all the other causes of patriotism and national fervor undiminished and uninjured, has added to our public duties the same feeling of necessity, the same sense of immediate self-interest, which in other countries actuates the members of a single family in their conduct toward each other.

Somewhat more than a year ago, I happened to be on a visit with a friend, in a small market-town* in the south-west of England, when one of the company turned the conversation to the

* Nether Stowey.—*Ed.*

weight of taxes and the consequent hardness of the times. I answered, that if the taxes were a real weight, and that in proportion to their amount, we must have been ruined long ago: for Mr. Hume, who had proceeded, as on a self-evident axiom, on the hypothesis, that the debt of a nation was the same as the debt of an individual, had declared our ruin arithmetically demonstrable, if the national debt increased beyond a certain sum. Since his time it has more than quntupled that sum, and yet— True, answered my friend, but the principle might be right, though he might have been mistaken in the time. But still, I rejoined, if the principle were right, the nearer we came to that given point, and the greater and the more active the pernicious cause became, the more manifest would its effects be. We might not be absolutely ruined, but our embarrassments would increase in some proportion to their cause. Whereas instead of being poorer and poorer, we are richer and richer. Will any man in his senses contend, that the actual labor and produce of the country has not only been decupled within half a century, but increased so prodigiously beyond that decuple as to make six hundred millions a less weight to us than fifty millions were in the days of our grandfathers? But if it really be so, to what can we attribute this stupendous progression of national improvement, but to that system of credit and paper currency, of which the national debt is both the reservoir and the water-works? A constant cause should have constant effects; but if you deem that this is some anomaly, some strange exception to the general rule, explain its mode of operation, make it comprehensible, how a cause acting on a whole nation can produce a regular and rapid increase of prosperity to a certain point, and then all at once pass from an angel of light into a dæmon of destruction! That an individual house may live more and more luxuriously upon borrowed funds, and that when the suspicions of the creditors are awakened, and their patience exhausted, the luxurious spendthrift may all at once exchange his palace for a prison—this I can understand perfectly: for I understand, whence the luxuries could be produced for the consumption of the individual house, and who the creditors might be, and that it might be both their inclination and their interest to demand the debt, and to punish the insolvent debtor. But who are a nation's creditors? The answer is, every man to every man. Whose possible interest could it be either to demand the principal, or to refuse his share toward the means of paying the interest? Not the merchant's: —for he would but provoke a crash of bankruptcy, in which his own house would as necessarily be included, as a single card in a house of cards. Not the landholder's;—for in the general destruction of all credit, how could he obtain payment for the produce of his estates? Not to mention the improbability that he would remain the undisturbed possessor in so direful a concussion —not to mention that on him must fall the whole weight of the public necessities—not to mention, that from the merchant's credit depends the ever-increasing value of his land and the readiest means of improving it. Neither could it be the laborer's interest;—for he must be either thrown out of employ, and lie like the fish in the bed of a river from which the water has been diverted, or have the value of his labor reduced to nothing by the irruption of eager competitors. But least of all could it be the wish of the lovers of liberty which must needs perish or be suspended, either by the horrors of anarchy, or by the absolute power, with which the government must be invested, in order to prevent them. In short, with the exception of men desperate from guilt or debt, or mad with the blackest ambition, there is no class or description of men who can have the least interest in producing or permitting a bankruptcy.

If then, neither experience has acquainted us with any national impoverishment or embarrassment from the increase of national debt, nor theory renders such efforts comprehensible;—for the predictions of Hume went on the false assumption, that a part only of the nation was interested in the preservation of the public credit;—on what authority are we to ground our apprehensions? Does history record a single nation, in which relatively to taxation there were no privileged or exempted classes, in which there were no compulsory prices of labor, and in which the interests of all the different classes and all the different districts, were mutually dependent and vitally co-organized, as in Great Britain,—has history, I say, recorded a single instance of such a nation being ruined or dissolved by the weight of taxation? In France there was no public credit, no communion of interests; its unprincipled government and the productive and taxable classes, were as two individuals with separate interests. Its bankruptcy and the consequences of it are sufficiently comprehensible. Yet the *cahiers*, or the instructions and complaints sent to the National Assembly, from the towns and provinces of France, an immense mass of documents indeed, but without examination and patient perusal of which, no man is entitled to write a history of the French revolution,—these proved, beyond contradiction, that the amount of the taxes was one only, and that a subordinate cause, of the revolutionary movement. Indeed, if the amount of the taxes could be disjoined from the mode of raising them, it might be fairly denied to have been a cause at all. Holland was taxed as heavily and as equally as ourselves; but was it by taxation that Holland was reduced to its present miseries?

The mode in which taxes are supposed to act on the marketableness of our manufactures in foreign marts, I shall examine on some future occasion, when I shall endeavor to explain in a more satisfactory way than has been hitherto done, to my apprehension at least, the real mode in which taxes act, and how and why, and to what extent, they affect the wealth, and what is of more consequence, the well-being of a nation. But in the present exigency, when the safety of the nation depends, on the one hand, on the sense which the people at large have of the comparative excellences of the laws and government, and on the firmness and wisdom of the legislators and enlightened classes in detecting, exposing, and removing its many particular abuses and corruptions on the other, right views on this subject of taxation are of such especial importance; and I have besides in my inmost nature such a loathing of factious falsehoods and mob-sycophancy, that is, the flattering of the multitude by informing against their betters;—that I can not but revert to that point of the subject from which I began, namely, that the weight of taxes is to be calculated not by what is paid, but by what is left. What matters it to a man, that he pays six times more taxes than his father did, if, notwithstanding, he with the same portion of exertion enjoys twice the comforts which his father did? Now this I affirm to be the case in general, throughout England, according to all the facts which I have collected during an examination of years, wherever I have travelled, and wherever I have been resident. I do not speak of Ireland, or the Lowlands of Scotland: and if I may trust to what I myself saw and heard there, I must even except the Highlands. In the conversation which I have spoken of as taking place in the south-west of England, by the assistance of one or other of the company, we went through every family in the town and neighborhood, and my assertion was found completely accurate, though the place had no one advantage over others, and many disadvantages,—that heavy one in particular, the non-residence and frequent change of its rectors,—the living being always given to one of the canons of Windsor, and resigned on the acceptance of better preferment. It was even asserted, and not only asserted but proved, by my friend,* who has from his earliest youth devoted a strong original understanding, and a heart warm and benevolent even to enthusiasm, to the service of the poor and the laboring class, that every sober laborer, in that part of England at least, who should not marry till thirty, might, without any hardship or extreme self-denial, commence housekeeping at that age, with from a hundred to a hundred and twenty pounds belonging to him. I have no doubt, that on seeing this essay, my friend will communicate to me the proof in detail. But the price of labor in the south-west of England is full one third less than in the greater number, if not all, of the northern counties. What then is wanting? Not the repeal of taxes, but the increased activity both of the gentry and clergy of the land, in securing the instruction of the lower classes. A system of education is wanting, such a system as that discovered, and to the blessings of thousands realized, by Dr. Bell, which I never am, or can be, weary of praising, while my heart retains any spark of regard for human nature, or of reverence for human virtue;—a system, by which in the very act of receiving knowledge, the best virtues and most useful qualities of the moral character are awakened, developed, and formed into habits. Were there a Bishop of Durham—no matter whether a temporal or a spiritual lord—in every county or half-county, and a clergyman enlightened with the views, and animated with the spirit, of Dr. Bell, in every parish, we might bid defiance to the present weight of taxes, and boldly challenge the whole world to show a peasantry as well fed and clothed as the English, or with equal chances of improving their situation, and of securing an old age of repose and comfort to a life of cheerful industry.

I will add one other anecdote, as it demonstrates incontrover-

* Thomas Poole.—*Ed.*

tibly the error of the vulgar opinion, that taxes make things really dear, taking in the whole of a man's expenditure. A friend of mine, who has passed some years in America, was questioned by an American tradesman, in one of their cities of the second class, concerning the names and number of our taxes and rates. The answer seemed perfectly to astound him : and he exclaimed, "How is it possible that men can live in such a country? In this land of liberty we never see the face of a tax-gatherer, nor hear of a duty, except in our sea-ports." My friend, who was perfect master of the question, made semblance of turning off the conversation to another subject : and then, without any apparent reference to the former topic, asked the American, for what sum he thought a man could live in such and such a style, with so many servants, in a house of such dimensions and such a situation (still keeping in his mind the situation of a thriving and respectable shopkeeper and householder in different parts of England), first supposing him to reside in Philadelphia or New York, and then in some town of secondary importance. Having received a detailed answer to these questions, he proceeded to convince the American, that notwithstanding all our taxes, a man might live in the same style, but with incomparably greater comforts, on the same income in London as in New York, and on a considerably less income in Exeter or Bristol, than in any American provincial town of the same relative importance. It would be insulting my readers to discuss on how much less a person may vegetate or brutalize in the back settlements of the republic, than he could live as a man, as a rational and social being, in an English village ; and it would be wasting time to inform him, that where men are comparatively few, and unoccupied land is in inexhaustible abundance, the laborer and common mechanic must needs receive—not only nominally, but really—higher wages than in a populous and fully occupied country. But that the American laborer is therefore happier, or even in possession of more comforts and conveniences of life than a sober or industrious English laborer or mechanic, remains to be proved. In conducting the comparison, we must not however exclude the operation of moral causes, when these causes are not accidental, but arise out of the nature of the country, and the constitution of the government and society. This being the case, take away from the American's wages all the taxes which his insolence, sloth, and attachment to spirituous liquors impose on him, and judge of the remainder by his house, his household furniture, and utensils—and if I have not been grievously deceived by those whose veracity and good sense I have found unquestionable in all other respects, the cottage of an honest English husbandman, in the service of an enlightened and liberal farmer, who is paid for his labor at the price usual in Yorkshire or Northumberland, would in the mind of a man in the same rank of life, who had seen a true account of America, make no impressions favorable to emigration. This, however, I confess, is a balance of morals rather than of circumstances: it proves, however, that where foresight and good morals exist, the taxes do not stand in the way of an industrious man's comforts.

Dr. Price almost succeeded in persuading the English nation, —for it is a curious fact, that the fancy of our calamitous situation is a sort of necessary sauce without which our real prosperity would become insipid to us—Dr. Price, I say, alarmed the country with pretended proofs that the island was in a rapid state of depopulation;—that England at the Revolution had been, Heaven knows how much more populous; and that in Queen Elizabeth's time, or about the Reformation, the number of inhabitants in England, might have been greater than even at the Revolution. My old mathematical master, a man of an uncommonly clear head, answered this blundering book of the worthy doctor's, and left not a stone unturned of the pompous cenotaph in which the effigy of the still living and bustling English prosperity lay interred. And yet so much more suitable was the doctor's book to the purposes of faction, and to the November mood of what is called the public, that Mr. Wales's pamphlet, though a master-piece of perspicacity as well as perspicuity, was scarcely heard of. This tendency to political nightmares in our countrymen, reminds me of a superstition, or rather nervous disease, not uncommon in the Highlands of Scotland, in which men, though broad awake, imagine they see themselves lying dead at a small distance from them. The act of Parliament for ascertaining the population of the empire has laid forever this uneasy ghost: and now, forsooth, we are on the brink of ruin from the excess of population, and he who would prevent the poor from rotting away in disease, misery, and wickedness, is an enemy to his country. A lately-deceased miser, of immense wealth, is reported to have been so delighted with this splendid discovery, as to have offered a handsome annuity to the author, in part of payment for this new and welcome piece of heart-armor. This, however, we may deduce from the fact of our increased population, that if clothing and food had actually become dearer in proportion to the means of procuring them, it would be as absurd to ascribe this effect to increased taxation, as to attribute the scantiness of fare, at a public ordinary, to the landlord's bill, when twice the usual number of guests had sat down to the same number of dishes. But the fact is notoriously otherwise, and every man has the means of discovering it in his own house and in that of his neighbors, provided that he makes the proper allowances for the disturbing forces of individual vice and imprudence. If this be the case, I put it to the consciences of our literary demagogues, whether a lie, for the purposes of creating public disunion and dejection, is not as much a lie, as one for the purpose of exciting discord among individuals. I entreat my readers to recollect, that the present question does not concern the effects of taxation on the public independence and on the supposed balance of the three constitutional powers, from which said balance, as well as from the balance of trade, I own, I have never been able to elicit one ray of common sense. That the nature of our constitution has been greatly modified by the funding system, I do not deny ;—whether for good or for evil, on the whole, will form part of my essay on the British constitution as it actually exists.

There are many and great public evils, all of which are to be lamented, some of which may, and ought to, be removed, and none of which can consistently with wisdom or honesty be kept concealed from the public. As far as these originate in false principles, or in the contempt or neglect of right ones, and as such belonging to the plan of The Friend, I shall not hesitate to make known my opinions concerning them, with the same fearless simplicity with which I have endeavored to expose the errors of discontent and the artifices of faction. But for the very reason that there are great evils, the more does it behoove us not to open out on a false scent.

I will conclude this essay with the examination of an article in a provincial paper of a recent date, which is now lying before me ; the accidental perusal of which occasioned the whole of the preceding remarks. In order to guard against a possible mistake,

I must premise, that I have not the most distant intention of defending the plan or conduct of our late expeditions, and should be grossly calumniated if I were represented as an advocate for carelessness or prodigality in the management of the public purse. The public money may or may not have been culpably wasted. I confine myself entirely to the general falsehood of the principle in the article here cited; for I am convinced, that any hopes of reform originating in such notions, must end in disappointment and public mockery.

"*ONLY A FEW MILLIONS!*

"We have unfortunately of late been so much accustomed to read of millions being spent in one expedition, and millions being spent in another, that a comparative insignificance is attached to an immense sum of money, by calling it only a few millions. Perhaps some of our readers may have their judgment a little improved by making a few calculations, like those below, on the millions which it has been estimated will be lost to the nation by the late expedition to Holland; and then, perhaps, they will be led to reflect on the many millions which are annually expended in expeditions, which have almost invariably ended in absolute loss.

"In the first place, with less money than it cost the nation to take Walcheren, &c. with the view of taking or destroying the French fleet at Antwerp, consisting of nine sail of the line, we could have completely built and equipped, ready for sea, a fleet of upwards of one hundred sail of the line.

"Or, secondly, a new town could be built in every county of England, and each town consist of upwards of 1000 substantial houses for a less sum.

"Or, thirdly, it would have been enough to give 100*l.* to 2000 poor families in every county in England and Wales.

"Or, fourthly, it would be more than sufficient to give a handsome marriage portion to 200,000 young women, who probably, if they had even less than 50*l.* would not long remain unsolicited to enter the happy state.

"Or, fifthly, a much less sum would enable the legislature to establish a life boat in every port in the United Kingdom, and provide for ten or twelve men to be kept in constant attendance on each; and 100,000*l.* could be funded, the interest of which to be applied in premiums to those who should prove to be particularly active in saving lives from wrecks, &c. and to provide for the widows and children of those men who may accidentally lose their lives in the cause of humanity.

"This interesting appropriation of ten millions sterling, may lead our readers to think of the great good that can be done by only a few millions."

The exposure of this calculation will require but a few sentences. These ten millions were expended, I presume, in arms, artillery, ammunition, clothing, provision, and the like, for about one hundred and twenty thousand British subjects: and I presume that all these consumables were produced by, and purchased from, other British subjects. Now during the building of these new towns for a thousand inhabitants each in every county, or the distribution of the hundred pound bank notes to the two thousand poor families, were the industrious ship-builders, clothiers, charcoal-burners, gunpowder-makers, gunsmiths, cutlers, cannon-founders, tailors, and shoemakers, to be left unemployed and starving ;—or our brave soldiers and sailors to have remained without food and raiment? And where is the proof, that these ten millions, which, observe, all remain in the kingdom, do not circulate as beneficially in the one way as they would in the other? Which is better? To give money to the idle, houses to those who do not ask for them, and towns to counties which have already perhaps too many, or to afford opportunity to the industrious to earn their bread, and to the enterprising to better their circumstances, and perhaps to found new families of independent proprietors? The only mode, not absolutely absurd, of considering the subject, would be, not by the calculation of the money expended, but of the labor of which the money is a symbol. But then the question would be removed altogether from the expedition : for assuredly, neither the armies were raised, nor the fleets built or manned for the sake of conquering the Isle of Walcheren, nor would a single regiment have been disbanded, nor a single sloop paid off, though the Isle of Walcheren had never existed. The whole dispute, therefore, resolves itself into this one question : whether our soldiers and sailors would not be better employed in making canals for instance, or cultivating waste lands, than in fighting or learning to fight; and the tradesman, in making gray coats instead of red or blue—and ploughshares instead of arms. When I reflect on the state of China and the moral character of the Chinese, I dare not positively affirm that it would be better. When the fifteen millions, which form our present population, shall have attained to the same general purity of morals and shall be capable of being governed by the same admirable discipline, as the society of the Friends, I doubt not that we should be all Quakers in this as in the other points of their moral doctrine. But were this transfer of employment desirable, is it practicable at present,—is it in our power? These men know, that it is not. What then does all their reasoning amount to? Nonsense.

ESSAY VIII.

I have not intentionally either hidden or disguised the truth, like an advocate ashamed of his client, or a bribed accomptant who falsifies the quotient to make the bankrupt's ledgers square with the creditor's inventory. My conscience forbids the use of falsehood and the arts of concealment: and were it otherwise, yet I am persuaded, that a system which has produced and protected so great prosperity, can not stand in need of them. If therefore honesty and the knowledge of the whole truth be the things you aim at, you will find my principles suited to your ends: and as I like not the democratic forms, so am I not fond of any others above the rest. That a succession of wise and godly men may be secured to the nation in the highest power, is that to which I have directed your attention in this essay, which if you will read, perhaps you may see the error of those principles which have led you into errors of practice. I wrote it purposely for the use of the multitude of well-meaning people, that are tempted in these times to usurp authority and meddle with government before they have any call from duty or tolerable understanding of its principles. I never intended it for learned men versed in politics; but for such as will be practitioners before they have been students.

BAXTER'S *Holy Commonwealth, or Political Aphorisms.*

THE metaphysical, or as I have proposed to call them, metapolitical reasoning hitherto discussed, belong to government in the abstract. But there is a second class of reasoners who argue for a change in our government from former usage, and from statutes still in force, or which have been repealed,—so these writers affirm—either through a corrupt influence, or to ward off temporary hazard or inconvenience. This class, which is rendered illustrious by the names of many intelligent and virtuous patriots, are advocates for reform in the literal sense of the word. They wish to bring back the government of Great Britain to a certain form, which they affirm it to have once possessed; and would melt the bullion anew in order to recast it in the original mould.

The answer to all arguments of this nature is obvious, and to my understanding appears decisive. These reformers assume the character of legislators or of advisers of the legislature, not that of law judges or of appellants to courts of law. Sundry statutes concerning the rights of electors, we will suppose,—still exist; so likewise do sundry statutes on other subjects,—on witchcraft for instance*—which change of circumstances have rendered obsolete, or increased information shown to be absurd. It is evident, therefore, that the expediency of the regulations prescribed by them, and their suitableness to the existing circumstances of the kingdom, must first be proved; and on this proof must be rested all rational claims for the enforcement of the statutes that have not, no less than for the re-enacting of those that have, been repealed. If the authority of the men who first enacted the laws in question, is to weigh with us, it must be on the presumption that they were wise men. But the wisdom of legislation consists in the adaptation of laws to circumstances. If then it can be proved, that the circumstances, under which those laws were enacted, no longer exist; and that other circumstances altogether different, and in some instances opposite, have taken their place; we have the best grounds for supposing, that if the men were now alive, they would not pass the same statutes. In other words, the spirit of the statute interpreted by the intention of the legislator would annul the letter of it. It is not indeed impossible, that by a rare felicity of accident the same law may apply to two sets of circumstances. But surely the presumption is, that regulations well adapted for the manners, the social distinctions, and the state of property, of opinion, and of external relations of England in the reign of Alfred, or even in that of Edward I., will not be well suited to Great Britain at the close of the reign of George III. For instance: at the time when the greater part of the cottagers and inferior farmers were in a state of villenage, when Sussex alone contained seven thousand, and the Isle of Wight twelve hundred, families of bondsmen, it was the law of the land that every freeman should vote in the assembly of the nation personally or by his representative. An act of Parliament in the year 1660 confirmed what a concurrence of causes had previously effected:—every Englishman is now born free, the laws of the land are the birthright of every native, and with the exception of a few

* Repealed now; but many other equally obsolete acts remain on the statute book, as illustrations of the principle in the text.—*Ed.*

honorary privileges all classes obey the same laws.* Now, argues one of our political writers, it being made the constitution of the land by our Saxon ancestors, that every freeman should have a vote, and all Englishmen being now born free, therefore, by the constitution of the land, every Englishman has now a right to a vote. How shall we reply to this without breach of that respect, to which the reasoner at least, if not the reasoning, is entitled? If it be the definition of a pun, that it is the confusion of two different meanings under the same or some similar sound, we might almost characterize this argument as being grounded on a grave pun. Our ancestors established the right of voting in a particular class of men, forming at that time the middle rank of society, and known to be all of them, or almost all, legal proprietors—and these were then called the freemen of England: therefore they established it in the lowest classes of society, in those who possess no property, because these two are now called by the same name! Under a similar pretext, grounded on the same precious logic, a Mameluke Bey extorted a large contribution from the Egyptian Jews: "These books, the Pentateuch, are authentic?" "Yes!" "Well, the debt then is acknowledged:—and now the receipt, or the money, or your heads! The Jews borrowed a large treasure from the Egyptians; but you are the Jews, and on you, therefore, I call for the re-payment." Besides, if a law is to be interpreted by the known intention of its makers, the Parliament in 1660, which declared all natives of England freemen, but neither altered nor meant thereby to alter the limitations of the right of election, did to all intents and purposes except that right from the common privileges of Englishmen, as Englishmen.

A moment's reflection may convince us, that every single statute is made under the knowledge of all the other laws, with which it is meant to co-exist, and by which its action is to be

* The reference is to the abolition of the military tenures at the Restoration. "For at length the military tenures, with all their heavy appendages (having during the usurpation been discontinued) were destroyed at one blow by the statute 12 Car. II. c. 24, which enacts that * * * all sorts of tenures, held by the king or others, be turned into free and common socage; save only tenures in frank-almoign, &c. A statute, which was a greater acquisition to the civil property of this kingdom than even *magna charta* itself." Blackst. Comm. II. c. 5.—*Ed.*

modified and determined. In the legislative as in the religious code the text must not be taken without the context. Now, I think, we may safely leave it to the reformers themselves to make choice between the civil and political privileges of Englishmen at present, considered as one sum total, and those of our ancestors in any former period of our history, considered as another, on the old principle, 'take one and leave the other; but whichever you take, take it all or none." Laws seldom become obsolete as long as they are both useful and practicable; but should there be an exception in any given law, there is no other way of reviving its validity but by convincing the existing legislature of its undiminished practicability and expedience; which in all essential points is the same as the recommending of a new law. And this leads me to the third class of the advocates of reform, those, namely, who leaving ancient statutes to lawyers and historians, and universal principles with the demonstrable deductions from them to the schools of logic, mathematics, theology, and ethics, rest all their measures, which they wish to see adopted, wholly on their expediency. Consequently, they must hold themselves prepared to give such proof, as the nature of comparative expediency admits, and to bring forward such evidence, as experience and the logic of probability can supply, that the plans which they recommend for adoption, are;—first, practicable; secondly, suited to the existing circumstances; and lastly, necessary or at least requisite, and such as will enable the government to accomplish more perfectly the ends for which it was instituted. These are the three indispensable conditions of all prudent change, the credentials, with which wisdom never fails to furnish her public envoys. Whoever brings forward a measure that combines this threefold excellence, whether in the cabinet, the senate, or by means of the press, merits emphatically the title of a patriotic statesman. Neither are they without a fair claim to respectful attention as state-counsellors, who fully aware of these conditions, and with a due sense of the difficulty of fulfilling them, employ their time and talents in making the attempt. An imperfect plan is not necessarily a useless plan: and in a complex enigma the greatest ingenuity is not always shown by him who first gives the complete solution. The dwarf sees farther than the giant, when he has the giant's shoulders to mount on.

Thus, as perspicuously as I could, I have exposed the erroneous principles of political philosophy, and pointed out the one only ground on which the constitution of governments can be either condemned or justified by wise men.

If I interpret aright the signs of the times, that branch of politics which relates to the necessity and practicability of infusing new life into our legislature, as the best means of securing talent and wisdom in the cabinet, will shortly occupy the public attention with a paramount interest. I would gladly, therefore, suggest the proper state of feeling, and the right preparatory notions with which this disquisition should be entered upon: and I do not know how I can effect this more naturally, than by relating the facts and circumstances which influenced my own mind. I can scarcely be accused of egotism, as in the communications and conversations which I am about to mention as having occurred to me during my residence abroad, I am no otherwise the hero of the tale, than as being the passive receiver or auditor.

To examine any thing wisely, two conditions are requisite first, a distinct notion of the desirable ends, in the complete accomplishment of which would consist the perfection of such a thing, or its ideal excellence; and, secondly, a calm and kindly mode of feeling, without which we shall hardly fail either to overlook, or not to make due allowances for, the circumstances which prevent these ends from being all perfectly realized in the particular thing which we are to examine. For instance, we must have a general notion what a man can be and ought to be, before we can fitly proceed to determine on the merits or demerits of any one individual. For the examination of our own government, I prepared my mind, therefore, by a short catechism, which I shall communicate in the next essay, and on which the letter and anecdotes that follow, will, I flatter myself, be found an amusing, if not an instructive, commentary.

ESSAY IX.

Hoc potissimum pacto felicem ac magnum regem se fore judicans; non si quam plurimis sed si quam optimis imperet. Proinde parum esse putat justis præsidiis regnum suum muniisse, nisi idem viris eruditione juxta ac vitæ integritate præcellentibus ditet atque honestet. Nimirum intelligit hæc demum esse vera regni decora, has veras opes: hanc veram et nullis unquam sæculis cessuram gloriam.—Erasmi Poncherio, Episc. Parisien. Epistola.

Judging that he will have employed the most effectual means of being a happy and powerful king, not by governing the most numerous but the most moral people. He deems it of small sufficiency to have protected the country by fleets and garrison, unless he shall at the same time enrich and illustrate it with men of eminent learning and sanctity. For these verily he conceives to be the true ornaments and wealth of his kingdom,—these its only genuine and imperishable glories.

In what do all states agree? A number of men—exert—powers—in union. Wherein do they differ? First, in the quality and quantity of the powers. One state possesses chemists, mechanists, mechanics of all kinds, men of science; the arts of war and peace; and its citizens naturally strong and of habitual courage. Another state may possess none or a few only of these, or the same more imperfectly. Or of two states possessing the same in equal perfection the one is more populous than the other, as in the instance of France and Switzerland. Secondly, in the more or less perfect union of these powers. Compare Mr. Leckie's valuable and authentic documents respecting the state of Sicily with the preceding essay on taxation. Thirdly, in the greater or less activity of exertion. Think of the papal state and its silent metropolis, and then of the county of Lancaster and the towns of Manchester and Liverpool. What is the condition indispensable to the exertion of powers in union by a number of men? A government. What are the ends of government? They are of two kinds, negative and positive. The negative ends of government are the protection of life, of personal freedom, of property, of reputation, and of religion, from foreign and from domestic attacks. The positive ends are;—

First, to make the means of subsistence more easy to each individual:—Secondly, that in addition to the necessaries of life he should derive from the union and division of labor a share of the comforts and conveniences which humanize and ennoble his nature; and at the same time the power of perfecting himself in his own branch of industry by having those things which he needs provided for him by others among his fellow-citizens; the tools and raw or manufactured materials necessary for his own employment being included. I knew a profound mathematician in Sicily, who had devoted a full third of his life to the discovery of the longitude, and who had convinced not only himself but the principal mathematicians of Messina and Palermo that he had succeeded: but neither throughout Sicily nor Naples could he find a single artist capable of constructing the instrument which he had invented:*—Thirdly, the hope of bettering his own condition and that of his children. The civilized man gives up those stimulants of hope and fear which constitute the chief charm of the savage life: and yet his Maker has distinguished him from the brute that perishes, by making hope an instinct of his nature, and an indispensable condition of his moral and intellectual progression. But a natural instinct constitutes a natural right, as far as its gratification is compatible with the equal rights of others. Hence our ancestors classed those who were bound to the soil (*adscriptitii glebæ*) and incapable by law of altering their condition from that of their parents, as bondsmen or villeins, however advantageously they might otherwise be situated. Reflect on the direful effects of castes in Hindostan, and then transfer yourself in fancy to an English cottage,—

* The good old man, who is poor, old, and blind, universally esteemed for the innocence and austerity of his life not less than for his learning, and yet universally neglected, except by persons almost as poor as himself, strongly reminded me of a German epigram on Kepler, which may be thus translated:—

No mortal spirit yet had clomb so high
As Kepler—yet his country saw him die
For very want! the minds alone he fed,
And so the bodies left him without bread.

The good old man presented me with the book in which he has described and demonstrated his invention: and I should with great pleasure transmit it to any mathematician who would feel an interest in examining it and communicating his opinion on its merits.

Where o'er the cradled infant bending
Hope has fix'd her wishful gaze,—

and the fond mother dreams of her child's future fortunes.—Who knows but he may come home a rich merchant, like such a one, or be a bishop or a judge? The prizes are indeed few and rare, but still they are possible: and the hope is universal, and perhaps occasions more happiness than even its fulfilment:—Lastly, the development of those faculties which are essential to his human nature by the knowledge of his moral and religious duties, and the increase of his intellectual powers in as great a degree as is compatible with the other ends of social union, and does not involve a contradiction. The poorest Briton possesses much and important knowledge, which he would not have had, if Luther, Calvin, Newton, and their compeers had not existed; but it is evident that the means of science and learning could not exist, if all men had a right to be made profound mathematicians or men of extensive erudition. Still instruction is one of the ends of government; for it is that only which makes the abandonment of the savage state an absolute duty: and that constitution is the best, under which the average sum of useful knowledge is the greatest, and the causes that awaken and encourage talent and genius, the most powerful and various.

These were my preparatory notions. The influences under which I proceeded to re-examine our own constitution, were the following, which I give, not exactly as they occurred, but in the order in which they will be illustrative of the different articles of the preceding paragraph. That we are better and happier than others is indeed no reason for our not becoming still better; especially as with states, as well as individuals, not to be progressive is to be retrograde. Yet the comparison will usefully temper the desire of improvement with love and a sense of gratitude for what we already are.

I. A LETTER RECEIVED, AT MALTA, FROM AN AMERICAN OFFICER OF HIGH RANK,* WHO HAS SINCE RECEIVED THE THANKS AND REWARDS OF CONGRESS FOR HIS SERVICES IN THE MEDITERRANEAN.

SIR, GRAND CAIRO, Dec. 13, 1804.

The same reason, which induced me to request letters of introduction to his Britannic Majesty's agents here, suggested the

* Decatur.—*Ed.*

propriety of showing an English jack at the main top-gallant mast-head, on entering the port of Alexandria on the 26th ult. The signal was recognized ; and Mr. B—— was immediately on board.

We found in port, a Turkish Vice Admiral, with a ship of the line, and six frigates; a part of which squadron is stationed there to preserve the tranquillity of the country; with just as much influence as the same number of pelicans would have on the same station.

On entering and passing the streets of Alexandria, I could not but notice the very marked satisfaction, which every expression and every countenance of all denominations of people, Turks and Frenchmen only excepted, manifested under an impression that we were the *avant-couriers* of an English army. They had conceived this from observing the English jack at our main, taking our flag perhaps for that of a feint, and because as is common enough everywhere, they were ready to believe what they wished. It would have been cruel to have undeceived them: consequently without positively assuming it, we passed in the character of Englishmen among the middle and lower orders of society, and as their allies among those of better information. Wherever we entered or wherever halted, we were surrounded by the wretched inhabitants; and stunned with their benedictions and prayers for blessings on us. "Will the English come? Are they coming? God grant the English may come! we have no commerce—we have no money—we have no bread! When will the English arrive?" My answer was uniformly, Patience! The same tone was heard at Rosetta as among the Alexandrians, indicative of the same dispositions; only it was not so loud, because the inhabitants are less miserable, although without any traits of happiness. On the fourth, we left that village for Cairo, and as well for our security as to facilitate our procurement of accommodations during our voyage, and our stay there, the resident directed his secretary, Capt. V——, to accompany us, and to give us lodgings in his house. We ascended the Nile leisurely, and calling at several villages, we plainly perceived that the national partiality, the strong and open expression of which proclaimed so loudly the feelings of the Egyptians of the sea-coast, was general throughout the country; and the prayers for the return of the English as earnest as universal.

On the morning of the sixth we went on shore at the village of Sabour. The villagers expressed an enthusiastic gladness at seeing red and blue uniforms and round hats;—(the French, I believe, wear three-cornered ones.) Two days before, five hundred Albanian deserters from the Viceroy's army had pillaged and left this village; at which they had lived at free quarters about four weeks. The famishing inhabitants were now distressed with apprehensions from another quarter. A company of wild Arabs were encamped in sight. They dreaded their ravages and apprized us of danger from them. We were eighteen in the party, well armed; and a pretty brisk fire which we raised among the numerous flocks of pigeons and other small fowl in the environs, must have deterred them from mischief, if, as is most probable, they had meditated any against us. Scarcely, however, were we on board and under weigh, when we saw these mounted marauders of the desert fall furiously upon the herds of camels, buffaloes, and cattle of the village, and drive many of them off wholly unannoyed on the part of the unresisting inhabitants, unless their shrieks could be deemed an annoyance. They afterwards attacked and robbed several unarmed boats, which were a few hours astern of us. The most insensible must surely have been moved by the situation of the peasants of that village. While we were listening to their complaints, they kissed our hands, and with prostrations to the ground, rendered more affecting by the inflamed state of the eyes almost universal among them, and which the new traveller might venially imagine to have been the immediate effect of weeping and anguish, they all implored English succor. Their shrieks at the assault of the wild Arabs seemed to implore the same still more forcibly, while it testified what multiplied reasons they had to implore it. I confess, I felt an almost insurmountable impulse to bring our little party to their relief, and might perhaps have done a rash act, had it not been for the calm and just observation of Captain V——, that "these were common occurrences, and that any relief which we could afford, would not merely be only temporary, but would exasperate the plunderers to still more atrocious outrages after our departure."

On the morning of the seventh we landed near a village. At our approach the villagers fled: signals of friendship brought some of them to us. When they were told that we were Englishmen, they flocked around us with demonstrations of joy, offered their services, and raised loud ejaculations for our establishment in the country. Here we could not procure a pint of milk for our coffee. The inhabitants had been plundered and chased from their habitations by the Albanians and desert Arabs, and it was but the preceding day, they had returned to their naked cottages.

Grand Cairo differs from the places already passed, only as the presence of the tyrant stamps silence on the lips of misery with the seal of terror. Wretchedness here assumes the form of melancholy; but the few whispers that are hazarded, convey the same feelings and the same wishes. And wherein does this misery and consequent spirit of revolution consist? Not in any form of government but in a formless despotism, an anarchy indeed,—for it amounts literally to an annihilation of every thing that can merit the name of government or justify the use of the word even in the laxest sense. Egypt is under the most frightful despotism, yet has no master. The Turkish soldiery, restrained by no discipline, seize every thing by violence, not only all that their necessities dictate, but whatever their caprices suggest. The Mamelukes, who dispute with these the right of domination, procure themselves subsistence by means as lawless though less insupportably oppressive; and the wild Arabs availing themselves of the occasion, plunder the defenceless wherever they find plunder. To finish the whole, the talons of the Viceroy fix on every thing which can be changed into currency, in order to find the means of supporting an ungoverned, disorganized banditti of foreign troops, who receive the harvest of his oppression, desert and betray him. Of all this rapine, robbery, and extortion, the wretched cultivators of the soil are the perpetual victims. A spirit of revolution is the natural consequence.

The reason the inhabitants of this country give for preferring the English to the French, whether true or false, is as natural as it is simple, and as influential as natural. "The English," say they, "pay for every thing,—the French pay nothing, and take every thing." They do not like this kind of deliverers.———

Well, thought I, after the perusal of this letter, the slave-trade,—which had not then been abolished,—is a dreadful crime, an English iniquity, and to sanction its continuance under full conviction and parliamentary confession of its injustice and inhumanity, is, if possible, still blacker guilt. Would that our discontents were for a while confined to our moral wants! Whatever may be the defects of our constitution, we have at least an effective government, and that too composed of men who were born with us and are to die among us. We are at least preserved from the incursions of foreign enemies: the intercommunion of interests precludes a civil war, and the volunteer spirit of the nation equally with its laws, gives to the darkest lanes of our crowded metropolis that quiet and security which the remotest villager at the cataracts of the Nile prays for in vain, in his mud hovel!

Not yet enslaved nor wholly vile,
O Albion, O my mother isle!
Thy valleys fair, as Eden's bowers,
Glitter green with sunny showers;
Thy grassy uplands' gentle swells
Echo to the bleat of flocks;—
Those grassy hills, those glitt'ring dells
Proudly ramparted with rocks,—
And ocean 'mid his uproar wild
Speaks safety to his island-child,
Hence for many a fearless age
Has social quiet loved thy shore;
Nor ever proud invader's rage
Or sack'd thy towers or stain'd thy fields with gore.*

II. Anecdote of Bonaparte.

Bonaparte, during his short stay at Malta, called out the Maltese regiments raised by the Knights, amounting to fifteen hundred of the stoutest young men of the islands. As they were drawn up on the parade, he informed them, in a bombastic harangue, that he had restored them to liberty; but in proof that his attachment to them was not bounded by this benefaction, he would now give them an opportunity of adding glory to freedom —and concluded by asking who of them would march forward to be his fellow-soldiers on the banks of the Nile, and oontribute a flower of Maltese heroism to the immortal wreaths of fame, with which he meant to crown the pyramids of Egypt! Not a man stirred: all gave a silent refusal. They were instantly surrounded by a regiment of French soldiers, marched to the Marino,

* Ode To the Departing Year. Poetical Works, VII. p. 103.—*Ed.*

forced on board the transports, and threatened with death if any one of them attempted his escape, or should be discovered in any part of the islands of Malta or Goza. At Alexandria they were always put in the front, both to save the French soldiery, and to prevent their running away; and of the whole number, fifty only survived to revisit their native country. From one of these survivors I first learned this fact, which was afterwards confirmed to me by several of his remaining comrades, as well as by the most respectable inhabitants of Valette.

This anecdote recalled to my mind an accidental conversation with an old countryman in a central district of Germany. I purposely omit names, because the day of retribution has come and gone by.* I was looking at a strong fortress in the distance, which formed a highly interesting object in a rich and varied landscape, and asked the old man, who had stopped to gaze at me, its name, adding—How beautiful it looks! "It may be well enough to look at," answered he, "but God keep all Christians from being taken thither!" He then proceeded to gratify the curiosity which he had thus excited, by informing me that the Baron —— had been taken out of his bed at midnight and carried to that fortress—that he was not heard of for nearly two years, when a soldier who had fled over the boundaries sent information to his family of the place and mode of his imprisonment. As I have no design to work on the feelings of my readers, I pass over the shocking detail: had not the language and countenance of my informant precluded such a suspicion, I might have supposed that he had been repeating some tale of horror from a romance of the dark ages. "What was his crime?" I asked.—"The report is," said the old man, "that in his capacity as minister he had remonstrated with the —— concerning the extravagance of his mistress, an outlandish countess; and that she in revenge persuaded the sovereign, that it was the Baron who had communicated to a professor at Göttingen the

* This anecdote refers to the transfer made by the Landgrave of Hesse-Cassel of a body of his troops to the service of Great Britain in the first American war:

—— and leagued with these
Each petty German princeling, nurs'd in gore;
Soul-harden'd barterers of human blood—
Death's prime slave-merchants—scorpion whips of fate!

Poetical Works, VII. p. 76.—*Ed.*

particulars of the infamous sale of some thousands of his subjects as soldiers." On the same day I discovered in the landlord of a small public-house one of the men who had been thus sold. He seemed highly delighted in entertaining an English gentleman, and in once more talking English after a lapse of so many years. He was far from regretting this incident in his life, but his account of the manner in which they were forced away accorded in so many particulars with Schiller's impassioned description of the same or a similar scene, in his tragedy of Cabal and Love, as to leave a perfect conviction on my mind, that the dramatic pathos of that description was not greater than its historic fidelity.

As I was thus reflecting, I glanced my eye on the leading paragraph of a London newspaper, containing much angry declamation, and some bitter truths, respecting our military arrangements. It were in vain, thought I, to deny that the influence of parliamentary interest, which prevents the immense patronage of the crown from becoming a despotic power, is not the most likely to secure the ablest commanders or the fittest persons for the management of our foreign empire. However, thank God! if we fight, we fight for our own king and country: and grievances which may be publicly complained of, there is some chance of seeing remedied.

III. A celebrated professor in a German university, showed me a very pleasing print, entitled, Toleration.—A Roman Catholic priest, a Lutheran divine, a Calvinist minister, a Quaker, a Jew, and a philosopher, were represented sitting round the same table, over which a winged figure hovered in the attitude of protection. "For this harmless print," said my friend, "the artist was imprisoned, and having attempted to escape, was sentenced to draw the boats on the banks of the Danube, with robbers and murderers: and there died in less than two months, from exhaustion and exposure. In your happy country, sir, this print would be considered as a pleasing scene from real life: for in every great town throughout your empire you may meet with the original." "Yes," I replied, "as far as the negative ends of government are concerned, we have no reason to complain. Our government protects us from foreign enemies, and our laws secure our lives, our personal freedom, our property, reputation, and religious rights, from domestic attacks. Our taxes, indeed, are enormous"

—"Oh! talk not of taxes," said my friend, "till you have resided in a country where the boor disposes of his produce to strangers for a foreign mart, not to bring back to his family the comforts and conveniences of foreign manufactures, but to procure that coin which his lord is to squander away in a distant land. Neither can I with patience hear it said, that your laws act only to the negative ends of government. They have a manifold positive influence, and their incorrupt administration gives a color to all your modes of thinking, and is one of the chief causes of your superior morality in private as well as public life."*

My limits compel me to strike out the different incidents which I had written as a commentary on the former three of the positive ends of government. To the moral feelings of my readers they might have been serviceable; but for their understandings they are superfluous. It is surely impossible to peruse those ends, and not admit that all three are realized under our government to a degree unexampled in any other old and long peopled country. The defects of our constitution, in which word I include the laws and customs of the land as well as its scheme of legislative and executive power, must exist, therefore, in the fourth, namely, the production of the highest average of general information, of general moral and religious principles, and the excitements and opportunities which it affords to paramount genius and heroic power in a sufficient number of its citizens. These are points in which it would be immorality to rest content with the presumption, however well founded, that we are better

* "The administration of justice throughout the continent is partial, venal, and infamous. I have, in conversation with many sensible men, met with something of content with their governments in all other respects than this; but upon the question of expecting justice to be really and fairly administered, every one confessed there was no such thing to be looked for. The conduct of the judges is profligate and atrocious. Upon almost every cause that comes before them interest is openly made with the judges; and woe betide the man, who, with a cause to support has no means of conciliating favor, either by the beauty of a handsome wife, or by other methods."—This quotation is confined in the original to France under the monarchy; I have extended the application, and adopted the words as comprising the result of my own experience: and I take this opportunity of declaring, that the most important part of Mr. Leckie's statement concerning Sicily, I myself know to be accurate, and am authorized by what I myself saw there, to rely on the whole as a fair and unexaggerated representation.

than others, if we are not what we ought to be ourselves, and are not using the means of improvement. The first question then is, What is the fact? The second upon the supposition of a defect or deficiency in one or all of these points, and that to a degree which may affect our power and prosperity, if not our absolute safety,—are the plans of legislative reform that have hitherto been proposed fit or likely to remove such defect, and supply such deficiency? The third and last question is,—Should there appear reason to deny or doubt this, are there any other means, and what are they? Of these points in the concluding essay of this section.

A French gentleman in the reign of Louis XIV. was comparing the French and English writers with all the boastfulness of national prepossession. "Sir!" replied an Englishman, better versed in the principles of freedom than the canons of criticism, "there are but two subjects worthy the human intellect, politics and religion, our state here and our state hereafter; and on neither of these dare you write." Long may the envied privilege be preserved to my countrymen of writing and talking concerning both! Nevertheless, it behooves us all to consider, that to write or talk concerning any subject, without having previously taken the pains to understand it, is a breach of duty which we owe to ourselves, though it may be no offence against the laws of the land. The privilege of talking and even publishing nonsense, is necessary in a free state; but the more sparingly we make use of it the better.

ESSAY X.

> Then we may thank ourselves,
> Who spell-bound by the magic name of peace
> Dream golden dreams. Go, warlike Briton, go,
> For the gray olive-branch change thy green laurels:
> Hang up thy rusty helmet, that the bee
> May have a hive, or spider find a loom!
> Instead of doubling drum and thrilling fife,
> Be lull'd in lady's lap with amorous flutes.
> But for Napoleon, know, he'll scorn this calm:
> The ruddy planet at his birth bore sway;
> Sanguine, adust, his humor, and wild fire
> His ruling element. Rage, revenge, and cunning
> Make up the temper of this captain's valor.

LITTLE prospective wisdom can that man obtain, who hurrying onward with the current, or rather torrent, of events, feels no interest in their importance, except as far as his curiosity is excited by their novelty; and to whom all reflection and retrospect are wearisome. If ever there were a time when the formation of just public principles becomes a duty of private morality; when the principles of morality in general ought to be made to bear on our public suffrages, and to affect every great national determination; when, in short, his country should have a place by every Englishman's fireside; and when the feelings and truths which give dignity to the fireside and tranquillity to the death-bed, ought to be present and influential in the cabinet and in the senate—that time is now with us. As an introduction to, and at the same time as a commentary on, the subject of international law, I have taken a review of the circumstances that led to the treaty of Amiens, and the recommencement of the war, more especially with regard to the occupation of Malta.

In a rich commercial state, a war seldom fails to become unpopular by length of continuance. The first, or revolution war, which towards its close, had become just and necessary, perhaps beyond any former example, had yet causes of unpopularity peculiar to itself. Exhaustion is the natural consequence of excessive stimulation, in the feelings of nations equally as in those of individuals. Wearied out by overwhelming novelties ; stunned, as it were, by a series of strange explosions ; sick too of hope long delayed ; and uncertain as to the real object and motive of the war, from the rapid change and general failure of its ostensible objects and motives : the public mind for many months preceding the signing of the preliminaries had lost all its tone and elasticity. The consciousness of mutual errors and mutual disappointments disposed the great majority of all parties to a spirit of diffidence and toleration, which, amiable as it may be in individuals, in a nation, and above all in an opulent and luxurious nation, is always too nearly akin to apathy and selfish indulgence. An unmanly impatience for peace became only not universal. After as long a resistance as the nature of our constitution and national character permitted, or even endured, the government applied at length the only remedy adequate to the greatness of the evil, a remedy which the magnitude of the evil justified, and which nothing but an evil of that magnitude could justify. At a high price they purchased for us the name of peace at a time when the views of France became daily more and more incompatible with our vital interests. Considering the peace as a mere truce of experiment, wise and temperate men regarded with complacency the treaty of Amiens, for the very reasons that would have insured the condemnation of any other treaty under any other circumstances. Its palpable deficiencies were its antidote ; or rather they formed its very essence, and declared at first sight, what alone it was, or was meant to be. Any attempt at that time, and in this treaty, to have secured Italy, Holland, and the German empire, would have been, in the literal sense of the word, preposterous. The nation would have withdrawn all faith in the pacific intentions of the ministers, if the negotiation had been broken off on a plea of this kind : for it had taken for granted the extreme desirableness, nay, the necessity of a peace, and, this once admitted, there would, no doubt, have been an absurdity in continuing the war for objects which the war furnished no means of realizing. If the First Consul had entered into stipulations with us respecting the continent, they would have been observed only as long as his interest from other causes might have dictated ;—they would have been signed with as much sincerity and observed with as much good faith, as the article actually inserted in the treaty of Amiens, respecting the integrity of the Turkish empire. This article indeed was wisely insisted on by us, because it affected both our national honor and the interests of our Indian empire immediately ; and still more, perhaps, because this of all others was the most likely to furnish an early proof of the First Consul's real dispositions. But deeply interested in the fate of the continent, as we are thought to be, it would nevertheless have been most idle to have abandoned a peace, upon the supposition of its being at all desirable, on the ground that the French government had refused that which would have been of no value had it been granted.

Indeed there results one serious disadvantage from insisting on the rights and interests of Austria, the Empire, Switzerland, &c. in a treaty between England and France, and, as it should seem, no advantage to counterbalance it. For so, any attack on those rights instantly pledges our character and national dignity to commence a war, however inexpedient it may happen to be, and however hopeless : while if a war be expedient, any attack on these countries by France furnishes a justifiable cause of war in its essential nature, and independently of all positive treaty. Seen in this light, the defects of the treaty of Amiens become its real merits. If the government of France made peace in the spirit of peace, then a friendly intercourse and the humanizing influences of commerce and reciprocal hospitality would gradually bring about in both countries the dispositions necessary for the calm discussion and sincere conclusion of a genuine, efficient, and comprehensive treaty. If the contrary proved the fact, the treaty of Amiens contained in itself the principles of its own dissolution. It was what it ought to be. If the First Consul had both meant and dealt fairly by us, the treaty would have led to a true settlement: but he acting as all prudent men expected that he would act, it supplied just reasons for the commencement of war, and at its decease left us, as a legacy, blessings that assuredly far outweighed our losses by the peace. It left us popular enthusiasm, national unanimity, and simplicity of object ; and removed one inconvenience which cleaved to the last war, by attaching to the right objects, and enlisting under their proper banners, the scorn and hatred of slavery, the passion for freedom, all the high thoughts and high feelings that connect us with the honored names of past ages; and inspire sentiments and language, to which our Hampdens, Sidneys, and Russels, might listen without jealousy.

The late peace then was negotiated by the government, ratified by the legislature, and received by the nation, as an experiment,—as the only means of exhibiting such proof as would be satisfactory to the people in their then temper; whether Bonaparte devoting his ambition and activity to the re-establishment of trade, colonial tranquillity, and social morals, in France, would abstain from insulting, alarming and endangering the British empire. And these thanks at least were due to the First Consul, that he did not long delay the proof. With more than papal insolence he issued edicts of anathema against us, and excommunicated us from all interference in the affairs of the continent. He insulted us still more indecently by pertinacious demands respecting our constitutional laws and rights of hospitality; by the official publication of Sebastiani's report; and by a direct personal outrage offered in the presence of all the foreign ministers to the king of England, in the person of his ambassador. He both insulted and alarmed us by a display of the most perfidious ambition in the subversion of the independence of Switzerland, in the avowal of designs against Egypt, Syria, and the Greek islands, and in the mission of military spies to Great Britain itself. And by forcibly maintaining a French army in Holland, he at once insulted, alarmed, and endangered us. What can render a war just—its expedience being pre-supposed—if insult, repeated alarm, and danger do not? And how can it be expedient for a rich, united, and powerful island-empire to remain in nominal peace and unresenting passiveness with an insolent neighbor, who has proved that to wage against it an unmitigated war of insult, alarm, and endangerment is both his temper and his system?

Many attempts were made by Mr. Fox to explain away the force of the greater number of the facts here enumerated: but the great fact, for which alone they have either force or meaning, the great ultimate fact, that Great Britain had been insulted, alarmed, and endangered by France, Mr. Fox himself expressly admitted. The opposers, however, of the present war concentre the strength of their cause in the following brief argument. Although we grant, say they, the grievances set forth in our manifesto to be as notorious as they are asserted to be, yet more notorious they can not be than that other fact which utterly annuls them as reasons for a war,—the fact, that ministers themselves regard them only as the pompous garnish of the dish. It stands on record, that Bonaparte might have purchased our silence forever, respecting these insults and injuries, by a mere acquiescence on his part in our retention of Malta. The whole treaty of Amiens is little more than a perplexed bond of compromise respecting Malta. On Malta we rested the peace: for Malta we renewed the war. So say the opposers of the present war. As its advocate I do not deny the fact as stated by them; but I hope to achieve all, and more than all, the purposes of such denial, by an explanation of the fact. The difficulty then resolves itself into two questions: first, in what sense of the words can we be said to have gone to war for Malta alone? Secondly, wherein does the importance of Malta consist? The answer to the second will be found in the notice of the life of Sir Alexander Ball, the liberator and political father of the Maltese, contained in a subsequent part of this work:* while the attempt to settle the first question, so as at the same time to elucidate the law of nations and its identity with the law of conscience, will occupy the remainder of the present essay.

I. IN WHAT SENSE CAN WE BE AFFIRMED TO HAVE RENEWED THE WAR FOR MALTA ALONE?

If we had known or could reasonably have believed, that the views of France were and would continue to be friendly or negative toward Great Britain, neither the subversion of the independence of Switzerland, nor the maintenance of a French army in Holland, would have furnished any prudent ground for war. For the only way by which we could have injured France, namely, the destruction of her commerce and navy, would increase her means of continental conquests, by concentrating all the resources and energies of the French empire in her military powers: while the losses and miseries which the French people would suffer in consequence, and their magnitude, compared with any advantages that might accrue to them from the extension of the name, France, were facts which, we knew by ex-

* See Essays 3, 4, 5, 6, of the third Landing Place.—*Ed.*

perience, would weigh as nothing with the existing government. Its attacks on the independence of its continental neighbors became motives to us for the recommencement of hostility, only as far as they gave proofs of a hostile intention toward ourselves, and facilitated the realizing of such intention. If any events had taken place, increasing the means of injuring this country, even though these events furnished no moral ground of complaint against France (such for instance, might be the great extension of her population and revenue, from freedom and a wise government), much more, if they were the fruits of iniquitous ambition, and therefore in themselves involved the probability of a hostile intention to us—then, I say, every after occurrence would become important, and both a just and expedient ground of war, in proportion, not to the importance of the thing in itself, but to the quantity of evident proof afforded by it to a hostile design in the government, by whose power our interests are endangered. If by demanding the immediate evacuation of Malta, when he had himself destroyed the security of its actual independence—on his promise of preserving which our pacific promises rested as on their sole foundation—and this too, after he had openly avowed such designs on Egypt, as not only in the opinion of our ministers, but in his own opinion, made it of the greatest importance to this country, that Malta should not be under French influence;—if by this conduct the First Consul exhibited a decisive proof of his intention to violate our rights and to undermine our national interests; then all his preceding actions on the continent became proofs likewise of the same intention; and any one* of these aggressions involved the meaning

* A hundred cases might be imagined which would place this assertion in its true light. Suppose, for instance, a country, according to the laws of which a parent might not disinherit a son without having first convicted him of some one of sundry crimes enumerated in a specific statute. Caius, by a series of vicious actions, has so nearly convinced his father of his utter worthlessness, that the father resolves, on the next provocation, to use the very first opportunity of legally disinheriting this son. The provocation occurs, and in itself furnishes this opportunity, and Caius is disinherited, though for an action much less glaring and intolerable than most of his preceding delinquencies had been. The advocates of Caius complain that he should be thus punished for a comparative trifle, so many worse misdemeanors having been passed over. The father replies: "This, his last action, is not the cause of the disinheritance; but the means of disinheriting

of the whole. Which of them was to determine us to war would be decided by other and prudential considerations. Had the First Consul acquiesced in our detention of Malta, he would thereby have furnished such proof of pacific intentions, as would have led to further hopes, would have lessened our alarm from his former acts of ambition, and relatively to us have altered in some degree their nature.

It should never be forgotten, that a parliament or national council is essentially different from a court of justice, alike in its objects and its duties. In the latter, the juror lays aside his private knowledge and his private connections, and judges exclusively according to the evidence adduced in the court: in the former, the senator acts upon his own internal convictions, and oftentimes upon private information, which it would be imprudent or criminal to disclose. Though his ostensible reason ought to be a true and just one, it is by no means necessary that it should be his sole or even his chief reason. In a court of justice, the juror attends to the character and general intentions of the accused party, exclusively, as adding to the probability of his having or not having committed the one particular action then in question. The senator, on the contrary, when he is to determine on the conduct of a foreign power, attends to particular actions, chiefly in proof of character and existing intentions. Now there were many and very powerful reasons why, though appealing to the former actions of Bonaparte, as confirmations of his hostile spirit and alarming ambition, we should nevertheless make Malta the direct object and final determinant of the war. Had we gone to war avowedly for the independence of Holland and Switzerland, we should have furnished Bonaparte with a colorable pretext for annexing both countries immediately to the French empire,* which, if he should do (as if his power

him. I punished him by it, rather than for it. In truth, it was not for any of his actions that I have thus punished him, but for his vices; that is, not so much for the injuries which I have suffered, as for the dispositions which these actions evinced: for the insolent and alarming intentions of which they are proofs. Now of this habitual temper, of these dangerous purposes, his last action is as true and complete a manifestation as any or all of his preceding offences; and it therefore may and must be taken as their common representative."

* The greater part of this essay was written in the year 1804, in Malta, at the request of Sir Alexander Ball.

continued he most assuredly would sooner or later) by a mere act of violence, and undisguised tyranny, there would follow a moral weakening of his power in the minds of men, which might prove of incalculable advantage to the independence and well-being of Europe ; but which, unfortunately, for this very reason, that it is not to be calculated, is too often disregarded by ordinary statesmen. At all events, it would have been made the plea for banishing, plundering, and perhaps murdering, numbers of virtuous and patriotic individuals, as being the partisans of the enemy of the continent. Add to this, that we should have appeared to have rushed into a war for objects which by war we could not hope to realize ; we should have exacerbated the misfortunes of the countries of which we had elected ourselves the champions ; and the war would have appeared a mere war of revenge and reprisal, a circumstance always to be avoided where it is possible. The ablest and best men in the Batavian republic, those who felt the insults of France most acutely, and were suffering from her oppressions the most severely, entreated our government, through their minister, not to make the state of Holland the great ostensible reason of the war. The Swiss patriots, too, believed that we could do nothing to assist them at that time, and attributed to our forbearance the comparatively timid use which France has made hitherto of her absolute power over that country. Besides, Austria, whom the changes on the continent much more nearly concerned than England, having refused all co-operation with us, there is reason to fear that an opinion, destructive of the one great blessing purchased by the peace, our national unanimity, would have taken deep root in the popular mind, namely, that these changes were mere pretexts. Neither should we forget, that the last war had left a dislike in our countrymen to continental interference, and a not unplausible persuasion, that where a nation has not sufficient sensibility as to its wrongs to commence a war against the aggressor, unbribed and ungoaded by Great Britain, a war begun by the government of such a nation, at the instance of our government, has little chance of other than a disastrous result, the character and revolutionary resources of the enemy considered. Whatever may be the strength or weakness of this argument, it is however certain, that there was a strong predilection in the British people for a cause indisputably and peculiarly British. And this feeling is not altogether ungrounded. In practical politics and the great expenditures of national power, we must not pretend to be too far-sighted : otherwise even a transient peace would be impossible among the European nations. To future and distant evils we may always oppose the various unforeseen events that are ripening in the womb of the future. Lastly, it is chiefly to immediate and unequivocal attacks on our own interests and honor, that we attach the notion of right with a full and efficient feeling. Now, though we may be first stimulated to action by probabilities and prospects of advantage, and though there is a perverse restlessness in human nature, which renders almost all wars popular at their commencement, yet a nation always needs a sense of positive right to steady its spirit. There is always needed some one reason, short, simple, and independent of complicated calculation, in order to give a sort of muscular strength to the public mind, when the power that results from enthusiasm, animal spirits, and the charm of novelty, shall have evaporated.

There is no feeling more honorable to our nature, and few that strike deeper root when our nature is happily circumstanced, than the jealousy concerning a positive right, independent of an immediate interest. To surrender, in our national character, the merest trifle that is strictly our right, the merest rock on which the waves will scarcely permit the sea-fowl to lay its eggs, at the demand of an insolent and powerful rival, on a shopkeeper's calculation of loss and gain, is in its final, and assuredly not very distant consequences, a loss of every thing—of national spirit, of national independence, and with these, of the very wealth for which the low calculation was made. This feeling in individuals, indeed, and in private life, is to be sacrificed to religion. Say rather, that by religion, it is transmuted into a higher virtue, growing on a higher and engrafted branch, yet nourished from the same root; that it remains in its essence the same spirit, but

> Made pure by thought, and naturalized in heaven;

and he who can not perceive the moral differences of national and individual duties, comprehends neither the one nor the other, and is not a whit the better Christian for being a bad patriot. Considered nationally, it is as if the captain of a man-of-war should strike and surrender his colors under the pretence, that it would be folly to risk the lives of so many good Christian sailors for the sake of a few yards of coarse canvas! Of such reasoners I take an indignant leave in the words of an obscure poet:—

Fear never wanted arguments: you do
Reason yourselves into a careful bondage,
Circumspect only to your misery.
I could urge freedom, charters, country, laws,
Gods, and religion, and such precious names—
Nay, what you value higher, wealth! But that
You sue for bondage, yielding to demands
As impious as they're insolent, and have
Only this sluggish aim,—to perish full!*

And here it is necessary to animadvert on a principle asserted by Lord Minto (in his speech, June 6th, 1803, and afterwards published at full length), that France had an undoubted right to insist on our abandonment at Malta, a right not given, but likewise not abrogated, by the treaty of Amiens. Surely in this effort of candor, his Lordship must have forgotten the circumstances on which he exerted it. The case is simply thus: the British government was convinced, and the French government admitted the justice of the conviction, that it was of the utmost importance to our interests, that Malta should remain uninfluenced by France. The French government bound itself down by a solemn treaty, that it would use its best endeavors, in conjunction with us, to secure this independence. This promise was no act of liberality, no generous free-gift, on the part of France—No! we purchased it at a high price. We disbanded our forces, we dismissed our sailors, and we gave up the best part of the fruits of our naval victories. Can it therefore with a shadow of plausibility be affirmed, that the right to insist on our evacuation of the island was unaltered by the treaty of Amiens, when this demand was strictly tantamount to our surrender of all the advantages which we had bought of France at so high a price,—tantamount to a direct breach on her part, not merely of a solemn treaty, but of an absolute bargain? It was not only the perfidy of unprincipled ambition—the demand was the fraudulent trick of a sharper. For what did France? She sold us the independence of Malta;—then exerted her power, and annihilated the very possibility of that independence, and lastly, demanded of us that we should leave it bound hand and foot for her to seize

* Cartwright. The Siege, or Love's Convert. Act I. sc. 1.—*Ed.*

without trouble, whenever her ambitious projects led her to regard such seizure as expedient. We bound ourselves to surrender it to the Knights of Malta—not surely to Joseph, Robert, or Nicholas, but to a known order, clothed with certain powers, and capable of exerting them in consequence of certain revenues. We found no such order. The men indeed and the name we found: and even so, if we had purchased Sardinia of its sovereign for so many millions of money, which through our national credit, and from the equivalence of our national paper to gold and silver, he might have agreed to receive in bank notes, and if he had received them—doubtless, he would have the bank-notes, even though immediately after our payment of them we had for this very purpose forced the Bank company to break. But would he have received the debt due to him? It is nothing more or less than a practical pun, as wicked though not quite so ludicrous, as the (in all senses) execrable pun of Earl Godwin, who requesting *basium* (a kiss) from the archbishop, thereupon seized on the archbishop's manor of Baseham.

A treaty is a writ of mutual promise between two independent states, and the law of promise is the same to nations as to individuals. It is to be sacredly performed by each party in that sense in which it knew and permitted the other party to understand it, at the time of the contract. Any thing short of this is criminal deceit in individuals, and in governments impious perfidy. After the conduct of France in the affair of the guarantees, and of the revenues of the order, we had the same right to preserve the island independent of France by a British garrison, as a lawful creditor has to the household goods of a fugitive and dishonest debtor.

One other assertion made by Lord Minto, in the same speech, bears so immediately on the plan of The Friend, as far as it proposed to investigate the principle of international, no less than of private morality, that I feel myself in some degree under an obligation to notice it. A treaty, says his lordship, ought to be strictly observed by a nation in its literal sense, even though the utter ruin of that nation should be the certain and foreknown consequence of that observance. Previously to any remarks of my own on this high flight of diplomatic virtue, we will hear what Harrington has said on this subject: "A man may devote himself to death or destruction to save a nation; but no nation will devote itself to death or destruction to save mankind. Machiavel is decried for saying, 'that no consideration is to be had of what is just or unjust, of what is merciful or cruel, of what is honorable or ignominious, in case it be to save a state or to preserve liberty :' which as to the manner of expression may perhaps be crudely spoken. But to imagine that a nation will devote itself to death or destruction any more after faith given, or an engagement thereto tending, than if there had been no engagement made or faith given, were not piety but folly."—Crudely spoken indeed, and not less crudely thought ; nor is the matter much mended by the commentator. Yet every man, who is at all acquainted with the world and its past history, knows that the fact itself is truly stated : and what is more important in the present argument, he can not find in his heart a full, deep, and downright verdict, that it should be otherwise. The consequences of this perplexity in the moral feelings are not seldom extensively injurious. For men hearing the duties which would be binding on two individuals living under the same laws insisted on as equally obligatory on two independent states, in extreme cases, where they see clearly the impracticability of realizing such a notion,—and having at the same time a dim half-consciousness, that two states can never be placed exactly on the same ground as two individuals,—relieve themselves from their perplexity by cutting what they can not untie, and assert that national policy can not in all cases be subordinated to the laws of morality ;—in other words, that a government may act with injustice, and yet remain blameless. This assertion was hazarded,—I record it with unfeigned regret,—by a minister of state, on the affair of Copenhagen. Tremendous assertion ! that would render every complaint, which we make, of the abominations of the French tyrant, hypocrisy, or mere incendiary declamation for the simple-headed multitude. But, thank God ! it is as unnecessary and unfounded, as it is tremendous. For what is a treaty ? A voluntary contract between two nations. So we will state it in the first instance. Now it is an impossible case, that any nation can be supposed by any other to have intended its own absolute destruction in a treaty, which its interests alone could have prompted it to make. The very thought is self-contradictory. Not only Athens (we will say) could not have intended this to have been understood in any specific promise made to

Sparta; but Sparta could never have imagined that Athens had so intended it. And Athens itself must have known, that had she even affirmed the contrary, Sparta could not have believed—nay, would have been under a moral obligation not to have believed her. Were it possible to suppose such a case—for instance, such a treaty made by a single besieged town, under an independent government as that of Numantia—it becomes no longer a state, but the act of a certain number of individuals voluntarily sacrificing themselves, each to preserve his separate honor. For the state was already destroyed by the circumstances which alone could make such an engagement conceivable.—But we have said, nations.—Applied to England and France, relatively to treaties, this is but a form of speaking. The treaty is really made by some half-dozen, or perhaps half a hundred individuals, possessing the government of these countries. Now it is a universally admitted part of the law of nations, that an engagement entered into by a minister with a foreign power, when it is known to this power that the minister in so doing has exceeded and contravened his instructions, is altogether nugatory. And is it to be supposed for a moment, that a whole nation, consisting perhaps of twenty millions of human souls, could ever have invested a few individuals, whom altogether for the promotion of its welfare it had intrusted with its government, with the right of signing away its existence?*

* See Paley's Moral and Political Philosophy, B. vi. c. 12.—*Ed.*

ESSAY XI.

Amicas reprehensiones gratissime accipiamus oportet; etiam si reprehendi non meruit opinio nostra, vel hanc propter causam, quod recte defendi potest. Si vero infirmitas vel humana vel propria, etiam cum veraciter arguitur, non potest non aliquantulum contristari, melius tumor dolet dum curatur, quam dum et parcitur et non sanatur. Hoc enim est quod acute vidit, qui dixit: utiliores esse plerumque inimicos objurgantes, quam amicos objurgare metuentes. Illi enim dum rixantur, dicunt aliquando vera quæ corrigamus: isti autem minorem, quam oportet, exhibent justitiæ libertatem, dum amicitiæ timent exasperare dulcedinem. AUGUSTIN. HIERONYMO.*

Censures, offered in friendliness, we ought to receive with gratitude: yea, though our opinions did not merit censure, we should still be thankful for the attack on them, were it only that it gives us an opportunity of successfully defending the same. For never doth an important truth spread its roots so wide or clasp the soil so stubbornly, as when it has braved the winds of controversy. There is a stirring and a far-heard music sent forth from the tree of sound knowledge, when its branches are fighting with the storm, which passing onward shrills out at once truth's triumph and its own defeat. But if the infirmity of human nature, or of our own constitutional temperament, can not, even when we have been fairly convicted of error, but suffer some small mortification, yet better suffer pain from its extirpation, than from the consequences of its continuance, and of the false tenderness that has withholden the remedy. This is what the acute observer had in his mind, who said, that upbraiding enemies were not seldom more profitable than friends afraid to find fault. For the former amidst their quarrelsome invectives may chance on some home truths, by which we may amend ourselves in consequence; while the latter from an over-delicate apprehension of ruffling the smooth surface of friendship shrink from its duties, and from the manly freedom which truth and justice demand.

ONLY a few privileged individuals are authorized to pass into the theatre without stopping at the door-keeper's box; but every

* August. Op. Tom. ii. Epist. xv. Ed. Basil. The original of the former part of the quotation, which is a good deal altered, stands thus:—*Ut et ego amicissimam reprehensionem gratissime accipiam, etiam si reprehendi non meruit quod recte defendi potest.* * * * * *Si vero infirmitas velut humana mea, etiam cum veraciter arguor, non potest non aliquantulum contristari, melius capitis tumor dolet, &c.*—Ed.

man of decent appearance may put down the play-price there, and thenceforward has as good a right as the managers themselves not only to see and hear, as far as his place in the house, and his own ears and eyes permit him, but likewise to express audibly his approbation or disapprobation of what may be going forward on the stage. If his feelings happen to be in unison with those of the audience in general, he may without breach of decorum persevere in his notices of applause or dislike, till the wish of the house is complied with. If he finds himself unsupported, he rests contented with having once exerted his common right, and on that occasion at least gives no further interruption to the amusement of those who feel differently from him. So it is, or so it should be, in literature. A few extraordinary minds may be allowed to pass a mere opinion;—though in point of fact those, who alone are entitled to this privilege, are ever the last to avail themselves of it. Add too, that even the mere opinions of such men may in general be regarded either as promissory notes, or as receipts referring to a former payment. But every man's opinion has a right to pass into the common auditory, if his reason for the opinion is paid down at the same time: for arguments are the sole current coin of intellect. The degree of influence to which the opinion is entitled should be proportioned to the weight and value of the reasons for it; and whether these are shillings or pounds sterling, the man, who has given them, remains blameless, provided he contents himself with the place to which they have entitled him, and does not attempt by strength of lungs to counterbalance its disadvantages, or expect to exert as immediate an influence in the back seats of the upper gallery, as if he had paid in gold and been seated in the stage box.

But unfortunately,—and here commence the points of difference between the theatric and the literary public,—in the great theatre of literature there are no authorized door-keepers: for our anonymous critics are self-elected. I shall not fear the charge of calumny if I add that they have lost all credit with wise men by unfair dealing: such as their refusal to receive an honest man's money, that is, his argument, because they anticipate and dislike his opinion, while others of suspicious character and the most unseemly appearance are suffered to pass without payment, or by virtue of orders which they have themselves distributed to known partisans. Sometimes the honest man's intellectual coin is refused under pretence that it is light or counterfeit, without any proof given either by the money scales, or by sounding the coin in dispute together with one of known goodness. We may carry the metaphor still farther. It is by no means a rare case, that the money is returned because it had a different sound from that of a counterfeit, the brassy blotches on which seemed to blush for the impudence of the silver wash in which they were inisled, and rendered the mock coin a lively emblem of a lie self-detected. Still oftener does the rejection take place by a mere act of insolence, and the blank assertion that the candidate's money is light or bad, is justified by a second assertion that he is a fool or knave for offering it.

The second point of difference explains the preceding, and accounts both for the want of established door-keepers in the auditory of literature, and for the practices of those, who under the name of reviewers volunteer this office. There is no royal mintage for arguments, no ready means by which all men alike, who possess common sense, may determine their value and intrinsic worth at the first sight or sound. Certain forms of natural logic indeed there are, the inobservance of which is decisive against an argument; but the strictest adherence to them is no proof of its actual, though an indispensable condition of its possible, validity. In the arguer's own conscience there is, no doubt, a certain value, and an infallible criterion of it, which applies to all arguments equally; and this is the sincere conviction of the mind itself. But for those to whom it is offered, there are only conjectural marks; yet such as will seldom mislead any man of plain sense, who is both honest and observant.

These characteristics I have attempted to comprise in a previous part of this work,* and to describe them more at large in the essays that follow, on the communication of truth. If the honest warmth, which results from the strength of the particular conviction, be tempered by the modesty which belongs to the sense of general fallibility; if the emotions, which accompany all vivid perceptions, are preserved distinct from the expression of personal passions, and from appeals to them in the heart of others; if the reasoner asks no respect for the opinion, as his opinion, but only in proportion as it is acknowledged by that reason, which is common to all men; and, lastly, if he supports an

* P. 41.—*Ed.*

opinion on no subject which he has not previously examined, and furnishes proof both that he possesses the means of inquiry by his education or the nature of his pursuits, and that he has endeavored to avail himself of those means; then, and with these conditions, every human being is authorized to make public the grounds of any opinion which he holds, and of course the opinion itself, as the object of them. Consequently, it is the duty of all men, not always indeed to attend to him, but, if they do, to attend to him with respect, and with a sincere as well as apparent toleration. I should offend against my own laws, if I disclosed at present the nature of my convictions concerning the degree, in which this virtue of toleration is possessed and practised by the majority of my contemporaries and countrymen. But if the contrary temper is felt and shown in instances where all those conditions have been observed, which have been stated at full in the preliminary essays that form the introduction to this work, and the chief of which I have just now recapitulated; I have no hesitation in declaring that whatever the opinion may be, and however opposite to the hearer's or reader's previous persuasions, one or other of all of the following defects must be taken for granted. Either the intolerant person is not master of the grounds on which his own faith is built; which, therefore, neither is nor can be his own faith, though it may very easily be his imagined interest, and his habit of thought. In this case he is angry, not at the opposition to truth, but at the interruption of his own indolence and intellectual slumber, or possibly at the apprehension, that his temporal advantages are threatened, or at least the ease of mind, in which he had been accustomed to enjoy them. Or, secondly, he has no love of truth for its own sake; no reverence for the divine command to seek earnestly after it, which command, if it had not been so often and solemnly given by revelation, is yet involved and expressed in the gift of reason, and in the dependence of all our virtues on its development. He has no moral and religious awe for freedom of thought, though accompanied both by sincerity and humility; nor for the right of free communication which is ordained by God, together with that freedom, if it be true that God has ordained us to live in society, and has made the progressive improvement of all and each of us to depend on the reciprocal aids, which directly or indirectly each supplies to all, and all to each. But if his alarm and his consequent intolerance, are occasioned by his eternal rather than temporal interests, and if, as is most commonly the case, he does not deceive himself on this point, gloomy indeed, and erroneous beyond idolatry, must have been his notions of the Supreme Being! For surely the poor heathen who represents to himself the divine attributes of wisdom, justice, and mercy, under multiplied and forbidden symbols in the powers of nature or the souls of extraordinary men, practises a superstition which (though at once the cause and effect of blindness and sensuality) is less incompatible with inward piety and true religious feeling than the creed of that man, who in the spirit of his practice, though not in direct words, loses sight of all these attributes, and substitutes instead of the adoptive and cheerful boldness, which our new alliance with God requires," a "servile and thrall-like fear."* Such fear-ridden and thence angry believers, or rather acquiescents, would do well to re-peruse the book of Job, and observe the sentence passed by the All-just on the friends of the sufferer, who had hoped, like venal advocates, to purchase the favor of God by uttering truths of which in their own hearts they had neither conviction nor comprehension. The truth from the lips did not atone for the lie in the heart, while the rashness of agony in the searching and bewildered complainant, was forgiven in consideration of his sincerity and integrity in not disguising the true dictates of his reason and conscience, but avowing his incapability of solving a problem by his reason, which before the Christian dispensation the Almighty was pleased to solve only by declaring it to be beyond the limits of human reason. Having insensibly passed into a higher and more serious style than I had first intended, I will venture to appeal to these self-obscurants, whose faith dwells in the land of the shadow of darkness, these

* *Milton Of Reformation in England*, B. i. *sub initio.* 'For in very deed, the superstitious man by his good-will is an atheist; but being scared from thence by the pangs and gripes of a boiling conscience, all in a pudder shuffles up to himself such a God and such a worship as is most agreeable to remedy his fear: which fear of his as also his hope, fixed only upon the flesh, renders likewise the whole faculty of his apprehension carnal; and all the inward acts of worship issuing from the native strength of the soul, run out lavishly to the upper skin, and there harden into a crust of formality. Hence men came to scan the Scriptures by the letter, and in the covenant of our redemption magnified the external signs more than the quickening power of the spirit.'—*Ibid.*—*Ed.*

papists without a pope, and protestants who protest only against all protesting; and will appeal to them in words which yet more immediately concern them as Christians, in the hope that they will lend a fearless ear to the learned apostle, when he both assures and labors to persuade them that they were called in Christ to all perfectness in spiritual knowledge and full assurance of understanding in the mystery of God. There can be no end without means: and God furnishes no means that exempt us from the task and duty of joining our own best endeavors. The original stock, or wild olive-tree of our natural powers, was not given us to be burned or blighted, but to be grafted on. We are not only not forbidden to examine and propose our doubts, so it be done with humility and proceed from a real desire to know the truth; but we are repeatedly commanded so to do; and with a most unchristian spirit must that man have read the preceding passages, if he can interpret any one sentence as having for its object to excuse a too numerous class, who, to use the words of St. Augustine, *quærunt non ut fidem sed ut infidelitatem inveniant;*—such as examine not to find reasons for faith, but pretexts for infidelity.

ESSAY XII.

Such is the iniquity of men, that they suck in opinions as wild asses do the wind, without distinguishing the wholesome from the corrupted air, and then live upon it at a venture: and when all their confidence is built upon zeal and mistake, yet therefore, because they are zealous and mistaken, they are impatient of contradiction. JEREMY TAYLOR.*

"IF," observes the eloquent bishop in the work, from which my motto is selected, "an opinion plainly and directly brings in a crime, as if a man preaches treason or sedition, his opinion is not his excuse. A man is nevertheless a traitor because he believes it lawful to commit treason; and a man is a murderer if he kills his brother unjustly, although he should think that he

* Epist. Dedicat. to the Liberty of Prophesying. Vol. vii. p. 409. Heber's edit.—*Ed.*

was doing God good service thereby. Matters of fact are equally judicable, whether the principle of them be from within or from without."*

To dogmatize a crime, that is, to teach it as a doctrine, is itself a crime, great or small as the crime dogmatized is more or less palpably so. "You say," said Sir John Cheke, addressing himself to the papists of his day, "that you rebel for your religion. First tell me, what religion is that which teaches you to rebel." As my object in the present section is to treat of tolerance and intolerance in the public bearings of opinions and their propagation, I shall embrace this opportunity of selecting the two passages, which I have been long inclined to consider as the most eloquent in our English literature, though each in a very different style of eloquence, as indeed the authors were as dissimilar in their bias, if not in their faith, as two bishops of the same church can well be supposed to have been. I think too, I may venture to add, that both the extracts will be new to a very great majority of my readers. For the length I make no apology. It was part of my plan to allot two essays of The Friend, the one to a selection from our prose writers, and the other from our poets; but in both cases from works that do not occur in our ordinary reading.

The following passages are both on the same subject;—the first from Jeremy Taylor;—the second from Bishop Bedell.

1. The rise and progress of a controversy, from the speculative opinion of an individual, to the revolution or intestine war of a nation.

"This is one of the inseparable characters of a heretic; he sets his whole communion and all his charity upon his article; for to be zealous in the schism, that is the characteristic of a good man, that is his note of Christianity; in all the rest he excuses you or tolerates you, provided you be a true believer; then you are one of the faithful, a good man and a precious, you are of the congregation of the saints, and one of the godly. All solifidians do thus; and all that do thus are solifidians, the church of Rome herself not excepted; for though in words she proclaims the possibility of keeping all the commandments; yet she dispenses easier with him that breaks them all, than with him that speaks one word against any of her articles, though but

* Liberty of Proph. s. 13.—*Ed.*

the least; even the eating of fish and forbidding flesh in Lent. So that it is faith they regard more than charity, a right belief more than a holy life; and for this you shall be with them upon terms easy enough, provided you go not a hair's breadth from any thing of her belief. For if you do, they have provided for you two deaths and two fires, both inevitable and one eternal. And this certainly is one of the greatest evils, of which the church of Rome is guilty: for this in itself is the greatest and unworthiest uncharitableness. But the procedure is of great use to their ends. For the greatest part of Christians are those that can not consider things leisurely and wisely, searching their bottoms and discovering their causes, or foreseeing events which are to come after; but are carried away by fear and hope, by affection and prepossession: and therefore the Roman doctors are careful to govern them as they will be governed. If you dispute, you gain, it may be, one, and lose five; but if you threaten them with damnation, you keep them in fetters; for they that are *in fear of death, are all their lifetime in bondage*,* saith the apostle: and there is in the world nothing so potent as fear of the two deaths which are the two arms and grapples of iron by which the church of Rome takes and keeps her timorous or conscientious proselytes. The easy protestant calls upon you from Scripture to do your duty, to build a holy life upon a holy faith, the faith of the apostles and first disciples of our Lord: he tells you if you err, and teaches ye the truth; and if ye will obey, it is well; if not, he tells you of your sin, and that all sin deserves the wrath of God; but judges no man's person, much less any states of men. He knows that God's judgments are righteous and true; but he knows also, that his mercy absolves many persons, who, in his just judgment, were condemned: and if he had a warrant from God to say, that he should destroy all the papists, as Jonas had concerning the Ninevites; yet he remembers that every repentance, if it be sincere, will do more, and prevail greater, and last longer than God's anger will. Besides these things, there is a strange spring, and secret principle in every man's understanding, that it is oftentimes turned about by such impulses, of which no man can give an account. But we all remember a most wonderful instance of it in the disputation between the two Reynoldses, John and William; the former of

* Heb. ii. 15.

which being a papist, and the latter a protestant, met and disputed, with a purpose to confute and to convert each other. And so they did: for those arguments which were used, prevailed fully against their adversary, and yet did not prevail with themselves. The papist turned protestant, and the protestant became a papist, and so remained to their dying day. Of which some ingenious person gave a most handsome account in the following excellent epigram:

Bella inter geminos plusquam civilia fratres
Traxerat ambiguus religionis apex.
Ille reformatæ fidei pro partibus instat;
Iste reformandam denegat esse fidem.
Propositis causæ rationibus, alter utrinque
Concurrere pares, et cecidere pares.
Quod fuit in votis, fratrem capit alter uterque;
Quod fuit in fatis, perdit uterque fidem.
Captivi gemini sine captivante fuerunt,
Et victor victi transfuga castra petit.
Quod genus hoc pugnæ est, ubi victus gaudet uterque,
Et tamen alteruter se superasse dolet?

But further yet, he considers the natural and regular infirmities of mankind; and God considers them much more; he knows that in man there is nothing admirable but his ignorance and weakness; his prejudice, and the infallible certainty of being deceived in many things: he sees that wicked men oftentimes know much more than many very good men; and that the understanding is not of itself considerable in morality, and effects nothing in rewards and punishments; it is the will only that rules man and can obey God. He sees and deplores it, that many men study hard and understand little; that they dispute earnestly and understand not one another at all; that affections creep so certainly, and mingle with their arguing, that the argument is lost, and nothing remains but the conflict of two adversaries' affections; that a man is so willing, so easy, so ready to believe what makes for his opinion, so hard to understand an argument against himself, that it is plain it is the principle within, not the argument without, that determines him. He observes also that all the world (a few individuals excepted) are unalterably determined to the religion of their country, of their family, of their society; that there is never any considerable change made, but what is made by war and empire, by fear and hope. He remembers that it is a rare thing to see a Jesuit of the Dominican opinion, or a Dominican (until of late) of the Jesuit; but every order gives laws to the understanding of their novices, and they never change. He considers there is such ambiguity in words, by which all lawgivers express their meaning; that there is such abstruseness in mysteries of religion, that some things are so much too high for us, that we can not understand them rightly; and yet they are so sacred, and concerning, that men will think they are bound to look into them, as far as they can; that it is no wonder if they quickly go too far, where no understanding, if it were fitted for it, could go far enough; but in these things it will be hard not to be deceived, since our words can not rightly express those things; that there is such variety of human understandings, that men's faces differ not so much as their souls; and that if there were not so much difficulty in things, yet they could not but be variously apprehended by several men. And hereto he considers, that in twenty opinions, it may be that not one of them is true; nay, whereas Varro reckoned that among the old philosophers there were eight hundred opinions concerning the *summum bonum*, that yet not one of them hit the right. He sees also that in all religions, in all societies, in all families, and in all things, opinions differ; and since opinions are too often begot by passion, by passions and violence they are kept; and every man is too apt to overvalue his own opinion; and out of a desire that every man should conform his judgment to his that teaches, men are apt to be earnest in their persuasion, and overact the proposition; and from being true as he supposes, he will think it profitable; and if you warm him either with confidence or opposition, he quickly tells you it is necessary; and as he loves those that think as he does, so he is ready to hate them that do not; and then secretly from wishing evil to him, he is apt to believe evil will come to him; and that it is just it should; and by this time the opinion is troublesome, and puts other men upon their guard against it; and then while passion reigns, and reason is modest and patient, and talks not loud like a storm, victory is more regarded than truth, and men call God into the party, and his judgments are used for arguments, and the threatenings of the Scripture are snatched up in haste, and men throw arrows, firebrands, and death, and by this time all the world is in an uproar. All this, and a thousand things more the English protestants considering deny not their communion to any Christian who desires it, and believes the apostles' creed, and is of the religion of the first four general councils; they hope well of all that live well; they receive into their bosom all true believers of what church soever; and for them that err, they instruct them, and then leave them to their liberty, to stand or fall before their own master."*

2. A doctrine not the less safe for being the more charitable.

"Christ our Lord hath given us, amongst others, two infallible notes to know the church. *My sheep*, saith he, *hear my voice*:† and again, *By this shall all men know that ye are my disciples, if ye have love one to another*.‡—What! shall we stand upon conjectural arguments from that which men say? We are partial to ourselves, malignant to our opposites. Let Christ be heard who be his, who not. And for the hearing of his voice—O that it might be the issue! But I see you decline it, therefore I leave it also for the present. That other is that which now I stand upon,—'the badge of Christ's sheep.' Not a likelihood, but a certain token whereby every man may know them: *by this*, saith he, *shall all men know that ye are my disciples if ye have charity one towards another*.—Thanks be to God, this mark of our Saviour is in us, which you with our schismatics and other enemies want. As Solomon found the true mother by her natural affection, that chose rather to yield to her adversary's plea, claiming her child, than endure that it should be cut in pieces; so may it soon be found at this day whether is the true mother. Ours, that faith, give her the living child and kill him not; or yours, that if she may not have it, is content it be killed rather than want of her will. 'Alas!' (saith ours even of those that leave her) 'these be my children! I have borne them to Christ in baptism: I have nourished them as I could with mine own breasts, his testaments. I would have brought them up to man's estate, as their free birth and parentage deserves. Whether it be their lightness or discontent, or her enticing words and gay shows, they leave me: they have found a better mother. Let them live yet, though in bondage. I shall have patience; I permit the care of them to their father; I beseech him to keep them that they do no evil. If they make their peace with him,

* Dissuasive from Popery. Part II.—B. i. s. 7.—*Ed.*

† John x. 27.—*Ed.* ‡ *Ib.* xiii. 35.—*Ed.*

I am satisfied : they have not hurt me at all.' 'Nay,' but saith yours, 'I sit alone as queen and mistress of Christ's family, he that hath not me for his mother, can not have God for his father. Mine, therefore, are these, either born or adopted ; and if they will not be mine, they shall be none. So without expecting Christ's sentence she cuts with the temporal sword, hangs, burns, draws, those that she perceives inclined to leave her, or have left her already. So she kills with the spiritual sword those that are subject not to her, yea, thousands of souls that not only have no means so to do, but many which never so much as have heard whether there be a pope of Rome or no. Let our Solomon be judge between them, yea, judge you, Mr. Waddesworth ! more seriously and maturely, not by guesses, but by the very mark of Christ, which wanting yourselves, you have unawares discovered in us : judge, I say, without passion and partiality, according to Christ's word, which is his flock, which is his church."*

ESSAY XIII.

ON THE LAW OF NATIONS.

Πρὸς πόλεως εὐδαιμονίαν καὶ δικαιοσύνην πάντα ἰδιώτον ἔμπροσθεν τέτακται φύσει· τούτων δὲ τὰ μὲν ἀνθρώπινα εἰς τὰ θεῖα, τὰ δὲ θεῖα εἰς τὸν ἡγεμόνα νοῦν ξύμπαντα δεῖ βλέπειν, οὐχ ὡς πρὸς ἀρετῆς τὶ μόριον, ἀλλὰ πρὸς ἀρετὴν ἐν ἀρεταῖς ἀεὶ ὑπομενοῦσαν, ὡς πρὸς νόμον τίνα νομοθετοῦντα. PLATO.

For all things that regard the well-being and justice of a state are pre-ordained and established in the nature of the individual. Of these it behooves that the merely human (the temporal and fluxional) should be referred and subordinated to the divine in man, and the divine in like manner to the Supreme Mind, so however that the state is not to regulate its actions by reference to any particular form and fragments of virtue, but must fix its eye on that virtue, which is the abiding spirit and (as it were) *substratum* in all the virtues, as on a law that is itself legislative.

It were absurd to suppose, that individuals should be under a law of moral obligation, and yet that a million of the same in-

* Letter to a friend who had deserted the Church of England for that of Rome.—*Ed.*

dividuals acting collectively or through representatives, should be exempt from all law: for morality is no accident of human nature, but its essential characteristic. A being altogether without morality is either a beast or a fiend, accordingly as we conceive this want of conscience to be natural or self-produced; a mere negation of goodness, or the consequence of rebellion to it. Yet were it possible to conceive a man wholly immoral, it would remain impossible to conceive him without a moral obligation to be otherwise; and none, but a madman, will imagine that the essential qualities of any thing can be altered by its becoming part of an aggregate; that a grain of corn, for instance, shall cease to contain flour, as soon as it is part of a peck or bushel. It is, therefore, grounded in the nature of the thing, and not by a mere fiction of the mind, that wise men, who have written on the law of nations, contemplate the several states of the civilized world, as so many individuals, and equally with the latter under a moral obligation to exercise their free agency within such bounds, as render it compatible with the existence of free agency in others. We may represent to ourselves this original free agency, as a right of common, the formation of separate states as an inclosure of this common, the allotments awarded severally to the co-proprietors as constituting national rights, and the law of nations as the common register-office of their title-deeds. But in all morality, though the principle, which is the abiding spirit of the law, remains perpetual and unaltered, even as that Supreme Reason in whom and from whom it has its being, yet the letter of the law, that is, the application of it to particular instances, and the mode of realizing it in actual practice, must be modified by the existing circumstances. What we should desire to do, the conscience alone will inform us; but how and when we are to make the attempt, and to what extent it is in our power to accomplish it, are questions for the judgment, and require an acquaintance with facts, and their bearings on each other. Thence the improvement of our judgment, and the increase of our knowledge, on all subjects included within our sphere of action, are not merely advantages recommended by prudence, but absolute duties imposed on us by conscience.

As the circumstances, then, under which men act as statesmen, are different from those under which they act as individuals, a proportionate difference must be expected in the practical rules by which their public conduct is to be determined. Let me not be misunderstood : I speak of a difference in the practical rules, not in the moral law itself, the means of administering in particular cases, and under given circumstances, which it is the sole object of these rules to point out. The spirit continues one and the same, though it may vary its form according to the element into which it is transported. This difference, with its grounds and consequences, it is the province of the philosophical publicist to discover and display : and exactly in this point (I speak with unfeigned diffidence) it appears to me that the writers on the law of nations,* whose works I have had the opportunity of studying, have been least successful.

In what does the law of nations differ from the laws enacted by a particular state for its own subjects ? The solution is evident. The law of nations, considered apart from the common principle of all morality, is not fixed or positive in itself, nor supplied with any regular means of being enforced. Like those duties in private life which, for the same reasons, moralists have entitled imperfect duties (though the most atrocious guilt may be involved in the omission or violation of them), the law of nations appeals only to the conscience and prudence of the parties concerned. Wherein then does it differ from the moral laws which the reason, considered as conscience, dictates for the conduct of individuals ? This is a more difficult question ; but my answer would be determined by, and grounded on, the obvious differences of the circumstances in the two cases. Remember then, that we are now reasoning, not as sophists or system-mongers, but as men anxious to discover what is right in order that we may practise it, or at least give our suffrage and the influence of our opinion in recommending its practice. We must therefore confine the question to those cases, in which honest men and real

* Grotius, Bynkerschoek, Puffendorf, Wolfe, and Vattel; to whose works I must add, as comprising whatever is most valuable in the preceding authors, with many important improvements and additions, Robinson's Reports of Cases in the Admiralty Court, under Sir W. Scott: to whom international law is under no less obligation than the law of commercial proceeding was to the late Lord Mansfield. As I have never seen Sir W. Scott, nor either by myself or my connections enjoy the honor of the remotest acquaintance with him, I trust that even by those who may think my opinion erroneous, I shall not at least be suspected of intentional flattery. 1817.

patriots can suppose any controversy to exist between real patriotism and common honesty. The objects of the patriot are, that his countrymen should, as far as circumstances permit, enjoy what the Creator designed for the enjoyment of animals endowed with reason, and of course that they should have it in their power to develop those faculties which were given them to be developed. He would do his best that every one of his countrymen should possess whatever all men may and should possess, and that a sufficient number should be enabled and encouraged to acquire those excellencies which, though not necessary or possible for all men, are yet to all men useful and honorable. He knows that patriotism itself is a necessary link in the golden chain of our affections and virtues, and turns away with indignant scorn from the false philosophy or mistaken religion, which would persuade him that cosmopolitism is nobler than nationality, the human race a sublimer object of love than a people; and that Plato, Luther, Newton, and their equals, formed themselves neither in the market nor the senate, but in the world, and for all men of all ages. True! But where, and among whom are these giant exceptions produced? In the wide empires of Asia, where millions of human beings acknowledge no other bond but that of a common slavery, and are distinguished on the map but by a name which themselves perhaps never heard, or hearing abhor? No! in a circle defined by human affections, the first firm sod within which becomes sacred beneath the quickened step of the returning citizen;—here, where the powers and interests of men spread without confusion through a common sphere, like the vibrations propagated in the air by a single voice, distinct yet coherent, and all uniting to express one thought and the same feeling;—here, where even the common soldier dares force a passage for his comrades by gathering up the bayonets of the enemy into his own breast, because his country expected every man to do his duty, and this not after he has been hardened by habit, but, as probably in his first battle; not reckless or hopeless, but braving death from a keener sensibility to those blessings which make life dear, to those qualities which render himself worthy to enjoy them;—here, where the royal crown is loved and worshiped as a glory around the sainted head of freedom;—where the rustic at his plough whistles with equal enthusiasm, "God save the King," and "Britons never shall be slaves," or, perhaps.

leaves one thistle unweeded in his garden, because it is the symbol of his dear native land;*—here, from within this circle defined, as light by shade, or rather as light within light, by its intensity,—here alone, and only within these magic circles, rise up the awful spirits, whose words are oracles for mankind, whose love embraces all countries, and whose voice sounds through all ages! Here, and here only, may we confidently expect those mighty minds to be reared and ripened, whose names are naturalized in foreign lands, the sure fellow-travellers of civilization, and yet render their own country dearer and more proudly dear to their own countrymen. This is indeed cosmopolitism, at once the nurseling and the nurse of patriotic affection. This, and this alone, is genuine philanthropy, which like the olive-tree, sacred to concord and to wisdom, fattens not exhausts the soil, from which it sprang, and in which it remains rooted. It is feebleness only which can not be generous without injustice, or just without ceasing to be generous. Is the morning star less brilliant, or does a ray less fall on the golden fruitage of the earth, because the moons of Saturn too feed their lamps from the same sun? Even Germany,—though curst with a base and hateful brood of nobles and princelings, cowardly and ravenous jackals to the very flocks intrusted to them as to shepherds, who hunt for the tiger and whine and wag their tails for his bloody offal—even Germany, the ever-changing boundaries of which superannuate the last year's map, and are altered as easily as the hurdles of a temporary sheep-fold, is still remembered with filial love and a patriot's pride, when the thoughtful German hears the names of Luther and Leibnitz. Ah! why, he sighs, why for herself in vain should my country have produced such a host of immortal

* I can not here refuse myself the pleasure of recording a speech of the poet Burns, related to me by the lady to whom it was addressed. Having been asked by her, why in his more serious poems he had not changed the two or three Scotch words which seemed only to disturb the purity of the style,—the poet with great sweetness, and his usual happiness in reply, answered that in truth it would have been better, but—

The rough bur-thistle spreading wide
  Amang the bearded bear,
I turn'd the weeder-clips aside
  An' spar'd the symbol dear.

An author may be allowed to quote from his own poems, when he does it with as much modesty and felicity as Burns did in this instance.

minds! Yea, even the poor enslaved, degraded, and barbarized Greek can still point to the harbor of Tenedos, and say,—"There lay our fleet when we were besieging Troy."

Reflect a moment on the past history of this wonderful people. What were they while they remained free and independent,—when Greece resembled a collection of mirrors set in a single frame, each having its own focus of patriotism, yet all capable, as at Marathon and Platea, of converging to one point and of consuming a common foe? What were they then? The fountains of light and civilization, of truth and of beauty, to all mankind! they were the thinking head, the beating heart, of the whole world! They lost their independence, and with their independence their patriotism; and became the cosmopolites of antiquity. It has been truly observed by the author of the work for which Palm was murdered, that, after the first acts of severity, the Romans treated the Greeks not only more mildly than their other slaves and dependents, but behaved to them even affectionately and with munificence. The victor nation felt reverentially the presence of the visible and invisible deities that gave sanctity to every grove, every fountain, and every forum. "Think," (writes Pliny to one of his friends) "that you are sent into the province of Achaia, that true and genuine Greece, where civilization, letters, even corn, are believed to have been discovered; that you are sent to administer the affairs of free states, that is, to men eminently free, who have retained their natural right by valor, by services, by friendship, lastly by treaty and by religion. Revere the gods their founders, the sacred influences represented in those gods; revere their ancient glory and this very old age which in man is venerable, in cities sacred. Cherish in thyself a reverence of antiquity, a reverence for their great exploits, a reverence even for their fables. Detract nothing from the liberty, or the dignity, or even the pretensions of any state; keep before thine eyes that this is the land which sent us our institutions, which gave us our laws, not after it was subjugated, but in compliance with our petition."* And what came out of these men, who were eminently free without patriotism, because without national independence? (which eminent freedom, however, Pliny himself, in the very next sentence, styles the shadow and *residuum*

* Lib. VIII. Ep. 24.—*Ed.*

of liberty.)* While they were intense patriots, they were the benefactors of all mankind, legislators for the very nation that afterwards subdued and enslaved them. When, therefore, they became pure cosmopolites, and no partial affections interrupted their philanthropy, and when yet they retained their country, their language, and their arts, what noble works, what mighty discoveries may we not expect from them? If the applause of a little city, the first-rate town of a country not much larger than Yorkshire, and the encouragement of a Pericles, produced a Phidias, a Sophocles, and a constellation of other stars scarcely inferior in glory, what will not the applause of the world effect, and the boundless munificence of the world's imperial masters? Alas! no Sophocles appeared, no Phidias was born; individual genius fled with national independence, and the best products were cold and laborious copies of what their fathers had thought and invented in grandeur and majesty. At length nothing remained, but dastardly and cunning slaves, who avenged their own ruin and degradation by assisting to degrade and ruin their conquerors; and the golden harp of their divine language remained only as the frame on which priests and monks spun their dirty cobwebs of sophistry and superstition!

If then in order to be men we must be patriots, and patriotism can not exist without national independence, we need no new or particular code of morals to justify us in placing and preserving our country in that relative situation which is most favorable to its independence. But the true patriot is aware that this object is not to be accomplished by a system of general conquest, such as was pursued by Philip of Macedon and his son, nor yet by the political annihilation of the one state, which happens to be its most formidable rival;—the unwise measure recommended by Cato, and carried into effect by the Romans in the instance of Carthage. Not by the latter;—for rivalry between two nations conduces to the independence of both, calls forth or fosters all the virtues by which national security is maintained;—and still less by the former; for the victor nation itself must at length, by the very extension of its own conquests, sink into a mere province; nay, it will most probably become the most abject portion of the empire, and the most cruelly oppressed, both because it will be

* *Quibus reliquam umbram et residuum libertatis nomen eripere, durum, ferum, barbarumque est.—Ib.*—Ed.

more feared and suspected by the common tyrant, and because it will be the sink and centre of his luxury and corruption. Even in cases of actual injury and just alarm the patriot sets bounds to the reprisal of national vengeance, and contents himself with such securities as are compatible with the welfare, though not with the ambitious projects of the nation, the aggressions of which had given the provocation: for as patriotism inspires no superhuman faculties, neither can it dictate any conduct which would require such. He is too conscious of his own ignorance of the future, to dare extend his calculations into remote periods; nor, because he is a statesman, arrogates to himself the cares of Providence and the government of the world. How does he know, but that the very independence and consequent virtues of the nation, which in the anger of cowardice he would fain reduce to absolute insignificance, and rob even of its ancient name, may in some future emergence be the destined guardians of his own country; and that the power which now alarms, may hereafter protect and preserve it? The experience of history authorizes to believe not only in the possibility, but even the probability, of such an event. An American commander,* who has deserved and received the highest honors which his grateful country, through her assembled representatives, could bestow upon him, once said to me with a sigh: In an evil hour for my country did the French and Spaniards abandon Louisiana to the United States. We were not sufficiently a country before: and should we ever be mad enough to drive the English from Canada and her other North American provinces, we shall soon cease to be a country at all. Without local attachment, without national honor, we shall resemble a swarm of insects that settle on the fruits of the earth to corrupt and consume them, rather than men who love and cleave to the land of their forefathers. After a shapeless anarchy and a series of civil wars, we shall at last be formed into many countries; unless the vices engendered in the process should demand further punishment, and we should previously fall beneath the despotism of some military adventurer, like a lion consumed by an inward disease, prostrate and helpless beneath the beak and talons of a vulture, or yet meaner bird of prey.†

* Decatur.—*Ed.*

† See Table Talk, VI. p. 398.—*Ed.*

ESSAY XIV.

"Ο, τι μὲν πρὸς τὸν τȣ̃ ὅλου πλοῦτον, μᾶλλον δὲ πρὸς τὶ φάντασμα πόλεως ἁπάσης, ὃ πανταχῇ καὶ οὐδαμῇ ἐϛὶ, φέρει μάθημα καὶ ἐπιτήδευμα, τοῦτο χρήσιμον καὶ σόφον τὶ δοξασθήσεται· τῶν δὲ ἄλλων καταγελᾷ ὁ πολιτικὸς. Ταύτην τὴν αἰτίαν χρὴ φάναι τοῦ μήτε ἄλλο καλὸν, μήτε τὰ πρὸς τὸν πόλεμον μεγαλοπρέπως ἀσκεῖν τὰς πόλεις, τῶν πολίτων μάλ' ἐνίοτε οὐκ ἀφυῶν ὄντων δυστυχούντων γε μήν. Πῶς λέγεις; Πῶς μὲν οὖν αὐτοὺς οὐ λέγοιμ' ἂν παράπαν δυστυχεῖς, οἷς γε ἀνάγκη διὰ βίου πεινῶσι τὴν ψυχὴν ἀεὶ τὴν αὐτῶν διεξελθεῖν.

Plato.*

Whatever study or doctrine bears upon the wealth of the whole, say rather on a certain phantom of a state in the whole, which is everywhere and nowhere, this shall be deemed most useful and wise; and all else is the state-craftsman's scorn. This we dare pronounce the cause why nations torpid on their dignity in general, conduct their wars so little in a grand and magnanimous spirit, while the citizens are too often wretched, though endowed with high capabilities by nature. How say you? Nay, how should I not call them wretched, who are under the unrelenting necessity of wasting away their life in the mere search after the means of supporting it?

In the preceding essay I treated of what may be wisely desired in respect to our foreign relations. The same sanity of mind will the true patriot display in all that regards the internal prosperity of his country. He will reverence not only whatever tends to make the component individuals more happy, and more worthy of happiness; but likewise whatever tends to bind them more closely together as a people;—that as a multitude of parts and functions make up one human body, so the whole multitude of his countrymen may, by the visible and invisible influences of religion, language, laws, customs, and the reciprocal dependence and re-action of trade and agriculture, be organized into one body politic. But much as he desires to see all become a whole, he

* *De Legibus*, viii.—The Greek is chiefly taken from the beginning of this book of the Laws; but it is not taken consecutively; some of the expressions are from other parts of Plato, and some seem to be the Author's own.—*Ed.*

places limits even to this wish, and abhors that system of policy which would blend men into a state by the dissolution of all those virtues which make them happy and estimable as individuals. Sir James Steuart, after stating the case of the vine-dresser, who is proprietor of a bit of land, on which grain (enough, and no more) is raised for himself and family, and who provides for their other wants, of clothing, salt, &c. by his extra labor as a vine-dresser, observes :—'From this example we discover the difference between agriculture exercised as a trade, and as a direct means of subsisting. We have the two species in the vine-dresser: he labors the vineyard as a trade, and his spot of ground for subsistence. We may farther conclude, that as to the last part he is only useful to himself; but as to the first, he is useful to the society and becomes a member of it; consequently were it not for his trade the state would lose nothing, although the vine-dresser and his land were both swallowed up by an earthquake.'*

Now this contains the sublime philosophy of the sect of economists. They worship a kind of nonentity under the different words, the state, the whole, the society, and so on, and to this idol they make bloodier sacrifices than ever the Mexicans did to Tescalipoca. All, that is, each and every sentient being in a given tract, are made diseased and vicious, in order that each may become useful to all, or the state, or the society,—that is, to the word, all, the word state, or the word society. The absurdity may be easily perceived by omitting the words relating to this idol—as for instance—in a former paragraph of the same (in most respects) excellent work: 'If it therefore happens that an additional number produced do no more than feed themselves, then I perceive no advantage gained from their production.'† What! No advantage gained by, for instance, ten thousand happy, intelligent, and immortal beings having been produced!—O yes! but no advantage to this society.—What is this society, this whole, this state? Is it any thing else but a word of convenience to express at once the aggregate of confederated individuals living in a certain district? Let the sum total of each man's happiness be supposed = 1000; and suppose ten thousand men produced, who neither made swords nor poison, nor found corn nor clothes for those who did—but who procured by their labor food and raiment for themselves, and for their children;—

* Polit. Econ. vol. i. c. 14.—*Ed.* † Ib.—*Ed.*

would not that society be richer by 10,000,000 parts of happiness? And think you it possible, that ten thousand happy human beings can exist together without increasing each other's happiness, or that it will not overflow into countless channels,* and diffuse itself through the rest of the society?

The poor vine-dresser rises from sweet sleep, worships his Maker, goes with his wife and children into his little plot—returns to his hut at noon, and eats the produce of the similar labor of a former day. Is he useful? No, not yet. Suppose then, that during the remaining hours of the day he endeavored to provide for his moral and intellectual appetites, by physical experiments and philosophical research, by acquiring knowledge for himself and communicating it to his wife and children. Would he be useful then? He useful! 'The state would lose nothing although the vine-dresser and his land were both swallowed up by an earthquake!' Well then, instead of devoting the latter half of each day to his closet, his laboratory, or to neighborly conversation, suppose he goes to the vineyard, and from the ground which would maintain in health, virtue, and wisdom, twenty of his fellow-creatures, helps to raise a quantity of liquor that will disease the bodies and debauch the souls of a hundred—Is he useful now? O yes! a very useful man, and a most excellent citizen.†

In what then does the law between state and state differ from that between man and man? For hitherto we seem to have discovered no variation. The law of nations is the law of common honesty, modified by the circumstances in which states differ from individuals. According to my best understanding, the difference may be reduced to this one point: that the influence of example in any extraordinary case, as the possible occasion of an action apparently like, though in reality very different, is of

* Well, and in the spirit of genuine philosophy, does the poet describe such beings as men

> Who being innocent do for that cause
> Bestir them in good deeds ———
>
> *Wordsworth.*

Providence, by the ceaseless activity which it has implanted in our nature, has sufficiently guarded against an innocence without virtue.

† So in Jollie's and Hutchinson's History of Cumberland, the writer speaks of a small estatesman, bred to a rural life, who can not betake himself from an indolent habit to manufacturing and labor!—*Introd.* p. 39, 1830.

considerable importance in the moral calculations of an individual; but of little, if any, in those of a nation. The reasons are evident. In the first place, in cases concerning which there can be any dispute between an honest man and a true patriot, the circumstances, which at once authorize and discriminate the measure, are so marked and peculiar and notorious, that it is incapable of being drawn into a precedent by any other state under dissimilar circumstances; except perhaps as a mere pretext for an action, which had been predetermined without reference to this authority, and which would have taken place, though it had never existed. But if so strange a thing should happen, as a second coincidence of the same circumstances, or of circumstances sufficiently similar to render the prior measure a fair precedent; then, if the one action was justifiable, so will the other be; and without any reference to the former, which in this case may be useful as a light, but can not be requisite as an authority. Secondly, in extraordinary cases it is ridiculous to suppose that the conduct of states will be determined by example. We know that they neither will, nor in the nature of things can, be determined by any other consideration but that of the imperious circumstances, which render a particular measure advisable. But lastly, and more important than all, individuals are and must be under positive laws: and so very great is the advantage which results from the regularity of legal decisions, and their consequent capability of being foreknown and relied upon, that equity itself must sometimes be sacrificed to it. For the very letter of a positive law is part of its spirit. But states neither are, nor can be, under positive laws. The only fixed part of the law of nations is the spirit: the letter of the law consists wholly in the circumstances to which the spirit of the law is applied. It is mere puerile declamation to rail against a country, as having imitated the very measures for which it had most blamed its ambitious enemy, if that enemy had previously changed all the relative circumstances which had existed for him, and therefore rendered his conduct iniquitous; but which, having been removed, however iniquitously, can not without absurdity be supposed any longer to control the measures of an innocent nation, necessitated to struggle for its own safety; especially when the measures in question were adopted for the very purpose of restoring those circumstances.

There are times when it would be wise to regard patriotism as a light that is in danger of being blown out, rather than as a fire which needs to be fanned by the winds of party spirit. There are times when party spirit, without any unwonted excess, may yet become faction; and though in general not less useful than natural in a free government, may under particular emergencies prove fatal to freedom itself. I trust I am writing to those who think with me, that to have blackened a ministry, however strong or rational our dislike may be of the persons who compose it, is a poor excuse and a miserable compensation for the crime of unnecessarily blackening the character of our country. Under this conviction, I request my reader to cast his eye back on my last argument, and then to favor me with his patient attention while I attempt at once to explain its purport and to show its cogency.

Let us transport ourselves in fancy to the age and country of the patriarchs, or, if the reader prefers it to some small colony uninfluenced by the mother country, which has not organized itself into a state, or agreed to acknowledge any one particular governor. We will suppose this colony to consist of from twenty to thirty households or separate establishments, differing greatly from each other in the number of retainers and in extent of possessions. Each household, however, possesses its own domain, the least equally with the greatest, in full right; and its master is an independent sovereign within his own boundaries. This mutual understanding and tacit agreement we may well suppose to have been the gradual result of many feuds, which had produced misery to all and real advantage to none; and that the same sober and reflecting persons, dispersed through the different establishments, who had brought about this state of things, had likewise coincided in the propriety of some other prudent and humane regulations, which from the authority of these wise men on points, in which they were unanimous, and from the evident good sense of the rules themselves, were acknowledged throughout the whole colony, though they were never voted into a formal law, though the determination of the cases, to which these rules were applicable, had not been intrusted to any recognized judge, nor their enforcement delegated to any particular magistrate. Of these virtual laws this, we may safely conclude, would be the chief: that as no man ought to interfere in the affairs of another against his will, so if any master of a household, instead of occupying himself with the improvement of his own fields and flocks, or with the better regulation of his own establishment, should be foolish and wicked enough to employ his children and servants in breaking down the fences and taking possession of the lands and property of a fellow-colonist, or in turning the head of the family out of his house, and forcing those that remained to acknowledge himself as their governor instead, and to obey whomever he might please to appoint as his deputy —it would then become the duty and the interest of the other colonists to join against the aggressor, and to do all in their power to prevent him from accomplishing his bad purposes, or to compel him to make restitution and compensation. The mightier the aggressor, and the weaker the injured party, the more cogent would the motive become for restraining the one and protecting the other. For it would be plain that he who was suffered to overpower, one by one, the weaker proprietors, and render the members of their establishment subservient to his will, must soon become an overmatch for those who were formerly his equals; and the mightiest would differ from the meanest only by being the last victim.

This allegoric fable faithfully portrays the law of nations and the balance of power among the European states. Let us proceed with it in the form of history. In the second or third generation the proprietors too generally disregarded the good old opinion, that what injured any could be of real advantage to none; and treated those, who still professed it, as fit only to instruct children in their catechism. By the avarice of some, the cowardice of others, and by the corruption and want of foresight in the greater part, the former state of things had been completely changed, and the tacit compact set at naught, the general acknowledgment of which had been so instrumental in producing this state and in preserving it, as long as it lasted. The stronger had preyed on the weaker, whose wrongs, however, did not remain long unavenged. For the same selfishness and blindness to the future, which had induced the wealthy to trample on the rights of the poorer proprietors, prevented them from assisting each other effectually, when they were themselves attacked, one after the other, by the most powerful of all; and from a concurrence of circumstances attacked so successfully, that of the whole colony few remained, that were not, directly or indirectly, the creatures and dependents of one overgrown establishment. Say rather, of its new master, an adventurer whom chance and poverty had brought thither, and who in better times would have been employed in the swine-yard, or the slaughter-house, from his moody temper and his aversion to all the arts that tended to improve either the land or those that were to be maintained by its produce. He was however eminent for other qualities, which were still better suited to promote his power among those degenerate colonists: for he feared neither God nor his own conscience. The most solemn oaths could not bind him; the most deplorable calamities could not awaken his pity; and when others were asleep, he was either brooding over some scheme of robbery and murder, or with a part of his banditti actually employed in laying waste his neighbor's fences, or in undermining the walls of their houses. His natural cunning, undistracted by any honest avocations, and meeting with no obstacle either in his head or heart, and above all, having been quickened and strengthened by constant practice and favored by the times with all conceivable opportunities, ripened at last into a surprising genius for oppression and tyranny: and, as we must distinguish him by some name, we will call him Misetes.* The only estate, which remained able to bid defiance to this common enemy, was that of Pamphilus,† superior to Misetes in wealth, and his equal in strength; though not in the power of doing mischief, and still less in the wish. Their characters were indeed perfectly contrasted: for it may be truly said, that throughout the whole colony there was not a single establishment which did not owe some of its best buildings, the increased produce of its fields, its improved implements of industry, and the general more decent appearance of its members, to the information given and the encouragements afforded by Pamphilus and those of his household. Whoever raised more than they wanted for their own establishment, were sure to find a ready purchaser in Pamphilus, and oftentimes for articles which they had themselves been before accustomed to regard as worthless, or even as nuisances; and they received in return things necessary or agreeable, and always in one respect at least useful, that they roused the purchaser to industry and its accompanying virtues. In this

* Bonaparte.—*Ed.* † England.—*Ed.*

intercommunion all were benefited : for the wealth of Pamphilus was increased by the increasing industry of his fellow-colonists, and their industry needed the support and encouraging influences of Pamphilus's capital. To this good man and his estimable household Misetes bore the most implacable hatred, and had publicly sworn that he would root him out ; the only sort of oath which he was not likely to break by any want of will or effort on his own part.

But fortunately for Pamphilus, his main property consisted of one compact estate divided from Misetes and the rest of the colony by a wide and dangerous river, with the exception of one small plantation which belonged to an independent proprietor whom we will name Lathrodacnus ;* a man of no influence in the colony, but much respected by Pamphilus. They were indeed relations by blood originally, and afterwards by intermarriages ; and it was to the power and protection of Pamphilus that Lathrodacnus owed his independence and prosperity, amid the general distress and slavery of the other proprietors. Not less fortunately did it happen, that the means of passing the river were possessed exclusively by Pamphilus and his above-mentioned kinsman ; and not only the boats themselves, but all the means of constructing and navigating them. As the very existence of Lathrodacnus, as an independent colonist, had no solid ground but in the strength and prosperity of Pamphilus ; and as the interests of the one in no respect interfered with those of the other ; Pamphilus for a considerable time remained without any anxiety, and looked on the river-craft of Lathrodacnus with as little alarm, as on those of his own establishment. It did not disquiet him, that Lathrodacnus had remained neutral in the quarrel. Nay, though many advantages, which in peaceful times would have belonged to Pamphilus, were now transferred to his neighbor, and had more than doubled the extent and profit of his concern, Pamphilus, instead of repining at this, was glad that some good at least to some one came out of the general evil. Great then was his surprise, when he discovered, that without any conceivable reason Lathrodacnus had employed himself in building and collecting a very unusual number of such boats, as were of no use to him in his traffic, but designed exclusively as ferry-boats ; and what was still stranger and more

* Denmark.—*Ed.*

alarming, that he chose to keep these in a bay on the other side of the river, opposite to the one small plantation, along-side of Pamphilus's estate, from which plantation Lathrodacnus derived the materials for building them. Willing to believe this conduct a transient whim of his neighbor's, occasioned partly by his vanity, and partly by envy (to which latter passion the want of a liberal education, and the not sufficiently comprehending the grounds of his own prosperity, had rendered him subject), Pamphilus contented himself for a while with urgent yet friendly remonstrances. The only answer, which Lathrodacnus vouchsafed to return, was, that by the law of the colony, which Pamphilus had made so many professions of revering, every proprietor was an independent sovereign within his own boundaries; that the boats were his own, and the opposite shore, to which they were fastened, part of a field which belonged to him; and, in short, that Pamphilus had no right to interfere with the management of his property, which, trifling as it might be, compared with that of Pamphilus, was no less sacred by the laws of the colony. To this uncourteous rebuff Pamphilus replied with a fervent wish, that Lathrodacnus could with more propriety have appealed to a law, as still subsisting, which, he well knew, had been effectually annulled by the unexampled tyranny and success of Misetes, together with the circumstances which had given occasion to the law, and made it wise and practicable. He further urged, that this law was not made for the benefit of any one man, but for the common safety and advantage of all:—that it was absurd to suppose that either he (Pamphilus) or Lathrodacnus himself, or any other proprietor, ever did or could acknowledge this law in the sense that it was to survive the very circumstances, of which it was the mere reflex. Much less could they have ever tacitly assented to it, if they had ever understood it as authorizing one neighbor to endanger the absolute ruin of another, who had perhaps fifty times the property to lose, and perhaps ten times the number of souls to answer for, and yet forbidding the injured person to take any steps in his own defence; and lastly, that this law gave no right without imposing a corresponding duty. Therefore if Lathrodacnus insisted on the rights given him by the law, he ought at the same time to perform the duties which it required, and join heart and hand with Pamphilus in his endeavors to defend his independence, to restore the former state of the colony, and with this to re-enforce the old law in opposition to Misetes who had enslaved the one and set at naught the other. So ardently was Pamphilus attached to the law, that excepting his own safety and independence there was no price which he would not pay, no sacrifice which he would not make for its restoration. His reverence for the very memory of the law was such, that the mere appearance of transgressing it would be a heavy affliction to him. In the hope therefore of gaining from the avarice of Lathrodacnus that consent which he could not obtain from his justice or neighborly kindness, he offered to give him in full right a plantation ten times the value of all his boats, and yet, whenever the colony should once more be settled, to restore the boats; if he would only permit Pamphilus to secure them during the present state of things, on his side of the river, retaining whatever he really wanted for the passage of his own household.

To all these persuasions and entreaties Lathrodacnus turned a deaf ear; and Pamphilus remained agitated and undetermined, till at length he received certain intelligence that Lathrodacnus had called a council of the chief members of his establishment, in consequence of the threats of Misetes, that he would treat him as the friend and ally of Pamphilus, if he did not declare himself his enemy. Partly for the sake of a large meadow belonging to him on the other side of the river which it was not easy to secure from the tyrant, but still more from envy and the irritable temper of a proud inferior, Lathrodacnus, and with him the majority of his advisers (though to the great discontent of the few wise heads among them) settled it finally that if he should be again pressed on this point by Misetes, he would join him and commence hostilities against his old neighbor and kinsman. It is indeed but too probable that he had long brooded over this scheme: for to what other end could he have strained his income, and over-worked his servants in building and fitting up such a number of passage-boats? As soon as this information was received by Pamphilus, and this from a quarter which it was impossible for him to discredit, he obeyed the dictates of self-preservation, took possession of the passage-boats by force, and brought them over to his own grounds; but without any further injury to Lathrodacnus, and still urging him to accept a compensation and continue in that amity which was so manifestly their common interest. Instantly a great outcry was raised against Pamphilus, who was charged in the bitterest terms with having first abused Misetes, and then imitated him in his worst acts of violence. In the calmness of a good conscience Pamphilus contented himself with the following reply: "Even so—if I were out on a shooting party with a Quaker for my companion, and saw coming on toward us an old footpad and murderer, who had made known his intention of killing me wherever he might meet me; and if my companion the Quaker would neither give me up his gun, nor even discharge it as (we will suppose) I had just before unfortunately discharged my own; if he would neither promise to assist me nor even promise to make the least resistance to the robber's attempt to disarm himself—you might call me a robber for wresting this gun from my companion, though for no other purpose but that I might at least do for myself what he ought to have done, but would not do either for or with me! Even so, and as plausibly, you might exclaim, O the hypocrite Pamphilus! Who has not been deafened with his complaints against robbers and footpads? and lo! he himself has turned footpad, and commenced by robbing his peaceful and unsuspecting companion of his double-barrelled gun!"

It is the business of The Friend to lay down principles, not to make the applications of them to particular, much less to recent cases. If any such there be to which these principles are fairly applicable, the reader is no less master of the facts than the writer of the present essay. If not, the principles remain; and I have finished the task which the plan of this work imposed on me, of proving the identity of international law and the law of morality in spirit, and the reasons of their difference in practice, in those extreme cases in which alone they have been allowed to differ.

POSTSCRIPT.

The preceding essay has more than its natural interest for me from the abuse, which it brought down on me as the defender of the attack on Copenhagen, and the seizure of the Danish fleet. The odium of the measure rested wholly on the commencement of hostilities without a previous declaration of war. Now it is remarkable, that in a work published many years before this event, Professor Beck had made this very point the subject of a particular chapter in his admirable comments on the Law of Nations: and every one of the circumstances stated by him as forming an exception to the moral necessity of previous declaration of war concurred in the Copenhagen expedition. I need mention two only. First, by the act or acts, which provoked the expedition, the party attacked had knowingly placed himself in a state of war. Let A stand for the Danish, B for the British government. A had done that which he himself was fully aware would produce immediate hostilities on the part of B, the moment it came to the knowledge of the latter. The act itself was a waging of war against B on the part of A. B therefore was the party attacked; and common sense dictates, that to resist and baffle an aggression requires no proclamation to justify it. I perceive a dagger aimed at my back, in consequence of a warning given me, just time enough to prevent the blow, knock the assassin down, and disarm him: and he reproaches me with treachery, because forsooth I had not sent him a challenge! Secondly, when the object which justifies and necessitates the war would be frustrated by the proclamation. For neither state nor individual can be presumed to have given either a formal or a tacit assent to any such modification of a positive right, as would suspend and virtually annul the right itself;—the right of self-preservation, for instance. This second exception will often depend on the existence of the first, and must always receive additional strength and clearness from it. That both of these exceptions appertained to the case in question, is now notorious. But at the time I found it necessary to publish the following comment, which I now adapt to The Friend, as illustrative of the fundamental principle of public justice; namely, that personal and national morality, ever one and the same, dictate the same measures under the same circumstances, and different measures only as far as the circumstances are different.

As my limits will not allow me to do more in the second, or ethical, section of The Friend, than to propose and develop my own system, without controverting the systems of others, I shall therefore devote the essay, which follows this postscript, to the consideration of the question: How far is the moral nature of an action constituted by its individual circumstances?

It was once said to me, when the Copenhagen affair was in dispute, "You do not see the enormity, because it is an affair between state and state: conceive a similar case between man and man, and you would both see and abhor it." Now, I was neither defending nor attacking the measure itself. My arguments were confined to the grounds which had been taken both in the arraigning of that measure and in its defence, because I thought both equally untenable. I was not enough master of facts to form a decisive opinion on the enterprise, even for my own mind; but I had no hesitation in affirming, that the principles, on which it was defended in the legislature, appeared to me fitter objects of indignant reprobàtion than the act itself. This having been premised, I replied to the assertion above stated, by asserting the direct contrary; namely, that were a similar case conceived between man and man, the severest arraigners of the measure would, on their grounds, find nothing to blame in it. How was I to prove this assertion? Clearly, by imagining some case between individuals living in the same relations toward each other, in which the several states of Europe exist or existed. My allegory, therefore, so far from being a disguise, was a necessary part of the main argument, a case in point, to prove the identity of the law of nations with the law of conscience. We have only to conceive individuals in the same relations as states, in order to learn that the rules emanating from international law, differ from those of private honesty, solely through the difference of the circumstances.

But why did I not avow the application of the principle to the seizure of the Danish fleet? Because I did not possess sufficient evidence to prove to others, or even to decide for myself, that my principle was applicable to this particular act. In the case of Pamphilus and Lathrodacnus, the prudence and necessity of the measure were certain; and, this taken for granted, I showed its perfect rightfulness. In the affair of Copenhagen, I had no doubt of our right to do as we did, the necessity supposed, or at least the extreme prudence of the measure; it being taken for granted that there existed a motive adequate to the action, and that the action was an adequate means of realizing the purpose.

But this I was not authorized to take for granted in the real, as I had been in the imaginary, case. I saw many reasons for the affirmative, and many for the negative. For the former, the certainty of a hostile design on the part of the Danes, the alarming state of Ireland, that vulnerable heel of the British Achilles, and the immense difference between military and naval superiority. Our naval power collectively might have defied that of the whole world; but it was widely scattered, and a combined operation from the Baltic, Holland, Brest, and Lisbon, might easily bring together a fleet double to that which we could have assembled against it during the short time that might be necessary to convey thirty or forty thousand men to Ireland. On the other hand, it seemed equally clear that Bonaparte needed sailors rather than ships; and that we took the ships and left him the Danish sailors, whose presence in the fleet at Antwerp turned the scale, perhaps, in favor of the worse than disastrous expedition to Walcheren.

But I repeat, that I had no concern with the measure itself; but only with the grounds or principles on which it had been attacked or defended. Those who attacked it declared that a right had been violated by us, and that no motive could justify such violation, however imperious that motive might be. In opposition to such reasoners, I proved, that no such right existed, or is deducible either from international law or the law of private morality. Those again who defended the seizure of the Danish fleet, conceded that it was a violation of right; but affirmed, that such violation was justified by the urgency of the motive. It was asserted (as I have before noticed in the introduction to the subject) that national policy can not in all cases be subordinated to the laws of morality; in other words, that a government may act with injustice, and yet remain blameless. To prove this assertion as groundless and unnecessary as it is tremendous, formed the chief object of the whole disquisition. I trust, then, that my candid judges will rest satisfied that it is not only my profession and pretext, but my constant plan and actual intention, to establish principles; that I refer to particular facts for no other purpose than that of giving illustration and interest to those principles; and that to invent principles with a view to particular cases, whether with the motive of attacking or defending a transitory cabinet, is a baseness which will scarcely be attributed to The Friend by any one who understands the work, even though the suspicion should not have been precluded by a knowledge of the author.

ESSAY XV.

Ja, ich bin der Atheist und Gottlose, der einer imaginären Berechnungslehre, einer blossen Einbildung von allgemeinen Folgen, die nie folgen können, zuwider—lügen will, wie Desdemona sterbend lag; lügen und betrügen will, wie der für Orest sich darstellende Pylades; Tempelraub unternehmen, wie David; ja, Aehren ausraufen am Sabbath, auch nur darum, weil mich hungert, und das Gesetz um des Menschen willen gemacht ist, nicht der Mensch um des Gesetzes willen.

Yes, I am that atheist, that godless person, who in opposition to an imaginary doctrine of calculation, to a mere ideal fabric of general consequences that can never be realized, would lie, as the dying Desdemona lied;* lie and deceive as Pylades when he personated Orestes; would commit sacrilege with David; yea and pluck ears of corn on the Sabbath, for no other reason than that I was fainting from lack of food, and that the law was made for man, and not man for the law. JACOBI'S LETTER TO FICHTE.

If there be no better doctrine,—I would add! Much and often have I suffered from having ventured to avow my doubts concerning the truth of certain opinions, which had been sanctified in the minds of my hearers by the authority of some reigning great name; even though, in addition to my own reasons, I had all the greatest names from the Reformation to the Revolution on my side. I could not, therefore, summon courage, without some previous pioneering, to declare publicly, that the principles of morality taught in the present work will be in direct opposition to the system of the late Dr. Paley. This confession I

* *Emilia.*—O who hath done
This deed?
Desd. Nobody; I myself; farewell;
Commend me to my kind lord.—O—farewell.
Othello.—You heard her say yourself, it was not I.
Emilia.—She said so; I must needs report the truth.
Othello.—She's, like a liar, gone to burning hell;
'twas I that killed her.
Emilia.—Oh! the more angel she!
Othello, Act v. scene 1.

should have deferred to a future time, if my opinions on the grounds of international morality had not been contradictory to a fundamental point in Paley's system of moral and political philosophy. I mean that chapter which treats of general consequences, as the chief and best criterion of the right or wrong of particular actions.* Now this doctrine I conceive to be neither tenable in reason nor safe in practice: and the following are the grounds of my opinion.

First; this criterion is purely ideal, and so far possesses no advantages over the former systems of morality; while it labors under defects, with which those are not justly chargeable. It is ideal: for it depends on, and must vary with, the notions of the individual, who, in order to determine the nature of an action, is to make the calculation of its general consequences. Here, as in all other calculation, the result depends on that faculty of the soul in the degrees of which men most vary from each other, and which is itself most affected by accidental advantages or disadvantages of education, natural talent, and acquired knowledge—the faculty, I mean, of foresight and systematic comprehension. But surely morality, which is of equal importance to all men, ought to be grounded, if possible, in that part of our nature which in all men may and ought to be the same,—in the conscience and the common sense. Secondly: this criterion confounds morality with law; and when the author adds, that in all probability the divine Justice will be regulated in the final judgment by a similar rule, he draws away the attention from the will, that is, from the inward motives and impulses which constitute the essence of morality, to the outward act; and thus changes the virtue commanded by the gospel into the mere legality, which was to be enlivened by it. One of the most persuasive, if not one of the strongest, arguments for a future state, rests on the belief, that although by the necessity of things our outward and temporal welfare must be regulated by our outward actions, which alone can be the objects and guides of human law, there must yet needs come a juster and more appropriate sentence hereafter, in which our intentions will be considered, and our happiness and misery made to accord with the grounds of our actions. Our fellow-creatures can only judge what we are by what we do; but in the eye of our Maker what we do is of no

* Moral and Political Philosophy. B. II. the first eight chapters.—*Ed.*

worth, except as it flows from what we are. Though the fig-tree should produce no visible fruit, yet if the living sap is in it, and if it has struggled to put forth buds and blossoms which have been prevented from maturing by inevitable contingencies of tempests or untimely frosts, the virtuous sap will be accounted as fruit; and the curse of barrenness will light on many a tree from the boughs of which hundreds have been satisfied, because the omniscient judge knows that the fruits were threaded to the boughs artificially by the outward working of base fear and selfish hopes, and were neither nourished by the love of God or of man, nor grew out of the graces engrafted on the stock by religion. This is not, indeed, all that is meant in the Apostle's use of the word, faith, as the sole principle of justification, but it is included in his meaning, and forms an essential part of it; and I can conceive nothing more groundless, than the alarm, that this doctrine may be prejudicial to outward utility and active well-doing. To suppose that a man should cease to be beneficent by becoming benevolent, seems to me scarcely less absurd, than to fear that a fire may prevent heat, or that a perennial fountain may prove the occasion of drought. Just and generous actions may proceed from bad motives, and both may, and often do, originate in parts, and, as it were, fragments of our nature. A lascivious man may sacrifice half his estate to rescue his friend from prison, for he is constitutionally sympathetic, and the better part of his nature happened to be uppermost. The same man shall afterwards exert the same disregard of money in an attempt to seduce that friend's wife or daughter. But faith is a total act of the soul: it is the whole state of the mind, or it is not at all; and in this consists its power, as well as its exclusive worth.

This subject is of such immense importance to the welfare of all men, and the understanding of it to the present tranquillity of many thousands at this time and in this country, that should there be one only of all my readers, who should receive conviction or an additional light from what is here written, I dare hope that a great majority of the rest would in consideration of that solitary effect think these paragraphs neither wholly uninteresting nor altogether without value. For this cause I will endeavor so to explain this principle, that it may be intelligible to the simplest capacity. The Apostle tells those who would substitute obedience for faith (addressing the man as obedience personified),

Know that *thou bearest not the root, but the root thee**—a sentence which, methinks, should have rendered all disputes concerning faith and good works impossible among those who profess to take the Scriptures for their guide. It would appear incredible, if the fact were not notorious, that two sects should ground and justify their opposition to each other, the one on the words of the Apostle, that we are justified by faith, that is, the inward and absolute ground of our actions; and the other on the declaration of Christ, that he will judge us according to our actions. As if an action could be either good or bad disjoined from its principle. As if it could be, in the Christian and only proper sense of the word, an action at all, and not rather a mechanic series of lucky or unlucky motions! Yet it may be well worth the while to show the beauty and harmony of these twin truths, or rather of this one great truth considered in its two principal bearings. God will judge each man before all men: consequently he will judge us relatively to man. But man knows not the heart of man; scarcely does any one know his own. There must therefore be outward and visible signs, by which men may be able to judge of the inward state; and thereby justify the ways of God to their own spirits, in the reward or punishment of themselves and their fellow-men. Now good works are these signs, and as such become necessary. In short there are two parties, God and the human race;—and both are to be satisfied. First, God, who seeth the root and knoweth the heart: therefore there must be faith, or the entire and absolute principle. Then man, who can judge only by the fruits: therefore that faith must bear fruits of righteousness, that principle must manifest itself by actions. But that which God sees, that alone justifies. What man sees, does in this life show that the justifying principle may be the root of the thing seen; but in the final judgment God's acceptance of these actions will show, that this principle actually was the root. In this world a good life is a presumption of a good man: his virtuous actions are the only possible, though

* Rom. xi. 18. But remember—a yet deeper and more momentous sense is conveyed in these words. Christ, the Logos, *Deitas objectiva*, centered humanity (always pre-existing in the *Pleroma*) in his life, and so became the light, that is, the reason of mankind. This eternal (that is, timeless) act he manifested in time—*σὰρξ ἐγένετο*, and dwelt among men, an individual man, in order that he might dwell in all his elect, as the root of the divine humanity in them.—1825.

still ambiguous, manifestations of his virtue: but the absence of a good life is not only a presumption, but a proof of the contrary, as long as it continues. Good works may exist without saving principles, and therefore can not contain in themselves the principle of salvation; but saving principles never did, never can, exist without good works. On a subject of such infinite importance, I have feared prolixity less than obscurity. Men often talk against faith, and make strange monsters in their imagination of those who profess to abide by the words of the Apostle interpreted literally: and yet in their ordinary feelings they themselves judge and act by a similar principle. For what is love without kind offices, wherever they are possible;—(and they are always possible, if not by actions commonly so called, yet by kind words, by kind looks; and, where even these are out of our power, by kind thoughts and fervent prayers)—yet what noble mind would not be offended, if he were supposed to value the serviceable offices equally with the love that produced them; or if he were thought to value the love for the sake of the services, and not the services for the sake of the love?

I return to the question of general consequences, considered as the criterion of moral actions. The admirer of Paley's system is required to suspend for a short time the objection, which, I doubt not, he has already made, that general consequences are stated by Paley as the criterion of the action, not of the agent. I will endeavor to satisfy him on this point, when I have completed my present chain of argument. It has been shown, that this criterion is no less ideal than that of any former system; that is, it is no less incapable of receiving any external experimental proof, compulsory on the understandings of all men, such as are the *criteria* exhibited in chemistry. Yet, unlike the elder systems of morality, it remains in the world of the senses, without deriving any evidence therefrom. The agent's mind is compelled to go out of itself in order to bring back conjectures, the probability of which will vary with the shrewdness of the individual. But this criterion is not only ideal; it is likewise imaginary. If we believe in a scheme of Providence, all actions alike work for good. There is not the least ground for supposing that the crimes of Nero were less instrumental in bringing about our present advantages, than the virtues of the Antonines. Lastly; the criterion is either nugatory or false. It is demonstrated, that the only real consequences can not be meant. The individual is to imagine what the general consequences would be, all other things remaining the same, if all men were to act as he is about to act. I scarcely need remind the reader, what a source of self-delusion and sophistry is here opened to a mind in a state of temptation. Will it not say to itself, I know that all men will not act so; and the immediate good consequences, which I shall obtain, are real, while the bad consequences are imaginary and improbable? When the foundations of morality have once been laid in outward consequences, it will be in vain to recall to the mind, what the consequences would be, were all men to reason in the same way: for the very excuse of this mind to itself is, that neither its action nor its reasoning is likely to have any consequences at all, its immediate object excepted. But suppose the mind in its sanest state. How can it possibly form a notion of the nature of an action considered as indefinitely multiplied, unless it has previously a distinct notion of the nature of the single action itself, which is the multiplicand? If I conceive a crown multiplied a hundred fold, the single crown enables me to understand what a hundred crowns are; but how can the notion hundred teach me what a crown is? For the crown substitute X. Y. or *abracadabra*, and my imagination may multiply it to infinity, yet remain as much at a loss as before. But if there be any means of ascertaining the action in and for itself, what further do we want? Would we give light to the sun, or look at our fingers through a telescope? The nature of every action is determined by all its circumstances: alter the circumstances and a similar set of motions may be repeated, but they are no longer the same or a similar action. What would a surgeon say, if he were advised not to cut off a limb, because if all men were to do the same, the consequences would be dreadful? Would not his answer be—"Whoever does the same under the same circumstances, and with the same motives, will do right; but if the circumstances and motives are different, what have I to do with it?" I confess myself unable to divine any possible use, or even meaning, in this doctrine of general consequences, unless it be, that in all our actions we are bound to consider the effect of our example, and to guard as much as possible against the hazard of their being misunderstood. I will not slaughter a lamb, or drown a litter of kittens, in the presence of my child of four years old, because the child can not understand my action, but will understand that his father has inflicted pain upon, and taken away life from, beings that had never offended him. All this is true, and no man in his senses ever thought otherwise. But methinks it is strange to state that as a criterion of morality, which is no more than an accessary aggravation of an action bad in its own nature, or a ground of caution as to the mode and time in which we are to do or suspend what is in itself good or innocent.

The duty of setting a good example is no doubt a most important duty; but the example is good or bad, necessary or unnecessary, accordingly as the action may be, which has a chance of being imitated. I once knew a small, but (in outward circumstances at least) respectable congregation, four fifths of whom professed that they went to church entirely for the example's sake; in other words to cheat each other and act a common lie! These rational Christians had not considered that example may increase the good or evil of an action, but can never constitute either. If it was a foolish thing to kneel when they were not inwardly praying, or to sit and listen to a discourse of which they believed little and cared nothing, they were setting a foolish example. Persons in their respectable circumstances do not think it necessary to clean shoes, that by their example they may encourage the shoe-black in continuing his occupation: and Christianity does not think so meanly of herself as to fear that the poor and afflicted will be a whit the less pious, though they should see reason to believe that those, who possessed the good things of the present life, were determined to leave all the blessings of the future for their more humble inferiors. If in this I have spoken with bitterness, let it be recollected that my subject is hypocrisy.

It is likewise fit, that in all our actions we should have considered how far they are likely to be misunderstood, and from superficial resemblances to be confounded with, and so appear to authorize, actions of a very different character. But if this caution be intended for a moral rule, the misunderstanding must be such as might be made by persons who are neither very weak nor very wicked. The apparent resemblances between the good action we were about to do and the bad one which might possibly be done in mistaken imitation of it, must be obvious; or that which makes them essentially different, must be subtle or recondite. For what is there which a wicked man blinded by his passions may not, and which a madman will not, misunderstand? It is ridiculous to frame rules of morality with a view to those who are fit objects only for the physician or the magistrate.

The question may be thus illustrated. At Florence there is an unfinished bust of Brutus, by Michel Angelo, under which a cardinal wrote the following distich:

Dum Bruti effigiem sculptor de marmore finxit,
In mentem sceleris venit, et abstinuit.

As the sculptor was forming the effigy of Brutus in marble, he recollected his act of guilt and refrained.

An English nobleman, indignant at this inscription, wrote immediately under it the following:

Brutum effinxisset sculptor, sed mente recursat
Multa viri virtus; sistit et obstupuit.

The sculptor would have framed a Brutus, but the vast and manifold virtue of the man flashed upon his thought: he stopped and remained in astonished admiration.

Now which is the nobler and more moral sentiment, the Italian cardinal's, or the English nobleman's? The cardinal would appeal to the doctrine of general consequences, and pronounce the death of Cæsar a murder, and Brutus an assassin. For (he would say) if one man may be allowed to kill another because he thinks him a tyrant, religious or political frenzy may stamp the name of tyrant on the best of kings: regicide will be justified under the pretence of tyrannicide, and Brutus be quoted as authority for the Clements and Ravailliacs.* From kings it may pass to generals and statesmen, and from these to any man whom an enemy or enthusiast may pronounce unfit to live. Thus we may have a cobbler of Messina in every city, and bravos in our streets as common as in those of Naples, with the name of Brutus on their stilettos.

The Englishman would commence his answer by commenting on the words "because he thinks him a tyrant." No! he would reply, not because the patriot thinks him a tyrant; but because

* Jacques Clement, a monk, who stabbed Henry III. of France, and François Ravailliac, an attorney, the well-known assassin of Henry IV.—*Ed.*

he knows him to be so, and knows likewise, that the vilest of his slaves can not deny the fact, that he has by violence raised himself above the laws of his country—because he knows that all good and wise men equally with himself abhor the fact. If there be no such state as that of being broad awake, or no means of distinguishing it when it exists; if because men sometimes dream that they are awake, it must follow that no man, when awake, can be sure that he is not dreaming; if because a hypochondriac is positive that his legs are cylinders of glass, all other men are to learn modesty, and cease to be certain that their legs are legs; what possible advantage can your criterion of general consequences possess over any other rule of direction? If no man can be sure that what he thinks a robber with a pistol at his breast demanding his purse, may not be a good friend inquiring after his health; or that a tyrant (the son of a cobbler perhaps, who at the head of a regiment of perjured traitors, has driven the representatives of his country out of the senate at the point of the bayonet, subverted the constitution which had trusted, enriched, and honored him, trampled on the laws which before God and man he had sworn to obey, and finally raised himself above all law) may not, in spite of his own and his neighbors' knowledge of the contrary, be a lawful king, who has received his power, however despotic it may be, from the kings his ancestors, who exercises no other power than what had been submitted to for centuries, and been acknowledged as the law of the country; on what ground can you possibly expect less fallibility, or a result more to be relied upon, in the same man's calculation of *your* general consequences? Would *he*, at least, find any difficulty in converting your criterion into an authority for his act? What should prevent a man, whose perceptions and judgments are so strangely distorted, from arguing, that nothing is more devoutly to be wished for, as a general consequence, than that every man, who by violence places himself above the laws of his country, should in all ages and nations be considered by mankind as placed by his own act out of the protection of law, and be treated by them as any other noxious wild beast would be? Do you think it necessary to try adders by a jury? Do you hesitate to shoot a mad dog, because it is not in your power to have him first tried and condemned at the Old Bailey? On the other hand, what consequence can be conceived more detestable, than one which would set a bounty on the most enormous crime in human nature, and establish it as a law of religion and morality that the accomplishment of the most atrocious guilt invests the perpetrator with impunity, and renders his person forever sacred and inviolable? For madmen and enthusiasts what avail your moral criterions? But as to your Neapolitan bravos, if the act of Brutus who

> In pity to the general wrong of Rome,
> Slew his best lover for the good of Rome,

authorized by the laws of his country, in manifest opposition to all selfish interest, in the face of the senate, and instantly presenting himself and his cause first to that senate, and then to the assembled commons, by them to stand acquitted or condemned—if such an act as this, with all its vast outjutting circumstances of distinction, can be confounded by any mind, not frantic, with the crime of a cowardly skulking assassin who hires out his dagger for a few crowns to gratify a hatred not his own, or even with the deed of that man who makes a compromise between his revenge and his cowardice, and stabs in the dark the enemy whom he dared not meet in the open field, or summon before the laws of his country—what actions can be so different, that they may not be equally confounded? The ambushed soldier must not fire his musket, lest his example should be quoted by the villain who, to make sure of his booty, discharges his piece at the unsuspicious passenger from behind a hedge. The physician must not administer a solution of arsenic to the leprous, lest his example should be quoted by professional poisoners. If no distinction, full and satisfactory to the conscience and common sense of mankind be afforded by the detestation and horror excited in all men, (even in the meanest and most vicious, if they are not wholly monsters) by the act of the assassin, contrasted with the fervent admiration felt by the good and wise in all ages when they mention the name of Brutus; contrasted with the fact that the honor or disrespect with which that name was spoken of, became an historic criterion of a nobler or a base age; and if it is in vain that our own hearts answer to the question of the poet—

> Is there among the adamantine spheres,
> Wheeling unshaken through the boundless void,
> Aught that with half such majesty can fill
> The human bosom, as when Brutus rose

Refulgent from the stroke of Cæsar's fate
Amid the crowd of patriots; and his arm
Aloft extending, like eternal Jove,
When guilt brings down the thunder, call'd aloud
On Tully's name, and shook his crimson sword,
And bade the father of his country, hail!
For lo! the tyrant prostrate on the dust
And Rome again is free!——————*

If, I say, all this be fallacious and insufficient, can we have any firmer reliance on a cold ideal calculation of imaginary general consequences, which, if they were general, could not be consequences at all: for they would be effects of the frenzy or frenzied wickedness, which alone could confound actions so utterly dissimilar? No! (would the ennobled descendant of our Russells or Sidneys conclude). No! calumnious bigot! never yet did a human being become an assassin from his own or the general admiration of the hero Brutus; but I dare not warrant, that villains might not be encouraged in their trade of secret murder, by finding their own guilt attributed to the Roman patriot, and might not conclude, that if Brutus be no better than an assassin, an assassin can be no worse than Brutus.

I request that the preceding be not interpreted as my own judgment on tyrannicide. I think with Machiavel and with Spinosa, for many and weighty reasons assigned by those philosophers, that it is difficult to conceive a case, in which a good man would attempt tyrannicide, because it is difficult to conceive one, in which a wise man would recommend it. In a small state, included within the walls of a single city, and where the tyranny is maintained by foreign guards, it may be otherwise; but in a nation or empire it is perhaps inconceivable, that the circumstances which made a tyranny possible, should not likewise render the removal of a tyrant useless. The patriot's sword may cut off the Hydra's head; but he possesses no brand to stanch the active corruption of the body, which is sure to re-produce a successor.

* Akenside. Pleasures of the Imagination, 2d ed. B. II. p. 361.—*Ed.*

"—— and shook the crimson sword
Of justice in his rapt, astonish'd eye,
And bade" &c.

So in the original. S. C.

I must now in a few words answer the objection to the former part of my argument (for to that part only the objection applies), namely, that the doctrine of general consequences was stated as the criterion of the action, not of the agent. I might answer, that the author himself had in some measure justified me in not noticing this distinction by holding forth the probability, that the Supreme Judge will proceed by the same rule. The agent may then safely be included in the action, if both here and hereafter the action only and its general consequences will be attended to. But my main ground of justification is, that the distinction itself is merely logical, not real and vital. The character of the agent is determined by his view of the action: and that system of morality is alone true and suited to human nature, which unites the intention and the motive, the warmth and the light, in one and the same act of mind. This alone is worthy to be called a moral principle. Such a principle may be extracted, though not without difficulty and danger, from the ore of the Stoic philosophy; but it is to be found unalloyed and entire in the Christian system, and is there called faith.*

ESSAY XVI.

THE following address was delivered at Bristol, in the month of February, 1795. The only omissions regard the names of persons; and I insert it here in support of the assertion made by me, in the beginning of Essay II. of this volume, and because this very address has been referred to in an infamous libel in proof of my former Jacobinism. Different as my present convictions are

* It may, perhaps, be not uninteresting to insert in this place a note which Mr. Coleridge wrote in his own copy of The Friend:—

'This last paragraph falls off from all the preceding. The reasoning is just, but it is dimly stated,—not brought out, nor urged to the point. Want of space was the original cause of this deficiency. The Friend appearing on stamped sheets, and the author having reached the sixteenth page in the treatment of the moral question, he was forced to compress the promised answer to the objection into the remainder of a single page;—and in the attempt slurred it over.' 22d June, 1829.—*Ed.*

on the subject of philosophical necessity, I have for this reason left the last paragraph unaltered.*

'Αεὶ γὰρ τῆς ἐλευθερίας ἐφίεμαι· πόλλα δὲ ἐν καὶ τοῖς φιλελευθέροις μισητὰ, ἀντελεύθερα.

For I am always a lover of liberty; but in those who would appropriate the title, I find too many points destructive of liberty and hateful to her genuine advocates.

Companies resembling the present will, from a variety of circumstances, consist chiefly of the zealous advocates for freedom. It will, therefore, be our endeavor, not so much to excite the torpid, as to regulate the feelings of the ardent: and above all, to evince the necessity of bottoming on fixed principles, that so we may not be the unstable patriots of passion or accident, nor hurried away by names of which we have not sifted the meaning, and by tenets of which we have not examined the consequences. The times are trying; and in order to be prepared against their difficulties, we should have acquired a prompt facility of adverting in all our doubts to some grand and comprehensive truth. In a deep and strong soil must that tree fix its roots, the height of which is to *reach to heaven, and the sight of it to the ends of all the earth.*

The example of France is indeed a warning to Britain. A nation wading to its rights through blood, and marking the track of freedom by devastation! Yet let us not embattle our feelings against our reason. Let us not indulge our malignant passions under the mask of humanity. Instead of railing with infuriate declamation against these excesses, we shall be more profitably employed in tracing them to their sources. French freedom is the beacon which if it guides to equality should show us likewise the dangers that throng the road.

The annals of the French revolution have recorded in letters of blood, that the knowledge of the few can not counteract the ignorance of the many; that the light of philosophy, when it is confined to a small minority, points out the possessors as the victims, rather than the illuminators, of the multitude. The pa-

* This speech, or lecture, was, with another on the then war with France, published in November, 1795, under the title *Conciones ad populum.* In this edition the author has made some alterations, but they are confined to the mere style.—*Ed.*

triots of France either hastened into the dangerous and gigantic error of making certain evil the means of contingent good, or were sacrificed by the mob, with whose prejudices and ferocity their unbending virtue forbade them to assimilate. Like Samson, the people were strong—like Samson, the people were blind. 'Those two massy pillars' of the temple of oppression, their monarchy and aristocracy,

> With horrible convulsion to and fro
> *They* tugg'd, *they* shook—till down they came and drew
> The whole roof after them with burst of thunder
> Upon the heads of all who sat beneath,
> Lords, ladies, captains, counsellors, *and* priests,
> Their choice nobility !*

The Girondists, who were the first republicans in power, were men of enlarged views and great literary attainments; but they seem to have been deficient in that vigor and daring activity, which circumstances made necessary. Men of genius are rarely either prompt in action or consistent in general conduct. Their early habits have been those of contemplative indolence; and the day-dreams, with which they have been accustomed to amuse their solitude, adapt them for splendid speculation, not temperate and practicable counsels. Brissot, the leader of the Gironde party, is entitled to the character of a virtuous man, and an eloquent speaker; but he was rather a sublime visionary, than a quick-eyed politician; and his excellences equally with his faults rendered him unfit for the helm in the stormy hour of revolution. Robespierre, who displaced him, possessed a glowing ardor that still remembered the end, and a cool ferocity that never either overlooked or scrupled the means. What this end was, is not known: that it was a wicked one, has by no means been proved. I rather think, that the distant prospect, to which he was travelling, appeared to him grand and beautiful; but that he fixed his eye on it with such intense eagerness as to neglect the foulness of the road. If, however, his first intentions were pure, his subsequent enormities yield us a melancholy proof, that it is not the character of the possessor which directs the power, but the power which shapes and depraves the character of the possessor. In Robespierre, its influence was assisted by the properties of his

* Samson Agonistes, with alterations in italics.—*Ed.*

disposition. Enthusiasm, even in the gentlest temper, will frequently generate sensations of an unkindly order. If we clearly perceive any one thing to be of vast and infinite importance to ourselves and all mankind, our first feelings impel us to turn with angry contempt from those, who doubt and oppose it. The ardor of undisciplined benevolence seduces us into malignity : and whenever our hearts are warm, and our objects great and excellent, intolerance is the sin that does most easily beset us. But this enthusiasm in Robespierre was blended with gloom, and suspiciousness, and inordinate vanity. His dark imagination was still brooding over supposed plots against freedom ;—to prevent tyranny he became a tyrant, and having realized the evils which he suspected, a wild and dreadful tyrant. And thus, his ear deafened to the whispers of conscience by the clamorous plaudits of the mob, he despotized in all the pomp of patriotism, and masqueraded on the bloody stage of revolution, a Caligula with the cap of liberty on his head.

It has been affirmed, and I believe with truth, that the system of terrorism, by suspending the struggles of contrariant factions, communicated an energy to the operations of the republic which had been hitherto unknown, and without which it could not have been preserved. The system depended for its existence on the general sense of its necessity, and when it had answered its end, it was soon destroyed by the same power that had given it birth—popular opinion. It must not however be disguised, that at all times, but more especially when the public feelings are wavy and tumultuous, artful demagogues may create this opinion : and they, who are inclined to tolerate evil as the means of contingent good, should reflect, that if the excesses of terrorism gave to the republic that efficiency and repulsive force which its circumstances made necessary, they likewise afforded to the hostile courts the most powerful support, and excited that indignation and horror which everywhere precipitated the subject into the designs of the ruler. Nor let it be forgotten that these excesses perpetuated the war in La Vendée, and made it more terrible, both by the accession of numerous partisans, who had fled from the persecution of Robespierre, and by inspiring the Chouans with fresh fury, and an unsubmitting spirit of revenge and desperation.

Revolutions are sudden to the unthinking only. Strange

rumblings and confused noises still precede these earthquakes and hurricanes of the moral world. The process of revolution in France has been dreadful, and should incite us to examine with an anxious eye the motives and manners of those, whose conduct and opinions seem calculated to forward a similar event in our own country. The oppositionists to "things as they are," are divided into many and different classes. To delineate them with an unflattering accuracy may be a delicate, but it is a necessary task, in order that we may enlighten, or at least be aware of, the misguided men who have enlisted under the banners of liberty, from no principles, or with bad ones: whether they be those, who

> admire they know not what,
> And know not whom, but as one leads to the other;—

or whether those,

> Whose end is private hate, not help to freedom,
> Adverse and turbulent when she would lead
> To virtue.

The majority of democrats appear to me to have attained that portion of knowledge in politics, which infidels possess in religion. I would by no means be supposed to imply that the objections of both are equally unfounded, but that they both attribute to the system which they reject, all the evils existing under it; and that both, contemplating truth and justice in the nakedness of abstraction, condemn constitutions and dispensations without having sufficiently examined the natures, circumstances, and capacities of their recipients.

The first class among the professed friends of liberty is composed of men, who unaccustomed to the labor of thorough investigation, and not particularly oppressed by the burthens of state, are yet impelled by their feelings to disapprove of its grosser depravities, and prepared to give an indolent vote in favor of reform. Their sensibilities not braced by the co-operation of fixed principles, they offer no sacrifices to the divinity of active virtue. Their political opinions depend with weathercock uncertainty on the winds of rumor, that blow from France. On the report of French victories they blaze into republicanism, at a tale of French excesses they darken into aristocrats. These dough-baked patriots are not, however, useless. This oscillation of political opinion will retard the day of revolution, and it will operate as a preventive to its excesses. Indecisiveness of character, though the effect of timidity, is almost always associated with benevolence.

Wilder features characterize the second class. Sufficiently possessed of natural sense to despise the priest, and of natural feeling to hate the oppressor, they listen only to the inflammatory harangues of some mad-headed enthusiast, and imbibe from them poison, not food; rage, not liberty. Unillumined by philosophy, and stimulated to a lust of revenge by aggravated wrongs, they would make the altar of freedom stream with blood, while the grass grew in the desolated halls of justice.

We contemplate those principles with horror. Yet they possess a kind of wild justice, well calculated to spread them among the grossly ignorant. To unenlightened minds, there are terrible charms in the idea of retribution, however savagely it be inculcated. The groans of the oppressor make fearful yet pleasant music to the ear of him, whose mind is darkness, and into whose soul the iron has entered.

This class, at present, is comparatively small—yet soon to form an overwhelming majority, unless great and immediate efforts are used to lessen the intolerable grievances of our poor brethren, and infuse into their sorely-wounded hearts the healing qualities of knowledge. For can we wonder that men should want humanity, who want all the circumstances of life that humanize? Can we wonder that with the ignorance of brutes, they should unite their ferocity? Peace and comfort be with these! But let us shudder to hear from men of dissimilar opportunities sentiments of similar revengefulness. The purifying alchemy of education may transmute the fierceness of an ignorant man into virtuous energy; but what remedy shall we apply to him whom plenty has not softened, whom knowledge has not taught benevolence? This is one among the many fatal effects which result from the want of fixed principles.

There is a third class among the friends of freedom, who possess not the wavering character of the first description, nor the ferocity last delineated. They pursue the interests of freedom steadily, but with narrow and self-centering views: they anticipate with exultation the abolition of privileged orders, and of acts that persecute by exclusion from the rights of citizenship. Whatever is above them they are most willing to drag down;

but every proposed alteration that would elevate their poorer brethren, they rank among the dreams of visionaries; as if there were any thing in the superiority of lord to gentleman so mortifying in the barrier, so fatal to happiness in the consequences, as the more real distinction of master and servant, of rich man and of poor. Wherein am I made worse by my ennobled neighbor? Do the childish titles of aristocracy detract from my domestic comforts, or prevent my intellectual acquisitions? But those institutions of society which should condemn me to the necessity of twelve hours' daily toil, would make my soul a slave, and sink the rational being in the mere animal. It is a mockery of our fellow-creatures' wrongs to call them equal in rights, when by the bitter compulsion of their wants we make them inferior to us in all that can soften the heart, or dignify the understanding. Let us not say that this is the work of time—that it is impracticable at present, unless we each in our individual capacities do strenuously and perseveringly endeavor to diffuse among our domestics those comforts and that illumination which far beyond all political ordinances are the true equalizers of men.

We turn with pleasure to the contemplation of that small but glorious band, whom we may truly distinguish by the name of thinking and disinterested patriots. These are the men who have encouraged the sympathetic passions till they have become irresistible habits, and made their duty a necessary part of their self-interest, by the long-continued cultivation of that moral taste which derives our most exquisite pleasures from the contemplation of possible perfection, and proportionate pain from the perception of existing depravity. Accustomed to regard all the affairs of man as a process, they never hurry and they never pause. Theirs is not that twilight of political knowledge which gives us just light enough to place one foot before the other: as they advance the scene still opens upon them, and they press right onward with a vast and various landscape of existence around them. Calmness and energy mark all their actions. Convinced that vice originates not in the man, but in the surrounding circumstances; not in the heart, but in the understanding; the Christian patriot is hopeless concerning no one;—to correct a vice or generate a virtuous conduct, he pollutes not his hands with the scourge of coercion; but by endeavoring to alter circumstances would remove, or by strengthening the intellect disarm, the temptation. The unhappy children of vice and folly, whose tempers are adverse to their own happiness as well as to the happiness of others, will at times awaken a natural pang; but he looks forward with gladdened heart to that glorious period when justice shall have established the universal fraternity of love. These soul-ennobling views bestow the virtues which they anticipate. He whose mind is habitually impressed with them soars above the present state of humanity, and may be justly said to dwell in the presence of the Most High.

> Would the forms
> Of servile custom cramp *the patriot's* power?
> Would sordid policies, the barbarous growth
> Of ignorance and rapine, bow *him* down
> To tame pursuits, to indolence and fear?
> Lo!—*he* appeals to nature, to the winds
> And rolling waves, the sun's unwearied course,
> The elements and seasons: all declare
> For what the Eternal Maker has ordain'd
> The powers of man: we feel within ourselves
> His energy divine: he tells the heart
> He meant, he made, us to behold and love
> What he beholds and loves, the general orb
> Of life and being—to be great like him,
> Beneficent and active.*

That general illumination should precede revolution, is a truth as obvious, as that the vessel should be cleansed before we fill it with a pure liquor. But the mode of diffusing it is not discoverable with equal facility. We certainly should never attempt to make proselytes by appeals to the selfish feelings, and consequently, should plead for the oppressed, not to them. The author of an essay on political justice considers private societies as the sphere of real utility;—that (each one illuminating those immediately beneath him), truth by a gradual descent may at last reach the lowest order. But this is rather plausible than just or practicable. Society as at present constituted does not resemble a chain that ascends in a continuity of links. Alas! between the parlor and the kitchen, the coffee-room and the tap, there is a gulf that may not be passed. He would appear to me to have adopted the best as well as the most benevolent mode of diffus-

* Akenside. Pleasures of Imagination, 1st edit. B. III. 615. The words in italics are altered.—*Ed.*

ing truth, who, uniting the zeal of the Methodist with the views of the philosopher, should be personally among the poor, and teach them their duties in order that he may render them susceptible of their rights.

Yet by what means can the lower classes be made to learn their duties, and urged to practise them? The human race may perhaps possess the capability of all excellence; and truth, I doubt not, is omnipotent to a mind already disciplined for its reception; but assuredly the over-worked laborer, skulking into an ale-house, is not likely to exemplify the one, or prove the other. In that barbarous tumult of inimical interests, which the present state of society exhibits, religion appears to offer the only means universally efficient. The perfectness of future men is indeed a benevolent tenet, and may operate on a few visionaries, whose studious habits supply them with employment, and seclude them from temptation. But a distant prospect, which we are never to reach, will seldom quicken our footsteps, however lovely it may appear; and a blessing, which not ourselves but posterity are destined to enjoy, will scarcely influence the actions of any—still less of the ignorant, the prejudiced, and the selfish.

Preach the Gospel to the poor. By its simplicity it will meet their comprehension, by its benevolence soften their affections, by its precepts it will direct their conduct, by the vastness of its motives insure their obedience. The situation of the poor is perilous: they are indeed both

> from within and from without
> Unarmed to all temptations.

Prudential reasonings will in general be powerless with them. For the incitements of this world are weak in proportion as we are wretched:—

> The world is not my friend, nor the world's law.
> The world has got no law to make me rich.

They too, who live from hand to mouth, will most frequently become improvident. Possessing no stock of happiness, they eagerly seize the gratifications of the moment, and snatch the froth from the wave as it passes by them. Nor is the desolate state of their families a restraining motive, unsoftened as they are by education, and benumbed into selfishness by the torpedo touch of extreme want. Domestic affections depend on association. We love an object if, as often as we see or recollect it, an agreeable sensation arises in our minds. But alas, how should he glow with the charities of father and husband, who gaining scarcely more than his own necessities demand, must have been accustomed to regard his wife and children, not as the soothers of finished labor, but as rivals for the insufficient meal? In a man so circumstanced the tyranny of the present can be overpowered only by the tenfold mightiness of the future. Religion will cheer his gloom with her promises, and by habituating his mind to anticipate an infinitely great revolution hereafter, may prepare it even for the sudden reception of a less degree of melioration in this world.

But if we hope to instruct others, we should familiarize our own minds to some fixed and determinate principles of action. The world is a vast labyrinth, in which almost every one is running a different way, and almost every one manifesting hatred to those who do not run the same way. A few indeed stand motionless, and not seeking to lead themselves or others out of the maze, laugh at the failures of their brethren. Yet with little reason: for more grossly than the most bewildered wanderer does he err, who never aims to go right. It is more honorable to the head, as well as to the heart, to be misled by our eagerness in the pursuit of truth, than to be safe from blundering by contempt of it. The happiness of mankind is the end of virtue, and truth is the knowledge of the means; which he will never seriously attempt to discover, who has not habitually interested himself in the welfare of others. The searcher after truth must love and be beloved; for general benevolence is a necessary motive to constancy of pursuit; and this general benevolence is begotten and rendered permanent by social and domestic affections. Let us beware of that proud philosophy, which affects to inculcate philanthropy while it denounces every home-born feeling by which it is produced and nurtured. The paternal and filial duties discipline the heart and prepare it for the love of all mankind. The intensity of private attachments encourages, not prevents, universal benevolence. The nearer we approach to the sun, the more intense his heat: yet what corner of the system does he not cheer and vivify?

The man who would find truth, mut likewise seek it with a

humble and simple heart, otherwise he will be precipitate and overlook it; or he will be prejudiced, and refuse to see it. To emancipate itself from the tyranny of association, is the most arduous effort of the mind, particularly in religious and political disquisitions. The assertors of the system have associated with it the preservation of order and public virtue; the oppugners, imposture and wars and rapine. Hence, when they dispute, each trembles at the consequences of the other's opinions instead of attending to his train of arguments. Of this, however, we may be certain, whether we be Christians or infidels, aristocrats or republicans, that our minds are in a state insusceptible of knowledge, when we feel an eagerness to detect the falsehood of an adversary's reasonings, not a sincere wish to discover if there be truth in them;—when we examine an argument in order that we may answer it, instead of answering because we have examined it.

Our opponents are chiefly successful in confuting the theory of freedom by the practices of its advocates; from our lives they draw the most forcible arguments against our doctrines. Nor have they adopted an unfair mode of reasoning. In a science the evidence suffers neither diminution nor increase from the actions of its professors; but the comparative wisdom of political systems depends necessarily on the manners and capacities of the recipients. Why should all things be thrown into confusion to acquire that liberty which a faction of sensualists and gamblers will neither be able nor willing to preserve?

A system of fundamental reform will scarcely be effected by massacres mechanized into revolution. We can not therefore inculcate on the minds of each other too often or with too great earnestness the necessity of cultivating benevolent affections. We should be cautious how we indulge the feelings even of virtuous indignation. Indignation is the handsome brother of anger and hatred. The temple of despotism, like that of Tescalipoca, the Mexican deity, is built of human skulls, and cemented with human blood;—let us beware that we be not transported into revenge while we are levelling the loathsome pile; lest when we erect the edifice of freedom we but vary the style of architecture, not change the materials. Let us not wantonly offend even the prejudices of our weaker brethren, nor by ill-timed and vehement declarations of opinion excite in them malignant feelings towards us. The energies of the mind are wasted in these intemperate effusions. Those materials of projectile force, which now carelessly scattered explode with an offensive and useless noise, directed by wisdom and union might heave rocks from their base,—or perhaps (apart from the metaphor) might produce the desired effect without the convulsion.

For this subdued sobriety of temper a practical faith in the doctrine of philosophical necessity seems the only preparative. That vice is the effect of error and the offspring of surrounding circumstances, the object therefore of condolence not of anger, is a proposition easily understood, and as easily demonstrated. But to make it spread from the understanding to the affections, to call it into action, not only in the great exertions of patriotism, but in the daily and hourly occurrences of social life, requires the most watchful attentions of the most energetic mind. It is not enough that we have once swallowed these truths:—we must feed on them, as insects on a leaf, till the whole heart be colored by their qualities, and show its food in every the minutest fibre.*

Finally, in the spirit of the Apostle,

Watch ye! Stand fast in the principles of which ye have been convinced! Quit yourselves like men! Be strong! Yet let all things be done in the spirit of love.

* I hope that this last paragraph, in all the fulness of its contrast with my present convictions, will start up before me whenever I speak, think, or feel intolerantly of persons on account of their doctrines and opinions.

30th Oct. 1818.

THE SECOND LANDING-PLACE:

OR ESSAYS INTERPOSED FOR AMUSEMENT, RETROSPECT, AND PREPARATION.

MISCELLANY THE SECOND.

Etiam a musis si quando animum paulisper abducamus, apud Musas nihilominus feriamur; at reclines quidem, at otiosas, at de his et illis inter se libere colloquentes.

THE SECOND LANDING-PLACE.

ESSAY I.

It were a wantonness, and would demand
Severe reproof if we were men whose hearts
Could hold vain dalliance with the misery
Even of the dead; contented thence to draw
A momentary pleasure, never mark'd
By reason, barren of all future good.
But we have known that there is often found
In mournful thoughts and always might be found
A power to virtue friendly. WORDSWORTH, M.S.

I KNOW not how I can better commence my second Landing-Place, as joining on to the section of Politics, than by the following proof of the severe miseries which misgovernment may occasion in a country nominally free. In the homely ballad of the Three Graves* I have attempted to exemplify the effect, which one painful idea, vividly impressed on the mind under unusual circumstances, might have in producing an alienation of the understanding; and in the parts hitherto published, I have endeavored to trace the progress to madness, step by step. But though the main incidents are facts, the detail of the circumstances is of my own invention; that is, not what I knew, but what I conceived likely to have been the case, or at least equivalent to it. In the tale that follows, I present an instance of the same causes acting upon the mind to the production of conduct as wild as that of madness, but without any positive or permanent loss of the reason or the understanding; and this in a real occurrence, real in all its parts and particulars. But in truth this tale overflows with a human interest, and needs no philosophical deduction to make it impressive. The account was

* Poet. Works, VII. p. 167.—*Ed.*

published in the city in which the event took place, and in the same year I read it, when I was in Germany, and the impression made on my memory was so deep, that though I relate it in my own language, and with my own feelings, and in reliance on the fidelity of my recollection, I dare vouch for the accuracy of the narration in all important particulars.

The imperial free towns of Germany are, with only two or three exceptions, enviably distinguished by the virtuous and primitive manners of the citizens, and by the parental character of their several governments. As exceptions, however, I must mention Aix la Chapelle, poisoned by French manners, and the concourse of gamesters and sharpers; and Nüremberg, the industrious and honest inhabitants of which deserve a better fate than to have their lives and properties under the guardianship of a wolfish and merciless oligarchy, proud from ignorance, and remaining ignorant through pride. It is from the small states of Germany that our writers on political economy might draw their most forcible instances of actually oppressive, and even mortal, taxation, and gain the clearest insight into the causes and circumstances of the injury. One other remark, and I proceed to the story. I well remember, that the event I am about to narrate, called forth, in several of the German periodical publications, the most passionate (and in more than one instance blasphemous) declamations concerning the incomprehensibility of the moral government of the world, and the seeming injustice and cruelty of the dispensations of Providence. But, assuredly, every one of my readers, however deeply he may sympathize with the poor sufferers, will at once answer all such declamations by the simple reflection, that no one of these awful events could possibly have taken place under a wise police and humane government, and that men have no right to complain of Providence for evils which they themselves are competent to remedy by mere common sense, joined with mere common humanity.

Maria Eleonora Schöning was the daughter of a Nüremberg wire-drawer. She received her unhappy existence at the price of her mother's life, and at the age of seventeen she followed, as the sole mourner, the bier of her remaining parent. From her thirteenth year she had passed her life at her father's sick-bed, the gout having deprived him of the use of his limbs, and seen the arch of heaven only when she went to fetch food or medicines. The discharge of her filial duties occupied the whole of her time and all her thoughts. She was his only nurse, and for the last two years they lived without a servant. She prepared his scanty meal, she bathed his aching limbs, and though weak and delicate from constant confinement and the poison of melancholy thoughts, she had acquired an unusual power in her arms, from the habit of lifting her old and suffering father out of and into his bed of pain. Thus passed away her early youth in sorrow: she grew up in tears, a stranger to the amusements of youth, and its more delightful schemes and imaginations. She was not, however, unhappy: she attributed, indeed, no merit to herself for her virtues, but for that reason were they the more her reward. The *peace which passeth all understanding* disclosed itself in all her looks and movements. It lay on her countenance, like a steady unshadowed moonlight: and her voice, which was naturally at once sweet and subtle, came from her, like the fine flute-tones of a masterly performer, which still floating at some uncertain distance, seem to be created by the player, rather than to proceed from the instrument. If you had listened to it in one of those brief sabbaths of the soul, when the activity and discursiveness of the thoughts are suspended, and the mind quietly eddies round, instead of flowing onward—(as at late evening in the spring I have seen a bat wheel in silent circles round and round a fruit-tree in full blossom, in the midst of which, as within a close tent of the purest white, an unseen nightingale was piping its sweetest notes)—in such a mood you might have half-fancied, half-felt, that her voice had a separate being of its own—that it was a living something, the mode of existence of which was for the ear only: so deep was her resignation, so entirely had it become the unconscious habit of her nature, and in all she did or said, so perfectly were both her movements and her utterance without effort, and without the appearance of effort! Her dying father's last words, addressed to the clergyman who attended him, were his grateful testimony, that during his long and sore trial his good Maria had behaved to him like an angel;—that the most disagreeable offices and the least suited to her age and sex, had never drawn an unwilling look from her, and that whenever his eye had met hers, he had been sure to see in it either the tear of pity or the sudden smile expressive of her affection and wish to cheer him. God (said he) will reward the good girl for all her long dutifulness to me! He departed during the inward prayer, which followed these his last words. His wish will be fulfilled in eternity; but for this world the prayer of the dying man was not heard.

Maria sat and wept by the grave, which now contained her father, her friend, the only bond by which she was linked to life. But while yet the last sound of his death-bell was murmuring away in the air, she was obliged to return with two revenue officers, who demanded entrance into the house, in order to take possession of the papers of the deceased, and from them to discover whether he had always given in his income, and paid the yearly income-tax according to his oath, and in proportion to his property.* After the few documents had been looked through and collated with the registers, the officers found, or pretended to find, sufficient proofs, that the deceased had not paid his tax proportionably, which imposed on them the duty to put all the effects under lock and seal. They therefore desired the maiden to retire to an empty room, till the Ransom Office had decided on the affair. Bred up in suffering, and habituated to immediate compliance, the affrighted and weeping maiden obeyed She hastened to the empty garret, while the revenue officers placed the lock and seal upon the other doors, and finally took away the papers to the Ransom Office.

Not before evening did the poor faint Maria, exhausted with weeping, rouse herself with the intention of going to her bed; but she found the door of her chamber sealed up and that she

* This tax called the *Losung* or ransom, in Nüremberg, was at first a voluntary contribution: every one gave according to his liking or circumstances. But in the beginning of the 15th century the heavy contributions levied for the service of the Empire forced the magistrates to determine the proportions and make the payment compulsory. Every citizen must yearly take what is called his ransom oath (*Losungseid*) that the sum paid by him has been in the strict determinate proportion to his property. On the death of any citizen, the Ransom Office, or commissioners for this income or property tax, possess the right to examine his books and papers, and to compare his yearly payment as found in their registers with the property he appears to have possessed during that time. If any disproportion is detected, if the yearly declarations of the deceased should have been inaccurate in the least degree, his whole effects are confiscated, and though he should have left wife and child, the state treasury becomes his heir

must pass the night on the floor of the garret. The officers had had the humanity to place at the door the small portion of food that happened to be in the house. Thus passed several days, till the officers returned with an order that Maria Eleonora Schöning should leave the house without delay, the commission court having confiscated the whole property to the city treasury. The father before he was bedridden had never possessed any considerable property; but yet, by his industry, had been able not only to keep himself free from debt, but to lay up a small sum for the evil day. Three years of evil days, three whole years of sickness, had consumed the greatest part of this; yet still enough remained not only to defend his daughter from immediate want, but likewise to maintain her till she could get into some service or employment, and should have recovered her spirits sufficiently to bear up against the hardships of life. With this thought her dying father comforted himself, and this hope too proved vain.

A timid girl, whose past life had been made up of sorrow and privation, she went indeed to solicit the commissioners in her own behalf; but these were, as is mostly the case on the continent, advocates—the most hateful class, perhaps, of human society, hardened by the frequent sight of misery, and seldom superior in moral character to English pettifoggers or Old Bailey Attorneys. She went to them, indeed, but not a word could she say for herself. Her tears and inarticulate sounds—for these her judges had no ears or eyes. Mute and confounded, like an unfledged dove fallen out from its mother's nest, Maria betook herself to her home, and found the house door too now shut upon her. Her whole wealth consisted in the clothes she wore. She had no relations to whom she could apply, for those of her mother had disclaimed all acquaintance with her, and her father was a Nether Saxon by birth. She had no acquaintance, for all the friends of old Schöning had forsaken him in the first year of his sickness. She had no play-fellow, for who was likely to have been the companion of a nurse in the room of a sick man? Surely, since the creation never was a human being more solitary and forsaken than this innocent poor creature, that now roamed about friendless in a populous city, to the whole of whose inhabitants her filial tenderness, her patient domestic goodness, and all her soft yet difficult virtues, might well have been the model :—

But homeless near a thousand homes she stood,
And near a thousand tables pin'd and wanted food !*

The night came, and Maria knew not where to find a shelter. She tottered to the church-yard of St. James' church in Nüremberg, where the body of her father rested. Upon the yet grassless grave she threw herself down ; and could anguish have prevailed over youth, that night she had been in heaven. The day came, and like a guilty thing, this guiltless, this good being, stole away from the crowd that began to pass through the church-yard, and hastening through the streets to the city-gate, she hid herself behind a garden hedge just beyond it, and there wept away the second day of her desolation. The evening closed in : the pang of hunger made itself felt amid the dull aching of self-wearied anguish, and drove the sufferer back again into the city. Yet what could she gain there ? She had not the courage to beg, and the very thought of stealing never occurred to her innocent mind. Scarce conscious whither she was going, or why she went, she found herself once more by her father's grave, as the last relic of evening faded away in the horizon.

I have sat for some minutes with my pen resting : I can scarce summon the courage to tell, what I scarce know whether I ought to tell. Were I composing a tale of fiction, the reader might justly suspect the purity of my own heart, and most certainly would have abundant right to resent such an incident, as an outrage wantonly offered to his imagination. As I think of the circumstance, it seems more like a distempered dream : but alas ! what is guilt so detestable other than a dream of madness, that worst madness, the madness of the heart ? I can not but believe, that the dark and restless passions must first have drawn the mind in upon themselves, and, as with the confusion of imperfect sleep, have in some strange manner taken away the sense of reality, in order to render it possible for a human being to perpetrate what it is too certain that human beings have perpetrated. The church-yards in most of the German cities, and too often, I fear, in those of our own country, are not more injurious to health than to mortality. Their former venerable character is no more. The religion of the place has followed its superstitions, and their darkness and loneliness tempt worse spirits to roam in them than

* Wordsworth's Female Vagrant.—*Ed.*

those whose nightly wanderings appalled the believing hearts of our brave forefathers. It was close by the new-made grave of her father that the meek and spotless daughter became the victim to brutal violence, which weeping, and watching, and cold, and hunger had rendered her utterly unable to resist. The monster left her in a trance of stupefaction, and into her right hand, which she had clenched convulsively, he had forced a half-dollar.

It was one of the darkest nights of autumn; in the deep and dead silence the only sounds audible were the slow blunt ticking of the church clock, and now and then the sinking down of bones in the nigh charnel house. Maria, when she had in some degree recovered her senses, sate upon the grave near which—not her innocence had been sacrificed, but—that which, from the frequent admonitions and almost the dying words of her father, she had been accustomed to consider as such. Guiltless, she felt the pangs of guilt, and still continued to grasp the coin which the monster had left in her hand, with an anguish as sore as if it had been indeed the wages of voluntary prostitution. Giddy and faint from want of food, her brain becoming feverish from sleeplessness, and this unexampled concurrence of calamities, this complication and entanglement of misery in misery, she imagined that she heard her father's voice bidding her leave his sight. His last blessings had been conditional, for in his last hours he had told her, that the loss of her innocence would not let him rest quiet in his grave. His last blessings now sounded in her ears like curses, and she fled from the church-yard as if a demon had been chasing her; and hurrying along the streets, through which it is probable her accursed violator had walked with quiet and orderly step* to

* It must surely have been after hearing of or witnessing some similar event or scene of wretchedness, that the most eloquent of our writers (I had almost said of our poets,) Jeremy Taylor, wrote the following paragraph, which at least in Longinus's sense of the word, we may place among the most sublime passages in English literature. "He that is no fool, but can consider wisely, if he be in love with this world, we need not despair but that a witty man might reconcile him with tortures, and make him think charitably of the rack, and be brought to admire the harmony that is made by a herd of evening wolves when they miss their draught of blood in their midnight revels. The groans of a man in a fit of the stone are worse than all these; and the distractions of a troubled conscience are worse than those groans: and yet a careless merry sinner is worse than all that. But if we could from one of the battlements of heaven espy, how many men and women

his place of rest and security, she was seized by the watchmen of the night—a welcome prey, as they receive in Nüremberg a reward from the police chest, for every woman they find in the streets after ten o'clock at night. It was midnight, and she was taken to the next watch-house.

The sitting magistrate, before whom she was carried the next morning, prefaced his first question with the most opprobrious title that ever belonged to the most hardened street-walkers, and which man born of woman should not address even to these, were it but for his own sake. The frightful name awakened the poor orphan from her dream of guilt, it brought back the consciousness of her innocence, but with it the sense likewise of her wrongs and of her helplessness. The cold hand of death seemed to grasp her, she fainted dead away at his feet, and was not without difficulty recovered. The magistrate was so far softened, and only so far, as to dismiss her for the present; but with a menace of sending her to the House of Correction if she were brought before him a second time. The idea of her own innocence now became uppermost in her mind; but mingling with the thought of her utter forlornness, and the image of her angry father, and, doubtless still in a state of bewilderment, she formed the resolution of drowning herself in the river Pegnitz—in order (for this was the shape which her fancy had taken) to throw herself at her father's feet, and to justify her innocence to him, in the world of spirits. She hoped, that her father would speak for her to the Saviour, and that she should be forgiven. But as she was passing through the suburb, she was met by a soldier's wife, who during the life-time of her father had been occasionally employed in the house as a chare-woman. This poor woman was startled at the disordered apparel, and more disordered

at this time lie fainting and dying for want of bread, how many young men are hewn down by the sword of war; how many poor orphans are now weeping over the graves of their father, by whose life they were enabled to eat; if we could but hear how many mariners and passengers are at this present in a storm, and shriek out because their keel dashes against a rock, or bulges under them; how many people there are that weep with want, and are mad with oppression, or are desperate by a too quick sense of a constant infelicity; in all reason we should be glad to be out of the noise and participation of so many evils. This is a place of sorrows and tears, of great evils and constant calamities: let us remove hence, at least in affections and preparations of mind." *Holy Dying*, ch. i. s. 5, with omissions.—*Ed.*

looks of her young mistress, and questioned her with such an anxious and heart-felt tenderness, as at once brought back the poor orphan to her natural feelings and the obligations of religion. As a frightened child throws itself into the arms of its mother, and hiding its head on her breast, half tells amid sobs what has happened to it, so did she throw herself on the neck of the woman who had uttered the first words of kindness to her since her father's death, and with loud weeping she related what she had endured and what she was about to have done, told her all her affliction and her misery, the wormwood and the gall. Her kind-hearted friend mingled tears with tears, pressed the poor forsaken one to her heart; comforted her with sentences out of the hymn-book: and with the most affectionate entreaties conjured her to give up her horrid purpose, for that life was short, and heaven was forever.

Maria had been bred up in the fear of God; she now trembled at the thought of her former purpose, and followed her friend Harlin, for that was the name of her guardian angel, to her home hard by. The moment she entered the door, she sank down and lay at her full length, as if only to be motionless in a place of shelter had been the fulness of delight. As when a withered leaf that has been long whirled about by the gusts of autumn, is blown into a cave or hollow tree, it stops suddenly, and all at once looks the very image of quiet—such might this poor orphan appear to the eye of a meditative imagination.

A place of shelter she had attained, and a friend willing to comfort her in all that she could: but the noble-hearted Harlin was herself a daughter of calamity, one who from year to year must lie down in weariness and rise up to labor; for whom this world provides no other comfort but the sleep which enables them to forget it; no other physician but death, which takes them out of it. She was married to one of the city guards, who, like Maria's father, had been long sick and bed-ridden. Him, herself, and two little children, she had to maintain by washing and charing;* and some time after Maria had been domesticated with them, Harlin told her that she herself had been once driven to a desperate thought by the cry of her hungry children, during

* I am ignorant, whether there be any classical authority for this word; but I know no other word that expresses occasional day-labor in the houses of others.

a want of employment, and that she had been on the point of killing one of the little ones, and of then surrendering herself into the hands of justice. In this manner, she had conceived, all would be well provided for; the surviving child would be admitted, as a matter of course, into the Orphan House, and her husband into the Hospital; while she herself would have atoned for her act by a public execution, and together with the child that she had destroyed, would have passed into a state of bliss. All this she related to Maria, and those tragic thoughts left but too deep and lasting impression on her mind. Weeks after, she herself renewed the conversation, by expressing to her benefactress her inability to conceive how it was possible for one human being to take away the life of another, especially that of an innocent little child. "For that reason," replied Harlin, "because it was so innocent and so good, I wished to put it out of this wicked world. Thinkest thou then, that I would have my head cut off for the sake of a wicked child? Therefore it was little Nan, that I meant to have taken with me, who, as you see, is always so sweet and patient; little Frank has already his humors and naughty tricks, and suits better for this world." This was the answer. Maria brooded awhile over it in silence, then passionately snatched the children up in her arms, as if she would protect them against their own mother.

For one whole year the orphan lived with the soldier's wife, and by their joint labors barely kept off absolute want. As a little boy (almost a child in size, though in his thirteenth year) once told me of himself, as he was guiding me up the Brocken, in the Hartz Forest, they had but "little of that, of which a great deal tells but for little." But now came the second winter, and with it came bad times, a season of trouble for this poor and meritorious household. The wife now fell sick: too constant and too hard labor, too scanty and too innutritious food, had gradually wasted away her strength. Maria redoubled her efforts in order to provide bread and fuel for their washing which they took in; but the task was above her powers. Besides, she was so timid and so agitated at the sight of strangers, that sometimes, with the best good-will, she was left without employment. One by one, every article of the least value which they possessed was sold off, except the bed on which the husband lay. He died just before the approach of spring; but about the same time the wife gave signs of convalescence. The physician, though almost as poor as his patients, had been kind to them: silver and gold had he none, but he occasionally brought a little wine, and often assured them that nothing was wanting to her perfect recovery, but better nourishment and a little wine every day. This, however, could not be regularly procured, and Harlin's spirits sank, and as her bodily pain left her she became more melancholy, silent, and self-involved. And now it was that Maria's mind was incessantly racked by the frightful apprehension, that her friend might be again meditating the accomplishment of her former purpose. She had grown as passionately fond of the two children as if she had borne them under her own heart; but the jeopardy in which she conceived her friend's salvation to stand —this was her predominant thought. For all the hopes and fears, which under a happier lot would have been associated with the objects of the senses, were transferred, by Maria, to her notions and images of a future state.

In the beginning of March, one bitter cold evening, Maria started up and suddenly left the house. The last morsel of food had been divided betwixt the two children for their breakfast: and for the last hour or more the little boy had been crying for hunger, while his gentler sister had been hiding her face in Maria's lap, and pressing her little body against her knees, in order by that mechanic pressure to dull the aching from emptiness. The tender-hearted and visionary maiden had watched the mother's eye, and had interpreted several of her sad and steady looks according to her preconceived apprehensions. She had conceived all at once the strange and enthusiastic thought, that she would in some way or other offer her own soul for the salvation of the soul of her friend. The money, which had been left in her hand, flashed upon the eye of her mind, as a single unconnected image: and faint with hunger and shivering with cold, she sallied forth—in search of guilt! Awful are the dispensations of the Supreme, and in his severest judgments the hand of mercy is visible. It was a night so wild with wind and rain, or rather rain and snow mixed together, that a famished wolf would have stayed in his cave, and listened to a howl more fearful than his own. Forlorn Maria! thou wast kneeling in pious simplicity at the grave of thy father, and thou becamest the prey of a monster. Innocent thou wast and without guilt didst thou remain. Now thou goest forth of thy own accord ;—but God will have pity on thee. Poor bewildered innocent! In thy spotless imagination dwelt no distinct conception of the evil which thou wentest forth to brave. To save the soul of thy friend was the dream of thy feverish brain, and thou wast again apprehended as an outcast of shameless sensuality, at the moment when thy too spiritualized fancy was busied with the glorified forms of thy friend and her little ones interceding for thee at the throne of the Redeemer!

At this moment her perturbed fancy suddenly suggested to her a new mean for the accomplishment of her purpose: and she replied to the night-watch, who with a brutal laugh bade her expect on the morrow the unmanly punishment, which to the disgrace of human nature the laws of some Protestant states inflict on female vagrants, that she came to deliver herself up as an infanticide. She was instantly taken before the magistrate through as wild and pitiless a storm as ever pelted on a houseless head,—through as black and tyrannous a night as ever aided the workings of a heated brain. Here she confessed that she had been delivered of an infant by the soldier's wife, Harlin, that she deprived it of life in the presence of Harlin, and according to a plan preconcerted with her, and that Harlin had buried it somewhere in the wood, but where she knew not. During this strange tale, she appeared to listen with a mixture of fear and satisfaction to the howling of the wind; and never sure could a confession of real guilt have been accompanied by a more dreadfully appropriate music. At the moment of her apprehension she had formed the scheme of helping her friend out of the world in a state of innocence. When the soldier's widow was confronted with the orphan, and the latter had repeated her confession to her face, Harlin answered in these words, "For God's sake, Maria! how have I deserved this of thee?" Then turning to the magistrate said, "I know nothing of this." This was the sole answer which she gave, and not another word could they extort from her. The instruments of torture were brought, and Harlin was warned, that if she did not confess of her own accord, the truth would be immediately forced from her. This menace convulsed Maria Schöning with affright; her intention had been to emancipate herself and her friend from a life of unmixed suffering, without the crime of suicide in either, and with no guilt at all on the part of her friend. The thought of her friend's being put to the torture had not occurred to her. Wildly and eagerly she pressed her friend's hands, already bound in preparation for the torture;—she pressed them in agony between her own, and said to her, "Anna, confess it! Anna, dear Anna! it will then be well with all of us! all, all of us! and Frank and little Nan will be put into the Orphan House!" Maria's scheme now passed, like a flash of lightning, through the widow's mind; she acceded to it at once, kissed Maria repeatedly, and then serenely turning her face to the judge, acknowledged that she had added to the guilt by so obstinate a denial, that all her friend had said was true, save only that she had thrown the dead infant into the river, and not buried it in the wood.

They were both committed to prison, and as they both persevered in their common confession, the process was soon made out and the condemnation followed the trial: and the sentence, by which they were both to be beheaded with the sword, was ordered to be put in force on the next day but one. On the morning of the execution, the delinquents were brought together, in order that they might be reconciled with each other, and join in common prayer for forgiveness of their common guilt.

But now Maria's thoughts took another turn. The idea that her benefactress, that so very good a woman, should be violently put out of life, and this with an infamy on her name which would cling forever to the little orphans, overpowered her. Her own excessive desire to die scarcely prevented her from discovering the whole plan; and when Harlin was left alone with her, and she saw her friend's calm and affectionate look, her fortitude was dissolved: she burst into loud and passionate weeping, and throwing herself into her friend's arms, with convulsive sobs she entreated her forgiveness. Harlin pressed the poor agonized girl to her arms; like a tender mother, she kissed and fondled her wet cheeks, and in the most solemn and emphatic tones assured her that there was nothing to forgive. On the contrary, she was her greatest benefactress and the instrument of God's goodness to remove her at once from a miserable world and from the temptation of committing a heavy crime. In vain. Her repeated promises, that she would answer before God for them both, could not pacify the tortured conscience of Maria, till at length the presence of the clergyman and the preparations for receiving the sacrament occasioning the widow to address her thus—"See, Maria! this is the body and blood of Christ, which takes away all sin! Let us partake together of this holy repast with full trust in God and joyful hope of our approaching happiness." These words of comfort, uttered with cheering tones, and accompanied with a look of inexpressible tenderness and serenity, brought back peace for a while to her troubled spirit. They communicated together, and on parting, the magnanimous woman once more embraced her young friend: then stretching her hand toward heaven, said, "Be tranquil, Maria! by to-morrow morning we are there, and all our sorrows stay here behind us."

I hasten to the scene of the execution: for I anticipate my reader's feelings in the exhaustion of my own heart. Serene and with unaltered countenance the lofty-minded Harlin heard the strokes of the death-bell, stood before the scaffold while the staff was broken over her, and at length ascended the steps, all with a steadiness and tranquillity of manner which was not more distant from fear than from defiance and bravado. Altogether different was the state of poor Maria: with shattered nerves and an agonizing conscience that incessantly accused her as the murderess of her friend, she did not walk but staggered towards the scaffold and stumbled up the steps. While Harlin, who went first, at every step turned her head round and still whispered to her, raising her eyes to heaven,—"But a few minutes, Maria! and we are there!" On the scaffold she again bade her farewell, again repeating, "Dear Maria! but one minute now, and we are together with God." But when she knelt down and her neck was bared for the stroke, the unhappy girl lost all self-command, and with a loud and piercing shriek she bade them hold and not murder the innocent. "She is innocent! I have borne false witness! I alone am the murderess!" She rolled herself now at the feet of the executioner, and now at those of the clergymen, and conjured them to stop the execution, declaring that the whole story had been invented by herself; that she had never brought forth, much less destroyed an infant; that for her friend's sake she made this discovery; that for herself she wished to die, and would die gladly, if they would take away her friend, and promise to free her soul from the dreadful agony of having murdered her friend by false witness. The executioner asked Harlin, if there were any truth in what Maria Schöning had said. The heroine answered with manifest reluctance: "Most assuredly she hath said the truth: I confessed myself guilty, because I wished to die and thought it best for both of us: and now that my hope is on the moment of its accomplishment, I can not be supposed to declare myself innocent for the sake of saving my life;—but any wretchedness is to be endured rather than that poor creature should be hurried out of the world in a state of despair."

The outcry of the attending populace prevailed to suspend the execution: a report was sent to the assembled magistrates, and in the mean time one of the priests reproached the widow in bitter words for her former false confession. "What," she replied sternly but without anger, "what would the truth have availed? Before I perceived my friend's purpose I did deny it: my assurance was pronounced an impudent lie: I was already bound for the torture, and so bound that the sinews of my hands started, and one of their worships in the large white peruke, threatened that he would have me stretched till the sun shone through me;—and that then I should cry out, Yes, when it was too late." The priest was hard-hearted or superstitious enough to continue his reproofs, to which the noble woman condescended no further answer. The other clergyman, however, was both more rational and more humane. He succeeded in silencing his colleague, and the former half of the long hour, which the magistrates took in making speeches on the improbability of the tale instead of re-examining the culprits in person, he employed in gaining from the widow a connected account of all the circumstances, and in listening occasionally to Maria's passionate descriptions of all her friend's goodness and magnanimity. For she had gained an influx of life and spirit from the assurance in her mind, both that she had now rescued Harlin from death and was about to expiate the guilt of her purpose by her own execution. For the latter half of the time the clergyman remained in silence, lost in thought, and momently expecting the return of the messenger. All that during the deep silence of this interval could be heard, was one exclamation of Harlin to her unhappy friend—"Oh! Maria! Maria! couldst thou but have kept up thy courage for another minute, we should have been now in heaven!" The messenger came back with an order from the magistrates—to proceed with the execution! With re-animated countenance

Harlin placed her neck on the block and her head was severed from her body amid a general shriek from the crowd. The executioner fainted after the blow, and the under hangman was ordered to take his place. He was not wanted. Maria was already gone: her body was found as cold as if she had been dead for some hours. The flower had been snapt in the storm, before the scythe of violence could come near it.

ESSAY II.

The history of times representeth the magnitude of actions and the public faces and deportment of persons, and passeth over in silence the smaller passages and motions of men and matters. But such being the workmanship of God, as he doth hang the greatest weight upon the smallest wires, *maxima e minimis suspendens;* it comes therefore to pass, that such histories do rather set forth the pomp of business than the true and inward resorts thereof. But lives, if they be well written, propounding to themselves a person to represent in whom actions both greater and smaller, public and private, have a commixture, must of necessity contain a more true, native, and lively representation. BACON.*

MANKIND in general are so little in the habit of looking steadily at their own meaning, or of weighing the words by which they express it, that the writer, who is careful to do both, will sometimes mislead his readers through the very excellence which qualifies him to be their instructor: and this with no other fault on his part, than the modest mistake of supposing in those, to whom he addresses himself, an intellect as watchful as his own. The inattentive reader adopts as unconditionally true, or perhaps rails at his author for having stated as such, what upon examination would be found to have been duly limited, and would so have been understood, if opaque spots and false refractions were as rare in the mental as in the bodily eye. The motto, for instance, to this paper has more than once served as an excuse and authority for huge volumes of biographical *minutiæ,* which render the real character almost invisible, like clouds of dust on a portrait, or the counterfeit frankincense which smoke-blacks the favorite idol of a

* Advancement of Learning, B. ii.—*Ed.*

Roman Catholic village. Yet Lord Bacon, by the expressions 'public faces' and 'propounding to themselves a person,' evidently confines the biographer to such facts as are either susceptible of some useful general inference, or tend to illustrate those qualities which distinguished the subject of them from ordinary men; while the passage in general was meant to guard the historian against considering, as trifles, all that might appear so to those who recognize no greatness in the mind, and can conceive no dignity in any incident, which does not act on their senses by its external accompaniments, or on their curiosity by its immediate consequences. Things apparently insignificant are recommended to our notice, not for their own sakes, but for their bearings or influences on things of importance: in other words, when they are insignificant in appearance only.

An inquisitiveness into the minutest circumstances and casual sayings of eminent contemporaries is indeed quite natural; but so are all our follies, and the more natural they are, the more caution should we exert in guarding against them. To scribble trifles even on the perishable glass of an inn window, is the mark of an idler; but to engrave them on the marble monument, sacred to the memory of the departed great, is something worse than idleness. The spirit of genuine biography is in nothing more conspicuous, than in the firmness with which it withstands the cravings of worthless curiosity, as distinguished from the thirst after useful knowledge. For, in the first place, such anecdotes as derive their whole and sole interest from the great name of the person concerning whom they are related, and neither illustrate his general character nor his particular actions, would scarcely have been noticed or remembered except by men of weak minds: it is not unlikely, therefore, that they were misapprehended at the time, and it is most probable that they have been related as incorrectly, as they were noticed injudiciously. Nor are the consequences of such garrulous biography merely negative For as insignificant stories can derive no real respectability from the eminence of the person who happens to be the subject of them, but rather an additional deformity of disproportion, they are apt to have their insipidity seasoned by the same bad passions that accompany the habit of gossiping in general; and the misapprehensions of weak men meeting with the misinterpretations of malignant men, have not seldom formed the groundwork of the most grievous calumnies. In the second place, these trifles are subversive of the great end of biography, which is to fix the attention, and to interest the feelings, of men on those qualities and actions which have made a particular life worthy of being recorded. It is, no doubt, the duty of an honest biographer, to portray the prominent imperfections as well as excellencies of his hero; but I am at a loss to conceive how this can be deemed an excuse for heaping together a multitude of particulars, which can prove nothing of any man that might not have been safely taken for granted of all men. In the present age (emphatically the age of personality) there are more than ordinary motives for withholding all encouragement from this mania of busying ourselves with the names of others, which is still more alarming as a symptom, than it is troublesome as a disease. The reader must be still less acquainted with contemporary literature than myself—a case not likely to occur—if he needs me to inform him that there are men, who trading in the silliest anecdotes, in unprovoked abuse and senseless eulogy, think themselves nevertheless employed both worthily and honorably, if only all this be done in good set terms, and from the press, and of public characters,—a class which has increased so rapidly of late, that it becomes difficult to discover what characters are to be considered as private. Alas! if these wretched misusers of language and the means of giving wings to thought,—the means of multiplying the presence of an individual mind,—alas! had they ever known, how great a thing the possession of any one simple truth is, and how mean a thing a mere fact is, except as seen in the light of some comprehensive truth; if they had but once experienced the unborrowed complacency, the inward independence, the homebred strength, with which every clear conception of the reason is accompanied; they would shrink from their own pages as at the remembrance of a crime. For a crime it is (and the man who hesitates in pronouncing it such, must be ignorant of what mankind owe to books, what he himself owes to them in spite of his ignorance), thus to introduce the spirit of vulgar scandal and personal inquietude into the closet and the library, environing with evil passions the very sanctuaries, to which we should flee for refuge from them. For to what do these publications appeal, whether they present themselves as biography or as anonymous criticism, but to the same feelings which the scandal-bearers and time-killers of ordinary life seek to gratify in themselves and their listeners? And both the authors and admirers of such publications, in what respect are they less truants and deserters from their own hearts, and from their appointed task of understanding and amending them, than the most garrulous female chronicler of the goings-on of yesterday in the families of her neighbors and townsfolk?

I have reprinted the following biographial sketch, partly indeed in the hope that it may be the means of introducing to the reader's knowledge, in case he should not have formed an acquaintance with them already, two of the most interesting biographical works in our language, both for the weight of the matter, and the *incuriosa felicitas* of the style. I refer to Roger North's Examen, and the Life of his brother, the Lord Keeper Guilford. The pages are all alive with the genuine idioms of our mother-tongue.

A fastidious taste, it is true, will find offence in the occasional vulgarisms, or what we now call slang, which not a few of our writers, shortly after the restoration of Charles II., seem to have affected as a mark of loyalty. These instances, however, are but a trifling drawback. They are not sought for, as is too often and too plainly done by L'Estrange, Collyer, Tom Brown, and their imitators. North never goes out of his way either to seek them or to avoid them; and in the main his language gives us the very nerve, pulse, and sinew of a hearty, healthy, conversational English.

This is my first reason for the insertion of this extract. My other and principal motive may be found in the kindly good-tempered spirit of the passage. But instead of troubling the reader with the painful contrast which so many recollections force on my own feelings, I will refer the character-makers of the present day to the letters of Erasmus and Sir Thomas More to Martin Dorpius, which are commonly annexed to the *Encomium Moriæ;* and then for a practical comment on the just and affecting sentiments of those two great men, to the works of Roger North, as proofs how alone an English scholar and gentleman will permit himself to delineate his contemporaries even under the strongest prejudices of party spirit, and though employed on the coarsest subjects. A coarser subject than the Chief Justice Saunders can not well be imagined; nor does North use his colors with a sparing or very delicate hand; and yet the final impression is that of kindness.

EXTRACT FROM NORTH'S LIFE OF THE LORD KEEPER GUILFORD.*

The Lord Chief Justice Saunders succeeded in the room of Pemberton. His character and his beginning were equally strange. He was at first no better than a poor beggar boy, if not a parish foundling, without known parents or relations. He had found a way to live by obsequiousness in Clement's Inn, as I remember, and courting the attorney's clerks for scraps. The extraordinary observance and diligence of the boy made the society willing to do him good. He appeared very ambitious to learn to write; and one of the attorneys got a board knocked up at a window on the top of a stair-case; and that was his desk, where he sat and wrote after copies of court and other hands the clerks gave him. He made himself so expert a writer that he took in business, and earned some pence by hackney-writing. And thus by degrees he pushed his faculties, and fell to forms, and, by books that were lent him, became an exquisite entering clerk; and, by the same course of improvement of himself, an able counsel, first in special pleading, then at large; and after he was called to the bar, had practice in the King's Bench court equal to any there. As to his person he was very corpulent and beastly; a mere lump of morbid flesh. He used to say, "By his troggs" (such a humorous way of talking he affected), "none could say he wanted issue of his body, for he had nine in his back." He was a fetid mass, that offended his neighbors at the bar in the sharpest degree. Those, whose ill-fortune it was to stand near him, were confessors, and, in summer-time, almost martyrs. This hateful decay of his carcass came upon him by continual sottishness; for to say nothing of brandy, he was seldom without a pot of ale at his nose, or near him. That exercise was all he used; the rest of his life was sitting at his desk or piping at home; and that home was a tailor's house in Butcher Row, called his lodging, and the man's wife was his nurse or worse; but by virtue of his money, of which he made little account, though he got a great deal, he soon became master of the family; and, being no changeling, he never removed,

* Edit. 1826, vol. ii. p. 41.—*Ed.*

but was true to his friends, and they to him, to the last hour of his life.

So much for his person and education. As for his parts, none had them more lively than he. Wit and repartee in an affected rusticity were natural to him. He was ever ready, and never at a loss; and none came so near as he to be a match for Serjeant Maynard. His great dexterity was in the art of special pleading, and he would lay snares that often caught his superiors who were not aware of his traps. And he was so fond of success for his clients, that, rather than fail, he would set the court hard with a trick: for which he met sometimes with a reprimand, which he would wittily ward off, so that no one was much offended with him. But Hale could not bear his irregularity of life; and for that, and suspicion of his tricks, used to bear hard upon him in the court. But no ill usage from the bench was too hard for his hold of business, being such as scarce any could do but himself. With all this, he had a goodness of nature and disposition in so great a degree, that he may be deservedly styled a philanthrope. He was a very Silenus to the boys, as, in this place I may term the students of the law, to make them merry whenever they had a mind to it. He had nothing of rigid or austere in him. If any near him at the bar grumbled at his stench, he ever converted the complaint into content and laughing with the abundance of his wit. As to his ordinary dealing, he was as honest as the driven snow was white; and why not, having no regard for money, or desire to be rich? And for good-nature and condescension, there was not his fellow. I have seen him for hours and half-hours together, before the court sat, stand at the bar with an audience of students over against him, putting of cases and debating so as suited their capacities, and encouraged their industry. And so in the Temple, he seldom moved without a parcel of youths hanging about him, and he merry and jesting with them.

It will be readily conceived that this man was never cut out to be a presbyter, or any thing that is severe and crabbed. In no time did he lean to faction, but did his business without offence to any. He put off officious talk of government or politics with jests, and so made his wit a *catholicon* or shield, to cover all his weak places or infirmities. When the court fell into a steady course of using the law against all kinds of offenders, this man was taken into the king's business; and had the part of drawing and perusal of almost all indictments and informations that were then to be prosecuted, with the pleadings thereon, if any were special; and he had the settling of the large pleadings in the *quo warranto* against London. His Lordship had no sort of conversation with him but in the way of business and at the bar; but once, after he was in the king's business, he dined with His Lordship, and no more. And there he showed another qualification he had acquired, and that was to play jigs upon a harpsichord; having taught himself with the opportunity of an old virginal of his landlady's; but in such a manner, not for defect, but figure, as to see him were a jest. The king, observing him to be of a free disposition, loyal, friendly, and without greediness or guile, thought of him to be the chief justice of the King's Bench at that nice time. And the ministry could not but approve of it. So great a weight was then at stake, as could not be trusted to men of doubtful principles, or such as any thing might tempt to desert them. While he sat in the court of King's Bench, he gave the rule to the general satisfaction of the lawyers. But his course of life was so different from what it had been, his business incessant, and withal crabbed, and his diet and exercise changed, that the constitution of his body, or head rather, could not sustain it, and he fell into an apoplexy and palsy, which numbed his parts; and he never recovered the strength of them. He outlived the judgment in the *quo warranto;* but was not present otherwise than by sending his opinion by one of the judges, to be for the king, who at the pronouncing of the judgment, declared it to the court accordingly, which is frequently done in like cases.

ESSAY III.

Proinde si videbitur, fingant isti me latrunculis interim animi causa lusisse, aut si malint, equitasse in arundine longa. Nam quæ tandem est iniquitas, cum omni vitæ instituto suos lusus concedamus, studiis nullum omnino lusum permittere: maxime si nugæ seria ducant, atque ita tractentur ludicra, ut ex his aliquanto plus frugis referat lector non omnino naris obesæ quam ex quorundam tetricis ac splendidis argumentis? ERASMUS.*

They may pretend, if they like, that I amuse myself with playing at fox and goose, or, if they prefer it, that I ride the cock-horse on my grandam's crutch. For is it not, I ask, very unfair, when every trade and profession is allowed its own sport and travesty, not to extend the same permission to literature;—especially if trifles are so handled, that a reader of tolerable quickness may occasionally derive from them more food for profitable reflection than from many a work of grand or gloomy argument?

IRUS, the forlorn Irus, whose nourishment consisted in bread and water, whose clothing was of one tattered mantle, and whose bed of an armful of straw, this same Irus, by a rapid transition of fortune, became the most prosperous mortal under the sun. It pleased the gods to snatch him at once out of the dust and to place him by the side of princes. He beheld himself in the possession of incalculable treasures. His palace excelled even the temple of the gods in the pomp of its ornaments; his least sumptuous clothing was of purple and gold, and his table might well have been named the compendium of luxury, the summary of all that the voluptuous ingenuity of men had invented for the gratification of the palate. A numerous train of admiring dependents followed him at every step; those to whom he vouchsafed a gracious look were esteemed already in the high road of fortune, and the favored individual who was permitted to kiss his hand appeared to be the object of common envy. The name of Irus sounding in his ears an unwelcome *memento* and perpetual reproach of his former poverty, he for this reason named himself

* *Præf. ad Moriæ Encom.*

Ceraunius, or the Lightning-flasher, and the whole people celebrated this splendid change of title by public rejoicings. The poet, who a few years ago had personified poverty itself under his former name of Irus, now made a discovery which had till that moment remained a profound secret, but was now received by all with implicit faith and warmest approbation. Jupiter, forsooth, had become enamored of the mother of Ceraunius, and assumed the form of a mortal in order to enjoy her love. Henceforward they erected altars to him, they swore by his name, and the priests discovered in the entrails of the sacrificial victim, that the great Ceraunius, this worthy son of Jupiter, was the sole pillar of the western world. Toxaris, his former neighbor, a man whom good fortune, unwearied industry, and rational frugality, had placed among the richest citizens, became the first victim of the pride of this new demi-god. In the time of his poverty Irus had repined at his luck and prosperity, and irritable from distress and envy, had conceived that Toxaris had looked contemptuously on him; and now was the time that Ceraunius would make him feel the power of him, whose father grasped the thunderbolt. Three advocates, newly admitted into the recently established order of the Cygnet, gave evidence that Toxaris had denied the gods, committed peculations on the sacred treasury, and increased his treasures by acts of sacrilege. He was hurried off to prison and sentenced to an ignominious death, and his wealth confiscated to the use of Ceraunius, the earthly representative of the deities. Ceraunius now found nothing wanting to his felicity but a bride worthy of his rank and blooming honors. The most illustrious of the land were candidates for his alliance. Euphorbia, the daughter of the noble Austrius, was honored with his final choice. To nobility of birth nature had added for Euphorbia, a rich dowry of beauty, a nobleness both of look and stature. The flowing ringlets of her hair, her lofty forehead, her brilliant eyes, her stately figure, her majestic gait, had enchanted the haughty Ceraunius: and all the bards told what the inspiring Muses had revealed to them, that Venus more than once had pined with jealousy at the sight of her superior charms. The day of espousal arrived, and the illustrious son of Jove was proceeding in pomp to the temple, when the anguish-stricken wife of Toxaris, with his innocent children, suddenly threw themselves at his feet, and with loud lamentations entreated him to spare the life of her husband. Enraged by this interruption, Ceraunius spurned her from him with his feet and—Irus awoke, and found himself lying on the same straw on which he had lain down, and with his old tattered mantle spread over him. With his returning reason, conscience too returned. He praised the gods and resigned himself to his lot. Ceraunius indeed had vanished, but the innocent Toxaris was still alive, and Irus poor yet guiltless.

Can my reader recollect no individual now on earth, who sometime or other will awake from his dream of empire, poor as Irus, with all the guilt and impiety of Ceraunius ?*

The reader will bear in mind, that this fable was written and first published, at the close of 1809 :—

ῥέχθεν δέ τε νήπιος ἔγνω.

CHRISTMAS WITHIN DOORS, IN THE NORTH OF GERMANY.

RATZEBURG, 1799.

There is a Christmas custom here which pleased and interested me.—The children make little presents to their parents, and to each other; and the parents to the children. For three or four months before Christmas the girls are all busy, and the boys save up their pocket-money, to make or purchase these presents. What the present is to be is cautiously kept secret, and the girls have a world of contrivances to conceal it—such as working when they are out on visits and the others are not with them; getting up in the morning before daylight, and the like. Then on the evening before Christmas-day, one of the parlors is lighted up by the children, into which the parents must not go. A great yew bough is fastened on the table at a little distance from the wall, a multitude of little tapers are fastened in the bough, but so as not to catch it till they are nearly burnt out, and colored paper hangs and flutters from the twigs. Under this bough the children lay out in great order the presents they mean for their parents, still concealing in their pockets what they intend for each other. Then the parents are introduced, and each presents his little gift, and then bring out the rest one by one from their pockets, and present them with kisses and embraces.

* Bonaparte.—*Ed.*

Where I witnessed this scene, there were eight or nine children, and the eldest daughter and the mother wept aloud for joy and tenderness; and the tears ran down the face of the father, and he clasped all his children so tight to his breast, it seemed as if he did it to stifle the sob that was rising within him. I was very much affected. The shadow of the bough and its appendages on the wall, and arching over on the ceiling, made a pretty picture; and then the raptures of the very little ones, when at last the twigs and their needles began to take fire and snap! O it was a delight for them!—On the next day, in the great parlor, the parents lay out on the table the presents for the children: a scene of more sober joy succeeds, as on this day, after an old custom, the mother says privately to each of her daughters, and the father to his sons, that which he has observed most praiseworthy and that which was most faulty in their conduct. Formerly, and still in all the smaller towns and villages throughout North Germany, these presents were sent by all the parents to some one fellow, who in high buskins, a white robe, a mask, and an enormous flax wig, personates *Knecht Rupert*, the servant Rupert. On Christmas night he goes round to every house and says, that Jesus Christ his master sent him thither;—the parents and elder children receive him with great pomp of reverence, while the little ones are most terribly frightened. He then inquires for the children, and according to the character which he hears from the parent, he gives them the intended present, as if they came out of heaven from Jesus Christ. Or, if they should have been bad children, he gives the parents a rod, and in the name of his master recommends them to use it frequently. About seven or eight years old the children are let into the secret, and it is curious to observe how faithfully they keep it.

CHRISTMAS OUT OF DOORS.

The whole lake of Ratzeburg is one mass of thick transparent ice, a spotless mirror of nine miles in extent. The lowness of the hills, which rise from the shores of the lake, precludes the awful sublimity of Alpine landscape, yet compensates for the want of it by beauties, of which this very lowness is a necessary condition. Yester-morning I saw the lesser lake completely hidden by mist; but the moment the sun peeped over the hill, the mist broke in the middle, and in a few seconds stood divided, leaving a broad road all across the lake; and between these two walls of mist the sunlight burnt upon the ice, forming a road of golden fire, intolerably bright, and the mist-walls themselves partook of the blaze in a multitude of shining colors. This is our second frost. About a month ago, before the thaw came on, there was a storm of wind; and during the whole night, such were the thunders and howlings of the breaking ice, that they have left a conviction on my mind, that there are sounds more sublime than any sight can be, more absolutely suspending the power of comparison, and more utterly absorbing the mind's self-consciousness in its total attention to the object working upon it. Part of the ice which the vehemence of the wind had shattered, was driven shoreward and froze anew. On the evening of the next day, at sunset, the shattered ice thus frozen, appeared of a deep blue, and in shape like an agitated sea; beyond this, the water that ran up between the great islands of ice which had preserved their masses entire and smooth, shone of a yellow green; but all these scattered ice-islands, themselves, were of an intensely bright blood color,—they seemed blood and light in union. On some of the largest of these islands, the fishermen stood pulling out their immense nets through the holes made in the ice for this purpose, and the men, their net-poles, and their huge nets, were a part of the glory; say rather, it appeared as if the rich crimson light had shaped itself into these forms, figures, and attitudes, to make a glorious vision in mockery of earthly things.

The lower lake is now all alive with skaters, and with ladies driven onward by them in their ice cars. Mercury, surely, was the first maker of skates, and the wings at his feet are symbols of the invention. In skating there are three pleasing circumstances; the infinitely subtle particles of ice which the skate cuts up, and which creep and run before the skate like a low mist, and in sunrise or sunset become colored; second, the shadow of the skater in the water, seen through the transparent ice; and third, the melancholy undulating sound from the skate, not without variety; and when very many are skating together, the sounds and the noises give an impulse to the icy trees, and the woods all round the lake tinkle.

Here I stop, having in truth transcribed the preceding in great measure, in order to present the lovers of poetry with a descriptive passage, extracted with the author's permission, from an unpublished poem on the growth and revolutions of an individual mind by Wordsworth :—

—an Orphic tale indeed,
A tale divine of high and passionate thoughts
To their own music chanted !*

GROWTH OF GENIUS FROM THE INFLUENCES OF NATURAL OBJECTS ON THE IMAGINATION IN BOYHOOD AND EARLY YOUTH.

Wisdom and spirit of the universe!
Thou soul, that art the eternity of thought!
And giv'st to forms and images a breath
And everlasting motion! not in vain,
By day or star-light, thus from my first dawn
Of childhood didst thou intertwine for me
The passions that build up our human soul,
Nor with the mean and vulgar works of man,
But with high objects, with enduring things,
With life and nature : purifying thus
The elements of feeling and of thought,
And sanctifying by such discipline
Both pain and fear, until we recognize
A grandeur in the beatings of the heart.
Nor was this fellowship vouchsaf'd to me
With stinted kindness. In November days
When vapors rolling down the valleys made
A lonely scene more lonesome; among woods
At noon, and 'mid the calm of summer nights,
When by the margin of the trembling lake,
Beneath the gloomy hills I homeward went
In solitude, such intercourse was mine;
'Twas mine among the fields both day and night,
And by the waters all the summer long.
And in the frosty season when the sun
Was set, and, visible for many a mile
The cottage windows through the twilight blazed,
I heeded not the summons :—happy time
It was indeed for all of us, to me
It was a time of rapture: clear and loud
The village clock toll'd six;—I wheel'd about
Proud and exulting, like an untir'd horse
That car'd not for its home.—All shod with steel
We hiss'd along the polish'd ice, in games

* Poetical Works, VII. p. 159.—*Ed.*

Confederate, imitative of the chase
And woodland pleasures, the resounding horn,
The pack loud bellowing, and the hunted hare.
So through the darkness and the cold we flew,
And not a voice was idle: with the din
Meanwhile the precipices rang aloud,
The leafless trees and every icy crag
Tinkled like iron, while the distant hills
Into the tumult sent an alien sound
Of melancholy—not unnoticed, while the stars,
Eastward, were sparkling clear, and in the west
The orange sky of evening died away.
  Not seldom from the uproar I retired
Into a silent bay or sportively
Glanc'd sideway, leaving the tumultuous throng,
To cut across the image of a star
That gleam'd upon the ice: and oftentimes
When we had given our bodies to the wind,
And all the shadowy banks on either side
Came sweeping through the darkness spinning still
The rapid line of motion, then at once
Have I reclined back upon my heels
Stopp'd short: yet still the solitary cliffs
Wheel'd by me even as if the earth had roll'd
With visible motion her diurnal round:
Behind me did they stretch in solemn train
Feebler and feebler, and I stood and watch'd
Till all was tranquil as a summer sea.

ESSAY IV.

Es ist fast traurig zu sehen, wie man von der Hebraischen Quellen so ganz sich abgewendet hat. In Ægyptens selbst dunkeln unenträthselbaren Hieroglyphen hat man den Schlüssel alter Weisheit suchen wollen; jetzt ist von nichts als Indiens Sprache und Weisheit die Rede; aber die Rabbinische Schriften liegen unerforscht. SCHELLING.

It is mournful to observe, how entirely we have turned our backs on the Hebrew sources. In the obscure, insolvable riddles of the Egyptian hieroglyphics the learned have been hoping to find the key of ancient doctrine, and now we hear of nothing but the language and wisdom of India, while the writings and traditions of the Rabbins are consigned to neglect without examination.

THE LORD HELPETH MAN AND BEAST.

DURING his march to conquer the world, Alexander the Macedonian came to a people in Africa, who dwelt, in a remote and secluded corner, in peaceful huts, and knew neither war nor conqueror. They led him to the hut of their chief, who received him hospitably, and placed before him golden dates, golden figs, and bread of gold. "Do you eat gold in this country?" said Alexander. "I take it for granted," replied the chief, "that thou wast able to find eatable food in thine own country. For what reason then art thou come among us?" "Your gold has not tempted me hither," said Alexander, "but I would willingly become acquainted with your manners and customs." "So be it," rejoined the other; "sojourn among us as long as it pleaseth thee." At the close of this conversation two citizens entered as into their court of justice. The plaintiff said, "I bought of this man a piece of land, and as I was making a deep drain through it I found a treasure. This is not mine, for I only bargained for the land, and not for any treasure that might be concealed beneath it: and yet the former owner of the land will not receive it." The defendant answered: "I hope I have a conscience as well as my fellow-citizen. I sold him the land with all its contingent, as well as existing advantages, and consequently the treasure inclusively."

The chief, who was at the same time their supreme judge, recapitulated their words, in order that the parties might see whether or no he understood them aright. Then after some reflection, said: "Thou hast a son, friend, I believe?" "Yes!" "And thou" (addressing the other) "a daughter?" "Yes!"—"Well, then, let thy son marry thy daughter, and bestow the treasure on the young couple for their marriage portion." Alexander seemed surprised and perplexed. "Think you my sentence unjust?" the chief asked him. "O no," replied Alexander, "but it astonishes me." "And how, then," rejoined the chief, "would the case have been decided in your country?" "To confess the truth," said Alexander, "we should have taken both parties into custody, and have seized the treasure for the king's use." "For the king's use!" exclaimed the chief, now in his turn astonished. "Does the sun shine on that country?"—"O yes!" "Does it rain there?"—"Assuredly." "Wonderful! but are there tame animals in the country that live on the grass and green herbs?" "Very many, and of many kinds." "Ay, that must be the cause," said the chief: "for the sake of those innocent animals the all-gracious Being continues to let the sun shine and the rain drop down on your country."

WHOSO HATH FOUND A VIRTUOUS WIFE HATH A GREATER TREASURE THAN COSTLY PEARLS.

Such a treasure had the celebrated teacher Rabbi Meir found. He sat during the whole of one Sabbath day in the public school, and instructed the people. During his absence from his house his two sons died, both of them of uncommon beauty and enlightened in the law. His wife bore them to her bed-chamber, laid them upon the marriage-bed, and spread a white covering over their bodies. In the evening Rabbi Meir came home. "Where are my two sons," he asked, "that I may give them my blessing?" "They are gone to the school," was the answer. "I repeatedly looked round the school," he replied, "and I did not see them there." She reached to him a goblet, he praised the Lord at the going out of the Sabbath, drank, and again asked:

"Where are my sons, that they too may drink of the cup of blessing?" "They will not be far off," she said, and placed food before him that he might eat. He was in a gladsome and genial mood, and when he had said grace after the meal, she thus addressed him: "Rabbi, with thy permission I would fain propose to thee one question." "Ask it then, my love!" he replied. "A few days ago, a person intrusted some jewels to my custody, and now he demands them: should I give them back?" "This is a question," said Rabbi Meir, "which my wife should not have thought it necessary to ask. What, wouldst thou hesitate or be reluctant to restore to every one his own?" "No," she replied; "but yet I thought it best not to restore them without acquainting thee therewith." She then led him to their chamber, and stepping to the bed, took the white covering from the dead bodies. "Ah, my sons, my sons," thus loudly lamented the father, "my sons, the light of mine eyes, and the light of my understanding. I was your father, but ye were my teachers in the law." The mother turned away and wept bitterly. At length she took her husband by the hand, and said, "Rabbi, didst thou not teach me that we must not be reluctant to restore that which was intrusted to our keeping? See, the Lord gave, the Lord hath taken away, and blessed be the name of the Lord!" "Blessed be the name of the Lord!" echoed Rabbi Meir, "and blessed be his name for thy sake too! For well it is written: Whoso hath found a virtuous wife hath a greater treasure than costly pearls: *she openeth her mouth with wisdom, and in her tongue is the law of kindness*."*

CONVERSATION OF A PHILOSOPHER WITH A RABBI.

"Your God in his book calls himself a jealous God, who can endure no other god beside himself, and on all occasions makes manifest his abhorrence of idolatry. How comes it then that he threatens and seems to hate the worshipers of false gods more than the false gods themselves." "A certain king," replied the Rabbi, "had a disobedient son. Among other worthless tricks of various kinds, he had the baseness to give his dogs his father's names and titles. Should the king show his anger on the prince or the dogs?" "Well turned," rejoined the philosopher: "but

* Prov. xxxi. 26.—*Ed.*

if your God destroyed the objects of idolatry he would take away the temptation to it." "Yea," retorted the Rabbi, "if the fools worshiped such things only as were of no further use than that to which their folly applied them, if the idol were always as worthless as the idolatry is contemptible. But they worship the sun, the moon, the host of heaven, the rivers, the sea, fire, air, and what not? Would you that the Creator, for the sake of these fools, should ruin his own works, and disturb the laws appointed to nature by his own wisdom? If a man steals grain and sows it, should the seed not shoot up out of the earth, because it was stolen? O no! the wise Creator lets nature run her own course: for her course is his own appointment. And what if the children of folly abuse it to evil? The day of reckoning is not far off, and men will then learn that human actions likewise re-appear in their consequences by as certain a law as the green blade rises up out of the buried corn-seed."*

* See Proben Rabbinischer Weisheit. Engel's Schriften, Bd. I. s. 297-306.—*Am. Ed.*

THE FRIEND.

SECTION THE SECOND.

ON THE GROUNDS OF MORALS AND RELIGION, AND THE DISCIPLINE OF THE MIND REQUISITE FOR A TRUE UNDERSTANDING OF THE SAME.

I know, the seeming and self-pleasing wisdom of our times consists much in cavilling and unjustly carping at all things that see light, and that there are many who earnestly hunt after the publike fame of learning and judgment by this easily trod and despicable path, which, notwithstanding, they tread with as much confidence as folly: for that, oftimes, which they vainly and unjustly brand with opprobrie, outlives their fate, and flourisheth when it is forgot that ever any such as they had being.—*Dedication to Lord Herbert of Ambrose Parey's Works by Thomas Johnson, the Translator*, 1634.

THE FRIEND.

INTRODUCTION.

Παρὰ Σέξτου——τὴν ἔννοιαν τοῦ κατὰ φύσιν ζῆν, καὶ τὸ σεμνὸν ἀπλάστως, ——ὥςε κολακείας μὲν πάσης προσηνεςέραν εἶναι τὴν ὁμιλίαν αὐτοῦ, αἰδεσιμώτατον δὲ παρ' αὐτὸν ἐκεῖνον τὸν καιρὸν εἶναι· καὶ ἅμα μὲν ἀπαθέςατον εἶναι, ἅμα δὲ φιλοςοργότατον· καὶ τὸ ἰδεῖν ἄνθρωπον σαφῶς ἐλάχιςον τῶν ἑαυτοῦ καλῶν ἡγούμενον τὴν αὐτοῦ πολυμαθίην. M. Antoninus.*

From Sextus, and from the contemplation of his character, I learned what it was to live a life in harmony with nature; and that seemliness and dignity of deportment, which insured the profoundest reverence at the very same time that his company was more winning than all the flattery in the world. To him I owe likewise that I have known a man at once the most dispassionate, and the most affectionate, and who of all his attractions set the least value on the multiplicity of his literary acquisitions.

TO THE EDITOR OF THE FRIEND.

Sir,

I hope you will not ascribe to presumption the liberty I take in addressing you on the subject of your work. I feel deeply interested in the cause you have undertaken to support; and my object in writing this letter is to describe to you, in part from my own feelings, what I conceive to be the state of many minds, which may derive important advantage from your instructions.

I speak, Sir, of those who, though bred up under our unfavorable system of education, have yet held at times some intercourse with nature, and with those great minds whose works have been moulded by the spirit of nature; who, therefore, when they pass from the seclusion and constraint of early study, bring with them into the new scene of the world much of the pure sensibility which is the spring of all that is greatly good in thought and ac-

* L. I. 9. But the passage is made up from, rather than found in, Antoninus.—*Ed.*

tion. To such the season of that entrance into the world is a season of fearful importance; not for the seduction of its passions, but of its opinions. Whatever be their intellectual powers, unless extraordinary circumstances in their lives have been so favorable to the growth of meditative genius, that their speculative opinions must spring out of their early feelings, their minds are still at the mercy of fortune: they have no inward impulse steadily to propel them: and must trust to the chances of the world for a guide. And such is our present moral and intellectual state, that these chances are little else than variety of danger. There will be a thousand causes conspiring to complete the work of a false education, and by inclosing the mind on every side from the influences of natural feeling, to degrade its inborn dignity, and finally bring the heart itself under subjection to a corrupted understanding. I am anxious to describe to you what I have experienced or seen of the dispositions and feelings that will aid every other cause of danger, and tend to lay the mind open to the infection of all those falsehoods in opinion and sentiment, which constitute the degeneracy of the age.

Though it would not be difficult to prove, that the mind of the country is much enervated since the days of her strength, and brought down from its moral dignity, it is not yet so forlorn of all good,—there is nothing in the face of the times so dark and saddening and repulsive—as to shock the first feelings of a generous spirit, and drive it at once to seek refuge in the elder ages of our greatness. There yet survives so much of the character bred up through long years of liberty, danger, and glory, that even what this age produces bears traces of those that are past, and it still yields enough of beautiful, and splendid, and bold, to captivate an ardent but untutored imagination. And in this real excellence is the beginning of danger: for it is the first spring of that excessive admiration of the age which at last brings down to its own level a mind born above it. If there existed only the general disposition of all who are formed with a high capacity for good, to be rather credulous of excellence than suspiciously and severely just, the error would not be carried far: but there are, to a young mind, in this country and at this time, numerous powerful causes concurring to inflame his disposition, till the excess of the affection above the worth of its object is beyond all computation. To trace these causes it will be necessary to follow the history of a pure and noble mind from the first moment of that critical passage from seclusion to the world, which changes all the circumstances of its intellectual existence, shows it for the first time the real scene of living men, and calls up the new feeling of numerous relations by which it is to be connected with them.

To the young adventurer in life, who enters upon his course with such a mind, every thing seems made for delusion. He comes with a spirit the dearest feelings and highest thoughts of which have sprung up under the influences of nature. He transfers to the realities of life the high wild fancies of visionary boyhood: he brings with him into the world the passions of solitary and untamed imagination, and hopes which he has learned from dreams. Those dreams have been of the great and wonderful and lovely, of all which in these has yet been disclosed to him: his thoughts have dwelt among the wonders of nature, and among the loftiest spirits of men, heroes, and sages, and saints;—those whose deeds, and thoughts, and hopes, were high above ordinary mortality, have been the familiar companions of his soul. To love and to admire has been the joy of his existence. Love and admiration are the pleasures he will demand of the world. For these he has searched eagerly into the ages that are gone; but with more ardent and peremptory expectation he requires them of that in which his own lot is cast: for to look on life with hopes of happiness is a necessity of his nature, and to him there is no happiness but such as is surrounded with excellence.

See first how this spirit will affect his judgment of moral character, in those with whom chance may connect him in the common relations of life. It is of those with whom he is to live, that his soul first demands this food of her desires. From their conversation, their looks, their actions, their lives, she asks for excellence. To ask from all and to ask in vain, would be too dismal to bear: it would disturb him too deeply with doubt and perplexity and fear. In this hope, and in the revolting of his thoughts from the possibility of disappointment, there is a preparation for self-delusion: there is an unconscious determination that his soul shall be satisfied; an obstinate will to find good everywhere. And thus his first study of mankind is a continued effort to read in them the expression of his own feelings. He catches at every uncertain show and shadowy resemblance of what he seeks; and unsuspicious in innocence, he is first won with those appearances of good which are in fact only false pretensions. But this error is not carried far: for there is a sort of instinct of rectitude, which, like the pressure of a talisman given to baffle the illusions of enchantment, warns a pure mind against hypocrisy. There is another delusion more difficult to resist and more slowly dissipated. It is when he finds, as he often will, some of the real features of excellence in the purity of their native form. For then his rapid imagination will gather round them all the kindred features that are wanting to perfect beauty; and make for him, where he could not find, the moral creature of his expectation; peopling, even from this human world, his little circle of affection with forms as fair as his heart desired for its love.

But when, from the eminence of life which he has reached, he lifts up his eyes, and sends out his spirit to range over the great scene that is opening before him and around him, the whole prospect of civilized life so wide and so magnificent;—when he begins to contemplate, in their various stations of power or splendor, the leaders of mankind, those men on whose wisdom are hung the fortunes of nations, those whose genius and valor wield the heroism of a people;—or those, in no inferior pride of place, whose sway is over the mind of society, chiefs in the realm of imagination, interpreters of the secrets of nature, rulers of human opinion;—what wonder when he looks on all this living scene, that his heart should burn with strong affection, that he should feel that his own happiness will be forever interwoven with the interests of mankind? Here then the sanguine hope with which he looks on life, will again be blended with his passionate desire of excellence; and he will still be impelled to single out some, on whom his imagination and his hopes may repose. To whatever department of human thought or action his mind is turned with interest, either by the sway of public passion or by its own impulse, among statesmen, and warriors, and philosophers, and poets, he will distinguish some favored names on which he may satisfy his admiration. And there, just as in the little circle of his own acquaintance, seizing eagerly on every merit they possess, he will supply more from his own credulous hope, completing real with imagined excellence, till living men, with all their imperfections, become to him the representatives of his perfect ideal creation;—till, multiplying his objects of reverence, as he enlarges his prospect of life, he will have surrounded himself with idols of his own hands, and his imagination will seem to discern a glory in the countenance of the age, which is but the reflection of its own effulgence.

He will possess, therefore, in the creative power of generous hope, a preparation for illusory and exaggerated admiration of the age in which he lives: and this predisposition will meet with many favoring circumstances, when he has grown up under a system of education like ours, which (as perhaps all education must that is placed in the hands of a distinct and embodied class, who therefore bring to it the peculiar and hereditary prejudices of their order) has controlled his imagination to a reverence of former times, with an unjust contempt of his own. For no sooner does he break loose from this control, and begin to feel, as he contemplates the world for himself, how much there is surrounding him on all sides, that gratifies his noblest desires, than there springs up in him an indignant sense of injustice, both to the age and to his own mind; and he is impelled warmly and eagerly to give loose to the feelings that have been held in bondage, to seek out and to delight in finding excellence that will vindicate the insulted world, while it justifies, too, his resentment of his own undue subjection, and exalts the value of his new found liberty.

Add to this, that secluded as he has been from knowledge, and, in the imprisoning circle of one system of ideas, cut off from his share in the thoughts and feelings that are stirring among men, he finds himself, at the first steps of his liberty, in a new intellectual world. Passions and powers which he knew not of start up in his soul. The human mind, which he had seen but under one aspect, now presents to him a thousand unknown and beautiful forms. He sees it, in its varying powers, glancing over nature with restless curiosity, and with impetuous energy striving forever against the barriers which she has placed around it; sees it with divine power creating from dark materials living beauty, and fixing all its high and transported fancies in imperishable forms. In the world of knowledge, and science, and art, and genius, he treads as a stranger: in the confusion of new sensations, bewildered in delights, all seems beautiful; all seems admirable. And therefore he engages eagerly in the pursuit of false or insufficient philosophy; he is won by the allurements of licentious art; he follows with wonder the irregular transports of undisciplined imagination. Nor, where the objects of his admiration are worthy, is he yet skilful to distinguish between the acquisitions which the age has made for itself, and that large proportion of its wealth which it has only inherited: but in his delight of discovery and growing knowledge, all that is new to his own mind seems to him newborn to the world. To himself every fresh idea appears instruction; every new exertion, acquisition of power: he seems just called to the consciousness of himself, and to his true place in the intellectual world; and gratitude and reverence towards those to whom he owes this recovery of his dignity, tend much to subject him to the dominion of minds that were not formed by nature to be the leaders of opinion.

All the tumult and glow of thought and imagination, which seize on a mind of power in such a scene, tend irresistibly to bind it by stronger attachment of love and admiration to its own age. And there is one among the new emotions which belong to its entrance on the world, one almost the noblest of all, in which this exaltation of the age is essentially mingled. The faith in the perpetual progression of human nature towards perfection gives birth to such lofty dreams, as secure to it the devout assent of the imagination; and it will be yet more grateful to a heart just opening to hope, flushed with the consciousness of new strength, and exulting in the prospect of destined achievements. There is, therefore, almost a compulsion on generous and enthusiastic spirits, as they trust that the future shall transcend the present, to believe that the present transcends the past. It is only on an undue love and admiration of their own age that they can build their confidence in the melioration of the human race. Nor is this faith, which, in some shape, will always be the creed of virtue, without apparent reason, even in the erroneous form in which the young adopt it. For there is a perpetual acquisition of knowledge and art, an unceasing progress in many of the modes of exertion of the human mind, a perpetual unfolding of virtues with the changing manners of society: and it is not for a young mind to compare what is gained with what has passed away; to discern that amidst the incessant intellectual activity of the race, the intellectual power of individual minds may be falling off; and that amidst accumulating knowledge lofty science may disappear; and still less, to judge, in the more complicated moral character of a people, what is progression, and what is decline.

Into a mind possessed with this persuasion of the perpetual progress of man, there may even imperceptibly steal both from the belief itself, and from many of the views on which it rests, something like a distrust of the wisdom of great men of former ages, and with the reverence, which no delusion will ever overpower in a pure mind, for their greatness, a fancied discernment of imperfection and of incomplete excellence, which wanted for its accomplishment the advantages of later improvements: there will be a surprise that so much should have been possible in times so ill prepared; and even the study of their works may be sometimes rather the curious research of a speculative inquirer, than the devout contemplation of an enthusiast,—the watchful and obedient heart of a disciple listening to the inspiration of his master.

Here then is the power of delusion that will gather round the first steps of a youthful spirit, and throw enchantment over the world in which it is to dwell;—hope realizing its own dreams; ignorance dazzled and ravished with sudden sunshine; power awakened and rejoicing in its own consciousness; enthusiasm kindling among multiplying images of greatness and beauty, and enamored, above all, of one splendid error; and, springing from all these, such a rapture of life and hope, and joy, that the soul, in the power of its happiness, transmutes things essentially repugnant to it, into the excellence of its own nature: these are the spells that cheat the eye of the mind with illusion. It is under these influences that a young man of ardent spirit gives all his love, and reverence, and zeal, to productions of art, to theories of science, to opinions, to systems of feeling, and to characters distinguished in the world, that are far beneath his own original dignity.

Now as this delusion springs not from his worse but his better nature, it seems as if there could be no warning to him from within of his danger: for even the impassioned joy which he draws at times from the works of nature, and from those of her mightier sons, and which would startle him from a dream of unworthy passion, serves only to fix the infatuation:—for those deep emotions, proving to him that his heart is uncorrupted, justify to him all its workings, and his mind, confiding and delighting in itself, yields to the guidance of its own blind impulses of pleasure. His chance, therefore, of security is the chance that the greater number of objects occurring to attract his honorable passions may be worthy of them. But we have seen that the whole power of circumstances is collected to gather round him such objects and influences as will bend his high passions to unworthy enjoyment. He engages in it with a heart and understanding unspoiled: but they can not long be misapplied with impunity. They are drawn gradually into closer sympathy with the falsehoods they have adopted, till, his very nature seeming to change under the corruption, there disappears from it the capacity of those higher perceptions and pleasures to which he was born: and he is cast off from the communion of exalted minds, to live and to perish with the age to which he has surrendered himself.

If minds under these circumstances of danger are preserved from decay and overthrow, it can seldom, I think, be to themselves that they owe their deliverance. It must be to a fortunate chance which places them under the influence of some more enlightened mind, from which they may first gain suspicion and afterwards wisdom. There is a philosophy, which, leading them by the light of their best emotions to the principles which should give life to thought and law to genius, will discover to them in clear and perfect evidence, the falsehood of the errors that have misled them, and restore them to themselves. And this philosophy they will be willing to hear and wise to understand; but they must be led into its mysteries by some guiding hand; for they want the impulse or the power to penetrate of themselves the recesses.

If a superior mind should assume the protection of others just beginning to move among the dangers I have described, it would probably be found, that delusions springing from their own virtuous activity were not the only difficulties to be encountered. Even after suspicion is awakened, the subjection to falsehood may be prolonged and deepened by many weaknesses both of the intellectual and moral nature; weaknesses that will sometimes shake the authority of acknowledged truth. There may be intellectual indolence; an indisposition in the mind to the effort of combining the ideas it actually possesses, and bringing into distinct form the knowledge, which in its elements is already its own: there may be, where the heart resists the sway of opinion, misgivings and modest self-mistrust in him who sees that, if he trusts his heart, he must slight the judgment of all around him: —there may be too habitual yielding to authority, consisting, more than in indolence or diffidence, in a conscious helplessness and incapacity of the mind to maintain itself in its own place against the weight of general opinion; and there may be too indiscriminate, too undisciplined, a sympathy with others, which by the mere infection of feeling will subdue the reason. There must be a weakness in dejection to him who thinks with sadness, if his faith be pure, how gross is the error of the multitude, and that multitude how vast;—a reluctance to embrace a creed that excludes so many whom he loves, so many whom his youth has revered;—a difficulty to his understanding to believe that those whom he knows to be, in much that is good and honorable, his superiors, can be beneath him in this which is the most important of all;—a sympathy pleading importunately at his heart to descend to the fellowship of his brothers, and to take their faith and wisdom for his own. How often, when under the impulses of those solemn hours, in which he has felt with clearer insight and deeper faith his sacred truths, he labors to win to his own belief those whom he loves, will he be checked by their indifference or their laughter! And will he not bear back to his meditations a painful and disheartening sorrow, a gloomy discontent in that faith which takes in but a portion of those whom he wishes to include in all his blessings? Will he not be enfeebled by a distraction of inconsistent desires, when he feels so strongly that the faith which fills his heart, the circle within which he would embrace all he loves—would repose all his wishes and hopes and enjoyments—is yet incommensurate with his affections?

Even when the mind, strong in reason and just feeling united, and relying on its strength, has attached itself to truth, how much is there in the course and accidents of life that is forever silently at work for its degradation. There are pleasures deemed harmless, that lay asleep the recollections of innocence: there are pursuits held honorable, or imposed by duty, that oppress the moral spirit: above all there is that perpetual connection with ordinary minds in the common intercourse of society; that restless activity of frivolous conversation, where men of all characters and all pursuits mixing together, nothing may be talked of that is not of common interest to all;—nothing, therefore, but those obvious thoughts and feelings that float over the surface of things; and all which is drawn from the depth of nature, all which impassioned feeling has made original in thought, would be misplaced and obtrusive. The talent that is allowed to show itself is that which can repay admiration by furnishing entertainment; and the display to which it is invited is that which flatters the vulgar pride of society, by abasing what is too high in excellence for its sympathy. A dangerous seduction to talents, which would make language, given to exalt the soul by the fervid expression of its pure emotions, the instrument of its degradation. And even when there is, as in the instance I have supposed, too much uprightness to choose so dishonorable a triumph, there is a necessity of manners, by which every one must be controlled who mixes much in society, not to offend those with whom he converses by his superiority; and whatever be the native spirit of a mind, it is evident that this perpetual adaptation of itself to others, this watchfulness against its own rising feelings, this studied sympathy with mediocrity, must pollute and impoverish the sources of its strength.

From much of its own weakness, and from all the errors of its misleading activities, may generous youth be rescued by the interposition of an enlightened mind; and in some degree it may be guarded by instruction against the injuries to which it is exposed in the world. His lot is happy who owes this protection to friendship; who has found in a friend the watchful guardian of his mind. He will not be deluded, having that light to guide; he will not slumber with that voice to inspire; he will not be desponding or dejected, with that bosom to lean on. But how many must there be whom Heaven has left unprovided, except in their own strength; who must maintain themselves, unassisted and solitary, against their own infirmities and the opposition of the world! For such there may yet be a protector. If a teacher should stand up in their generation, conspicuous above the multitude in superior power, and still more in the assertion and proclamation of disregarded truth;—to him, to his cheering or summoning voice, all those would turn, whose deep sensibility has been oppressed by the indifference, or misled by the seduction of the times. Of one such teacher who has been given to our own age you have described the power when you said, that in his annunciation of truths he seemed to speak in thunders. I believe that mighty voice has not been poured out in vain; that there are hearts that have received into their inmost depths all its varying tones; and that even now, there are many to whom the name of Wordsworth calls up the recollection of their weakness and the consciousness of their strength.

To give to the reason and eloquence of one man this complete control over the minds of others, it is necessary, I think, that he should be born in their own times. For thus whatever false opinion of pre-eminence is attached to the age becomes at once a title of reverence to him; and when with distinguished powers he sets himself apart from the age, and above it, as the teacher of high but ill-understood truths, he will appear at once to a generous imagination in the dignity of one whose superior mind outsteps the rapid progress of society, and will derive from illusion itself the power to disperse illusions. It is probable too, that he who labors under the errors I have described, might feel the power of truth in a writer of another age, yet fail in applying the full force of his principles to his own times; but when he receives them from a living teacher, there is no room for doubt or misapplication. It is the errors of his own generation that are denounced; and whatever authority he may acknowledge in the instructions of his master, strikes, with inevitable force, at his veneration for the opinions and characters of his own times. And finally there will be gathered round a living teacher, who speaks to the deeper soul, many feelings of human love that will place the infirmities of the heart peculiarly under his control; at the same time that they blend with and animate the attachment to his cause. So that there will flow from him something of the peculiar influence of a friend: while his doctrines will be embraced and asserted and vindicated with the ardent zeal of a disciple, such as can scarcely be carried back to distant times, or connected with voices that speak only from the grave.

I have done what I proposed. I have related to you as much as I have had opportunities of knowing of the difficulties from within and from without, which may oppose the natural development of true feeling and right opinion in a mind formed with some capacity for good; and the resources which such a mind may derive from an enlightened contemporary writer. If what I have said be just, it is certain that this influence will be felt more particularly in a work, adapted by its mode of publication to address the feelings of the time, and to bring to its readers repeated admonition and repeated consolation.

I have, perhaps, presumed too far in trespassing on your attention, and in giving way to my own thoughts; but I was unwilling to leave any thing unsaid which might induce you to consider with favor the request I was anxious to make, in the name of all whose state of mind I have described, that you would at times regard us more particularly in your instructions. I can not judge to what degree it may be in your power to give the truth you teach a control over understandings that have matured their strength in error; but in our class I am sure you will have docile learners.

MATHETES.*

The Friend might rest satisfied that his exertions thus far have not been wholly unprofitable, if no other proof had been given of their influence, than that of having called forth the foregoing letter, with which he has been so much interested, that he could not deny himself the pleasure of communicating it to his readers. In answer to his correspondent, it need scarcely here be repeated, that one of the main purposes of his work is to weigh, honestly and thoughtfully, the moral worth and intellectual power of the age in which we live; to ascertain our gain and our loss; to determine what we are in ourselves positively, and what we are compared with our ancestors; and thus, and by every other means within his power, to discover what may be hoped for future times, what and how lamentable are the evils to be feared, and how far there is cause for fear. If this attempt should not be made wholly in vain, my ingenious correspondent, and all who are in a state of mind resembling that of which he gives so lively a picture, will be enabled more readily and surely to distinguish false from legitimate objects of admiration: and thus may the personal errors which he would guard against be more effectually prevented or removed by the development of general truth for a general purpose, than by instructions specifically adapted to himself or to the class of which he is the able representative. There is a life and spirit in knowledge which we extract from truths scattered for the benefit of all, and which the mind by its own

* This letter was, as the Editor is informed, the joint composition of the present Professor Wilson and his friend, Mr. Alexander Blair.—*Ed.*

activity, has appropriated to itself,—a life and spirit, which is seldom found in knowledge communicated by formal and direct precepts, even when they are exalted and endeared by reverence and love for the teacher.

Nevertheless, though I trust that the assistance which my correspondent has done me the honor to request, will in course of time flow naturally from my labors, in a manner that will best serve him, I can not resist the inclination to connect, at present, with his letter a few remarks of direct application to the subject of it; remarks, I say,—for to such I shall confine myself,—independent of the main point out of which his complaint and request both proceed; I mean the assumed inferiority of the present age in moral dignity and intellectual power to those which have preceded it. For if the fact were true, that we had even surpassed our ancestors in the best of what is good, the main part of the dangers and impediments which my correspondent has feelingly portrayed, could not cease to exist for minds like his, nor indeed would they be much diminished; as they arise out of the constitution of things, from the nature of youth, from the laws that govern the growth of the faculties, and from the necessary condition of the great body of mankind. Let us throw ourselves back to the age of Elizabeth, and call up to mind the heroes, the warriors, the statesmen, the poets, the divines, and the moral philosophers, with which the reign of the virgin queen was illustrated. Or if we be more strongly attracted by the moral purity and greatness, and that sanctity of civil and religious duty, with which the tyranny of Charles I. was struggled against, let us cast our eyes, in the hurry of admiration, round that circle of glorious patriots: but do not let us be persuaded, that each of these, in his course of discipline, was uniformly helped forward by those with whom he associated, or by those whose care it was to direct him. Then, as now, existed objects to which the wisest attached undue importance; then, as now, judgment was misled by factions and parties, time wasted in controversies fruitless, except as far as they quickened the faculties; then, as now, minds were venerated or idolized, which owed their influence to the weakness of their contemporaries rather than to their own power. Then, though great actions were wrought, and great works in literature and science produced, yet the general taste was capricious, fantastical, or grovelling; and in this point, as in all others, was youth subject to delusion, frequent in proportion to the liveliness of the sensibility, and strong as the strength of the imagination. Every age hath abounded in instances of parents, kindred, and friends, who, by indirect influence of example, or by positive injunction and exhortation, have diverted or discouraged the youth, who, in the simplicity and purity of nature, had determined to follow his intellectual genius through good and through evil, and had devoted himself to knowledge, to the practice of virtue and the preservation of integrity, in slight of temporal rewards. Above all, have not the common duties and cares of common life at all times exposed men to injury from causes the action of which is the more fatal from being silent and unremitting, and which, wherever it was not jealously watched and steadily opposed, must have pressed upon and consumed the diviner spirit?

There are two errors into which we easily slip when thinking of past times. One lies in forgetting in the excellence of what remains the large overbalance of worthlessness that has been swept away. Ranging over the wide tracts of antiquity, the situation of the mind may be likened to that of a traveller* in some unpeopled part of America, who is attracted to the burial-place of one of the primitive inhabitants. It is conspicuous upon an eminence, "a mount upon a mount!" He digs into it, and finds that it contains the bones of a man of mighty stature; and he is tempted to give way to a belief, that as there were giants in those days, so all men were giants. But a second and wiser thought may suggest to him that this tomb would never have forced itself upon his notice, if it had not contained a body that was distinguished from others,—that of a man who had been selected as a chieftain or ruler for the very reason that he surpassed the rest of his tribe in stature, and who now lies thus conspicuously inhumed upon the mountain-top, while the bones of his followers are laid unobtrusively together in their burrows upon the plain below. The second habitual error is, that in this comparison of ages we divide time merely into past and present, and place these in the balance to be weighed against each other; not considering that the present is in our estimation not more than a period of thirty years, or half a century at most, and that the past is a mighty accumulation of many such periods, perhaps the

* See Ashe's Travels in America

whole of recorded time, or at least the whole of that portion of it in which our own country has been distinguished. We may illustrate this by the familiar use of the words ancient and modern, when applied to poetry. What can be more inconsiderate or unjust than to compare a few existing writers with the whole succession of their progenitors? The delusion, from the moment that our thoughts are directed to it, seems too gross to deserve mention; yet men will talk for hours upon poetry, balancing against each other the words ancient and modern, and be unconscious that they have fallen into it.

These observations are not made as implying a dissent from the belief of my correspondent, that the moral spirit and intellectual powers of this country are declining; but to guard against unqualified admiration, even in cases where admiration has been rightly fixed, and to prevent that depression which must necessarily follow, where the notion of the peculiar unfavorableness of the present times to dignity of mind has been carried too far. For in proportion as we imagine obstacles to exist out of ourselves to retard our progress, will, in fact, our progress be retarded. Deeming, then, that in all ages an ardent mind will be baffled and led astray in the manner under contemplation, though in various degrees, I shall at present content myself with a few practical and desultory comments upon some of those general causes, to which my correspondent justly attributes the errors in opinion, and the lowering or deadening of sentiment, to which ingenuous and aspiring youth is exposed. And first, for the heart-cheering belief in the perpetual progress of the species towards a point of unattainable perfection. If the present age do indeed transcend the past in what is most beneficial and honorable, he that perceives this, being in no error, has no cause for complaint; but if it be not so, a youth of genius might, it should seem, be preserved from any wrong influence of this faith by an insight into a simple truth, namely, that it is not necessary, in order to satisfy the desires of our nature, or to reconcile us to the economy of providence, that there should be at all times a continuous advance in what is of highest worth. In fact it is not, as a writer of the present day has admirably observed, in the power of fiction to portray in words, or of the imagination to conceive in spirit, actions or characters of more exalted virtue, than those which thousands of years ago have existed upon earth, as we know from the records of authentic history. Such is the inherent dignity of human nature, that there belong to it sublimities of virtues which all men may attain, and which no man can transcend: and though this be not true in an equal degree of intellectual power, yet in the persons of Plato, Demosthenes, and Homer, and in those of Shakspeare, Milton, and Lord Bacon, were enshrined as much of the divinity of intellect as the inhabitants of this planet can hope will ever take up its abode among them. But the question is not of the power or worth of individual minds, but of the general moral or intellectual merits of an age, or a people, or of the human race. Be it so. Let us allow and believe that there is a progress in the species towards unattainable perfection, or whether this be so or not, that it is a necessity of a good and greatly-gifted nature to believe it; surely it does not follow that this progress should be constant in those virtues and intellectual qualities, and in those departments of knowledge, which in themselves absolutely considered are of most value, things independent and in their degree indispensable. The progress of the species neither is nor can be like that of a Roman road in a right line. It may be more justly compared to that of a river, which, both in its smaller reaches and larger turnings, is frequently forced back towards its fountains by objects which can not otherwise be eluded or overcome; yet with an accompanying impulse that will insure its advancement hereafter, it is either gaining strength every hour, or conquering in secret some difficulty, by a labor that contributes as effectually to further it in its course, as when it moves forward uninterrupted in a line, direct as that of the Roman road with which I began the comparison.

It suffices to content the mind, though there may be an apparent stagnation, or a retrograde movement in the species, that something is doing which is necessary to be done, and the effects of which will in due time appear; that something is unremittingly gaining, either in secret preparation or in open and triumphant progress. But in fact here, as everywhere, we are deceived by creations which the mind is compelled to make for itself; we speak of the species not as an aggregate, but as endued with the form and separate life of an individual. But human kind,—what is it else than myriads of rational beings in various degrees obedient to their reason; some torpid, some aspiring; some in eager chase to the right hand, some to the left; these wasting down their moral nature, and these feeding it for immortality? A whole generation may appear even to sleep, or may be exasperated with rage,—they that compose it, tearing each other to pieces with more than brutal fury. It is enough for complacency and hope, that scattered and solitary minds are always laboring somewhere in the service of truth and virtue; and that by the sleep of the multitude the energy of the multitude may be prepared; and that by the fury of the people the chains of the people may be broken. Happy moment was it for England when her Chaucer, who has rightly been called the morning-star of her literature, appeared above the horizon; when her Wicliffe, like the sun, shot orient beams through the night of Romish superstition! Yet may the darkness and the desolating hurricane which immediately followed in the wars of York and Lancaster, be deemed in their turn a blessing, with which the land has been visited.

May I return to the thought of progress, of accumulation, of increasing light, or of any other image by which it may please us to represent the improvement of the species? The hundred years that followed the usurpation of Henry IV., were a hurling-back of the mind of the country, a dilapidation, an extinction; yet institutions, laws, customs, and habits, were then broken down, which would not have been so readily, nor perhaps so thoroughly destroyed by the gradual influence of increasing knowledge; and under the oppression of which, if they had continued to exist, the virtue and intellectual prowess of the succeeding century could not have appeared at all, much less could they have displayed themselves with that eager haste, and with those beneficent triumphs, which will to the end of time be looked back upon with admiration and gratitude.

If the foregoing obvious distinctions be once clearly perceived, and steadily kept in view, I do not see why a belief in the progress of human nature towards perfection should dispose a youthful mind, however enthusiastic, to an undue admiration of his own age, and thus tend to degrade that mind.

But let me strike at once at the root of the evil complained of in my correspondent's letter. Protection from any fatal effect of seductions and hindrances which opinion may throw in the way of pure and high-minded youth, can only be obtained with certainty at the same price by which every thing great and good is obtained, namely, steady dependence upon voluntary and self-originating effort, and upon the practice of self-examination, sincerely aimed at and rigorously enforced. But how is this to be expected from youth? Is it not to demand the fruit when the blossom is barely put forth, and is hourly at the mercy of frosts and winds? To expect from youth these virtues and habits, in that degree of excellence to which in mature years they may be carried, would indeed be preposterous. Yet has youth many helps and aptitudes for the discharge of these difficult duties, which are withdrawn for the most part from the more advanced stages of life. For youth has its own wealth and independence; it is rich in health of body and animal spirits, in its sensibility to the impressions of the natural universe, in the conscious growth of knowledge, in lively sympathy and familiar communion with the generous actions recorded in history, and with the high passions of poetry; and, above all, youth is rich in the possession of time, and the accompanying consciousness of freedom and power. The young man feels that he stands at a distance from the season when his harvest is to be reaped; that he has leisure and may look around, and may defer both the choice and the execution of his purposes. If he makes an attempt and shall fail, new hopes immediately rush in, and new promises. Hence, in the happy confidence of his feelings, and in the elasticity of his spirit, neither worldly ambition, nor the love of praise, nor dread of censure, nor the necessity of worldly maintenance, nor any of those causes which tempt or compel the mind habitually to look out of itself for support; neither these, nor the passions of envy, fear, hatred, despondency, and the rankling of disappointed hopes (all which in after-life give birth to, and regulate, the efforts of men and determine their opinions), have power to preside over the choice of the young, if the disposition be not naturally bad, or the circumstances have not been in an uncommon degree unfavorable.

In contemplation, then, of this disinterested and free condition of the youthful mind, I deem it in many points peculiarly capable of searching into itself, and of profiting by a few simple questions, such as these that follow. Am I chiefly gratified by the exertion of my power from the pure pleasure of intellectual activity, and from the knowledge thereby acquired? In other words, to what degree do I value my faculties and my attainments for their own sakes? or are they chiefly prized by me on account of the distinction which they confer, or the superiority which they give me over others? Am I aware that immediate influence and a general acknowledgment of merit are no necessary adjuncts of a successful adherence to study and meditation in those departments of knowledge which are of most value to mankind;—that a recompense of honors and emoluments is far less to be expected; in fact, that there is little natural connection between them? Have I perceived this truth; and, perceiving it, does the countenance of philosophy continue to appear as bright and beautiful in my eyes?—Has no haze bedimmed it? Has no cloud passed over and hidden from me that look which was before so encouraging? Knowing that it is my duty, and feeling that it is my inclination, to mingle as a social being with my fellow-men; prepared also to submit cheerfully to the necessity that will probably exist of relinquishing, for the purpose of gaining a livelihood, the greatest portion of my time to employments where I shall have little or no choice how or when I am to act; have I, at this moment, when I stand as it were upon the threshold of the busy world, a clear intuition of that pre-eminence in which virtue and truth (involving in this latter word the sanctities of religion) sit enthroned above all denominations and dignities which, in various degrees of exaltation, rule over the desires of men? Do I feel that, if their solemn mandates shall be forgotten, or disregarded, or denied the obedience due to them when opposed to others, I shall not only have lived for no good purpose, but that I shall have sacrificed my birth-right as a rational being; and that every other acquisition will be a bane and a disgrace to me? This is not spoken with reference to such sacrifices as present themselves to the youthful imagination in the shape of crimes, acts by which the conscience is violated; such a thought, I know, would be recoiled from at once, not without indignation; but I write in the spirit of the ancient fable of Prodicus, representing the choice of Hercules. Here is the World, a female figure approaching at the head of a train of willing or giddy followers: her air and deportment are at once careless, remiss, self-satisfied, and haughty: and there is Intellectual Prowess, with a pale cheek and serene brow, leading in chains Truth, her beautiful and modest captive. The one makes her salutation with a discourse of ease, pleasure, freedom, and domestic tranquillity; or, if she invite to labor, it is labor in the busy and beaten tract, with assurance of the complacent regards of parents, friends, and of those with whom we associate. The promise also may be upon her lip of the huzzas of the multitude, of the smile of kings, and the munificent rewards of senates. The other does not venture to hold forth any of these allurements; she does not conceal from him whom she addresses the impediments, the disappointments, the ignorance and prejudice which her follower will have to encounter, if devoted, when duty calls, to active life; and if to contemplative, she lays nakedly before him a scheme of solitary and unremitting labor, a life of entire neglect perhaps, or assuredly a life exposed to scorn, insult, persecution, and hatred; but cheered by encouragement from a grateful few, by applauding conscience, and by a prophetic anticipation, perhaps, of fame—a late, though lasting consequence. Of these two, each in this manner soliciting you to become her adherent, you doubt not which to prefer; but oh! the thought of moment is not preference, but the degree of preference; the passionate and pure choice, the inward sense of absolute and unchangeable devotion.

I spoke of a few simple questions. The question involved in this deliberation is simple, but at the same time it is high and awful; and I would gladly know whether an answer can be returned satisfactory to the mind. We will for a moment suppose that it can not; that there is a startling and a hesitation. Are we then to despond,—to retire from all contest,—and to reconcile ourselves at once to cares without a generous hope, and to efforts in which there is no more moral life than that which is found in the business and labors of the unfavored and unaspiring many? No. But if the inquiry have not been on just grounds satisfactorily answered, we may refer confidently our youth to that nature of which he deems himself an enthusiastic follower, and one who wishes to continue no less faithful and enthusiastic. We would tell him that there are paths which he has not trodden; recesses which he has not penetrated; that there is a beauty which he has not seen, a pathos which he has not felt, a sublimity to which he hath not been raised. If he have trembled because there has occasionally taken place in him a lapse of which he is conscious; if he foresee open or secret attacks, which he has had intimations that he will neither be strong enough to resist, nor watchful enough to elude, let him not hastily ascribe this weakness, this deficiency, and the painful apprehensions accompanying them, in any degree to the virtues or noble qualities with which youth by nature is furnished ; but let him first be assured, before he looks about for the means of attaining the insight, the discriminating powers, and the confirmed wisdom of manhood, that his soul has more to demand of the appropriate excellencies of youth, than youth has yet supplied to it ; that the evil under which he labors is not a superabundance of the instincts and the animating spirit of that age, but a falling short, or a failure. But what can he gain from this admonition ? He can not recall past time ; he can not begin his journey afresh ; he can not untwist the links by which, in no undelightful harmony, images and sentiments are wedded in his mind. Granted that the sacred light of childhood is and must be for him no more than a remembrance. He may, notwithstanding, be remanded to nature, and with trustworthy hopes, founded less upon his sentient than upon his intellectual being ; to nature, as leading on insensibly to the society of reason, but to reason and will, as leading back to the wisdom of nature. A re-union, in this order accomplished, will bring reformation and timely support ; and the two powers of reason and nature, thus reciprocally teacher and taught, may advance together in a track to which there is no limit.

We have been discoursing (by implication at least) of infancy, childhood, boyhood, and youth, of pleasures lying upon the unfolding intellect plenteously as morning dew-drops,—of knowledge inhaled insensibly like the fragrance,—of dispositions stealing into the spirit like music from unknown quarters,—of images uncalled for and rising up like exhalations,—of hopes plucked like beautiful wild flowers from the ruined tombs that border the highways of antiquity, to make a garland for a living forehead ;—in a word, we have been treating of nature as a teacher of truth through joy and through gladness, and as a creatress of the faculties by a process of smoothness and delight. We have made no mention of fear, shame, sorrow, nor of ungovernable and vexing thoughts ; because, although these have been and have done mighty service, they are overlooked in that stage of life when youth is passing into manhood—overlooked, or forgotten. We now apply for the succor which we need to a faculty that works after a different course ; that faculty is reason ; she gives more spontaneously, but she seeks for more ; she works by thought through feeling ; yet in thoughts she begins and ends.

A familiar incident may elucidate this contrast in the operations of nature, may render plain the manner in which a process of intellectual improvements, the reverse of that which nature pursues, is by reason introduced. There never perhaps existed a school-boy, who, having, when he retired to rest, carelessly blown out his candle, and having chanced to notice, as he lay upon his bed in the ensuing darkness, the sullen light which had survived the extinguished flame, did not, at some time or other, watch that light as if his mind were bound to it by a spell. It fades and revives, gathers to a point, seems as if it would go out in a moment, again recovers its strength, nay becomes brighter than before : it continues to shine with an endurance, which in its apparent weakness is a mystery ; it protracts its existence so long, clinging to the power which supports it, that the observer, who had lain down in his bed so easy-minded, becomes sad and melancholy ; his sympathies are touched ; it is to him an intimation and an image of departing human life ; the thought comes nearer to him ; it is the life of a venerated parent, of a beloved brother or sister, or of an aged domestic, who are gone to the grave, or whose destiny it soon may be thus to linger, thus to hang upon the last point of mortal existence, thus finally to depart and be seen no more. This is nature teaching seriously and sweetly through the affections, melting the heart, and, through that instinct of tenderness, developing the understanding. In this instance the object of solicitude is the bodily life of another. Let us accompany this same boy to that period between youth and manhood, when a solicitude may be awakened for the moral life of himself. Are there any powers by which, beginning with a sense of inward decay that affects not however the natural life, he could call to mind the same image and hang over it with an equal interest as a visible type of his own perishing spirit ? Oh ! surely, if the being of the individual be under his own care, if it be his first care, if duty begin from the point of accountableness to our conscience, and, through that, to God and human nature ; if without such primary sense of duty, all secondary care of teacher, of friend, or parent, must be baseless and fruitless ; if, lastly, the motions of the soul transcend in worth those of the animal functions, nay, give to them their sole value; then truly are there such powers; and the image of the dying taper may be recalled and contemplated, though with no sadness in the nerves, no disposition to tears, no unconquerable sighs, yet with a melancholy in the soul, a sinking inward into ourselves from thought to thought, a steady remonstrance, and a high resolve. Let then the youth go back, as occasion will permit, to nature and to solitude, thus admonished by reason, and relying upon this newly acquired support. A world of fresh sensations will gradually open upon him as his mind puts off its infirmities, and as instead of being propelled restlessly towards others in admiration, or too hasty love, he makes it his prime business to understand himself. New sensations, I affirm, will be opened out, pure, and sanctioned by that reason which is their original author; and precious feelings of disinterested, that is self-disregarding, joy and love may be regenerated and restored; and, in this sense, he may be said to measure back the track of life he has trodden.

In such disposition of mind let the youth return to the visible universe, and to conversation with ancient books, and to those, if such there be, which in the present day breathe the ancient spirit; and let him feed upon that beauty which unfolds itself, not to his eye as it sees carelessly the things which can not possibly go unseen, and are remembered or not as accident shall decide, but to the thinking mind, which searches, discovers, and treasures up, infusing by meditation into the objects with which it converses an intellectual life, whereby they remain planted in the memory, now and forever. Hitherto the youth, I suppose, has been content for the most part to look at his own mind, after the manner in which he ranges along the stars in the firmament with naked unaided sight: let him now apply the telescope of art, to call the invisible stars out of their hiding-places; and let him endeavor to look through the system of his being, with the organ of reason, summoned to penetrate, as far as it has power, in discovery of the impelling forces and the governing laws.

These expectations are not immoderate; they demand nothing more than the perception of a few plain truths; namely, that knowledge, efficacious for the production of virtue, is the ultimate end of all effort, the sole dispenser of complacency and repose A perception also is implied of the inherent superiority of contemplation to action. The Friend does not in this contradict his own words, where he has said heretofore, that 'doubtless to act is nobler than to think.'* In those words, it was his purpose to censure that barren contemplation, which rests satisfied with itself in cases where the thoughts are of such quality that they may, and ought to, be embodied in action. But he speaks now of the general superiority of thought to action; as proceeding and governing all action that moves to salutary purposes; and, secondly, as leading to elevation, the absolute possession of the individual mind, and to a consistency or harmony of the being within itself, which no outward agency can reach to disturb or to impair; and lastly, as producing works of pure science; or of the combined faculties of imagination, feeling, and reason; works which, both from their independence in their origin upon accident, their nature, their duration, and the wide spread of their influence, are entitled rightly to take place of the noblest and most beneficent deeds of heroes, statesmen, legislators, or warriors.

Yet, beginning from the perception of this established superiority, we do not suppose that the youth, whom we wish to guide and encourage, is to be insensible to those influences of wealth, or rank, or station, by which the bulk of mankind are swayed. Our eyes have not been fixed upon virtue which lies apart from human nature, or transcends it. In fact there is no such virtue. We neither suppose nor wish him to undervalue or slight these distinctions as modes of power, things that may enable him to be more useful to his contemporaries; nor as gratifications that may confer dignity upon his living person, and, through him, upon those who love him; nor as they may connect his name, through a family to be founded by his success, in a closer chain of gratitude with some portion of posterity, who shall speak of him as among their ancestry, with a more tender interest than the mere general bond of patriotism or humanity would supply. We suppose no indifference to, much less a contempt of, these rewards; but let them have their due place; let it be ascertained, when the soul is searched into, that they are only an auxiliary motive to exertion, never the principal or originating force. If this be too much to expect from a youth who, I take for granted, possesses no ordinary endowments, and whom circumstances with respect to the more dangerous passions have favored, then, indeed, must the noble spirit of the country be wasted away; then would

* Ante, p. 172.—*Ed.*

our institutions be deplorable, and the education prevalent among us utterly vile and debasing.

But my correspondent, who drew forth these thoughts, has said rightly, that the character of the age may not without injustice be thus branded. He will not deny that, without speaking of other countries, there is in these islands, in the departments of natural philosophy, of mechanic ingenuity, in the general activities of the country, and in the particular excellence of individual minds, in high stations civil or military, enough to excite admiration and love in the sober-minded, and more than enough to intoxicate the youthful and inexperienced. I will compare, then, an aspiring youth, leaving the schools in which he has been disciplined, and preparing to bear a part in the concerns of the world, I will compare him in this season of eager admiration, to a newly-invested knight appearing with his blank unsignalized shield, upon some day of solemn tournament, at the court of the Faery-queen, as that sovereignty was conceived to exist by the moral and imaginative genius of our divine Spenser. He does not himself immediately enter the lists as a combatant; but he looks round him with a beating heart, dazzled by the gorgeous pageantry, the banners, the impresses, the ladies of overcoming beauty, the persons of the knights, now first seen by him, the fame of whose actions is carried by the traveller, like merchandise, through the world, and resounded upon the harp of the minstrel. But I am not at liberty to make this comparison. If a youth were to begin his career in such an assemblage, with such examples to guide and to animate, it will be pleaded, there would be no cause for apprehension; he could not falter, he could not be misled. But ours is, notwithstanding its manifold excellences, a degenerate age; and recreant knights are among us far outnumbering the true. A false Gloriana in these days imposes worthless services, which they who perform them, in their blindness, know not to be such; and which are recompensed by rewards as worthless, yet eagerly grasped at, as if they were the immortal guerdon of virtue.

I have in this declaration insensibly overstepped the limits which I had determined not to pass: let me be forgiven; for it is hope which hath carried me forward. In such a mixed assemblage as our age presents, with its genuine merit and its large overbalance of alloy, I may boldly ask into what errors, either with respect to person or thing, could a young man fall, who had sincerely entered upon the course of moral discipline which has been recommended, and to which the condition of youth, it has been proved, is favorable? His opinions could nowhere deceive him beyond the point up to which, after a season, he would find that it was salutary for him to have been deceived. For as that man can not set a right value upon health who has never known sickness, nor feel the blessing of ease who has been through his life a stranger to pain, so can there be no confirmed and passionate love of truth for him who has not experienced the hollowness of error. Range against each other as advocates, oppose as combatants, two several intellects, each strenuously asserting doctrines which he sincerely believes; but the one contending for the worth and beauty of that garment which the other has outgrown and cast away. Mark the superiority, the ease, the dignity, on the side of the more advanced mind, how he overlooks his subject, commands it from centre to circumference, and hath the same thorough knowledge of the tenets which his adversary, with impetuous zeal, but in confusion also, and thrown off his guard at every turn of the argument, is laboring to maintain. If it be a question of the fine arts (poetry for instance) the riper mind not only sees that his opponent is deceived; but, what is of far more importance, sees how he is deceived. The imagination stands before him with all its imperfections laid open; as duped by shows, enslaved by words, corrupted by mistaken delicacy and false refinement, as not having even attended with care to the reports of the senses, and therefore deficient grossly in the rudiments of its own power. He has noted how, as a supposed necessary condition, the understanding sleeps in order that the fancy may dream. Studied in the history of society, and versed in the secret laws of thought, he can pass regularly through all the gradations, can pierce infallibly all the windings, which false taste through ages has pursued, from the very time when first, through inexperience, heedlessness, or affectation, the imagination took its departure from the side of truth, its original parent. Can a disputant thus accoutred be withstood?—one to whom, further, every movement in the thoughts of his antagonist is revealed by the light of his own experience; who, therefore, sympathizes with weakness gently, and wins his way by forbearance; and hath, when needful, an irresistible power of onset, arising from gratitude to the truth which he vindicates, not merely as a positive good for mankind, but as his own especial rescue and redemption.

I might here conclude: but my correspondent towards the close of his letter, has written so feelingly upon the advantages to be derived, in his estimation, from a living instructor, that I must not leave this part of the subject without a word of direct notice. The Friend cited, some time ago,* a passage from the prose works of Milton, eloquently describing the manner in which good and evil grow up together in the field of the world almost inseparably; and insisting, consequently, upon the knowledge and survey of vice as necessary to the constituting of human virtue, and the scanning of error to the confirmation of truth.

If this be so, and I have been reasoning to the same effect in the preceding paragraph, the fact, and the thoughts which it may suggest, will, if rightly applied, tend to moderate an anxiety for the guidance of a more experienced or superior mind. The advantage, where it is possessed, is far from being an absolute good: nay, such a preceptor, ever at hand, might prove an oppression not to be thrown off, and a fatal hindrance. Grant that in the general tenor of his intercourse with his pupil he is forbearing and circumspect, inasmuch as he is rich in that knowledge (above all other necessary for a teacher) which can not exist without a liveliness of memory, preserving for him an unbroken image of the winding, excursive, and often retrograde course, along which his own intellect has passed. Grant that, furnished with these distinct remembrances, he wishes that the mind of his pupil should be free to luxuriate in the enjoyments, loves, and admirations appropriated to its age; that he is not in haste to kill what he knows will in due time die of itself; or be transmuted, and put on a nobler form and higher faculties otherwise unattainable. In a word, that the teacher is governed habitually by the wisdom of patience waiting with pleasure. Yet perceiving how much the outward help of art can facilitate the progress of nature, he may be betrayed into many unnecessary or pernicious mistakes where he deems his interference warranted by substantial experience. And in spite of all his caution, remarks may drop insensibly from him which shall wither in the mind of his pupil a generous sympathy, destroy a sentiment of

* Ante, p. 77.—*Ed.*

approbation or dislike, not merely innocent but salutary; and for the inexperienced disciple how many pleasures may be thus cut off, what joy, what admiration, and what love! While in their stead are introduced into the ingenuous mind misgivings, a mistrust of its own evidence, dispositions to affect to feel where there can be no real feeling, indecisive judgments, a superstructure of opinions that has no base to support it, and words uttered by rote with the impertinence of a parrot or a mocking-bird, yet which may not be listened to with the same indifference, as they can not be heard without some feeling of moral disapprobation.

These results, I contend, whatever may be the benefit to be derived from such an enlightened teacher, are in their degree inevitable. And by this process, humility and docile dispositions may exist towards the master, endued as he is with the power which personal preference confers; but at the same time they will be liable to overstep their due bounds, and to degenerate into passiveness and prostration of mind. This towards him; while, with respect to other living men, nay even to the mighty spirits of past times, there may be associated with such weakness a want of modesty and humility. Insensibly may steal in presumption and a habit of sitting in judgment in cases where no sentiment ought to have existed by diffidence or veneration. Such virtues are the sacred attributes of youth; its appropriate calling is not to distinguish in the fear of being deceived or degraded, not to analyze with scrupulous minuteness, but to accumulate in genial confidence; its instinct, its safety, its benefit, its glory, is to love, to admire, to feel, and to labor. Nature has irrevocably decreed, that our prime dependence in all stages of life after infancy and childhood have been passed through (nor do I know that this latter ought to be excepted) must be upon our own minds; and that the way to knowledge shall be long, difficult, winding, and oftentimes returning upon itself.

What has been said is a mere sketch, and that only of a part of the interesting country into which we have been led; but my correspondent will be able to enter the paths that have been pointed out. Should he do this and advance steadily for a while, he needs not fear any deviations from the truth which will be finally injurious to him. He will not long have his admiration fixed upon unworthy objects; he will neither be clogged nor drawn aside by the love of friends or kindred, betraying his understanding through his affections; he will neither be bowed down by conventional arrangements of manners producing too often a lifeless decency; nor will the rock of his spirit wear away in the endless beating of the waves of the world; neither will that portion of his own time, which he must surrender to labors by which his livelihood is to be earned or his social duties performed, be unprofitable to himself indirectly, while it is directly useful to others; for that time has been primarily surrendered through an act of obedience to a moral law established by himself, and therefore he moves then also along the orbit of perfect liberty.

Let it be remembered, that the advice requested does not relate to the government of the more dangerous passions, or to the fundamental principles of right and wrong as acknowledged by the universal conscience of mankind. I may therefore assure my youthful correspondent, if he will endeavor to look into himself in the manner which I have exhorted him to do, that in him the wish will be realized, to him in due time the prayer granted, which was uttered by that living teacher of whom he speaks with gratitude as of a benefactor, when in his character of philosophical poet, having thought of morality as implying in its essence voluntary obedience, and producing the effect of order, he transfers in the transport of imagination, the law of moral to physical natures, and having contemplated, through the medium of that order, all modes of existence as subservient to one spirit, concludes his address to the power of duty in the following words:

> To humbler functions, awful power!
> I call thee: I myself commend
> Unto thy guidance from this hour;
> Oh, let my weakness have an end!
> Give unto me, made lowly wise,
> The spirit of self-sacrifice;
> The confidence of reason give,
> And in the light of truth thy bondman let me live!*

This reply to Mathetes was written by Mr. Wordsworth.—*Ed.*

THE FRIEND.

ESSAY I.

We can not but look up with reverence to the advanced natures of the naturalists and moralists in highest repute amongst us, and wish they had been heightened by a more noble principle, which had crowned all their various sciences with the principal science, and in their brave strayings after truth helpt them to better fortune than only to meet with her handmaids, and kept them from the fate of Ulysses, who wandering through the shades met all the ghosts, yet could not see the queen.—*J. H.* (JOHN HALL?) *his Motion to the Parliament of England concerning the Advancement of Learning.*

THE preceding section, ending with the second Landing Place, had for its express object the principles of our duty as citizens, or morality as applied to politics. According to his scheme there remained for The Friend first, to treat of the principles of morality generally, and then of those of religion. But since the commencement of this edition,* the question has repeatedly arisen in my mind, whether morality can be said to have any principle distinguishable from religion, or religion any substance divisible from morality. Or should I attempt to distinguish them by their objects, so that morality were the religion which we owe to things and persons of this life, and religion our morality toward God and the permanent concerns of our own souls, and those of our brethren;—yet it would be evident, that the latter must involve the former, while any pretence to the former without the latter would be as bold a mockery as, if having withholden an estate from the rightful owner, we should seek to appease our conscience by the plea, that we had not failed to bestow alms on him in his beggary. It was never my purpose, and it does not appear the want of the age, to bring together the rules and inducements of

* The second.—*Ed.*

worldly prudence. But to substitute these for the laws of reason and conscience, or even to confound them under one name, is a prejudice, say rather a profanation, which I became more and more reluctant to flatter by even an appearance of assent, though it were only in a point of form and technical arrangement.

At a time, when my thoughts were thus employed, I met with a volume of old tracts, published during the interval from the captivity of Charles I. to the restoration of his son. Since my earliest manhood it had been among my fondest regrets, that a more direct and frequent reference had not been made by our historians to the books, pamphlets, and flying sheets of that momentous period, during which all the possible forms of truth and error (the latter being themselves for the greater part caricatures of truth) bubbled up on the surface of the public mind, as in the ferment of a chaos. It would be difficult to conceive a notion or a fancy, in politics, ethics, theology, or even in physics and physiology, not anticipated by the men of that age ;—in this as in most other respects sharply contrasted with the products of the French revolution, which was scarcely more characterized by its sanguinary and sensual abominations than (to borrow the words of an eminent living poet) by

> A dreary want at once of books and men.*

The parliament's army was not wholly composed of mere fanatics. There was no mean proportion of enthusiasts ; and that enthusiasm must have been of no ordinary grandeur, which could draw from a common soldier, in an address to his comrades, such a dissuasive from acting in the cruel spirit of fear, and such sentiments, as are contained in the following passage, which I would rescue from oblivion,† both for the honor of our forefathers, and in proof of the difference between the republicans of that period, and the democrats, or rather demagogues, of the present. It is as follows :

"I judge it ten times more honorable for a single person, in

* Wordsworth.

† The more so because every year consumes its quota. The late Sir Wilfred Lawson's predecessor, from some pique or other, left a large and unique collection of the pamphlets published from the commencement of the civil war to the Restoration to his butler, and it supplied the chandlers' and druggists' shops of Penrith and Kendal for many years.

witnessing a truth to oppose the world in its power, wisdom, and authority, this standing in its full strength, and he singly and nakedly, than fighting many battles by force of arms, and gaining them all. I have no life but truth; and if truth be advanced by my suffering, then my life also. If truth live, I live; if justice live, I live; and these can not die, but by any man's suffering for them are enlarged, enthroned. Death can not hurt me. I sport with him, am above his reach. I live an immortal life. What we have within, that only can we see without. I can not see death; and he that hath not this freedom is a slave. He is in the arms of that, the phantom of which he beholdeth and seemeth to himself to flee from. Thus, you see that the king hath a will to redeem his present loss. You see it by means of the lust after power in your own hearts. For my part I condemn his unlawful seeking after it. I condemn his falsehood and indirectness therein. But if he should not endeavor the restoring of the kingliness to the realm, and the dignity of its kings, he were false to his trust, false to the majesty of God that he is intrusted with. The desire of recovering his loss is justifiable. Yea, I should condemn him as unbelieving and pusillanimous, if he should not hope for it. But here is his misery and yours too at present, that ye are unbelieving and pusillanimous, and are, both alike, pursuing things of hope in the spirit of fear. Thus you condemn the parliament for acknowledging the king's power so far as to seek to him by a treaty; while by taking such pains against him you manifest your own belief that he hath a great power;—which is a wonder, that a prince despoiled of all his authority, naked, a prisoner, destitute of all friends and helps, wholly at the disposal of others, tied and bound too with all obligations that a parliament can imagine to hold him, should yet be such a terror to you, and fright you into such a large remonstrance, and such perilous proceedings to save yourselves from him. Either there is some strange power in him, or you are full of fear that are so affected with a shadow.

"But as you give testimony to his power, so you take a course to advance it; for there is nothing that hath any spark of God in it, but the more it is suppressed, the more it rises. If you did indeed believe, that the original of power were in the people, you would believe likewise that the concessions extorted from the king would rest with you. And, doubtless, such of them as in righteousness ought to have been given would do so, but that your violent courses disturb the natural order of things, in which they still tend to their centre. These courses, therefore, so far from being the way to secure what we have got, are the way to lose them, and (for a time at least) to set up princes in a higher form than ever. For all things by force compelled from their nature will fly back with the greater earnestness on the removal of that force; and this, in the present case, must soon weary itself out, and hath no less an enemy in its own satiety than in the disappointment of the people.

"Again, you speak of the king's reputation, and do not consider that the more you crush him, the sweeter the fragrance that comes from him. While he suffers, the spirit of God and glory rests upon him. There is a glory and a freshness sparkling in him by suffering, an excellency that was hidden, and which you have drawn out. And naturally men are ready to pity sufferers. When nothing will gain me, affliction will. I confess his sufferings make me a royalist, who never cared for him. He that doth and can suffer shall have my heart; you had it while you suffered. But now your severe punishment of him for his abuses in government, and your own usurpations, will not only win the hearts of the people to the oppressed suffering king, but provoke them to rage against you, as having robbed them of the interest which they had in his royalty. For the king is in the people, and the people in the king. The king's being is not solitary, but as he is in union with his people, who are his strength in which he lives; and the people's being is not naked, but an interest in the greatness and wisdom of the king who is their honor which lives in them. And though you will disjoin yourselves from kings, God will not, neither will I. God is king of kings, kings' and princes' God, as well as people's, theirs as well as ours, and theirs eminently (as the speech enforces, God of Israel, that is, Israel's God above all other nations, and so king of kings), by a near and special kindred and communion. Kingliness agrees with all Christians, who are indeed Christians. For they are themselves of a royal nature, made kings with Christ, and can not but be friends to it, being of kin to it; and if there were not kings to honor, they would want one of the appointed objects whereon to bestow that fulness of honor which is in their breasts. A virtue would lie unemployed within them, and in prison, pining and restless from the want of its outward correlative. It is a bastard religion, that is inconsistent with the majesty and the greatness of the most splendid monarch. Such spirits are strangers from the kingdom of heaven. Either they know not the glory in which God lives; or they are of narrow minds that are corrupt themselves, and not able to bear greatness, and so think that God will not, or can not, qualify men for such high places with correspondent and proportionable power and goodness. Is it not enough to have removed the malignant bodies which eclipsed the royal sun, and mixed their bad influences with his, and would you extinguish the sun itself to secure yourselves? O! this is the spirit of bondage to fear, and not of love and a sound mind. To assume the office and the name of champions for the common interest, and of Christ's soldiers, and yet to act for self-safety is so poor and mean a thing that it must needs produce most vile and absurd actions, the scorn of the old pagans, but for Christians who in all things are to love their neighbor as themselves, and God above both, it is of all affections the unworthiest. Let me be a fool and boast, if so I may show you, while it is yet time, a little of that rest and security which I and those of the same spirit enjoy, and which you have turned your backs upon; self, like a banished thing, wandering in strange ways. First, then, I fear no party, or interest, for I love all, I am reconciled to all, and therein I find all reconciled to me. I have enmity to none but the son of perdition. It is enmity begets insecurity: and while men live in the flesh, and in enmity to any party, or interest, in a private, divided, and self good, there will be, there can not but be, perpetual wars; except that one particular should quite ruin all other parts and live alone, which the universal must not, will not, suffer. For to admit a part to devour and absorb the others, were to destroy the whole, which is God's presence therein; and such a mind in any part doth not only fight with another part, but against the whole. Every faction of men, therefore, striving to make themselves absolute, and to owe their safety to their strength, and not to their sympathy, do directly war against God who is love, peace, and a general good, gives being to all and cherishes all, and, therefore, can have neither peace nor security. But we being enlarged into the largeness of God, and comprehending all things in our bosoms by the divine spirit, are at rest with all, and delight in all; for we know nothing but what is, in its essence, in our own hearts. Kings, nobles, are much beloved of us, because they are in us, of us, one with us, we as Christians being kings and lords by the anointing of God."

But such sentiments, it will be said, are the flights of speculative minds. Be it so; yet to soar is nobler than to creep. We attach, likewise, some value to a thing for its mere infrequency. And speculative minds, alas! have been rare, though not equally rare, in all ages and countries of civilized men. With us the very word seems to have abdicated its legitimate sense. Instead of designating a mind so constituted and disciplined as to find in its own wants and instincts an interest in truths for their truth's sake, it is now used to signify a practical schemer, one who ventures beyond the bounds of experience in the formation and adoption of new ways and means for the attainment of wealth or power. To possess the end in the means, as it is essential to morality in the moral world, and the contra-distinction of goodness from mere prudence, so is it, in the intellectual world, the moral constituent of genius, and that by which true genius is contra-distinguished from mere talent.*

The man of talent, who is, if not exlusively, yet chiefly and characteristically a man of talent, seeks and values the means wholly in relation to some object not therein contained. His means may be peculiar; but his ends are conventional, and common to the mass of mankind. Alas! in both cases alike, in that of genius, as well as in that of talent, it too often happens, that this diversity in the quality of their several intellects, extends to the feelings and impulses properly and directly moral, to their dispositions, habits, and maxims of conduct. It characterizes not the intellect alone, but the whole man. The one substitutes prudence for virtue, legality in act and demeanor for warmth and purity of heart, and too frequently becomes jealous, envious, a coveter of other men's good gifts, and a detractor from their merits, openly or secretly, as his fears or his passions chance to preponderate.†

* See the note to this essay. p. 384.—*Ed.*

† According to the principles of Spurzheim's cranioscopy (a scheme, the indicative or gnomonic parts of which have a stronger support in facts than the theory in reason or common sense) we should find in the skull of such an individual the organs of circumspection and appropriation disproportion-

The other, on the contrary, might remind us of the zealots for legitimate succession after the decease of our sixth Edward, who not content with having placed the rightful sovereign on the throne, would wreak their vengeance on "the meek usurper," who had been seated on it by a will against which she had herself been the first to remonstrate. For with that unhealthful preponderance of impulse over motive, which, though no part of genius, is too often its accompaniment, he lives in continued hostility to prudence, or banishes it altogether; and thus deprives virtue of her guide and guardian, her prime functionary, yea, the very organ of her outward life. Hence a benevolence that squanders its shafts and still misses its aim, or resembles the charmed bullet that, levelled at the wolf, brings down the shepherd. Hence desultoriness, extremes, exhaustion—

> And thereof cometh in the end despondency and madness!*

Let it not be forgotten, however, that these evils are the disease of the man, while the records of biography furnish ample proof, that genius, in the higher degree, acts as a preservative against them; more remarkably, and in more frequent instances, when the imagination and preconstructive power have taken a scientific or philosophic direction; as in Plato, indeed in almost all the first-rate philosophers, in Kepler, Milton, Boyle, Newton, Leibnitz, and Berkeley. At all events, a certain number of speculative minds is necessary to a cultivated state of society, as a condition of its progressiveness; and nature herself has provided against any too great increase in this class of her productions. As the gifted masters of the divining rod to the ordinary miners, and as the miners of a country to the husbandmen, mechanics, and artisans, such is the proportion of the *trismegisti* to the sum total of speculative minds, even of those, I mean, that are truly such; and of

ately large and prominent compared with those of ideality and benevolence. It is certain that the organ of appropriation, or (more correctly) the part of the skull asserted to be significant of that tendency and correspondent to the organ, is strikingly large in a cast of the head of the famous Dr. Dodd; and it was found of equal dimensions in a literary man, whose skull puzzled the cranioscopist more than it did me. Nature, it should seem, makes no distinction between manuscripts and money-drafts, though the law does.

* Wordsworth.

these again, to the remaining mass of useful laborers and operatives in science, literature, and the learned professions.

This train of thought brings to my recollection a conversation with a friend of my youth, an old man of humble estate; but in whose society I had great pleasure. The reader will, I hope, pardon me if I embrace the opportunity of recalling old affections, afforded me by its fitness to illustrate the present subject. A sedate man he was, and had been a miner from his boyhood. Well did he represent the olden time, when every trade was a mystery and had its own guardian saint; when the sense of self-importance was gratified at home, and ambition had a hundred several lotteries, in one or other of which every freeman had a ticket, and the only blanks were drawn by sloth, intemperance, or inevitable calamity; when the detail of each art and trade (like the oracles of the prophets, interpretable in a double sense) was ennobled in the eyes of its professors by being spiritually improved into symbols and mementos of all doctrines and all duties, and every craftsman had, as it were, two versions of his Bible, one in the common language of the country, another in the acts, objects, and products of his own particular craft. There are not many things in our elder popular literature, more interesting to me than those contests, or eclogues, between workmen for the superior worth and dignity of their several callings, which used to be sold at our village-fairs, in stitched sheets, neither untitled nor undecorated, though without the superfluous cost of a separate title-page.

With this good old miner I was once walking through a cornfield at harvest-time, when that part of the conversation, to which I have alluded, took place. "At times," said I, "when you were delving in the bowels of the arid mountain or foodless rock, it must have occurred to your mind as a pleasant thought, that in providing the scythe and the sword you were virtually reaping the harvest and protecting the harvest-man." "Ah!" he replied with a sigh, that gave a fuller meaning to his smile, "out of all earthly things there come both good and evil;—the good through God, and the evil from the evil heart. From the look and weight of the ore I learned to make a near guess, how much iron it would yield; but neither its heft, nor its hues, nor its breakage would prophesy to me, whether it was to become a thievish pick-lock, a murderer's dirk, a slave's collar, or the woodman's axe, the feeding plough-share, the defender's sword, or the mechanic's tool.

So, perhaps, my young friend, I have cause to be thankful, that the opening upon a fresh vein gives me a delight so full as to allow no room for other fancies, and leaves behind it a hope and a love that support me in my labor, even for the labor's sake."

As, according to the eldest philosophy, life being in its own nature aeriform, is under the necessity of renewing itself by inhaling the connatural, and therefore assimilable, air, so is it with the intelligential soul with respect to truth; for it is itself of the nature of truth. *Γενομένη ἐκ θεωρίας, καὶ θέαμα θεῖον, φύσιν ἔχειν φιλοθεάμονα ὑπάρχει.** But the occasion and brief history of the decline of true speculative philosophy, with the origin of the separation of ethics from religion, I must defer to the following number.

NOTE.

As I see many good, and can anticipate no ill consequences in the attempt to give distinct and appropriate meanings to words hitherto synonymous, or at least of indefinite and fluctuating application, if only the proposed sense be not passed upon the reader as the existing and authorized one, I shall make no other apology for the use of the word, Talent, in this preceding essay and elsewhere in my works than by annexing the following explanation.

I have been in the habit of considering the qualities of intellect, the comparative eminence in which characterizes individuals and even countries, under four kinds—Genius, Talent, Sense, and Cleverness. The first I use in the sense of most general acceptance, as the faculty which adds to the existing stock of power and knowledge by new views, new combinations; by discoveries not accidental but anticipated, or resulting from anticipation. In short, I define Genius, as originality in intellectual construction; the moral accompaniment, and actuating principle of which consists, perhaps, in the carrying on of the freshness and feelings of childhood into the powers of manhood.

By Talent, on the other hand, I mean the comparative facility of acquiring, arranging, and applying the stock furnished by others, and already existing in books or other conservatories of intellect.

By Sense I understand that just balance of the faculties which is to the judgment what health is to the body. The mind seems to act at once and altogether by a synthetic rather than an ana-

* Plotinus. *Ennead.* III. l. 8. s. 3, slightly altered.—*Ed.*

lytic process: even as the outward senses, from which the metaphor is taken, perceive immediately, each as it were by a peculiar tact or intuition, without any consciousness of the mechanism by which the perception is realized. This is often exemplified in well-bred, unaffected, and innocent women. I know a lady, on whose judgment, from constant experience of its rectitude, I could rely almost as on an oracle. But when she has sometimes proceeded to a detail of the grounds and reasons for her opinion, then, led by similar experience, I have been tempted to interrupt her with—"I will take your advice," or, "I shall act on your opinion; for I am sure you are in the right. But as to the *fors* and *becauses*, leave them to me to find out." The general accompaniment of sense is a disposition to avoid extremes, whether in theory or in practice, with a desire to remain in sympathy with the general mind of the age or country, and a feeling of the necessity and utility of compromise. If genius be the initiative, and talent the administrative, sense is the conservative, branch in the intellectual republic.

By Cleverness (which I dare not with Dr. Johnson call a low word, while there is a sense to be expressed which it alone expresses) I mean a comparative readiness in the invention and use of means, for the realizing of objects and ideas—often of such ideas, which the man of genius only could have originated, and which the clever man perhaps neither fully comprehends nor adequately appreciates, even at the moment that he is prompting or executing the machinery of their accomplishment. In short, cleverness is a sort of genius for instrumentality. It is the brain in the hand. In literature, cleverness is more frequently accompanied by wit, genius and sense by humor.

If I take the three great countries of Europe, in respect of intellectual character, namely, Germany, England, and France, I should characterize them in the following way;—premising only that in the first line of the first two tables I mean to imply that genius, rare in all countries, is equal in both of these, the instances equally numerous; not, therefore, contra-distinguishing either from the other, but both from the third country. We can scarcely avoid considering a Cervantes and Calderon as in some sort characteristic of the nation which produced them. In the last war we felt it in the hope, which the recollection of these names inspired. But yet it can not, equally with the qualities placed as second and third in each table, be called a national characteristic; though, in the appropriation of these likewise, we refer exclusively to the intellectual portion of each country.

GERMANY.
Genius,
Talent,
Fancy.*

ENGLAND.
Genius,
Sense,
Humor.

FRANCE.
Cleverness,
Talent,
Wit.

So again with regard to the forms and effects, in which the qualities manifest themselves intellectually.

GERMANY.
Idea, or law anticipated,†
Totality,‡
Distinctness.

ENGLAND.
Law discovered,§
Selection,
Clearness.

* The latter chiefly as exhibited in wild combination and in pomp of ornament. Imagination is implied in genius.

† This, as co-ordinate with genius in the first table, applies likewise to the few only; and conjoined with the two following qualities, as more general characteristics of German intellect, includes or supposes, as its consequences and accompaniments, speculation, system, method; which in a somewhat lower class of minds appear as nationality (or a predilection for *noumena, mundus intelligibilis*, as contra-distinguished from *phænomena*, or *mundus sensibilis*), scheme, arrangement, orderliness.

‡ In totality I imply encyclopædic learning, exhaustion of the subject treated of, and the passion for completion and the love of the complete.

§ It might have been expressed;—the contemplation of ideas objectively, as existing powers, while the German of equal genius is predisposed to contemplate law subjectively, with anticipation of a correspondent in nature.

France.

Theory invented,
Particularity,*
Palpability.

Lastly, we might exhibit the same qualities in their moral, religious, and political manifestations: in the cosmopolitism of Germany, the contemptuous nationality of the Englishman, and the ostentatious and boastful nationality of the Frenchman. The craving of sympathy marks the German; inward pride the Englishman; vanity the Frenchman. So again, enthusiasm, visionariness seems the tendency of the German; zeal, zealotry of the English; fanaticism of the French. But the thoughtful reader will find these and many other characteristic points contained in, and deducible from, the relations which the mind of the three countries bears to time.

Germany.

Past and Future.

England.

Past and Present.

France.

The Present.

A whimsical friend of mine, of more genius than discretion, characterizes the Scotchman of literature (confining his remark, however, to the period since the union) as a dull Frenchman and a superficial German. But when I recollect the splendid excep-

* Tendency to individualize, embody, insulate, as instanced in the advocacy of the vitreous and the resinous fluids instead of the positive and negative forces of the power of electricity. Thus, too, it was not sufficient that oxygen was the principal, and with one exception, the only then known acidifying substance; the power and principle of acidification must be embodied, and as it were impersonated and hypostasized in this gas. Hence the idolism of the French, here expressed in one of its results, namely, palpability. Ideas and a Frenchman are incompatible terms; but I confine the remark to the period from the latter half of the reign of Louis XIV. Ideas, I say, are here out of the question; but even the conceptions of a Frenchman;—whatever he admits to be conceivable must be likewise, according to him, imageable, and the imageable must be fancied tangible—the non-apparency of either or both being accounted for by the disproportion of our senses, not by the nature of the objects.

tions of Hume, Robertson, Smollett, Reid, Thomson (if this last instance be not objected to as favoring of geographical pedantry, that truly amiable man and genuine poet having been born but a few furlongs from the English border), Dugald Stewart, Burns, Walter Scott, Hogg, and Campbell—not to mention the very numerous physicians and prominent dissenting ministers, born or bred beyond the Tweed ;—I hesitate in recording so wild an opinion, which derives its plausibility, chiefly from the circumstance so honorable to our northern sister, that Scotchmen generally have more, and a more learned, education than the same ranks in other countries, below the first class ; but in part likewise, from the common mistake of confounding the general character of an emigrant, whose objects are in one place and his best affections in another, with the particular character of a Scotchman : to which we may add, perhaps, the clannish spirit of provincial literature, fostered undoubtedly by the peculiar relations of Scotland, and of which therefore its metropolis may be a striking, but is far from being a solitary instance.

ESSAY II.

Ἡ ὅδος κάτω.
The road downward. Heraclit. *Fragment.*

Amour *de moi-même, mais bien calculé*—was the motto and maxim of a French philosopher. Our fancy inspirited by the more imaginative powers of hope and fear enables us to present to ourselves the future as the present, and thence to accept a scheme of self-love for a system of morality. And doubtless, an enlightened self-interest would recommend the same course of outward conduct, as the sense of duty would do ; even though the motives in the former case had respect to this life exclusively. But to show the desirableness of an object, or the contrary, is one thing ; to excite the desire, to constitute the aversion, is another : the one being to the other as a common guide-post to the "chariot instinct with spirit," which at once directs and conveys ; or employing a more familiar image, we may compare the rule of self-interest to a watch with an excellent hour-plate, hand, and regulator, but without its spring and wheel-work. Nay, where its sufficiency and exclusive validity are adopted as the maxim (*regula maxima*) of morality, it would be a fuller and fairer comparison to say, that the maxim of self-interest stands in a familiar relation to the law of conscience or universal selfless reason, as the dial to the sun, which indicates its path by intercepting its radiance.*

But let it be granted, that in certain individuals from a happy evenness of nature, formed into a habit by the strength of education, the influence of example, and by favorable circumstances in general, the actions diverging from self-love as their centre should be precisely the same as those produced from the Christian principle, which requires of us that we should place our self and our neighbor at an equal distance, and love both alike as modes in which we realize and exhibit the love of God above all;—wherein would the difference be then? I answer boldly,—even in that, for which all actions have their whole worth and their main value,—in the agents themselves. So much indeed is this of the very substance of genuine morality, that wherever the latter has given way in the general opinion to a scheme of ethics founded on utility, its place is soon challenged by the spirit of honor. Paley, who degrades the spirit of honor into a mere club-law among the higher classes originating in selfish convenience, and enforced by the penalty of excommunication from the society which habit had rendered indispensable to the happiness of the individuals, has misconstrued it not less than Shaftesbury, who extols it as the noblest influence of noble natures. The spirit of honor is more indeed than a mere conventional substitute for honesty. For to take the word in a sense, which no man of honor would acknowledge, may be allowed to the writer of satires, but not to the moral philosopher. But, on the other hand, instead of being a finer form of moral life, it may be more truly de-

* Here are two syllogisms, having equivalent practical conclusions, yet not only different, but even contradistinguished. I. It is my duty to love all men: but I am myself a man: *ergo*, it is my duty to love myself equally with others. II. It is my nature to love myself: but I can not realize this impulse of nature, without acting to others as if I loved them equally with myself: *ergo*, it is my duty to love myself by acting towards others as if I loved them equally with myself. Dec. 1820.

scribed as the shadow or ghost of virtue deceased. Honor implies a reverence for the invisible and supersensual in our nature, and so far it is virtue ; but it is a virtue that neither understands itself nor its true source, and is therefore often unsubstantial, not seldom fantastic, and always more or less capricious. Abstract the notion from the lives of Lord Herbert of Cherbury, or Henry IV. of France ; and then compare it with the 1 Cor. xiii. and the epistle to Philemon, or rather with the realization of this fair ideal in the character of St. Paul* himself. I know not a better test. Nor can I think of any investigation, that would be more instructive where it would be safe, but none likewise of greater delicacy from the probability of misinterpretation, than a history of the rise of honor in the European monarchies as connected with the corruptions of Christianity, and an inquiry into the specific causes of the inefficacy which has attended the combined efforts of divines and moralists against the practice and obligation of duelling.

Of a widely different character from this moral *αἵρεσις*, yet as a derivative from the same root, we may contemplate the heresies of the Gnostics in the early ages of the church, and of the

* This has struck the better class even of infidels. Collins, one of the most learned of our English deists, is said to have declared, that contradictory as miracles appeared to his reason, he would believe in them notwithstanding, if it could be proved to him that St. Paul had asserted any one as having been worked by himself in the modern sense of the word, miracle ; adding, "St. Paul was so perfect a gentleman and a man of honor !" When I call duelling, and similar aberrations of honor, a moral heresy, I refer to the force of the Greek *αἵρεσις*, as signifying a principle or opinion taken up by the will for the will's sake, as a proof and pledge to itself of its own power of self-determination, independent of all other motives. In the gloomy gratification derived or anticipated from the exercise of this awful power,—the condition of all moral good while it is latent and hidden, as it were in the centre, but the essential cause of fiendish guilt, when it makes itself existential and peripheric, *si quando in circumferentiam erumpat ;* (in both cases I have purposely adopted the language of the old mystic theosophers)—I find the only explanation of a moral phenomenon not very uncommon in the last moments of condemned felons ; namely, the obstinate denial, not of the main guilt, which might be accounted for by ordinary motives, but of some particular act, which had been proved beyond all possibility of doubt, and attested by the criminal's own accomplices and fellow-sufferers in their last confessions ; and this too an act, the non-perpetration of which, if believed, could neither mitigate the sentence of the law, nor even the opinions of men after the sentence had been carried into execution.

family of love, with other forms of Antinomianism, since the Reformation to the present day. But lest in uttering truth I should convey falsehood and fall myself into the error which it is my object to expose, it will be requisite to distinguish an apprehension of the whole of a truth, even where that apprehension is dim and indistinct, from a partial perception of the same rashly assumed as a perception of the whole. The first is rendered inevitable in many things for many, in some points for all, men from the progressiveness no less than from the imperfection of humanity, which itself dictates and enforces the precept, Believe that thou mayest understand.* The most knowing must at times be content with the *facit* of a sum too complex or subtle for us to follow nature through the antecedent process. Hence in subjects not under the cognizance of the senses wise men have always attached a high value to general and long-continued assent, as a presumption of truth. After all the subtle reasonings and fair analogies which logic and induction could supply to a mighty intellect, it is yet on this ground that the Socrates of Plato mainly rests his faith in the immortality of the soul, and the moral government of the universe. It had been holden by all nations in all ages, but with deepest conviction by the best and wisest men, as a belief connatural with goodness and akin to prophecy. The same argument is adopted by Cicero, as the principal ground of his adherence to divination. *Gentem quidem nullam video, neque tam humanam atque doctam, neque tam immanem tamque barbaram, quæ non significari futura, et a quibusdam intelligi prædicique posse censeat.*† I confess, I can

* The Greek verb, συνίεναι, which we render by the word, understand, is literally the same as our own idiomatic phrase, to go along with.

† *De Divinat.* Lib. I. s. i. I find indeed no people or nation, however civilized and cultivated, or however wild and barbarous, who have not deemed that there are antecedent signs of future events, and some men capable of understanding and predicting them.

I am tempted to add a passage from my own translation of Schiller's Wallenstein, the more so that the work has been long ago used up, as "winding sheets for pilchards," or extant only by (as I would fain flatter myself) the kind partiality of the trunk-makers: though with exception of works for which public admiration supersedes or includes individual commendations, I scarce remember a book that has been more honored by the express attestations in its favor of eminent and even of popular *literati*, among whom I take this opportunity of expressing my acknowledgments to the author of Waverley, Guy Mannering, &c. How (asked Ulysses, ad-

never read the *De Divinatione* of this great orator, statesman, and patriot, without feeling myself inclined to consider this opinion as an instance of the second class, namely, of fractional truths integrated by fancy, passion, accident, and that preponderance of the positive over the negative in the memory, which makes it no less tenacious of coincidences than forgetful of failures. Still I should not fear to be its advocate under the following limitation ; *non nisi de rebus divinis datur divinatio.*

I am indeed firmly persuaded, that no doctrine was ever widely diffused among various nations through successive ages,

dressing his guardian goddess) shall I be able to recognize Proteus in the swallow that skims round our houses, whom I have been accustomed to behold as a swan of Phœbus, measuring his movements to a celestial music? In both alike, she replied, thou canst recognize the god.

So supported, I dare avow that I have thought my translation worthy of a more favorable reception from the public and its literary guides and purveyors. But when I recollect that a much better and very far more valuable work, Mr. Cary's incomparable translation of Dante, had very nearly met with the same fate, I lose all right, and I trust, all inclination, to complain ;—an inclination, which the mere sense of its folly and uselessness will not always suffice to preclude. (1817.—*Ed.*)

Countess. What dost thou not believe, that oft in dreams
A voice of warning speaks prophetic to us?
Wallenstein. There is no doubt that there exist such voices;
Yet I would not call them
Voices of warning, that announce to us
Only the inevitable. As the sun,
Ere it is risen, sometimes paints its image
In the atmosphere, so often do the spirits
Of great events stride on before the events,
And in to-day already walks to-morrow.
That which we read of the Fourth Henry's death
Did ever vex and haunt me, like a tale
Of my own future destiny. The king
Felt in his breast the phantom of the knife,
Long ere Ravaillac arm'd himself therewith.
His quiet mind forsook him: the phantasma
Started him in his Louvre, chas'd him forth
Into the open air. Like funeral knells
Sounded that coronation festival;
And still with boding sense he heard the tread
Of those feet, that even then were seeking him
Throughout the streets of Paris. *Death of Wallenstein*, act v. sc. i.
Poetical Works, VII. p. 667.

and under different religions (such, for instance, as the tenets of original sin and redemption, those fundamental articles of every known religion professing to have been revealed), which is not founded either in the nature of things, or in the necessities of human nature. Nay, the more strange and irreconcilable such a doctrine may appear to the understanding, the judgments of which are grounded on general rules abstracted from the world of the senses, the stronger is the presumption in its favor. For whatever satirists may say, or sciolists imagine, the human mind has no predilection for absurdity. I would even extend the principle (proportionately I mean) to sundry tenets, that from their stangeness or dangerous tendency appear only to be generally reprobated, as eclipses, in the belief of barbarous tribes, are to be frightened away by noises and execrations; but which rather resemble the luminary itself in this one respect, that after a longer or shorter interval of occultation, they are still found to re-emerge. It is these, the re-appearance of which (*nomine tantum mutato*) from age to age gives to ecclesiastical history a deeper interest than that of romance and scarcely less wild for every philosophic mind. I am far from asserting that such a doctrine (the Antinomian, for instance, or that of a latent mystical sense in the words of Scripture and the works of nature, according to Origen and Emanuel Swedenborg) shall be always the best possible, or not a distorted and dangerous, as well as partial, representation of the truth on which it is founded. For the same body casts strangely different shadows in different positions and different degrees of light. But I dare, and do, affirm that it always does shadow out some important truth, and from it derives its main influence over the faith of its adherents, obscure as their perception of this truth may be, and though they may themselves attribute their belief to the supernatural gifts of the founder, or the miracles by which his preaching had been accredited. See Wesley's Journal for proofs. But we have the highest possible authority, that of Scripture itself, to justify us in putting the question,—whether miracles can, of themselves, work a true conviction in the mind. There are spiritual truths which must derive their evidence from within, which whoever rejects, *neither will he believe though a man were to rise from the dead* to confirm them. And under the Mosaic law a miracle in attestation of a false doctrine subjected the miracle-worker to death; and whether the miracle was really or only seemingly supernatural, makes no difference in the present argument, its power of convincing, whatever that power may be, whether great or small, depending on the fulness of the belief in its miraculous nature. *Est quibus esse videtur.* Or rather, that I may express the same position in a form less likely to offend, is not a true efficient conviction of a moral truth, is not *the creating of a new heart*, which collects the energies of a man's whole being in the focus of the conscience, the one essential miracle, the same and of the same evidence to the ignorant and the learned, which no superior skill can counterfeit, human or demoniacal? Is it not emphatically that leading of the Father, without which no man can come to Christ? Is it not that implication of doctrine in the miracle and of miracle in the doctrine, which is the bridge of communication between the senses and the soul;—that predisposing warmth which renders the understanding susceptible of the specific impression from the historic, and from all other outward, seals of testimony? Is not this the one infallible criterion of miracles, by which a man can know whether they be of God? The abhorrence in which the most savage or barbarous tribes hold witchcraft, in which however their belief is so intense* as even to control the springs of life,—is not this abhorrence of witchcraft under so full a conviction of its reality a proof, how little of divine, how little fitting to our nature, a miracle is, when insulated from spiritual truths, and disconnected from religion as its end? What then can we think of a theological theory, which adopting a scheme of prudential legality, common to it with "the sty of Epicurus," as far at least as the springs of moral action are concerned, makes its whole religion consist in the belief of miracles! As well might the poor African prepare for himself a fetisch by plucking out the eyes from the eagle or the lynx, and enshrining the same, worship in them the power of vision. As the tenet of professed Christians (I speak of the principle not of the men, whose hearts will always more or less correct the errors of their understandings) it is even more absurd, and the pretext for such a religion more inconsistent than the religion itself. For they profess to

* I refer the reader to Hearn's Travels among the Copper Indians, and to Bryan Edward's account of the Oby in the West Indies, grounded on judicial documents and personal observation.

derive from it their whole faith in that futurity, which if they had not previously believed on the evidence of their own consciences, of Moses and the Prophets, they are assured by the great Founder and Object of Christianity, that neither will they believe it, in any spiritual and profitable sense, though a man should rise from the dead.

For myself, I can not resist the conviction, built on particular and general history, that the extravagances of Antinomianism and Solifidianism are little more than the counteractions to this Christian paganism;—the play, as it were, of antagonist muscles. The feelings will set up their standard against the understanding, whenever the understanding has renounced its allegiance to the reason: and what is faith, but the personal realization of the reason by its union with the will? If we would drive out the demons of fanaticism from the people, we must begin by exercising the spirit of Epicureanism in the higher ranks, and restore to their teachers the true Christian enthusiasm,* the vivifying influences of the altar, the censer, and the sacrifice. They must neither be ashamed of, nor disposed to explain away, the articles of prevenient and auxiliary grace, nor the necessity of being born again to the life from which our nature had become apostate.† They must administer indeed the necessary medicines to the sick, the motives of fear as well as of hope; but they must not withhold from them the idea of health, or conceal from them that the medicines for the sick are not the diet of the healthy. Nay, they must make it a part of the curative process to induce the patient, on the first symptoms of recovery, to look forward with prayer and aspiration to that state, in which perfect love shutteth out fear. Above all, they must not seek to make the mysteries of faith what the world calls rational by theories of original sin and redemption borrowed analogically from the imperfection of human law-courts and the coarse contrivances of state expedience.

Among the numerous examples with which I might enforce

* The original meaning of the Greek, *ἐνθουσιασμὸς* is,—the influence of the divinity such as was supposed to take possession of the priest during the performance of the services at the altar.

Δίζεο σὺ ψυχῆς ὀχετὸν, ὅθεν ἤ τίνι τάξει
Σώματι θητεύσας, ἐπὶ τάξιν ἀφ' ἧς ἐῤῥύσθης
Αὖθις ἀναστήσεις, ἱερῷ Λόγῳ ἔργον ἑνώσας.
Zoroastr. Oracula Initio. Edit. Opsopæi. 1599.—*Ed.*

this warning, I refer, not without reluctance, to the most eloquent and one of the most learned of our divines; a rigorist, indeed, concerning the authority of the Church, but a Latitudinarian in the articles of its faith; who stretched the latter almost to the advanced posts of Socinianism, and strained the former to a hazardous conformity with the assumptions of the Roman hierarchy. With what emotions must not a pious mind peruse such passages as the following:—"It (death) reigned upon them whose sins therefore would not be so imputed as Adam's was; because there was no law with an express threatening given to them as was to Adam; but although it was not wholly imputed upon their own account, yet it was imputed upon their's and Adam's. For God was so exasperated with mankind, that being angry he would still continue that punishment to lesser sins and sinners, which he only had first threatened to Adam; and so Adam brought it upon them. * * * * The case is this. Jonathan and Michal were Saul's children. It came to pass, that seven of Saul's issue were to be hanged; all equally innocent, equally culpable.* David took the five sons of Michal, for she had left him unhandsomely. Jonathan was his friend, and therefore he spared his son Mephibosheth. Here it was indifferent as to the guilt of the persons" (observe, no guilt was attached to either of them) "whether David should take the sons of Michal or of Jonathan; but it is likely that, as upon the kindness which David had to Jonathan, he spared his son, so upon the just provocation of Michal, he made that evil to fall upon them, of which they were otherwise capable; which, it may be, they should not have suffered, if their mother had been kind. Adam was to God, as Michal to David."† And this, with many passages equally gross, occurs in a refutation of the doctrine of original sin, on the ground of its incongruity with reason, and its incompatibility with God's justice! "Exasperated" with those whom the Bishop has elsewhere, in the same treatise, declared to have been "innocent and most unfortunate"—the two things that most conciliate love and pity! Or, if they did not remain innocent, yet, those whose abandonment to a mere nature, while they were subjected to a law above

* These two words are added without the least ground in Scripture, according to which (2 Samuel, xxi.) no charge was laid to them but that they were the children of Saul, and sacrificed to a point of state expedience.

† Jeremy Taylor's Doctrine and Practice of Repentance, c. vi. s. 1.—*Ed.*

nature, he affirms to be the irresistible cause that they, one and all, did sin ;—and this at once illustrated and justified by one of the worst actions of an imperfect mortal! So far could the resolve to coerce all doctrines within the limits of the individual's power of comprehension, and the prejudices of an Arminian against the Calvinist preachers, carry a highly-gifted and exemplary divine. Let us be on our guard, lest similar effects should result from the zeal, however well-grounded in some respects, against the Church Calvinists of our days. My own belief is, perhaps, equi-distant from that of both parties, the Grotian and the Genevan. But, confining my remark exclusively to the doctrines and the practical deductions from them, I could never read Bishop Taylor's Tract on the doctrine and practice of Repentance, without being tempted to characterize high Calvinism as (comparatively) a lamb in wolf's skin, and strict Arminianism as approaching to the reverse.

Actuated by these motives, I have devoted the following essay to a brief history of the rise and occasion of the Latitudinarian system in its birth-place in Greece, and to a faithful exhibition both of its parentage and its offspring. The reader will find it strictly correspondent to the motto of both essays, ἡ ὁδὸς κάτω—the way downwards.

ESSAY III.

ON THE ORIGIN AND PROGRESS OF THE SECT OF SOPHISTS IN GREECE.

Ἡ ὁδὸς κάτω·
The road downwards. HERACLIT. *Fragment.*

As Pythagoras, declining the title of the wise man, is said to have first named himself philosopher, or lover of wisdom, so Protagoras, followed by Gorgias, Prodicus, and others, found even the former word too narrow for his own opinion of himself, and first assumed the title of sophist ;—this word originally signifying one who possesses the power of making others wise, a wholesale and retail dealer in wisdom;—a wisdom-monger, in the same sense as we say, an iron-monger. In this, and not in their abuse of the arts of reasoning, have Plato and Aristotle placed the essential of the sophistic character. Their sophisms were indeed its natural products and accompaniments, but must yet be distinguished from it, as the fruits from the tree. *Ἔμπορός τις—κάπηλος—τὰ μαθήματα περιάγων κατὰ τὰς πόλεις, καὶ πωλοῦντες καὶ καπηλεύοντες*—a vender, a market-man, in moral and intellectual knowledges (*connoissances*)—one who hires himself out or puts himself up at auction, as a carpenter and upholsterer to the heads and hearts of his customers—such are the phrases by which Plato at once describes and satirizes the proper sophist.* Nor does the Stagyrite fall short of his great master and rival in the reprobation of these professors of wisdom, or differ from him in the grounds of it. He, too, gives the baseness of the motives joined with the impudence and delusive nature of the pretence, as the generic character.†

Next to this pretence of selling wisdom and eloquence, they were distinguished by their itinerancy. Athens was, indeed, their great emporium and place of resort, but by no means their domicile. Such were Protagoras, Gorgias, Prodicus, Hippias, Polus, Callicles, Thrasymachus, and a whole host of sophists *minorum gentium*: and though many of the tribe, like the Euthydemus and Dionysodorus, so dramatically portrayed by Plato, were mere empty disputants, sleight-of-word jugglers, this was far from being their common character. Both Plato and Aristotle repeatedly admit the brilliancy of their talents and the extent of their acquirements. The following passage from the Timæus of the former will be my best commentary as well as authority. "The race of sophists, again, I acknowledge for men of no common powers, and of eminent skill and experience in many and various kinds of knowledge, and these too not seldom truly fair and ornamental of our nature; but I fear that somehow, as being itinerants from city to city, loose from all permanent ties of house and home, and everywhere aliens, they shoot wide of the proper

* See the Protagoras, s. 12; and the *καπηλικὸν, αὐτοπωλικὸν, μαθηματοπωλικὸν γένος*, of the Sophistes, s. 21.—*Ed.*

† See Aristot. *De Reprehensione Sophist.* Ἔστὶ γὰρ ἡ σαφιστικὴ, φαινομένη σοφία· οὖσα δὲ μή· καὶ ὁ σοφιστὴς, χρηματιστὴς ἀπὸ φαινομένης σοφίας, ἀλλ' οὐκ οὔσης. Ib. c. 2.—*Ed.*

aim of man, whether as philosopher or as citizen." The few remains of Zeno the Eleatic, his paradoxes against the reality of motion, are mere identical propositions spun out into a sort of whimsical conundrums, as in the celebrated paradox entitled Achilles and the Tortoise, the whole plausibility of which rests on the trick of assuming a *minimum* of time while no *minimum* is allowed to space, joined with that of exacting from *intelligibilia*, *νούμενα*, the conditions peculiar to objects of the senses *φαινόμενα* or *αἰσθανόμενα*.* The passages still extant from the works of Gorgias, on the other hand, want nothing but the form† of a premiss to undermine by a legitimate *deductio ad absurdum* all the philosophic systems that had been hitherto advanced, with

* Place a tortoise 20 paces before Achilles, and suppose the fleetness of Achilles to that of the tortoise to be as 20 to 1. Whilst Achilles moves 20 paces, the tortoise moves 1; whilst he moves the 21st pace, she gains the 20th part of the 22d pace; whilst he gains this 20th part of the 22d pace, she gains the 20th part of the next 20th part of the same 22d pace; and so on *in infinitum*. See Aristotle's solution, or attempt at it, in the Physics VI. c. 9, which consists chiefly in applying an infinite divisibility of the moments of time to the assumed infinite divisibility of the parts of matter. *Τοῦτο δὲ ἐστι ψεῦδος· οὐ γὰρ σύγκειται ὁ χρόνος ἐκ τῶν νῦν ὄντων ἀδιαιρέτων ὥσπερ οὐδ' ἄλλο μέγεθος οὐδέν.*—Ib.

"I had remarked to him" (Mr. Coleridge), says Mr. De Quincey, "that the sophism, as it is usually called, but the difficulty, as it should be called, of Achilles and the Tortoise, which had puzzled all the sages of Greece, was, in fact, merely another form of the perplexity which besets decimal fractions; that, for example, if you throw ⅔ into a decimal form, it will never terminate, but be ·666666, &c., *ad infinitum*. 'Yes,' Coleridge replied; 'the apparent absurdity in the Grecian problem arises thus,—because it assumes the infinite divisibility of space, but drops out of view the corresponding infinity of time.' There was a flash of lightning, which illuminated a darkness that had existed for twenty-three centuries."—Tait's Mag. Sept. 1834, p. 514.

I apprehend, however, that this part of the solution, such as it is, is substantially what Aristotle means in his remark on the Zenonian paradox; but the latter part, namely, the detection of the sophism of applying to an idea conditions only properly applicable to sensuous *phænomena*, belongs to Mr. Coleridge himself.—*Ed.* [The solution is given by Leibnitz; also in a Letter to Mr. Foucher. *Opp. ed. Erdmann*, I. p. 115. S. C.]

† Namely, if either the world itself as an animated whole, according to the Italian school; or if atoms, according to Democritus; or any one primal element, as water or fire, according to Thales or Empedocles; or if a *nous*, as explained by Anaxagoras; be assumed as the absolutely first: then, &c.

the exception of the Heraclitic, and of that too as it was generally understood and interpreted. Yet Zeno's name was, and ever will be holden in reverence by philosophers; for his object was as grand as his motives were honorable,—that of assigning limits to the claims of the senses, and subordinating them to the pure reason; while Gorgias will ever be cited as an instance of prostituted genius from the immoral nature of his object and the baseness of his motives. These, and not his sophisms, constituted him a sophist, a sophist whose eloquence and logical skill rendered him only the more pernicious.

Soon after the repulse of the Persian invaders, and as a heavy counterbalance to the glories of Marathon and Platæa, we may date the commencement of that corruption first in private and next in public life, which displayed itself more or less in all the free states and communities of Greece, but most of all in Athens. The causes are obvious, and such as in popular republics have always followed, and are themselves the effects of, that passion for military glory and political preponderance, which may well be called the bastard and the parricide of liberty. In reference to the fervid but light and sensitive Athenians, we may enumerate, as the most operative, the giddiness of sudden aggrandizement; the more intimate connection and frequent intercourse with the Asiatic states; the intrigues with the court of Persia; the intoxication of the citizens at large, sustained and increased by the continued allusions to their recent exploits, in the flatteries of the theatre, and the funeral panegyrics; the rage for amusement and public shows; and lastly the destruction of the Athenian constitution by the ascendency of its democratic element. During the operation of these causes at an early period of the process, and no unimportant part of it, the sophists made their first appearance. Some of these applied the lessons of their art in their own persons, and traded for gain and gainful influence in the character of demagogues and public orators; but the greater number offered themselves as instructors, in the arts of persuasion and temporary impression, to as many as could come up to the high prices, at which they rated their services. *Νέων πλουσίων θήρα σοφιστική**—(these are Plato's words)—hireling hunters of the young and rich,—they offered to the vanity of youth and the ambition of wealth a substitute for that authority,

* Sophistes, s. 17.—*Ed.*

which by the institutions of Solon had been attached to high birth and property, or rather to the moral discipline, the habits, attainments, and directing motives, on which the great legislator had calculated (not indeed as necessary or constant accompaniments, but yet) as the regular and ordinary results of comparative opulence and renowned ancestry.

The loss of this stable and salutary influence was to be supplied by the arts of popularity. But in order to the success of this scheme, it was necessary that the people themselves should be degraded into a populace. The cupidity for dissipation and sensual pleasure in all ranks had kept pace with the increasing inequality in the means of gratifying it. The restless spirit of republican ambition, engendered by their success in a just war, and by the romantic character of that success, had already formed a close alliance with luxury; with luxury, too, in its early and most vigorous state, when it acts as an appetite to enkindle, and before it has exhausted and dulled the vital energies by the habit of enjoyment. But this corruption was now to be introduced into the citadel of the moral being, and to be openly defended by the very arms and instruments, which had been given for the purpose of preventing or chastising its approach. The understanding was to be corrupted by the perversion of the reason, and the feelings through the medium of the understanding. For this purpose all fixed principles, whether grounded on reason, religion, law, or antiquity, were to be undermined, and then, as now, chiefly by the sophistry of submitting all positions alike, however heterogeneous, to the criterion of the mere understanding;—the sophists meantime disguising or concealing the fact, that the rules which alone they applied were abstracted from the objects of the senses, and applicable exclusively to things of quantity and relation. At all events, the minds of men were to be sensualized; and even if the arguments themselves failed, yet the principles so attacked were to be brought into doubt by the mere frequency of hearing all things doubted, and the most sacred of all now openly denied, and now insulted by sneer and ridicule. For by the constitution of our nature, as far as it is human nature, so awful is truth, that as long as we have faith in its attainability and hopes of its attainment, there exists no bribe strong enough to tempt us wholly and permanently from our allegiance.

Religion, in its widest sense, signifies the act and habits of reverencing the invisible, as the highest both in ourselves and in nature. To this the senses and their immediate objects are to be made subservient, the one as its organs, the other as its exponents; and as such, therefore, having on their own account no true value, because no inherent worth. They are, in short, a language; and taken independently of their representative function, from words they become mere empty sounds, and differ from noise only by exciting expectations which they can not gratify—fit ingredients of the idolatrous charm, the potent *abracadabra*, of a sophisticated race, who had sacrificed the religion of faith to the superstition of the senses, a race of animals, in whom the presence of reason is manifested solely by the absence of instinct.

The same principle, which in its application to the whole of our being becomes religion, considered speculatively is the basis of metaphysical science, that, namely, which requires an evidence beyond that of sensible concretes, which latter the ancients generalized in the word, *physica*, and therefore, prefixing the preposition μετά, beyond or transcending, named the superior science, metaphysics. The invisible was assumed as the supporter of the apparent, τῶν φαινομένων—as their substance, a term which, in any other interpretation, expresses only the striving of the imaginative power under conditions that involve the necessity of its frustration. If the invisible be denied, or (which is equivalent) considered invisible from the defect of the senses and not in its own nature, the sciences even of observation and experiment lose their essential *copula*. The component parts can never be reduced into an harmonious whole, but must owe their systematic arrangement to the accidents of an ever-shifting perspective. Much more then must this apply to the moral world disjoined from religion. Instead of morality, we can at best have only a scheme of prudence, and this too a prudence fallible and short-sighted; for were it of such a kind as to be *bona fide* coincident with morals in reference to the agent as well as to the outward action, its first act would be that of abjuring its own usurped primacy. By celestial observations alone can even terrestrial charts be constructed scientifically.

The first attempt, therefore, of the sophists was to separate ethics from the faith in the invisible, and to stab morality through the side of religion; an attempt to which the idolatrous polytheism of Greece furnished too many facilities. To the zeal with which he counteracted this plan by endeavors to purify and ennoble that popular belief, which, from obedience to the laws, he did not deem himself permitted to subvert, Socrates owed his martyr-cup of hemlock. Still while any one principle of morality remained, religion in some form or other must remain inclusively. Therefore, as they commenced by assailing the former through the latter, so did they continue their warfare by reversing the operation. The principle was confounded with the particular acts, in which under the guidance of the understanding or judgment it was to manifest itself.

Thus the rule of expediency, which properly belonged to one and the lower part of morality, was made to be the whole. And so far there was at least a consistency in this; for in two ways only could it subsist. It must either be the mere servant of religion, or its usurper and substitute. Viewed as principles, they were so utterly heterogeneous, that by no grooving could the two be fitted into each other; by no intermediate could they be preserved in lasting adhesion. The one or the other was sure to decompose the cement. We can not have a stronger historical authority for the truth of this statement than the words of Polybius, in which he attributes the ruin of the Greek states to the frequency of perjury, which they had learned from the sophists to laugh at as a trifle that broke no bones, nay, as in some cases, an expedient and justifiable exertion of the powers given us by nature over our own words, without which no man could have a secret that might not be extorted from him by the will of others. In the same spirit the sage and observant historian attributes the growth and strength of the Roman republic to the general reverence of the invisible powers, and the consequent horror in which the breaking of an oath was holden. This he states as the *causa causarum*, as the ultimate and inclusive cause, of Roman grandeur.

Under such convictions, therefore, as the sophists labored with such fatal success to produce, it needed nothing but the excitement of the passions under circumstances of public discord to turn the arguments of expedience and self-love against the whole scheme of morality founded on them, and to procure a favorable hearing for the doctrines, which Plato attributes to the sophist

Callicles.* The passage is curious, and might be entitled, a Jacobin head, a genuine antique, in high preservation. "By nature," exclaims this Napoleon of old, "the worse off is always the more infamous, that, namely, which suffers wrong; but according to the law it is the doing of wrong. For no man of noble spirit will let himself be wronged; this a slave only endures, who is not worth the life he has, and under injuries and insults can neither help himself nor those that belong to him. Those, who first made the laws, were, in my opinion, feeble creatures, which in fact the greater number of men are; or they would not remain entangled in these spider-webs. Such, however, being the case, laws, honor, and ignominy were all calculated for the advantage of the law-makers. But in order to frighten away the stronger, whom they could not coerce by fair contest, and to secure greater advantages for themselves than their feebleness could otherwise have procured, they preached up the doctrine, that it was base and contrary to right to wish to have any thing beyond others; and that in this wish consisted the essence of injustice. Doubtless it was very agreeable to them, if being creatures of a meaner class they were allowed to share equally with their natural superiors. But nature dictates plainly enough another code of right, namely, that the nobler and stronger should possess more than the weaker and more pusillanimous. Where the power is, there lies the substantial right. The whole realm of animals, nay the human race itself as collected in independent states and nations, demonstrates that the stronger has a right to control the weaker for his own advantage. Assuredly, they have the genuine notion of right, and follow the law of nature, though truly not that which is holden valid in our governments. But the minds of our youths are preached away from them by declamations on the beauty and fitness of letting themselves be mastered, till by these verbal conjurations the noblest nature is tamed and cowed, like a young lion born and bred in a cage. Should a man with full untamed force but once step forward, he would break all your spells and conjurations, trample your contra-natural laws under his feet, vault into the seat of supreme power, and in a splendid style make the right of nature be valid among you."

* See the speech of Callicles in the Gorgias:—*φύσει μὲν γὰρ πᾶν αἴσχιόν ἐστιν ὅ περ καὶ κάκιον, π. τ. λ.*—*Ed.*

It would have been well for mankind, if such had always been the language of sophistry. A selfishness, that excludes partnership, all men have an interest in repelling. Yet the principle is the same: and if for power we substitute pleasure and the means of pleasure, it is easy to construct a system well fitted to corrupt natures, and the more mischievous in proportion as it is less alarming. As long as the spirit of philosophy reigns in the learned and highest class, and that of religion in all classes, a tendency to blend and unite will be found in all objects of pursuit, and the whole discipline of mind and manners will be calculated in relation to the worth of the agents. With the prevalence of sophistry, when the pure will (if indeed the existence of a will be admitted in any other sense than as the temporary main current in the wide gust-eddying stream of our desires and aversions)—with this prevalence of sophistry, when the pure will is ranked among the means to an alien end, instead of being itself the one absolute end, in the participation of which all other things are worthy to be called good, commences the epoch of division and separation. Things are rapidly improved, persons as rapidly deteriorated; and for an indefinite period the powers of the aggregate increase, as the strength of the individual declines. Still, however, sciences may be estranged from philosophy, the practical from the speculative, and one of the two at least may remain. Music may be divided from poetry, and both may continue to exist, though with diminished influence. But religion and morals cannot be disjoined without the destruction of both: and that this does not take place to the full extent, we owe to the frequency with which both take shelter in the heart, and that men are always better or worse than the maxims which they adopt or concede.

To demonstrate the hollowness of the present system, and to deduce the truth from its sources, is not possible for me without a previous agreement as to the principles of reasoning in general. The attempt could neither be made within the limits of the present work, nor would its success greatly affect the immediate moral interests of the majority of the readers for whom this work was especially written. For as sciences are systems on principles, so in the life of practice is morality a principle without a system. Systems of morality are in truth nothing more than the old books of casuistry generalized, even of that casuistry, which the genius of Protestantism gradually worked off from itself like a heterogeneous humor, together with the practice of auricular confession;—a fact the more striking, because in both instances it was against the intention of the first teachers of the Reformation; and the revival of both was not only urged, but provided for, though in vain, by no less men than Bishops Saunderson and Jeremy Taylor.

But there is yet another prohibitory reason; and this I can not convey more effectually than in the words of Plato to Dionysius:

*'Αλλὰ ποῖον τι μὴν τοῦτ' ἐςιν, ὦ παῖ Διονυσίου καὶ Δωρίδος, τὸ ἐρώτημα, ὃ πάντων αἴτιόν ἐςι κακῶν; μᾶλλον δὲ ἡ περὶ τούτου ὠδὶς ἐν τῇ ψυχῇ εγγιγνομένη, ἣν εἰ μή τις ἐξαιρεθήσεται, τῆς ἀληθείας ὄντως οὐ μήποτε τύχῃ.**

But what a question is this, which you propose, O, son of Dionysius and Doris!—what is the origin and cause of all evil? But rather is the darkness and travail concerning this that thorn in the soul, which unless a man shall have had removed, never can he partake of the truth that is verily and indeed truth.

Yet that I may fulfil the original scope of The Friend, I shall attempt to provide the preparatory steps for such an investigation in the following essays on the principles of method common to all investigations; which I here present, as the basis of my future philosophical and theological writings, and as the necessary introduction to the same. And in addition to this, I can conceive no object of inquiry more appropriate, none which, commencing with the most familiar truths, with facts of hourly experience, and gradually winning its way to positions the most comprehensive and sublime, will more aptly prepare the mind for the reception of specific knowledge, than the full exposition of a principle which is the condition of all intellectual progress, and which may be said even to constitute the science of education, alike in the narrowest and in the most extensive sense of the word. Yet as it is but fair to let the public know beforehand, what the genius of my philosophy is, and in what spirit it will be applied by me, whether in politics or religion, I conclude with the following brief history of the last hundred and thirty years by a lover of Old England.

Wise and necessitated confirmation and explanation of the law of England, erroneously entitled The English Revolution of

* *Epist. Dionysio. II.—Ed.*

1688; mechanical philosophy, hailed as a kindred movement, and espoused, as a common cause, by the partisans of the revolution in the state.

The consequence is, or was, a system of natural rights instead of social and hereditary privileges; acquiescence in historic testimony substituted for faith, and yet the true historical feeling, the feeling of being an historical people, generation linked to generation by ancestral reputation, by tradition, by heraldry,—this noble feeling, I say, openly stormed or perilously undermined.

Imagination excluded from poesy, and fancy paramount in physics; the eclipse of the ideal by the mere shadow of the sensible; subfiction for supposition. *Plebs pro senatu populoque;* the wealth of nations for the well-being of nations, and of man.

Anglo-mania in France followed by revolution in America; constitution of America appropriate, perhaps, to America, but elevated from a particular experiment to a universal model. The word constitution altered to mean a capitulation, a treaty, imposed by the people on their own government, as on a conquered enemy; hence giving sanction to falsehood and universality to anomaly.

Despotism, despotism, despotism, of finance in statistics, of vanity in social converse, of presumption and overweening contempt of the ancients in individuals.

French Revolution; pauperism, revenue laws, government by clubs, committees, societies, reviews, and newspapers.

Thus it is that a nation first sets fire to a neighboring nation; then catches fire and burns backward.

Statesmen should know that a learned class is an essential element of a state, at least of a Christian state. But you wish for general illumination! You begin with the attempt to popularize learning and philosophy; but you will end in the plebification of knowledge. A true philosophy in the learned class is essential to a true religious feeling in all classes.

In fine, religion, true or false, is and ever has been the moral centre of gravity in Christendom, to which all other things must and will accommodate themselves.

ESSAY IV.

῞Ο δὲ μετὰ ταῦτα δίκαιόν ἐϛι ποιεῖν, ἄκουε, ἵνα σοι καὶ ἀποκρίνωμαι ὃ σὺ ἐρωτᾷς, πῶς χρὴ ἔχειν ἐμὲ καὶ σὲ πρὸς ἀλλήλους. Εἰ μὲν ὅλως φιλοσοφίας καταπεφρόνηκας, ἐᾶν χαίρειν· εἰ δὲ παρ' ἑτέρου ἀκήκοας ἢ αὐτὸς βελτίονα εὕρηκας τῶν παρ' ἐμοί, ἐκεῖνα τίμα· εἰ δ' ἄρα τὰ παρ' ἡμῶν σοι ἀρέσκει, τιμητέον καὶ ἐμὲ μάλιϛα.

PLATO.*

Hear then what are the terms on which you and I ought to stand toward each other. If you hold philosophy altogether in contempt, bid it farewell. Or if you have heard from any other person, or have yourself found out a better than mine, then give honor to that, whichever it be. But if the doctrine taught in these our works please you, then it is but just that you should honor me too in the same proportion.

WHAT is that which first strikes us, and strikes us at once, in a man of education, and which, among educated men, so instantly distinguishes the man of superior mind, that (as was observed with eminent propriety of the late Edmund Burke) "we can not stand under the same archway during a shower of rain, without finding him out?" Not the weight or novelty of his remarks ; not any unusual interest of facts communicated by him ; for we may suppose both the one and the other precluded by the shortness of our intercourse, and the triviality of the subjects. The difference will be impressed and felt, though the conversation should be confined to the state of the weather or the pavement. Still less will it arise from any peculiarity in his words and phrases. For if he be, as we now assume, a well-educated man as well as a man of superior powers, he will not fail to follow the golden rule of Julius Cæsar, *insolens verbum, tanquam scopulum, evitare.* Unless where new things necessitate new terms, he will avoid an unusual word as a rock. It must have been among the earliest lessons of his youth, that the breach of this precept, at all times hazardous, becomes ridiculous in the topics of ordinary conversation. There remains but one other

* *Epist. Dionysio. II.—Ed.*

point of distinction possible; and this must be, and in fact is, the true cause of the impression made on us. It is the unpremeditated and evidently habitual arrangement of his words, grounded on the habit of foreseeing, in each integral part, or (more plainly) in every sentence, the whole that he then intends to communicate. However irregular and desultory his talk, there is method in the fragments.

Listen, on the other hand, to an ignorant man, though perhaps shrewd and able in his particular calling, whether he be describing or relating. We immediately perceive, that his memory alone is called into action; and that the objects and events recur in the narration in the same order, and with the same accompaniments, however accidental or impertinent, in which they had first occurred to the narrator. The necessity of taking breath, the efforts of recollection, and the abrupt rectification of its failures, produce all his pauses; and with exception of the "and then," the "and there," and the still less significant, "and so," they constitute likewise all his connections.

Our discussion, however, is confined to method as employed in the formation of the understanding, and in the constructions of science and literature. It would indeed be superfluous to attempt a proof of its importance in the business and economy of active or domestic life. From the cotter's hearth or the workshop of the artisan to the palace or the arsenal, the first merit, that which admits neither substitute nor equivalent, is, that everything be in its place. Where this charm is wanting, every other merit either loses its name, or becomes an additional ground of accusation and regret. Of one, by whom it is eminently possessed, we say proverbially, he is like clock-work. The resemblance extends beyond the point of regularity, and yet falls short of the truth. Both do, indeed, at once divide and announce the silent and otherwise indistinguishable lapse of time. But the man of methodical industry and honorable pursuits does more; he realizes its ideal divisions, and gives a character and individuality to its moments. If the idle are described as killing time, he may be justly said to call it into life and moral being, while he makes it the distinct object not only of the consciousness, but of the conscience. He organizes the hours, and gives them a soul; and that, the very essence of which is to fleet away, and evermore to have been, he takes up into his own permanence, and communicates to it the imperishableness of a spiritual nature. Of the *good and faithful servant*, whose energies, thus directed, are thus methodized, it is less truly affirmed, that he lives in time, than that time lives in him. His days, months, and years, as the stops and punctual marks in the records of duties performed, will survive the wreck of worlds, and remain extant when time itself shall be no more.

But as the importance of method in the duties of social life is incomparably greater, so are its practical elements proportionably obvious, and such as relate to the will far more than to the understanding. Henceforward, therefore, we contemplate its bearings on the latter.

The difference between the products of a well-disciplined and those of an uncultivated understanding, in relation to what we will now venture to call the science of method, is often and admirably exhibited by our great dramatist. I scarcely need refer my readers to the Clown's evidence, in the first scene of the second act of Measure for Measure, or to the Nurse in Romeo and Juliet. But not to leave the position, without an instance to illustrate it, I will take the easy-yielding Mrs. Quickly's relation of the circumstances of Sir John Falstaff's debt to her:—

FALSTAFF. What is the gross sum that I owe thee?

HOST. Marry, if thou wert an honest man, thyself and the money too. Thou didst swear to me upon a parcel-gilt goblet, sitting in my Dolphin chamber, at the round table, by a sea-coal fire, upon Wednesday in Whitsun week, when the prince broke thy head for liking his father to a singing-man of Windsor; thou didst swear to me then, as I was washing thy wound, to marry me and make me my lady thy wife. Canst thou deny it? Did not goodwife Keech, the butcher's wife, come in then and call me gossip Quickly?—coming in to borrow a mess of vinegar; telling us she had a good dish of prawns; whereby thou didst desire to eat some; whereby I told thee they were ill for a green wound, &c.*

And this, be it observed, is so far from being carried beyond the bounds of a fair imitation, that the poor soul's thoughts and sentences are more closely interlinked than the truth of nature would have required, but that the connections and sequence, which the habit of method can alone give, have in this instance a substitute in the fusion of passion. For the absence of method, which characterizes the uneducated, is occasioned by an habitual

* Henry IV. Pt. II. act ii. sc. 1.—*Ed*

submission of the understanding to mere events and images as such, and independent of any power in the mind to classify or appropriate them. The general accompaniments of time and place are the only relations which persons of his class appear to regard in their statements. As this constitutes their leading feature, the contrary excellence, as distinguishing the well-educated man, must be referred to the contrary habit. Method, therefore, becomes natural to the mind which has been accustomed to contemplate not things only, or for their own sake alone, but likewise and chiefly the relations of things, either their relations to each other, or to the observer, or to the state and apprehension of the hearers. To enumerate and analyze these relations, with the conditions under which alone they are discoverable, is to teach the science of method.

The enviable results of this science, when knowledge has been ripened into those habits which at once secure and evince its possession, can scarcely be exhibited more forcibly as well as more pleasingly, than by contrasting with the former extract from Shakspeare the narration given by Hamlet to Horatio of the occurrences during his proposed transportation to England, and the events that interrupted his voyage :—

Ham. Sir, in my heart there was a kind of fighting
That would not let me sleep: methought, I lay
Worse than the mutines in the bilboes. Rashly,
And praised be rashness for it——Let us know,
Our indiscretion sometimes serve us well,
When our deep plots do fail: and that should teach us,
There's a divinity that shapes our ends,
Rough-hew them how we will.
Hor. That is most certain.
Ham. Up from my cabin,
My sea-gown scarf'd about me, in the dark
Grop'd I to find out them; had my desire;
Finger'd their packet; and, in fine, withdrew
To my own room again: making so bold,
My fears forgetting manners, to unseal
Their grand commission; where I found, Horatio,
A royal knavery; an exact command—
Larded with many several sorts of reasons,
Importing Denmark's health, and England's too,
With, ho! such bugs and goblins in my life—
That on the supervise, no leisure bated,

No, not to stay the grinding of the axe,
My head should be struck off!
  HOR. Is't possible?
  HAM. Here's the commission;—read it at more leisure.*

Here the events, with the circumstances of time and place, are all stated with equal compression and rapidity, not one introduced which could have been omitted without injury to the intelligibility of the whole process. If any tendency is discoverable, as far as the mere facts are in question, it is the tendency to omission: and, accordingly, the reader will observe in the following quotation that the attention of the narrator is called back to one material circumstance, which he was hurrying by, by a direct question from the friend to whom the story is communicated, "How was this sealed?" But by a trait which is indeed peculiarly characteristic of Hamlet's mind, ever disposed to generalize, and meditative if to excess (but which, with due abatement and reduction, is distinctive of every powerful and methodizing intellect), all the digressions and enlargements consist of reflections, truths, and principles of general and permanent interest, either directly expressed or disguised in playful satire.

——————— I sat me down;
Devis'd a new commission; wrote it fair.
I once did hold it, as our statists do,
A baseness to write fair, and labored much
How to forget that learning; but, sir, now
It did me yeoman's service. Wilt thou know
The effect of what I wrote?
  HOR. Ay, good my lord.
  HAM. An earnest conjuration from the king,—
As England was his faithful tributary;
As love between them, like the palm, might flourish;
As peace should still her wheaten garland wear,
And stand a comma 'tween their amities,
And many such like ases of great charge—
That on the view and knowing of their contents,
Without debatement further, more or less,
He should the bearers put to sudden death,
No shriving time allowed.
  HOR. How was this seal'd?
  HAM. Why, even in that was heaven ordinant.
I had my father's signet in my purse,

* Act v. sc. 2.

Which was the model of that Danish seal:
Folded the writ up in the form of the other;
Subscribed it; gave't the impression; placed it safely,
The changeling never known. Now, the next day
Was our sea-fight; and what to this was sequent,
Thou know'st already.
Hor. So Guildenstern and Rosencrantz go to't?
Ham. Why, man, they did make love to this employment.
They are not near my conscience: their defeat
Doth by their own insinuation grow.
'Tis dangerous when the baser nature comes
Between the pass and fell incensed points
Of mighty opposites.*

It would, perhaps, be sufficient to remark of the preceding passage, in connection with the humorous specimen of narration,

Fermenting o'er with frothy circumstance,

in Henry IV., that if, overlooking the different value of the matter in each, we considered the form alone, we should find both immethodical,—Hamlet from the excess, Mrs. Quickly from the want, of reflection and generalization; and that method, therefore, must result from the due mean or balance between our passive impressions and the mind's own re-action on the same. Whether this re-action do not suppose or imply a primary act positively originating in the mind itself, and prior to the object in order of nature, though co-instantaneous with it in its manifestation, will be hereafter discussed. But I had a further purpose in thus contrasting these extracts from our myriad-minded bard, μυριονοῦς ἀνηρ. I wished to bring forward, each for itself, these two elements of method, or, to adopt an arithmetical term, its two main factors.

Instances of the want of generalization are of no rare occurrence in real life: and the narrations of Shakspeare's Hostess and the Tapster differ from those of the ignorant and unthinking in general by their superior humor, the poet's own gift and infusion, not by their want of method, which is not greater than we often meet with in that class, of which they are the dramatic representatives. Instances of the opposite fault, arising from the excess of generalization and reflection in minds of the opposite class, will, like the minds themselves, occur less frequently in the course

* Act v. sc. 2.

of our own personal experience. Yet they will not have been wanting to our readers, nor will they have passed unobserved, though the great poet himself (ὁ τὴν ἑαυτοῦ ψυχὴν ὥσει ὕλην τινα ἀσώματον μορφαῖς ποικιλαῖς μορφώσας*) has more conveniently supplied the illustrations. To complete, therefore, the purpose aforementioned, that of presenting each of the two components as separately as possible, I chose an instance in which, by the surplus of its own activity, Hamlet's mind disturbs the arrangement, of which that very activity had been the cause and impulse.†

Thus exuberance of mind, on the one hand, interferes with the forms of method; but sterility of mind, on the other, wanting the spring and impulse to mental action, is wholly destructive of method itself. For in attending too exclusively to the relations which the past or passing events and objects bear to general truth, and the moods of his own thought, the most intelligent man is sometimes in danger of overlooking that other relation, in which they are likewise to be placed to the apprehension and sympathies of his hearers. His discourse appears like soliloquy intermixed with dialogue. But the uneducated and unreflecting talker overlooks all mental relations, both logical and psychological; and consequently precludes all method which is not purely accidental. Hence the nearer the things and incidents in time and place, the more distant, disjointed, and impertinent to each other, and to any common purpose, will they appear in his narration: and this from the want of a staple, or starting-post, in the narrator himself; from the absence of the leading thought, which, borrowing a phrase from the nomenclature of legislation, I may not inaptly call the initiative. On the contrary, where the habit of method is present and effective, things the most remote and diverse in time, place, and outward circumstance, are brought into mental contiguity and succession, the more striking as the less expected. But while I would impress the necessity of this habit, the illustrations adduced give proof that in undue preponderance, and when the prerogative of the mind is stretched into despotism, the discourse may degenerate into the grotesque or the fantastical.

* He that moulded his own soul, as some incorporeal material, into various forms.—THEMISTIUS.

† See the criticism on the character of Hamlet in the Lectures upon Shakspeare and other Dramatists. IV. p. 144.—*Ed.*

With what a profound insight into the constitution of the human soul is this exhibited to us in the character of the Prince of Denmark, where flying from the sense of reality, and seeking a reprieve from the pressure of its duties in that ideal activity, the overbalance of which, with the consequent indisposition to action, is his disease, he compels the reluctant good sense of the high yet healthful-minded Horatio to follow him in his wayward meditation amid the graves!

HAM. To what base uses we may return, Horatio! Why may not imagination trace the noble dust of Alexander till he find it stopping a bung-hole?

HOR. 'Twere to consider too curiously, to consider so.

HAM. No, 'faith, not a jot; but to follow him thither with modesty enough, and likelihood to lead it: As thus; Alexander died, Alexander was buried, Alexander returneth to dust; the dust is earth; of earth we make loam: And why of that loam whereto he was converted, might they not stop a beer-barrel?

Imperious Cæsar, dead, and turn'd to clay,
Might stop a hole to keep the wind away!*

But let it not escape our recollection, that when the objects thus connected are proportionate to the connecting energy, relatively to the real, or at least to the desirable, sympathies of mankind; it is from the same character that we derive the genial method in the famous soliloquy, "To be, or not to be"†—which, admired as it is, and has been, has yet received only the first-fruits of the admiration due to it.

We have seen that from the confluence of innumerable impressions in each moment of time the mere passive memory must needs tend to confusion; a rule, the seeming exceptions to which (the thunder-bursts in Lear, for instance) are really confirmations of its truth. For, in many instances, the predominance of some mighty passion takes the place of the guiding thought, and the result presents the method of nature, rather than the habit of the individual. For thought, imagination (and I may add, passion), are, in their very essence, the first, connective, the latter coadunative: and it has been shown, that if the excess lead to method misapplied, and to connections of the moment, the absence, or marked deficiency, either precludes method altogether, both form and substance; or (as the following extract will exemplify) retains the outward form only.

* Act v. sc. 1.

† Act iii. sc. 1.

My liege and Madam, to expostulate
What majesty should be, what duty is,
Why day is day, night night, and time is time,
Were nothing but to waste night, day and time.
Therefore—since brevity is the soul of wit,
And tediousness the limbs and outward flourishes,—
I will be brief. Your noble son is mad:
Mad call I it; for to define true madness,
What is't, but to be nothing else but mad!
But let that go.
  QUEEN. More matter with less art.
  POL. Madam, I swear, I use no art at all.
That he is mad, 'tis true: 'tis true, 'tis pity:
And pity 'tis, 'tis true: a foolish figure;
But farewell it, for I will use no art.
Mad let us grant him then: and now remains,
That we find out the cause of this effect,
Or rather say the cause of this defect:
For this effect defective comes by cause.
Thus it remains, and the remainder thus
Perpend.*

Does not the irresistible sense of the ludicrous in this flourish of the soul-surviving body of old Polonius's intellect, not less than in the endless confirmations and most undeniable matters of fact of Tapster Pompey or the hostess of the tavern prove to our feelings, even before the word is found which presents the truth to our understandings, that confusion and formality are but the opposite poles of the same null-point?

It is Shakspeare's peculiar excellence, that throughout the whole of his splendid picture-gallery (the reader will excuse the acknowledged inadequacy of this metaphor), we find individuality everywhere, mere portrait nowhere. In all his various characters, we still feel ourselves communing with the same nature, which is everywhere present as the vegetable sap in the branches, sprays, leaves, buds, blossoms, and fruits, their shapes, tastes, and odors. Speaking of the effect, that is, his works themselves, we may define the excellence of their method as consisting in that just proportion, that union and interpenetration, of the universal and the particular, which must ever pervade all works of decided genius and true science. For method implies a progressive transition, and it is the meaning of the word in the original language. The Greek μέθοδος is literally a way or path

* Act ii. sc. 2.

of transit. Thus we extol the Elements of Euclid, or Socrates' discourse with the slave in the Menon of Plato,* as methodical, a term which no one who holds himself bound to think or speak correctly, would apply to the alphabetical order or arrangement of a common dictionary. But as without continuous transition there can be no method, so without a preconception there can be no transition with continuity. The term, method, can not therefore, otherwise than by abuse, be applied to a mere dead arrangement, containing in itself no principle of progression.

ESSAY V.

Scientiis idem quod plantis. Si planta aliqua uti in animo habeas, de radice quid fiat, nil refert: si vero transferre cupias in aliud solum, tutius est radicibus uti quam surculis. Sic traditio, quæ nunc in usu est, exhibet plane tanquam truncos (pulchros illos quidem) scientiarum; sed tamen absque radicibus fabro lignario certe commodos, at plantatori inutiles. Quod si, disciplinæ ut crescant, tibi cordi sit, de truncis minus sis solicitus: ad id curam adhibe, ut radices illæsæ, etiam cum aliquantulo terræ adhærentis, extrahantur: dummodo hoc pacto et scientiam propriam revisere, vestigiaque cognitionis tuæ remetiri possis; et eam sic transplantare in animum alienum, sicut crevit in tuo.

BACON.†

It is with sciences as with trees. If it be your purpose to make some particular use of the tree, you need not concern yourself about the roots. But if you wish to transfer it into another soil, it is then safer to employ the roots than the scions. Thus the mode of teaching most common at present exhibits clearly enough the trunks, as it were, of the sciences, and those too of handsome growth; but nevertheless, without the roots, valuable and convenient as they undoubtedly are to the carpenter, they are useless to the planter. But if you have at heart the advancement of education, as that which proposes to itself the general discipline of the mind for its end and aim, be less anxious concerning the trunks, and let it be your care, that the roots should be extracted entire, even though a small portion of the soil should adhere to them: so that at all events you may be able, by this mean, both to review your own scientific acquirements, re-measuring

---

* Λέγε γάρ μοι σύ· οὐ τὸ μὲν τετράπουν τοῦτο ἡμῖν ἐστὶ χωρίον; κ. τ. λ.—*Ed.*

† *De Augment. Scient.* vi. c. 2, with some verbal alterations and transposition.—*Ed.*

as it were the steps of your knowledge for your own satisfaction, and at the same time to transplant it into the minds of others, just as it grew in your own.

It has been observed, in a preceding page, that the relations of objects are prime materials of method, and that the contemplation of relations is the indispensable condition of thinking methodically. It becomes necessary therefore to add, that there are two kinds of relation, in which objects of mind may be contemplated. The first is that of law, which, in its absolute perfection, is conceivable only of the Supreme Being, whose creative idea not only appoints to each thing its position, but in that position, and in consequence of that position, gives it its qualities, yea, gives it its very existence, as that particular thing. Yet in whatever science the relation of the parts to each other and to the whole is predetermined by a truth originating in the mind, and not abstracted or generalized from observation of the parts, there we affirm the presence of a law, if we are speaking of the physical sciences, as of astronomy for instance; or the presence of fundamental ideas, if our discourse be upon those sciences, the truths of which, as truths absolute, not merely have an independent origin in the mind, but continue to exist in and for the mind alone.* Such, for instance, is geometry, and such are the ideas of a perfect circle, of asymptotes, and the like.

I have thus assigned the first place in the science of method to law; and first of the first, to law, as the absolute kind which, comprehending in itself the substance of every possible degree, precludes from its conception all degree, not by generalization, but by its own plenitude. As such, therefore, and as the sufficient cause of the reality correspondent thereto, I contemplate it as exclusively an attribute of the Supreme Being, inseparable from the idea of God; adding, however, that from the contemplation of law in this its only perfect form, must be derived all true insight into all other grounds and principles necessary to method, as the science common to all sciences, which in each, in the words of Plato, τυγχάνει ὂν ἄλλο αὐτῆς τῆς ἐπιστήμης. Alienated from this intuition or steadfast faith, ingenious men may produce

* Here I have fallen into an error. The terms, idea and law, are always correlative. Instead of geometrical ideas, I ought to have said theorems;—not theories—but θεωρήματα, the intelligible products of contemplation, intellectual objects in the mind, and of and for the mind exclusively.—1829.

schemes conducive to the peculiar purposes of particular sciences, but no scientific system.

But though I can not enter on the proof of this assertion, I dare not remain exposed to the suspicion of having obtruded a mere private opinion, as a fundamental truth. The authorities are such, that my only difficulty is occasioned by their number. The following extract from Aristocle's (preserved with other interesting fragments of the same writer by Eusebius of Cæsarea) is as explicit as peremptory. *'Εφιλοσόφησε δὲ Πλάτων, εἰ καὶ τις ἄλλος τῶν πώποτε, γνησίως καὶ τελείως. 'Ηξίου δὲ μὴ δύνασθαι τὰ ἀνθρώπινα κατιδεῖν ἡμᾶς, εἰ μὴ τὰ θεῖα πρότερον ὀφθείη.** And Plato himself in his Republic, happily still extant, evidently alludes to the same doctrine. For personating Socrates in the discussion of a most important problem, namely, whether political justice is or is not the same as private honesty, after many inductions, and much analytic reasoning, he breaks off with these words—*καὶ εὖ γ' ἴσθι, ὦ Γλαύκων, ὡς ἡ ἐμὴ δόξα, ἀκριβῶς μὲν τοῦτο ἐκ τοιούτων μεθόδων, οἵαις νῦν ἐν τοῖς λόγοις χρώμεθα, οὐ μή ποτε λάβωμεν· ἀλλὰ γὰρ μακροτέρα καὶ πλείων ὁδὸς ἡ ἐπὶ τοῦτο ἄγουσα*† —not however, he adds, precluding the former (the analytic and inductive, to wit) which have their place likewise, in which (but as subordinate to the other) they are both useful and requisite. If any doubt could be entertained as to the purport of these words, it would be removed by the fact stated by Aristotle,‡ that Plato had discussed the problem, whether in order to scientific ends we must set out from principles or ascend towards them: in other words, whether the synthetic or analytic be the right method. But as no such question is directly discussed in the published

* *Præparat. Evangel.* xi. c. 3.—*Ed.* Plato, who philosophized legitimately and perfectively, if ever any man did in any age, held it for an axiom, that it is not possible for us to have an insight into things human (that is, the nature and relations of man, and the objects presented by nature for his investigation,) without a previous contemplation or intellectual vision of things divine; that is, of truths that are to be affirmed concerning the absolute, as far as they can be made known to us.

† *De Republica*, iv. But know well, O Glaucon, as my firm persuasion, that by such methods, as we have hitherto used in this inquisition, we can never attain to a satisfactory insight: for it is a longer and ampler way that conducts to this.

‡ Εὖ *γὰρ καὶ* Πλάτων *ἠπόρει τοῦτο καὶ ἐζήτει, πότερον ἀπὸ τῶν ἀρχῶν, ἢ ἐπὶ τὰς ἀρχάς, ἐστιν ἡ ὁδός.—Ethic. Nicom.* I. c. 2.—*Ed.*

works of the great master, Aristotle must either have received it orally from Plato himself, or have found it in the ἄγραφα δόγματα, the private text-books or manuals constructed by his select disciples, and intelligible to those only who like themselves had been intrusted with the esoteric, or interior and unveiled, doctrines of Platonism. Comparing this therefore with the writings, which he held it safe or not profane to make public, we may safely conclude, that Plato considered the investigation of truth *à posteriori* as that which is employed in explaining the results of a more scientific process to those, for whom the knowledge of the results was alone requisite and sufficient ; or in preparing the mind for legitimate method, by exposing the insufficiency or self-contradictions of the proofs and results obtained by the contrary process. Hence, therefore, the earnestness with which the genuine Platonists afterwards opposed the doctrine (that all demonstration consists of identical propositions) advanced by Stilpo, and maintained by the Megaric school, who denied the synthesis, and, like Hume and others in recent times, held geometry itself to be merely analytical.

The grand problem, the solution of which forms, according to Plato, the final object and distinctive character of philosophy, is this : for all that exists conditionally (that is, the existence of which is inconceivable except under the condition of its dependency on some other as its antecedent) to find a ground that is unconditional and absolute, and thereby to reduce the aggregate of human knowledge to a system. For the relation common to all being known, the appropriate orbit of each becomes discoverable, together with its peculiar relations to its concentrics in the common sphere of subordination. Thus the centrality of the sun having been established, and the law of the distances of the planets from the sun having been determined, we possess the means of calculating the distance of each from the other. But as all objects of sense are in continual flux, and as the notices of them by the senses must, as far as they are true notices, change with them, while scientific principles or laws are no otherwise principles of science than as they are permanent and always the same, the latter were appropriated to the pure reason, either as its products or as* implanted in it. And now the remarkable

* Which of these two doctrines was Plato's own opinion, it is hard to say. In many passages of his works, the latter (that is, the doctrine of in-

fact forces itself on our attention, namely, that the material world is found to obey the same laws as had been deduced independently from the reason; and that the masses act by a force, which can not be conceived to result from the component parts, known or imaginable. In magnetism, electricity, galvanism, and in chemistry generally, the mind is led instinctively, as it were, to regard the working powers as conducted, transmitted, or accumulated by the sensible bodies, and not as inherent. This fact has, at all times, been the stronghold alike of the materialists and of the spiritualists, equally solvable by the two contrary hypotheses, and fairly solved by neither. In the clear and masterly* re-

nate, or rather of connate, ideas) seems to be it; but from the character and avowed purpose of these works, as addressed to a promiscuous public, therefore preparatory, and for the discipline of the mind, rather than directly doctrinal, it is not improbable that Plato chose it as the more popular representation, and as belonging to the poetic drapery of his *philosophemata*.

* I can conceive no better remedy for the overweening self-complacency of modern philosophy than the annulment of its pretended originality. The attempt has been made by Dutens (*Rêcherches sur l'origine des dêcouvertes attribuêes aux Modernes.* 1766.—*Ed.*), but he failed in it by flying to the opposite extreme. When he should have confined himself to the philosophies, he extended his attack to the sciences, and even to the main discoveries of later times; and thus instead of vindicating the ancients, he became the calumniator of the moderns; as far at least as detraction is calumny. A splendid and most instructive course of lectures might be given, comprising the origin and progress, the fates and fortunes of philosophy from Pythagoras to Locke, with the lives and succession of the philosophers in each sect; tracing the progress of speculative science chiefly in relation to the gradual development of the human mind, but without omitting the favorable or inauspicious influence of circumstances and the accidents of individual genius. The main divisions would be, 1. From Thales and Pythagoras to the appearance of the Sophists: 2. And of Socrates;—the character and effects of Socrates' life and doctrines illustrated in the instances of Xenophon, as his most faithful representative, and of Antisthenes or the Cynic sect as the one partial view of his philosophy, and of Aristippus or the Cyrenaic sect as the other and opposite extreme: 3. Plato, and Platonism: 4. Aristotle and the Peripatetic school: 5. Zeno and Stoicism, Epicurus and Epicureanism, with the effects of these in the Roman republic and empire: 6. The rise of the Eclectic or Alexandrian philosophy, the attempt to set up a pseudo-Platonic polytheism against Christianity, the degradation of philosophy itself into mysticism and magic, and its final disappearance, as philosophy, under Justinian: 7. The resumption of the Aristotelian philosophy in the thirteenth

view of the elder philosophies, which must be ranked among the most splendid proofs of his judgment no less than of his genius, and more expressly in the critique on the atomic or corpuscular doctrine of Democritus and his followers as the one extreme, and in that of the pure rationalism of Zeno the Eleatic as the other, Plato has proved incontrovertibly that in both alike the basis is too narrow to support the superstructure; that the grounds of both are false or disputable; and that, if these were conceded, yet neither the one nor the other scheme is adequate to the solution of the problem,—namely, what is the ground of the coincidence between reason and experience; or between the laws of matter and the ideas of the pure intellect. The only answer which Plato deemed the question capable of receiving, compels the reason to pass out of itself and seek the ground of this agreement in a supersensual essence, which being at once the ideal of the reason and the cause of the material world, is the pre-establisher of the harmony in and between both. Religion therefore is the ultimate aim of philosophy, in consequence of which philosophy itself becomes the supplement of the sciences, both as the convergence of all to the common end, namely wisdom; and as supplying the copula, which, modified in each in the comprehension of its parts in one whole, is in its principles common to all, as integral parts of one system. And this is method, itself a distinct science, the immediate offspring of philosophy, and the link or mordant by which philosophy becomes scientific, and the sciences philosophical.

ESSAY VI.

'Απάντων ζητοῦντες λόγον ἔξωθεν ἀναιροῦσι λόγον.

The second relation is that of theory, in which the existing forms and qualities of objects, discovered by observation or experiment, suggest a given arrangement of many under one point of view; and this not merely or principally in order to facilitate the

century, and the successive re-appearance of the different ancient sects from the restoration of literature to our own times.

remembrance, recollection, or communication of the same; but for the purposes of understanding, and in most instances of controlling them. In other words, all theory supposes the general idea of cause and effect. The scientific arts of medicine, chemistry, and physiology in general, are examples of a method hitherto founded on this second sort of relation.

Between these two lies the method in the fine arts, which belongs indeed to this second or external relation, because the effect and position of the parts is always more or less influenced by the knowledge and experience of their previous qualities; but which, nevertheless, constitutes a link connecting the second form of relation with the first. For in all that truly merits the name of poetry in its most comprehensive sense, there is a necessary predominance of the ideas, that is, of that which originates in the artist himself, and a comparative indifference of the materials. A true musical taste is soon dissatisfied with the harmonica or any similar instrument of glass or steel, because the body of the sound (as the Italians phrase it), or that effect which is derived from the materials, encroaches too far on the effect from the proportions of the notes, or that which is given to music by the mind. To prove the high value as well as the superior dignity of the first relation, and to evince, that on this alone a perfect method can be grounded, and that the methods attainable by the second are at best but approximations to the first, or tentative exercises in the hope of discovering it, forms the first object of the present disquisition.

These truths I have (as the most pleasing and popular mode of introducing the subject) hitherto illustrated from Shakspeare. But the same truths, namely the necessity of a mental initiative to all method, as well as a careful attention to the conduct of the mind in the exercise of method itself, may be equally, and here, perhaps, more characteristically, proved from the most familiar of the sciences. We may draw our elucidation even from those which are at present fashionable among us; from botany or from chemistry. In the lowest attempt at a methodical arrangement of the former science, that of artificial classification for the preparatory purpose of nomenclature, some antecedent must have been contributed by the mind itself; some purpose must be in view; or some question at least must have been proposed to nature, grounded, as all questions are, upon some idea of the answer ; as for instance, the assumption that—"two great sexes animate the world."* For no man can confidently conceive a fact to be universally true who does not with equal confidence anticipate its necessity, and who does not believe that necessity to be demonstrable by an insight into its nature, whenever and wherever such insight can be obtained. We acknowledge, we reverence, the obligations of botany to Linnæus, who, adopting from Bartholinus, Sebastian Vaillant, and others, the sexuality of plants, grounded thereon a scheme of classific and distinctive marks, by which one man's experience may be communicated to others, and the objects safely reasoned on while absent, and recognized as soon as and wherever they are met with. He invented a universal character for the language of botany chargeable with no greater imperfections than are to be found in the alphabets of every particular language. As for the study of the ancients, so for that of the works of nature, an accidence and a dictionary are the first and indispensable requisites ; and to the illustrious Swede, botany is indebted for both. But neither was the central idea of vegetation itself, by the light of which we might have seen the collateral relations of the vegetable to the inorganic and to the animal world, nor the constitutive nature and inner necessity of sex itself, revealed to Linnæus.† Hence, as in

* Par. Lost, viii. 151.—*Ed.*

† The word nature has been used in two senses, actively and passively; energetic, or *forma formans*, and material, or *forma formata*. In the first (the sense in which the word is used in the text) it signifies the inward principle of whatever is requisite for the reality of a thing, as existent: while the essence or essential property, signifies the inner principle of all that appertains to the possibility of a thing. Hence, in accurate language, we say the essence of a mathematical circle or other geometrical figure, not the nature; because in the conception of forms purely geometrical there is no expression or implication of their real existence. In the second or material sense of the word nature, we mean by it the sum total of all things, as far as they are objects of our senses, and consequently of possible experience; the aggregate of *phænomena*, whether existing for our outward senses, or for our inner sense. The doctrine concerning material nature would therefore (the word physiology being both ambiguous in itself, and already otherwise appropriated) be more properly entitled phænomenology, distinguished into its two grand divisions, somatology and psychology. The doctrine concerning energetic nature is comprised in the science of dynamics; the union of which with phænomenology, and the alliance of both with the sciences of the possible, or of the conceivable, namely, logic and mathematics, constitute natural philosophy.

all other cases where the master light is missing, so in this, the reflective mind avoids Scylla only to lose itself in Charybdis. If we adhere to the general notion of sex, as abstracted from the more obvious modes and forms in which the sexual relation manifests itself, we soon meet with whole classes of plants to which it is found inapplicable. If arbitrarily, we give it indefinite extension, it is dissipated into the barren truism, that all specific products suppose specific means of production. Thus a growth and a birth are distinguished by the mere verbal definition, that the latter is a whole in itself, the former not: and when we would apply even this to nature, we are baffled by objects (the flower polypus, for example, and many others) in which each is the other. All that can be done by the most patient and active industry, by the widest and most continuous researches; all that the amplest survey of the vegetable realm, brought under immediate contemplation by the most stupendous collections of species and varieties, can suggest; all that minutest dissection and exactest chemical analysis, can

Having thus explained the term nature, I now more especially entreat the reader's attention to the sense in which here, and everywhere through this essay, I use the word idea. I assert, that the very impulse to universalize any *phænomenon* involves the prior assumption of some efficient law in nature, which in a thousand different forms is evermore one and the same, entire in each, yet comprehending all, and incapable of being abstracted or generalized from any number of *phænomena*, because it is itself pre-supposed in each and all as their common ground and condition, and because every definition of a *genus* is the adequate definition of the lowest species alone, while the efficient law must contain the ground of all in all. It is attributed, never derived. The utmost we ever venture to say is, that the falling of an apple suggested the law of gravitation to Sir I. Newton. Now a law and an idea are correlative terms, and differ only as object and subject, as being and truth.

Such is the doctrine of the Novum Organum of Lord Bacon, agreeing (as I shall more largely show in the text) in all essential points with the true doctrine of Plato, the apparent differences being for the greater part occasioned by the Grecian sage having applied his principles chiefly to the investigation of the mind, and the method of evolving its powers, and the English philosopher to the development of nature. That our great countryman speaks too often detractingly of the divine philosopher must be explained, partly by the tone given to thinking minds by the Reformation, the founders and fathers of which saw in the Aristotelians, or schoolmen, the antagonists of Protestantism, and in the Italian Platonists the despisers and secret enemies of Christianity itself; and partly, by his having formed his notions of Plato's doctrine from the absurdities and phantasms of his misinterpreters, rather than from an unprejudiced study of the original works.

unfold; all that varied experiment and the position of plants and of their component parts in every conceivable relation to light, heat (and whatever else we distinguish as imponderable substances), to earth, air, water, to the supposed constituents of air and water, separate and in all proportions—in short, all that chemical agents and re-agents can disclose or adduce;—all these have been brought, as conscripts, into the field, with the completest accoutrement, in the best discipline, under the ablest commanders. Yet after all that was effected by Linnæus himself, not to mention the labors of Gesner,* Cæsalpinus,† Ray,‡ Tournefort,§ and the other heroes who preceded the general adoption of the sexual system, as the basis of artificial arrangement;—after all the successive toils and enterprises of Hedwig,‖ Jussieu, Mirbel,¶ Sir James Smith, Knight, Ellis, and others,—what is botany at this present hour? Little more than an enormous nomenclature; a huge catalogue, well arranged, and yearly and monthly augmented, in various editions, each with its own scheme of technical memory and its own conveniences of reference. A dictionary in which (to carry on the metaphor) an Ainsworth arranges the contents by the initials; a Walker by the endings; a Scapula by the radicals; and a Cominius by the similarity of the uses and purposes. The terms system, method, science, are mere improprieties of courtesy, when applied to a mass enlarging by endless appositions, but without a nerve that oscillates, or a pulse that throbs, in sign of growth or inward sympathy. The innocent amusement, the healthful occupation, the ornamental accomplishment of amateurs (most honorable indeed and deserving of all praise as a preventive substitute for the stall, the kennel, and the subscription-room), it has yet to expect the devotion and energies of the philosopher.

* Conrad G. who died in 1568. See his Letters.—*Ed.*

† *Libri* xv. *De Plantis.*—*Ed.*

‡ *Methodus Plantarum nova.* 1682. *Historia Plantarum.* 1686-7-1704. —*Ed.*

§ *Elémens de Botanique; ou, Méthode pour connaître les Plantes.* 1694. —*Ed.*

‖ *Theoria generationis et fructificationis plantarum cryptogamicarum Linnæi.* 1784. *Cryptogamia.* 1787.—*Ed.*

¶ *Histoire générale et particulière des plantes; ou, Traité de physiologie végétale. Exposition de la théorie de l'organisation végétale.* 1805. *Elémens de physiologie végétale et de botanique.* 1815.—*Ed.*

So long back as the first appearance of Dr. Darwin's *Phytologia*, I, then* in earliest manhood, presumed to hazard the opinion, that the physiological botanists were hunting in a false direction, and sought for analogy where they should have looked for antithesis. I saw, or thought I saw, that the harmony between the vegetable and animal world, was not a harmony of resemblance, but of contrast; and that their relation to each other was that of corresponding opposites. They seemed to me, whose mind had been formed by observation, unaided, but at the same time unenthralled, by partial experiment, as two streams from the same fountain indeed, but flowing the one due west, and the other direct east, and that consequently, the resemblance would be as the proximity, greatest in the first and rudimental products of vegetable and animal organization. Whereas, according to the received notion, the highest and most perfect vegetable, and the lowest and rudest animal forms, ought to have seemed the links of the two systems, which is contrary to fact. Since that time, the same idea has dawned in the minds of philosophers capable of demonstrating its objective truth by induction of facts in an unbroken series of correspondences in nature. From these men, or from minds enkindled by their labors, we may hope hereafter to receive it, or rather the yet higher idea to which it refers us, matured into laws of organic nature, and thence to have one other splendid proof, that with the knowledge of law alone dwell power and prophecy, decisive experiment, and, lastly, a scientific method, that dissipating with its earliest rays the gnomes of hypothesis and the mists of theory may, within a single generation, open out on the philosophic seer discoveries that had baffled the gigantic, but blind and guideless, industry of ages.

Such, too, is the case with the assumed indecomponible substances of the laboratory. They are the symbols of elementary powers, and the exponents of a law, which, as the root of all these powers, the chemical philosopher, whatever his theory may be, is instinctively laboring to extract. This instinct, again, is itself but the form, in which the idea, the mental correlative of the law, first announces its incipient germination in his own mind: and hence proceeds the striving after unity of principle through all the diversity of forms, with a feeling resembling that

* 1801. The *Zoonomia* was published in 1793.—*Ed.*

which accompanies our endeavors to recollect a forgotten name; when we seem at once to have and not to have it; which the memory feels but can not find. Thus, as "the lunatic, the lover, and the poet,"* suggest each the other to Shakspeare's Theseus, as soon as his thoughts present to him the one form, of which they are but varieties; so water and flame, the diamond, the charcoal, and the mantling champagne, with its ebullient sparkles, are convoked and fraternized by the theory of the chemist. This is, in truth, the first charm of chemistry, and the secret of the almost universal interest excited by its discoveries. The serious complacency which is afforded by the sense of truth, utility, performance, and progression, blends with and ennobles the exhilarating surprise and the pleasurable sting of curiosity, which accompany the propounding and the solving of an enigma. It is the sense of a principle of connection given by the mind, and sanctioned by the correspondency of nature. Hence the strong hold which in all ages chemistry has had on the imagination. If in Shakspeare we find nature idealized into poetry, through the creative power of a profound yet observant meditation, so through the meditative observation of a Davy, a Wollaston, or a Hatchett;

——— By some connatural force,
Powerful at greatest distance to unite
With secret amity things of like kind,

we find poetry, as it were, substantiated and realized in nature,—yea, nature itself disclosed to us, *geminam istam naturam, quæ fit et facit, et creat et creatur*, as at once the poet and the poem.

* Mids. Night's Dream, act v. sc. 1.—*Ed.*

ESSAY VII.

Ταυτῇ τόινῦν διαίρω χῶρις μὲν, οὓς νῦν δὴ ἔλεγες φιλοθεάμονάς τε, καὶ φιλοτέχνους, καὶ πρακτίκους, καὶ χῶρις αὖ περὶ ὧν ὁ λόγος, οὓς μόνους ἀν τὶς ὄρθως προσείποι φιλοσόφους, ὡς μὲν γιγνώσκοντας, τίνος ἔςιν ἐπιςήμμ ἑκάςη πούτων τῶν ἐπιςήμων, ὁ τυγχάνει ὂν ἄλλο αὐτῆς τῆς ἐπιςήμης· PLATO.

In the following then I distinguish, first, those whom you indeed may call philotheorists, or philotechnists, or practicians, and secondly those whom alone you may rightly denominate philosophers, as knowing what the science of all these branches of science is, which may prove to be something more than the mere aggregate of the knowledge in any particular science.

FROM Shakspeare to Plato, from the philosophic poet to the poetic philosopher, the transition is easy, and the road is crowded with illustrations of our present subject. For of Plato's works, the larger and more valuable portion have all one common end, which comprehends and shines through the particular purpose of each several dialogue; and this is to establish the sources, to evolve the principles, and exemplify the art of method. This is the clue, without which it would be difficult to exculpate the noblest productions of the divine philosopher from the charge of being tortuous and labyrinthine in their progress, and unsatisfactory in their ostensible results. The latter indeed appear not seldom to have been drawn for the purpose of starting a new problem, rather than that of solving the one proposed as the subject of the previous discussion. But with the clear insight that the purpose of the writer is not so much to establish any particular truth, as to remove the obstacles, the continuance of which is preclusive of all truth, the whole scheme assumes a different aspect, and justifies itself in all its dimensions. We see, that to open anew a well of springing water, not to cleanse the stagnant tank, or fill, bucket by bucket, the leaden cistern; that the education of the intellect, by awakening the principle and method of self-development, was his proposed object, not any specific information that can be conveyed into it from without;—not to assist in storing the passive mind with the various sorts of knowledge most in request, as if the human soul were a mere repository or banqueting-room, but to place it in such relations of circumstance as should gradually excite the germinal power that craves no knowledge but what it can take up into itself, what it can appropriate, and reproduce in fruits of its own. To shape, to dye, to paint over, and to mechanize the mind, he resigned, as their proper trade, to the sophists, against whom he waged open and unremitting war. For the ancients, as well as the moderns, had their machinery for the extemporaneous mintage of intellects, by means of which, off-hand, as it were, the scholar was enabled to make a figure on any and all subjects, on any and all occasions. They too had their glittering vapors, which (as the comic poet tells us) fed a host of sophists—

μεγάλαι θεαὶ ἀνδράσιν ἀργοῖς,
αἵπερ γνώμην, καὶ διάλεξιν, καὶ νοῦν ἡμῖν παρέχουσι,
*καὶ τερατείαν, καὶ περίλεξιν, καὶ κροῦσιν, καὶ κατάληψιν.**

Great goddesses are they to lazy folks,
Who pour down on us gifts of fluent speech,
Sense most sententious, wonderful fine effect,
And how to talk about it and about it,
Thoughts brisk as bees, and pathos soft and thawy.

In fine, as improgressive arrangement is not method, so neither is a mere mode or set fashion of doing a thing. Are further facts required? I appeal to the notorious fact that zoology, soon after the commencement of the latter half of the last century, was falling abroad, weighed down and crushed, as it were, by the inordinate number and manifoldness of facts and *phænomena* apparently separate, without evincing the least promise of systematizing itself by any inward combination, any vital interdependence, of its parts. John Hunter, who appeared at times almost a stranger to the grand conception, which yet never ceased to work in him as his genius and governing spirit, rose at length in the horizon of physiology and comparative anatomy. In his printed works, the one directing thought seems evermore to flit before him, twice or thrice only to have been seized, and after a momen-

* *Aristoph. Nubes.* 316, &c.—*Ed.*

tary detention to have been again let go: as if the words of the charm had been incomplete, and it had appeared at its own will only to mock his calling. At length, in the astonishing preparations for his museum, he constructed it for the scientific apprehension out of the unspoken alphabet of nature. Yet notwithstanding the imperfection in the annunciation of the idea, how exhilarating have been the results! I dare appeal to* Abernethy, to Everard Home, to Hatchett, whose communication to Sir Everard on the egg and its analogies, in a recent paper of the latter (itself of high excellence) in the Philosophical Transactions, I may point out as being, in the proper sense of the term, the development of a fact in the history of physiology, and to which I refer as exhibiting a luminous instance of what I mean by the discovery of a central *phænomenon*. To these I appeal, whether whatever is grandest in the views of Cuvier be not either a reflection of this light or a continuation of its rays, well and wisely directed through fit *media* to the appropriate object.†

We have seen that a previous act and conception of the mind is indispensable even to the mere semblances of method; that neither fashion, mode, nor orderly arrangement can be produced without a prior purpose, and a pre-cogitation *ad intentionem ejus quod quæritur*, though this purpose may have been itself excited, and this pre-cogitation itself abstracted from the perceived likenesses and differences of the objects to be arranged. But it has likewise been shown, that fashion, mode, ordonnance, are not method, inasmuch as all method supposes a principle of unity with progression; in other words, progressive transition without breach of continuity. But such a principle, it has been proved,

* Since this was written, Mr. Abernethy has realized this anticipation, dictated solely by my wishes, and at the time justified only by my general admiration of Mr. A.'s talents and principles, and composed without the least knowledge that he was then actually engaged in proving the assertion here hazarded, at large and in detail. See his eminent Treatise on Physiology, 1821.

† Nor should it be wholly unnoticed, that Cuvier, who, I understand, was not born in France, and is not of unmixed French extraction, had prepared himself for his illustrious labors (as I learn from a reference in the first chapter of his great work, and should have concluded from the general style of thinking, though the language betrays suppression, as of one who doubted the sympathy of his readers or audience) in a very different school of methodology and philosophy than any which Paris could have afforded.

can never in the sciences of experiment or in those of observation be adequately supplied by a theory built on generalization. For what shall determine the mind to abstract and generalize one common point rather than another;—and within what limits, from what number of individual objects, shall the generalization be made? The theory must still require a prior theory for its own legitimate construction. With the mathematician the definition makes the object, and pre-establishes the terms which, and which alone, can occur in the after-reasoning. If a circle be found not to have the *radii* from the centre to the circumference perfectly equal, which in fact it would be absurd to expect of any material circle, it follows only that it was not a circle; and the tranquil geometrician would content himself with smiling at the *quid pro quo* of the simple objector. A mathematical *theoria seu contemplatio* may therefore be perfect. For the mathematician can be certain that he has contemplated all that appertains to his proposition. The celebrated Euler, treating on some point respecting arches, makes this curious remark:—"All experience is in contradiction to this; *sed potius fidendum est analysi;* but this is no reason for doubting the analysis." The words sound paradoxical; but in truth mean no more than this, that the properties of space are not less certainly the properties of space because they can never be entirely transferred to material bodies. But in physics, that is, in all the sciences which have for their objects the things of nature, and not the *entia rationis*—more philosophically, intellectual acts and the products of those acts, existing exclusively in and for the intellect itself—the definition must follow, and not precede, the reasoning. It is representative not constitutive, and is indeed little more than an abbreviature of the preceding observation, and the deductions therefrom. But as the observation, though aided by experiment, is necessarily limited and imperfect, the definition must be equally so. The history of theories, and the frequency of their subversion by the discovery of a single new fact, supply the best illustrations of this truth.*

* The following extract from a most respectable scientific Journal contains an exposition of the impossibility of a perfect theory in physics, the more striking because it is directly against the purpose and intention of the writer. I content myself with one question,—what if Kepler, what if Newton in his investigations concerning the tides, had holden themselves

As little can a true scientific method be grounded on an hypothesis, unless where the hypothesis is an exponential image or picture-language of an idea which is contained in it more or less clearly; or the symbol of an undiscovered law, like the characters of unknown quantities in algebra, for the purpose of submitting the *phænomena* to a scientific *calculus*. In all other instances, it is itself a real or supposed *phænomenon*, and therefore a part of the problem which it is to solve. It may be among the foundation-stones of the edifice, but can never be the ground.

But in experimental philosophy, it may be said how much do we not owe to accident? Doubtless: but let it not be forgotten, that if the discoveries so made stop there; if they do not excite some master idea; if they do not lead to some law (in whatever dress of theory or hypothesis the fashions and prejudices of the time may disguise or disfigure it);—the discoveries may remain for ages limited in their uses, insecure and unproductive. How many centuries, we might have said *millennia*, have passed, since the first accidental discovery of the attraction and repulsion of

bound to this canon, and, instead of propounding a law, had employed themselves exclusively in collecting materials for a theory?

"The magnetic influence has long been known to have a variation which is constantly changing; but that change is so slow, and at the same time so different in various parts of the world, that it would be in vain to seek for the means of reducing it to established rules, until all its local and particular circumstances are clearly ascertained and recorded by accurate observations made in various parts of the globe. The necessity and importance of such observations are now pretty generally understood, and they have been actually carrying on for some years past; but these (and by parity of reason the incomparably greater number that remain to be made) must be collected, collated, proved, and afterwards brought together into one focus before ever a foundation can be formed upon which any thing like a sound and stable theory can be constituted for the explanation of such changes." *Journal of Science and the Arts*, No. vii. p. 103.

An intelligent friend, on reading the words "into one focus," observed: "But what and where is the lens?" I however fully agree with the writer. All this and much more must have been achieved before "a sound and stable theory" could be "constituted;"—which even then (except as far as it might occasion the discovery of a law) might possibly explain (*ex plicis plana reddere*), but never account for, the facts in question. But the most satisfactory comment on these and similar assertions would be afforded by a matter of fact history of the rise and progress, the accelerating and retarding *momenta*, of science in the civilized world.

light bodies by rubbed amber! Compare the interval with the progress made within less than a century, after the discovery of the *phænomena* that led immediately to a theory of electricity. That here as in many other instances, the theory was supported by insecure hypotheses; that by one theorist two heterogeneous fluids are assumed, the vitreous and the resinous; by another, a *plus* and *minus* of the same fluid; that a third considers it a mere modification of light; while a fourth composes the electrical *aura* of oxygen, hydrogen, and caloric;—this does but place the truth we have been evolving in a stronger and clearer light. For abstract from all these suppositions, or rather imaginations, that which is common to, and involved in, them all; and we shall have neither notional fluid or fluids, nor chemical compounds, nor elementary matter,—but the idea of two—opposite—forces, tending to rest by *equilibrium*. These are the sole factors of the *calculus*, alike in all the theories. These give the law, and in it the method, both of arranging the *phænomena* and of substantiating appearances into facts of science; with a success proportionate to the clearness or confusedness of the insight into the law. For this reason, I anticipate the greatest improvements in the method, the nearest approaches to a system of electricity, from these philosophers, who have presented the law most purely, and the correlative idea as an idea;—those, namely, who, since the year 1798, in the true spirit of experimental dynamics, rejecting the imagination of any material substrate, simple or compound, contemplate in the *phænomena* of electricity the operation of a law which reigns through all nature, the law of polarity, or the manifestation of one power by opposite forces;—who trace in these appearances, as the most obvious and striking of its innumerable forms, the agency of the positive and negative poles of a power essential to all material construction; the second, namely, of the three primary principles, for which the beautiful and most appropriate symbols are given by the mind in the three ideal dimensions of space.*

The time is, perhaps, nigh at hand, when the same comparison between the results of two unequal periods,—the interval between the knowledge of a fact, and that from the discovery of

* "Perhaps the attribution or analogy may seem fanciful at first sight, but I am in the habit of realizing to myself magnetism as length, electricity as breadth, and galvanism as depth." *Table Talk*, VI. 284.—*Ed.*

the law,—will be applicable to the sister science of magnetism. But how great the contrast between magnetism and electricity at the present moment! From remotest antiquity, the attraction of iron by the magnet was known and noticed; but, century after century, it remained the undisturbed property of poets and orators. The fact of the magnet and the fable of the phœnix stood on the same scale of utility. In the thirteenth century, or perhaps earlier, the polarity of the magnet, and its communicability to iron, were discovered; and soon suggested a purpose so grand and important, that it may well be deemed the proudest trophy ever raised by accident* in the service of mankind,—the invention of the compass. But it led to no idea, to no law, and consequently to no method: though a variety of *phænomena*, as startling as they are mysterious, have forced on us a presentiment of its intimate connection with all the great agencies of nature; of a revelation, in ciphers, the key to which is still wanting. I can recall no event of human history that impresses the imagination more deeply than the moment when Columbus,† on an un-

* If accident it were; if the compass did not obscurely travel to us from the remotest east; if its existence there does not point to an age and a race, to which scholars of highest rank in the world of letters, Sir W. Jones, Bailly, Schlegel have attached faith. That it was known before the æra generally assumed for its invention, and not spoken of as a novelty, has been proved by Mr. Southey and others: (See the *Omniana*, vol. i. p. 210. No. 108,—where Mr. Southey quotes a passage from the *Partidas* (1250–7), very distinctly referring to the mariner's needle.—*Ed.*)

† It can not be deemed alien from the purposes of this disquisition, if I am anxious to attract the attention of my readers to the importance of speculative meditation, even for the worldly interests of mankind; and to that concurrence of nature and historic event with the great revolutionary movements of individual genius, of which so many instances occur in the study of history;—to point out how nature, or that which in nature itself is more than nature, seems to come forward in order to meet, to aid, and to reward every idea excited by a contemplation of her methods in the spirit of filial care, and with the humility of love. It is with this view that I extract the following lines from an ode of Chiabrera's, which, in the strength of the thought and the lofty majesty of the poetry, has but "few peers in ancient or in modern song."

Certo da cor, ch' alto destin non scelse,
Son l' imprese magnanime neglette;
Ma le bell' alme alle bell' opre elette
Sanno gioir nelle fatiche eccelse;
Nè biasmo popolar, frale catena,
Spirto d' onore, il suo cammin raffrena.

known ocean, first perceived one of these startling facts, the change of the magnetic needle.

In what shall we seek the cause of this contrast between the rapid progress of electricity and the stationary condition of magnetism? As many theories, as many hypotheses, have been advanced in the latter science as in the former. But the theories and fictions of the electricians contained an idea, and all the same idea, which has necessarily led to method; implicit indeed, and only regulative hitherto, but which requires little more than the dismission of the imagery to become constitutive like the ideas of the geometrician. On the contrary, the assumptions of the magnetists (as for instance, the hypothesis that the planet itself is one vast magnet, or that an immense magnet is concealed within it, or that of a concentric globe within the earth, revolving on its own independent axis), are but repetitions of the same fact or *phænomenon* looked at through a magnifying glass; the reiteration of the problem, not its solution. The naturalist, who can not or will not see, that one fact is often worth a thousand, as including them all in itself, and that it first makes all the other facts,—who has not the head to comprehend, the soul to reverence, a central experiment or observation (what the Greeks would perhaps have called a *protophænomenon*),—will never receive an auspicious answer from the oracle of nature.

Cosi lunga stagion per modi indegni
Europa disprezzò l'inclita speme,
Schernendo il vulgo e seco i regi insieme,
Nudo nocchier promettitor di regni;
Ma per le sconosciute onde marine
L' invitta prora ei pur sospinse al fine.
Qual uom, che torni alla gentil consorte,
Tal ei da sua magion spiegò l'antenne;
L' ocean corse, e i turbini sostenne,
Vinse le crude immagini di morte;
Poscia, dell' ampio mar spenta la guerra,
Scorse la dianzi favolosa terra.
Allor dal cavo pin scende veloce,
E di grand' orma il nuovo mondo imprime;
Nè men ratto per l'aria erge sublime,
Segno del ciel, l'insuperabil croce;
E porge umile esempio, onde adorarla
Debba sua gente. CHIABRERA, P. I. 12.

ESSAY VIII.

> The soul doth give
> Brightness to the eye: and some say, that the sun
> If not enlighten'd by th' Intelligence
> That doth inhabit it, would shine no more
> Than a dull clod of earth.
>
> CARTWRIGHT'S *Lady-Errant*, act iii. sc. iv.

IT is strange, yet characteristic of the spirit that was at work during the latter half of the last century, and of which the French revolution was, I hope, the closing monsoon, that the writings of Plato should be accused of estranging the mind from sober experience and substantial matter of fact, and of debauching it by fictions and generalities;—Plato, whose method is inductive throughout, who argues on all subjects not only from, but in and by, inductions of facts;—who warns us indeed against that usurpation of the senses, which quenching the *lumen siccum* of the mind, sends it astray after individual cases for their own sakes—against that *tenuem et manipularem experientiam*, which remains ignorant even of the transitory relations, to which the *pauca particularia* of its idolatry not seldom owe their fluxional existence;—but who so far oftener, and with such unmitigated hostility, pursues the assumptions, abstractions, generalities, and verbal legerdemain of the sophists! Strange, but still more strange, that a notion so groundless should be entitled to plead in its behalf the authority of Lord Bacon, from whom the Latin words in the preceding sentence are taken, and whose scheme of logic, as applied to the contemplation of nature, is Platonic throughout, and differing only in the mode, which in Lord Bacon is dogmatic, that is, assertory, in Plato tentative, and (to adopt the Socratic phrase) obstetric. I am not the first, or even among the first, who have considered Bacon's studied depreciation of the ancients, with his silence, or worse than silence, concerning the merits of his contemporaries, as the least amiable, the least exhilarating, side in the character of our illustrious countryman. His detractions from the divine Plato it is more easy to explain than to justify or even to palliate; and that he has merely retaliated Aristotle's own unfair treatment of his predecessors and contemporaries, may lessen the pain, but should not blind us to the injustice of the aspersions on the name and works of that philosopher. The most eminent of our recent zoologists and mineralogists have acknowledged with respect, and even with expressions of wonder, the performances of Aristotle, as the first clearer and breaker-up of the ground in natural history. It is indeed scarcely possible to peruse the treatise on colors,* falsely ascribed to Theophrastus, the scholar and successor of Aristotle, after a due consideration of the state and means of science at that time, without resenting the assertion, that he had utterly enslaved his investigations in natural history to his own system of logic (*logicæ suæ prorsus mancipavit.*)† Nor let it be forgotten that the sunny side of Lord Bacon's character is to be found neither in his inductions, nor in the application of his own method to particular *phænomena* or particular classes of physical facts, which are at least as crude for the age of Gilbert,‡ Galileo, and Kepler, as Aristotle's for that of Philip and Alexander. Nor is it to be found in his recommendation (which is wholly independent of his inestimable principles of scientific method) of tabular collections of particulars. Let any unprejudiced naturalist turn to Lord Bacon's questions and proposals for the investigation of single problems; to his Discourse on the Winds; or to the almost comical caricature of this scheme in the Method of improving Natural Philosophy, by Robert Hooke (the history of whose multifold inventions, and indeed of his whole philosophical life, is the best answer to the scheme, if a scheme so palpably impracticable needs any answer),—and put it to his conscience, whether any desirable end could be hoped for from such a process; or inquire of his own experience, or historical recollections, whether any important discovery was ever made in this way.§ For though Bacon never so far deviates from his

* The Περὶ Χρωμάτων is not now, I believe, considered genuine.—*Ed.*

† Nov. Org. Aph. LIV.

‡ William Gilbert died in 1603. His works are De Magnete, &c. 1600, and De Mundo, &c. 1651.—*Ed.*

§ I refer the reader to Hooke's Posthumous Works (Hooke died in 1702. —*Ed.*) published under the auspices of the Royal Society, by their Secre-

own principles, as not to admonish the reader that the particulars are to be thus collected, only that by careful selection they may be concentrated into universals; yet so immense is their number, and so various and almost endless the relations in which each is to be separately considered, that the life of an antediluvian patriarch would have been expended, and his strength and spirits wasted, in merely polling the votes, and long before he could have commenced the process of simplification, or have arrived in sight of the law which was to reward the toils of the over-tasked Psyche.*

tary, Richard Waller, and especially to the pages from p. 22 to 42 inclusive, as containing the preliminary knowledge requisite or desirable for the naturalist, before he can form "even a foundation upon which any thing like a sound and stable theory can be constituted." As a small specimen of this appalling catalogue of preliminaries with which he is to make himself conversant, take the following:—The history of potters, tobacco-pipe-makers, glaziers, glass-grinders, looking-glass-makers or foilers, spectacle-makers and optic-glass-makers, makers of counterfeit pearl and precious stones, bugle-makers, lamp-blowers, color-makers, color-grinders, glass-painters, enamellers, varnishers, color-sellers, painters, limners, picture-drawers, makers of baby-heads, of little bowling-stones or marbles, fustian-makers (*quære* whether poets are included in this trade) music-masters, tinsey-makers, and taggers;—the history of schoolmasters, writing-masters, printers, book-binders, stage-players, dancing-masters, and vaulters, apothecaries, chirurgeons, seamsters, butchers, barbers, laundresses, and cosmetics, &c. (the true nature of which being actually determined) will hugely facilitate our inquiries in philosophy.

As a summary of Dr. R. Hooke's multifarious recipe for the growth of science may be fairly placed that of the celebrated Dr. Watts for the improvement of the mind, which was thought by Dr. Knox to be worthy of insertion in the Elegant Extracts, vol. ii. p. 456, under the head of

DIRECTIONS CONCERNING OUR IDEAS.

"Furnish yourselves with a rich variety of ideas. Acquaint yourselves with things ancient and modern; things natural, civil, and religious; things of your native land, and of foreign countries; things domestic and national; things present, past, and future; and above all, be well acquainted with God and yourselves; with animal nature, and the workings of your own spirits. Such a general acquaintance with things will be of very great advantage."

* See the beautiful allegoric tale of Cupid and Psyche, in the original of Apuleius, (*De Asino aureo*, L. iv. v. vi.—*Ed.*) The tasks imposed on her by the jealousy of her mother-in-law, and the agency by which they are at length self-performed, are noble instances of that hidden wisdom, "where more is meant than meets the ear."

I yield to none in grateful veneration of Lord Bacon's philosophical writings. I am proud of his very name, as a lover of knowledge; and as an Englishman, I am almost vain of it. But I may not permit the honest workings of national attachment to degenerate into the jealous and indiscriminate partiality of clanship. Unawed by such as praise and abuse by wholesale, I dare avow that there are points in the character of our Verulam, from which I turn to the life and labors of John Kepler,* as from gloom to sunshine. The beginning and the close of his life were clouded by poverty and domestic troubles, while the intermediate years were comprised within the most tumultuous period of the history of his country, when the furies of religious and political discord had left neither eye, ear, nor heart for the muses. But Kepler seemed born to prove that true genius can overpower all obstacles. If he gives an account of his modes of proceeding, and of the views under which they first occurred to his mind, how unostentatiously and *in transitu*, as it were, does he introduce himself to our notice; and yet never fails to present the living germ out of which the genuine method, as the inner form of the tree of science, springs up! With what affectionate reverence does he express himself of his master and immediate predecessor, Tycho Brahe; with what zeal does he vindicate his services against posthumous detraction! How often and how gladly does he speak of Copernicus;—and with what fervent tones of faith and consolation does he proclaim the historic fact that the great men of all ages have prepared the way for each other, as pioneers and heralds! Equally just to the ancients and to his contemporaries, how circumstantially, and with what exactness of detail, does Kepler demonstrate that Euclid Copernicizes—*ὡς πρὸ Κοπερνικου κοπερινκίζει Εὐκλείδης*,—how elegant the compliments which he addresses to Porta, and with what cordiality he thanks him for the invention of the *camera obscura*, as enlarging his views into the laws of vision! But while I can not avoid contrasting this generous enthusiasm with Lord Bacon's cold and invidious treatment of Gilbert, and his assertion that the works of Plato and Aristotle had been carried down the stream of time, like straws, by their levity alone, when things of weight and worth had sunk to the bottom;—still in the founder of a rev-

* Born 1571, ten years after Lord Bacon: died 1630, four years after the death of Bacon.

olution, scarcely less important for the scientific, and even for the commercial, world than that of Luther for the world of religion and politics, we must allow much to the heat of protestation, much to the vehemence of hope, and much to the vividness of novelty. Still more must we attribute to the then existing and actual state of the Platonic and Peripatetic philosophies, or rather to the dreams or verbiage which then passed current as such. Had Bacon but attached to their proper authors the schemes and doctrines which he condemns, our illustrious countryman would, in this point, at least, have needed no apology. And surely no lover of truth, conversant with the particulars of Lord Bacon's life, with the very early, almost boyish, age at which he quitted the university, and the manifold occupations and anxieties in which his public and professional duties engaged, and his courtly,—alas! his servile, prostitute, and mendicant—ambition entangled him, in his after-years, will be either surprised or offended, though I should avow my conviction, that he had derived his opinions of Plato and Aristotle from any source, rather than from a dispassionate and patient study of the originals themselves. At all events it will be no easy task to reconcile many passages in the *De Augmentis*, and the *Redargutio Philosophiarum*, with the author's own fundamental principles, as established in his *Novum Organum;* if we attach to the words the meaning which they may bear, or even, in some instances, the meaning which might appear to us, in the present age, more obvious; instead of the sense in which they were employed by the professors, whose false premises and barren methods Bacon was at that time controverting. And this historical interpretation is rendered the more necessary by his fondness for point and antithesis in his style, where we must often disturb the sound in order to arrive at the sense. But with these precautions;—and if, in collating the philosophical works of Lord Bacon with those of Plato, we, in both cases alike, separate the grounds and essential principles of their philosophic systems from the inductions themselves; no inconsiderable portion of which, in the British sage, as well as in the divine Athenian, is neither more nor less crude and erroneous than might be anticipated from the infant state of natural history, chemistry, and physiology, in their several ages; and if we moreover separate the principles from their practical application, which in both is not seldom impracticable, and, in our countryman, not always reconcilable with the principles themselves;—we shall not only extract that from each which is for all ages, and which constitutes their true systems of philosophy, but shall convince ourselves that they are radically one and the same system;—in that, namely, which is of universal and imperishable worth, the science of method, and the grounds and conditions of the science of method.

ESSAY IX.

A great authority may be a poor proof, but it is an excellent presumption: and few things give a wise man a truer delight than to reconcile two great authorities, that had been commonly but falsely held to be dissonant.
STAPYLTON.

UNDER a deep impression of the importance of the truths I have essayed to develop, I would fain remove every prejudice that does not originate in the heart rather than in the understanding. For truth, says the wise man, will not enter a malevolent spirit.

To offer or to receive names in lieu of sound arguments, is only less reprehensible than an ostentatious contempt of the great men of former ages; but we may well and wisely avail ourselves of authorities, in confirmation of truth, and above all, in the removal of prejudices founded on imperfect information. I do not see, therefore, how I can more appropriately conclude this first, explanatory and controversial section of the inquiry, than by a brief statement of our renowned countryman's own principles of method, conveyed for the greater part in his own words. Nor do I see, in what more precise form I can recapitulate the substance of the doctrines asserted and vindicated in the preceding pages. For I rest my strongest pretensions to a calm and respectful perusal, in the first instance, on the fact, that I have only reproclaimed the coinciding prescripts of the Athenian Verulam, and the British Plato—*genuinam scilicet Platonis dialecticem, et methodologiam principialem.*

FRANCISCI DE VERULAMIO.

In the first instance, Lord Bacon equally with myself demands what I have ventured to call the intellectual or mental initiative, as the motive and guide of every philosophical experiment; some well-grounded purpose, some distinct impression of the probable results, some self-consistent anticipation as the ground of the *prudens quæstio*, the forethoughtful query, which he affirms to be the prior half of the knowledge sought, *dimidium scientiæ*. With him, therefore, as with me, an idea is an experiment proposed, an experiment is an idea realized. For so, though in other words, he himself informs us: *neque id molimur tam instrumentis quam experimentis; etenim experimentorum longe major est subtilitas quam sensus ipsius, licet instrumentis exquisitis adjuti. De iis loquimur experimentis, quæ ad intentionem ejus quod quæritur perite et secundum artem excogitata et apposita sunt. Itaque perceptioni sensus immediatæ ac propriæ non multum tribuimus: sed eo rem deducimus, ut sensus tantum de experimento, experimentum de re, judicet.* This last sentence is, as the attentive reader will have himself detected, one of those faulty verbal antitheses not unfrequent in Lord Bacon's writings. Pungent antitheses, and the analogies of wit in which the resemblance is too often more indebted to the double or equivocal sense of a word, than to any real conformity* in the thing or image, form the *dulcia vitia* of his style, the Dalilahs of our philosophical Samson. But in this instance, as indeed throughout all his works, the meaning is clear and evident;—namely, that the sense can apprehend, through the organs of sense, only the *phænomena* evoked by the experiment: *vis vero mentis ea, quæ experimentum excogitaverat, de re judicet*: that is, that power which out of its own conceptions had shaped the experiment, must alone determine the true import of the *phænomena*. If again we ask, what it is which gives birth to the question, and then *ad intentionem quæstionis suæ experimentum excogitat, unde de re judicet*, the answer is,—*lux intellectus, lumen siccum*, the pure and impersonal reason, freed from all the various idols

* Thus (to take the first instance that occurs), Bacon says, that some knowledges, like the stars, are so high that they give no light. Where the word, "high," means "deep or sublime," in the one case, and "distant" in the other.

enumerated by our great legislator of science (*idola tribus, specus, fori, theatri*); that is, freed from the limits, the passions, the prejudices, the peculiar habits of the human understanding, natural or acquired; but above all, pure from the arrogance, which leads man to take the forms and mechanism of his own mere reflective faculty, as the measure of nature and of Deity. In this indeed we find the great object both of Plato's and of Lord Bacon's labors. They both saw that there could be no hope of any fruitful and secure method, while forms, merely subjective, were presumed as the true and proper moulds of objective truth. This is the sense in which Lord Bacon uses the phrases, *intellectus humanus, mens hominis,* so profoundly and justly characterized in the preliminary essay to the *Novum Organum.** And with all right and propriety did he so apply them: for this was, in fact, the sense in which the phrases were applied by the teachers, whom he is controverting; by the doctors of the schools, and the visionaries of the laboratory. To adopt the bold but happy phrase of a late ingenious French writer, it is the *homme particulier*, as contrasted with *l'homme général,* against which, Heraclitus and Plato, among the ancients, and among the moderns, Bacon and Stewart (rightly understood), warn and preadmonish the sincere inquirer. Most truly, and in strict consonance with his two great predecessors, does our immortal Verulam teach, that the human understanding, even independently of the causes that always, previously to its purification by philosophy, render it more or less turbid or uneven, *sicut speculum inæquale rerum radios ex figura et sectione propria immutat*:† that our understanding not only reflects the objects subjectively, that is, substitutes for the inherent laws and properties of the objects the relations which the objects bear to its own particular constitution; but that in all its conscious presentations and reflexes, it is itself only a *phænomenon* of the inner sense, and requires the same corrections as the appearances transmitted by the outward senses. But that there is potentially, if not actually, in every rational being, a somewhat, call it what you will, the pure reason, the spirit, *lumen siccum*, νοῦς, φῶς νοερὸν, intellectual intuition, or the like,—and that in this are to be found the indispensable conditions of all science, and scientific research, whether meditative, contemplative, or experimental,—is often expressed,

* *Distributio Operis.*—Ed.

† *Nov. Org. Distrib. Operis.*—Ed.

and everywhere supposed, by Lord Bacon. And that this is not only the right but the possible nature of the human mind, to which it is capable of being restored, is implied in the various remedies prescribed by him for its diseases, and in the various means of neutralizing or converting into useful instrumentality the imperfections which can not be removed. There is a sublime truth contained in his favorite phrae, *idola intellectus.* He thus tells us, that the mind of man is an edifice not built with human hands, which needs only be purged of its idols and idolatrous services to become the temple of the true and living Light. Nay, he has shown and established the true criterion between the ideas and the *idola* of the mind; namely, that the former are manifested by their adequacy to those ideas in nature, which in and through them are contemplated. *Non leve quiddam interest inter humanæ mentis idola et divinæ mentis ideas, hoc est, inter placita quædam inania et veras signaturas atque impressiones factas in creaturis, prout inveniuntur.** Thus the difference, or rather distinction, between Plato and Lord Bacon is simply this: that philosophy being necessarily bipolar, Plato treats principally of the truth, as it manifests itself at the ideal pole, as the science of intellect (*de mundo intelligibili*); while Bacon confines himself, for the most part, to the same truth, as it is manifested at the other or material pole, as the science of nature (*de mundo sensibili*). It is as necessary, therefore, that Plato should direct his inquiries chiefly to those objective truths that exist in and for the intellect alone, the images and representatives of which we construct for ourselves by figure, number, and word; as that Lord Bacon should attach his main concern to the truths which have their signatures in nature, and which (as he himself plainly and often asserts) may indeed be revealed to us through and with, but never by the senses, or the faculty of sense. Otherwise, indeed, instead of being more objective than the former (which they are not in any sense, both being in this respect the same), they would be less so, and, in fact, incapable of being insulated from the *idola tribus* (*quæ*) *sunt fundata in ipsa natura humana, atque in ipsa tribu seu gente hominum. Falso enim asseritur sensum humanum esse mensuram rerum; quin contra, omnes perceptiones tam sensus quam mentis, sunt*

* *Nov. Org.* P. II. *Summ.* 23.—*Ed.*

*ex analogia hominis, non ex analogia universi.** Hence too, it will not surprise us, that Plato so often calls ideas living laws, in which the mind has its whole true being and permanence; or that Bacon, *vice versa*, names the laws of nature ideas; and represents what I have in a former part of this disquisition called facts of science and central *phænomena*, as signatures, impressions, and symbols of ideas. A distinguishable power self-affirmed, and seen in its unity with the Eternal Essence, is, according to Plato, an idea: and the discipline, by which the human mind is purified from its idols (εἴδωλα), and raised to the contemplation of ideas, and thence to the secure and ever-progressive, though never-ending, investigation of truth and reality by scientific method, comprehends what the same philosopher so highly extols under the title of dialectic. According to Lord Bacon, as describing the same truth seen from the opposite point, and applied to natural philosophy, an idea would be defined as—*intuitio sive inventio, quæ in perceptione sensus non est (ut quæ puræ et sicci luminis intellectioni est propria) idearum divinæ mentis, prout in creaturis per signaturas suas sese patefaciant.* "That (saith the judicious Hooker) which doth assign unto each thing the kind, that which doth moderate the orce and power, that which doth appoint the form and measure, of working, the same we term a law."†

We can now, as men furnished with fit and respectable credentials, proceed to the historic importance and practical application of method, under the deep and solemn conviction, that without this guiding light neither can the sciences attain to their full evolution, as the organs of one vital and harmonious body, nor that most weighty and concerning of all sciences, the science of education, be understood in its first elements, much less display its powers, as the *nisus formativus*‡ of social man, as the

* *Nov. Org.* P. II. *Summ.* 41.—*Ed.*

† *Eccl. Pol.* B. I. 2.—*Ed.*

‡ So our medical writers commonly translate Professor Blumenbach's *Bildungstrieb*, the *vis plastica*, or *vis vitæ formatrix*, of the elder physiologists, and the life or living principle of John Hunter, the profoundest, I had almost said the only, physiological philosopher of the latter half of the preceding century. For in what other sense can we understand his assertion, that this principle or agent is independent of organization, which yet it animates, sustains, and repairs, or the purport of that magnificent commentary on his system, the Hunterian Museum? The Hunterian idea

appointed protoplast of true humanity. Never can society comprehend fully, and in its whole practical extent, the permanent distinction, and the occasional contrast, between cultivation and civilization ; never can it attain to a due insight into the momentous fact, fearfully as it has been, and even now is, exemplified in a neighbor country, that a nation can never be a too cultivated, but may easily become an over-civilized race : never, I repeat, can this sanative and preventive knowledge take up its

of a life or vital principle independent of the organization, yet in each organ working instinctively towards its preservation, as the ants or termites in repairing the nests of their own fabrication, demonstrates that John Hunter did not, as Stahl and others had done, individualize, or make an *hypostasis* of the principles of life, as a something manifestable *per se*, and consequently itself a *phænomenon ;* the latency of which was to be attributed to accidental, or at least contingent causes, as for example, the limits or imperfection of our senses, or the inaptness of the *media ;* but that herein he philosophized in the spirit of the purest Newtonians, who in like manner refused to hypostasize the law of gravitation into an ether, which even if its existence were conceded, would need another gravitation for itself. The Hunterian position is a genuine philosophic idea, the negative test of which, as of all ideas is, that it is equi-distant from an *ens logicum* or abstraction, an *ens repræsentativum* or generalization, and an *ens phantasticum* or imaginary thing or *phænomenon.**

Is not the progressive enlargement, the boldness without temerity, of chirurgical views and chirurgical practice since Hunter's time to the present day, attributable, in almost every instance, to his substitution of what may perhaps be called experimental dynamics, for the mechanical notions, or the less injurious traditional empiricism, of his predecessors ? And this, too, though the light is still struggling through a cloud, and though it is shed on many who see either dimly or not at all the idea from which it is eradiated ? Willingly would I designate, what I have elsewhere called the mental initiative, by some term less obnoxious to the anti-Platonic reader, than this of idea—obnoxious, I mean, as soon as any precise and peculiar sense is attached to the sound. Willingly would I exchange the term, might it be done without sacrifice of the import : and did I not see, too, clearly, that it is the meaning, not the word, which is the object of that aversion, which, fleeing from inward alarm, tries to shelter itself in outward contempt ; which is at once folly and a stumbling-block to the partisans of a crass and sensual materialism, the advocates of the *nihil nisi ab extra :*—

They shrink in, as moles,
Nature's mute monks, live mandrakes of the ground,
Creep back from light, then listen for its sound ;
See but to dread, and dread they know not why,
The natural alien of their negative eye !

Poet. Works, VII. p. 196.

* Theory of Life. I. App. C.—*Am. Ed.*

abode among us, while we oppose ourselves voluntarily to that grand prerogative of our nature, a hungering and thirsting after truth, as the appropriate end of our intelligential, and its point of union with our moral nature; but therefore after truth, that must be found within us before it can be intelligibly reflected back on the mind from without, and a religious regard to which is indispensable, both as guide and object to the just formation of the human being, poor and rich: while, in a word, we are blind to the master-light, which I have already presented in various points of view, and recommended by whatever is of highest authority with the venerators of the ancient, and the adherents of modern philosophy.

ESSAY X.

Πολυμαθιη νόον οὐ διδάσκει.—Εἶναι γὰρ ἓν τὸ σοφὸν, ἐπίςασθαι γνώμην ἤτε ἐγκυβερνήσει πάντα διὰ πάντων. HERACLITUS.*

The effective education of the reason is not to be supplied by multifarious acquirements: for there is but one knowledge that merits to be called wisdom, a knowledge that is one with a law which shall govern all in and through all.

HISTORICAL AND ILLUSTRATIVE.

THERE is still preserved in the Royal Observatory at Richmond the model of a bridge, constructed by the late justly celebrated Mr. Atwood (at that time, however, in the decline of life), in the confidence that he had explained the wonderful properties of the arch as resulting from the compound action of simple wedges, or of the rectilinear solids of which the material arch was composed; and of which supposed discovery, his model was to exhibit ocular proof. Accordingly, he took a sufficient number of wedges of brass highly polished. Arranging these at first on a skeleton arch of wood, he then removed this scaffolding or support; and the bridge not only stood firm, without any cement between the squares, but he could take away any given portion of them, as a third or a half, and appending a correspondent

* *Diogen. Laert.* ix. c. 1, s. 2.—*Ed.*

weight, at either side, the remaining part stood as before. Our venerable sovereign, who is known to have had a particular interest and pleasure in all works and discoveries of mechanic science or ingenuity, looked at it for awhile steadfastly, and, as his manner was, with quick and broken expressions of praise and courteous approbation, in the form of answers to his own questions. At length, turning to the constructor, he said, "But, Mr. Atwood, you have presumed the figure. You have put the arch first in this wooden skeleton. Can you build a bridge of the same wedges in any other figure? A strait bridge, or with two lines touching at the apex? If not, is it not evident, that the bits of brass derive their continuance in the present position from the property of the arch, and not the arch from the property of the wedge? The objection was fatal, the justice of the remark not to be resisted; and I have ever deemed it a forcible illustration of the Aristotelian axiom, with respect to all just reasoning, that the whole is of necessity prior to its parts; nor can I conceive a more apt illustration of the scientific principles I have already laid down.

All method supposes a union of several things to a common end, either by disposition, as in the works of man; or by convergence, as in the operations and products of nature. That we acknowledge a method, even in the latter, results from the religious instinct which bids us "find tongues in trees; books in the running streams; sermons in stones; and good (that is, some useful end answering to some good purpose) in every thing." In a self-conscious and thence reflecting being, no instinct can exist without engendering the belief of an object corresponding to it, either present or future, real or capable of being realized; much less the instinct, in which humanity itself is grounded;—that by which, in every act of conscious perception, we at once identify our being with that of the world without us, and yet place ourselves in contra-distinction to that world. Least of all can this mysterious pre-disposition exist without evolving a belief that the productive power,* which in nature acts as nature, is essentially one (that

* Obscure from too great compression. The sense is, that the productive power, or *vis naturans*, which in the sensible world, or *natura naturata*, is what we mean by the word, nature, when we speak of the same as an agent, is essentially one, &c. In other words, idea and law are the subjective and objective poles of the same magnet, that is, of the same living and energiz-

is, of one kind) with the intelligence, which is in the human mind above nature; however disfigured this belief may become by accidental forms or accompaniments, and though like heat in the thawing of ice, it may appear only in its effects. So universally has this conviction leavened the very substance of all discourse, that there is no language on earth in which a man can abjure it as a prejudice, without employing terms and conjunctions that suppose its reality, with a feeling very different from that which accompanies a figurative or metaphorical use of words. In all aggregates of construction therefore, which we contemplate as wholes, whether as integral parts or as a system, we assume an intention, as the initiative, of which the end is the correlative.

Hence proceeds the introduction of final causes in the works of nature equally as in those of man. Hence their assumption, as constitutive and explanatory, by the mass of mankind; and the employment of the presumption, as an auxiliary and regulative principle, by the enlightened naturalist, whose office it is to seek, discover, and investigate the efficient causes. Without denying, that to resolve the efficient into the final may be the ultimate aim of philosophy, he, of good right, resists the substitution of the latter for the former, as premature, presumptuous, and preclusive of all science; well aware, that those sciences have been most progressive, in which this confusion has been either precluded by the nature of the science itself, as in pure mathematics, or avoided by the good sense of its cultivator. Yet even he admits a teleological ground in physics and physiology; that is, the presumption of a something analogous to the casualty of the human will, by which, without assigning to nature, as nature, a conscious purpose, he may yet distinguish her agency from a blind and lifeless mechanism. Even he admits its use,

ing reason. What an idea is in the subject, that is, in the mind, is a law in the object, that is, in nature. But throughout these essays, the want of illustrative examples, and varied exposition is, I am conscious, the main defect, and it was occasioned by the haunting dread of being tedious. But O! the cold water that was thrown on me, chiefly from those from whom I ought to have received warmth and encouragement! "Who, do you expect, will read this," &c.—But, vanity as it may appear, it is nevertheless true, and uttered with feelings the most unlike those of self-conceit, that it has been my mistake through life to be looking up to those whom I ought to have been looking at, nay (in some instances) down upon.—June 23d, 1829.

and, in many instances, its necessity, as a regulative principle; as a ground of anticipation, for the guidance of his judgment and for the direction of his observation and experiment;—briefly in all that preparatory process, which the French language so happily expresses by *s'orienter*, to find out the east for one's self. When the naturalist contemplates the structure of a bird, for instance, the hollow cavity of the bones, the position of the wings for motion, and of the tail for steering its course, and the like, he knows indeed that there must be a correspondent mechanism, as the *nexus effectivus;* but he knows, likewise, that this will no more explain the particular existence of the bird, than the principles of cohesion could inform him why of two buildings one is a palace and the other a church. Nay, it must not be overlooked, that the assumption of the *nexus effectivus* itself originates in the mind, as one of the laws under which alone it can reduce the manifold of the impression from without into unity, and thus contemplate it as one thing; and could never (as hath been clearly proved by Mr. Hume) have been derived from outward experience, in which it is indeed presupposed as a necessary condition. *Notio nexus causalis non oritur, sed supponitur, a sensibus.* Between the purpose and the end the component parts are included, and thence receive their position and character as means, that is, parts contemplated as parts. It is in this sense, that I will affirm that the parts, as means to an end, derive their position, and therein their qualities (or character)—nay, I dare add, their very existence, as particular things,—from the antecedent method, or self-organizing purpose; upon which therefore I have dwelt so long.

I am aware that it is with our cognitions as with our children. There is a period in which the method of nature is working for them; a period of aimless activity and unregulated accumulation, during which it is enough if we can preserve them in health and out of harm's way. Again, there is a period of orderliness, of circumspection, of discipline, in which we purify, separate, define, select, arrange, and settle the nomenclature of communication. There is also a period of dawning and twilight, a period of anticipation, affording trials of strength. And all these, both in the growth of the sciences and in the mind of a rightly-educated individual, will precede the attainment of a scientific method. But, notwithstanding this, unless the importance of the latter be felt and acknowledged, unless its attainment be looked forward to and from the very beginning prepared for, there is little hope and small chance that any education will be conducted aright; or will ever prove in reality worth the name.

Much labor, much wealth may have been expended, yet the final result will too probably warrant the sarcasm of the Scythian traveller: *Væ! quantum nihili!* and draw from a wise man the earnest recommendation of a full draught from Lethe, as the first and indispensable preparative for the waters of the true Helicon. Alas! how many examples are now present to my memory, of young men the most anxiously and expensively be-schoolmastered, be-tutored, be-lectured, any thing but educated; who have received arms and ammunition, instead of skill, strength, and courage; varnished rather than polished; perilously over-civilized, and most pitiably uncultivated! And all from inattention to the method dictated by nature herself, to the simple truth, that as the forms in all organized existence, so must all true and living knowledge proceed from within; that it may be trained, supported, fed, excited, but can never be infused, or impressed.

Look back on the history of the sciences. Review the method in which providence has brought the more favored portion of mankind to their present state. Lord Bacon has justly remarked, *antiquitas sæculi juventus mundi**—antiquity of time is the youth of the world and of science. In the childhood of the human race, its education commenced with the cultivation of the moral sense; the object proposed being such as the mind only could apprehend, and the principle of obedience being placed in the will. The appeal in both was made to the inward man. *Through faith we understand that the worlds were framed by the word of God; so that things which are seen were not made of things which do appear.* The solution of *phænomena* can never be derived from *phænomena.* Upon this ground the writer of the epistle to the Hebrews (c. xi.) is not less philosophical than eloquent. The aim, the method throughout was, in the first place, to awaken, to cultivate, and to mature the truly human in human nature, in and through itself, or as independently as possible of the notices derived from sense, and of the motives that had reference to the sensations; till the time should arrive when the senses themselves might be allowed to present

* Advancement of Learning, B. i.—*Ed.*

symbols and attestations of truths, learnt previously from deeper and inner sources. Thus the first period of the education of our race was evidently assigned to the cultivation of humanity itself, or of that in man, which of all known embodied creatures he alone possesses, the pure reason, as designed to regulate the will. And by what method was this done? First, by the excitement of the idea of their Creator as a spirit, of an idea which they were strictly forbidden to realize to themselves under any image; and secondly, by the injunction of obedience to the will of a super-sensual Being. Nor did the method stop here. For, unless we are equally to contradict Moses and the New Testament, in compliment to the paradox of a Warburton, the rewards of their obedience were placed at a distance. For the time present they equally with us were to endure, as seeing him who is invisible. Their bodies they were taught to consider as fleshly tents, which as pilgrims they were bound to pitch wherever the invisible Director of their route should appoint, however barren or thorny the spot might appear. *Few and evil have the days of the years of my life been,** says the aged Israel. But that life was but his pilgrimage, and he trusted in the promises.

Thus were the very first lessons in the divine school assigned to the cultivation of the reason and of the will; or rather of both as united in faith. The common and ultimate object of the will and of the reason was purely spiritual, and to be present in the mind of the disciple—μόνον ἐν ἰδέᾳ, μηδαμῆ εἰδωλικῶς, that is, in the idea alone, and never as an image or imagination. The means too, by which the idea was to be excited, as well as the symbols by which it was to be communicated, were to be, as far as possible, intellectual.

Those, on the contrary, who wilfully chose a mode opposite to this method, who determined to shape their convictions and deduce their knowledge from without, by exclusive observation of outward and sensible things as the only realities, became, it appears, rapidly civilized. They built cities, invented musical instruments, were artificers in brass and in iron, and refined on the means of sensual gratification, and the conveniencies of courtly intercourse. They became the great masters of the agreeable, which fraternized readily with cruelty and rapacity; these being, indeed, but alternate moods of the same sensual selfishness.

* Gen. xlvii. 9.

Thus, both before and after the flood, the vicious of mankind receded from all true cultivation, as they hurried towards civilization. Finally, as it was not in their power to make themselves wholly beasts, or to remain without a semblance of religion ; and yet continuing faithful to their original maxim, and determined to receive nothing as true, but what they derived, or believed themselves to derive from their senses, or (in modern phrase) what they could prove *à posteriori*, they became idolaters of the heavens and the material elements. From the harmony of operation they concluded a certain unity of nature and design, but were incapable of finding in the facts any proof of a unity of person. They did not, in this respect, pretend to find what they must themselves have first assumed. Having thrown away the clusters, which had grown in the vineyard of revelation, they could not, as later reasoners, by being born in a Christian country, have been enabled to do, hang the grapes on thorns, and then pluck them as the native growth of the bushes. But the men of sense of the patriarchal times, neglecting reason and having rejected faith, adopted what the facts seemed to involve and the most obvious analogies to suggest. They acknowledged a whole beehive of natural gods : but while they were employed in building a temple* consecrated to the material heavens, it pleased divine wisdom to send on them a confusion of lip accompanied with the usual embitterment of controversy, where all parties are in the wrong, and the grounds of quarrel are equally plausible on all sides. As the modes of error are endless, the hundred forms of polytheism had each its group of partisans who, hostile or alienated, thenceforward formed separate tribes kept aloof from each

* I am far from being a Hutchinsonian, nor have I found much to respect in the twelve volumes of Hutchinson's works, either as biblical comment or natural philosophy ; though I give him credit for orthodoxy and good intentions. But his interpretation of the first nine verses of Genesis xi. seems not only rational in itself, and consistent with after accounts of the sacred historian, but proved to be the literal sense of the Hebrew text. His explanation of the cherubim is pleasing and plausible : I dare not say more. Those who would wish to learn the most important points of the Hutchinsonian doctrine in the most favorable form, and in the shortest possible space, I can refer to Duncan Forbes's Letter to a Bishop. If my own judgment did not withhold my assent, I should never be ashamed of a conviction holden, professed, and advocated by so good and wise a man as Duncan Forbes.

other by their ambitious leaders. Hence arose, in the course of a few centuries, the diversity of languages, which has sometimes been confounded with the miraculous event that was indeed its first and principal, though remote, cause.

Following next, and as the representative of the youth and approaching manhood of the human intellect, we have ancient Greece, from Orpheus, Linus, Musæus, and the other mythological bards, or perhaps the brotherhoods impersonated under those names,* to the time when the republics lost their independence, and their learned men sank into copyists and commentators of the works of their forefathers. That I include these as educated under a distinct providential, though not miraculous, dispensation, will surprise no one, who reflects that in whatever has a permanent operation on the destinies and intellectual condition of mankind at large—that in all which has been manifestly employed as a co-agent in the mightiest revolution of the moral world, the propagation of the gospel; and in the intellectual progress of mankind, in the restoration of philosophy, science, and the ingenuous arts—it were irreligion not to acknowledge the hand of Divine providence. The periods, too, join on to each other. The earliest Greeks took up the religious and lyrical poetry of the Hebrews; and the schools of the prophets were, however partially and imperfectly, represented by the mysteries, derived through the corrupt channel of the Phœnicians. With these secret schools of physiological theology the mythical poets were doubtless in connection; and it was these schools, which prevented polytheism from producing all its natural barbarizing effects. The mysteries and the mythical hymns and pæans shaped themselves gradually into epic poetry and history on the one hand, and into the ethical tragedy and philosophy on the other. Under their protection, and that of a youthful liberty secretly controlled by a species of internal theocracy, the sciences

* "I have no doubt whatever that *Homer* is a mere concrete name for the rhapsodies of the Iliad. Of course there was *a* Homer, and twenty besides. * * * * I have the firmest conviction that Homer is a mere traditional synonyme with, or figure for, the Iliad. You can not conceive for a moment, any thing about the poet, as you call him, apart from that poem. Difference in men there was in degree, but not in kind; one man was, perhaps, a better poet than another; but he was a poet upon the same ground and with the same feelings as the rest." *Table Talk*, VI. pp. 312, 400.—*Ed.*

and the sterner kinds of the fine arts, namely, architecture and statuary, grew up together;—followed, indeed, by painting, but a statuesque and austerely idealized painting, which did not degenerate into mere copies of the sense, till the process, for which Greece existed, had been completed. Contrast the rapid progress and perfection of all the products, which owe their existence and character to the mind's own acts, intellectual or imaginative, with the rudeness of their application to the investigation of physical laws and *phænomena:* then contemplate the Greeks (Γραῖοι ἀεὶ παῖδες) as representing a portion only of the education of man; and the conclusion is inevitable.

In the education of the mind of the race, as in that of the individual, each different age and purpose requires different objects and different means; though all dictated by the same principle, tending toward the same end, and forming consecutive parts of the same method. But if the scale taken be sufficiently large to neutralize or render insignificant the disturbing forces of accident, the degree of success is the best criterion by which to appreciate both the wisdom of the general principle, and the fitness of the particular objects to the given epoch or period. Now it is a fact, for the greater part of universal acceptance, and attested as to the remainder by all that is of highest fame and authority, by the great, wise, and good, during a space of at least seventeen centuries—weighed against whom the opinions of a few distinguished individuals, or the fashion of a single age, must be holden light in the balance,—it is a fact, I say, that whatever could be educed by the mind out of its own essence, by attention to its own acts and laws of action, or as the products of the same; and whatever likewise could be reflected from material masses transformed as it were into mirrors, the excellence of which is to reveal, in the least possible degree, their own original forms and natures;—all these, whether arts or sciences, the ancient Greeks carried to an almost ideal perfection: while in the application of their skill and science to the investigation of the laws of the sensible world, and the qualities and composition of material concretes, chemical, mechanical, or organic, their essays were crude and improsperous, compared with those of the moderns during the early morning of their strength, and even at the first re-ascension of the light. But still more striking will the difference appear, if we contrast the physiological schemes and fancies of the Greeks with their own discoveries in the region of the pure intellect, and with their still unrivalled success in the arts of imagination. In the aversion of their great men from any practical use of their philosophic discoveries, as in the well-known instance of Archimedes, the soul of the world was at work; and the few exceptions were but a rush of billows driven shoreward by some chance gust before the hour of tide, instantly retracted, and leaving the sands bare and soundless long after the momentary glitter had been lost in evaporation.

The third period, that of the Romans, was devoted to the preparations for preserving, propagating, and realizing the labors of the preceding; to war, empire, law. To this we may refer the defect of all originality in the Latin poets and philosophers, on the one hand, and on the other, the predilection of the Romans for astrology, magic, divination in all its forms. It was the Roman instinct to appropriate by conquest and to give fixure by legislation. And it was the bewilderment and prematurity of the same instinct which restlessly impelled them to materialize the ideas of the Greek philosophers, and to render them practical by superstitious uses.

Thus the Hebrews may be regarded as the fixed mid point of the living line, toward which the Greeks as the ideal pole, and the Romans as the material, were ever approximating; till the coincidence and final synthesis took place in Christianity, of which the Bible is the law, and Christendom the *phænomenon*. So little confirmation from history, from the process of education planned and conducted by unerring Providence, do those theorists receive, who would at least begin (too many, alas! both begin and end) with the objects of the senses; as if nature herself had not abundantly performed this part of the task, by continuous, irresistible enforcements of attention to her presence, to the direct beholding, to the apprehension and observation, of the objects that stimulate the senses;—as if the cultivation of the mental powers, by methodical exercise of their own forces, were not the securest means of forming the true correspondents to them in the functions of comparison, judgment, and interpretation.

ESSAY XI.

Sapimus animo, fruimur anima: sine animo animo est debilis.
L. Accii Fragmenta.

As there are two wants connatural to man, so are there two main directions of human activity, pervading in modern times the whole civilized world; and constituting and sustaining that nationality which yet it is their tendency, and, more or less, their effect, to transcend and to moderate,—trade and literature. These were they, which, after the dismemberment of the old Roman world, gradually reduced the conquerors and the conquered at once into several nations and a common Christendom. The natural law of increase and the instincts of family may produce tribes, and, under rare and peculiar circumstances, settlements and neighborhoods; and conquest may form empires. But without trade and literature, mutually commingled, there can be no nation; without commerce and science, no bond of nations. As the one hath for its object the wants of the body, real or artificial, the desires for which are for the greater part, nay, as far as the origination of trade and commerce is concerned, altogether excited from without; so the other has for its origin, as well as for its object, the wants of the mind, the gratification of which is a natural and necessary condition of its growth and sanity. And the man (or the nation, considered according to its predominant character as one man) may be regarded under these circumstances, as acting in two forms of method, inseparably co-existent, yet producing very different effects accordingly as one or the other obtains the primacy; the senses, the memory, and the understanding (that is, the retentive, reflective, and judicial functions of his mind) being common to both methods. As is the rank assigned to each in the theory and practice of the governing classes, and, according to its prevalence in forming the foundation of their public habits and opinions, so will be the outward and inward life of the people at large: such will the nation be. In tracing the epochs, and alternations of their relative sovereignty or subjection, consists the philosophy of history. In the power of distinguishing and appreciating their several results consists the historic sense. And that under the ascendency of the mental and moral character the commercial relations may thrive to the utmost desirable point, while the reverse is ruinous to both, and sooner or later effectuates the fall or debasement of the country itself—this is the richest truth obtained for mankind by historic research; though unhappily it is the truth, to which a rich and commercial nation listens with most reluctance and receives with least faith. Where the brain and the immediate conductors of its influence remain healthy and vigorous, the defects and diseases of the eye will most often admit either of a cure or a substitute. And so is it with the outward prosperity of a state, where the well-being of the people possesses the primacy in the aims of the governing classes, and in the public feeling. But what avails the perfect state of the eye,

> Though clear
> To outward view of blemish or of spot,*

where the optic nerve is paralyzed by a pressure on the brain? And even so is it not only with the well-being, but ultimately with the prosperity of a people, where the former is considered (if it be considered at all) as subordinate and secondary to wealth and revenue.

In the pursuits of commerce the man is called into action from without, in order to appropriate the outward world, as far as he can bring it within his reach, to the purposes of his senses and sensual nature. His ultimate end is appearance and enjoyment. Where on the other hand the nurture and evolution of humanity is the final aim, there will soon be seen a general tendency toward, an earnest seeking after, some ground common to the world and to man, therein to find the one principle of permanence and identity, the rock of strength and refuge, to which the soul may cling amid the fleeting surge-like objects of the senses. Disturbed as by the obscure quickening of an inward birth; made restless by swarming thoughts, that, like bees when they first miss the queen and mother of the hive, with vain dis-

* Milton, Sonnet to Cyriack Skinner.—*Ed.*

cursion seek each in the other what is the common need of all; man sallies forth into nature—in nature, as in the shadows and reflections of a clear river, to discover the originals of the forms presented to him in his own intellect. Over these shadows, as if they were the substantial powers and presiding spirits of the stream, Narcissus-like, he hangs delighted: till finding nowhere a representative of that free agency which yet is a fact of immediate consciousness sanctioned and made fearfully significant by his prophetic conscience, he learns at last that what he seeks he has left behind, and that he but lengthens the distance as he prolongs the search. Under the tutorage of scientific analysis, haply first given to him by express revelation,

E cœlo descendit, *Γνῶθι σεαυτὸν*,*

he separates the relations that are wholly the creatures of his own abstracting and comparing intellect, and at once discovers and recoils from the discovery, that the reality, the objective truth, of the objects he has been adoring, derives its whole and sole evidence from an obscure sensation, which he is alike unable to resist or to comprehend, which compels him to contemplate as without and independent of himself what yet he could not contemplate at all, were it not a modification of his own being.

Earth fills her lap with pleasures of her own;
Yearnings she hath in her own natural kind,
And, even with something of a mother's mind,
And no unworthy aim
The homely nurse doth all she can
To make her foster-child, her inmate man,
Forget the glories he hath known,
And that imperial palace whence he came.
* * * * * * *
O joy! that in our embers
Is something that doth live,
That nature yet remembers
What was so fugitive!
The thought of our past years in me doth breed
Perpetual benedictions: not indeed
For that which is most worthy to be blest;
Delight and liberty, the simple creed
Of childhood, whether busy or at rest,
With new-fledged hope still fluttering in his breast:—

* Juv. xi. 27.—*Ed.*

Not for these I raise
The song of thanks and praise;
But for those obstinate questionings
Of sense and outward things,
Fallings from us, vanishings;
Blank misgivings of a creature
Moving about in worlds not realized,
High instincts, before which our mortal nature
Did tremble like a guilty thing surprised!
But for those first affections,
Those shadowy recollections,
Which, be they what they may,
Are yet the fountain light of all our day,
Are yet a master light of all our seeing;
Uphold us—cherish—and have power to make
Our noisy years seem moments in the being
Of the eternal silence: truths that wake,
To perish never;
Which neither listlessness, nor mad endeavor,
Nor man nor boy,
Nor all that is at enmity with joy,
Can utterly abolish or destroy!
Hence, in a season of calm weather,
Though inland far we be,
Our souls have sight of that immortal sea
Which brought us hither;
Can in a moment travel thither—
And see the children sport upon the shore,
And hear the mighty waters rolling evermore.

WORDSWORTH.*

Long indeed will man strive to satisfy the inward querist with the phrase, laws of nature. But though the individual may rest content with the seemly metaphor, the race can not. If a law

* *Intimations of immortality from recollections of early childhood.—Ed.* During my residence in Rome I had the pleasure of reciting this sublime ode to the illustrious Baron Von Humboldt, then the Prussian minister at the papal court, and now at the court of St. James. By those who knew and honored both the brothers, the talents of the ambassador were considered equal to those of the scientific traveller, his judgment superior. I can only say, that I know few Englishmen, whom I could compare with him in the extensive knowledge and just appreciation of English literature and its various epochs. He listened to the ode with evident delight, and as evidently not without surprise, and at the close of the recitation exclaimed, "And is this the work of a living English poet? I should have attributed it to the age of Elizabeth, not that I recollect any writer, whose style it resembles; but rather with wonder, that so great and original a poet should

of nature be a mere generalization, it is included in the above as an act of the mind. But if it be other and more, and yet manifestable only in and to an intelligent spirit, it must in act and substance be itself spiritual: for things utterly heterogeneous can have no intercommunion. In order therefore to the recognition of himself in nature man must first learn to comprehend nature in himself, and its laws in the ground of his own existence. Then only can he reduce *phænomena* to principles; then only will he have achieved the method, the self-unravelling clue, which alone can securely guide him to the conquest of the former;—when he has discovered in the basis of their union the necessity of their differences, in the principle of their continuance the solution of their changes. It is the idea alone of the common centre, of the universal law, by which all power manifests itself in opposite yet interdependent forces—(*ἡ γὰρ δυὰς ἀεὶ παρὰ μονάδι κάθηται, καὶ νοεραῖς ἀστράπτει τομαῖς*)—which enlightening inquiry, multiplying experiment, and at once inspiring humility and perseverance will lead him to comprehend gradually and progressively the relation of each to the other, of each to all, and of all to each.

Imagine the unlettered African, or rude yet musing Indian, poring over an illuminated manuscript of the inspired volume, with the vague yet deep impression that his fates and fortunes are in some unknown manner connected with its contents. Every tint, every group of characters, has its several dream. Say that after long and dissatisfying toils, he begins to sort, first the paragraphs that appear to resemble each other, then the lines, the words—nay, that he has at length discovered that the whole is formed by the recurrence and interchanges of a limited number of ciphers, letters, marks, and points, which, however, in the very height and utmost perfection of his attainment, he makes twentyfold more numerous than they are, by classing every different form of the same character, intentional or accidental, as a separate element. And the whole is without soul or substance, a talisman of superstition, a mockery of science: or employed

have escaped my notice." Often as I repeat passages from it to myself, I recur to the words of Dante:

Canzon! io credo, che saranno radi
Color che tua ragion intendan bene:
Tanto lor parli faticoso ed alto.

perhaps at last to feather the arrows of death, or to shine and flutter amid the plumes of savage vanity. The poor Indian too truly represents the state of learned and systematic ignorance—arrangement guided by the light of no leading idea, mere orderliness without method.

But see! the friendly missionary arrives. He explains to him the nature of written words, translates them for him into his native sounds, and thence into the thoughts of his heart—how many of these thoughts then first evolved into consciousness, which yet the awakening disciple receives, and not as aliens! Henceforward, the book is unsealed for him; the depth is opened out; he communes with the spirit of the volume as with a living oracle. The words become transparent, and he sees them as though he saw them not.

I have thus delineated the two great directions of man and society with their several objects and ends. Concerning the conditions and principles of method appertaining to each, I have affirmed (for the facts hitherto adduced have been rather for illustration than for evidence, to make the position distinctly understood rather than to enforce the conviction of its truth); that in both there must be a mental antecedent; but that in the one it may be an image or conception received through the senses, and originating from without, the inspiriting passion or desire being alone the immediate and proper offspring of the mind; while in the other the initiative thought, the intellectual seed, must itself have its birth-place within, whatever excitement from without may be necessary for its germination. Will the soul thus awakened neglect or undervalue the outward and conditional causes of her growth? Far rather, might I dare borrow a wild fancy from the Mantuan bard, or the poet of Arno, will it be with her, as if a stem or trunk, suddenly endued with sense and reflection, should contemplate its green shoots, their leafits and budding blossoms, wondered at as then first noticed, but welcomed nevertheless as its own growth: while yet with undiminished gratitude, and a deepened sense of dependency, it would bless the dews and the sunshine from without, deprived of the awakening and fostering excitement of which, its own productivity would have remained forever hidden from itself, or felt only as the obscure trouble of a baffled instinct.

Hast thou ever raised thy mind to the consideration of existence, in and by itself, as the mere act of existing? Hast thou ever said to thyself thoughtfully, It is! heedless in that moment, whether it were a man before thee, or a flower, or a grain of sand,—without reference, in short, to this or that particular mode or form of existence? If thou hast indeed attained to this, thou wilt have felt the presence of a mystery, which must have fixed thy spirit in awe and wonder. The very words,—there is nothing! or,—There was a time, when there was nothing! are self-contradictory. There is that within us which repels the proposition with as full and instantaneous a light, as if it bore evidence against the fact in the right of its own eternity.

Not to be, then, is impossible: to be, incomprehensible. If thou hast mastered this intuition of absolute existence, thou wilt have learnt likewise, that it was this, and no other, which in the earlier ages seized the nobler minds, the elect among men, with a sort of sacred horror. This it was which first caused them to feel within themselves a something ineffably greater than their own individual nature. It was this which, raising them aloft, and projecting them to an ideal distance from themselves, prepared them to become the lights and awakening voices of other men, the founders of law and religion, the educators and foster-gods of mankind. The power, which evolved this idea of being, being in its essence, being limitless, comprehending its own limits in its dilatation, and condensing itself into its own apparent mounds—how shall we name it? The idea itself, which like a mighty billow at once overwhelms and bears aloft—what is it? Whence did it come? In vain would we derive it from the organs of sense: for these supply only surfaces, undulations, phantoms. In vain from the instruments of sensation: for these furnish only the chaos, the shapeless elements of sense. And least of all may we hope to find its origin, or sufficient cause, in the moulds and mechanism of the understanding, the whole purport and functions of which consist in individualization, in outlines and differencings by quantity and relation. It were wiser to seek substance in shadow, than absolute fulness in mere negation.

I have asked then for its birth-place in all that constitutes our relative individuality, in all that each man calls exclusively himself. It is an alien of which they know not: and for them the question itself is purposeless, and the very words that convey it are as sounds in an unknown language, or as the vision of heaven and earth expanded by the rising sun, which falls but as warmth on the eyelids of the blind. To no class of *phænomena* or particulars can it be referred, itself being none; therefore, to no faculty by which these alone are apprehended. As little dare we refer it to any form of abstraction or generalization; for it has neither co-ordinate nor *analogon;* it is absolutely one; and that it is, and affirms itself to be, is its only predicate. And yet this power, nevertheless, is;—in supremacy of being it is;*—and he for whom it manifests itself in its adequate idea, dare as little arrogate it to himself as his own, can as little appropriate it either totally or by partition, as he can claim ownership in the breathing air, or make an inclosure in the cope of heaven.† He bears witness of it to his own mind, even as he describes life and light: and, with the silence of light, it describes itself and dwells in us only as far as we dwell in it. The truths which it manifests are such as it alone can manifest, and in all truth it manifests itself. By what name then canst thou call a truth so manifested? Is it not revelation? Ask thyself whether thou canst attach to that latter word any consistent meaning not included in the idea of the former. And the manifesting power, the source and the correlative of the idea thus manifested—is it not God? Either thou knowest it to be God, or thou hast called an idol by that awful name. Therefore in the most appropriate, no less than in the highest, sense of the word were the earliest teachers

* To affirm that reason is, is the same as to affirm that reason is being, or that the true being is reason, Ὁ Λόγος.—Hence, the reason or law of a thing constitutes its actual being, the ground of its reality.—1829.

† And yet this same IS, is the essential predicate of the correspondent object of this power. What must we infer? Even this;—that the object and subject are one;—that the reason is being;—the supreme reason the supreme Being; and that the antithesis of truth and being is but the result of the polarizing property of all finite mind, for which unity is manifested only by correspondent opposites. Here do we stop? Woe to us, if we do! Better that we had never begun. A deeper yet must be sought for,—even the absolute Will, the Good, the superessential source of being, and in the eternal act of self-affirmation, the I Am, the Father—who with the only-begotten *Logos* (word, idea, supreme mind, *pleroma*, the word containing every word that proceedeth from the mouth of the Most Highest) and with the Spirit proceeding, is the one only God from everlasting to everlasting. —1829.

of humanity inspired. They alone were the true seers of God, and therefore prophets of the human race.

Look round you, and you behold everywhere an adaptation of means to ends. Meditate on the nature of a being whose ideas are creative, and consequently more real, more substantial than the things that, at the height of their creaturely state, are but their dim reflexes ;* and the intuitive conviction will arise that in such a being there could exist no motive to the creation of a machine for its own sake; that, therefore, the material world must have been made for the sake of man, at once the high-priest and representative of the Creator, as far as he partakes of that reason in which the essences of all things co-exist in all their distinctions yet as one and indivisible. But I speak of man in his idea, and as subsumed in the divine humanity, in whom alone God loved the world.

In all inferior things from the grass on the house-top to the giant tree of the forest; from the gnats that swarm in its shade, and the mole that burrows amid its roots to the eagle which builds in its summit, and the elephant which browses on its branches, we behold—first, a subjection to universal laws by which each thing belongs to the whole, as interpenetrated by the powers of the whole; and, secondly, the intervention of particular laws by which the universal laws are suspended or tempered for the weal and sustenance of each particular class. Hence and thus we see too that each species, and each individual of every species, becomes a system, a world of its own. If then we behold this economy everywhere in the irrational creation, shall we not hold it probable that by some analogous intervention a similar temperament will have been effected for the rational and moral?

* If I may not rather resemble them to the resurgent ashes, with which (according to the tales of the later alchemists) the substantial forms of bird and flower made themselves visible as,

τὰ κακῆς ὕλης βλαςήματα χρηςὰ καὶ ἐσθλά.

And let me be permitted to add, in especial reference to this passage, a premonition quoted from the same work (*Zoroastris Oracula Magica*),

Ἃ Νοῦς λέγει, τῷ νοοῦντι δὴ πȣ λέγει.

Of the flower apparitions so solemnly affirmed by Sir K. Digby, Kercher, Helmont, and others, see a full and most interesting account in Southey's Omniana (vol. ii. p. 82. Spectral Flowers.—*Ed.*), with a probable solution of this chemical marvel.

Are we not entitled to expect some appropriate agency in behalf of the presiding and alone progressive creature? To presume some especial provision for the permanent interest of the creature destined to move and grow towards that divine humanity which we have learnt to contemplate as the final cause of all creation, and the centre in which all its lines converge?

To discover the mode of intervention requisite for man's development and progression, we must seek then for some general law, by the untempered and uncounteracted action of which man's development and progression would be prevented and endangered. But this we shall find in that law of his understanding and fancy, by which he is impelled to abstract the changes and outward relations of matter and to arrange them under the form of causes and effects. And this was necessary, as the condition under which alone experience and intellectual growth are possible. But, on the other hand, by the same law he is inevitably tempted to misinterpret a constant precedence into positive causation, and thus to break and scatter the one divine and invisible life of nature into countless idols of the sense; and falling prostrate before lifeless images, the creatures of his own abstraction, is himself sensualized, and becomes a slave to the things of which he was formed to be the conqueror and sovereign. From the fetisch of the imbruted African to the soul-debasing errors of the proud fact-hunting materialist we may trace the various ceremonials of the same idolatry, and shall find selfishness, hate, and servitude as the results. If therefore by the overruling and suspension of the phantom-cause of this superstition; if by separating effects from their natural antecedents; if by presenting the *phænomena* of time (as far as is possible) in the absolute forms of eternity; the nursling of experience should, in the early period of his pupilage, be compelled by a more impressive experience to seek in the invisible life alone for the true cause and invisible *nexus* of the things that are seen, we shall not demand the evidences of ordinary experience for that which, if it ever existed, existed as its antithesis and for its counteraction. Was it an appropriate mean to a necessary end? Has it been attested by lovers of truth; has it been believed by lovers of wisdom? Do we see throughout all nature the occasional intervention of particular agencies in counter-check of universal laws? (And of what other definition is a miracle susceptible?) These are the questions: and if to these our answers must be affirmative, then we too will acquiesce in the traditions of humanity, and yielding as to a high interest of our own being, will discipline ourselves to the reverential and kindly faith, that the guides and teachers of mankind were the hands of power, no less than the voices of inspiration: and little anxious concerning the particular forms, proofs, and circumstances of each manifestation we will give an historic credence to the historic fact, that men sent by God have come with signs and wonders on the earth.

If it be objected, that in nature, as distinguished from man, this intervention of particular laws is, or with the increase of science will be, resolvable into the universal laws which they had appeared to counterbalance, we will reply: Even so it may be in the case of miracles; but wisdom forbids her children to antedate their knowledge, or to act and feel otherwise or further than they know. But should that time arrive, the sole difference, that could result from such an enlargement of our view, would be this;—that what we now consider as miracles in opposition to ordinary experience, we should then reverence with a yet higher devotion as harmonious parts of one great complex miracle, when the antithesis between experience and belief would itself be taken up into unity of intuitive reason.

And what purpose of philosophy can this acquiescence answer? A gracious purpose, a most valuable end; if it prevent the energies of philosophy from being idly wasted, by removing the contrariety without confounding the distinction between philosophy and faith. The philosopher will remain a man in sympathy with his fellow-men. The head will not be disjoined from the heart, nor will speculative truth be alienated from practical wisdom. And vainly without the union of both shall we expect an opening of the inward eye to the glorious vision of that existence which admits of no question out of itself, acknowledges no predicate but the I AM IN THAT I AM! *Θαυμάζοντες φιλοσοφοῦμεν· φιλοσοφήσαντες θαμβοῦμεν.* In wonder (*τῷ θαυμάζειν*) says Aristotle, does philosophy begin; and in astoundment (*τῷ θαμβεῖν*) says Plato, does all true philosophy finish. As every faculty, with every the minutest organ of our nature, owes its whole reality and comprehensibility to an existence incomprehensible and groundless, because the ground of all comprehension; not without the union of all that is essential in all the functions of our spirit, not without an emotion tranquil from its very intensity, shall we worthily contemplate in the magnitude and integrity of the world that life-ebullient stream which breaks through every momentary embankment, again, indeed, and evermore to embank itself, but within no banks to stagnate or be imprisoned.

But here it behooves us to bear in mind, that all true reality has both its ground and its evidence in the will, without which as its complement science itself is but an elaborate game of shadows, begins in abstractions and ends in perplexity. For considered merely intellectually, individuality, as individuality, is only conceivable as with and in the universal and infinite, neither before nor after it. No transition is possible from one to the other, as from the architect to the house, or the watch to its maker. The finite form can neither be laid hold of by, nor can it appear to, the mere speculative intellect as any thing of itself real, but merely as an apprehension, a frame-work which the human imagination forms by its own limits, as the foot measures itself on the snow; and the sole truth of which we must again refer to the divine imagination, in virtue of its omniformity. For even as thou art capable of beholding the transparent air as little during the absence as during the presence of light, so canst thou behold the finite things as actually existing neither with nor without the substance. Not without,—for then the forms cease to be, and are lost in night: not with it,—for it is the light, the substance shining through it, which thou canst alone really see.

The ground-work, therefore, of all pure speculation is the full apprehension of the difference between the contemplation of reason, namely, that intuition of things which arises when we possess ourselves, as one with the whole, which is substantial knowledge, and that which presents itself when transferring reality to the negations of reality, to the ever-varying frame-work of the uniform life, we think of ourselves as separated beings, and place nature in antithesis to the mind, as object to subject, thing to thought, death to life. This is abstract knowledge, or the science of the mere understanding. By the former, we know that existence is its own predicate, self-affirmation, the one attribute in which all others are contained, not as parts, but as manifestations. It is an eternal and infinite self-rejoicing, self-loving, with a joy unfathomable, with a love all-comprehensive. It is absolute; and the absolute is neither singly that which affirms, nor that which is affirmed; but the identity and living *copula* of both.

On the other hand, by the abstract knowledge which belongs to us as finite beings, and which leads to a science of delusion, then only, when it would exist for itself instead of being the instrument of the former—(even as the former is equally hollow and yet more perilously delusive, where it is not radicated in a deeper ground) when it would itself, I say, be its own life and verity, instead of being, as it were, a translation of the living word into a dead language, for the purposes of memory, arrangement, and general communication,—it is by this abstract knowledge that the understanding distinguishes the affirmed from the affirming. Well if it distinguish without dividing! Well if by distinction it add clearness to fulness, and prepare for the intellectual re-union of the all in one in that eternal Reason whose fulness hath no opacity, whose transparency hath no *vacuum*.

If we thoughtfully review the three preceding paragraphs, we shall find the conclusion to be;—that the dialectic intellect by the exertion of its own powers exclusively can lead us to a general affirmation of the supreme reality of an absolute being. But here it stops. It is utterly incapable of communicating insight or conviction concerning the existence or possibility of the world, as different from Deity. It finds itself constrained to identify, more truly to confound, the Creator with the aggregate of his creature, and, cutting the knot which it can not untwist, to deny altogether the reality of all finite existence, and then to shelter itself from its own dissatisfaction, its own importunate queries, in the wretched evasion that of nothings, no solution can be required; till pain haply, and anguish, and remorse, with bitter scoff and moody laughter inquire;—Are we then indeed nothings?—till through every organ of sense nature herself asks;—How and whence did this sterile and pertinacious nothing acquire its plural number?—*Unde quæso, hæc nihili in nihila tam portentosa transnihilatio?*—and lastly;—What is that inward mirror, in which these nothings have at least relative existence? The inevitable result of all consequent reasoning, in which the intellect refuses to acknowledge a higher or deeper ground than it can itself supply, and weens to possess within itself the centre of its own system, is—and from Zeno the Eleatic to Spinosa, and from Spinosa to the Schellings, Okens and their adherents, of the present day, ever has been—pantheism under one or other of its modes, the least repulsive of which differs from the rest, not in its consequences, which are one and the same in all, and in all alike are practically atheistic, but only as it may express the striving of the philosopher himself to hide these consequences from his own mind. This, therefore, I repeat, is the final conclusion. All speculative disquisition must begin with postulates, which the conscience alone can at once authorize and substantiate: and from whichever point the reason may start, from the things which are seen to the one invisible, or from the idea of the absolute one to the things that are seen, it will find a chasm, which the moral being only, which the spirit and religion of man alone, can fill up.

Thus I prefaced my inquiry into the science of method with a principle deeper than science, more certain than demonstration. For that the very ground, saith Aristotle, is groundless or self-grounded, is an identical proposition. From the indemonstrable flows the sap that circulates through every branch and spray of the demonstration. To this principle I referred the choice of the final object, the control over time, or, to comprise all in one, the method of the will. From this I started, or rather seemed to start; for it still moved before me, as an invisible guardian and guide, and it is this the re-appearance of which announces the conclusion of the circuit, and welcomes me at the goal. Yea (saith an enlightened physician), there is but one principle, which alone reconciles the man with himself, with others, and with the world; which regulates all relations, tempers all passions, gives power to overcome or support all suffering, and which is not to be shaken by aught earthly, for it belongs not to the earth; namely, the principle of religion, the living and substantial faith *which passeth all understanding*, as the cloud-piercing rock, which overhangs the stronghold of which it had been the quarry and remains the foundation. This elevation of the spirit above the semblances of custom and the senses to a world of spirit, this life in the idea, even in the supreme and godlike, which alone merits the name of life, and without which our organic life is but a state of somnambulism; this it is which affords the sole sure anchorage in the storm, and at the same time the substantiating principle of all true wisdom, the satisfactory solution of all the contradictions of human nature, of the whole riddle of the world.

This alone belongs to and speaks intelligibly to all alike, the learned and the ignorant, if but the heart listens. For alike present in all, it may be awakened, but it can not be given. But let it not be supposed, that it is a sort of knowledge : no ! it is a form of BEING, or indeed it is the only knowledge that truly *is*, and all other science is real only so far as it is symbolical of this. The material universe, saith a Greek philosopher, is but one vast complex *mythus*, that is, symbolical representation, and mythology the *apex* and complement of all genuine physiology. But as this principle can not be implanted by the discipline of logic, so neither can it be excited or evolved by the arts of rhetoric. For it is an immutable truth, that what comes from the heart, that alone goes to the heart; what proceeds from a divine impulse, that the godlike alone can awaken.

THE THIRD LANDING-PLACE:

OR

ESSAYS MISCELLANEOUS.

Etiam a Musis si quando animum paulisper abducamus, apud Musas nihilominus feriamur; at reclines quidem, at otiosas, at de his et illis inter se libere colloquentes.

THE THIRD LANDING-PLACE.

ESSAY I.

Fortuna plerumque est veluti gàlaxia quarundam obscurarum virtutum sine nomine. BACON.

Fortune is for the most part but a galaxy or milky-way, as it were, of certain obscure virtues without a name.

DOES fortune favor fools? Or how do you explain the origin of the proverb, which, differently worded, is to be found in all the languages of Europe?

This proverb admits of various explanations according to the mood of mind in which it is used. It may arise from pity, and the soothing persuasion that Providence is eminently watchful over the helpless, and extends an especial care to those who are not capable of caring for themselves. So used, it breathes the same feeling as 'God tempers the wind to the shorn lamb'—or the more sportive adage, that 'the fairies take care of children and tipsy folk.' The persuasion itself, in addition to the general religious feeling of mankind, and the scarcely less general love of the marvellous, may be accounted for from our tendency to exaggerate all effects that seem disproportionate to their visible cause and all circumstances that are in any way strongly contrasted with our notions of the persons under them. Secondly, it arises from the safety and success which an ignorance of danger and difficulty sometimes actually assists in procuring; inasmuch as it precludes the despondence, which might have kept the more foresighted from undertaking the enterprise, the depression which would retard its progress, and those overwhelming influences of terror in cases where the vivid perception of the danger constitutes the greater part of the danger itself. Thus men are said to have swooned and even died at the sight of a narrow bridge, over which they had ridden the night before in perfect safety; or at tracing their footmarks along the edge of a precipice which the darkness had concealed from them. A more obscure cause, yet not wholly to be omitted, is afforded by the undoubted fact, that the exertion of the reasoning faculties tends to extinguish or bedim those mysterious instincts of skill, which, though for the most part latent, we nevertheless possess in common with other animals.

Or the proverb may be used invidiously: and folly in the vocabulary of envy or baseness may signify courage and magnanimity. Hardihood and fool-hardiness are indeed as different as green and yellow, yet will appear the same to the jaundiced eye. Courage multiplies the chances of success by sometimes making opportunities, and always availing itself of them; and in this sense fortune may be said to favor fools by those, who, however prudent in their own opinion, are deficient in valor and enterprise. Again: an eminently good and wise man, for whom the praises of the judicious have procured a high reputation even with the world at large, proposes to himself certain objects, and adapting the right means to the right end attains them: but his objects not being what the world calls fortune, neither money nor artificial rank, his admitted inferiors in moral and intellectual worth, but more prosperous in their worldly concerns, are said to have been favored by fortune, and he slighted: although the fools did the same in their line as the wise man in his: they adapted the appropriate means to the desired end and so succeeded. In this sense the proverb is current by a misuse, or a *catachresis* at least, of both the words, fortune and fools.

But, lastly, there is, doubtless, a true meaning attached to fortune, distinct both from prudence and from courage; and distinct too from that absence of depressing or bewildering passions, which (according to my favorite proverb, 'extremes meet,') the fool not seldom obtains in as great perfection by his ignorance, as the wise man by the highest energies of thought and self-discipline. Luck has a real existence in human affairs from the infinite number of powers that are in action at the same time, and from the co-existence of things contingent and accidental (such as to us at least are accidental) with the regular appearances and general laws of nature. A familiar instance will make these words intelligible. The moon waxes and wanes according to a necessary law. The clouds likewise, and all the manifold appearances connected with them, are governed by certain laws no less than the phases of the moon. But the laws which determine the latter are known and calculable, while those of the former are hidden from us. At all events, the number and variety of their effects baffle our powers of calculation; and that the sky is clear or obscured at any particular time, we speak of, in common language, as a matter of accident. Well! at the time of the full moon, but when the sky is completely covered with black clouds, I am walking on in the dark, aware of no particular danger: a sudden gust of wind rends the cloud for a moment, and the moon emerging discloses to me a chasm or precipice, to the very brink of which I had advanced my foot. This is what is meant by luck, and according to the more or less serious mood or habit of our mind we exclaim, how lucky! or, how providential! The co-presence of numberless *phænomena*, which from the complexity or subtlety of their determining causes are called contingencies, and the co-existence of these with any regular or necessary *phænomenon* (as the clouds with the moon for instance) occasion coincidences, which, when they are attended by any advantage or injury, and are at the same time incapable of being calculated or foreseen by human prudence, form good or ill luck. On a hot sunshiny afternoon came on a sudden storm and spoilt the farmer's hay: and this is called ill luck. We will suppose the same event to take place, when meteorology shall have been perfected into a science, provided with unerring instruments; but which the farmer had neglected to examine. This is no longer ill luck, but imprudence. Now apply this to our proverb. Unforeseen coincidences may have greatly helped a man, yet if they have done for him only what possibly from his own abilities he might have effected for himself, his good luck will excite less attention and the instance be less remembered. That clever men should attain their objects seems natural, and we neglect the circumstances that perhaps produced that success of themselves without the intervention of skill or foresight; but we dwell on the fact and remember it as something strange, when the same happens to a weak or ignorant man. So too, though the latter should fail in his undertakings from concurrences that might have happened to the wisest man, yet his failure being no more than might have been expected and accounted for from his folly, it lays no hold on our attention, but fleets away among the other distinguished waves in which the stream of ordinary life murmurs by us, and is forgotten. Had it been as true as it was notoriously false, that those all-embracing discoveries, which have shed a dawn of science on the art of chemistry, and give no obscure promise of some one great constitutive law, in the light of which dwell dominion and the power of prophecy; if these discoveries, instead of having been as they really were, preconcerted by meditation, and evolved out of his own intellect, had occurred by a set of lucky accidents to the illustrious father and founder of philosophic alchemy: if they had presented themselves to Davy exclusively in consequence of his luck in possessing a particular galvanic battery; if this battery, as far as Davy was concerned, had itself been an accident, and not (as in point of fact it was) desired and obtained by him for the purpose of insuring the testimony of experience to his principles, and in order to bind down material nature under the inquisition of reason, and force from her, as by torture, unequivocal answers to prepared and preconceived questions;—yet still they would not have been talked of or described, as instances of luck, but as the natural results of his admitted genius and known skill. But should an accident have disclosed similar discoveries to a mechanic at Birmingham or Sheffield, and if the man should grow rich in consequence, and partly by the envy of his neighbors, and partly with good reason, be considered by them as a man below *par* in the general powers of his understanding; then, "O what a lucky fellow!—Well, Fortune does favor fools—that's certain!—It is always so!"—And forthwith the exclaimer relates half a dozen similar instances. Thus accumulating the one sort of facts and never collecting the other, we do, as poets in their diction, and quacks of all denominations do in their reasoning, put a part for the whole, and at once soothe our envy and gratify our love of the marvellous, by the sweeping proverb, 'Fortune favors fools.'

ESSAY II.

Quod me non movet æstimatione:
Verum est μνημόσυνον mei sodalis. CATULLUS.*

It interests me not by any conceit of its value; but it is a remembrance of my honored friend.

THE philosophic ruler, who secured the favors of fortune by seeking wisdom and knowledge in preference to them, has pathetically observed—The heart knoweth its own bitterness; and there is a joy in which the stranger intermeddleth not. A simple question founded on a trite proverb, with a discursive answer to it, would scarcely suggest to an indifferent person any other notion than that of a mind at ease, amusing itself with its own activity. Once before (I believe about this time last year) I had taken up the old memorandum-book, from which I transcribed the preceding essay, and it had then attracted my notice by the name of the illustrious chemist mentioned in the last illustration. Exasperated by the base and cowardly attempt which had been made to detract from the honors due to his astonishing genius, I had slightly altered the concluding sentences, substituting the more recent for his earlier discoveries; and without the most distant intention of publishing what I then wrote, I had expressed my own convictions for the gratification of my own feelings, and finished by tranquilly paraphrasing into a chemical allegory the Homeric adventure of Menelaus with Proteus. Oh! with what different feelings, with what a sharp and sudden emotion did I re-peruse the same question yester-morning, having by accident opened the book at the page upon which it was written. I was moved: for it was Admiral Sir Alexander Ball who first proposed the question to me, and the particular satisfaction which he expressed, had occasioned me to note down the substance of my reply. I was moved: because to this conversation I was indebted for the friendship and confidence with which he after-

* XII.—*Ed.*

wards honored me; and because it recalled the memory of one of the most delightful mornings I ever passed; when, as we were riding together, the same person related to me the principal events of his own life, and introduced them by adverting to this conversation. It recalled, too, the deep impression left on my mind by that narrative, the impression, that I had never known any analogous instance, in which a man so successful had been so little indebted to fortune, or lucky accidents, or so exclusively both the architect and builder of his own success. The sum of his history may be comprised in this one sentence: *Hæc, sub numine nobismet fecimus, sapientia duce, fortuna permittente.* (These things, under God, we have done for ourselves, through the guidance of wisdom, and with the permission of fortune.) Luck gave him nothing: in her most generous moods, she only worked with him as with a friend, not for him as for a fondling; but more often she simply stood neuter, and suffered him to work for himself. Ah! how could I be otherwise than affected by whatever reminded me of that daily and familiar intercourse with him, which made the fifteen months from May 1804, to October 1805, in many respects, the most memorable and instructive period of my life?—Ah! how could I be otherwise than most deeply affected, when there was still lying on my table the paper which, the day before, had conveyed to me the unexpected and most awful tidings of this man's death,—his death in the fulness of all his powers, in the rich autumn of ripe yet undecaying manhood? I once knew a lady, who after the loss of a lovely child continued for several days in a state of seeming indifference, the weather, at the same time, as if in unison with her, being calm, though gloomy; till one morning a burst of sunshine breaking in upon her, and suddenly lighting up the room where she was sitting, she dissolved at once into tears, and wept passionately. In no very dissimilar manner did the sudden gleam of recollection at the sight of this memorandum act on myself. I had been stunned by the intelligence, as by an outward blow, till this trifling incident startled and disentranced me; the sudden pang shivered through my whole frame; and if I repressed the outward shows of sorrow, it was by force that I repressed them, and because it is not by tears that I ought to mourn for the loss of Sir Alexander Ball.

He was a man above his age: but for that very reason the

age has the more need to have the master-features of his character portrayed and preserved. This I feel it my duty to attempt, and this alone: for having received neither instructions nor permission from the family of the deceased, I can not think myself allowed to enter into the particulars of his private history, strikingly as many of them would illustrate the elements and composition of his mind. For he was indeed a living confutation of the assertion attributed to the Prince of Condé, that no man appeared great to his *valet de chambre*—a saying which, I suspect, owes its currency less to its truth, than to the envy of mankind and the misapplication of the word, great, to actions unconnected with reason and free will. It will be sufficient for my purpose to observe that the purity and strict propriety of his conduct, which precluded rather than silenced calumny, the evenness of his temper and his attentive and affectionate manners, in private life, greatly aided and increased his public utility: and, if it should please Providence, that a portion of his spirit should descend with his mantle, the virtues of Sir Alexander Ball, as a master, a husband, and a parent, will form a no less remarkable epoch in the moral history of the Maltese than his wisdom, as a governor, has made in that of their outward circumstances. That the private and personal qualities of a first magistrate should have political effects, will appear strange to no reflecting Englishman, who has attended to the workings of men's minds during the first ferment of revolutionary principles, and must therefore have witnessed the influence of our own sovereign's domestic character in counteracting them. But in Malta there were circumstances which rendered such an example peculiarly requisite and beneficent. The very existence, for so many generations, of an order of lay celibates in that island, who abandoned even the outward shows of an adherence to their vow of chastity, must have had pernicious effects on the morals of the inhabitants. But when it is considered too that the knights of Malta had been for the last fifty years or more a set of useless idlers, generally illiterate,*—for they thought litera-

* The personal effects of every knight were, after his death, appropriated to the Order, and his books, if he had any, devolved to the public library. This library therefore, which has been accumulating from the time of their first settlement in the island, is a fair criterion of the nature and degree of their literary studies, as an average. Even in respect to

ture no part of a soldier's excellence; and yet effeminate,—for they were soldiers in name only: when it is considered, that they were, moreover, all of them aliens, who looked upon themselves not merely as of a superior rank to the native nobles, but as beings of a different race (I had almost said, species), from the Maltese collectively; and finally that these men possessed exclusively the government of the island; it may be safely concluded that they were little better than a perpetual influenza, relaxing and diseasing the hearts of all the families within their sphere of influence. Hence the peasantry, who fortunately were below their reach, notwithstanding the more than childish ignorance in which they were kept by their priests, yet compared with the middle and higher classes, were both in mind and body as ordinary men compared with dwarfs. Every respectable family had some one knight for their patron, as a matter of course; and to him the honor of a sister or a daughter was sacrificed, equally as a matter of course.* But why should I thus disguise the truth? Alas! in nine instances out of ten, this patron was the common paramour of every woman in the family. Were I composing a state-memorial, I should abstain from all allusion to moral good or evil, as not having now first to learn, that with diplomatists and with practical statesmen of every denomination, it would preclude all attention to its other contents, and have no result but that of securing for its author's name the official private mark of exclusion or dismission, as a weak or suspicious person. But among those for whom I am now writing, there are, I trust, many who will think it not the feeblest reason for rejoicing in our possession of Malta, and not the least worthy motive for wishing its retention, that one source of human misery and corruption has been dried up. Such persons will hear the name of Sir Alexander Ball with additional reverence, as of one who has made the protection of Great Britain a double blessing to the Maltese, and broken *the bonds of iniquity*, as well as unlocked the fetters of political oppression.

When we are praising the departed by our own fire-sides, we dwell most fondly on those qualities which had won our personal

works of military science, it is contemptible—as the sole public library of so numerous and opulent an order, most contemptible—and in all other departments of literature it is below contempt.

* See Table Talk, VI. p. 509.—*Ed.*

affection, and which sharpen our individual regrets. But when impelled by a loftier and more meditative sorrow, we would raise a public monument to their memory, we praise them appropriately when we relate their actions faithfully; and thus preserving their example for the imitation of the living, alleviate the loss, while we demonstrate its magnitude. My funeral eulogy of Sir Alexander Ball must therefore be a narrative of his life; and this friend of mankind will be defrauded of honor in proportion as that narrative is deficient and fragmentary. It shall, however, be as complete as my information enables, and as prudence and a proper respect for the feelings of the living permit, me to render it. His fame (I adopt the words of our elder writers) is so great throughout the world that he stands in no need of an encomium; and yet his worth is much greater than his fame. It is impossible not to speak great things of him, and yet it will be very difficult to speak what he deserves. But custom requires that something should be said; it is a duty and a debt which we owe to ourselves and to mankind, not less than to his memory; and I hope his great soul, if it hath any knowledge of what is done here below, will not be offended at the smallness even of my offering.

Ah! how little, when among the subjects of The Friend I promised "characters met with in real life," did I anticipate the sad event, which compels me to weave on a cypress branch those sprays of laurel which I had destined for his bust, not his monument! He lived as we should all live; and, I doubt not, left the world as we should all wish to leave it. Such is the power of dispensing blessings, which Providence has attached to the truly great and good, that they can not even die without advantage to their fellow-creatures; for death consecrates their example; and the wisdom, which might have been slighted at the council-table, becomes oracular from the shrine. Those rare excellencies, which make our grief poignant, make it likewise profitable; and the tears, which wise men shed for the departure of the wise, are among those that are preserved in heaven. It is the fervent aspiration of my spirit, that I may so perform the task which private gratitude, and public duty impose on me, that, "as God hath cut this tree of paradise down from its seat of earth, the dead trunk may yet support a part of the declining temple, or at least serve to kindle the fire on the altar."*

* Jer. Taylor.

ESSAY III.

Si partem tacuisse velim, quodcumque relinquam,
Majus erit. Veteres actus, primamque juventam
Prosequar? Ad sese mentem præsentia ducunt.
Narrem justitiam? Resplendet gloria Martis.
Armati referam vires? Plus egit inermis. CLAUDIAN.*

If I desire to pass over a part in silence, whatever I omit, will seem the most worthy to have been recorded. Shall I pursue his old exploits and early youth? His recent merits recall the mind to themselves. Shall I dwell on his justice? The glory of the warrior rises before me resplendent. Shall I relate his strength in arms? He performed yet greater things unarmed.

"THERE is something," says Harrington,† "first in the making of a commonwealth, then in the governing of it, and last of all in the leading of its armies, which, though there be great divines, great lawyers, great men in all ranks of life, seems to be peculiar only to the genius of a gentleman. For so it is in the universal series of story, that if any man has founded a commonwealth, he was first a gentleman." Such also, he adds, as have got any fame as civil governors, have been gentlemen, or persons of known descents. Sir Alexander Ball was a gentleman by birth; a younger brother of an old and respectable family in Gloucestershire. He went into the navy at an early age from his choice, and as he himself told me, in consequence of the deep impression and vivid images left on his mind by the perusal of Robinson Crusoe. It is not my intention to detail the steps of his promotion, or the services in which he was engaged as a subaltern. I recollect many particulars indeed, but not the dates, with such distinctness as would enable me to state them (as it would be necessary to do if I stated them at all) in the order of time. These dates might, perhaps, have been procured from other sources; but incidents that are neither characteristic nor instructive, even such as would

* De Laud. Stilic. i. 13.—*Ed.* † Preliminaries to Oceana, p. i.—*Ed.*

be expected with reason in a regular life, are no part of my plan; while those which are both interesting and illustrative I have been precluded from mentioning, some from motives which have been already explained, and others from still higher considerations. The most important of these may be deduced from a reflection with which he himself once concluded a long and affecting narration; namely, that no body of men can for any length of time be safely treated otherwise than as rational beings; and that, therefore, the education of the lower classes was of the utmost consequence to the permanent security of the empire, even for the sake of our navy. The dangers, apprehended from the education of the lower classes, arose (he said) entirely from its not being universal, and from the unusualness in the lowest classes of those accomplishments, which he, like Dr. Bell, regarded as one of the means of education, and not as education itself.* If, he observed, the lower classes in general possessed but one eye or one arm, the few who were so fortunate as to possess two would naturally become vain and restless, and consider themselves as entitled to a higher situation. He illustrated this by the faults attributed to learned women, and that the same objections were formerly made to educating women at all; namely, that their knowledge made them vain, affected, and neglectful of their proper duties. Now that all women of condition are well-educated, we hear no more of these apprehensions, or observe any instances to justify them. Yet if a lady understood the Greek one-tenth part as well as the whole circle of her acquaintances understood the French language, it would not surprise us to find her less pleasing from the consciousness of her superiority in the possession of an unusual advantage. Sir Alexander Ball quoted the speech of an old admiral, one of whose two great wishes was to have a ship's crew composed altogether of serious Scotchmen. He spoke with great reprobation of the vulgar notion, the worse man, the better sailor. Courage, he said, was the natural product of familiarity with danger, which thoughtlessness would oftentimes turn into foolhardiness; and that he had always found the most usefully brave

* Which consists in educing, or to adopt Dr. Bell's own expression, eliciting the faculties of the human mind, and at the same time subordinating them to the reason and conscience; varying the means of this common end according to the sphere and particular mode, in which the individual is likely to act and become useful.

sailors the gravest and most rational of his crew. The best sailor he had ever had, first attracted his notice by the anxiety which he expressed concerning the means of remitting some money which he had received in the West Indies to his sister in England; and this man, without any tinge of methodism, was never heard to swear an oath, and was remarkable for the firmness with which he devoted a part of every Sunday to the reading of his Bible. I record this with satisfaction as a testimony of great weight, and in all respects unexceptionable; for Sir Alexander Ball's opinions throughout life remained unwarped by zealotry, and were those of a mind seeking after truth in calmness and complete self-possession. He was much pleased with an unsuspicious testimony furnished by Dampier. "I have particularly observed," writes this famous old navigator,* "there and in other places, that such as had been well-bred, were generally most careful to improve their time, and would be very industrious and frugal where there was any probability of considerable gain; but on the contrary, such as had been bred up in ignorance and hard labor, when they came to have plenty would extravagantly squander away their time and money in drinking and making a bluster." Indeed, it is a melancholy proof, how strangely power warps the minds of ordinary men, that there can be a doubt on this subject among persons who have been themselves educated. It tempts a suspicion, that unknown to themselves they find a comfort in the thought that their inferiors are something less than men: or that they have an uneasy half-consciousness that, if this were not the case, they would themselves have no claim to be their superior. For a sober education naturally inspires self-respect. But he who respects himself will respect others; and he who respects both himself and others, must of necessity be a brave man. The great importance of this subject, and the increasing interest which good men of all denominations feel in the bringing about of a national education, must be my excuse for having entered so minutely into Sir Alexander Ball's opinions on this head, in which, however, I am the more excusable, being now on that part of his life which I am obliged to leave almost a blank.

During his lieutenancy, and after he had perfected himself in the knowledge and duties of a practical sailor, he was compelled by the state of his health to remain in England for a considerable

* Vol. II. P. ii. p. 89.—*Ed.*

length of time. Of this he industriously availed himself for the acquirement of substantial knowledge from books; and during his whole life afterwards, he considered those as his happiest hours, which, without any neglect of official or professional duty, he could devote to reading. He preferred, indeed he almost confined himself to, history, political economy, voyages and travels, natural history, and latterly agricultural works: in short, to such books as contain specific facts, or practical principles capable of specific application. His active life, and the particular objects of immediate utility, some one of which he had always in his view, precluded a taste for works of pure speculation and abstract science, though he highly honored those who were eminent in these respects, and considered them as the benefactors of mankind, no less than those who afterwards discovered the mode of applying their principles, or who realized them in practice. Works of amusement, as novels, plays, and the like did not appear even to amuse him; and the only poetical composition, of which I have ever heard him speak, was a manuscript* poem written by one of my friends, which I read to his lady in his presence. To my surprise he afterwards spoke of this with warm interest; but it was evident to me, that it was not so much the poetic merit of the composition that had interested him, as the truth and psychological insight with which it represented the practicability of reforming the most hardened minds, and the various accidents which may awaken the most brutalized person to a recognition of his nobler being. I will add one remark of his own knowledge acquired from books, which appears to me both just and valuable. The prejudice against such knowledge, he said, and the custom of opposing it to that which is learnt by practice, originated in those times when books were almost confined to theology and to logical and metaphysical subtleties; but that at present there is scarcely any practical knowledge, which is not to be found in books: the press is the means by which intelligent men now converse with each other, and persons of all classes and all pursuits convey, each the contribution of his individual experience. It was therefore, he said as absurd to hold book-knowledge at present in contempt, as it would be for a man to avail himself only of his own eyes and

* Though it remains, I believe, unpublished, I can not resist the temptation of recording that it was Mr. Wordsworth's Peter Bell. 1817.

ears, and to aim at nothing which could not be performed exclusively by his own arms. The use and necessity of personal experience consisted in the power of choosing and applying what had been read, and of discriminating by the light of analogy the practicable from the impracticable, and probability from mere plausibility. Without a judgment matured and steadied by actual experience, a man would read to little or perhaps to bad purpose; but yet that experience, which in exclusion of all other knowledge has been derived from one man's life, is in the present day scarcely worthy of the name—at least for those who are to act in the higher and wider spheres of duty. An ignorant general, he said, inspired him with terror; for if he were too proud to take advice he would ruin himself by his own blunders; and if he were not, by adopting the worst that was offered. A great genius may indeed form an exception; but we do not lay down rules in expectation of wonders. A similar remark I remember to have heard from an officer, who to eminence in professional science and the gallantry of a tried soldier, adds all the accomplishments of a sound scholar and the powers of a man of genius.

One incident, which happened at this period of Sir Alexander's life, is so illustrative of his character, and furnishes so strong a presumption that the thoughtful humanity by which he was distinguished was not wholly the growth of his latter years, that, though it may appear to some trifling in itself, I will insert it in this place, with the occasion on which it was communicated to me. In a large party at the Grand Master's palace, I had observed a naval officer of distinguished merit listening to Sir Alexander Ball, whenever he joined in the conversation, with so marked a pleasure, that it seemed as if his very voice, independently of what he said, had been delightful to him: and once as he fixed his eyes on Sir Alexander Ball, I could not but notice the mixed expression of awe and affection, which gave a more than common interest to so manly a countenance. During his stay in the island, this officer honored me not unfrequently with his visits; and at the conclusion of my last conversation with him, in which I had dwelt on the wisdom of the Governor's*

* Such Sir Alexander Ball was in reality, and such was his general appellation in the Mediterranean: I adopt this title, therefore, to avoid the ungraceful repetition of his own name on the one hand, and on the other the confusion which might arise from the use of his real title, namely, "His

conduct in a recent and difficult emergency, he told me that he considered himself as indebted to the same excellent person for that which was dearer to him than his life. "Sir Alexander Ball," said he, "has (I dare say) forgotten the circumstance; but when he was Lieutenant Ball, he was the officer whom I accompanied in my first boat-expedition, being then a midshipman and only in my fourteenth year. As we were rowing up to the vessel which we were to attack, amid a discharge of musketry, I was overpowered by fear, my knees trembled under me, and I seemed on the point of fainting away. Lieutenant Ball, who saw the condition I was in, placed himself close beside me, and still keeping his countenance directed toward the enemy, took hold of my hand, and pressing it in the most friendly manner, said in a low voice, 'Courage, my dear boy! don't be afraid of yourself! you will recover in a minute or so—I was just the same, when I first went out in this way.' Sir," added the officer to me, "it was as if an angel had put a new soul into me. With the feeling, that I was not yet dishonored, the whole burthen of agony was removed; and from that moment I was as fearless and forward as the oldest of the boat's crew, and on our return the lieutenant spoke highly of me to our captain. I am scarcely less convinced of my own being, than that I should have been what I tremble to think of, if, instead of his humane encouragement, he had at that moment scoffed, threatened, or reviled me. And this was the more kind in him, because, as I afterwards understood, his own conduct in his first trial had evinced to all appearances the greatest fearlessness, and that he said this therefore only to give me heart, and restore me to my own good opinion." This anecdote, I trust, will have some weight with those who may have lent an ear to any of those vague calumnies from which no naval commander can secure his good name, who, knowing the paramount necessity of regularity and strict discipline in a ship of war, adopts an appropriate plan

Majesty's civil Commissioner for the island of Malta and its Dependencies; and Minister Plenipotentiary to the Order of St. John." This is not the place to expose the timid and unsteady policy which continued the latter title, or the petty jealousies which interfered to prevent Sir Alexander Ball from having the title of Governor, from one of the very causes which rendered him fittest for the office.

(See *Table Talk*, VI. p. 507.—*Ed.*)

for the attainment of these objects, and remains constant and immutable in the execution. To an Athenian, who, in praising a public functionary, had said that every one either applauded him or left him without censure, a philosopher replied—"How seldom then must he have done his duty!"

Of Sir Alexander Ball's character, as Captain Ball, of his measures as a disciplinarian, and of the wise and dignified principle on which he grounded those measures, I have already spoken in a former part of this work,* and must content myself therefore with entreating the reader to re-peruse that passage as belonging to this place, and as a part of the present narration. Ah! little did I expect at the time I wrote that account, that the motives of delicacy, which then impelled me to withhold the name, would so soon be exchanged for the higher duty which now justifies me in adding it! At the thought of such events the language of a tender superstition is the voice of nature itself, and those facts alone presenting themselves to our memory which had left an impression on our hearts, we assent to and adopt the poet's pathetic complaint:

——— O, Sir! the good die first,
And those whose hearts are dry as summer dust,
Burn to the socket.†———

Thus that the humane plan described in the pages now referred to, a system in pursuance of which the captain of a man of war uniformly regarded his sentences not as dependent on his own will, or to be affected by the state of his feelings at the moment, but as the pre-established determinations of known laws, and himself as the voice of the law in pronouncing the sentence, and its delegate in enforcing the execution, could not but furnish occasional food to the spirit of detraction, must be evident to every reflecting mind. It is indeed little less than impossible, that he, who in order to be effectively humane determines to be inflexibly just, and who is inexorable to his own feelings when they would interrupt the course of justice; who looks at each particular act by the light of all its consequences, and as the representative of ultimate good or evil, should not sometimes be charged with tyranny by weak minds. And it is too certain that the calumny will be willingly believed and eagerly propa-

* Essay p. 157.—*Ed.*

† Excursion, B. I.—*Ed.*

gated by all those, who should shun the presence of an eye keen in the detection of imposture, incapacity, and misconduct, and of a resolution as steady in their exposure. We soon hate the man whose qualities we dread, and thus have a double interest, an interest of passion as well as of policy, in decrying and defaming him. But good men will rest satisfied with the promise made to them by the Divine Comforter, that by her children shall wisdom be justified.

ESSAY IV.

——— the generous spirit, who, when brought
Among the tasks of real life, hath wrought
Upon the plan that pleased his childish thought;
Whose high endeavors are an inward light
That make the path before him always bright;
Who doomed to go in company with pain,
And fear and bloodshed, miserable train!
Turns his necessity to glorious gain;
By objects, which might force the soul to abate
Her feeling, rendered more compassionate. WORDSWORTH.*

AT the close of the American war, Captain Ball was intrusted with the protection and convoying of an immense mercantile fleet to America, and by his great prudence and unexampled attention to the interests of all and each, he endeared his name to the American merchants, and laid the foundation of that high respect and predilection which both the Americans and their government ever afterwards entertained for him. My recollection does not enable me to attempt any accuracy in the date or circumstances, or to add the particulars, of his services in the West Indies and on the coast of America. I now therefore merely allude to the fact with a prospective reference to opinions and circumstances, which I shall have to mention hereafter. Shortly after the general peace was established, Captain Ball, who was now a married man, passed some time with his lady in France, and, if I mistake not, at Nantes. At the same time, and in the

* The Christian Warrior.—*Ed.*

same town, among the other English visitors, Lord (then Captain) Nelson happened to be one. In consequence of some punctilio, as to whose business it was to pay the compliment of the first call, they never met, and this trifling affair occasioned a coldness between the two naval commanders, or in truth a mutual prejudice against each other. Some years after, both their ships being together close off Minorca and near Port Mahon, a violent storm nearly disabled Nelson's vessel, and in addition to the fury of the wind, it was night-time and the thickest darkness. Captain Ball, however, brought his vessel at length to Nelson's assistance, took his ship in tow, and used his best endeavors to bring her and his own vessel into Port Mahon. The difficulties and the dangers increased. Nelson considered the case of his own ship as desperate, and that unless she was immediately left to her own fate, both vessels would inevitably be lost. He, therefore, with the generosity natural to him, repeatedly requested Captain Ball to let him loose; and on Ball's refusal he became impetuous, and enforced his demand with passionate threats. Ball then himself took the speaking-trumpet, which the fury of the wind and waves rendered necessary, and with great solemnity and without the least disturbance of temper, called out in reply, "I feel confident that I can bring you in safe; I therefore must not, and, by the help of Almighty God! I will not leave you!" What he promised he performed; and after they were safely anchored, Nelson came on board of Ball's ship, and embracing him with all the ardor of acknowledgment, exclaimed—"a friend in need is a friend indeed!" At this time and on this occasion commenced that firm and perfect friendship between these two great men, which was interrupted only by the death of the former. The pleasing task of dwelling on this mutual attachment I defer to that part of the present sketch which will relate to Sir Alexander Ball's opinions of men and things. It will be sufficient for the present to say, that the two men, whom Lord Nelson especially honored, were Sir Thomas Troubridge and Sir Alexander Ball; and once, when they were both present, on some allusion made to the loss of his arm, he replied, "Who shall dare tell me that I want an arm, when I have three right arms—this (putting forward his own left one) and Ball and Troubridge?"

In the plan of the battle of the Nile it was Lord Nelson's design, that Captains Troubridge and Ball should have led up the attack. The former was stranded; and the latter, by accident of the wind, could not bring his ship into the line of battle till some time after the engagement had become general. With his characteristic forecast and activity of (what may not improperly be called) practical imagination, he had made arrangements to meet every probable contingency. All the shrouds and sails of the ship, not absolutely necessary for its immediate management, were thoroughly wetted and so rolled up, that they were as hard and as little inflammable as so many solid cylinders of wood; every sailor had his appropriate place and function, and a certain number were appointed as the firemen, whose sole duty it was to be on the watch if any part of the vessel should take fire: and to these men exclusively the charge of extinguishing it was committed. It was already dark when he brought his ship into action, and laid her along-side the French *L'Orient*. One particular only I shall add to the known account of the memorable engagement between these ships, and this I received from Sir Alexander Ball himself. He had previously made a combustible preparation, but which, from the nature of the engagement to be expected, he had purposed to reserve for the last emergency. But just at the time when, from several symptoms, he had every reason to believe that the enemy would soon strike to him, one of the lieutenants, without his knowledge, threw in the combustible matter; and this it was that occasioned the tremendous explosion of that vessel, which, with the deep silence and interruption of the engagement which succeeded to it, has been justly deemed the sublimest war incident recorded in history. Yet the incident which followed, and which has not, I believe, been publicly made known, is scarcely less impressive, though its sublimity is of a different character. At the renewal of the battle, Captain Ball, though his ship was then on fire in three different parts, laid her along-side a French eighty-four; and a second, longer obstinate contest began. The firing on the part of the French ship having at length for some time slackened, and then altogether ceased, and yet no sign given of surrender, the first lieutenant came to Captain Ball and informed him that the hearts of his men were as good as ever, but that they were so completely exhausted, that they were scarcely capable of lifting an arm. He asked, therefore, whether, as the enemy had now ceased firing, the men might be permitted to lie down by their guns for a short time. After some reflection, Sir Alexander acceded to the proposal, taking of course the proper precautions to rouse them again at the moment he thought requisite. Accordingly, with the exception of himself, his officers, and the appointed watch, the ship's crew lay down, each in the place to which he was stationed, and slept for twenty minutes. They were then roused; and started up, as Sir Alexander expressed it, more like men out of an ambush than from sleep, so co-instantaneously did they all obey the summons! They recommenced their fire, and in a few minutes the enemy surrendered; and it was soon after discovered, that during that interval, and almost immediately after the French ship had first ceased firing, the crew had sunk down by their guns, and there slept, almost by the side, as it were, of their sleeping enemy.

ESSAY V.

Whose powers shed round him in the common strife
Or mild concerns of ordinary life
A constant influence, a peculiar grace;
But who if he be called upon to face
Some awful moment, to which heaven has join'd
Great issues, good or bad for human kind,
Is happy as a lover, is attired
With sudden brightness like a man inspired;
And through the heat of conflict keeps the law
In calmness made, and sees what he foresaw.

WORDSWORTH.*

AN accessibility to the sentiments of others on subjects of importance often accompanies feeble minds, yet it is not the less a true and constituent part of practical greatness, when it exists wholly free from that passiveness to impression which renders counsel itself injurious to certain characters, and from that weakness of heart which, in the literal sense of the word, is always craving advice. Exempt from all such imperfections, say rather in perfect harmony with the excellencies that preclude them, this openness to the influxes of good sense and information, from

* The Christian Warrior.—*Ed.*

whatever quarter they might come, equally characterized Lord Nelson and Sir Alexander Ball, though each displayed it in the way best suited to his natural temper. The former with easy hand collected, as it passed by him, whatever could add to his own stores, appropriated what he could assimilate, and levied subsidies of knowledge from all the accidents of social life and familiar intercourse. Even at the jovial board, and in the height of unrestrained merriment, a casual suggestion, that flashed a new light on his mind, changed the boon-companion into the hero and the man of genius; and with the most graceful transition he would make his company as serious as himself. When the taper of his genius seemed extinguished, it was still surrounded by an inflammable atmosphere of its own, and rekindled at the first approach of light, and not seldom at a distance which made it seem to flame up self-revived. In Sir Alexander Ball, the same excellence was more an affair of system: and he would listen even to weak men, with a patience, which, in so careful an economist of time, always demanded my admiration, and not seldom excited my wonder. It was one of his maxims, that a man may suggest what he can not give: adding, that a wild or silly plan had more than once, from the vivid sense and distinct perception of its folly, occasioned him to see what ought to be done in a new light, or with a clearer insight. There is, indeed, a hopeless sterility, a mere negation of sense and thought, which, suggesting neither difference nor contrast, can not even furnish hints for recollection. But on the other hand, there are minds so whimsically constituted, that they may sometimes be profitably interpreted by contraries, a process of which the great Tycho Brahe is said to have availed himself in the case of the little lackwit, who used to sit and mutter at his feet while he was studying. A mind of this sort we may compare to a magnetic needle, the poles of which had been suddenly reversed by a flash of lightning, or other more obscure accident of nature. It may be safely concluded, that to those whose judgment or information he respected, Sir Alexander Ball did not content himself with giving access and attention. No! he seldom failed of consulting them whenever the subject permitted any disclosure; and where secrecy was necessary, he well knew how to acquire their opinion without exciting even a conjecture concerning his immediate object.

Yet, with all this readiness of attention, and with all this zeal in collecting the sentiments of the well-informed, never was a man more completely uninfluenced by authority than Sir Alexander Ball, never one who sought less to tranquillize his own doubts by the mere suffrage and coincidence of others. The ablest suggestions had no conclusive weight with him, till he had abstracted the opinion from its author, till he had reduced it into a part of his own mind. The thoughts of others were always acceptable, as affording him at least a chance of adding to his materials for reflection; but they never directed his judgment, much less superseded it. He even made a point of guarding against additional confidence in the suggestions of his own mind, from finding that a person of talents had formed the same conviction, unless the person, at the same time, furnished some new argument, or had arrived at the same conclusion by a different road. On the latter circumstance he set an especial value and, I may almost say, courted the company and conversation of those, whose pursuits had least resembled his own, if he thought them men of clear and comprehensive faculties. During the period of our intimacy, scarcely a week passed, in which he did not desire me to think on some particular subject, and to give him the result in writing. Most frequently by the time I had fulfilled his request, he would have written down his own thoughts, and then, with the true simplicity of a great mind, as free from ostentation as it was above jealousy, he would collate the two papers in my presence, and never expressed more pleasure than in the few instances, in which I had happened to light on all the arguments and points of view which had occurred to himself, with some additional reasons which had escaped him. A single new argument delighted him more than the most perfect coincidence, unless, as before stated, the train of thought had been very different from his own, and yet just and logical. He had one quality of mind, which I have heard attributed to the late Mr. Fox, that of deriving a keen pleasure from clear and powerful reasoning for its own sake, a quality in the intellect which is nearly connected with veracity and a love of justice in the moral character.*

* It may not be amiss to add, that the pleasure from the perception of truth was so well poised and regulated by the equal or greater delight in utility, that his love of real accuracy was accompanied with a proportionate dislike of that hollow appearance of it, which may be produced by turns of phrase, words placed in balanced antithesis, and those epigrammatic points

Valuing in others merits which he himself possessed, Sir Alexander Ball felt no jealous apprehension of great talent. Unlike those vulgar functionaries, whose place is too big for them, a truth which they attempt to disguise from themselves, and yet feel, he was under no necessity of arming himself against the natural superiority of genius by factitious contempt and an industrious association of extravagance and impracticability with every deviation from the ordinary routine; as the geographers in the middle ages used to designate, on their meagre maps, the greater part of the world, as deserts or wildernesses inhabited by griffins and chimæras. Competent to weigh each system or project by its own arguments, he did not need these preventive charms and cautionary amulets against delusion. He endeavored to make talent instrumental to his purposes in whatever shape it appeared, and with whatever imperfections it might be accompanied; but wherever talent was blended with moral worth, he sought it out, loved and cherished it. If it had pleased Providence to preserve his life, and to place him on the same course on which Nelson ran his race of glory, there are two points in which Sir Alexander Ball would most closely have resembled his illustrious friend. The first is, that in his enterprises and engagements he would have thought nothing done, till all had been done that was possible:

Nil actum reputans, si quid superesset agendum.

The second, that he would have called forth all the talent and virtue that existed within his sphere of influence, and created a band of heroes, a gradation of officers, strong in head and strong in heart, worthy to have been his companions and his successors in fame and public usefulness.

Never was greater discernment shown in the selection of a fit

that pass for subtle and luminous distinctions with ordinary readers, but are most commonly translatable into mere truisms or trivialities, if indeed they contain any meaning at all. Having observed in some casual conversation, that though there were doubtless masses of matter unorganized, I saw no ground for asserting a mass of unorganized matter; Sir A. B. paused, and then said to me, with that frankness of manner which made his very rebukes gratifying, "The distinction is just, and, now I understand you, abundantly obvious; but hardly worth the trouble of your inventing a puzzle of words to make it appear otherwise." I trust the rebuke was not lost on me.

agent, than when Sir Alexander Ball was stationed off the coast of Malta to intercept the supplies destined for the French garrison, and to watch the movements of the French commanders, and those of the inhabitants who had been so basely betrayed into their power. Encouraged by the well-timed promises of the English captain, the Maltese rose through all their casals (or country towns) and themselves commenced the work of their emancipation, by storming the citadel at Città Vecchia, the ancient metropolis of Malta, and the central height of the island. Without discipline, without a military leader, and almost without arms, these brave peasants succeeded, and destroyed the French garrison by throwing them over the battlements into the trench of the citadel. In the course of this blockade, and of the tedious siege of Valetta, Sir Alexander Ball displayed all that strength of character, that variety and versatility of talent, and that sagacity, derived in part from habitual circumspection, but which, when the occasion demanded it, appeared intuitive and like an instinct; at the union of which, in the same man, one of our oldest naval commanders once told me, "he could never exhaust his wonder." The citizens of Valetta were fond of relating their astonishment, and that of the French, at Captain Ball's ship wintering at anchor out of the reach of the guns, in a depth of fathom unexampled, on the assured impracticability of which the garrison had rested their main hope of regular supplies. Nor can I forget, or remember, without some portion of my original feeling, the solemn enthusiasm with which a venerable old man, belonging to one of the distant casals, showed me the sea coomb, where their father Ball (for so they commonly called him), first landed; and afterwards pointed out the very place, on which he first stepped on their island, while the countenances of his town's-men, who accompanied him, gave lively proofs that the old man's enthusiasm was the representative of the common feeling.

There is no reason to suppose, that Sir Alexander Ball was at any time chargeable with that weakness so frequent in Englishmen, and so injurious to our interests abroad, of despising the inhabitants of other countries, of losing all their good qualities in their vices, of making no allowance for those vices, from their religious or political impediments, and still more of mistaking for vices a mere difference of manners and customs. But if ever he had any of this erroneous feeling, he completely freed himself from it by living among the Maltese during their arduous trials, as long as the French continued masters of the capital. He witnessed their virtues, and learned to understand in what various shapes and even disguises the valuable parts of human nature may exist. In many individuals, whose littleness and meanness in the common intercourse of life would have stamped them at once as contemptible and worthless with ordinary Englishmen, he had found such virtues of disinterested patriotism, fortitude, and self-denial, as would have done honor to an ancient Roman.

There exists in England a gentlemanly character, a gentlemanly feeling, very different even from that which is the most like it, the character of a well-born Spaniard, and unexampled in the rest of Europe. This feeling probably originated in the fortunate circumstance, that the titles of our English nobility follow the law of their property, and are inherited by the eldest sons only. From this source, under the influences of our constitution and of our astonishing trade, it has diffused itself in different modifications through the whole country. The uniformity of our dress among all classes above that of the day-laborer, while it has authorized all classes to assume the appearance of a gentleman, has at the same time inspired the wish to conform their manners, and still more their ordinary actions in social intercourse, to their notions of the gentlemanly, the most commonly received attribute of which character is a certain generosity in trifles. On the other hand, the encroachments of the lower classes on the higher, occasioned and favored by this resemblance in exteriors, by this absence of any cognizable marks of distinction, have rendered each class more reserved and jealous in their general communion, and far more than our climate, or natural temper, have caused that haughtiness and reserve in our outward demeanor, which is so generally complained of among foreigners. Far be it from me to depreciate the value of this gentlemanly feeling ; I respect it in all its forms and varieties, from the House of Commons to the gentlemen in the one shilling gallery. It is always the ornament of virtue, and oftentimes a support ; but it is a wretched substitute for it. Its worth, as a moral good, is by no means in proportion to its value, as a social advantage. These observations are not irrelevant : for to the want of reflection, that this diffusion of gentlemanly feeling among us is not the growth of our moral excellence, but the effect of various accidental advantages peculiar to England; to our not considering that it is unreasonable and uncharitable to expect the same consequences, where the same causes have not existed to produce them; and, lastly, to our proneness to regard the absence of this character (which, as I have before said, does, for the greater part, and, in the common apprehension, consist in a certain frankness and generosity in the detail of action) as decisive against the sum total of personal or national worth; we must, I am convinced, attribute a large portion of that conduct, which in many instances has left the inhabitants of countries conquered or appropriated by Great Britain, doubtful whether the various solid advantages which they derived from our protection and just government were not bought dearly by the wounds inflicted on their feelings and prejudices, by the contemptuous and insolent demeanor of the English as individuals. The reader who bears this remark in mind, will meet, in the course of this narrative, more than one passage that will serve as its comment and illustration.

It was, I know, a general opinion among the English in the Mediterranean, that Sir Alexander Ball thought too well of the Maltese, and did not share in the enthusiasm of Britons concerning their own superiority. To the former part of the charge, I shall only reply at present, that a more venial and almost desirable fault could scarcely be attributed to a governor, than that of a strong attachment to the people whom he was sent to govern The latter part of the charge is false, if we are to understand by it, that he did not think his countrymen superior on the whole to the other nations of Europe; but it is true, as far as relates to his belief, that the English thought themselves still better than they are; that they dwelt on, and exaggerated their national virtues, and weighed them by the opposite vices of foreigners, instead of the virtues which those foreigners possessed, and they themselves wanted. Above all, as statesmen, we must consider qualities by their practical uses. Thus he entertained no doubt that the English were superior to all others in the kind and the degree of their courage, which is marked by far greater enthusiasm than the courage of the Germans and northern nations, and by a far greater steadiness and self-subsistency than that of the French. It is more closely connected with the character of the individual. The courage of an English army (he used to say) is the sum total of the courage which the individual soldiers bring with them to it, rather than of that which they derive from it. This remark of Sir Alexander's was forcibly recalled to my mind when I was at Naples. A Russian and an English regiment were drawn up together in the same square :—" See," said a Neapolitan to me, who had mistaken me for one of his countrymen, " there is but one face in that whole regiment, while in that" (pointing to the English) " every soldier has a face of his own." On the other hand, there are qualities scarcely less requisite to the completion of the military character, in which Sir A. did not hesitate to think the English inferior to the continental nations ; as for instance, both in the power and the disposition to endure privations ; in the friendly temper necessary, when troops of different nations are to act in concert ; in their obedience to the regulations of their commanding officers, respecting the treatment of the inhabitants of the countries through which they are marching, as well as in many other points, not immediately connected with their conduct in the field ; and, above all, in sobriety and temperance. During the siege of Valetta, especially during the sore distress to which the besiegers were for some time exposed from the failure of provision, Sir Alexander Ball had an ample opportunity of observing and weighing the separate merits and demerits of the native and of the English troops ; and surely since the publication of Sir John Moore's campaign, there can be no just offence taken, though I should say, that before the walls of Valetta, as well as in the plains of Galicia, an indignant commander might, with too great propriety, have addressed the English soldiery in the words of an old dramatist—

> Will you still owe your virtues to your bellies?
> And only then think nobly when y'are full?
> Doth fodder keep you honest? Are you bad
> When out of flesh? And think you't an excuse
> Of vile and ignominious actions, that
> Y'are lean and out of liking?*

From the first insurrectionary movement to the final departure of the French from the island, though the civil and military powers and the whole of the island, save Valetta, were in the hands of the peasantry, not a single act of excess can be charged against the Maltese, if we except the razing of one house at

* Cartwright, Love's Convert, act i. sc. 1.

Città Vecchia belonging to a notorious and abandoned traitor, the creature and hireling of the French. In no instance did they injure, insult, or plunder, any one of the native nobility, or employ even the appearance of force toward them, except in the collection of the lead and iron from their houses and gardens, in order to supply themselves with bullets: and this very appearance was assumed from the generous wish to shelter the nobles from the resentment of the French, should the patriotic efforts of the peasantry prove unsuccessful. At the dire command of famine the Maltese troops did indeed once force their way to the ovens, in which the bread for the British soldiery was baked, and were clamorous that an equal division should be made. I mention this unpleasant circumstance, because it brought into proof the firmness of Sir Alexander Ball's character, his presence of mind, and generous disregard of danger and personal responsibility, where the slavery or emancipation, the misery or the happiness, of an innocent and patriotic people were involved; and because his conduct in this exigency evinced that his general habits of circumspection and deliberation were the results of wisdom and complete self-possession, and not the easy virtues of a spirit constitutionally timorous and hesitating. He was sitting at a table with the principal British officers, when a certain general addressed him in strong and violent terms concerning this outrage of the Maltese, reminding him of the necessity of exerting his commanding influence in the present case, or the consequences must be taken. "What," replied Sir Alexander Ball, "would you have us do? Would you have us threaten death to men dying with famine? Can you suppose that the hazard of being shot will weigh with whole regiments acting under a common necessity? Does not the extremity of hunger take away all difference between men and animals? and is it not as absurd to appeal to the prudence of a body of men starving, as to a herd of famished wolves? No, general, I will not degrade myself or outrage humanity by menacing famine with massacre! More effectual means must be taken." With these words he rose and left the room, and having first consulted with Sir Thomas Troubridge, he determined at his own risk on a step, which the extreme necessity warranted, and which the conduct of the Neapolitan court amply justified. For this court, though terror-striken by the French, was still actuated by hatred to the English and a jealousy of their power in the Mediterranean; and this in so strange and senseless a manner, that we must join the extremes of imbecility and treachery in the same cabinet, in order to find it comprehensible.* Though the very existence of Naples and Sicily, as a nation, depended wholly and exclusively on British support; though the royal family owed their personal safety to the British fleet; though not only their dominions and their rank, but the liberty and even the lives of Ferdinand and his family, were interwoven with our success: yet with an infatuation scarcely credible, the most affecting representations of the distress of the besiegers, and of the utter insecurity of Sicily if the French remained possessors of Malta, were treated with neglect; and urgent remonstrances for the permission of importing corn from Messina were answered only by sanguinary edicts precluding all supply. Sir Alexander Ball sent for his first lieutenant, and gave him orders to proceed immediately to the port of Messina, and there to seize and bring with him to Malta the ships laden with corn, of the number of which Sir Alexander had received accurate information. These orders were executed without delay, to the great delight and profit of the ship owners and proprietors; the necessity of raising the siege was removed; and the author of the measure waited in calmness for the consequences that might result to himself personally. But not a complaint, not a murmur, proceeded from the court of Naples. The sole result was, that the governor of Malta became an especial object of its hatred, its fear, and its respect.

The whole of this tedious siege, from its commencement to the

* It can not be doubted, that the sovereign himself was kept in a state of delusion. Both his understanding and his moral principles are far better than could reasonably be expected from the infamous mode of his education: if indeed the systematic preclusion of all knowlndge, and the unrestrained indulgence of his passions, adopted by the Spanish court for the purposes of preserving him dependent, can be called by the name of education. Of the other influencing persons in the Neapolitan government, Mr. Leckie has given us a true and lively account. It will be greatly to the advantage of the present narrative, if the reader should have previously perused Mr. Leckie's pamphlet on the state of Sicily: the facts which I shall have occasion to mention hereafter will reciprocally confirm and be confirmed by the documents furnished in that most interesting work; in which I see but one blemish of importance, namely, that the author appears too frequently to consider justice and true policy as capable of being contradistinguished.

signing of the capitulation, called forth into constant activity the rarest and most difficult virtues of a commanding mind; virtues of no show or splendor in the vulgar apprehension, yet more infallible characteristics of true greatness than the most unequivocal displays of enterprise and active daring. Scarcely a day passed, in which Sir Alexander Ball's patience, forbearance, and inflexible constancy, were not put to the severest trial. He had not only to remove the misunderstandings that arose between the Maltese and their allies, to settle the differences among the Maltese themselves, and to organize their efforts: he was likewise engaged in the more difficult and unthankful task of counteracting the weariness, discontent, and despondency, of his own countrymen;—a task, however, which he accomplished by management and address, and an alternation of real firmness with apparent yielding. During many months he remained the only Englishman who did not think the siege hopeless, and the object worthless. He often spoke of the time in which he resided at the country seat of the grand master at St. Antonio, four miles from Valetta, as perhaps the most trying period of his life. For some weeks Captain Vivian was his sole English companion, of whom, as his partner in anxiety, he always expressed himself with affectionate esteem. Sir Alexander Ball's presence was absolutely necessary to the Maltese, who, accustomed to be governed by him, became incapable of acting in concert without his immediate influence. In the outburst of popular emotion, the impulse, which produces an insurrection, is for a brief while its sufficient pilot; the attraction constitutes the cohesion, and the common provocation, supplying an immediate object, not only unites, but directs, the multitude. But this first impulse had passed away, and Sir Alexander Ball was the one individual who possessed the general confidence. On him they relied with implicit faith: and even after they had long enjoyed the blessings of British government and protection, it was still remarkable with what childlike helplessness they were in the habit of applying to him, even in their private concerns. It seemed as if they thought him made on purpose to think for them all. Yet his situation at St. Antonio was one of great peril: and he attributed his preservation to the dejection, which had now begun to prey on the spirits of the French garrison, and which rendered them unenterprising and almost passive, aided by the dread which the nature of the country inspired. For subdivided as it was into small fields, scarcely larger than a cottage-garden, and each of these little squares of land inclosed with substantial stone walls; these too from the necessity of having the fields perfectly level, rising in tiers above each other; the whole of the inhabited part of the island was an effective fortification for all the purposes of annoyance and offensive warfare. Sir Alexander Ball exerted himself successfully in procuring information respecting the state and temper of the garrison, and by the assistance of the clergy and the almost universal fidelity of the Maltese, contrived that the spies in the pay of the French should be in truth his own most confidential agents. He had already given splendid proofs that he could outfight them; but here, and in his after diplomatic intercourse previously to the recommencement of the war, he likewise out-witted them. He once told me with a smile, as we were conversing on the practice of laying wagers, that he was sometimes inclined to think that the final perseverance in the siege was not a little due to several valuable bets of his own, he well knowing at the time, and from information which himself alone possessed, that he should certainly lose them. Yet this artifice had a considerable effect in suspending the impatience of the officers, and in supplying topics for dispute and conversation. At length, however, the two French frigates, the sailing of which had been the subject of these wagers, left the great harbor on the 24th of August, 1800, with a part of the garrison; and one of them soon became a prize to the English. Sir Alexander Ball related to me the circumstances which occasioned the escape of the other; but I do not recollect them with sufficient accuracy to dare repeat them in this place. On the 15th of September following, the capitulation was signed, and after a blockade of two years the English obtained possession of Valetta, and remained masters of the whole island and its dependencies.

Anxious not to give offence, but more anxious to communicate the truth, it is not without pain that I find myself under the moral obligation of remonstrating against the silence concerning Sir Alexander Ball's services or the transfer of them to others. More than once has the latter roused my indignation in the reported speeches of the House of Commons; and as to the former, I need only state that in Rees's Encyclopædia there is an historical article of considerable length under the word Malta, in which

Sir Alexander's name does not once occur! During a residence of eighteen months in that island, I possessed and availed myself of the best possible means of information, not only from eye-witnesses, but likewise from the principal agents themselves. And I now thus publicly and unequivocally assert, that to Sir A. Ball pre-eminently—and if I had said, to Sir A. Ball alone, the ordinary use of the word under such circumstances would bear me out—the capture and the preservation of Malta were owing, with every blessing that a powerful mind and a wise heart could confer on its docile and grateful inhabitants. With a similar pain I proceed to avow my sentiments on this capitulation, by which Malta was delivered up to his Britannic Majesty and his allies, without the least mention made of the Maltese. With a warmth honorable both to his head and his heart, Sir Alexander Ball pleaded, as not less a point of sound policy than of plain justice, that the Maltese, by some representative, should be made a party in the capitulation, and a joint subscriber in the signature. They had never been the slaves or the property of the Knights of St. John, but freemen and the true landed proprietors of the country, the civil and military government of which, under certain restrictions, had been vested in that order, yet checked by the rights and influences of the clergy and the native nobility, and by the customs and ancient laws of the island. This trust the Knights had, with the blackest treason and the most profligate perjury, betrayed and abandoned. The right of government of course reverted to the landed proprietors and the clergy. Animated by a just sense of this right, the Maltese had risen of their own accord, had contended for it in defiance of death and danger, had fought bravely, and endured patiently. Without undervaluing the military assistance afterwards furnished by Great Britain (though how scanty this was before the arrival of General Pigot is well known), it remained undeniable, that the Maltese had taken the greatest share both in the fatigues and in the privations consequent on the siege; and that had not the greatest virtues and the most exemplary fidelity been uniformly displayed by them, the English troops (they not being more numerous than they had been for the greater part of the two years) could not possibly have remained before the fortifications of Valetta, defended as that city was by a French garrison which greatly outnumbered the British besiegers. Still less could there have been the least hope of ultimate success; as if any part of the Maltese peasantry had been friendly to the French, or even indifferent, if they had not all indeed been most zealous and persevering in their hostility towards them, it would have been impracticable so to blockade that island as to have precluded the arrival of supplies. If the siege had proved unsuccessful, the Maltese were well aware that they should be exposed to all the horrors which revenge and wounded pride could dictate to an unprincipled, rapacious, and sanguinary soldiery; and now that success had crowned their efforts, was this to be their reward, that their own allies were to bargain for them with the French as for a herd of slaves, whom the French had before purchased from a former proprietor? If it be urged, reasoned Sir A. B., that there is no established government in Malta, is it not equally true that through the whole population of the island there is not a single dissentient;—and thus that the chief inconvenience, which an established authority is to obviate, is virtually removed by the admitted fact of their unanimity? And have they not a bishop and a dignified clergy, their judges and municipal magistrates, who were at all times sharers in the power of the government, and now, supported by the unanimous suffrage of the inhabitants, have a rightful claim to be considered as its representatives? Will it not be oftener said than answered, that the main difference between French and English injustice rests in this point alone, that the French seized on the Maltese without any previous pretences of friendship, while the English procured possession of the island by means of their friendly promises, and by the co-operation of the natives afforded in confident reliance on these promises? The impolicy of refusing the signature on the part of the Maltese was equally evident; since such refusal could answer no one purpose but that of alienating their affections by a wanton insult to their feelings. For the Maltese were not only ready but desirous and eager to place themselves at the same time under British protection, to take the oath of loyalty as subjects of the British crown, and to acknowledge their island to belong to it. These representations, however, were overruled: and I dare affirm, from my own experience in the Mediterranean, that our conduct in this instance aggravated the impression which had been made at Corsica, Minorca, and elsewhere, and was often referred to by men of reflection in Sicily, who have more than once said to me, "a connection with Great Britain, with the consequent extension and security of our commerce, are indeed great blessings: but who can rely on their permanence; or that we shall not be made to pay bitterly for our zeal as partisans of England, whenever it shall suit its plans to deliver us back to our old oppressors?"

ESSAY VI.

The way of ancient ordnance, though it winds,
Is yet no devious way. Straight forward goes
The lightning's path; and straight the fearful path
Of the cannon-ball. Direct it flies and rapid,
Shattering that it may reach, and shattering what it reaches
My son! the road the human being travels,
That, on which blessing comes and goes, doth follow
The river's course, the valley's playful windings,
Curves round the corn-field and the hill of vines,
Honoring the holy bounds of property!
——————————There exists
A higher than the warrior's excellence. WALLENSTEIN.*

CAPTAIN BALL'S services in Malta were honored with his sovereign's approbation, transmitted in a letter from the secretary Dundas, and with a baronetcy. A thousand pounds† were at

* Part I. act 1. sc. 4.—*Ed.*

† I scarce know whether it be worth mentioning, that this sum remained undemanded till the spring of the year 1805: at which time, during an examination of the treasury accounts, I observed the circumstance and noticed it to the governor, who had suffered it to escape altogether from his memory, for the latter years at least. The value attached to the present by the receiver, must have depended on his construction of its purpose and meaning: for, in a pecuniary point of view, the sum was not a moiety of what Sir Alexander had expended from his private fortune during the blockade. His immediate appointment to the government of the island, so earnestly prayed for by the Maltese, would doubtless have furnished a less questionable proof that his services were as highly estimated by the ministry as they were graciously accepted by his sovereign. But this was withholden as long as it remained possible to doubt, whether great talents, joined to local experience, and the confidence and affection of the inhabi-

the same time directed to be paid him from the Maltese treasury. The best and most appropriate addition to the applause of his king and his country, Sir Alexander Ball found in the feelings and faithful affection of the Maltese. The enthusiasm manifested in reverential gestures and shouts of triumph whenever their friend and deliverer appeared in public, was the utterance of a deep feeling, and in nowise the mere ebullition of animal sensibility; which is not indeed a part of the Maltese character. The truth of this observation will not be doubted by any person, who has witnessed the religious processions in honor of the favorite saints, both at Valetta and at Messina or Palermo, and who must have been struck with the contrast between the apparent apathy, or at least the perfect sobriety, of the Maltese, and the fanatical agitations of the Sicilian populace. Among the latter, each man's soul seems hardly containable in his body, like a prisoner, whose jail is on fire, flying madly from one barred outlet to another; while the former might suggest the suspicion, that their bodies were on the point of sinking into the same slumber with their understandings. But their political deliverance was a thing that came home to their hearts, and intertwined itself with their most impassioned recollections, personal and patriotic. To Sir Alexander Ball exclusively the Maltese themselves attributed their emancipation: on him too they rested their hopes of the future. Whenever he appeared in Valetta, the passengers on each side, through the whole length of the street, stopped, and remained uncovered till he had passed: the very clamors of the market-place were hushed at his entrance, and then exchanged for shouts of joy and welcome. Even after the lapse of years he never appeared in any of their casals,* which did not lie in the direct road between Valetta and St. Antonio, his summer residence, but the women and children, with

tants, might not be dispensed with in the person intrusted with that government. *Crimen ingrati animi quod magnis ingeniis haud raro objicitur sæpius nil aliud est quam perspicacia quædam in causam beneficii collati.*

* It was the governor's custom to visit every casal throughout the island once, if not twice, in the course of each summer; and during my residence there, I had the honor of being his constant, and most often his only companion, in these rides; to which I owe some of the happiest and most instructive hours of my life. In the poorest house of the most distant casal two rude paintings were sure to be found: a picture of the Virgin and Child; and a portrait of Sir Alexander Ball.

such of the men who were not at labor in their fields, fell into ranks, and followed or preceded him, singing the Maltese song which had been made in his honor, and which was scarcely less familiar to the inhabitants of Malta and Gozo, than God save the King to Britons. *When he went to the gate through the city, the young men refrained talking; and the aged arose and stood up. When the ear heard, then it blessed him; and when the eye saw him, it gave witness to him; because he delivered the poor that cried, and the fatherless, and those that had none to help them. The blessing of them that were ready to perish came upon him; and he caused the widow's heart to sing for joy.*

These feelings were afterwards amply justified by his administration of the government; and the very excesses of their gratitude on their first deliverance proved, in the end, only to be acknowledgments antedated. For some time after the departure of the French, the distress was so general and so severe, that a large portion of the lower classes became mendicants, and one of the greatest thoroughfares of Valetta still retains the name of "*Nix Mangiare Stairs*," from the crowd who used there to assail the ears of the passengers with the cries of "*nix mangiare*," or "nothing to eat," the former word *nix* being the low German pronunciation of *nichts*, nothing. By what means it was introduced into Malta, I know not; but it became the common vehicle both of solicitation and refusal, the Maltese thinking it an English word, and the English supposing it to be Maltese. I often felt it as a pleasing remembrancer of the evil day gone by, when a tribe of little children, quite naked, as is the custom of that climate, and each with a pair of gold ear-rings in its ears, and all fat and beautifully proportioned, would suddenly leave their play, and, looking round to see that their parents were not in sight, change their shouts of merriment for "*nix mangiare!*" awkwardly imitating the plaintive tones of mendicancy; while the white teeth in their little swarthy faces gave a splendor to the happy and confessing laugh, with which they received the good-humored rebuke or refusal, and ran back to their former sport.

In the interim between the capitulation of the French garrison and Sir Alexander Ball's appointment as his Majesty's civil commissioner for Malta, his zeal for the Maltese was neither suspended, nor unproductive of important benefits. He was enabled to remove many prejudices and misunderstandings; and to persons of no inconsiderable influence gave juster notions of the true importance of the island to Great Britain. He displayed the magnitude of the trade of the Mediterranean in its existing state; showed the immense extent to which it might be carried, and the hollowness of the opinion, that this trade was attached to the south of France by any natural or indissoluble bond of connection. I have some reason likewise for believing, that his wise and patriotic representations prevented Malta from being made the seat of, and pretext for, a numerous civil establishment, in hapless imitation of Corsica, Ceylon, and the Cape of Good Hope. It was at least generally rumored, that it had been in the contemplation of the ministry to appoint Sir Ralph Abercrombie as governor, with a salary of £10,000 a year, and to reside in England, while one of his countrymen was to be the lieutenant-governor, at £5,000 a year; to which were to be added a long *et cetera* of other offices and places of proportional emolument. This threatened appendix to the state calendar may have existed only in the imagination of the reporters, yet inspired some uneasy apprehensions in the minds of many well-wishers to the Maltese, who knew that—for a foreign settlement at least, and one too possessing in all the ranks and functions of society an ample population of its own—such a stately and wide-branching tree of patronage, though delightful to the individuals who are to pluck its golden apples, sheds, like the manchineel, unwholesome and corrosive dews on the multitude who are to rest beneath its shade. It need not, however, be doubted, that Sir Alexander Ball would exert himself to preclude any such intention, by stating and evincing the extreme impolicy and injustice of the plan, as well as its utter inutility, in the case of Malta. With the exception of the governor and of the public secretary, both of whom undoubtedly should be natives of Great Britain, and appointed by the British government, there was no civil office that could be of the remotest advantage to the island which was not already filled by the natives, and the functions of which none could perform so well as they. The number of inhabitants (he would state) was prodigious compared with the extent of the island, though from the fear of the Moors one fourth of its surface remained unpeopled and uncultivated. To deprive, therefore, the middle and lower classes of such places as they had been accustomed to hold, would be cruel; while the places holden by the nobility were, for the greater part, such as none but natives could perform the duties of. By any innovation we should affront the higher classes and alienate the affections of all, not only without any imaginable advantage but with the certainty of great loss. Were Englishmen to be employed, the salaries must be increased four-fold, and would yet be scarcely worth acceptance; and in higher offices, such as those of the civil and criminal judges, the salaries must be augmented more than ten-fold. For, greatly to the credit of their patriotism and moral character, the Maltese gentry sought these places as honorable distinctions, which endeared them to their fellow-countrymen, and at the same time rendered the yoke of the order somewhat less grievous and galling. With the exception of the Maltese secretary, whose situation was one of incessant labor, and who at the same time performed the duties of law counsellor to the government, the highest salaries scarcely exceeded £100 a year, and were barely sufficient to defray the increased expenses of the functionaries for an additional equipage, or one of more imposing appearance. Besides, it was of importance that the person placed at the head of that government should be looked up to by the natives, and possess the means of distinguishing and rewarding those who had been most faithful and zealous in their attachment to Great Britain, and hostile to their former tyrants. The number of the employments to be conferred would give considerable influence to his Majesty's civil representative, while the trifling amount of the emolument attached to each precluded all temptation of abusing it.

Sir Alexander Ball would likewise, it is probable, urge, that the commercial advantages of Malta, which were most intelligible to the English public, and best fitted to render our retention of the island popular, must necessarily be of very slow growth, though finally they would become great, and of an extent not to be calculated. For this reason, therefore, it was highly desirable that the possession should be, and appear to be, at least inexpensive. After the British Government had made one advance for a stock of corn sufficient to place the island a year before hand, the sum total drawn from Great Britain need not exceed 25, or at most £30,000 annually; excluding of course the expenditure connected with our own military and navy, and the repair of the fortifications, which latter expense ought to be much less than at Gibraltar, from the multitude and low wages of the laborers in Malta, and from the softness and admirable quality of the stone. Indeed much more might safely be promised on the assumption that a wise and generous system of policy would be adopted and persevered in. The monopoly of the Maltese corn-trade by the government formed an exception to a general rule, and by a strange, yet valid, anomaly in the operations of political economy, was not more necessary than advantageous to the inhabitants. The chief reason is, that the produce of the island itself barely suffices for one fourth of its inhabitants, although fruits and vegetables form so large a part of their nourishment. Meantime the harbors of Malta, and its equi-distance from Europe, Asia, and Africa, gave it a vast and unnatural importance in the present relations of the great European powers, and imposed on its government, whether native or dependent, the necessity of considering the whole island as a single garrison, the provisioning of which could not be trusted to the casualties of ordinary commerce. What is actually necessary is seldom injurious. Thus in Malta bread is better and cheaper on an average than in Italy or the coast of Barbary: while a similar interference with the corn-trade in Sicily impoverishes the inhabitants and keeps the agriculture in a state of barbarism. But the point in question is the expense to Great Britain. Whether the monopoly be good or evil in itself, it remains true, that in this established usage, and in the gradual inclosure of the uncultivated district, such resources exist as without the least oppression might render the civil government in Valetta independent of the Treasury at home, finally taking upon itself even the repair of the fortifications, and thus realize one instance of an important possession that costs the country nothing.

But now the time arrived, which threatened to frustrate the patriotism of the Maltese themselves and all the zealous efforts of their disinterested friend. Soon after the war had for the first time become indisputably just and necessary, the people at large, and a majority of independent senators, incapable, as it might seem, of translating their fanatical anti-Jacobinism into a well-grounded, yet equally impassioned, anti-Gallicanism, grew impatient for peace, or rather for a name, under which the most terrific of all wars would be incessantly waged against us. Our conduct was not much wiser than that of the weary traveller, who having proceeded half-way on his journey, procured a short rest for himself by getting up behind a chaise which was going the contrary road. In the strange treaty of Amiens, in which we neither recognized our former relations with France, nor with the other European powers, nor formed any new ones, the compromise concerning Malta formed the prominent feature: and its nominal re-delivery to the Order of St. John was authorized in the minds of the people by Lord Nelson's opinion of its worthlessness to Great Britain in a political or naval view. It is a melancholy fact, and one that must often sadden a reflective and philanthropic mind, how little moral considerations weigh even with the noblest nations, how vain are the strongest appeals to justice, humanity, and national honor unless when the public mind is under the immediate influence of the cheerful or vehement passions, indignation or avaricious hope. In the whole class of human infirmities there is none, that makes such loud appeals to prudence, and yet so frequently outrages its plainest dictates, as the spirit of fear. The worst cause conducted in hope is an overmatch for the noblest managed by despondence: in both cases an unnatural conjunction that recalls the old fable of Love and Death, taking each the arrows of the other by mistake. When islands that had courted British protection in reliance upon British honor, are with their inhabitants and proprietors abandoned to the resentment which we had tempted them to provoke, what wonder, if the opinion becomes general, that alike to England as to France, the fates and fortunes of other nations are but the counters, with which the bloody game of war is played: and that notwithstanding the great and acknowledged difference between the two governments during possession, yet the protection of France is more desirable because it is more likely to endure? for what the French take, they keep. Often both in Sicily and Malta have I heard the case of Minorca referred to, where a considerable portion of the most respectable gentry and merchants (no provision having been made for their protection on the re-delivery of that island to Spain) expiated in dungeons the warmth and forwardness of their predilection for Great Britain.

It has been by some persons imagined that Lord Nelson was considerably influenced, in his public declaration concerning the value of Malta, by ministerial flattery, and his own sense of the great serviceableness of that opinion to the persons in office. This supposition is, however, wholly false and groundless. His lordship's opinion was indeed greatly shaken afterwards, if not changed; but at that time he spoke in strictest correspondence with his existing convictions. He said no more than he had often previously declared to his private friends: it was the point on which, after some amicable controversy, his lordship and Sir Alexander Ball had "agreed to differ." Though the opinion itself may have lost the greatest part of its interest, and except for the historian is, as it were, superannuated; yet the grounds and causes of it, as far as they arose out of Lord Nelson's particular character, and may perhaps tend to re-enliven our recollection of a hero so deeply and justly beloved, will forever possess an interest of their own. In an essay, too, which purports to be no more than a series of sketches and fragments, the reader, it is hoped, will readily excuse an occasional digression, and a more desultory style of narration than could be tolerated in a work of regular biography.

Lord Nelson was an admiral every inch of him. He looked at everything, not merely in its possible relations to the naval service in general, but in its immediate bearings on his own squadron; to his officers, his men, to the particular ships themselves his affections were as strong and ardent as those of a lover. Hence though his temper was constitutionally irritable and uneven, yet never was a commander so enthusiastically loved by men of all ranks from the captain of the fleet to the youngest ship-boy. Hence too the unexampled harmony which reigned in his fleet year after year, under circumstances that might well have undermined the patience of the best balanced dispositions, much more of men with the impetuous character of British sailors. Year after year, the same dull duties of a wearisome blockade and of doubtful policy; little if any opportunity of making prizes; and the few prizes, which accident might throw in the way, of little or no value; and when at last the occasion presented itself which would have compensated for all, then a disappointment as sudden and unexpected as it was unjust and cruel, and the cup dashed from their lips!—Add to these trials the sense of enterprises checked by feebleness and timidity elsewhere, not omitting the tiresomeness of the Mediterranean sea, sky, and climate ; and the unjarring and cheerful spirit of affectionate brotherhood, which linked together the hearts of that whole squadron, will appear not less wonderful to us than admirable and affecting. When the resolution was taken of commencing hostilities against Spain, before any intelligence was sent to Lord Nelson, another admiral, with two or three ships of the line, was sent into the Mediterranean, and stationed before Cadiz, for the express purpose of intercepting the Spanish prizes. The admiral despatched on this lucrative service gave no information to Lord Nelson of his arrival in the same sea, and five weeks elapsed before his lordship became acquainted with the circumstance. The prizes thus taken were immense. A month or two sufficed to enrich the commander and officers of this small and highly-favored squadron : while to Nelson and his fleet the sense of having done their duty, and the consciousness of the glorious services which they had performed were considered, it must be presumed, as an abundant remuneration for all their toils and long-suffering ! It was indeed an unexampled circumstance, that a small squadron should be sent to the station which had been long occupied by a large fleet, commanded by the darling of the navy, and the glory of the British empire, to the station where this fleet had for years been wearing away in the most barren, repulsive, and spirit-trying service, in which the navy can be employed ; and that this minor squadron should be sent independently of, and without any communication with, the commander of the former fleet, for the express and solitary purpose of stepping between it and the Spanish prizes, and as soon as this short and pleasant service was performed, of bringing home the unshared booty with all possible caution and despatch. The substantial advantages of naval service were perhaps deemed of too gross a nature for men already rewarded with the grateful affections of their own countrymen, and the admiration of the whole world. They were to be awarded, therefore, on a principle of compensation to a commander less rich in fame, and whose laurels, though not scanty, were not yet sufficiently luxuriant to hide the golden crown which is the appropriate ornament of victory in the bloodless war of commercial capture. Of all the wounds which were ever inflicted on Nelson's feelings (and there were not a few), this was the deepest—this rankled most. "I had thought," (said the gallant man, in a letter written in the first sense of the affront)

"I fancied—but nay, it must have been a dream, an idle dream—yet I confess it, I did fancy, that I had done my country service; and thus they use me. It was not enough to have robbed me once before of my West-Indian harvest; now they have taken away the Spanish; and under what circumstances, and with what pointed aggravations! Yet, if I know my own thoughts, it is not for myself, or on my own account chiefly, that I feel the sting and the disappointment. No! it is for my brave officers; for my noble-minded friends and comrades—such a gallant set of fellows! such a band of brothers! My heart swells at the thought of them!"——

This strong attachment of the heroic admiral to his fleet, faithfully repaid by an equal attachment on their part to their admiral, had no little influence in attuning their hearts to each other; and when he died it seemed as if no man was a stranger to another: for all were made acquaintances by the rights of a common anguish. In the fleet itself, many a private quarrel was forgotten, no more to be remembered; many, who had been alienated, became once more good friends; yea, many a one was reconciled to his very enemy, and loved, and (as it were) thanked him, for the bitterness of his grief, as if it had been an act of consolation to himself in an intercourse of private sympathy. The tidings arrived at Naples on the day that I returned to that city from Calabria: and never can I forget the sorrow and consternation that lay on every countenance. Even to this day there are times when I seem to see, as in a vision, separate groups and individual faces of the picture. Numbers stopped and shook hands with me, because they had seen the tears on my cheek, and conjectured that I was an Englishman; and several, as they held my hand, burst themselves into tears. And though it may excite a smile, yet it pleased and affected me, as a proof of the goodness of the human heart struggling to exercise its kindness in spite of prejudices the most obstinate, and eager to carry on its love and honor into the life beyond life, that it was whispered about Naples that Lord Nelson had become a good Catholic before his death. The absurdity of the fiction is a sort of measurement of the fond and affectionate esteem which had ripened the pious wish of some kind individual, through all the gradations of possibility and probability, into a confident assertion believed and affirmed by hundreds. The feelings of Great Britain on this awful event have been described well and worthily by a living poet, who has happily blended the passion and wild transitions of lyric song with the swell and solemnity of epic narration :

——Thou art fall'n ; fall'n, in the lap
Of victory. To thy country thou cam'st back,
Thou, conqueror, to triumphal Albion cam'st
A corse ! I saw before thy hearse pass on
The comrades of thy perils and renown.
The frequent tear upon their dauntless breasts
Fell. I beheld the pomp thick gather'd round
The trophied car that bore thy grac'd remains
Thro' arm'd ranks, and a nation gazing on.
Bright glow'd the sun and not a cloud distain'd
Heaven's arch of gold, but all was gloom beneath.
A holy and unutterable pang
Thrill'd on the soul. Awe and mute anguish fell
On all.—Yet high the public bosom throbb'd
With triumph. And if one, 'mid that vast pomp,
If but the voice of one had shouted forth
The name of Nelson,—thou hadst pass'd along,
Thou in thy hearse to burial pass'd, as oft
Before the van of battle, proudly rode
Thy prow, down Britain's line, shout after shout
Rending the air with triumph, ere thy hand
Had lanc'd the bolt of victory.*

I introduced this digression with an apology, yet have extended it so much further than I had designed, that I must once more request my reader to excuse me. It was to be expected (I have said) that Lord Nelson would appreciate the isle of Malta from its relations to the British fleet on the Mediterranean station. It was the fashion of the day to style Egypt the key of India, and Malta the key of Egypt. Nelson saw the hollowness of this metaphor ; or if he only doubted its applicability in the former instance, he was sure that it was false in the latter. Egypt might or might not be the key of India ; but Malta was certainly not the key of Egypt. It was not intended to keep constantly two distinct fleets in that sea ; and the largest naval force at Malta would not supersede the necessity of a squadron off Toulon. Malta does not lie in the direct course from Toulon to Alexandria : and from the nature of the winds (one time taken with another) the comparative length of the voyage to the latter port will be found far

* Sotheby's Saul.—*Ed.*

less than a view of the map would suggest, and in truth of little practical importance. If it were the object of the French fleet to avoid Malta in its passage to Egypt, the port-admiral of Valetta would in all probability receive his first intelligence of its course from Minorca or the squadron off Toulon, instead of communicating it. In what regarded the re-fitting and provisioning of the fleet, either on ordinary or extraordinary occasions, Malta was as inconvenient as Minorca was advantageous, not only from its distance (which yet was sufficient to render it almost useless in cases of the most pressing necessity, as after a severe action or injuries of tempest) but likewise from the extreme difficulty, if not impracticability, of leaving the harbor of Valetta with a N. W. wind, which often lasts for weeks together. In all these points his lordship's observations were perfectly just; and it must be conceded by all persons acquainted with the situation and circumstances of Malta, that its importance, as a British possession, if not exaggerated on the whole, was unduly magnified in several important particulars. Thus Lord Minto, in a speech delivered at a country meeting and afterwards published, affirmed, that upon the supposition (which no one could consider as unlikely to take place) that the court of Naples should be compelled to act under the influence of France, and that the Barbary powers were unfriendly to us, either in consequence of French intrigues or from their own caprice and insolence, there would not be a single port, harbor, bay, creek, or road-stead in the whole Mediterranean, from which our men of war could obtain a single ox or a hogshead of fresh water,—unless Great Britain retained possession of Malta. The noble speaker seems not to have been aware, that under the circumstances supposed by him, Odessa too being closed against us by a Russian war, the island of Malta itself would be no better than a vast almshouse of 75,000 persons, exclusively of the British soldiers, all of whom must be regularly supplied with corn and salt meat from Great Britain or Ireland. The population of Malta and Gozo exceeds 100,000; while the food of all kinds produced on the two islands would barely suffice for one-fourth of that number. The deficiency is supplied by the growth and spinning of cotton, for which corn could not be substituted from the nature of the soil, or were it attempted, would produce but a small proportion of the quantity which the cotton raised on the same fields and spun* into thread, enables the Maltese to purchase;—not to mention that the substitution of grain for cotton would leave half of the inhabitants without employment. As to live stock, it is quite out of the question, if we except the pigs and goats, which perform the office of scavengers in the streets of Valetta and the towns on the other side of the Porto Grande.

Against these latter arguments Sir A. Ball placed the following considerations. It had been long his conviction, that the Mediterranean squadron should be supplied by regular store-ships, the sole business of which should be that of carriers for the fleet. This he recommended as by far the most economic plan, in the first instance. Secondly, beyond any other it would secure a system and regularity in the arrival of supplies. And, lastly, it would conduce to the discipline of the navy, and prevent both ships and officers from being out of the way on any sudden emergence. If this system were introduced, the objections to Malta, from its great distance, and the like, would have little force. On the other hand, the objections to Minorca he deemed irremovable. The same disadvantages which attended the getting out of the harbor of Valetta, applied to vessels getting into Port Mahon; but while fifteen hundred or two thousand British troops might be safely intrusted with the preservation of Malta, the troops for the defence of Minorca must ever be in proportion to those which the enemy may be supposed likely to send against it. It is so little favored by nature or by art, that the possessors stand merely on the level with the invaders. *Cæteris paribus*, if there were 12,000 of the enemy landed, there must be an equal number to repel them; nor could the garrison, or any part of it be spared for any sudden emergence without risk of losing the

* The Maltese cotton is naturally of a deep buff, or dusky orange color, and, by the laws of the island, must be spun before it can be exported. I have heard it asserted by persons apparently well informed on the subject, that the raw material would fetch as high a price as the thread, weight for weight; the thread from its coarseness being applicable to few purposes. It is manufactured likewise for the use of the natives themselves into a coarse nankin, which never loses its color by washing and is durable beyond any clothing I have ever known or heard of. The cotton seed is used as a food for the cattle that are not immediately wanted for the market: it is very nutritious, but changes the fat of the animal into a kind of suet, congealing quickly, and of an adhesive substance.

island. Previously to the battle of Marengo, the most earnest representations were made to the governor and commander at Minorca by the British admiral, who offered to take on himself the whole responsibility of the measure, if he would permit the troops at Minorca to join our allies. The governor felt himself compelled to refuse his assent. Doubtless, he acted wisely, for responsibility is not transferable. The fact is introduced in proof of the defenceless state of Minorca, and its constant liability to attack. If the Austrian army had stood in the same relation to eight or nine thousand British soldiers at Malta, a single regiment would have precluded all alarms, as to the island itself, and the remainder have perhaps changed the destiny of Europe. What might not, almost I would say, what must not eight thousand Britons have accomplished at the battle of Marengo, nicely poised as the fortunes of the two armies are now known to have been? Minorca too is alone useful or desirable during a war, and on the supposition of a fleet off Toulon. The advantages of Malta are permanent and national. As a second Gibraltar, it must tend to secure Gibraltar itself; for if by the loss of that one place we could be excluded from the Mediterranean, it is difficult to say what sacrifices of blood and treasure the enemy would deem too high a price for its conquest. Whatever Malta may or may not be respecting Egypt, its high importance to the independence of Sicily can not be doubted, or its advantages, as a central station, for any portion of our disposable force. Neither is the influence which it will enable us to exert on the Barbary powers to be wholly neglected. I shall only add, that during the plague at Gibraltar, Lord Nelson himself acknowledged that he began to see the possession of Malta in a different light.

Sir Alexander Ball looked forward to future contingencies as likely to increase the value of Malta to Great Britain. He foresaw that the whole of Italy would become a French province, and he knew that the French government had been long intriguing on the coast of Barbary. The Dey of Algiers was believed to have accumulated a treasure of fifteen millions sterling, and Bonaparte had actually duped him into a treaty, by which the French were to be permitted to erect a fort on the very spot where the ancient Hippo stood, the choice between which and the Hellespont as the site of New Rome is said to have perplexed the judgment of Constantine. To this he added an additional point of connection with Russia, by means of Odessa, and on the supposition of a war in the Baltic, a still more interesting relation to Turkey, and the Morea, and the Greek islands.—It had been repeatedly signified to the British government, that from the Morea and the countries adjacent, a considerable supply of ship timber and naval stores might be obtained, such as would at least greatly lessen the pressure of a Russian war. The agents of France were in full activity in the Morea and the Greek islands, the possession of which by that government would augment the naval resources of the French to a degree of which few are aware, who have not made the present state of commerce of the Greeks an object of particular attention. In short, if the possession of Malta were advantageous to England solely as a convenient watch-tower, as a centre of intelligence, its importance would be undeniable.

Although these suggestions did not prevent the signing away of Malta at the peace of Amiens, they doubtless were not without effect, when the ambition of Bonaparte had given a full and final answer to the grand question : can we remain in peace with France ? I have likewise reason to believe, that Sir Alexander Ball baffled by exposure an insidious proposal of the French government, during the negotiations that preceded the recommencement of the war—that the fortifications of Malta should be entirely dismantled, and the island left to its inhabitants. Without dwelling on the obvious inhumanity and flagitious injustice of exposing the Maltese to certain pillage and slavery from their old and inveterate enemies the Moors, he showed that the plan would promote the interests of Bonaparte even more than his actual possession of the island, which France had no possible interest in desiring, except as the means of keeping it out of the hands of Great Britain.

But Sir Alexander Ball is no more. I still cling to the hope that I may yet be enabled to record his good deeds more fully and regularly ; that then, with a sense of comfort not without a subdued exultation, I may raise heaven-ward from his honored tomb the glistening eye of a humble but ever grateful friend.

APPENDIX.

APPENDIX.

A.

PROSPECTUS OF THE FRIEND, (EXTRACTED FROM A LETTER TO A CORRESPONDENT.)

It is not unknown to you, that I have employed almost the whole of my life in acquiring, or endeavoring to acquire, useful knowledge by study, reflection, observation, and by cultivating the society of my superiors in intellect, both at home and in foreign countries. You know, too, that at different periods of my life I have not only planned, but collected the materials for, many works on various and important subjects; so many indeed, that the number of my unrealized schemes and the mass of my miscellaneous fragments have often furnished my friends with a subject of raillery, and sometimes of regret and reproof. Waiving the mention of all private and accidental hinderances, I am inclined to believe that this want of perseverance has been produced in the main by an over-activity of thought, modified by a constitutional indolence, which made it more pleasant to me to continue acquiring, than to reduce what I had acquired to a regular form. Add, too, that almost daily throwing off my notices or reflections in desultory fragments, I was still tempted onward by an increasing sense of the imperfection of my knowledge, and by the conviction that, in order fully to comprehend and develop any one subject, it was necessary that I should make myself master of some other, which again as regularly involved a third, and so on with an ever-widening horizon. Yet one habit, formed during long absences from those with whom I could converse with full sympathy, has been of advantage to me;—that of daily noting down in my memorandum or common-place books both incidents and observations;—whatever had occurred to me from without, and all the flux and reflux of my mind within itself. The number of these notices and their tendency, miscellaneous as they were, to one common end—(*quid sumus et quid futuri gignimur*, what we are and what we are born to become; and thus from the end of our being to deduce its proper objects)—first encouraged me to undertake the weekly essay, of which you will consider this letter as the *prospectus*.

Not only did the plan seem to accord better than any other with the nature of my own mind, both in its strength and in its weakness; but, conscious that in upholding some principles both of taste and philosophy, adopted by the great men of Europe, from the middle of the fifteenth till toward the close of the seventeenth century, I must run counter to many prejudices of many of my readers (for old faith is often modern heresy), I perceived too in a periodical essay the most likely means of winning instead of forcing my way. The truth supposed on my side, the shock of the first day might be so far lessened by the reflections of succeeding days, as to procure for my next week's essay a less hostile reception than it would have met with had it been only the next chapter of a present volume. I hoped to disarm the mind of those feelings, which preclude conviction by contempt, and, as it were, fling the door in the face of reasoning by a presumption of its absurdity. A motive too for honorable ambition was supplied by the fact, that every periodical paper of the kind now attempted, which had been conducted with zeal and ability, was not only well received at the time, but has become permanently, and in the best sense of the word, popular. By honorable ambition I mean the strong desire to be useful, aided by the wish to be generally acknowledged to have been so. As I feel myself actuated in no ordinary degree by this desire, so the hope of realizing it appears less and less presumptuous to me since I have received from men of highest rank and established character in the republic of letters, not only strong encouragements as to my own fitness for the undertaking, but likewise promises of support from their own stores.

The object of The Friend, briefly and generally expressed, is—to uphold those truths and those merits, which are founded in the nobler and permanent parts of our nature, against the caprices of fashion and such pleasures as either depend on transitory and accidental causes, or are pursued from less worthy impulses. The chief subjects of my own essays will be:

The true and sole ground of morality or virtue, as distinguished from prudence:

The origin and growth of moral impulses, as distinguished from external and immediate motives:

The necessary dependence of taste on moral impulses and habits, and the nature of taste (relative to judgment in general and to genius) defined, illustrated, and applied. Under this head I comprise the substance of the Lectures given, and intended to have been given, at the Royal Institution on the distinguished English poets, in illustration of the general principles of poetry; together with suggestions concerning the affinity of the fine arts to each other, and the principles common to them all;—architecture; gardening; dress; music; painting; poetry:

The opening out of new objects of just admiration in our own language, and information as to the present state and past history of Swedish, Danish, German, and Italian literature,—to which, but as supplied by a friend, I may add the Spanish, Portuguese, and French —as far as the same has not been already given to English readers, or is not to be found in common French authors:

Characters met with in real life;—anecdotes and results of my own life and travels, as far as they are illustrative of general moral laws, and have no direct bearing on personal or immediate politics:

Education in its widest sense, private and national:

Sources of consolation to the afflicted in misfortune, or disease, or dejection of mind, from the exertion and right application of the reason, the imagination, and the moral sense; and new sources of enjoyment opened out, or an attempt (as an illustrious friend once expressed the thought to me) to add sunshine to daylight, by making the happy more happy. In the words "Dejection of mind" I refer particularly to doubt or disbelief of the moral government of the world, and the grounds and arguments for the religious hopes of human nature.

Such are the chief subjects in the development of which I hope to realize, to a certain extent, the great object of my essays. It will assuredly be my endeavor, by as much variety as is consistent with that object, to procure entertainment for my readers as well as instruction: yet I feel myself compelled to hazard the confession, that such of my readers as make the latter the paramount motive for their encouragement of The Friend, will receive the largest portion of the former. I have heard it said of a young lady,—"if you are told, before you see her, that she is handsome, you will think her ordinary; if that she is ordinary, you will think her handsome." I may perhaps apply this remark to my own essays. If instruction and the increase of honorable motives and virtuous impulses be chiefly expected, there will, I would fain hope, be felt no deficiency of amusement; but I must submit to be thought dull by those who seek amusement only. The Friend will be distinguished from its celebrated predecessors, the Spectator and the like, as to its plan, chiefly by the greater length of the separate essays, by their closer connection with each other, and by the predominance of one object, and the common bearing of all to one end.

It would be superfluous to state, that I shall receive with gratitude any communications addressed to me: but it may be proper to say, that all remarks and criticisms in praise or dispraise of my contemporaries (to which, however, nothing but a strong sense of moral interest will ever lead me) will be written by myself only; both because I can not have the same certainty concerning the motives of others, and because I deem it fit, that such strictures should always be attended by the name of their author, and that one and the same person should be solely responsible for the insertion as well as composition of the same.

B.

COMMENCEMENT OF NO. I.

If it be usual with writers in general to find the first paragraph of their works that which has given them the most trouble with the least satisfaction, The Friend may be allowed to feel the difficulties and anxiety of a first introduction in a more than ordinary degree. He is embarrassed by the very circumstances that discriminate the plan and purposes of the present weekly paper from those of its periodical brethren, as well as from its more dignified literary relations, which come forth at once and in full growth from their parents. If it had been my ambition to have copied its whole scheme and fashion from the great founders of the race, the Tatler and Spectator, I should indeed have exposed my essays to a greater hazard of unkind comparison. An imperfect imitation is often felt as a contrast. On the other hand, however, the very names and descriptions of the fictitious characters, which I had proposed to assume in the course of my work, would have put me at once in possession of the stage; and my first act have opened with a procession of masks. Again, if I were composing one work on one given object, the same acquaintance with its grounds and bearings, which had authorized me to publish my opinions, would, with its principles or fundamental facts, have supplied me with my best and most appropriate commencement. More easy still would my task have been, had I planned The Friend chiefly as a vehicle for a weekly descant on public characters and political parties. My perfect freedom from all warping influences; the distance which permitted a distinct view of the game, yet secured me from its passions; the liberty of the press; and its especial importance at the present period from whatever event or topic might happen to form the great interest of the day; in short, the *recipe* was ready to my hand, and it was framed so skilfully, and has been practised with such constant effect, that it would have been affectation to have deviated from it. For originality for its own sake merely is idle at the best, and sometimes monstrous. Excuse me, therefore, gentle reader! if borrowing from my title a right of anticipation, I avail myself of the privileges of a friend before I have earned them; and waiving the ceremony of a formal introduction, permit me to proceed at once to the subject, trite indeed and familiar as the first lessons of childhood; which yet must be the foundation of my future superstructure with all its ornaments, the hidden root of the tree, I am attempting to rear, with all its branches and boughs. But if from it I have deduced my strongest moral motives for this undertaking, it has at the same time been applied in suggesting the most formidable obstacle to my success,—as far, I mean, as my plan alone is concerned, and not the talents necessary for its completion.

Conclusions drawn from facts which subsist in perpetual flux, without definite place or fixed quantity, must always be liable to plausible objections, nay, often to unanswerable difficulties; and yet, having their foundation in uncorrupted feeling, are assented to by mankind at large, and in all ages, as undoubted truths. As our notions concerning them are almost equally obscure, so are our convictions almost equally vivid, with those of our life and individuality. Regarded with awe as guiding principles by the founders of law and religion, they are the favorite objects of attack with mock philosophers, and the demagogues in church, state, and literature; and the denial of them has in all times, though at various intervals, formed heresies and systems, which, after their day of wonder, are regularly exploded, and again as regularly revived when they have re-acquired novelty by courtesy of oblivion.

Among these universal persuasions we must place the sense of a self-contradicting principle in our nature, or a disharmony in the different impulses that constitute it;—of a something which essentially distinguishes man both from all other animals that are known to exist, and from the idea of his own nature, or conception of the original man. In health and youth we may indeed connect the glow and buoyance of our bodily sensations with the words of a theory, and imagine that we hold it with a firm belief. The pleasurable heat which the blood or the breathing generates, the sense of external reality which comes with the strong grasp of the hand, or the vigorous tread of the foot, may indifferently become associated with the rich eloquence of a Shaftesbury, imposing on us man's possible perfections for his existing nature; or with the cheerless and hardier impieties of a Hobbes, while cutting the Gordian knot he denies the reality of either vice or virtue, and explains away the mind's self-reproach into a distempered ignorance, an epidemic affection of the human nerves and their habits of motion.

"Vain wisdom all, and false philosophy!"

I shall hereafter endeavor to prove, how distinct and different the sensation of positiveness is from the sense of certainty;—the turbulent heat of temporary fermentation from the mild warmth of essential life. Suffice it for the present to affirm, to declare it at least, as my own creed, that whatever humbles the heart, and forces the mind inward, whether it be sickness, or grief, or remorse, or the deep yearnings of love [and there have been children of affliction for whom all these have met and made up one complex suffering], in proportion as it acquaints us with the thing we are, renders us docile to the concurrent testimony of our fellow-men in all ages and in all nations. From Pascal in his closet resting the arm, which supports his thoughtful brow, on a pile of demonstrations, to the poor pensive Indian that seeks the missionary in the American wilderness, the humiliated self-examinant feels that there is evil in our nature as well as good;—an evil and a good, for a just analogy to which he questions all other natures in vain. It is still the great definition of humanity, that we have a conscience, which no mechanic compost, no chemical combination of mere appetence, memory and understanding, can solve; which is indeed an element of our being;—a conscience, unrelenting yet not absolute; which we may stupefy but can not delude; which we may suspend but can not annihilate; although we may perhaps find a treacherous counterfeit in the very quiet which we derive from its slumber, or its entrancement.

Of so mysterious a *phænomenon* we might expect a cause as mysterious. Accordingly, we find this [cause be it, or condition, or necessary accompaniment] involved and implied in the fact, which it alone can explain. For if our permanent consciousness did not reveal to us our free-agency, we should yet be obliged to deduce it, as a necessary inference, from the fact of our conscience: or rejecting both the one and the other, as mere illusions of internal feelings, forfeit all power of thinking consistently with our actions, or acting consistently with our thought, for any single hour during our whole lives. But I am proceeding farther than I had wished or intended. It will be long ere I shall dare flatter myself that I have won the confidence of my reader sufficiently to require of him that effort of attention, which the regular establishment of this truth would require.

After the brief season of youthful hardihood, and the succeeding years of unceasing fluctuation, after long-continued and patient study of the most celebrated works in the languages of ancient and modern Europe, in defence or denial of this prime article of human faith, which (save to the trifler or the worldling) no frequency of discussion can superannuate, I at length satisfied my own mind by arguments, which placed me on firm land. This one conviction, determined, as in a mould, the form and feature of my whole system in religion and morals, and even in literature. These arguments were not suggested to me by books, but forced on me by reflection on my own being, and observation of the ways of those about me, especially of little children. And as they had the power of fixing the same persuasion in some valuable minds, much interested, and not unversed in the controversy, and from the manner probably rather than the substance, appeared to them in some sort original—[for oldest reasons will put on an impressive semblance of novelty, if they have indeed been drawn from the fountain-head of genuine self-research]—and since the arguments are neither abstruse, nor dependent on a long chain of deductions, nor such as suppose previous habits of metaphysical disquisition; I shall deem it my duty to state them with what skill I can, at a fitting opportunity, though rather as the biographer of my own sentiments than a legislator of the opinions of other men.

At present, however, I give it merely as an article of my own faith, closely connected with all my hopes of melioration in man, and leading to the methods by which alone I hold any fundamental or permanent melioration practicable;—that there is evil distinct from error and from pain, an evil in human nature which is not wholly grounded in the limitation of our understandings. And this, too, I believe to operate equally in subjects of taste, as in the higher concerns of morality. Were it my conviction, that our follies, vice, and misery, have their entire origin in miscalculation from ignorance, I should act irrationally in attempting other task than that of adding new lights to the science of moral arithmetic, or new facility to its acquirement. In other words, it would have been my worthy business to have set forth, if it were in my power, an improved system of book-keeping for the ledgers of calculating self-love. If, on the contrary, I believed our nature fettered to all its wretchedness of head and heart, by an absolute and innate necessity, at least by a necessity which no human power, no efforts of reason or eloquence could remove or lessen [no, nor even prepare the way for such removal or diminution]; I should then yield myself at once to the admonitions of one of my correspondents [unless, indeed, it should better suit my humor to do nothing than nothings, *nihil quam nihili*], and deem it even presumptuous to aim at other or higher object than that of amusing, during some ten minutes in every week, a small portion of the reading public.

CONCLUSION OF NO. I.

Previously to my ascent of Etna, as likewise of the Brocken in North-Germany, I remember to have amused myself with examining the album or manuscript, presented to travellers at the first stage of the mountain, in which, on their return, their fore-runners had sometimes left their experience, and more often disclosed or betrayed their own characters. Something like this I have endeavored to do relatively to my great predecessors in periodical literature, from the

Spectator to the Mirror, or whatever later work of excellence there may be. But the distinction between my proposed plan and all and each of theirs, I must defer to a future essay. From all other works The Friend is sufficiently distinguished, either by the very form and intervals of its publication, or by its avowed exclusion of the events of the day, and of all personal politics.

For a detail of the principal subjects, which I have proposed to myself to treat in the course of this work, I must refer to the *Prospectus*,—printed at the end of this sheet. But I own I am anxious to explain myself more fully on the delicate subjects of religion and politics. Of the former perhaps it may, for the present, be enough to say that I have confidence in myself, that I shall neither directly nor indirectly attack its doctrines or mysteries, much less attempt basely to undermine them by allusion, or tale, or anecdote. What more I might dare promise of myself, I reserve for another occasion. Of politics, however, I have many motives to declare my intentions more explicitly. It is my object to refer men to principles in all things; in literature, in the fine arts, in morals, in legislation, in religion. Whatever, therefore, of a politic nature may be reduced to general principles, necessarily, indeed, dependent on the circumstances of a nation internal and external, yet not especially connected with this year or the preceding—this I do not exclude from my scheme. Thinking it a sort of duty to place my readers in full possession, both of my opinions and the only method in which I can permit myself to recommend them, and aware, too, of many calumnious accusations, as well as gross misapprehensions of my political creed, I shall dedicate my second number entirely to the views, which a British subject, in the present state of his country, ought to entertain of its actual and existing constitution of government. If I can do no positive good, I may perhaps aid in preventing others from doing harm. But all intentional allusions to particular persons, all support of, or hostility to, particular parties or factions, I now and forever utterly disclaim. My principles command this abstinence, my tranquillity requires it:—

Tranquillity! *thou* better name
Than all the family of fame, &c.
* * * * *

But I have transgressed a rule, which I had intended to have established for myself, that of never troubling my readers with my own verses:

Ite hinc Camœnæ! vos quoque, ite, suaves,
Dulces Camœnæ! Nam (fatebimur verum)
Dulces fuistis: et tamen meas chartas
Revisitote; sed pudenter et raro.

I shall, indeed, very rarely and cautiously, avail myself of this privilege. For long and early habits of exerting my intellect in metrical composition have not so enslaved me, but that for some years

I have felt, and deeply felt, that the poet's high functions were not my proper assignment;—that many may be worthy to listen to the strains of Apollo, neighbors of the sacred choir, and able to discriminate, and feel, and love its genuine harmonies; yet not therefore called to receive the harp in their own hands, and join in the concert. I am content and gratified, that Spenser, Shakspeare, Milton, have not been born in vain for me: and I feel it as a blessing, that even among my contemporaries I know one at least, who has been deemed worthy of the gift; who has received the harp with reverence, and struck it with the hand of power.

C.

COMMENCEMENT OF NO. II.

Conscious that I am about to deliver my sentiments on a subject of the utmost delicacy, to walk

per ignes
Suppositos cineri doloso,

I have been tempted by my fears to preface them with a motto of unusual length, from an authority equally respected by both of the opposite parties. I have selected it from an orator, whose eloquence has taken away for Englishmen all cause of humiliation from the names of Demosthenes and Cicero: from a statesman, who has left to our language a bequest of glory unrivalled, and all his own, in the keen-eyed, yet far-sighted genius, with which he has almost uniformly made the most original and profound general principles of political wisdom, and even recondite laws of human passions, bear upon particular measures and events. While of the harangues of Pitt, Fox, and their elder compeers, on the most important occurrences, we retain a few unsatisfactory fragments alone, the very flies and weeds of Burke shine to us through the purest amber, imperishably enshrined, and valuable from the precious material of their embalmment. I have extracted the passage from that Burke whose latter exertions have rendered his works venerable, as oracular voices from the sepulchre of a patriarch, to the upholders of government and society in their existing state and order; but from a speech delivered by him while he was the most beloved, the proudest name with the more anxious friends of liberty (I distinguish them in courtesy by the name of their own choice, not as implying any enmity to true freedom in the characters of their opponents); while he was the darling of those, who, believing mankind to have been improved, are desirous to give to forms of government a similar progression.

From the same anxiety, I have been led to introduce my opinions on this most hazardous subject by a preface of a somewhat personal character. And though the title of my address is general, yet, I own, I direct myself more particularly to those among my readers, who, from various printed and unprinted calumnies, have judged most unfavorably of my political tenets; and to those, whose favor I have chanced to win in consequence of a similar, though not equal, mistake. To both I affirm, that the opinions and arguments I am about to detail, have been the settled convictions of my mind for the last ten or twelve years, with some brief intervals of fluctuation, and those only in lesser points, and known only to the companions of my fireside. From both and from all my readers, I solicit a gracious attention to the following explanations; first, on the congruity of this number with the general plan and object of The Friend, and secondly on the charge of arrogance, which may be adduced against the author for the freedom with which, in this number, and in others that will follow, on other subjects, he presumes to dissent from men of established reputation, or even to doubt of the justice with which the public laurel crown, as symbolical of the first class of genius and intellect, has been awarded to sundry writers since the Revolution, and permitted to wither around the brows of our elder benefactors, from Hooker to Sir Philip Sidney, and from Sir Philip Sidney to Jeremy Taylor and Stillingfleet.

First, then, as to the consistency of the subject of the following essay with the proposed plan of my work, let something be allowed to honest personal motives, a justifiable solicitude to stand well with my contemporaries in those points, in which I have remained unreproached by my own conscience. *Des aliquid famæ.* A reason of far greater importance is derived from the well-grounded complaint of sober minds, concerning the mode by which political opinions of greatest hazard have been, of late years, so often propagated. This evil can not be described in more just and lively language than in the words of Paley, which, though by him applied to infidelity, hold equally true of the turbulent errors of political heresy. They are "served up in every shape that is likely to allure, surprise, or beguile the imagination; in a fable, a tale, a novel, a poem; in interspersed and broken hints; remote and oblique surmises; in books of travels, of philosophy, of natural history; in a word, in any form, rather than the right one, that of a professed and regular disquisition."* Now, in claiming for The Friend a fair chance of unsuspected admission into the families of Christian believers and quiet subjects, I can not but deem it incumbent on me to accompany my introduction with a

* Moral and Polit. Philosophy, B. V. c. 9.—*Ed.*

full and fair statement of my own political system;—not that any considerable portion of my essays will be devoted to politics in any shape, for rarely shall I recur to them, except as far as they may happen to be involved in some point of private morality; but that the encouragers of this work may possess grounds of assurance, that no tenets of a different tendency from these I am preparing to state, will be met in it. I would fain hope, that even those persons to whose political opinions I may run counter, will not be displeased at seeing the possible objections to their creed calmly set forth by one who, equally with themselves, considers the love of true liberty as a part both of religion and morality, as a necessary condition of their general predominance, and ministering to the same blessed purposes. The development of my persuasions, relatively to religion in its great essentials, will occupy a following number, in which, and throughout these essays, my aim will be, seldom, indeed, to enter the temple of revelation (much less of positive institution), but to lead my readers to its threshold, and to remove the prejudices with which the august edifice may have been contemplated from ill chosen and unfriendly points of view.

But, independently of this motive, I deem the subject of politics, so treated as I intend to treat it, strictly congruous with my general plan. For it was and is my prime object to refer men in all their actions, opinions, and even enjoyments, to an appropriate rule, and to aid them with all the means I possess, by the knowledge of the facts on which such rule grounds itself. The rules of political prudence do, indeed, depend on local and temporary circumstances in a much greater degree than those of morality, or even those of taste. Still, however, the circumstances being known, the deductions obey the same law, and must be referred to the same arbiter. In a late summary reperusal of our more celebrated periodical essays, by the contemporaries of Addison and those of Johnson, it appeared to me that the objects of the writers were, either to lead the reader from gross enjoyments and boisterous amusements, by gradually familiarizing them with more quiet and refined pleasures; or to make the habits of domestic life and public demeanor more consistent with decorum and good sense, by laughing away the lesser follies and freaks of self-vexation, or to arm the yet virtuous mind with horror of the direr crimes and vices, by exemplifying their origin, progress, and results, in affecting tales and true or fictitious biography; or where, as in the Rambler, it is intended to strike a yet deeper note, to support the cause of religion and morality by eloquent declamation and dogmatic precept, such as may with propriety be addressed to those, who require to be awakened rather than convinced, whose conduct is incongruous with their own sober convictions; in short, to practical not speculative heretics. Revered forever be the names of these great and good men! Immortal be their fame; and may love, and honor, and docility of heart in their readers constitute its essentials! Not without cruel injustice should I be accused or suspected of a wish to underrate their merits, because, in journeying toward the same end, I have chosen a different road. Not wantonly, however, have I ventured even on this variation. I have decided on it in consequence of all the observations which I have made on my fellow-creatures, since I have been able to observe in calmness the present age, and to compare its *phænomena* with the best indications we possess of the character of the ages before us.

My time since earliest manhood has been pretty equally divided between deep retirement, with little other society than that of one family, and my library, and the occupations and intercourse of [comparatively at least] public life both abroad and in the British metropolis. But in fact the deepest retirement, in which a well-educated Englishman of active feelings, and no misanthrope, can live at present, supposes few of the disadvantages and negations, which a similar place of residence would have involved a century past. Independently of the essential knowledge to be derived from books, children, housemates, and neighbors, however few and humble,—newspapers, their advertisements, speeches in parliament, law courts, and public meetings, reviews, magazines, obituaries, and [as affording occasional commentaries on all these] the diffusion of uniform opinions, behavior, and appearance, of fashions in things external and internal, have combined to diminish, and often to render evanescent, the distinctions between the enlightened inhabitants of the great city, and the scattered hamlet. From all the facts, however, that have occurred as subjects of reflection within the sphere of my experience, be they few or numerous, I have fully persuaded my own mind, that formerly men were worse than their principles, but that at present the principles are worse than the men. For the former half of the proposition I might, among a thousand other more serious and unpleasant proofs, appeal even to the Spectators and Tatlers. It would not be easy, perhaps, to detect in them any great corruption or debasement of the main foundations of truth and goodness; yet a man —I will not say of delicate mind and pure morals, but—of common good manners, who means to read an essay, which he has opened upon at hazard in these volumes to a mixed company, will find it necessary to take a previous survey of its contents. If stronger illustration be required, I would refer to one of Shadwell's comedies, in connection with its dedication to the Duchess of Newcastle, encouraged as he says, by the high delight with which her Grace had listened to the author's private recitation of the manuscript in her closet. A writer of the present day, who should dare address such a composition to a virtuous matron of high rank, would secure general infamy, and run no small risk of Bridewell or the pillory. Why need I add the plays and poems of Dryden, contrasted with his serious prefaces and declarations of his own religious and moral opinions? Why the little success, except among the heroes and heroines of fashionable life, of the two or three living writers of prurient love-odes [if I may be forgiven for thus profaning the word love] and novels, at once terrific and libidinous? These gentlemen erred both in place and time, and have understood the temper of their age and country as ill as the precepts of that Bible, which, notwithstanding the atrocious blasphemy of one of them, the great majority of their countrymen peruse with safety to their morals, if not improvement.

The truth of the latter half of the proposition in its favorable part is evidenced by the general anxiety on the subject of education, the solicitous attention paid to several late works on its general principles, and the unexpected sale of the very numerous large and small volumes, published for the use of parents and instructors, and for the children given or intrusted to their charge. The first ten or twelve leaves of our old almanac books, and the copper-plates of old ladies' magazines, and similar publications, will afford, in the fashions and head-dresses of our grandmothers, contrasted with the present simple ornaments of women in general, a less important, but not less striking elucidation of my meaning. The wide diffusion of moral information, in no slight degree owing to the volumes of our popular essayists, has undoubtedly been on the whole beneficent. But above all, the recent events [say, rather, tremendous explosions], the thunder and earthquakes, and deluge of the political world, have forced habits of great thoughtfulness on the minds of men; particularly in our own island, where the instruction has been acquired without the stupefying influences of terror or actual calamity. We have been compelled to acknowledge [what our fathers would have perhaps called it want of liberality to assert], the close connection between private libertinism and national subversion. To those familiar with the state and morals, and the ordinary subjects of after-dinner conversation, at least among the young men in Oxford and Cambridge, only twenty or twenty-five years back, I might with pleasure point out, in support of my thesis, the present state of our two universities, which has rather superseded, than been produced by any additional vigilance or austerity of discipline.

The unwelcome remainder of the proposition, the "feet of iron and clay," the unsteadiness, or falsehood, or abasement of the principles, which are taught and received by the existing generation, it is the chief purpose and general business of The Friend to examine, to evince, and [as far as my own forces extend, increased by the contingents which, I flatter myself, will be occasionally furnished by abler patrons of the same cause] to remedy or alleviate. That my efforts will effect little, I am fully conscious; but by no means admit, that little is to be effected. The squire of low degree may announce the approach of puissant knight, yea, the giant may even condescend to lift up the feeble dwarf, and permit it to blow the horn of defiance on his shoulders.

Principles, therefore, their subordination, their connection, and their application, in all the divisions of our duties and of our pleasures—this is my chapter of contents. May I not hope for a candid interpretation of my motive, if I again recur to the possible apprehension on the part of my readers, that The Friend,

> O'erlaid with black, staid wisdom's hue,

with eye fixed in abstruse research, and brow of perpetual wrinkle, is to frown away the light-hearted graces, and unreproved pleasures; or invite his guests to a dinner of herbs in a hermit's cell; if I affirm, that my plan does not in itself exclude either impassioned style or interesting narrative, tale, or allegory, or anecdote; and that the defect will originate in my abilities, not in my wishes or efforts, if I fail to bring forward,

> Due at *my* hour prepared
> For dinner savory fruits, of taste to please
> True appetite—
> *In* order, so contrived as not to mix
> Tastes, not well joined, inelegant, but bring
> Taste after taste upheld with kindliest change.*

D.

NO. V.

The comparison of the English with the Anglo-American newspapers will best evince the difference between a lawless press [lawless, at least, in practice and by connivance], and a press at once protected and restrained by law.

IBID.

Chrysippus, in one of his Stoical Aphorisms, presented by Cicero,† says:—Nature has given to the hog a soul instead of salt, in order to keep it from putrefying. This holds equally true of man considered as an animal. Modern physiologists have substituted the words vital power [*vis vitæ*] for that of soul, and not without good reason: for, from the effect we may fairly deduce the inherence of a power pro-

* Par. Lost, V. 303, 333.—*Ed.*

† *De Natura Deorum*, II; s. 64.—*Ed.*

ducing it, but are not entitled to hypostasise this power, that is, to affirm it to be an individual substance, any more than the steam in the steam-engine, the power of gravitation in the watch, or the magnetic influence in the lodestone. If the machine consist of parts mutually dependent, as in the time-piece or the hog, we can not dispart without destroying it: if otherwise, as in a mass of lodestone and in the *polypus*, the power is equally divisible with the substance. The most approved definition of a living substance is, that its vitality consists in the susceptibility of being acted upon by external stimulants, joined to the necessity of reaction, and in the due balance of this action and reaction, the healthy state of life consists. We must, however, further add the power of acquiring habits, and facilities by repetition. This being the generical idea of life, is common to all living beings: but taken exclusively, it designates the lowest class, plants and plant-animals. An addition to the mechanism gives locomotion. A still costlier and more complex apparatus diversely organizes the impressions received from the external powers, that fall promiscuously on the whole surface. The light shines on the whole face, but it receives form and relation only in the eyes; in them it is organized. To these organs of sense we suppose, by analogy from our own experience, sensation attached, and these sensuous impressions acting on other parts of the machine framed for other stimulants included in the machine itself, namely, the organs of appetite; and these again working on the instruments of locomotion, and on those by which the external substances corresponding to the sensuous impressions can be acted upon [the mouth, teeth, talons, and the like], constitute our whole idea of the perfect animal. More than this Des Cartes denied to all other animals but man, and to man himself as an animal: for that this truly great man considered animals insensible, or rather insensitive, machines, though commonly asserted, and that in books of highest authority, is an error, and the charge was repelled with disdain by himself, in a letter to Dr. Henry More, which, if I mistake not, is annexed to the small edition of More's Ethics.

The strict analogy, however, between certain actions of sundry animals and those of mankind, forces upon us the belief that they possess some share of a higher faculty; which, however closely united with life in one person, can yet never be educed out of the mere idea of vital power. Indeed, if we allow any force to the universal opinion, and almost instinct, concerning the difference between plants and animals, we must hold even sensation as a fresh power added to his *vis vitæ*, unless we would make an end of philosophy, by comprising all things in each thing, and thus denying that any one power of the universe can be affirmed to be itself and not another. However this may be, the understanding or regulative faculty is manifestly distinct from life and sensation; its junction being to take up the passive affections into distinct thought of the sense, according to its own essential forms.* These forms, however, as they are first awakened by impressions from the senses, so have they no substance or meaning unless in their application to objects of the senses: and if we would remove from them, by careful abstraction, all the influences and intermixtures of a yet far higher faculty [self-consciousness, for instance], it would be difficult, if at all possible, to distinguish its functions from those of instinct, of which it would be no inapt definition, that it is a more or less limited understanding without self-consciousness, or spontaneous origination. Besides this, the understanding with all its axioms of sense, its anticipations of apperception, and its analogies of experience, has no appropriate object, but the material world in relation to our worldly interests. The far-sighted prudence of man, and the more narrow, but at the same time far more certain and effectual, cunning of the fox, are both no other than a nobler substitute for salt, in order that the hog may not putrefy before its destined hour.

E.

NO. XII.

He who taketh the side of justice maketh the land prosperous: he who withdraweth from the same is an accomplice in its destruction.

Rabbi Assi was sick, lay on his bed surrounded by his disciples, and prepared himself for death. His nephew came unto him, and found him weeping. "Wherefore weepest thou, Rabbi?" he asked. "Must not every look which thou castest back on thy past life, bring a thought of joy to thee? Hast thou not then sufficiently studied, not sufficiently taught the sacred law? Lo! thy disciples here are proofs of the contrary. Hast thou then been backward in practising the works of righteousness? Every man is satisfied that thou hast not. And thy humility was the crown of all thy virtues! Never wouldst thou suffer thyself to be elected the judge of the district, anxiously as the whole district wished it." "It is even this, my son," answered

* Aristotle, the first systematic anatomist of the mind, constructed the first numeration table of these innate forms or faculties (not innate ideas or notions) under the names of Categories: which table, though both incomplete and erroneous, remains an unequivocal proof of his penetration and philosophical genius. The best and most orderly arrangement of the original forms of the understanding, the moulds as it were both of our notions and judgments concerning the notices of the senses, is that of quantity, quality, relation, and mode, each consisting of three kinds. There is but one possible way of making an enumeration of them interesting or even endurable to the general reader: the history of the origin of certain useful inventions in machinery in the minds of the inventors.

Rabbi Assi, "which now troubles me. I had it in my power to exercise right and justice among the children of men, and out of mistaken humility, I did not avail myself thereof. Whoso withdraweth himself from justice is an accomplice in the ruin of the land."

F.

NO. XIV.

DURING my second term at Cambridge, I had for my own amusement commenced a work on the plan of the well-known Miseries of Human Life, at least with the same title; for by its title only, and the pleasure expressed by all who have spoken to me of it, am I acquainted with that publication. But at the same time I had meant to add, as an appendix, a catalogue *raisonné* of the sights, incidents, and employments, that leave us better men than they found us; or, to use my original phrase, of the things that do a man's heart good. If the seventeen or eighteen years that have elapsed since that period, would enable me greatly to extend and diversify the former list, the latter, as more properly the offspring of experience and reflection, would be augmented in a still larger proportion. Among the *addenda* to this second catalogue I should rank foremost, a long winter evening devoted to the re-perusal of the letters of far-distant, or deceased friends. I suppose the person so employed to be one, whose time is seldom at his own disposal, and that he finds himself alone in a quiet house, the other inmates of which are absent on some neighborly visit. I have been led to this observation by the numerous letters (many of which had all the pleasure of novelty for me, joined with the more tender charm of awakened recollection) from The Friend, with a slight sketch of whose character I have introduced the present number under the name, which he went by among his friends and familiars, of Satyrane,* the Idoloclast, or breaker of idols.

A few seasons ago, I made the tour of the northern counties with him and three other companions. His extensive erudition, his energetic and all too subtle intellect, the opulence of his imagination, and above all, his inexhaustible store of anecdotes, which always appeared to us the most interesting when of himself, and his passionate love of mountain imagery, which often gave an eloquence to his looks and made his very silence intelligible, will forever endear the

* The attentive reader will of course see that Satyrane is the author himself, and that this extract contains one of the many sketches of his own character, scattered throughout his writings.

remembrance of that tour to the survivors. Various were our discussions, most often with him, but sometimes [when we had split our party for a few hours] concerning him and his opinions; not a few of which appeared, to some of us at least, sufficiently paradoxical, though there was nothing which he bore with less patience than the hearing them thus characterized. Many and various were our topics, often suggested by the objects and occurrences of the moment, and often occasioned by the absence of other interest. O Satyrane! who would not have lost the sense of time and fatigue in thy company? How often, after a walk of fifteen or twenty miles, on rough roads and through a dreary or uninteresting country, have we seen our proposed resting-place with a sort of pleasant surprise, all joining in the same question—"Who would have thought we had walked so far?" And then, perhaps, we examined our watches, as if half in doubt, or perhaps to contrast the length of time which had thus slipped away from us, with our own little sense of its lapse. These discussions, and the marked difference of our several characters (though we were all old acquaintances, and, with one exception, all of us fellow-Cantabs), suggested to us the plan of a joint work, to be entitled, "Travelling Conversations." Since that time I have often renewed this scheme in my mind, and pleased myself with the thought of realizing it. Independently of the delightful recollections, the lively portraiture and inward music, which would enliven my own fancy during the composition, it appeared to me to possess the merit of harmonizing an indefinite variety of matter by that unity of interest, which would arise from the characters remaining the same throughout, while the tour itself would supply the means of introducing the most different topics by the most natural connections. We had agreed to call each other by the names of our walking-sticks, each of which happened to be of a different wood; Satyrane, however, excepted, who was well pleased to be called among us by his old college name, and not displeased with his learned *agnomen*, when we used with mock solemnity to entreat a short reprieve for our prejudices from him, under the lofty title of "Puissant and most redoubtable Idoloclastes." I flatter myself that the readers of The Friend will consent to travel over the same road with the same fellow-tourist. High, indeed, will be my gratification, if they should hereafter think of the walk and talk with The Friend's Satyrane, Holly, Larch, Hickory and Sycamore, with a small portion of the delight with which they have accompanied the Spectator to his club, and made acquaintance with Will Honeycomb, and the inimitable Sir Roger de Coverley. From any imitation, indeed, I am precluded by the nature and object of my work; and for many reasons, the persons whom I introduce, must be distinguished by their sentiments, their different kinds of information, and their different views of life and society, rather than by any prominent individuality of humor in their personal characters. What they were to myself they will be to my reader; glasses of different colors and various degrees of power, through which truth and error, happiness and misery, may be contemplated.

From his earliest youth, Satyrane had derived his highest pleasures from the admiration of moral grandeur and intellectual energy; and, during the whole of his short life, he had a greater and more heartfelt delight in the superiority of other men to himself, than men in general derive from the belief of their own. His readiness to imagine a superiority where it did not exist, was, indeed, for many years, his predominant weakness. His pain from the perception of inferiority in others, whom he had heard spoken of with any respect, was unfeigned and involuntary, and perplexed him, as a something which he did not comprehend. In the child-like simplicity of his nature, he talked to all men as if they were, at least, his equals in knowledge and talents; and his familiars record many a whimsical anecdote, and many a ludicrous incident, connected with this habit of his of scattering the good seed on unreceiving soils. When he was at length compelled to see and acknowledge the true state of the morals and intellect of his contemporaries, his disappointment was severe, and his mind, always thoughtful, became pensive and almost gloomy: for to love and sympathize with mankind was a necessity of his nature. Hence, as if he sought a refuge from his own sensibility, he attached himself to the most abstruse researches, and seemed to derive his purest delight from subjects that exercised the strength and subtlety of his understanding, without awakening the feelings of his heart. When I first knew him, and for many years after, this was all otherwise. The sun never shone on a more joyous being. The Letters of earliest date, which I possess of his, were written to a common friend, and contain the accounts of his first travels. That I may introduce him to my readers in his native and original character, I now place before them his first letter, written on his arrival at Hamburgh.* I have only to premise, that Satyrane was incapable of ridiculing a foreigner merely for speaking English imperfectly; but the extravagant vanity that could prompt a man, so speaking and pronouncing, to pride himself on his excellence as a linguist, is as honest a subject of light satire, as an old coquette, or as a beau of threescore and ten, exposing the infirmities of old age in a reel on his wedding-day.

* The Letter here alluded to was published in the author's "Literary Life."

G.

PRELIMINARY TO NO. XXI.

Ante quod est in me, postque ——
* * * * * *
Omnis habet geminas, hinc atque hinc, janua frontes,
E quibus hæc populum spectat; at illa larem.
Utque sedens vester primi prope limina tecti
Janitor egressus introitusque videt;
Sic ego —— OVID.*

† I HAVE always looked forward to the present number of The Friend as its first proper starting post; for the twenty numbers preceding I regarded as a preparatory heat, in order to determine whether or no I should be admitted, as a candidate, on that longer course, on which alone the speed and strength of the racer can be fairly proved.

* * * * * *

I was not so ignorant of mankind as to expect that my essays would be found interesting in the hurry and struggle of active life. All the passions which are there at work it was my object to preclude: and I distinctly foresaw, that by rejecting all appeals to personal passions, and party spirit, and all interest grounded wholly on the cravings of curiosity, and the love of novelty for its own sake, I at the same time precluded three fourths of the ordinary readers of periodical publications, whether reviews, magazines, or newspapers. I might, however, find dispersedly what I could not hope to meet with collectively. I thought it not improbable, that there might be individuals, scattered throughout the kingdom, to whom the very absence of such stimulants would prove a recommendation to the work; and that, when the existence of such a work was generally known, a sufficient number of persons, able and willing to patronize it, might gradually be collected.

* * * * * *

I ought to have made it a condition, that a notice of six weeks should be given of the intention to discontinue the work;—but this I neglected from unwise delicacy, an habitual turning away from all thoughts relating to money, and, from a self-flattering persuasion that those, who, after the perusal of my *Prospectus*, had determined on giving the work a trial, would be sensible of the difficulties it had to struggle with, and whether satisfied or not with its style of execution, yet for the earnest wish of The Friend, not only to please them,

* Fast. I. 114, 135, &c.—*Ed.*

† The following passages are extracted from an address by Mr. Coleridge to his subscribers, and to the readers of The Friend in general.—*Ed.*

but to please them in such a way as might leave them permanently better pleased with themselves, would be disposed rather to lessen than increase them.

* * * * * *

Among other things of the kind, a person, signing himself "Carlyol," has addressed a threatening and abusive letter to me from Dover. I shall not tell him that such an act was ungentlemanly, unmanly, and unchristian, for this would be to him the same "learned non*sence* and unintelligible jar*gin*" for which he abuses me; but some other points I may venture to press on his attention. First, that it was a lack of common honesty in him to write a letter with a fictitious signature, and not pay the postage: secondly, that it was injudicious to address the letter to me, as the editor of the Courier is alone responsible for the appearance of the passages which have offended him, and the other admirers of Bonaparte in that paper: thirdly, that there is one branch of learning without which learning itself can not be railed at with common decency, namely, spelling: and lastly, that unintelligibility is a very equivocal charge. It certainly may arise from the author, especially if he should chance to be deficient in that branch of erudition last mentioned; but it may likewise, and often does, arise from the reader, and this from more than one cause. He may have an idiotic understanding, and what is far more common, as well as incomparably more lamentable, he may have an idiotic heart. To this last cause must we attribute the commission of such crimes as provoke the vengeance of the law, by men who can not but have heard from the pulpit truths and warnings, which, though evident to their understandings, were, unhappily for them, religious nonsense and unintelligible jargon to their bad hearts. And I feel it my duty to press on my correspondent's reflection the undoubted fact, that a man may be quite fool enough to be a rogue, and yet not appear fool enough to save him from the legal consequences of his roguery.

IBID.

During the composition of this last paragraph,* I have been aware that I shall appear to have been talking arrogantly, and with an unwarrantable assumption of superiority; but a moment's reflection will enable my reader to acquit me of this charge, as far as it is, or ought to be a charge. He will recollect that I have been giving the history of my own mind; and that, if it had been my duty to believe, that the main obstacle to the success of my undertaking existed not in the minds of others, but in my own insufficiency and inferiority, I ought not to have undertaken it at all. To a sincere and sensible

* On thought and attention contained in Essay 2, p. 27.—*Ed.*

mind it can not but be disgusting, to find an author writing on subjects, to the investigation of which he professes to have devoted the greater portion of his life, and yet appealing to all his readers promiscuously, as his full and competent judges, and thus soliciting their favor by a mock modesty, which either convicts him of gross hypocrisy, or the most absurd presumption. For what can be conceived at once more absurd and psesumptuous, than for a man to write and publish books for the instruction of those who are wiser than himself, more learned, and more judicious? Humility, like all other virtues, must exist in harmony with truth. My heart bears me witness that I would gladly give up all the pleasures which I can ever derive from literary reputation, could I receive instead of them a deep conviction, that The Friend has failed in pleasing no one, whose own superiority had not rendered the essays tiresome, because superfluous. And why should that be deemed a mark of self-sufficiency in an author, which would be thought only common sense in a musician or a painter, namely, the supposition that he understands and can practise those arts, to which he has devoted his best faculties during life, in consequence of a particular predilection for them, better than the mass of mankind, who have given their time and thoughts to other pursuits? There is one species of presumption among authors which is truly hateful, and which betrays itself, when writers, who, in their prefaces, have prostrated themselves before the superiority of their readers as supreme judges, will yet, in their works, pass judgments on Plato, Milton, Shakspeare, Spenser, and their compeers, in blank assertions and a peremptory *ipse-dixi*, and with a grossness of censure, which a sensible schoolmaster would not apply to the exercises of the youths in his upper forms. I need no outward remembrances of my own inferiority, but I possess them on almost every shelf of my library; and the very book which I am now using as my writing-desk (Lord Bacon's *Novum Organum*) inspires an awe and heartfelt humility, which I would not exchange for all the delight which Bonaparte can enjoy at the moment that his crowned courtiers hail him emperor of emperors, and lord paramount of the West.

As the week, which is to decide on the continuance of The Friend, coincides with the commencement of the new year, the present address has not inappropriately taken its character from the two-faced god to whom the first month is indebted for its name; it being in part retrospective, and in part prospective. Among the various reasons which Ovid, in the passage from which I have taken my motto, has made Janus himself assign for his bifront appearance, he has omitted the most obvious intention of the emblem, that of instructing his worshipers to commence the new year with a religious, as well as prudential, review of their own conduct, and its consequences during the past year; and thus to look onward to the year before them with wiser plans, and with strengthened or amended resolutions. I will apply this to my own conduct as far as it concerns the present publication; and having already sufficiently informed the reader of the general plan which I had proposed to myself, I will now, with the same simplicity, communicate my own calm judgment on the manner in which that plan has been so far realized and the outline filled up. My first number bears marks of the effort and anxiety with which it was written, and is composed less happily than I could wish. It assuredly had not the cheerful winning aspect, which a door-keeper, presenting the bill of fare, ought to possess. Its object, however, was so far answered, as it announced distinctly the fundamental position or grand postulate on which the whole superstructure, with all its supporting beams and pillars, was to rest. I call it a postulate, not only because I deferred the proofs, but because, in strictness, it was not susceptible of any proof from without. The sole possible question was—Is it, or is it not, a fact?—and for the answer every human being must be referred to his own consciousness.

* * * * * *

If man be a free agent, his good and evil must not be judged according to the nature of his outward actions, or the mere legality of his conduct, but by the final motive and intention of the mind. Now the final motive of an intelligent will is a principle: and consequently to refer the opinions of men to principles (that is to absolute and necessary, instead of secondary and contingent, grounds) is the best and only secure way of referring the feelings of men to their proper objects. In the union of both consists the perfection of the human character.

The same subject was illustrated in my second essay, and reasons assigned from the peculiar circumstances of the age, and the present state of the minds of men, for giving this particular direction to their serious studies, instead of the more easy and attractive mode of instruction adapted by my illustrious predecessors in periodical literature. At the same time, being conscious how many authorities of recent, but for that reason more influential reputation I must of necessity contravene in the support and application of my principles, both in criticism and philosophy, I thought it requisite to state the true nature of presumption and arrogance, and thus, if it were possible, preclude the charge in cases where I had not committed the offence. The object of the next four numbers was to demonstrate the innoxiousness of truth, if only the conditions were preserved which the reason and conscience dictated; to show at large what those conditions were which ought to regulate the conduct of the individual in the communication of truth; and by what principles the civil law ought to be governed in the punishment of libels. Throughout the whole of these numbers, and more especially in the latter two, I again, and again recalled the attention of the reader to the paramount importance of principles, alike for their moral and their intellectual, for their private and national, consequences; the importance, I say, of principles of reason, as distinct from, and paramount to, the maxims of prudence, even for prudence' sake. Some of my readers will probably have seen this subject supported by other and additional arguments in my seventh letter, 'On the grounds of hope for a people warring against Armies,' published during the last month, in the Courier.

In the mean time I was aware, that in thus grounding my opinions in literature, morals and religion, I should frequently use the same or similar language, as had been applied by Rousseau, the French physiocratic philosophers, and their followers in England, to the nature and rightful origin of civil government. The remainder of my work, therefore, hitherto has been devoted to the purpose of averting this mistake, as far as I have not been compelled by the general taste of my readers to interrupt the systematic progress of the plan by essays of a lighter kind, or which at least required a less effort of attention. In truth, since my twelfth number, I have not had courage to renew any subject which did require attention. The way to be admired is to tell the reader what he knew before, but clothed in a statelier phraseology, and embodied in apt and lively illustrations. To attempt to make a man wiser is of necessity to remind him of his ignorance, and in the majority of instances, the pain actually felt is so much greater than the pleasure anticipated, that it is natural that men should attempt to shelter themselves from it by contempt or neglect. For a living writer is yet *sub judice:* and if we can not follow his conceptions or enter into his feelings, it is more consoling to our pride, as well as more agreeable to our indolence, to consider him as lost beneath, than as soaring out of our sight above us. *Itaque ad agitur, ut ignorantia etiam ab ignominia liberetur.* Happy is that man, who can truly say, with Giordano Bruno, and whose circumstances at the same time permit him to act on the sublime feeling;—

Procedat nudus, quem non ornant nubila,
Sol: non conveniunt quadrupedum phaleræ
Humano dorso. Porro veri species
Quæsita, inventa, et patefacta, me efferat.
Etsi nullus intelligat,
Si cum natura sapio et sub numine,
Id vere plusquam satis est.

Should the number of subscribers remaining on my list be sufficient barely to pay the expenses of the publication, I shall assuredly proceed in the present form, at least till I have concluded all the subjects which have been left imperfect in the preceding essays. And this, as far as I can at present calculate, will extend the present volume to the twenty-eighth or perhaps thirtieth number. The first place will be given to 'Fragments and sketches of the life of the late Admiral Sir Alexander Ball.' I shall next finish the important subject left incomplete at the ninth number, and demonstrate that despotism and barbarism are the natural result of a national attempt to realize anti-feudalism, or the system of philosophical jacobinism. This position will be illustrated and exemplified at each step by the present state of France; and the essay will conclude with a detailed analysis of the character of Bonaparte, promised by the author so many years ago in the Morning Post, as a companion to the character of Mr. Pitt, which I have been requested by men of the highest reputation in the philosophical and literary world, to republish in a more permanent form. In the third place, I shall conduct the subject of taxation to a conclusion, my essay on which has been grossly misunderstood. These misconceptions and misrepresentations I shall use my best efforts to remove; and then develop the influences of taxation and a national debt, on the foreign trade of Great Britain: and lastly [the only mournful part of the tale], on the principles and intellectual habits of the country. And the volume, whether it be destined to stand alone or as the first of a series, will conclude with a philosophical examination of the British constitution in all its branches, separately and collectively. To the next, or twenty-first number, I shall annex a note of explanation requested by many intelligent readers, concerning my use of the words 'reason' and 'understanding,' as far as is requisite for the full comprehension of the political essays from the seventh to the eleventh numbers. But as I am not likely to receive back my list of subscribers from London within less than ten days, and must till then remain ignorant of the names of those who may have given orders for the discontinuance of The Friend, I am obliged to suspend the publication for one week. I can not conclude this address without expressions of gratitude to those who have written me letters of encouragement and respect; but at the same time entreat, that in their friendly efforts to serve the work by procuring new names for it, they will apply to such only as, they have cause to believe, will be actually pleased with a work of this kind. Such only can be of real advantage to The Friend: and even if it were otherwise, he ought not to wish it. An author's success should always depend on feelings inspired exclusively by his writings, and on the sense of their having been useful to the person who recommends them. On this supposition, and on this only, such recommendation becomes a duty.

IBID.

NO. XXI.

As to myself, and my own present attempt to record the life and character of the late Admiral Sir Alexander Ball, I have already stated that I consider myself as debarred from all circumstances, not appertaining to his conduct or character as a public functionary that involve the names of the living for good or for evil. Whatever facts and incidents I relate of a private nature, must for the most part concern Sir Alexander Ball exclusively, and as an insulated individual. But I needed not this restraint. It will be enough for me, still as I write, to recollect the form and character of Sir Alexander Ball himself, to represent to my own feelings the inward contempt, with which he would have abstracted his mind from worthless anecdotes and petty personalities;—a contempt rising into indignation, if ever an illustrious name were used as the thread to string them upon. If this recollection be my Socratic demon to warn and to check me, I shall on the other hand derive encouragement from the remembrance of the tender patience, the sweet gentleness, with which he was wont to tolerate the tediousness of well-meaning men; and the inexhaustible attention, the unfeigned interest, with which he would listen for hours, where the conversation appealed to reason, and like the bee made honey while it murmured.

H.

NO. XXII.

To the doctrine of retribution after death the philosopher made the following objection. "When the soul is disunited from the body, to which will belong the guilt of the offences committed during life? Certainly not to the body; for this, when the soul takes its departure, lies like a clod of earth, and without the soul would never have been capable of offending: and as little would the soul have defiled itself with sin but for its union with the flesh. Which of the two then is the proper object of the divine justice?" "God's wisdom only," answered the Rabbi, "fully comprehends the way of his justice. Yet the mortal may without offence, if with humility, strive to render the same intelligible to himself and his fellows. A householder had in his fruit garden two servants, the one lame and the other blind. Yonder, said the lame man to the blind, on those trees I see most delicious fruit hang, take me on thy shoulders and we will pluck thereof. This they did, and thus robbed their benefactor who had maintained them, as unprofitable servants, out of his mere goodness and compassion. The master discovered the theft, and called the two ingrates to account. Each threw off the blame from himself, the one urging in his defence his incapability of seeing the fruit, and the other the want of power to get at it. What did the master of the house do? He placed the lame man upon the blind, and punished them in the same posture in which they had committed the offence. So will the Judge of the world do with the soul and body of man."

www.ingramcontent.com/pod-product-compliance
Lightning Source LLC
LaVergne TN
LVHW021243110826
845150LV00002B/396

* 9 7 8 1 4 2 5 5 6 1 4 5 1 *